AMSCO'S
Preparing
for the SAT
in Critical Reading
and Writing

HENRY I. CHRIST

AMSCO SCHOOL PUBLICATIONS, INC.
315 Hudson Street / New York, N.Y. 10013

Henry I. Christ has had a long and distinguished career as writer, editor, teacher, and supervisor. A specialist in language, literature, and composition, he has written more than a hundred textbooks in the field of English, including many published by Amsco. For nearly ten years, he was the editor of the teachers' magazine *High Points*. He has been active in professional organizations and has held office at the local, state, and national levels. A frequent speaker at English conventions and workshops throughout the United States, he has also lectured on educational television and frequently participated in curriculum development and evaluation. His latest trade books are *Shakespeare for the Modern Reader* and *Lexicon for Lovers of Language*.

Marie E. Christ has worked with Henry I. Christ as a partner throughout his writing career. She has provided many practical suggestions and usable materials. As always, her good judgment, common sense, and hard work played a major role in the development and preparation of this book.

Grateful acknowledgment is made to **Duncan Searl** for reading the manuscript and providing valuable input.

Special acknowledgment is made to **Mike Ross**, the editor of this project, who supervised the book at every stage, and kept the process moving. His calm good sense and confidence prevailed throughout.

Please visit our Web site at:
www.amscopub.com

Text and Cover Design: Merrill Haber

Text Composition: Publishing Synthesis

Cartoon Illustrations: Hadel Studio

When ordering this book, please specify:
either **R 312 W** or **AMSCO'S PREPARING FOR THE SAT IN CRITICAL READING AND WRITING**

ISBN 978-1-56765-124-9
NYC Item 56765-124-8

CONTENTS

DIVISION B   READING COMPREHENSION   175

DIVISION C   MASTERY TESTS/ CRITICAL READING   347

DIVISION D   WRITING   389

DIVISION E   MASTERY TESTS / WRITING   495

DIVISION F ANSWERS

INTRODUCTION

Preparing to Take the Scholastic Assessment Test (SAT)

You are consulting this book because you are planning to take the SAT. You may be wondering how to go about preparing for the test or hoping that some magic formula may be found here for obtaining a high score.

When Pharaoh Ptolemy I asked the philosopher Euclid whether there might be some easy way to learn geometry, Euclid is reported to have told him, "There is no royal road to geometry."

Nor is there a royal road to success on the SAT. What can you do? How can you prepare for so formidable a challenge? With so little time and so much at stake, how should you go about preparing for the SAT? Can any book provide the crucial help you need for this task?

Even if you have little time to prepare, there are some steps to take. You have not lived your life in a scholastic and cultural vacuum. You have been developing many skills throughout your life. Suggestions later in this introduction (pages xii-xiii) consider some of the short-term and long-term steps you may take.

Amsco's Preparing for the SAT in Critical Reading and Writing accepts the point of view that a crash course in amassing knowledge is impractical preparation. What *is* practical, however, is learning how to use the resources you already have and to develop certain key concepts and insights that will be helpful when you sit down to take the SAT.

This book is NOT a cram course. It is, instead, a program with specific major goals:

1. To develop writing, critical reading and critical thinking skills.

2. To explain test strategy in general and the SAT strategy in particular.

3. To demonstrate how you can put this strategy to good use.

4. To show you how to reach into your experiences for insights and answers.

5. To provide certain organizing principles that will help you to handle SAT questions.

6. To supply key information, like a detailed study of contexts and roots, that will repay a hundred times over the time you spend on mastery.

7. To build language power, not merely amass bits of knowledge.

8. To teach an awareness of language conventions and provide practice in accepted usage.

9. To develop increased proficiency in writing.

10. To be useful beyond the SAT, providing a source book and reference volume for the years ahead.

Doing well on the SAT is one goal. Doing well in later life is another. This book has been planned to help you with both. Cram courses have limited value beyond the demands of the present. A full program for the years ahead is much to be preferred. Keep the book for reference in later life.

A New Millennium

Whether the third millennium began on January 1, 2000, or January 1, 2001, the dramatic changeover aroused many fears and stimulated many hopes for a new day, after the discords of a troubled century. Computers, those willing servants and unyielding masters, had to be brought into line to prevent a worldwide meltdown. That all went well is a tribute to human resourcefulness and prudence.

Despite technological advances, certain verities remain. The world needs competent, rational, thoughtful human beings, capable of adapting to new challenges and unfamiliar situations. The ability to read, to reason, to function in a complicated world are qualities of paramount importance. Preparing to take the SAT sharpens those abilities. The SAT is not a casual test of marginal value. It rewards those candidates who give promise of benefiting from a college education and ultimately becoming a success in the larger world. You can become a member of this group.

How Does This Book Help?

1. It has as its major goal the building of language power, not the amassing of bits of knowledge—soon to be forgotten.

2. It analyzes in detail the kinds of questions on the SAT and provides detailed explanations of strategy.

3. It provides direct and specific help in handling questions involving vocabulary power. It develops strategies that will help you to approach new and unfamiliar words intelligently.

4. It stresses important matters like figurative language and allusions. It reviews and amplifies the subject matter, with abundant examples.

5. It provides extensive help in the area of roots, prefixes, and suffixes, with sample words, reviews, applications, and summaries.

6. The structure of the book is pedagogically sound. It is a-self-teaching text. Trial tests, examples, explanations, reviews, and summaries develop sound strategies for approaching SAT questions. A glance at the contents will give some idea of the book's teaching strategy.

7. The diagnostic tests and the mastery tests have cross-references to text pages where help can be found in answering the questions.

8. It provides ample practice in all areas of grammar and usage, with many activities similar to those on the SAT.

9. It encourages the writing of strong essays using the skills developed throughout the book.

10. By providing answers for all questions and detailed analyses for a great many, it provides self-teaching opportunities throughout. Thoughtful evaluation of a question is the key to competence. Check the table of contents for the location of answers not covered in strategies.

How Is the Book Organized?

The book is divided into six major divisions:

Division A: Vocabulary

Division B: Reading Comprehension

Division C: Mastery Tests / Critical Reading

Division D: Writing

Division E: Mastery Tests / Writing

Division F: Answers

Divisions A, B, and D are divided into *sections* specializing in the specific concepts and skills needed for the SAT. Each subsection in Divisions A and B follows a sound procedure. Subsections in Division D are presented in handbook form.

1. The topic is introduced and explained.

2. A *Trial Test* gives immediate practice in trying out the skill. Answers and analysis of the Trial Test provide further help.

3. A typical SAT question is introduced—called *Problem* in the text.

4. The problem is analyzed and a *Strategy* outlined to solve it.

5. *Review* provides additional drill and application.

6. A *Summary* pulls together the teaching points and reviews the information.

7. Frequent cross references reinforce those teaching points.

How Is Each Kind of Question Handled?

Sentence Completions. As the phrase *sentence completion* implies, you will meet sentences with gaps to be filled. Choosing the right answer depends upon your understanding of the total context, a concept fully developed in this book.

There are two different types of sentence completion questions. The first type is a straightforward vocabulary-in-context question. The second type combines vocabulary and reasoning. Understanding the sentence is as important as knowing the vocabulary.

In one form or another, vocabulary plays a major role throughout the SAT. The book provides ample assistance in mastering the basics.

Reading Comprehension Questions. This is a crucial area meriting a great deal of pretest attention. The reading test also tests vocabulary words as they are used in the passage. Since reading depends upon vocabulary—which is essential for all SAT questions—this entire book provides preparation for the reading test.

The reading passages run from 125–850 words. They include materials from the humanities, social sciences, natural sciences, and narratives. They concentrate more on the ability to make inferences than on the simpler identification of details. In addition, a pair of passages requires students to draw comparisons, point out contrasts, and identify supporting elements. See page 175 for a further discussion of the SAT reading test.

Though not every subject appeals to every person, the passages in this book, like those on the SAT, have been chosen because of their general interest. You will find them interesting as well as challenging.

To prepare for the test, take the reading tests in the book. Study the analyses. Read books, newspapers, and magazines that include complex ideas. Look for reading material that challenges you to think. When you read a passage, look for those specific words that contradict or support each choice.

Identifying Sentence Errors, Improving Sentences, and **Improving Paragraphs.** Each of these exercises test your awareness of standard usage and an appreciation of concise, effective writing. The testing techniques provide an opportunity to evaluate many kinds of errors. Analyses of the answers, pages 556–558, can lead to mastery of all the points tested. Always take the test first, before checking the answers.*

Short-Term Preparation for the SAT

Can anything be done at a late date to help you do well on the SAT? It's never too late to do something.

1. Concentrate on learning how the test works.

2. Follow the advice beginning with "long-term preparation" below.

3. Review the *Contents* pages of this book. Are there areas you consider yourself particularly weak in? Concentrate most of your time in these areas.

4. Read the introduction to each section (e.g., Section I, page 24) and go over *Problem* and *Strategy* (e.g., page 25) whenever possible. These will provide information in capsule form.

*Consult the table of contents for the placement of answers for 11 activities in this book. Problems are answered in the text.

5. Read the summary of each section (e.g., page 30).

6. Take the *Critical Reading Mastery Test* (page 351) to find out what your special strengths and weaknesses are. Study the answers and analyses (pages 537–540). Take as many of these as you can for practice.

7. Check the *Writing Mastery Test* (page 499) in the same way, to get an overview of the challenges ahead. Answers are on 562–563.

8. Focus on your weaknesses in the time remaining before the test.

Long-Term Preparation for the SAT

Long-term preparation is the ideal way to face the SAT. Getting a good education is the best way to prepare for a Power Test.

1. Try to broaden your reading. Choose some challenging books as well as entertaining ones. Figure out what the author means. Read between the lines.

2. Keep a vocabulary notebook or better yet a card file. List new words that challenge you. Don't interrupt your reading to look up every word, or you'll soon be discouraged. Make a brief note of the word's context and read on. Look up meanings later.

3. Tackle this book systematically. If you are in a class studying this text, your teacher will assign sections or suggest work to be done on your own. Starting on page 568, Amsco School Publications supplies to teachers suggested syllabi for getting maximum advantage from this book.

4. If you are not using this book in class, you will find it a self-teaching text. Questions are answered and analyzed in the book itself.

5. Set up a schedule, perhaps several hours a week at specified times.

6. Concentrate first on your areas of greatest weakness, but don't saturate yourself to the point of irritation. Occasionally work in other areas. Enjoy your strengths.

7. If you have enough time to proceed throughout the book, you will find cumulative reviews that refresh your memory about areas you've visited.

8. Several months before the SAT, begin trying your hand at the mastery tests. Pinpoint areas that still need attention while you still have time to do something constructive.

9. Don't put off the bulk of your study till the last minute. Cramming can be self-defeating.

Getting Ready to Take the Test

1. Set up a schedule of preparation with some time devoted each day to the project.

2. Don't cram. Probably, not a single last-minute fact will help on the exam.

3. Before the test, review key strategies as outlined in the *Introduction*. Go over the types of questions asked on the SAT. Be sure you are familiar with the test's structure. Take another look at the *Mastery Tests* (pages 351–387, 499–511) to see how questions may be arranged.

4. Keep yourself in good physical condition. The test is a nervous and physical drain.

5. Try to relax, especially the day before. Get a good night's sleep.

6. Become familiar with the way in which answers are recorded.

7. Arrive in plenty of time. Leave time for possible emergencies: traffic jams, flat tires, uncertain directions.

At the Test

1. Have a watch with you to gauge your allotment of time. Don't spend too much time on any one question. If you are stumped, go on to the next question. If you have time, go back for another look; since you may write on the test booklet, check a question you want to go back to. In a multiple-choice question, put a line through answers you've ruled out, so that you don't have to go back over those rejected answers on a rerun. Use the booklet in any constructive way you can. Use it as scratch paper, if you like.

2. Timing is an individual matter. If you are especially strong in vocabulary, you may sail through these, taking a quarter of the time another might take. One rough bit of advice is to allot, on average, about 30–40 seconds for a shorter question and 70–75 for a reading question, including the time spent for reading the passage. Thus, the time allotment is about twice as much for reading questions as for the others.

3. Take the shorter questions first. Run through these, nailing down as many as possible. If you are stumped on one, check it on the question booklet and move on. If you have time, go back, but don't use up too much time on any one question. You will probably discover that the sentence completions and analogies are arranged in the order of difficulty.

4. Read the directions carefully and follow them, noting the time allotted for the section you are tackling.

5. Since you will be penalized a fraction for incorrect answers, don't guess if you have absolutely *no* clue. If, however, you can definitely eliminate one wrong answer, you should probably guess among the others. You have raised the possible percentage a bit. An educated

guess is wise, but not a know-nothing stab. See the example ("When Guessing Helps") below.

6. Check your answer sheet to make sure that you are putting your answers in the right places. If you skip a question, be sure you skip a space on your answer sheet. Don't find yourself at the end with three additional spaces after you think you have put all answers in the right spots.

7. Keep moving, but don't rush. Haste can truly make waste. Occasionally take a deep relaxing breath. If you have devices for calming yourself down, use them. Don't panic.

8. Always look for the *best* answer. Some reading questions have several *possible* answers. You must choose the best. Although first impressions are frequently the right ones, these first impressions may prompt you to choose the first "right" answer that you come to. Snap judgments may be wrong. Always check *all* the alternatives before you answer a question.

9. Think positively. Keep cool. Don't suddenly become defeatist. Remember that there is no such thing as a failing mark. There is no magic number that you must reach to "pass." You may omit a number of answers and still do well. Give yourself the best chance. Do the best that you can with the resources you have. That's all you can be expected to do.

Good luck!

Postscript: When Guessing Helps

The following example demonstrates the strategy of guessing. Three students take the following test item. Who should guess?

EXAMPLE

Though ostensibly a put-down in its good-natured ribbing, the average "Celebrity Roast" turns out to be more of a _____ in reality.

   (A) critique
   (B) masquerade
   (C) eulogy
   (D) debacle
   (E) calamity

Student A hasn't the faintest idea. All answers look equally good. A should *not* guess.

Student B notices that because of *though,* the blank requires a word contrasted with *put-down.* B thus eliminates (E) altogether, but isn't too sure of the others. Even with one answer definitely eliminated B *should* guess.

Student C isn't sure of the answer but he does recall that *eu* appears in the word *euphemism,* just met in an English class. Realizing that *eu,* meaning "good," "well," may be the opposite of *put-down,* C *should* guess. The guess is a sound one. Though *eulogy,* a "speech of praise," is often delivered at a funeral, it is also appropriate in other contexts, as here.

A Note on Entering Answers

For convenience in machine scoring, the SAT supplies ovals to be blacked in. Here is a typical format.

EXAMPLE

Martha's Vineyard, once a sleepy vacation spot for _____ visitors, has now become a _____ mecca for hordes of sun-worshiping tourists.

(A) myriad . . quiet
(B) impoverished . . weary
(C) discriminating . . bustling
(D) impetuous . . depressing
(E) curious . . pensive

(A) (B) ● (D) (E)

This method, efficient for quick scoring, is unsuitable for the drill and analysis offered in this book. It uses a slightly different format.

EXAMPLE

Martha's Vineyard, once a sleepy vacation spot for _____ visitors, has now become a _____ mecca for hordes of sun-worshiping tourists.

(A) myriad . . quiet
(B) impoverished . . weary
(C) discriminating . . bustling
(D) impetuous . . depressing
(E) curious . . pensive

C

Take the following test for an advance look at what the SAT looks like. Find out which areas you are strong in. These areas won't require much work in the weeks ahead. Also find out which areas are most difficult for you. **Page numbers in parentheses refer you to specific areas of this book that explain and illustrate the testing point of each question.**

Complete Diagnostic Test for Critical Reading

For each question in this section, select the best answer from among the choices given.

Each sentence below has one or two blanks, each blank indicating that something has been omitted. Beneath the sentence are five lettered words or sets of words labeled A through E. Choose the word or set of words that best fits the meaning of the sentence as a whole.

EXAMPLE

Although its publicity has been _____, the film itself is intelligent, well-acted, handsomely produced, and altogether _____.
(A) tasteless .. respectable
(B) extensive .. moderate
(C) sophisticated .. spectacular
(D) risqué .. crude
(E) perfect .. spectacular

A

(pages 24–30)

1. Sharon expressed some _____ when she read that the stones in the Great Pyramid could build a(n) _____ wall around France ten feet high and nine inches wide.
   (A) consternation .. rock
   (B) apathy .. ugly
   (C) incredulity .. substantial
   (D) intransigence .. massive
   (E) exhilaration .. permanent

1 ___

(pages 24–30)

2. The *Information Please Almanac* is not only a _____ of relevant statistics but also a _____ of odd and specialized information, like aids to solving crossword puzzles.
   (A) compilation .. repository
   (B) compendium .. muddle
   (C) hodgepodge .. debacle
   (D) collection .. signpost
   (E) potpourri .. collaboration

2 ___

(pages 24–30)

3. Behavioral psychology suggests that our actions are _____ largely by conditioned responses to environmental _____.
   (A) influenced . . anomalies
   (B) described . . reports
   (C) improved . . successes
   (D) motivated . . suitability
   (E) determined . . stimuli

   3 ____

(pages 43–47)

4. The _____ beauty of California's Monterey coast is a combination of superb shoreline, dense forests of Monterey pines and cypresses, and _____ stands of windblown trees clinging tenaciously to rocky headlands.
   (A) famous . . lush
   (B) exquisite . . sparse
   (C) attractive . . murky
   (D) subtle . . towering
   (E) superb . . decaying

   4 ____

(pages 43–47)

5. Shortly after opening to high expectations, London's Millennium Bridge was closed down because as people walked on it, the bridge bounced and vibrated _____.
   (A) minimally
   (B) musically
   (C) naturally
   (D) disconcertingly
   (E) lethargically

   5 ____

(pages 35–39)

6. With his usual _____, beginning in 1786, Noah Webster _____ tirelessly for three years to have the new republic adopt his simplified spelling plan.
   (A) pathos . . traveled
   (B) pertinacity . . campaigned
   (C) megalomania . . meditated
   (D) unawareness . . barnstormed
   (E) fervor . . procrastinated

   6 ____

(pages 30–34)

7. Some scientists believe that popular _____ and _____ have reached dangerous proportions in this supposedly scientific age.
   (A) impassivity . . inquisitiveness
   (B) skepticism . . conviction
   (C) divination . . opportunism
   (D) sophistication . . trustworthiness
   (E) gullibility . . naiveté

   7 ____

(pages 24–30)

8. In one of the most _____ areas on earth, Mongolian nomads manage to _____ for the most part on mare's milk and the meat of fat-tailed sheep.
   (A) rigorous . . nibble
   (B) fertile . . celebrate
   (C) inhospitable . . subsist
   (D) well-traveled . . flourish
   (E) desolate . . luxuriate

   8 ____

(pages 24–30)

9. The schedule of operas in 25 American cities _____ the _____ pronouncements that opera is dead.
   (A) belies . . premature
   (B) advertises . . unenthusiastic
   (C) reinforces . . confident
   (D) promulgates . . pompous
   (E) accepts . . pervasive

   9 ____

For each question in this section, select the best answer from among the choices given.

Each passage below is followed by questions based on its content. Answer the questions following each passage on the basis of what is stated or implied in that passage and in any introductory material that may be provided.

This brief passage suggests how a person's worth should be measured.

1 Any man may play his part in the mummery, and act the honest man on the scaffolding; but to be right within, in his own bosom, where all is allowed, where all is
5 concealed—there's the point! The next step is to be so in our own home, in our ordinary actions, of which we need render no account to any man, where there is no study, no make-believe.

(pages 304–307)
10. The most important phrase in the selection is
    (A) on the scaffolding
    (B) to be right within
    (C) where all is concealed
    (D) in our own home
    (E) no study

10 ____

The following passage talks about the influence of language upon the lives of peoples past and present.

Toward the end of the last century people began to speak of languages as being "born," producing "daughter" languages, and eventually "dying"—undoubtedly because the
5 metaphor of a living organism came naturally to a generation that had recently learned about Darwinian evolution. Some languages were also thought to "give birth" to weak mutations, in which case euthana-
10 sia could always be practiced upon them by the eternally vigilant guardians of correct usage. The metaphor of language as a living organism persists to this day, but it is inherently false. A language does not live or
15 die. And unless it is to be considered merely a code to be broken (like Egyptian or Mayan hieroglyphics) or an intellectual pastime (like speaking Latin), a language has no life apart from the lives of the people who speak
20 it.
Today a more fitting metaphor might be the "ecology" of language—the web formed by strands uniting the kind of language spoken, its history, the social conventions of
25 the community in which it is spoken, the influence of neighboring languages, and even the physical environment in which the language is spoken. This metaphor empha-sizes that the function of language is to
30 relate its speakers to one another and to the world they live in. Eskimo, for example, is a language whose grammar makes it difficult to express certain ideas but very easy to say other things. It is spoken in the
35 particular physical environment of the Arctic Circle, which makes it understandable that this language should have a large vocabulary for describing different kinds of snow and seals. Its vocabulary has also been
40 influenced by the presence of neighboring Indian tribes and of Europeans. And the strategies for using the language are unconscious conventions of the social environment into which native speakers are
45 born—a speech community with its own ideas about the "rightness" or "wrongness" of whatever is said.
An Eskimo's language affords him a tremendous, possibly infinite, number of ways
50 he can communicate whatever he wishes to say—whether it be to impart information, to convince someone of the rightness of his cause, or just to be sociable. But in actuality his choice of exactly what he will say at any
55 particular moment is much more limited because his environment severely restricts

the strategies he can use. He will express the same thought differently in the igloo than he will on a hunt. And he will uncon-
60 sciously be influenced by his relationship to his listener, the role he intends to play in his society, whether or not an audience is present, and so on—with theresult that out of the many possible things he might
65 say, only a few choices are acceptable at the moment. Everything I have stated about the Eskimo holds true for speakers of other languages any place on earth.

(pages 178–181)

11. Which of the following best expresses the main idea of the passage?
    (A) An Eskimo's language affords him a tremendous, possibly infinite, number of ways he can communicate.
    (B) A language has no life apart from the lives of the people who speak it.
    (C) The Eskimo's vocabulary has been influenced by the presence of neighboring Indian tribes and of Europeans.
    (D) A language is part of the ecology and culture of the people who speak it.
    (E) Some ideas are easily expressed in some languages but not others.
                                    11 ____

(page 68)

12. In lines 9–10, *euthanasia* is an example of _____.
    (A) language misuse
    (B) irony
    (C) connotation
    (D) prose poetry
    (E) grammatical excess
                                    12 ____

(pages 202–205)

13. Although an Eskimo has a tremendous number of ways he can communicate, he is nevertheless restricted by his _____.
    (A) environment
    (B) education
    (C) desire to display his virtuosity
    (D) success or failure in hunting
    (E) status in his group
                                    13 ____

(pages 239–243)

14. All the following terms are mentioned EXCEPT _____.
    (A) igloo
    (B) Arctic Circle
    (C) whale
    (D) Egyptian hieroglyphics
    (E) Latin
                                    14 ____

(pages 189–191)

15. The selection suggests that the author _____.
    (A) supports the metaphor of language as a living organism
    (B) is equally at home among Eskimo or other groups
    (C) would support the reintroduction of Latin into the high school curriculum
    (D) would like to live among the Eskimos to study this fascinating speech community
    (E) is not judgmental about the superiority or inferiority of any language
                                    15 ____

(pages 189–191)

16. The selection suggests that in an unfamiliar speech community, a visitor might _____.

(A) be too assertive
(B) resent the differences
(C) stay briefly and leave
(D) find other speech patterns funny
(E) misconstrue intended meanings

16 ____

The following excerpt from a short story suggests the turmoil of late adolescence and an infatuation that flares up almost instantaneously.

It was eight o'clock on a warm September evening, and all the bells of Harvard were striking the hour. Elgin Smith, tired of studying, was standing on the steps of
5 Widener Library—those wide, Roman, inconvenient steps—blinking his eyes and staring into the distance, because that was supposed to refresh the corneas and the retina. He was thinking, but not of his
10 schoolwork. He was thinking of what it would be like to fall in love, to worship a girl and to put his life at her feet. He despised himself, because he feared he was incapable of passion and he believed that only pas-
15 sionate people were worthwhile and all other kinds were shallow. He was taking courses in English Literature, in German Literature, in Italian Literature, in History, ancient and medieval, and every one
20 of them was full of incidents that he thought mocked him, since they seemed to say that the meaning of life, the peak of existence, the core of events was one certain emotion, to which he was a stranger, and for which
25 he was very likely too rational. Therefore, he stood on the steps of Widener, so cracked by longing that it seemed only gravity held him together.

He was very tall, six feet three, and gan-
30 gling. He had a small head, curiously shaped (his roommate, Dimitri, sometimes accused him of looking like a wedge of cheese), and a hooked nose. He wanted to be a professor in the field of comparative
35 philology, and he believed in Beauty. He studied all the time, and there were mo-

ments when he was appalled by how hard he worked. He was known for his crying in movies. He was not unathletic.
40 Somehow, he had become convinced that he was odd and that only odd girls liked him, pitiable girls who couldn't do any better, and this singed his pride.

It was his fate that this particular night
45 he should see a girl walking up the steps of Widener Library. She was of medium height and had black hair cut short; she was wearing a light-colored coat that floated behind her because she was walking so fast,
50 nearly running, but not quite; and the curve of her forehead and the way her eyes were set took Elgin's breath away. She was so pretty and carried herself so well and had a look of such healthy and arrogant self-sat-
55 isfaction that Elgin sighed and thought here was the sort of not odd girl who could bestow indescribable benefits on any young man she liked—and on his confidence. She was that very kind of girl, that far from
60 unhappy, that world-contented kind, he believed would never fall for him.

She carried her books next to her bosom. Elgin's eyes followed her up the steps; and then his head turned, his nostrils distended
65 with emotion; and she was gone, vanished into Widener.

"Surely this year," he thought, looking up at the sky. "Now that I'm almost nineteen." He stretched out his arms, and the leaves
70 on the trees, already growing dry at the approach of autumn, rustled in the breezes.

He thought about that girl once or twice

in the days that followed, but the longing for her didn't really take root until he saw
75 her again, two weeks later, at a Radcliffe Jolly-Up in Cabot Hall. It was in one of the dimly lit common rooms, where couples were indefatigably dancing in almost total darkness. Elgin was swaying in place (he
80 was not a good dancer) with a girl who helped him on his German, when he caught sight of his Widener Library vision. When the next dance began, he wound through the couples looking for her, to cut in on her,
85 but when he drew near her, he turned and walked over to the wall, where he caught his breath and realized he was frightened.

This was the stroke that fatally wounded him. Knowing he was frightened of that
90 girl, he longed for her, the way men who think they are cowards long for war so they can prove they're not. Or perhaps it was some other reason. The girl had a striking appearance; there was her youth and her
95 proud, clean look to recommend her.

But whatever the reason, he did begin to think about her in earnest. She rose up in clouds of brilliant light in his head whenever he came across certain words in his
100 reading. ("Mistress" was one, "beautiful" another; you can guess the rest.) He did a paper on "The Unpossessable Loved One in Troubadour Poetry." When he walked through the Yard on his way to classes, his
105 eyes revolved nervously and never rested, searching all the faces on all the walks in the hope of seeing her. In fact, on his walks to classes he looked so disordered that a number of his friends asked him if he was
110 feeling ill, and it pleased Elgin, after the first two times this happened, to reply that he was. He was ill with longing.

At night, before going to the dining hall for supper, he would put on his bathrobe
115 and slip down to the pool in the basement of Adams House. There, under the wooden beams, he would swim angrily from one end of the pool to the other, faster and faster, until his arms ached. Then he would take a
120 cold shower.

When he slept, he dreamed of carnage, horses, and speeding automobiles. He went to French movies and ground his knees against the seat in front of him. He laughed
125 at himself, and decided to break this absurd habit he had got into of thinking all the time about this girl he had never met, but he didn't quite succeed. At last, he admitted to himself that he was in love with her; and
130 one night, sleeping in his lower bunk while Dimitri breathed heavily over his head, he had tears in his eyes because he was so foolish and did desire that girl whom he had seen the two times mentioned and only twice more besides.

(pages 189–191; 257–262)

17. Elgin's attitude can best be described as _____.
- (A) self-critical
- (B) overbearing
- (C) disdainful
- (D) condescending
- (E) apathetic

17 ____

(pages 181–184)

18. A good title for the selection is _____.
- (A) The Perils of Politeness
- (B) Obsession at First Sight
- (C) Love at Harvard
- (D) The Onset of Adolescence
- (E) Courage and Cowardice

18 ____

(pages 239–243)

19. All the following are courses mentioned in the passage EXCEPT
_____.
    (A) German Literature
    (B) Ancient History
    (C) Behavioral Psychology
    (D) Medieval History
    (E) Italian Literature

    19 ____

(pages 189–191; 257–262)

20. The girl on the steps of Widener Library is _____.
    (A) chosen as the prettiest girl on campus
    (B) a close friend of Dimitri
    (C) in several of Elgin's classes
    (D) idealized by Elgin
    (E) secretly admiring Elgin from afar

    20 ____

(pages 189–191)

21. That *beauty* is capitalized in line 35 suggests that Elgin _____.
    (A) may give up philology for aesthetics
    (B) is a better-than-average art critic
    (C) seeks out the artistic in Ancient History
    (D) has decorated his room with prints
    (E) emphasizes the abstract

    21 ____

(pages 189–191; 257–262)

22. Elgin's paper on the poetry of the troubadours _____.
    (A) was probably for a course in German Literature
    (B) was part of a plan to meet the girl
    (C) had autobiographical elements
    (D) reduced his longing to meet the girl
    (E) aroused Dimitri's scorn

    22 ____

(pages 202–205)

23. Which of the following best describes the girl as she is portrayed in the selection?
    (A) healthy, self-confident
    (B) striking, talkative
    (C) proud, unkind
    (D) pretty, blond
    (E) athletic, restless

    23 ____

(pages 189–191; 257–262)

24. Elgin's infatuation _____.
    (A) caused brief but severe consequences
    (B) made the girl uncomfortable
    (C) caused him to fail English Literature
    (D) made him look ill
    (E) caused him to speak to the girl at a dance

    24 ____

(pages 202–205)

25. The girl in Elgin's German class was
_____.
    (A) Elgin's secret love
    (B) one of the students Elgin tutored
    (C) a friend of the girl on the steps
    (D) an admirer of Italian Literature
    (E) a temporary partner at the dance

    25 ____

Section 2

For each question in this section, select the best answer.

Each sentence below has one or two blanks, each blank indicating that something has been omitted. Beneath the sentence are five lettered words or sets of words labeled A through E. Choose the word or set of words that *best* fits the meaning of the sentence as a whole.

EXAMPLE

Although its publicity has been _____, the film itself is intelligent, well-acted, handsomely produced, and altogether _____.
(A) tasteless . . respectable
(B) extensive . . moderate
(C) sophisticated . . amateur
(D) risqué . . crude
(E) perfect . . spectacular

<u>A</u>

(pages 24–30)

1. Sunflower seeds from an isolated valley in the Grand Canyon fortunately display a(n) _____ to a rust fungus _____ sunflower crops around the world.
   (A) dispensation . . enriching
   (B) genetic puzzle . . destroying
   (C) susceptibility . . affecting
   (D) immunity . . devastating
   (E) weakness . . revitalizing

   1 ____

(pages 52–57)

2. "If I seemed to _____ your _____," said Holmes, "I was merely trying to jog your memory a little."
   (A) impugn . . veracity
   (B) stifle . . curiosity
   (C) arouse . . wonder
   (D) quell . . hostility
   (E) enjoy . . repartee

   2 ____

(pages 30–34)

3. With a telltale _____ in his eye and a _____ in his voice, Morris slyly declared, "Don't talk when I'm interrupting."
   (A) flash . . rumble
   (B) note . . grating
   (C) twinkle . . chuckle
   (D) wink . . catch
   (E) tear . . sneer

   3 ____

(pages 39–43)

4. In their incredible 100-mile runs, the Tarahumara Indians of Mexico's Grand Canyon are as _____ as an Arctic tern on its _____ journey from the northern hemisphere to the south.
   (A) insulated . . chilly
   (B) concentrated . . stormy
   (C) serene . . dreaded
   (D) jaded . . motivated
   (E) indefatigable . . protracted

   4 ____

(pages 52–57)

5. Although the beneficial nematode is
   no bigger than a dust mite, its
   _____ appetite soon _____
   grubs, cutworms, and weevils.
   (A) disproportionate . . outnumbers
   (B) fortuitous . . demolishes
   (C) languid . . undermines
   (D) greedy . . irritates
   (E) voracious . . exterminates

5 ____

(pages 52–57)

6. Even when animals are _____ by
   unusual weather or any other alter-
   ations in their environment, they can
   undergo _____ changes in their
   populations.
   (A) disturbed . . statistical
   (B) unperturbed . . unpredictable
   (C) impacted . . significant
   (D) untroubled . . superficial
   (E) clustered . . indeterminate

6 ____

(pages 47–51)

7. According to Bernard De Voto, Presi-
   dent James K. Polk has been un-
   fairly underestimated, _____, and
   _____ by historians.
   (A) overlooked . . eulogized
   (B) underrated . . misjudged
   (C) neglected . . reappraised
   (D) confirmed . . castigated
   (E) depreciated . . rehabilitated

7 ____

(pages 47–51)

8. So-called "killer bees" have been la-
   beled _____ and even _____,
   but their bad reputation has been
   largely unearned.
   (A) bloodthirsty . . deadly
   (B) social . . disagreeable
   (C) unrelenting . . efficacious
   (D) superabundant . . harmless
   (E) feisty . . unvarying

8 ____

(pages 35–39)

9. The Chunnel between England and
   France is actually three tunnels, the
   middle of which is used as a safety
   _____ and escape route in case of
   fire or other _____.
   (A) process . . distraction
   (B) idea . . derailing
   (C) alternative . . emergency
   (D) procedure . . conflagration
   (E) trial . . combustion

9 ____

(pages 39–43)

10. From London to Delhi, the _____
   tomato has been as _____ a food
   as the potato and corn, other intro-
   ductions from the New World.
   (A) tantalizing . . bland
   (B) ubiquitous . . celebrated
   (C) tangy . . starchy
   (D) aromatic . . insipid
   (E) commonplace . . inspired

10 ____

The two passages below are followed by questions based on their content and on the relationship between the two passages. Answer the questions on the basis of what is stated or implied in the passages and in any introductory material that may be provided.

Television has brought sports vividly into every home. Each sport has its adherents. Two of the more articulate fans have their say in the following two passages. Answers are on page 517.

Passage 1
Baseball is the ideal spectator sport. The playing field is wide open, visible from every seat in the stands. The action is unhurried, with periods of intense action to vary the
5 pace. The knowledgeable spectator enjoys

strategy: the placement of outfielders for a strong left-handed batter; the position of infielders when bases are loaded; the decision to take a called strike during certain
10 situations; a risky hit-and-run attempt to upset the pitcher. The players demonstrate their grace and skill in a double play, a leaping catch in centerfield just below the stands, a slide beneath the catcher at home
15 plate. The game is not limited by rigid time constraints. A team can still rally from the depths to win the game.

Passage 2
1   Football is the ideal spectator sport. The physical contact emphasizes that this is a 60-minute war, waged by giant warriors in Star Trek outfits. The complexity of the
5 game satisfies the fans, who appreciate the many facets: the work of the opposing lines, the plays generated by the offense, and the counterattacks mounted by the defense. As in baseball, the spectator must follow the
10 ball, but, unlike baseball, the ball isn't where all the action is. Expecting a pass, the wide receivers are evading linebackers and cornerbacks, while the halfback is running off tackle. It is a game of deception pre-
15 sented with finely honed skills at every position.

(pages 189–191; 305–306)

11. The authors of both paragraphs _____.
    (A) emphasize the importance of physical contact
    (B) lukewarmly praise the opposing sport
    (C) grudgingly admit the weaknesses of their own choice
    (D) obviously prefer the sport they are describing
    (E) secretly enjoy the other sport
    11 ____

(pages 202–205; 305–306)

12. The author of Passage 1 _____.
    (A) considers the hit-and-run more exciting than the double play
    (B) places major emphasis on the visibility of all the action
    (C) believes in the superiority of left-handed batters
    (D) wishes for a speedier game
    (E) extols managerial skill
    12 ____

(pages 189–191; 305–306)

13. A major advantage of baseball over football is _____.
    (A) the greater skill of the participants
    (B) the almost constant tension
    (C) disregard of the clock
    (D) the greater number of play possibilities
    (E) the infrequency of disputes
    13 ____

(pages 202–205; 305–306)

14. The author of Passage 2 _____.
(A) implies that kicking is a major part of the game
(B) believes that defense wins games more often than offense
(C) doesn't consider the importance of the time limit
(D) thinks that football is easier to appreciate than baseball
(E) considers the complexity of football a major strength

14 ____

The passage below is followed by questions based on its content. Answer the questions on the basis of what is *stated* or *implied* in the passage and in any introductory material.

The following passage discusses the importance of clockmakers in the advancement of scientific knowledge.

Precisely because the clock did not start as a practical tool shaped for a single purpose, it was destined to be the mother of machines. The clock broke down the walls
5 between kinds of knowledge, ingenuity, and skill, and clockmakers were the first consciously to apply the theories of mechanics and physics to the making of machines. Progress came from the collaboration of sci-
10 entists—Galileo, Huygens, Hooke, and others—with craftsmen and mechanics.

Since clocks were the first modern measuring machines, clockmakers became the pioneer scientific-instrument makers. The
15 enduring legacy of the pioneer clockmakers, though nothing could have been further from their minds, was the basic technology of machine tools. The two prime examples are the gear (or toothed wheel) and the
20 screw. The introduction of the pendulum, by Galileo and then by Huygens, made it possible for clocks to be ten times more accurate than they had been, but this could be accomplished only by precisely divided and pre-
25 cisely cut toothed wheels. Clockmakers developed new, simpler, and more precise techniques both for dividing the circumference of a circular metal plate into equal units and for cutting the gear teeth with an effi-
30 cient profile. Clocks also required precision screws, which in turn required the improvement of the metal lathe.

Gears were, of course, the essential connective tissue in a mechanical clock. The
35 teeth in the wheels within the clock were not apt to be accurately spaced or cleanly cut if they were hand-hewn. The first gear-cutting machine of which we have any record is the work of an Italian craftsman,
40 Juanelo Torriano of Cremona (1501–1575), who went to Spain in 1540 to make an elegant large planetary clock for Emperor Charles V. Torriano spent twenty years planning a timepiece with eighteen hun-
45 dred gear wheels and then three and a half years building it. "So every day (not counting holidays)," his friend reported, "he had to make . . . more than three wheels that were different in size, number and shape of
50 teeth, and in the way in which they are placed and engaged. But in spite of the fact that this speed is miraculous, even more astounding is a most ingenious lathe that he invented . . . to carve out with a file iron
55 wheels to the required dimension and degree of uniformity of the teeth . . . no wheel was made twice because it always came out right the first time." During Torriano's lifetime his "lathe" was already being used by
60 other clockmakers. It appears to have become the model for the "wheel-cutting engines" used by English and French clockmakers in the seventeenth century, when timepieces were reaching a wider
65 market. Without such a device it would have been impossible for clocks to be made in large numbers for the commercial market. With such a gear-cutting machine, it was possible to make countless other ma-
70 chines and scientific instruments.

The screw, like the gear, was essential for a new world of machines. Its prototypes, like those of the gear, go back to the time of Archimedes or before. An ancient Greek
75 scientist, Hero, may have devised a screw-cutting tool. But making a simple screw long remained a difficult operation. Until the mid-nineteenth century, when finally screws were made with points, it was al-
80 ways necessary in advance to prepare a hole for the full length of the screw.

(pages 181–184)

15. A phrase from the selection that is most suitable for a title is _____.
    (A) The improvement of the metal lathe
    (B) Theories of mechanics and physics
    (C) The mother of machines
    (D) Wheel-cutting engines
    (E) The basic technology of machine tools

    15 ____

(pages 206–208)

16. The introduction of the pendulum can be attributed to _____.
    (A) Galileo and Hooke
    (B) Torriano and Huygens
    (C) Hooke and Galileo
    (D) Archimedes and Hero
    (E) Huygens and Galileo

    16 ____

(pages 189–191)

17. Clockmakers can be considered pioneers because they _____.
    (A) provided practical applications for scientific theories
    (B) disregarded previous knowledge and started anew
    (C) arranged for widespread distribution of their newest timepieces
    (D) found a use for ungainly wooden gears
    (E) disproved outmoded theories expounded by Archimedes

    17 ____

(page 226)

18. The author's style may best be characterized as _____.
    (A) intentionally disturbing
    (B) businesslike and informative
    (C) dense and argumentative
    (D) unnecessarily wordy
    (E) chatty

    18 ____

(pages 189–191)

19. Because of its nature and purpose, a clock needed parts that were characterized by _____.
    (A) artistry
    (B) lightness
    (C) precision
    (D) functionality
    (E) availability

    19 ____

(pages 202–205)

20. The most important element of Torriano's method of building his complicated clock was the _____.
    (A) toothed wheel
    (B) wooden screw
    (C) 1000 gear wheels
    (D) metal lathe
    (E) correspondence with Huygens

    20 ____

(pages 202–205)

21. The successful mass production of clocks can be attributed to the achievements of _____.
   (A) Archimedes
   (B) Charles V
   (C) Hero
   (D) Torriano
   (E) an anonymous genius

21 ____

(pages 202–205)

22. Clocks became more widely available _____.

   (A) because of the promotional efforts of Hooke
   (B) when Hero became active
   (C) before "wheel-cutting engines" were used
   (D) in the seventeenth century
   (E) in the mid-nineteenth century

22 ____

(pages 189–191)

23. At the time of Archimedes _____.
   (A) forms of the screw and the gear were known
   (B) perfect gears were already in use, but not screws
   (C) rivalry between Hero and Archimedes stifled progress
   (D) the first metal screw was developed
   (E) mechanical clocks were just beginning to come into existence

23 ____

(pages 202–205)

24. The invention of the pendulum increased a clock's _____.
   (A) durability
   (B) appearance
   (C) accuracy
   (D) barter value
   (E) speed

24 ____

(pages 24–30)

25. *Prototypes* as used in line 72 means _____.
   (A) inferior imitations
   (B) original models
   (C) descendants
   (E) rivals
   (E) machines

25 ____

(pages 202–205)

26. Torriano's efforts in completing his clock were successful because he _____.
   (A) was inspired by French clockmakers
   (B) created effective wooden wheels
   (C) worked under the constant vigilance of Emperor Charles V
   (D) adhered closely to the principles of Archimedes
   (E) invented a gear-cutting machine

26 ____

Section 3

3 3 3

The passages below are followed by questions based on their content. Answer the questions on the basis of what is stated or implied in the passage and any introductory material that may be provided.

The following passage takes an unusual attitude toward the hierarchy of cruelties.

To bereave a man of life, or by violence to confiscate his estate without accusation or trial, would be so gross and notorious an act of despotism as must at once convey the

5 alarm of tyranny throughout the whole nation; but confinement of the person, by secretly hurrying him off to jail, where his
sufferings are unknown or forgotten, is a
less public, a less striking, and therefore a
10 more *dangerous engine* of arbitrary government.

(pages 202–205; 304–307)

1. In the hierarchy of crime against hu-
manity, the highest place is accorded
to _____.
   (A) expropriating an estate unjustly
   (B) corrupt trial procedures
   (C) secret imprisonment
   (D) violence
   (E) murder

   1 ____

For each question in this section, select the best answer from among the choices given.

The two passages below are followed by questions based on their content and on the relationship between the two passages. Answer the questions on the basis of what is *stated* or *implied* in the passages and in any introductory material that may be provided.

In Passage 1, the author takes a dim view of pre-election polls for political office. The author of the second passage finds much to admire and little to condemn in the efforts of pollsters to keep the American public informed.

Passage 1

The intrusive polls of recent years have poisoned the political climate and subverted the aims of democracy. The entire political process is tainted by the daily rat-
5 ings changes, as though a presidential election is a day on Wall Street or an afternoon at the racetrack. For those who bet on horses, minute-to-minute changes indicate, by the odds posted, which horse is favored
10 and which might as well take the day off. Presidential races now seem similar, with constant changes in the expected percentages favoring a particular candidate.

Harmless? No. A major danger is that
15 fewer voters may go to the polls because they feel that the election has already been settled. If their candidate is winning in the polls, why waste a pleasant Tuesday afternoon voting to assure what is already assured? If their can-
20 didate is behind, why waste that same afternoon in a hopeless cause? In an article in *American Heritage*, Bernard A. Weisberger reports, "Some countries even forbid the publication of poll results immediately before the
25 election or projections until the last voting booth is closed."

There are two separate elements in Weisberger's statement: the polls before the election and the projections of winners on
30 the night of the election. The former might run into First Amendment considerations in America. The second might encounter geographical problems.

On the latter point: withholding projec-
35 tions in a country as large as the United States would require that voters wait until the wee hours of the next morning for results. But why not? Voters in the 2000 presidential election had to wait weeks to find
40 out who had won. Projections are an inexact science at best. In that 2000 election, Al Gore was at first projected to win the crucial electoral votes of Florida. Then the projection was reversed, and George W. Bush was
45 the projected winner. On the basis of this projection, Al Gore conceded the election. Then some discrepancies in the vote count were discovered, and Gore withdrew his concession. From then on, legal battles de-
50 layed the naming of the president for many weeks. So much for projections.

Pre-election polls, however, are another matter. This daily polling procedure could be eliminated by general consensus. How-
55 ever, such a consensus is probably doubtful. Nevertheless, an examination of the place of polls in American life can still be helpful.

What would be the advantage of giving up polls? For one thing, as noted already, it might minimize some of the notorious American voter apathy generated by knowing who will win anyway. There is another serious problem. Some commentators believe that constant poll-taking tempts candidates to modify their strategies, and ultimately their goals, in trying to following the polls instead of leading.

Still another disadvantage is the reluctance of financial backers to provide funds for an able candidate who is lower in the polls. Why support a candidate who is projected a loser?

Polling may have a legitimate place in consumer surveys, but choosing a president is another matter. If we must have polls, educate the public to recognize their pitfalls and misleading messages.

Passage 2

Polls are not a recent invention. As early as 1824, straw polls purported to indicate the way the political wind was blowing. In 1856, the *Chicago Tribune* polled 24 veterans of the War of 1812 and recorded their responses as predicting the election of John C. Fremont to the presidency. Like many future polls, this poll was flawed. James Buchanan was elected.

In modern times, two outstanding blunders by pollsters cast the entire philosophy of polling in doubt. In 1936, a magazine called the *Literary Digest* predicted the election of Alfred Landon. Franklin D. Roosevelt won in a landslide. In 1948, polls predicted the election of Thomas E. Dewey. Harry S. Truman won.

These two setbacks condemned the flaws, not the philosophy of polls. They exposed two major defects that modern pollsters try to avoid. In the 1936 poll, an unrepresentative sample was counted. In the 1948 poll, pollsters stopped surveying shortly before Election Day. They missed last-minute shifts and late decisions by previously undecided voters.

The entire philosophy of poll-taking rests on the assumption that a truly representative sample, even though a small percentage of the total number of prospective voters, will accurately indicate how the rest will vote.

Perhaps the outstanding example of accuracy in polling was the presidential election of 2000. As Election Day approached, the pollsters were confounded. They refused to pick a winner. George W. Bush and Al Gore were neck and neck. The crucial electoral vote of Florida eventually decided the election . . . by a hair.

Could polls have played a positive role in this scenario? They accurately predicted the closeness of the race. That should have alerted election supervisors in every county to make sure that electoral procedures were well thought out and not vulnerable to later second guesses. As it turned out, slipshod procedures did taint the election process. Paying attention to the polls might have averted this calamity.

Despite the *ifs* associated with taking the pulse of public opinion, pollsters claim that polls are healthy. Kathleen A. Frankovic, director of polling at CBS News, said, "Polls both inform and elevate the level of public discussion . . . reporting public opinion polls tells readers and viewers that their opinions are important." She added, "Poll bashing . . . is an antidemocratic fix, an elitist solution . . . a surrender to the notion that only some people's opinions matter." If democracy is enacting the will of the people, the pollsters vitalize democracy by reporting people's goals and deep-seated fears.

Surveys have been around for generations. The *Fortune Survey* had, as long ago as 1935, analyzed the financial climate at the time. Polling has not been reserved for political campaigns. It has helped to determine social and economic trends, forestalling negative or misguided decisions. Polling is here to stay because it provides a valuable public service.

(pages 24–30)

2. As used in lines 2–3, *subverted* means _____.
(A) reinvigorated
(B) overturned
(C) clarified
(D) advertised
(E) altered

2 ____

(pages 189–191)

3. Some countries forbid the posting of election poll results close to Election Day because _____.
(A) the polls are at least 20% inaccurate
(B) last-minute wagering may disrupt the process itself
(C) polls are manipulated to favor one candidate or another
(D) rioting may occur at the polling booths
(E) voters may be unduly influenced

3 ____

(pages 181–189; 291–303)

4. Which of the following titles best summarizes the content of Passage 1?
(A) Polling—an American Invention
(B) Projecting Election Results
(C) The Trouble with Polling
(D) The Early Failures of Polling
(E) The American Electoral Process

4 ____

(pages 202–205; 291–303)

5. One roadblock in the way of banning polls in America is _____.
(A) the First Amendment
(B) America's geography
(C) voter apathy
(D) the example of other countries
(E) incompetent election supervisors

5 ____

(pages 231–234; 291–303)

6. In Passage 1, the author is making a distinction between _____.
(A) good and bad politicians
(B) elections of 1936 and 2000
(C) projections and polling
(D) voter apathy and electioneering
(E) economic and social forces

6 ____

(pages 176–178; 291–303)

7. Which of the following elections best reflected the accuracy of polls?
(A) 1824
(B) 1856
(C) 1936
(D) 1948
(E) 2000

7 ____

(pages 202–205; 291–303)

8. The author of Passage 2 feels that the polls, properly used in 2000, could have _____.
(A) decided the president by the second day after the election
(B) assisted justices in handing down their opinions
(C) helped count the ballots in key counties
(D) averted confusion in election precincts
(E) saved the candidates millions of dollars

8 ____

(pages 236–239; 291–303)

9. "Straw polls purported to indicate the way the political wind was blowing" is an example of _____.
(A) exaggeration
(B) metaphor
(C) equivocation
(D) irony
(E) double entendre

9 ____

(pages 202–205; 291–303)

10. The failure of the *Literary Digest* poll
_____.

(A) was apparent even before election

(B) caused Harry S. Truman to rejoice

(C) suggested that Franklin D. Roosevelt would outlaw polls if he were elected

(D) can ultimately be blamed on inadequate sampling

(E) surprisingly provided the *Literary Digest* with favorable publicity

10 _____

(pages 176–178; 291–303)

11. The authors of both passages would agree that _____.

(A) polls advance the cause of democracy

(B) polls ultimately cast a shadow over the election process

(C) candidates are unaware of the frequent polls

(D) polls can be wrong

(E) the electoral college should be replaced by the popular vote

11 _____

(pages 197–200; 291–303)

12. While the author of Passage 2 is most concerned with the accuracy of the polls, the author of Passage 1 is most concerned with _____.

(A) the dishonesty of elected officials

(B) irresponsibility at the Cabinet level

(C) voter apathy

(D) candidates retaining Congressional seats while running for public office

(E) limitations on First Amendment rights

12 _____

(pages 202–205; 291–303)

13. Kathleen A. Frankovic and Bernard A. Weisberger would probably _____.

(A) take opposing positions on the value of pre-election polling

(B) accept a voluntary suspension of polling a week before a presidential election

(C) volunteer to count ballots in a close, disputed election

(D) critique the strategy of senatorial campaigns

(E) support a ban on projections until the last poll has closed

13 _____

(pages 209–212)

14. Which of the following were all 20th century presidential candidates?

(A) Fremont, Landon, Dewey

(B) Landon, Dewey, Roosevelt

(C) Buchanan, Dewey, Truman

(D) Fremont, Truman, Buchanan

(E) Landon, Roosevelt, Cleveland

14 _____

Division A

Vocabulary

Remember . . . When Preparing for the SAT

- Rely upon your built-in knowledge of words, the experiences you have already had with language. This book will show you how to use this built-in knowledge and how to expand your current vocabulary.

- Do not rely on studying long lists of difficult words. Unless you use the words soon afterward, you will probably forget them. Besides, the word lists you study may not contain any of the words on the test you will take.

- Master the skills of test-taking. This book will show you how.

The Sentence-Completion Segment

The next several pages will increase your vocabulary skills and help prepare you for the sentence-completion questions on the SAT. A knowledge of vocabulary is basic to success on these questions, but reasoning ability is also called for. The following pages will consider both vocabulary and reasoning ability.

Directions for the Sentence-Completion Segment

On the SAT, the directions for sentence-completion tests have the following wording.

> Each sentence below has one or two blanks, each blank indicating that something has been omitted. Beneath the sentence are five lettered words or sets of words labeled A through E. Choose the word or set of words that, when inserted in the sentence, best fits the meaning of the sentence as a whole.
>
> EXAMPLE
>
> Spiders, considered by many to be a _____, kill a hundred times their number in insects and help maintain the balance of nature.
> (A) freak
> (B) bête-noire
> (C) curiosity
> (D) champion
> (E) vertebrate
>
>

The ovals in the box above are the marking devices used by the SAT. See page xvi for an explanation of the method used in this book.

Vocabulary-Based Test Items

In the SAT, there are two basic types of sentence-completion items: those that call principally for your familiarity with key test words and "logic-based" questions that test your reasoning ability as well.

1. The dancer in the skeleton costume struck a(n) _____ note at the masked ball.
   (A) benign
   (B) omnipotent
   (C) macabre
   (D) lackluster
   (E) vacuous

A sentence of this sort presents few clues to the meaning of the omitted word. You may have a good idea of the probable effect of the costume on the other dancers, but you still need some knowledge of vocabulary. *Benign* (A), meaning "kindly," doesn't fit. *Omnipotent* (B), "all powerful," is also incorrect. It is unlikely that a dramatic skeleton outfit would qualify as *lackluster* (D), "dull." *Vacuous* (E), "stupid," makes little sense. Under certain conditions, perhaps with intended irony, some of the four rejected alternatives might fit, but the SAT requires you to choose the *best*, most sensible word. *Macabre* (C), meaning "gruesome" or "ghastly," sensibly completes the sense of the sentence.

2. When awakened suddenly from a deep sleep, Gordon tended to be _____ and his reply _____.
   (A) merciless . . roguish
   (B) pompous . . punctilious
   (C) uneasy . . dilatory
   (D) brusque . . laconic
   (E) grateful . . chivalrous

Sometimes the vocabulary-based question has two blanks, as in this example. The sentence here is not complicated or difficult, but knowing the meanings of the suggested alternatives is quite important. Try reading the sentence to yourself, substituting the suggested alternatives for the blanks.

(A) When awakened suddenly from a deep sleep, Gordon tended to be <u>merciless</u> and his reply <u>roguish</u>.

    It's conceivable that Gordon might be angry enough to be *merciless,* but then his reply would not be *roguish.*

(B) When awakened suddenly from a deep sleep, Gordon tended to be <u>pompous</u> and his reply <u>punctilious</u>.

    This is a sentence in which neither word in the pair makes sense.

(C) When awakened suddenly from a deep sleep, Gordon tended to be <u>uneasy</u> and his reply <u>dilatory</u>.

    These words could be stretched to make an offbeat kind of sense, but would this be the best answer?

(D) When awakened suddenly from a deep sleep, Gordon tended to be <u>brusque</u> and his reply <u>laconic</u>.

    Now we have it. Both words make sense, aptly suggesting an irritated ex-sleeper! But we haven't checked the last pair.

(E) When awakened suddenly from a deep sleep, Gordon tended to be <u>grateful</u> and his reply <u>chivalrous</u>.

    As in (C), this answer has a kind of sense in a special, perhaps humorous, situation, but when matched with (D), it is obviously inferior.

Logic-Based Test Items

Though long sentences look forbidding, they are sometimes easier to handle than shorter ones. If you keep your wits about you, you will often find that the extra words provide more clues.

3. After twelve days of fruitless debate, the jury reached an unbreakable _____ and had to be dismissed by the judge.

(A) contract
(B) conviction
(C) acquittal
(D) annulment
(E) impasse

The sentence provides the needed clues if you follow the reasoning. *Twelve days* is a long time for deliberations. The phrase suggests disagreement in the jury room. *Fruitless debate* states without qualification that nothing has been accomplished. *Unbreakable* carries along the sense of inaction. *Dismissed by the judge* provides the clinching information. The jury was deadlocked, unable to reach a verdict.

Even if the word *impasse* is unfamiliar to you, the sentence tells you that (E) is the correct choice if only by a strategy of elimination. Each of the other words suggests some kind of decision, a possibility ruled out by the original sentence.

(E) After twelve days of fruitless debate, the jury reached an unbreakable impasse and had to be dismissed by the judge.

Now the sentence makes sense.

4. Murray cultivated a(n) _____ personality, but his charming manner toward those he considered his equals contrasted with his _____ behavior toward all others.

(A) gracious . . condescending
(B) delightful . . sociable
(C) debonair . . affable
(D) unnatural . . vicious
(E) indifferent . . complicated

Sometimes this type of sentence-completion question also has two blanks, as in the example above.

(A) Murray cultivated a gracious personality, but his charming man-ner toward those he considered his equals contrasted with his condescending behavior toward all others.

This sentence works. *But* tells us that Murray's charm was superficial. The first word in the pair is positive in connotation; the second, negative. Important words like *but* are discussed on pages 52–53. The transitional function words are essential to the structure of the sentence.

For one reason or another, the other possible answers do not work. In (B) the second word, *sociable,* makes no sense when preceded by *but.* Both alternatives in (C) are positive, a distortion of the sense of the sentence. Both alternatives in (D) are negative, equally unsuitable answers. Neither word in the (E) pair makes much sense.

Note that though the sentence is rather long, its structure becomes readily apparent upon examination. It consists of three clauses: two coordinate clauses and one subordinate clause.

Coordinate:
  "Murray . . personality"
  "But . . others"

Subordinate:
  "[that] he . . equals

The subordinate (adjective) clause is nestled inside the second coordinate clause.

When you read a sentence with comprehension, you do not consciously identify clauses and phrases. Your knowledge of English sentence structure, acquired from childhood on, helps you to analyze a sentence quite unconsciously and to put sequences in order.

This introduction to the sentence-completion segment of the SAT is intended to suggest the general types of questions presented. In the following pages, you will have many opportunities to try your skill at handling sentence-completion items.

Section I: Context Clues

How did you learn that a **lane** is a narrow road, that a **platter** is a kind of dish, and that a **glove** is a hand covering? You probably never looked these words up in a dictionary. You learned them through experience, through hearing the words in a certain situation, a *context*.

Here, put on these **gloves** when you go out. It's cold outside.

You learned the word **glove** without having it defined for you. Nearly all common words are learned through the context of experience. Even words like **hope, love, friendship**, and **justice** are mastered in much the same way.

Here is another example.

That's not **fair**.

If you hear that expression applied to certain situations, you soon decide what is **fair** and what is **unfair.**

You have learned new words in your reading, too. Consider this sentence.

The sailors caught a dozen **pompano** and made a beach fire for a fish fry at sunset.

Even if you had never seen the word **pompano** before, you would know, from the context, that the pompano is a fish. The words surrounding **pompano**, the word's context, provide all the clues you need.

Each time you use a word in a new context, you sharpen your understanding of the word. One reading will often provide enough clues to learn a new word. The image created will also help you remember the word.

How will learning to use context clues help you in taking the SAT? One section of the test, the sentence-completion question, relies heavily on context clues for deriving the correct answer, but context helps elsewhere as well. First, let's sample a few easier sentences to familiarize you with the context clues in action and to analyze techniques for handling words. Next you will examine some actual test questions.

Context Clue 1: The Entire Sentence

This clue is a common one, but it sometimes requires some thought and ingenuity to make an intelligent guess with word meanings.

A. The **incessant** traffic noise outside my hotel window, though not loud, gave me scarcely a moment's sleep throughout the night.

What kind of noise would keep someone from sleeping? A loud noise would present a problem, but the sentence specifically says "not loud." What other quality of noise would interfere with sleep? Some kind of persistent noise. Is the noise in the quoted sentence occasional, or steady and continuous? "Gave me scarcely a moment's sleep" suggests that the noise is steady. It never stops. If the sentence had said the noise "interrupted my sleep," we might infer that the sound comes and goes. But the sentence tells us the noise "gave me scarcely a moment's sleep."

Therefore, **incessant** means "never stopping." As you will see later, the spelling of **incessant** provides some other clues to meaning, clues that help you nail down the meaning.

   B. As a result of the new owner's surprisingly **indolent** ways, the formerly flourishing farm sank into neglect and failure.

What ways would cause a farm to sink into "neglect and failure"? Certainly not careful, energetic, or efficient ways. A neglected farm is not worked enough. If it is not worked enough, the owner must be either lazy or physically unable to do the work. What is the best guess here? The word "surprisingly" suggests that everyone expected the new owner to do a good job. Apparently, the owner was not ill or physically incapacitated in any way. Therefore, he or she must be lazy. **Indolent** means "lazy."

Problem

Bill Cosby showed a keen understanding of family life, providing a(n) _____ role model for other parents to use.

(A) embarrassing (D) dogmatic
(B) confused   (E) positive
(C) superficial

Strategy. The expression *keen understanding of family life* suggests that Cosby's influence would be a good one. Such awareness immediately eliminates the negative (A), (B), and (C). Both (D) and (E) are possible, but the tone of *keen understanding* does not suit (D). It does suit (E).

    (E)   Bill Cosby showed a keen understanding of family life, providing a positive role model for other parents to use.

TRIAL TEST

Take the following short test to make sure you understand this kind of context clue. Write the letter of the word or words that have the same meaning as the boldfaced word.

After the flood the policyholders took some comfort in knowing that they would be **compensated** for their losses.
   (A) charged   (D) called
   (B) forgiven   (E) repaid
   (C) prepared

                  E

If the policyholders were comforted, then the correct choice is (E).

1. Through the binoculars we could **discern** two hikers on the ridge of Mt. Jefferson.
   (A) call to   (D) report
   (B) see   (E) wave to
   (C) photograph
               1 ___

2. Because the plan seemed **feasible**, the explorers put it into operation.
   (A) detailed   (D) workable
   (B) exciting   (E) commonplace
   (C) premeditated
               2 ___

3. After the **cessation** of hostilities, an unaccustomed calm settled over the city.
   (A) stopping   (D) description
   (B) expansion (E) denunciation
   (C) eruption
               3 ___

4. The medication **assuaged** the pain and permitted Charles a few hours of sleep.
   (A) localized   (D) recalled
   (B) varied   (E) lessened
   (C) inflamed
               4 ___

5. Bonnie made a **grimace** when she sipped the vinegar instead of the cider.
   (A) curtsy
   (B) prepared speech
   (C) distorted face
   (D) backbend
   (E) agitated dance step
               5 ___

6. In the tennis tournament, Jeanne slapped a hard volley to the corner, and Linda quickly **retaliated** with a smash down the line.
   (A) struck quietly
   (B) exclaimed bitterly
   (C) objected strenuously
   (D) found excuses
   (E) returned like for like
               6 ___

7. Mel couldn't conceal his **chagrin** when he tripped awkwardly in front of Betty.
   (A) embarrassment (D) expression
   (B) sense of humor (E) curiosity
   (C) delight
               7 ___

8. The March robin has always been the traditional **harbinger** of spring.
   (A) bird   (D) friend
   (B) forerunner (E) latecomer
   (C) lover
               8 ___

9. Pru worked **assiduously** throughout the night and completed her term report in time for morning class.
   (A) cheerfully   (D) industriously
   (B) thoughtlessly (E) prayerfully
   (C) frequently
               9 ___

10. In a relatively brief career, Jesse James **perpetrated** many crimes.

(A) committed
(B) solved
(C) reported
(D) permitted
(E) witnessed

10 ___

Now examine an actual test question. The question requires you to select the word or set of words that *best* completes the sentence.

Problem
Susan did not resent the arduous work, for she believed that every _____ that demands thought, attention, and independent judgment _____ the quality of daily life.
(A)   task . . heightens
(B)   profession . . belittles
(C)   hobby . . undercuts
(D)   folly . . exalts
(E)   diversion . . disrupts

Strategy. Here is a helpful first step. Finish the sentence with *your own words* before looking at the answers suggested. Taking this first step gives you some feeling for the structure of the completed sentence and helps with judging possible alternatives. Then evaluate the alternatives provided.

If you are unfamiliar with a word in the sentence, examine the context and make an intelligent guess. If, for example, you don't know the word *arduous,* you will find a lot of help in the context, or the other words, in the sentence. The sentence suggests that arduous work might be resented, for a special point is made of the fact that Susan did not resent it. What kind of work might be resented? A good guess is *hard work. Arduous* probably means "hard to do." But even if you did not determine the meaning of *arduous* exactly, you could still figure out that arduous work might be considered unpleasant. This judgment would assist in choosing the correct answer.

How do the various alternatives fit?

Choice *(A)* Try out the first pair.

Susan did not resent the arduous work, for she believed that every *task* that demands thought, attention, and independent judgment *heightens* the quality of daily life.

Task is obviously a good choice, for it is clearly related to "work" in the preceding clause. How does *heightens* also fit into the scheme? Sometimes in questions of this kind the first alternative may work, but the second one may not. Or the reverse may be true. If *heightens* is an unfamiliar word to you, the word within it is a clue. The word *height* is associated with intensity. The height of indignation, for example, is an intense form of indignation. *Heightens* probably means "make more intense." Does the word make sense in the completed sentence? Obviously it does. A demanding task improves the quality of everyday living.

Notice that now the entire sentence makes sense. Susan did not resent hard work because she realized that challenging tasks make living richer. These two words *(task* and *heightens)* fit admirably well. But the directions say to select the words that <u>best</u> complete the sentence. Perhaps there are other words that do an even better job.

Choice *(B)* If you insert *profession* and *belittles,* you run into problems. *Profession* isn't as good a word as *task,* but it does make sense. However, what of *belittles? Belittles* destroys the meaning of the sentence. *Belittle,* clearly meaning "make little," makes nonsense of Susan's attitude. Choice *(B)* then is incorrect.

Choice *(C)* If you insert *hobby* into the first blank, you have a barely possible answer but not so good an answer as that in *(A).* The required word should involve arduous work. A task certainly involves arduous work, as does a profession. A *hobby* might involve arduous work, but *hobby* is a leisure-time activity. Go on to *undercuts.* This presents the same problem as *belittles* in *(B).* Even if you are not precisely sure of the meaning of *undercut* ("to make less effective"), you can still be sure the idea is negative. The barely possible *hobby* and the unsuitable *undercuts* make this a poor choice.

Choice *(D)* If you insert *folly* into the first blank, you run into trouble immediately. *Folly* runs counter to the idea of work. Susan accepts work but not folly. Besides, *folly* doesn't demand "thought, attention, and independent judgment." You can reject this choice immediately, but just to be sure, you ought to try out the second word in the second blank. If you know that *exalts* means "raises up, glorifies," you have verified your guess that *(D)* is incorrect. If you do not know the meaning of *exalts,* you have still rejected *(D)* because *folly* doesn't make sense. Thus far no alternative is as good as *(A).*

Choice *(E)* The first choice in *(E)* is *diversion,* a hard word. You can guess at the meaning by looking at the little word within the bigger one and noting related words (*divert, diverse, diversity*). A strategy for handling this skill is discussed later (page 83). Fortunately, however, you don't have to waste too much time, for if one alternative in the pair is incorrect, the answer is incorrect. Look at *disrupts. Disrupts* (meaning "breaks up, disturbs") is a fairly common word, but even if it is unfamiliar to you, you can guess that a word beginning with *dis* may well be a negative word. *Dislike, displease,* and *disloyal* are all negative words. The context of the entire sentence requires a positive word here. Why else would Susan not resent the arduous work? A *diversion* that disturbs or lessens the quality of everyday life would <u>not</u> be Susan's choice.

The preceding analysis shows certain things.

1. You don't have to know every word to get the answer correct.

2. By a process of elimination, you can often find the best answer. Quite often it is enough to guess intelligently at only one of the choices.

3. The context of the sentence AS A WHOLE is the crucial element in the answer. Just ask: "What words make best sense when inserted into the blanks?"

Although we have taken a lot of time to analyze each choice carefully, you will not need to spend as much time in deciding upon your answer. Trying out all alternatives rapidly and in succession often gives you a feeling for the sentence as a whole. Quite often the correct answer will jump from the page. At other times, a little more careful evaluation will be necessary.

REVIEW   *(Answers to Review Tests begin on page 534.)*

Write the letter of the word or words that have the same meaning as the boldfaced word.

1. The group of **ornithologists** went on lengthy bird-watching hikes.
   (A) dental specialists
   (B) champion spellers
   (C) bird experts
   (D) story collectors
   (E) bone doctors

   1 ___

2. A victim is doomed because there is no known **antidote** for the rare snake-bite.
   (A) amusing story
   (B) appetizer
   (C) old furniture
   (D) remedy
   (E) deer

   2 ___

3. The audience was shrieking with laughter, but no one could discover the reason for such **levity**.
   (A) frivolity
   (B) tax
   (C) riverbank
   (D) floating in air
   (E) controlling device

   3 ___

4. No one knew the reason for the sudden, **prodigious** increase in real estate values in so short a time.
   (A) small
   (B) enormous
   (C) average
   (D) disappointing
   (E) expected

   4 ___

5. The play *Blithe* Spirit is about a non-threatening, fun-loving ghost.
   (A) ghostly
   (B) athletic
   (C) deteriorated
   (D) cheerful
   (E) flexible

   5 ___

6. Totally absorbed in the computer program, the students were **oblivious to** the hallway noises.
   (A) unaware of
   (B) antagonistic toward
   (C) concerned about
   (D) absorbed in
   (E) distracted by

   6 ___

7. Because of the **plethora** of jobs and housing in the area, everyone was well off.
   (A) curse
   (B) plentiful supply
   (C) lack
   (D) lung disease
   (E) blessing

   7 ___

8. The press club did a hilarious **parody** of the candidates' debate, called "The State of Disunion."
   (A) talking bird
   (B) abnormal distrust
   (C) contradictory statement
   (D) one-celled creature
   (E) humorous imitation

   8 ___

9. At its **apogee** the satellite reached its maximum distance of 480 miles from earth.
   (A) words of regret
   (B) vicious attack
   (C) farthest point
   (D) lack of interest
   (E) window opening

   9 ___

10. The job is too much responsibility for a **callow** youngster, hardly out of school.
    (A) thick-skinned
    (B) immature
    (C) lily-like
    (D) rich in food energy
    (E) experienced

    10 ___

SUMMARY

Context Clue 1: The Entire Sentence

When you deal with the problem in an SAT question, there are strategies to use. Often the entire sentence provides clues to the meaning of a word in that sentence.

1. Complete the sentence with *your own words* before looking at the choices.

2. Then go ahead and work with the choices provided.

3. If you are not familiar with a word, examine the word's context. Then make an intelligent choice.

Context Clue 2: Pairing

Problem

The 13th-century carved ivory and bronze portrait busts of Benin in West Africa are _____ designed and competently modeled.

(A) irregularly
(B) skillfully
(C) properly

(D) strangely
(E) fortunately

Strategy. This example emphasizes the importance of getting the *best* answer, not just an acceptable answer. (A) and (E) seem out of the running and may be rejected at once, but the others can fit and still make sense. The conjunction *and* is intended to link equivalent items. Which word is closest in association to *competently?* The answer is (B) *skillfully. Properly* (C) makes a judgment without much meaning. What is a "properly" carved ivory? *Strangely* (D) is certainly a possibility, but without additional context, the reader must stick with (B). In answering sentence-completion questions, check whether a pair of words suggests the meaning.

> (B)   The 13th-century carved ivory and bronze portrait busts of Benin in West Africa are skillfully designed and competently modeled.

Since writers often repeat themselves slightly to make a point, watch out for paired words. If you don't know the first word, you'll probably know the second.

> Pauline was an **ardent**, enthusiastic collector of old Roman coins.

Since the words *ardent* and *enthusiastic* are paired and descriptive of the same person, you have good reason to believe they are related. *Enthusiastic,* a common word, provides a substantial clue to the less common word *ardent.*

TRIAL TEST

Take the following trial test to make sure you understand this type of context clue. Write the letter of your answer in the space at the right.

Benedict Arnold at last was **perfidious,** faithless to the ideals he once professed.
  (A) fastidious   (D) egotistical
  (B) talented   (E) treacherous
  (C) relentless

$$\dfrac{\quad E \quad}{}$$

"Faithless" makes clear that **perfidious** means *treacherous (E).*

---

1. Perry has a colorful, **flamboyant** style of dress that sets him apart.
   (A) drab   (D) happy
   (B) showy   (E) irritating
   (C) conservative

   1 __

2. The audience's **acclamation** gratified the soloist, who liked the obvious approval of her performance.
   (A) interest   (D) applause
   (B) participation   (E) coolness
   (C) evaluation

   2 __

3. Scrooge's actions were mean and **despicable**.
   (A) aware
   (B) unpredictable
   (C) generous
   (D) desperate
   (E) unkind

   3 __

4. The lawyer **demurred**, disapproving the suggested settlement.
   (A) objected (D) orated
   (B) chuckled (E) sat down
   (C) consented

   4 ___

5. It is not unusual for a young child to live in **reveries** and daydreams.
   (A) nurseries (D) prayers
   (B) realities (E) misgivings
   (C) fantasies

   5 ___

6. The treasurer's reports were always **concise** and to the point.
   (A) elaborate
   (B) uninformative
   (C) funny
   (D) brief
   (E) labored

   6 ___

7. The mountain climb proved too **arduous** and difficult for the inexperienced members of the party.
   (A) monotonous (D) chilly
   (B) strenuous (E) rocky
   (C) unexpected

   7 ___

8. To **malign** someone, to tell an evil lie about him, might lay the speaker open to charges of slander.
   (A) wrong (D) irritate
   (B) advertise (E) discuss
   (C) report

   8 ___

9. The inhabitants of the besieged city endured **privation** and hardship unknown in peacetime.
   (A) fury (D) experiences
   (B) want (E) repetition
   (C) excitement

   9 ___

10. Ever since he failed the math test, Greg has been **morose** and ill-tempered.
    (A) excitable (D) speechless
    (B) resigned (E) gloomy
    (C) vicious

    10 ___

Problem

Ms. Wilton urged patience and _____ in dealing with the protesters rather than the unyielding attitude the administration had adopted.

(A) obstinacy (D) compromise
(B) desperation (E) retaliation
(C) arrogance

Strategy. Here "patience" is obviously being paired with the word needed in the blank. How does each of the alternatives fit as a possible member of the pair?

Choice *(A) Obstinacy* doesn't fit the blank too well. *Obstinacy* (remember the adjective *obstinate*) means "stubbornness." Stubbornness does not go well with patience.

Choice *(B) Desperation* is a poor match as well. *Desperation* (remember *desperate),* like *obstinacy,* does not go well with patience.

Choice *(C) Arrogance* clashes with patience. Arrogant persons are rarely patient, for they want their way—immediately.

Choice *(D) Compromise* is a good match. Patient people are not overbearing or in a hurry. They are willing to take time, to see other sides, to make adjustments in their own viewpoints. *Compromise* seems like the answer, but make sure by looking at the last possibility.

Choice *(E) Retaliation* conflicts directly with patience. To *retaliate,* to "strike back," may come after patience has been exhausted, but it does not match patience.

Compromise (D) is obviously the right answer. Notice that this sentence also provides other clues. The sentence as a whole calls for a positive word in the blank.

As you work with context clues, you will often find several in one sentence, all helping you to learn the unfamiliar word.

REVIEW

Write the letter of the word or words that have the same meaning as the boldfaced word.

1. The combination of high inflation and low employment was a **paradox**, a pairing of opposite conditions.
   (A) heavenly place
   (B) example
   (C) established custom
   (D) contradiction
   (E) illustrative story

   1 ___

2. The Delmarva Peninsula **comprises**, or includes, parts of three states: Delaware, Maryland, and Virginia.
   (A) agrees to
   (B) contains
   (C) obeys; follows
   (D) promises
   (E) understands

   2 ___

3. With the sandals, gym shorts, and cap, the white shirt and tie were indeed **incongruous**, hopelessly out of place.
   (A) without ability
   (B) without a name
   (C) inappropriate
   (D) disrespectful
   (E) colorful

   3 ___

4. One warning of an earthquake is a display of uncommon, **unwonted** behavior of animals.
   (A) brilliant
   (B) unusual
   (C) angered
   (D) irreverent
   (E) colorful

   4 ___

5. The news of the fare increase was received with **vituperation** and abusive remarks.
   (A) a sense of humor
   (B) a healthful food element
   (C) bitter scolding
   (D) surgery
   (E) approval

   5 ___

6. There was an unspoken, **tacit** agreement that all expenses would be shared.
   (A) diplomatic; courteous
   (B) silent; understood
   (C) maneuverable
   (D) touching
   (E) debatable

   6 ___

7. Money had not been a problem for Gale since she came into the bequest, or **legacy**, from her aunt.
   (A) old tale
   (B) inheritance
   (C) veterans' group
   (D) lawsuit
   (E) readable writing

   7 ___

8. It isn't worth all the trouble to get a measly, **paltry** 20-cent refund.
   (A) small
   (B) pale
   (C) unexpected
   (D) trembling
   (E) warm

   8 ___

9. The house in the expensive new neighborhood seemed showy and **ostentatious**.
   (A) swinging to and fro
   (B) banished; shut out
   (C) modest
   (D) pretentious; done to attract attention
   (E) absorbent

   9 ___

10. After the business failed, the owner was **destitute**, without a penny to his name.
    (A) very sad
    (B) deserted
    (C) very poor
    (D) dried out
    (E) like a tyrant

    10 ___

SUMMARY
Context Clue 2: Pairing

1. Be on the lookout for paired words or ideas. (Writers often repeat themselves to make a point.)

2. If you don't know one of the words or ideas, you may know the other.

Context Clue 3: | Direct Explanation

Problem
All our farm animals had been _____ by the year 2000 B.C.; but since that time no new animals have been added to the farmer's workforce. (A) described   (D) noticed (B) domesticated   (E) captured (C) painted

Strategy. The sentence here deals with the practical uses of animals, as the last two words disclose. Therefore the best answer is (B) *domesticated*. The other answers make some kind of sense, but not one of these answers is relevant to the second clause: "but . . . workforce."

    (B)   All our farm animals had been domesticated by the year 2000 B.C., but since that time no new animals have been added to the farmer's workforce.

Surprisingly often, a tricky word will actually be explained in the same sentence in which it appears.

    Greg was so **avaricious** he refused to spend money even for necessities and almost starved among his collection of gold coins.

The sentence provides the explanation of **avaricious**. Someone who hoards money unwisely, who refuses to spend even for necessities, is "greedy to the point of sickness." There you have the definition of *avaricious*.

Sometimes an appositive provides the direct explanation you need.

    Hedonism, the pursuit of pleasure at all costs, may lead to misery.

The appositive phrase, "the pursuit of pleasure at all costs," clearly tells the meaning of **hedonism**. It defines the word in context.

Sometimes a participial phrase provides helpful clues to the meaning of a word.

    Gazelles are **herbivorous**, eating only grasses and other vegetation.

The participial phrase, "eating only grasses and other vegetation," tells the meaning of **herbivorous**. It, too, defines the word in context.

TRIAL TEST

Take the following trial test to make sure you understand this type of context clue. Underline the word or words that explain the boldfaced word. Write the letter of your answer in the space at the right.

Jud's remarks served to **exacerbate** the problem, making a solution more remote than ever.
- (A) slightly ease
- (B) make worse
- (C) clearly reveal
- (D) cleverly explain
- (E) repeat

_____ B

"Making a solution more remote than ever" explains **exacerbate**. The correct answer is *make worse (B)*.

1. Jody lived a **sedentary** life, rarely engaging in exercise or even leaving the house for a walk along the colorful streets near his home.
   - (A) lively   (D) inactive
   - (B) varied   (E) interesting
   - (C) puzzling

   1 ___

2. Each wave of frantic buying and selling in the stock market tends to **subside**, or settle down, after a short time.
   - (A) calm down   (D) explode
   - (B) whirl about   (E) recover
   - (C) stir up

   2 ___

3. In carpentry, Chuck is a model of **ineptitude,** hitting a finger with a hammer and sawing a crooked line.
   - (A) humor   (D) surprise
   - (B) clumsiness   (E) discontent
   - (C) failure to plan

   3 ___

4. A 20-degree day can feel like ten below zero, depending on the wind **velocity**, the speed at which it is blowing.
   - (A) heat
   - (B) unpredictability
   - (C) agreement
   - (D) good fortune
   - (E) rapidity

   4 ___

5. Among the high-risk group are fairly inactive adults with a **predilection**, or taste, for cholesterol-rich foods.
   - (A) amusement   (D) preference
   - (B) necessity   (E) portion
   - (C) accuracy

   5 ___

6. Senator Fogg launched into his usual **harangue**, an endless lecture on the frightful conditions everywhere.
   - (A) long, ranting speech
   - (B) exclamation of pleasure
   - (C) humorous comment
   - (D) obvious lie
   - (E) dessert

   6 ___

7. When they heard the Prime Minister's proposals, the members were **derisive,** hooting and howling their displeasure.
   - (A) violent   (D) silent
   - (B) scornful   (E) secure
   - (C) joyous

   7 ___

8. A portion of the sign **protrudes** be-
   yond the corner of the building, pre-
   senting an obstacle for every passerby.
   (A) becomes visible
   (B) is being constructed
   (C) twists
   (D) sticks out
   (E) reappears

   8 ___

9. The assassination of the Archduke Ferdinand **precluded** a peaceful solution,
   making unavoidable the mass slaughter of World War I.
   (A) foretold   (D) presented
   (B) unfolded   (E) suggested
   (C) prevented

   9 ___

10. Mr. Allen was **parsimonious** by na-
    ture, miserly and thrifty to the point of
    excess.
    (A) thoughtful
    (B) clever
    (C) stingy
    (D) small
    (E) suspicious

    10 ___

Problem

Meteors become _____ only after they
enter the atmosphere, for it is then that
they begin to burn and leave their luminous trails.

(A) incandescent   (D) reflective
(B) invisible   (E) elemental
(C) illusionary

Strategy. Quite often, a clause beginning with "for" (meaning "because" or "since") actually explains the point of the previous clause.

I screamed, for the pain was intense.

Similarly, in the test sentence, the "for" clause says specifically that meteors "burn and leave luminous trails." If the word "luminous" is new to you, you have the word *illuminate* to fall back on. Also, when something burns, it is usually bright.

Choice *(A) Incandescent* might be a familiar word to you because of the incandescent electric light bulb. This seems like a good answer because the "for" clause has just told you that the meteors burn and leave bright trails.

Choice *(B) Invisible* is incorrect. If meteors burn brightly, they can't be invisible.

Choice *(C) Illusionary* suggests trickery or deception, from the word *illusion*. But there's nothing tricky or deceptive about the meteor's bright trail.

One meaning of choice *(D) Reflective* doesn't make sense in the sentence. The other meaning is a possibility: "throwing back light." However, it doesn't fit as well as Choice *(A)*.

Choice *(E) Elemental* has nothing to do with brightness.

Note that the sense of the entire sentence is also a clue to meaning here.

Quite often a subordinate clause actually explains the point of the main clause.

> The Congressional committee sought to investigate **covert actions**, which had been concealed illegally from the American public.

This time the "which" clause explains that **covert actions** deal with illegal concealment.

REVIEW

Write the letter for the word or words that have the same meaning as the boldfaced word in each sentence.

1. Some citizens continue to live in **abject** poverty, with no way to escape from it.
   (A) conforming   (D) forgiven
   (B) hopeless   (E) temporary
   (C) sudden

   1. ___

2. "Waste not, want not" is an old **maxim**, a tried and true bit of advice.
   (A) wise saying
   (B) greatest amount
   (C) person who knows everything
   (D) woman in charge
   (E) grown-up person

   2 ___

3. In combat, a large tent may house an **infirmary**, a hospital for the injured.
   (A) shaky place
   (B) kind of tent
   (C) treatment place
   (D) illness
   (E) endless distance

   3 ___

4. Only a trained eye can **discern**, or tell the difference between, a high and low quality diamond.
   (A) disagree   (D) control; train
   (B) recognize   (E) throw away
   (C) rule out

   4. ___

5. The entire school was run by a small, **arrogant** group, who lorded it over the rest of the students.
   (A) well-spoken
   (B) aromatic
   (C) haughty; scornful
   (D) romantic
   (E) disorderly; confused

   5 ___

6. Wherever the terrorist went, he was a **firebrand**, who stirred up the people to revolt and strike.
   (A) good speaker (D) newscaster
   (B) messenger   (E) troublemaker
   (C) friend

   6 ___

7. In the 14th century, the Black Death was **rampant** in Europe, raging unchecked through the crowded cities.
(A) unrestrained
(B) unfortunate
(C) unexpected
(D) unforced
(E) unpopular

7 ___

8. The comic John Paul entered with his hat **askew**, for it perched at an impossible angle on his head.
(A) colorful
(B) upside down
(C) reversed
(D) crooked
(E) untouched

8 ___

9. The counsel for the defense took strong exception to the prosecutor's **derogatory** comments, which humiliated the defendant and prejudiced the case against him.
(A) unfavorable and disparaging
(B) generous but sarcastic
(C) fierce and cruel
(D) unexpected and partial
(E) thoughtless and indefinite

9 ___

10. A book jacket often gives a **synopsis** of the plot, summarizing the major events.
(A) grammatical system
(B) condensation
(C) combination
(D) artificiality
(E) simultaneous event

10 ___

SUMMARY
Context Clue 3: Direct Explanation

For help with this kind of context clue, look for:

1. An appositive: an explanatory word or phrase set off by a comma or a pair of commas.

2. A participial phrase explaining the meaning of the key word.

3. An explanation beginning with *for,* meaning "because" or "since."

4. An explanation provided by a subordinate clause.

Context Clue 4: Comparison

Problem

The ruins of Pompeii reveal a city as _____ as any pleasant resort city in the modern world.

(A) tragic
(B) flamboyant
(C) poorly run
(D) polluted
(E) comfortable

Strategy. The comparison tells all. Pompeii is compared with a modern pleasant resort city. *Pleasant* suggests that the basis of comparison is positive, not negative. Thus (C) and (D) should be eliminated. Pompeii is certainly a tragic memory, but *tragic* (A) conflicts with *pleasant*. *Flamboyant* (B) is nowhere suggested. The remaining alternative, (E), makes sense.

    (E) The ruins of Pompeii reveal a city as comfortable as any pleasant resort city in the modern world.

Sometimes a sentence will reveal the meaning of an unfamiliar word by including a helpful comparison.

    In attacking the problem, Sandy was as **diligent** as a bee gathering honey.

A characteristic of a "bee gathering honey" is single-minded devotion to the task. The comparison tells us Sandy was hard-working and industrious.

TRIAL TEST

Take the following trial test to make sure you understand this type of context clue. Write the letter of your answer in the space at the right.

After the hostage was **liberated**, he felt as free as a bird.
    (A) embarrassed
    (B) let go
    (C) educated
    (D) changed
    (E) understood

                    B

"As free as a bird" tells how a hostage that is "liberated" will feel if he is *let go. (B)*

1. Dundee often displays the **irascibility** of a wasp whose nest has been disturbed.
    (A) subtle charm
    (B) cowardly behavior
    (C) quickness to anger
    (D) inventive genius
    (E) sweetness

                  1 ___

2. With the subtlety of a hammer smashing an eggshell, Frank **bludgeoned** everyone to agree.
    (A) asked   (D) destroyed
    (B) elected   (E) bullied
    (C) calmed

                  2 ___

3. The interior of the building was as **murky** as winter twilight with an overcast sky.
    (A) brilliant   (D) colorful
    (B) cold   (E) odorous
    (C) gloomy

                  3 ___

4. Pete's **incessant** interruptions had all the qualities of endless drops from a leaky faucet.
    (A) irrelevant   (D) exaggerated
    (B) sharp   (E) ill-tempered
    (C) continuing

                  4 ___

5. When the dinner bell is sounded, Carl moves with the **alacrity** of a startled lizard.
(A) quick motion (D) resourcefulness
(B) intelligence (E) body language
(C) grace

5 ___

6. Jan's costume was as **incongruous** as an evening dress at a picnic.
(A) dazzling (D) indecisive
(B) pleasing (E) unavailing
(C) unsuitable

6 ___

7. Maz's retorts had all the **caustic** charm of a corrosive acid.
(A) biting (D) bewildering
(B) witty (E) immortal
(C) delightful

7 ___

8. The moped's tracks in the sand were as **sinuous** as a snake's trail.
(A) unpleasant (D) loathsome
(B) intriguing (E) winding
(C) easily read

8 ___

9. The senator's **tirade** in Congress was like a mother's scolding of a naughty son.
(A) stay (D) absenteeism
(B) denunciation (E) explanation
(C) filibuster

9 ___

10. After two weeks I was as **ravenous** as a tiger on a starvation diet.
(A) angry (D) prepared
(B) upset (E) blissful
(C) hungry

10 ___

Problem

Just as congestion plagues every important highway, so it _____ the streets of every city.

(A) delimits (D) obviates
(B) delays (E) destroys
(C) clogs

Strategy. The comparison with *as* helps determine the answer to this question. The sentence compares congestion on the rural highways and on the city streets. The second clause must follow the sense of the first clause. The word *plague* is obviously negative. It tells us that congestion slows traffic on highways. The second clause must suggest that congestion slows traffic on city streets. Look at the choices.

Choice *(A) Delimits* has nothing to do with "congestion" in a physical sense. It means "fix the limits of," but the meaning has little to do with the sentence.

Choice *(B) Delays* has the right suggestion. Traffic does cause delays. But streets are not delayed. "Delaying the streets of every city" doesn't make sense.

Choice *(C) Clogs* strikes the right note at once. *Congestion* suggests clogging. This alternative fits perfectly.

Choice *(D) Obviates* has the right negative tone, but it doesn't fit into the sentence. We can *clog* streets; we cannot *obviate* ("get rid of") them.

Choice *(E) Destroys* is hopelessly overstated. *Congestion* doesn't destroy the streets. It may destroy the peace of mind of the drivers, but it doesn't destroy the streets. The correct answer, *clogs (C)*, was suggested by the comparison in the two clauses.

REVIEW

Write the letter of the word or words that have the same meaning as the boldfaced word in each sentence.

1. Melissa served the luncheon with the **dexterity** of a professional magician.
   (A) clumsiness   (D) foolishness
   (B) skillfulness   (E) forgetfulness
   (C) slowness

   1 ___

2. The chain-reaction accident on the freeway threw everyone into a state of **consternation**, like the frenzied activity of ants when a shovel is thrust into an ant colony.
   (A) utter confusion (D) incompetence
   (B) total calm   (E) preservation
   (C) seeing stars

   2 ___

3. It the transit authority raises fares any more, the public will become as **restive** as a crowd waiting for a fight to break out.
   (A) relaxed
   (B) highly amused
   (C) supportive
   (D) completely restored
   (E) restless

   3 ___

4. On the hot, hazy afternoon, we felt as **torpid** as a cat snoozing in the sun.
   (A) hot   (D) punished
   (B) energetic   (E) injured
   (C) sluggish

   4 ___

5. With the **impartiality** of a computer following its program, a competent judge makes a decision based on clear-cut evidence and facts.
   (A) impatience
   (B) fairness; not favoring either side
   (C) disorderliness
   (D) slowness
   (E) joyfulness

   5 ___

6. The shop windows filled with merchandise were as **tantalizing** to us as rich, tasty foods are to a dieter.
   (A) confusing   (D) tempting
   (B) actual   (E) disgusting
   (C) meddling

   6 ___

7. Old Mr. Scaggs is as **parsimonious** as a miser counting his pennies.
   (A) generous   (D) happy
   (B) exact   (E) outgoing
   (C) stingy

   7 ___

8. The speaker's opening remarks were as **trite** as a third-rate verse on a flowery greeting card.
   (A) literate   (D) ordinary
   (B) splendid   (E) memorable
   (C) moving

   8 ___

9. Craig's abruptly quitting the committee was an **impetuous** act, like a child throwing a tantrum.
(A) thoughtful; careful
(B) profitable
(C) foolish; rash
(D) mature
(E) tiresome; boring

9 ___

10. The Hollidays' response to the invitation was as **tentative** as a cat's sniffing of some unfamiliar food.
(A) keyed up
(B) hesitant; uncertain
(C) soft
(D) decisive; sure
(E) fast; quick

10 ___

SUMMARY

Context Clue 4:   Comparison

1. Comparisons can suggest meanings. If you don't know a word, you will probably know the compared word or meaning.

2. "As" or "like" often begins a comparison.

Context Clue 5:   Contrast

Problem

At the time of the Revolutionary War, Philadelphia was a well-populated metropolis, not an unimportant _____.

(A) community   (D) backwater
(B) capital   (E) resort
(C) diocese

Strategy. The negative *not* (pages 52–53) controls the answer. The blank is contrasted with *well-populated metropolis.* The word most obviously contrasted is *backwater* (D). Note that for one reason or another the other alternatives are faulty. *Community* (A) is rather general; it doesn't contrast particularly with *metropolis. Capital* (B) clashes with *unimportant. Diocese* (C) is a religious term, not parallel with *metropolis. Resort* is a possibility, but it is not so perfectly suited as *backwater.* The advice is worth repeating: choose the *best* answer, not just a *possible* answer.

(D)   At the time of the Revolutionary War, Philadelphia was a well-populated metropolis, not an unimportant backwater.

Another form of comparison—what might be called a *negative comparison*—is contrast. Contrast frequently provides a clue to meaning.

> The actions of the speaker served to **nullify** the effect of the suggestion, not to support it.

The contrast beginning with *not* tells what the key word **nullify** is not. *Support* is opposed to **nullify**. The speaker obviously did his best to oppose the suggestion.

> Though the firecracker looked **innocuous**, it contained enough powder to shatter a small building.

The contrast suggested by *though* tells us **innocuous** means "innocent, not dangerous."

TRIAL TEST

Take the following trial test to make sure you understand this type of context clue. Write the letter of your answer in the space at the right.

At one moment Prue seems to be sunk in **melancholy**; the next moment she changes and becomes bright and cheerful.
  (A) gloom
  (B) wit
  (C) fierce discussion
  (D) argument
  (E) sleep

  A

"Bright" and "cheerful" contrast with **melancholy**. The contrast makes clear that **melancholy** means *gloom (A)*.

1. The relationship between the twins was **discordant**, not harmonious.
   (A) careless   (D) curious
   (B) conflicting   (E) interesting
   (C) musical

   1 __

2. Carla did not make a **unilateral** decision; instead, she invited all participants to share in decision making.
   (A) one-sided
   (B) foolish
   (C) single
   (D) universally disapproved
   (E) ill-considered

   2 __

3. Hayes made a **ludicrous** suggestion, but the other members took the proposal seriously.
   (A) meaty   (D) solemn
   (B) vigorous   (E) pleasant
   (C) laughable

   3 __

4. When Miss Webster gets hold of an idea, she is **tenacious**, never weak and changing.
   (A) offensive   (D) adaptable
   (B) fickle   (E) persistent
   (C) friendly

   4 __

5. At times, Mr. Collins is **penurious**; at others, generous.
   (A) penny-wise (D) contributory
   (B) stingy (E) weary
   (C) helpful

   5 ___

6. Jeremy is not **infallible**; he makes many errors.
   (A) always right
   (B) sometimes uncertain
   (C) generally persuasive
   (D) optimistic
   (E) never arbitrary

   6 ___

7. In this uncertain weather, the bees may be either active or **dormant.**
   (A) irritable (D) indecisive
   (B) quiet (E) unprofitable
   (C) frivolous

   7 ___

8. Too often, fame is **ephemeral**, not lasting.
   (A) livelong (D) living
   (B) lively (E) lifelike
   (C) short-lived

   8 ___

9. Joella's efforts with a clarinet range from **cacophony** to a blissful blending of sounds.
   (A) ingenuity (D) harsh sounds
   (B) improvisation (E) surprise
   (C) symphony

   9 ___

10. Midge's explanation did not **placate** her partner; it angered him.
    (A) interest (D) eliminate
    (B) trick (E) soothe
    (C) arouse

    10 ___

Problem

Alice was annoyed that, although Edgar accepted the _____ of her argument, he would not _____ that her conclusion was correct.

(A) logic . . concede
(B) absurdity . . require
(C) sequence . . predict
(D) existence . . preclude
(E) feasibility . . dispute

Strategy. The contrast suggested by the *although* clause is the key to answer this question. The contrast is between acceptance and rejection. Edgar accepted some aspect of Alice's argument, but he obviously rejected her conclusion. Sometimes it is easy to overlook important little words. The key word *not* plays an important part in the analysis.

Choice *(A)* Try the sentence, substituting the alternatives suggested. Alice was annoyed that, although Edgar accepted the *logic* of her argument, he would not *concede* that her conclusion was correct.

That sounds good! Every now and then, the first choice seems the best. The contrast now makes sense. Edgar accepted the logic of Alice's argument, but he wouldn't accept her conclusion. This lack of consistency might well annoy someone! The contrast between acceptance and rejection is clear if we substitute the two words suggested. But examine the remaining choices.

Choice *(B)* The first alternative, *absurdity,* tends to discredit this pair. One is unlikely to accept *absurdity.* The second alternative, *require,* doesn't make sense.

Choice *(C)* The first alternative, *sequence,* is a possibility, though not nearly as good a choice as *logic* in *(A).* The second alternative, *predict,* is inadequate. Why would Edgar make a prediction? The alternatives are clearly not as good as those in *(A).*

Choice *(D) Existence* is a weak alternative, but *preclude* is even more unlikely.

Choice *(E) Dispute* is the clue to this answer. If Edgar did not dispute the conclusion, Alice would not have been annoyed.

The correct answer, *(A),* was indicated by the contrast suggested by the two clauses.

REVIEW

Write the letter of the word or words that have the same meaning as the boldfaced word in each sentence.

1. In a pressroom, the roar of machinery is **perpetual**, but the rumbling is easier to bear than an occasional sudden burst of sound.
   (A) brief   (D) harmful
   (B) constant   (E) puzzling
   (C) periodic

   1 ___

2. They say that Robin Hood took from the **affluent** and gave to the poor.
   (A) flowing   (D) rich
   (B) sick   (E) soaked
   (C) engaged

   2 ___

3. An organization that prevents cruelty to animals is a **benevolent** organization.
   (A) kindly   (D) neutral
   (B) unkind   (E) large
   (C) neglectful

   3 ___

4. Jennifer has an unusual **aptitude** for playing the piano, but a total inability to play any other instrument.
   (A) viewpoint
   (B) height
   (C) appreciation
   (D) talent
   (E) enjoyment

   4 ___

5. Although everyday folklore says that dogs and cats dislike one another, many of them are clearly **affectionate** toward one another.
   (A) sweet
   (B) catching
   (C) loving
   (D) candied
   (E) harmful

   5 ___

6. The owner of the famous restaurant greeted every guest **cordially**; there was nothing unpleasant or unfriendly about the place.
   (A) coldly
   (B) huffily
   (C) warmly
   (D) hastily
   (E) indifferently

   6 ___

7. Although the salespersons seemed honest, their "promises" about the product were **deceptive.**
   (A) misleading
   (B) straightforward
   (C) deep; penetrating
   (D) true
   (E) clear

   7 ___

8. A cat can be loving and gentle, but it can attack an enemy with astonishing strength and **ferocity.**
   (A) speed   (D) viciousness
   (B) honesty   (E) intelligence
   (C) perfection

   8 ___

9. Even though the picnic lunch was **sufficient**, everyone could have eaten more.
   (A) bountiful   (D) healthful
   (B) adequate   (E) unbearable
   (C) delicious

   9 ___

10. Although you might not call Harvey **obese**, he is not slim either.
    (A) skinny   (D) athletic
    (B) jolly   (E) healthy
    (C) fat

    10 ___

SUMMARY
Context Clue 5: Contrast

1. A contrast is a *negative comparison*. It tells what something is *not*.

2. Look for contrast words: **not, although, though, never, instead, but, either-or**, etc.

Context Clue 6: Sequence

Problem

Hitler's Nazi party began as a small, ruthless minority, took control of the government, and then _____ every method, legal or illegal, to extend its power and control the populace.

(A) disclosed   (D) commandeered
(B) disavowed   (E) promised
(C) exploited

Strategy. There is a sequence of events reported in the sentence: *began, took control,* and the blank. *Disclosed* (A) is unlikely, especially with the inclusion of *illegal* and *ruthless. Disavowed* (B) runs counter to the sense of the sentence. *Commandeered* (D) is too obvious a word for a clever, ruthless group. Besides, it is usually used for physical objects. *Promised* (E) *illegal methods* would not be a likely strategy. Only *exploited* (C) captures the essential meaning of the sentence.

(C) Hitler's Nazi party began as a small, ruthless minority, took control of the government, and then exploited every method, legal or illegal, to extend its power and control the populace.

Sometimes the way in which items are arranged in a sentence provides a clue to meaning. In the Gettysburg Address, Abraham Lincoln said, "We cannot dedicate—we cannot consecrate—we cannot hallow—this ground." The sequence of items clearly indicates a rise in intensity. *Dedicate* is a strong word to honor the ground where the soldiers are buried. *Consecrate* is stronger. *Hallow* is stronger still.

The article I read is weak, tasteless, really **insipid.**

The grouping of adjectives suggests a progression from the mild word *weak* to the stronger word **insipid.**

TRIAL TEST

Take the following trial test to make sure you understand this type of context clue. Write the letter of your answer in the space at the right.

The Halloween costume looked eerie and strange enough by day; at night it was positively **grotesque.**
   (A) handsome
   (B) well made
   (C) timely
   (D) fantastic
   (E) commonplace

                                    D

The phrasing shows a sequence from *eerie* and *strange* to **grotesque. Grotesque** is apparently a stronger word than *eerie* and *strange.* **Grotesque** means *fantastic (D).*

---

1. When facing a math problem, Grover is slow, even **obtuse.**
   (A) witty   (D) dull
   (B) secure   (E) well-rounded
   (C) thorough

                                    1 ___

2. Leora's creative style requires that she first **improvise** freely and later revise carefully.
   (A) write slowly
   (B) read intensively
   (C) compose offhand
   (D) copy slavishly
   (E) carry homeward

                                    2 ___

3. The prices of articles at the fair were much too high, ranging from steep to **exorbitant.**
   (A) modest   (D) surprising
   (B) reasonable   (E) low
   (C) excessive

   3 ___

4. At the party, Lon's behavior was at first merely irritating, but later it became **obnoxious.**
   (A) offensive   (D) positive
   (B) funny   (E) serious
   (C) cruel

   4 ___

5. Climbing on the lower slopes of Everest was challenging, but crossing ice fields on the upper slopes was truly **arduous.**
   (A) satisfying   (D) improbable
   (B) strenuous   (E) simple
   (C) comical

   5 ___

6. The characters in Dina's novel were more than dull; they were **stereotyped.**
   (A) composed in haste
   (B) tried beforehand
   (C) painted from life
   (D) copied from another novel
   (E) stamped from a mold

   6 ___

7. The inconveniences most travelers consider merely **irksome** Sam finds unbearable.
   (A) annoying   (D) inevitable
   (B) expected   (E) preventable
   (C) enjoyable

   7 ___

8. The visual effects in the average horror movie are no longer mildly frightening; they must be **gruesome**.
   (A) unpleasant   (D) hideous
   (B) interesting   (E) colorful
   (C) bitter

   8 ___

9. The approaches to the Grand Canyon are magnificent, but the Canyon itself is **unparalleled.**
   (A) unexpected
   (B) incomparable
   (C) deep
   (D) speechless
   (E) incomprehensible

   9 ___

10. My day started wild and gradually became more and more **frenetic.**
    (A) even
    (B) frantic
    (C) picturesque
    (D) normal
    (E) independent

    10 ___

Problem

In order to make the best use of available human resources, we must first _____ and then _____ human talents.

(A) educate . . equalize
(B) decompose . . rebuild
(C) revitalize . . discern
(D) discover . . develop
(E) produce . . accrue

Strategy. The sequence suggested by "first" and "and then" is the key to this question. Obviously the second alternative is an outgrowth of the first. This is how the alternatives work.

Choice *(A) Educate* seems like a fairly good alternative until we notice that "talents" is probably the object of the verb. We don't educate "talents." We educate *people.* The second alternative, *equalize,* is impractical and out of keeping with the suggestion "to make the best use of available human resources."

Choice *(B)* Why would anyone wish to *decompose,* break down, human talents? What would be the point of breaking them down only to rebuild them? This pair is unsatisfactory.

Choice (C) Revitalize sounds acceptable, but *discern* is inappropriate. We want to do more than look at human talents after we've revitalized them.

Choice *(D)* The sequence here makes sense. We first *discover* the talents and then *develop* them. Steps 1 and 2 are logical and reasonable.

Choice *(E)* We don't *produce* human talents. We *discover* and *develop* them. Some students might choose *accrue* because they don't know its meaning and think it just might be the right answer. The word means "to grow," but it doesn't take an object. Besides, the first alternative, *produce,* is clearly incorrect.

Since *(D)* is so obviously correct, none of the other alternatives make a strong showing. It is wise to check them anyway, even if rapidly. Here, the sequence is the clue to meaning.

REVIEW

Write the letter for the word or words that have the same meaning as the boldfaced word in each sentence.

1. A back injury is not just painful; it can be **excruciating.**
   (A) left out
   (B) unpleasant
   (C) extremely painful
   (D) forgiven; pardoned
   (E) rejected

   1 ___

2. Taking inventory is a difficult, **onerous** task.
   (A) one of a kind
   (B) ongoing; continuous
   (C) all-knowing
   (D) burdensome; oppressive
   (E) unrepeated

   2 ___

3. Scott may be lazy, but his brother is downright **lethargic.**
   (A) leathery; tough
   (B) very strong
   (C) extremely sluggish
   (D) very heavy
   (E) deadly

   3 ___

4. The officials were stubbornly against changing any rules, but they were **adamantly** opposed to easing the entrance requirements.
   (A) moderately
   (B) addictively
   (C) increasingly
   (D) unyieldingly
   (E) confusedly

   4 ___

5. The plump dog became **corpulent** after figuring out how to open the dog food container.
   (A) very fat
   (B) incorporated
   (C) correctable
   (D) proven
   (E) very certain

   5 ___

6. During the long hike, the youngsters quickly became hungry and eventually became **ravenous.**
   (A) unstrung
   (B) very hungry
   (C) very beautiful
   (D) eaten up
   (E) destroyed

   6 ___

7. A heavy, gas-guzzling sedan may be outdated, but a horse and buggy is **archaic.**
   (A) very cold
   (B) no longer used
   (C) very difficult
   (D) very enthusiastic
   (E) more recent

   7 ___

8. First the accused asked the judge for a light sentence; then he **implored** him to be set free.
   (A) detested completely
   (B) suggested indirectly
   (C) punished severely
   (D) pleaded urgently
   (E) placed firmly

   8 ___

9. Forgetting to thank the participants was a bad mistake, but leaving their names out of the program was an **egregious** one.
   (A) self-centered
   (B) equalizing
   (C) conceited
   (D) sociable; outgoing
   (E) outrageous

   9 ___

10. Most of the committee meetings were private ones, but one was so **clandestine** it was never revealed to the public.
   (A) very secretive
   (B) very quiet
   (C) very noisy
   (D) very unpleasant
   (E) very clear

   10 ___

SUMMARY
Context Clue 6: Sequence

Words arranged in sequence show an increase in intensity. If you know just one of the words, you can figure out the rest.

Context Clue 7: Function Words

Problem
_____ Julius Caesar who said, "I came, I saw, I conquered," Romeo might have said of Juliet, "I came, I saw, I was conquered."

    (A) With   (D) Unlike
    (B) Following   (E) Besides
    (C) Admiring

Strategy. This sentence highlights the importance of a connecting word, a preposition. Since the supposed Romeo quotation is critically different from the Julius Caesar quotation, the blank must demonstrate this difference. Only *Unlike* (D) qualifies. (A) and (B) run counter to the meaning. (C) is remotely possible, but not so good as (D). *Besides* (E) expresses a relationship not suggested in the sentence.

    (D) Unlike Julius Caesar who said, "I came, I saw, I conquered," Romeo might have said of Juliet, "I came, I saw, I was conquered."

In English, nouns and verbs are heavyweight words. They carry the burden of meaning in most sentences. Even a simple sentence like "Wasps sting" shows how important nouns and verbs can be. Just two words tell volumes.

Adjectives and adverbs are also strong content words, as they describe, limit, and qualify the powerful nouns and verbs. "Angry wasps sting mercilessly" paints a strong picture.

Because these four content words (nouns, verbs, adjectives, and adverbs) are so overpowering, we sometimes overlook other important words, like prepositions and conjunctions, words that show connections and relationships. These other words provide the glue that holds the content words together. Without the important *function words,* as they are sometimes called, sentences would not hang together.

    After Claude had skied, he put his skis **in** the rack **near** the front door **and** went **inside** the lodge.

In the preceding sentence, the content words provide most of the essential information, but they do not tell when and where. Words like **after, in, near, and,** and **inside** are needed to convey the message.

Often the meaning of a sentence hangs on a simple word like **not, but,** or **then.**

The following sampling of these function words will suggest the extent of their influence in creating sentences.

CAUSE-EFFECT: **as, because, for, if, since, so that, yet**

DEGREE: **somewhat, too, very**

PLACE: **above, along, across, around, at, behind, beside, below, beyond** (and many others)

OPPOSITE DIRECTION: **although, but, however, nevertheless, otherwise, unless**

SAME DIRECTION: **and, also, as well, besides**

TIME: **after, before, during, meanwhile, then, when, while, till, until**

NUMBERS: **few, less, many, more, some, one** (and other numerals)

NEGATIVE: **no, not, nobody, no one, neither**

Buddy's room was **chaotic**. It did have a certain informal charm.

These two sentences provide very little help in suggesting the meaning of **chaotic**. In the context provided, **chaotic** might mean almost anything favorable, from "masculine" to "beautiful." We cannot make an intelligent guess.

Notice what happens when two seemingly unimportant words, **somewhat** and **but**, are inserted into the sentence.

Buddy's room was **somewhat chaotic, but** it did have a certain informal charm.

Now the meaning of **chaotic** can be guessed at. The word **but** suggests that the room's charm is unexpected. Therefore **chaotic** must be a negative word, but **somewhat** softens the blow. The room is not **chaotic**; it is **somewhat chaotic**.

If, in spite of everything, the room has "a certain informal charm," we might reasonably guess that **chaotic** means "upset, disordered." *Informal* becomes an important clue to the meaning of **chaotic**, but the two words **but** and **somewhat** put us on the right track.

Function words are crucially important. Review the importance of **rather than** in the test question for Context Clue 2 (pages 32–33) and the importance of **first** and **and then** in the test question for Context Clue 6 (pages 49–50).

TRIAL TEST

Take the following trial test to make sure you understand this type of context clue. Write the letter of your answer on the line at the right.

Her knowledge and **expertise** in the field of computer science qualified her for the job.
- (A) beauty
- (B) wealth
- (C) specialized skill
- (D) acting ability
- (E) dress

C

You should have noticed the function word *and,* which shows that knowledge is related to expertise. *Expertise* must mean *specialized skill, (C),* since the other choices are not in the same direction as knowledge.

---

1. Because the father was **domineering,** the children rebelled and left home.
   - (A) weak but pleasant
   - (B) indifferent
   - (C) wittily charming
   - (D) humorously fanciful
   - (E) strongly controlling

   1 ___

2. If there is further **diminution** of club funds, we'll have to increase next year's dues.
   - (A) advertising   (D) spread
   - (B) decrease   (E) theft
   - (C) expansion

   2 ___

3. A long drought threatened the community water supply, but a series of heavy rains **replenished** much of the water in the reservoir.
   - (A) drained   (D) refilled
   - (B) polluted   (E) wasted
   - (C) dissipated

   3 ___

4. Because Ted is so **gullible**, his friends like to tell him wild stories and exaggerated anecdotes.
   - (A) funny   (D) birdlike
   - (B) agreeable   (E) excitable
   - (C) believing

   4 ___

5. The editor replaced many tired words and expressions in an attempt to make the report sound less **hackneyed**.
   - (A) commonplace   (D) unsound
   - (B) vivid   (E) grim
   - (C) critical

   5 ___

6. I'll be left in a **quandary** unless you give me more help in choosing the right course.
   - (A) time of decision
   - (B) trick of fate
   - (C) expression of hope
   - (D) state of uncertainty
   - (E) call for action

   6 ___

7. Although Barbara is **meticulous** in matters of personal grooming, she is careless in keeping her checkbook account.
   - (A) somewhat slovenly
   - (B) too cowardly
   - (C) very careful
   - (D) occasionally gentle
   - (E) rather casual

   7 ___

8. Since she had been caught in a heavy downpour, Beth looked **disheveled** when she came into the house.
   - (A) angry   (D) adorned
   - (B) puzzled   (E) tired
   - (C) untidy

   8 ___

9. Until the roof leaked rainwater onto the dirt floor of the barn, we had been able to keep the stables **immaculate**.

(A) spotless   (D) locked
(B) wide open   (E) colorful
(C) dressy

9 __

10. If I cannot **rectify** my mistake, I'll resign as club president.

(A) explain   (D) clarify
(B) correct   (E) magnify
(C) conceal

10 __

Problem

Because even the briefest period of idleness bored and exasperated her, she _____ worked at some project or activity.

(A) constantly   (D) cynically
(B) reluctantly   (E) languidly
(C) occasionally

Strategy. "Because" is the key to the answer. Cause and effect are at work. The way in which she works at a project or activity is a result of her boredom and exasperation.

Choice *(A) Constantly* seems to fit the sentence well. The "because" clause tells us she cannot stand even the briefest period of idleness. Therefore, when she works, she'll avoid even a brief period of idleness—in short, *constantly,* all the time.

Choice *(B) Reluctantly* is directly opposed to the sense of the sentence. If she is bored by idleness, she won't be reluctant to work. She'll be eager to do so.

Choice *(C) Occasionally* does consider the time problem, but boredom at even brief periods of idleness suggests occasional work will not be enough.

Choice *(D) Cynically* suggests an attitude, a bitter attitude, but there is nothing in the sentence to suggest such an attitude. She won't overcome her boredom by being cynical.

Choice *(E) Languidly* also suggests an attitude and a manner of weakness, sluggishness. But she is a dynamo of activity, as the *because* clause suggests.

Constantly is clearly the best answer, indeed the only answer possible.

REVIEW

Write the letter of the word or words that have the same meaning as the boldfaced word in each sentence.

1. We wished the day of surprises would go on forever, but such pleasures are usually **transitory**.
   (A) expected   (D) surprising
   (B) lasting   (E) elated
   (C) short-lived
                                    1 ___

2. Although the topic was **abstruse**, Stephanie was able to write about it simply and clearly.
   (A) easy to understand
   (B) hard to understand
   (C) blunt; insensitive
   (D) very simple
   (E) badly treated
                                    2 ___

3. No one thought their intentions were **bellicose** until their troops stormed the city.
   (A) peaceful   (D) beautiful
   (B) stormy   (E) warlike
   (C) ugly
                                    3 ___

4. After the **sardonic** reviews in the news media, nobody bothered to see the movie.
   (A) fishy   (D) praising
   (B) scornful   (E) neutral
   (C) positive
                                    4 ___

5. Because of the **salubrious** food and climate at the resort, everyone felt wonderful after staying there.
   (A) sloppy   (D) healthful
   (B) salty   (E) unpleasant
   (C) moist
                                    5 ___

6. Even though the professor is **erudite** in his subject, he doesn't know the first thing about everyday matters like balancing a checkbook or driving a car.
   (A) uninformed   (D) scholarly
   (B) rude   (E) impractical
   (C) incorrect
                                    6 ___

7. Because the fashion show displayed only the **quintessence** of the new styles, only the best designers could participate.
   (A) finest   (D) hint
   (B) worst   (E) selection
   (C) fifth
                                    7 ___

8. The youngsters had only a **nebulous** understanding of the opera, but they did enjoy the lavish staging and costumes.
   (A) complete   (D) marvelous
   (B) vague   (E) necessary
   (C) lavish
                                    8 ___

9. Because Stan is so **gregarious**, he always seems to be in the center of activity, surrounded by people.
   (A) very deceitful (D) tan
   (B) growing   (E) outrageous
   (C) sociable
                                    9 ___

10. After Lincoln **emancipated** the slaves, many of them still had to stay with their former masters.
    (A) underfed   (D) imprisoned
    (B) mistreated   (E) employed
    (C) set free
                                    10 ___

SUMMARY
Context Clue 7: Function Words

1. Nouns, verbs, adjectives, and adverbs are heavyweight words, giving basic meanings.

2. Function words (**because, somewhat, above, although,** etc.) change, intensify, and redirect the basic meanings.

3. Often the meaning of a sentence depends on one function word.

Context Clues: Review Test

The sentences below provide context clues to word meanings. From the group of words below, select a word to replace each boldface word. Write the word on the line at the right.

deceit	hateful	overelaborate	soaked
equivalent	made poor	peculiarities	timid
excessive	nobody	pierced	turned aside
fortress	noisy speech	poisonous	wearing away
harsh	overcrowding	punishment	yellowish

1. Because of her own high standards of morality, Marilyn spurned the **duplicity** of her comrades.   1. _____
2. The trader had a virtual monopoly on salt, and he charged **exorbitant** prices for it.   2. _____
3. From a **nonentity**, Jackson rose to the highest honor America can grant.   3. _____
4. He feared **retribution** for his evil deeds.   4. _____
5. The terms were **tantamount** to complete surrender.   5. _____
6. They stormed the **citadel** with arrows.   6. _____
7. There was such **congestion** in the halls that members could scarcely move.   7. _____
8. The tax plan of the nobles **impoverished** the peasantry, draining away all wealth.   8. _____
9. Soil **erosion** stripped the topsoil from some of our richest land.   9. _____
10. Far from being **diffident**, she has boldly stepped into the limelight.   10. _____
11. The tips of the shoes were **perforated**, the holes being at regular intervals.   11. _____
12. To the newcomer, the Northeast winters were **rigorous** and severe.   12. _____

13. After long confinement in the dungeon, he emerged with a thin frame and **sallow** complexion.

13. _____

14. She rushed into the house from the storm, her clothing thoroughly **saturated**.

14. _____

15. The mob growled menacingly as they listened to the speaker's unrestrained **harangue**.

15. _____

16. The theft from the poor widow made the crime even more **heinous**.

16. _____

17. The escaping fumes were not **noxious** but actually beneficial to the animals in the laboratory.

17. _____

18. Despite Thomson's odd **quirks**, people are very fond of him.

18. _____

19. The carved ceiling was too **ornate**, displeasing in its lack of simplicity.

19. _____

20. Jonathan never once **deviated** from the course he had set for himself early in life.

20. _____

Context Clues: Summary

Review these context clues from time to time. If you understand how context helps you learn new words, you'll do better on the vocabulary sections of the SAT. You'll also do better on the reading sections. As a special bonus, you'll become a more efficient general reader and student.

Clue 1 **The Entire Sentence**

Use your own words first to make an intelligent guess with word meanings; then examine the whole sentence as a context clue.

The first **tremor** of the earthquake rattled the dishes and bounced the pots together.

Clue 2 **Pairing**

If you don't know one word in a pair, you may know the other.

Jefferson is so **dogmatic** and opinionated, no one cares to discuss anything with him.

Clue 3 **Direct Explanation**

The test sentence may give an explanation directly, in an appositive, in a participial phrase, in an explanation beginning with **for**, or in one provided by a subordinate clause.

Pittsburgh is at the **confluence** of the Allegheny and Monongahela rivers, where the two flow together to form the Ohio.

Clue 4   **Comparison**

The compared word or meaning can be a clue; **as** or **like** are clue words.

When Doreen has a task to do, she is as **assiduous** as a bee on a nectar-gathering expedition.

Clue 5   **Contrast**

A contrast, or a *negative* comparison, tells what something is *not:* some contrast words—**not, although, though, never, instead, but, either . . . or**.

Paul felt he was a **nonentity**, not a person of real importance.

Clue 6   **Sequence**

Words in sequence show an increase in intensity; if you know one of the words, you can figure out the rest.

At the beginning Curren worried about Becker's serves, but they became even harder, more accurate, and **formidable** as the match went on.

Clue 7   **Function Words**

Often the meaning of a sentence depends on one function word. (See pages 52–53 for a sampling of function words.)

When the stranger struck the first awful blow, Tom **retaliated** with all his might.

Section II: Word Clues

Word Clue 1: Connotation and Denotation

Problem
Many people daydream of owning a modest _____ someday in the woods or at the seashore.
(A) abode   (D) hovel
(B) aerie   (E) shack
(C) cabin

Strategy. All alternatives identify a kind of dwelling, but the task is to select the most suitable. *Abode* (A) is too general. *Aerie* (B) suggests a dwelling in a high place, perhaps on a peak, unlikely at the seashore. (D) and (E) have negative connotations. Daydreamers have more positive hopes. *Cabin* (C) fits the slot best.

(C)   Many people daydream of owning a modest cabin someday in the woods or at the seashore.

"I'd like you to meet my mommy."

"I'd like you to meet my mother."

"Mommy" and "mother" mean the same person, but the words seem quite different. An adult talks freely about his or her "mother" but rarely uses the word "mommy" outside the home. "Mommy" seems to belong to an earlier period of life. It is a word used by younger children or by adults in the company of small children. It has an altogether different tone from "mother."

Words have many meanings, but all these meanings can usually be divided into two broad types: (1) dictionary meanings and (2) suggested meanings. The first kind of meaning is called denotation; the second is called connotation. The denotations (dictionary meaning) of "mommy" and "mother" are pretty much the same. The connotations (suggested meanings), however, are quite different. "Mother" is more formal, more general, more applicable to many situations, even to other living creatures. "Mommy" has the flavor of childhood and expresses a certain tone and meaning.

The world of childhood is filled with words that have very special connotations, words like *choo-choo, ducky,* and *kitty.* Childhood words make especially good illustrations of connotation because they are so dramatically different from more adult words like *train, duck,* and *cat.* Sometimes words are rich in connotations for one individual and not another. *Snake* has a very negative connotation for the average camper and a very positive connotation for a naturalist.

No two words are exactly alike. As we shall see later, no two words—even close synonyms—are exactly the same, but many pairs of words are fairly close in meaning. Their denotations are similar, but their connotations may be further apart. *Vision* and *sight* have similar denotations and are listed as synonyms. But they may have widely different connotations.

"That movie star is a vision."

"That movie star is a sight."

If you have a feeling for connotation as well as denotation, you'll do better in all portions of the verbal part of the SAT.

Dan and Merle are friendly (adversaries, antagonists, foes, rivals) for the affections of the new student in class.

All four words suggest that Dan and Merle are competing. The trick is to select the word with the most appropriate *tone.* The sentence says the competition is friendly. The strongly negative connotation of *adversaries, antagonists,* and *foes* is too powerful for friendship. *Rival* is more neutral. *Friendly rivalry* is more likely than *friendly antagonism.*

The spectators were gripped by sudden (consternation, dismay, dread, panic) and stampeded when the cry of "Fire!" was raised.

All four words suggest both fear and upset. The choice becomes a matter of connotation. *Consternation, dismay,* and *dread* are less overpowering than *panic. Dismay* and *dread* suggest long-term worry or concern. *Consternation* suggests fear that leads to inactivity. *Panic,* on the other hand, suggests wild, uncontrolled action.

As a word is used, and as a connotation becomes more widespread, the connotation may become part of the dictionary definition. The word *appease* was once a fairly neutral word. It meant simply "to quiet, to satisfy." In the expression "to appease one's appetite," the word is still neutral. But just before and during World War II, the word *appeasement* came to mean "giving in to the demands of a hostile power." It became a very negative word, and the growing negative connotation eventually became included in the dictionary definition.

TRIAL TEST

Take the following trial test to make sure you understand this type of word clue. Write the letter for the word that best completes the meaning in each sentence.

The new nations of Africa were _____ of their rights and their hard-won independence.

    (A) suspicious   (D) unconcerned
    (B) jealous   (E) weary
    (C) fearful

                          B

  Since *jealous* suggests a desire to hold onto what one has, *(B)* is the correct answer.

1. The ex-champion's muscles became _____ from lack of exercise.
    (A) delicate
    (B) flabby
    (C) flimsy
    (D) limp
    (E) loose

                    1 ____

2. The photographer specialized in _____ camera shots.
    (A) frank
    (B) open
    (C) candid
    (D) plain
    (E) blunt

                    2 ____

3. The characters in this novel are _____ and bear no intentional resemblance to actual people.
    (A) fabulous
    (B) mythical
    (C) legendary
    (D) imagined
    (E) fictitious

                    3 ____

4. A mild _____ blew in out of the west.
    (A) breeze
    (B) blast
    (C) tempest
    (D) tornado
    (E) gale

                    4 ____

5. Medieval monks spent a great deal of time _____ ancient manuscripts.
    (A) imitating
    (B) mocking
    (C) aping
    (D) copying
    (E) matching

                    5 ____

6. When the four racing cars crashed, the spectators were stricken by sudden _____ and ran in all directions.
    (A) dismay
    (B) panic
    (C) consternation
    (D) dread
    (E) anxiety

                    6 ____

7. The owner was unreasonable because he expected nothing short of _____ in his employees.
    (A) merit
    (B) excellence
    (C) virtue
    (D) quality
    (E) perfection

                    7 ____

8. Although she had been away for years, when Sheila approached her house, everything suddenly seemed to become _____.
(A) confidential
(B) intimate
(C) familiar
(D) exciting
(E) commonplace

8 ____

9. After a week in the desert without food and very little water, the returning hiker looked _____.
(A) haggard
(B) wan
(C) weak
(D) weary
(E) thin

9 ____

10. Three blocks of houses were burned in one great _____.
(A) blaze
(B) fire
(C) combustion
(D) burning
(E) conflagration

10 ____

Problem

The World Cup matches in the United States in 1994 _____ what had been, up to then, only a _____ interest in soccer.

(A) intensified . . . resurgent
(B) rejected . . . quiescent
(C) increased . . . modest
(D) explained . . . vigorous
(E) derided . . . dormant

Strategy. The word *only* plays a major qualifying role in the sentence. Since it precedes *interest,* we must assume that the modifier of *interest* is not positive. Words with positive connotations like *resurgent* and *vigorous* counteract the effect of *only.* Thus, we may eliminate (A) and (D), no matter what the first word in each pair is. The other second alternatives—*quiescent, modest,* and *dormant*—are possible with *only.* Then we must look at the first word in each pair.

Common sense suggests that an important event like holding the World Cup soccer matches would not have a negative effect on soccer. *Rejected* and *derided do* have negative connotations and may be eliminated. That leaves but one possible pair: *increased, modest.* Let's substitute the suggested answers to see how they fit.

The World Cup matches in the United States in 1994 increased what had been, up to then, only a modest interest in soccer.

They fit perfectly. In sentences of this type, the SAT question will often give similar words as alternatives to be chosen. In this test question, *dormant* and *quiescent* are related. Either would fill the blank satisfactorily, but the first word in each pair is unsuitable. *Intensified* and *increased* are also related words, but *intensified* is coupled with the obviously incorrect *resurgent*. Our strategy has two steps: (1) first, use context clues for unfamiliar words; (2) then, if this plan doesn't help, examine the connotations of similar words.

Problem

The actors _____, outrageously over-playing the farcical roles that required restraint, not _____.

- (A) grimaced ... license
- (B) pranced ... denial
- (C) orated ... rejection
- (D) mumbled ... amplification
- (E) dawdled ... creativity

Strategy. The word *overplaying* dominates the sentence. It suggests immediately that both paired words must have *negative* connotations. *Amplification* has a neutral connotation, and *creativity* has a positive connotation. Thus, we may eliminate (D) and (E). It is true that *mumbled* and *dawdled* are indeed negative and are therefore possibilities, but their paired words are unacceptable. On a closer look, you'll also note that the paired words in (D) actually contradict each other. *Orated* and *pranced* are also possible, but their paired words—*denial* and *rejection*—are unsuitable. By a process of elimination, we come to (A). Though *grimaced* and *license* may be the most unfamiliar words of the ten, thoughtful analysis leaves this pair as the answer.

The actors grimaced, outrageously overplaying the farcical roles that required restraint, not license.

This question shows that even unfamiliar words need not prevent you from finding the correct answer.

REVIEW

Write the letter for the word that makes best sense in each sentence.

---

1. Garment sizes for the gowns were pe-tite, small, medium, and _____.
   - (A) loose
   - (B) baggy
   - (C) big
   - (D) large
   - (E) overgrown

   1 ____

2. Some wrinkle-free fabrics are made of _____ fibers.
   - (A) fake
   - (B) phony
   - (C) unreal
   - (D) synthetic
   - (E) counterfeit

   2 ____

3. The moisturizing cream is supposed to make the complexion less _____.
(A) limp
(B) dry
(C) soft
(D) mushy
(E) slippery

3 ____

4. Many mobile homes are surprisingly _____.
(A) palatial
(B) roomy
(C) immense
(D) cavernous
(E) enormous

4 ____

5. The rude audience's idle _____ was annoying.
(A) discourse
(B) chatter
(C) discussion
(D) debate
(E) speech

5 ____

6. The constant urban problem is _____ streets and parkways.
(A) infested
(B) overflowing
(C) congested
(D) congealed
(E) stuffed

6 ____

7. Buying defective merchandise hurriedly is a bit _____.
(A) rash
(B) foolish
(C) insane
(D) slothful
(E) tiresome

7 ____

8. The important executive _____ into the room.
(A) strode
(B) trudged
(C) wandered
(D) fell
(E) stumbled

8 ____

9. Millions of viewers _____ the championship game.
(A) ogled
(B) glanced at
(C) stared at
(D) noticed
(E) watched

9 ____

10. Homeowners must _____ their property from theft.
(A) barricade
(B) militarize
(C) arm
(D) protect
(E) isolate

10 ____

SUMMARY

Word Clue 1: Connotation and Denotation

No two words are exactly alike. Words have many meanings, but all meanings can usually be divided into two types: dictionary meanings called *denotation* and suggested meanings called *connotation*.

House and *home* are sometimes used interchangeably, but *home* has far richer connotations than *house*. "There's no place like a house" is not quite the same as "There's no place like home."

Recognizing connotation is especially helpful in answering reading comprehension questions on the SAT.

Word Clue 2: | Figurative Language

Problem

He was suddenly thrown into a fit of despair, his faith in himself infirm, his self-confidence _____.

(A) shattered
(B) soaring
(C) unassailable
(D) inflated
(E) delayed

Strategy. As it happens, all the alternatives provided are examples of figurative language. They are all metaphors. *Shattered* suggests breakage. *Soaring* suggests flight. *Unassailable* suggests conflict. *Inflated* suggests increase. *Delayed* suggests obstruction. Which implied comparison is most suitable here?

Two clues help: "fit of despair" and "infirm faith." Someone who is in despair and of infirm faith has lost his self-confidence. Which figurative meaning suggests the loss? *Shattered* fits. Self-confidence might well crumble and be lost. Quickly check the others to be sure.

Soaring and *unassailable* do not fit at all. They are positive words and suggest the wrong picture. *Inflated* also suggests an improvement in self-confidence, the opposite of the meaning we need. *Delayed* is a milder word than *shattered*. It suggests that self-confidence is slightly affected, but despair suggests something more drastic. *(A) Shattered,* the correct answer, uses a physical picture to make the point more strongly.

> March comes in like a *lion* and goes out like a *lamb*.

> When Ellen heard the news, her eyes *danced* and her smile *sparkled*.

In the sample sentences, March does not really resemble a lamb or a lion. Ellen's eyes don't actually dance, nor does her smile sparkle. These examples of "it is what it isn't" are good illustrations *of figurative language,* or *figures of speech*.

SIMILE

The March sentence provides an example of **simile** (SIM uh lee), the comparison of unlike things by using *like* or *as*. Some similes like *white as snow* and *sweet as sugar* have long since worn out their usefulness, and are avoided by careful speakers and writers. However, other phrases startle us by their freshness and appropriateness: *as lonesome as a bell buoy at sea.*

METAPHOR

In the Ellen sentence, *danced* and *sparkled* are examples of **metaphor** (MET uh for), comparisons without *like* or *as*. Metaphor is the poetry of everyday life. We can speak scarcely a sentence without using metaphor, either obvious or concealed. Action metaphors are everywhere, as we *run up* a bill, *skirt* a topic, *win* approval, *hold down* a job, *catch* a cold, *kill* time, *flock* to a new idea, *find* a solution, or *go over* an answer. We may call a person a *rock,* a *tower of strength,* or a *chameleon.* We talk of an *arm* of the sea, the *eye* of a hurricane, the *teeth* of a gale, a *shoulder* of a mountain, or an *elbow* of land. Flowers are often gems of metaphor: *lady's slipper, baby's breath, buttercup, larkspur, Queen Anne's lace, snow-on-the-mountain, jewelweed.* The English language is incredibly rich in metaphor. Metaphors often appear in sentence completion and reading comprehension questions.

Though simile and metaphor are most familiar, there are other kinds of figurative language.

PERSONIFICATION

Personification (per SAHN uh fi KAY shun) gives some human traits to things not human. *Duty* calls. *Truth* cries out. *War* stalks the land. *Joy* flees the house. *Happiness* grows. *Justice* is sometimes blind. *Democracy* encourages citizen participation in government. *Violins* cry, and *trombones* wail. Personification is usually easy to identify.

METONYMY

Metonymy (met ON uh me) substitutes one word for another closely associated with it. If we say, "The kettle is boiling," we're using metonymy. The kettle itself isn't boiling; it's the water inside. "Kettle" is used to represent water. Other examples of metonymy follow.

> The *pen is mightier than the sword.*
> (pen = writing; sword = force and violence)

> I like the new *dish* you cooked.
> (dish = food in the dish)

> No man can live by *bread* alone.
> (bread = food and the physical needs for survival)

SYNECDOCHE

Synecdoche (sin ECK duh kee) also relies on association. Synecdoche substitutes a part for the whole or the whole for a part. If we talk about hired *hands,* we really mean *laborers.* If we take a *head* count, we are really counting *people.* If a store sign says, "Now Hiring Smiling Faces," the owner is looking for new employees, not just faces.

HYPERBOLE

Hyperbole (high PURR buh lee) is exaggeration for effect. When someone says, "I ran a thousand miles before breakfast," *thousand miles* is certainly exaggerated! Occasional hyperbole is effective, but some speakers overuse this device. "I was *absolutely famished.* I drank *gallons* of water and gulped down a *ton* of hamburgers." Like all strong statements, hyperbole is most effective in small doses.

UNDERSTATEMENT

Understatement, the opposite of hyperbole, may also be used for emphasis.

> This dessert *isn't bad* at all! (It's excellent.)

> After staying awake for 36 hours, I was a *little tired.* (I was exhausted.)

IRONY

Irony is intentionally using words to say one thing and imply something quite the opposite. Suppose you take a clock apart and can't get it back together again. You might then say, "I guess I'm just a *skilled mechanic,"* and mean the opposite. *Skilled mechanic* is an example of irony. Satire and sarcasm belong to the irony family.

Review of Figurative Language

A single expression may combine two or more figures of speech. Personification is closely related to metaphor. "Truth may whisper and falsehood shout." *Truth* and *falsehood* are personified. *Whisper* and *shout* are metaphors. No person or thing is actually whispering or shouting. "Buddy laughed till he burst" is certainly hyperbole. *Burst* is also a metaphor.

If you become sensitive to figurative language, you will be better able to handle the vocabulary and reading questions on the SAT. You'll also enrich all your reading and listening.

Notice how the same action may be reported differently. A clumsy young man enters a room, trips over a rug, breaks a priceless lamp, and pours coffee over an expensive sofa. He is unhurt, however. What are some reactions an observer might make?

You're *like a bull in a china shop!* (Simile)

You're a clumsy *clown!* (Metaphor)

Destruction enters our quiet room! (Personification)

Oh, mighty *toe!* (Synecdoche)

You've just ruined *everything* in this room! (Hyperbole)

You had a *bit of a fall,* didn't you? (Understatement)

My, but you're an *agile* person! (Irony)

TRIAL TEST

Write the letter for the name of the figurative language in boldface in each of the following sentences.

(A) Simile
(B) Metaphor
(C) Personification

(D) Synecdoche
(E) Hyperbole
(F) Understatement

(G) Irony
(H) Metonymy

When I broke the expensive butter dish, I **died** of embarrassment.

_E_

Died is an exaggeration. This is an example of hyperbole _(E)._

---

1. Jean stepped back from the rattle-snake in the path **like a mouse jumping away from a cat.**

    1 __

2. The **eyes** of the potato are really buds.

    2 __

3. Isn't all this rainy weather, with its hordes of mosquitoes, **a lot of fun!**

    3 __

4. Mr. Acton **hit the roof** when he saw the dent in his new car.

    4 __

5. We call our dog **"the nose"** because he can smell food a mile away.

    5 __

6. **Gloom** makes few friends.

    6 __

7. In reading the passage, I **stumbled** over the first word.

    7 __

8. It was as cold as the **north side of a January gravestone by starlight.**

    8 __

9. My six weeks in the hospital caused me a **bit of inconvenience.**

    9 __

10. **Love** conquers all.

    10 __

Problem

Ballet is known to be _____; once you go, you are likely to find yourself going again and again, loving the performances more each time.

(A) addictive
(B) erratic
(C) expendable
(D) anticlimactic
(E) interminable

Strategy. Once again, figurative language is the key to the correct answer. *Addictive* is a word used originally for physical bondage to a habit. Drug addiction, for example, suggests a powerful need involving slavery to narcotics. But addiction, through metaphor, has acquired much wider uses. People say they're addicted to jogging, to square dancing, to tennis, or a host of other activities. Though addiction to jogging is quite different from addiction to drugs, there are enough points of similarity to make the comparison effective, especially the compulsive need to participate almost daily.

The sentence provides several clues, as is so often the case. "Going again and again" emphasizes the repetition. "Loving the performances" suggests the joy. Alternatives *(B)* to *(E)* are too negative or have the wrong tone for the sentence. Only *(A)*, with its appropriate figurative meaning, is suitable as an answer.

REVIEW

Write the letter for the name of the figurative language in boldface in each sentence.

(A) Simile
(B) Metaphor
(C) Personification

(D) Synecdoche
(E) Hyperbole
(F) Understatement

(G) Irony
(H) Metonymy

1. The entire **theater burst into laughter.**

   1 ___

2. When she stumbled over the doorsill and fell flat, she earned the title **Miss Graceful.**

   2 ___

3. Suddenly the child was **as quiet as a mouse.**

   3 ___

4. Late as usual, Dexter had an alibi **that was a mile long.**

   4 ___

5. The flight across the ocean was **as smooth as silk**.

   5 ___

6. The old **house told** us of happier days.

   6 ___

7. The humid, 100-degree day was **not especially refreshing.**

   7 ___

8. The command was given: **"All hands on deck."**

   8 ___

9. Her delicate **laughter rippled** through the air.

   9 ___

10. They talked and talked, while **ten thousand people were waiting** to use the phone.

    10 ___

SUMMARY

Word Clue 2: Figurative Language

SIMILE: comparison with **like** or **as**
   Gray-haired Saturn, **quiet as a stone.** (John Keats)

METAPHOR: implied comparison
   I felt a **cleavage** in my mind. (Emily Dickinson)

PERSONIFICATION: representing an object or idea as a person
   Love laughs at locksmiths. (George Colman)

METONYMY: use of a word for another closely associated word
   This hairy meteor did announce
   The fall of **sceptres** and of **crowns.** (Samuel Butler)

SYNECDOCHE: use of the part for the whole, or the reverse
   We dispatch you for bearers of this greeting to old **Norway.**
   (William Shakespeare)

HYPERBOLE: exaggeration for effect
   At every word a reputation **dies.** (Alexander Pope)

UNDERSTATEMENT: emphasis by saying less than is meant
   The report of my death was **an exaggeration.** (Mark Twain)

IRONY: saying one thing and implying the opposite
   Stick close to your desks and never go to sea,
   And you all may be **Rulers of the Queen's Navee**. (W. S. Gilbert)

Mastering the types of figurative language will help you to answer many of the vocabulary test items on the SAT.

Word Clue 3: Synonym Discrimination

Are you happy at this moment? How would you describe your happiness? Are you *cheerful, contented, elated, exuberant, joyful, jubilant, pleased, satisfied?* The English language supplies synonyms by the dozens. We have so many words with similar meanings because English has roots in many languages. Greek, Latin, Celtic, Anglo-Saxon, German, French, Italian— the roll call sounds like a list of the world's languages, dead and living.

Two main streams, the native Anglo-Saxon and Norman, came together when the Normans under William the Conqueror overran England. But before and since, English has borrowed from Latin, Greek, and other sources to provide enrichment unparalleled in the world's languages. New coinages and borrowings occur today, enriching the treasure of English.

Notice how many degrees of happiness are suggested in the opening group of synonyms. *Happy* is a general word including many degrees of feeling. Some of the other words are more specific. *Elated, exuberant,* and *jubilant* suggest greater joy than *happy*. *Contented, pleased,* and *satisfied* suggest a moderate degree of happiness. *Cheerful* puts more emphasis on the obvious display of happiness. A person might be *happy* and not show anything. But *a cheerful* person makes an impression.

Although synonyms have generally similar meanings, no two words are interchangeable in all situations. Denotations and connotations vary enough to make every word slightly different from any other word. Synonyms may be as close as *pardon* and *excuse,* and still be different. We may say, "Pardon me" or "Excuse me," and the words seem interchangeable. But a prison inmate may be *pardoned,* not *excused.*

Look at another group of synonyms. *Gleam, glitter, glow, shimmer,* and *sparkle* all refer to light, but each word has a specific application of its own. A beacon may *gleam* in the wilderness but not *glitter* or *shimmer.* Certain metals may *glitter* with reflected light but not *gleam.* Embers may *glow* after a fire has died down but not *sparkle.* Beautiful eyes may *sparkle* but not *glow.* Water may *shimmer* in moonlight but not *gleam.* And so it goes for all groups of synonyms. Subtle differences determine suitability for a given context.

> The lawyer brought on a surprise witness in an attempt to aid the almost hopeless cause of his (client, customer, patient, patron).

All four words apply to a person who pays others for a service, but we use the word *client* with "lawyer." A doctor has a *patient.* A store has a *customer.* A theater has a *patron.*

> The landlord went to court to get an order to (dismiss, eliminate, evict, expel) the tenant from the apartment.

All four words have something to do with getting rid of something or someone. The word used for the removal of a tenant from occupancy is **evict**.

Problem

A truly _____ historian of science, Meyer neither _____ the abilities of the scientists she presents nor condescends to them.

(A) unbiased .. scrutinizes
(B) objective .. inflates
(C) impressionable .. patronizes
(D) reverent .. admires
(E) analytic .. evaluates

Strategy. Answer *(E)* is incorrect. If the historian is *analytic,* she will not fail to *evaluate.* Answer *(D)* is incorrect. If the historian is *reverent,* she will not fail to *admire.* Answer *(C)* is incorrect. If the historian is *impressionable,* the answer *patronizes* does not fit. It has nothing to do with being impressionable or not being impressionable.

Answers *(A)* and *(B)* have words somewhat similar in meaning: *unbiased* and *objective.* When this situation occurs, look closely at the second alternative: *scrutinizes* or *inflates.* This time, the two function words, *neither* and *nor,* suggest a comparison. We already know that the historian doesn't condescend to the scientists. If she doesn't condescend, then she also doesn't inflate their abilities.

Substitute the correct alternatives and look at the sentence again.

A truly **objective** historian of science, Meyer neither **inflates** the abilities of the scientists she presents nor condescends to them.

You might be led astray by thinking *unbiased* fits reasonably well in the first blank. The historian *is* probably *unbiased,* but *objective* is better. It has just the right meaning to fit here: "impersonal" and "fair." The clincher is the second alternative, *inflates.* It's opposed to "condescends" and keyed to **objective.**

TRIAL TEST

Write the letter for the word that is most appropriate in each sentence.

The thirsty travelers thought they saw a pond of water in the shimmering sand, but the pond proved to be a _____.
  (A) daydream
  (B) mistake
  (C) vision
  (D) mirage
  (E) fantasy

  _____D_____

All alternatives suggest that the travelers were deceived, but the specific word for a trick-of-the-eye in the desert is *mirage (D).*

1. Young Mozart _____ concertos, sonatas, and symphonies before he was thirteen.
  (A) constructed
  (B) composed
  (C) created
  (D) prepared
  (E) produced

  1 ____

2. When planning her landscaping, Anne decided upon a(n) _____ bed along the driveway.
  (A) eternal
  (B) everlasting
  (C) perpetual
  (D) perennial
  (E) fadeless

  2 ____

3. Citizens who fail to cooperate with law agencies _____ justice.
   (A) counteract
   (B) obstruct
   (C) repress
   (D) restrict
   (E) inhibit

   3 ____

4. Very little food is needed to _____ Owen's appetite.
   (A) glut
   (B) cloy
   (C) cram
   (D) satisfy
   (E) gorge

   4 ____

5. The boss sent around a brief _____ reminding employees of the changed office hours.
   (A) catalog
   (B) enumeration
   (C) memorandum
   (D) inscription
   (E) register

   5 ____

6. Yvonne's _____ athletic ability almost guarantees her success as a tennis player.
   (A) native
   (B) inbred
   (C) internal
   (D) ingrained
   (E) indispensable

   6 ____

7. Upon arising, Norm follows a rigid _____ each morning.
   (A) habit
   (B) routine
   (C) custom
   (D) fashion
   (E) practice

   7 ____

8. The two roads _____ in the outskirts of Springfield.
   (A) mingled
   (B) mixed
   (C) intertwined
   (D) merged
   (E) fused

   8 ____

9. The _____ edition of Shakespeare's plays exactly reproduces the look of the First Folio.
   (A) facsimile
   (B) duplicate
   (C) sample
   (D) copy
   (E) imitation

   9 ____

10. Sandra's _____ mannerisms are charming, not unpleasant.
    (A) impudent
    (B) defiant
    (C) pert
    (D) haughty
    (E) overbearing

    10 ____

Problem

He angrily _____ Plato as more consistently _____ than any other philosopher on all questions involving physical science, politics, ethics, or education.

(A) approved .. debatable
(B) defended .. refuted
(C) condemned .. wrong
(D) quoted .. brilliant
(E) derided .. acceptable

Strategy. The answers have two sets of similar words: *condemned* and *derided*, *approved* and *defended*. You will have to make a further analysis to find the correct answer.

Some answers can be rejected because they contradict themselves.

Answer *(A)* is incorrect. If he *approved* Plato, Plato would not be consistently *debatable*.

Answer *(B)* is incorrect. If he *defended* Plato, Plato would not be consistently *refuted*.

Answer *(D)* is incorrect. He wouldn't be *quoting* Plato "angrily" if Plato were more *brilliant* than any other philosopher.

Answer *(E)* is incorrect. If he *derided* Plato "angrily," he would not consider Plato *acceptable*.

Answer *(C)* fits perfectly. He angrily *condemned* Plato because he considered Plato so *wrong*. Both parts fit. Note that both *derided* and *condemned* are similarly negative. *Condemned* wins out because of the second alternative, *wrong*.

Sometimes close pairs like *condemned* and *derided* can lead you astray. In situations like these, the answer is usually found elsewhere, especially in the second alternative.

REVIEW

A. Following each sentence are three word choices in parentheses. Write the words in the spaces where they make best sense in the sentence.

1. The _____ hadn't done any real _____ to the body tissues, though the _____ was considerable. (damage, pain, wound)

2. She was _____ though perhaps not _____. Her every motion was _____. (beautiful, graceful, pretty)

3. He _____ his goal in life when he _____ the 440-yard race. The coaches all agreed that he had _____ the victory. (attained, earned, won)

4. His costume was so _____ and his manner of speaking so _____ that all of us considered him extremely _____. (comical, witty, grotesque)

5. Good, _____ food, prepared under _____ conditions, is influential in keeping us _____. (healthy, sanitary, wholesome)

6. Charles renounced the _____ of the French nobility he hated, and adopted the _____ of Darnay to conceal his real _____ of Evremonde. (name, pseudonym, title)

7. In a(n) _____ Ford, like the knights of _____ times, the _____ suitor for the hand of the town widow rode forth. (antiquated, elderly, olden)

8. The circus people considered it a great _____ for the aerialists to attempt their daring _____ at every _____. (achievement, feat, performance)

9. A petty _____ led to a long and bitter _____ that brought _____ to the little town. (feud, quarrel, strife)

10. The _____ whistles and the _____ crowd made for a _____ celebration. (boisterous, loud, shrill)

B. Many of our commonest words often have a number of colorful and discriminating synonyms. From the list of words below select a word to fill a blank in each of the following sentences.

distinguished   peered   stared
gazed   recognized   surveyed
glowered   scanned
observed   scrutinized

1. The travelers _____ in the distance the familiar towers of home.

2. The art dealer _____ the painting for any traces of retouching.

3. The angry knight _____ at his opponent before the battle.

4. The visitors _____ at the famous painting for a long time in admiration.

5. Deep in thought, she _____ unseeingly out of the window.

6. Her eye _____ the magazine hurriedly.

7. The small boy _____ eagerly through the knothole in an effort to see the baseball game.

8. He _____ the changes in society without alarm.

9. At that distance, her eye just _____ the climbers on the ridge.

10. From her viewpoint on top of Mt. Washington, she _____ the entire countryside.

SUMMARY
Word Clue 3: Synonym Discrimination

Synonyms are words of similar meaning, but no two words are always interchangeable. When you meet synonyms that need to be discriminated, consider connotation (pages 60–61). Try the words out in sentences of your own to see where a word fits or doesn't fit.

If you cannot see the difference between *inability* and *disability,* for example, try them out in a sentence. "Pete may have had a physical disability, but this meant no inability to play golf." If you interchange the words, the sentence doesn't work.

Synonym discrimination is especially helpful in sentence completion, analogy, and reading comprehension questions on the SAT.

Word Clue 4:   Associated Words

Problem
Aunt Ellen's specialized skills included weaving, knitting, embroidering, needlepoint, and _____.   (A) cooking   (B) refinishing   (C) painting   (D) crocheting   (E) sculpting

Strategy. It's obvious that all five answers might reasonably be assigned to Aunt Ellen, but in the context of grouping, the best answer is *crocheting* (D), another needlework skill.

   (D) Aunt Ellen's specialized skills include weaving, knitting, embroidering, needlepoint, and crocheting.

When your life experience expands, so does your vocabulary. If you become interested in watching football, you soon learn what these words mean: *clipping, cornerback, pass interference, blitz, bomb,* and *touchback.* You know where the *end zone* is and what the *hash marks* are used for. You discover that a *goal line stand* is not a wooden structure, a *nose guard* is not part of a helmet, and a *quarterback sack* is not a kind of bag. Once you become interested in any new subject, you soon learn a great many new words.

Reading a book about the sea introduces you to words like *tiller, forecastle, boom, tack, jib, port,* and *starboard.* If you join a theater group, you learn what *upstage, downstage,* and *stage left* mean. If you collect coins, you meet *numismatist, mint, obverse,* and *uncirculated.* Carpentry brings you into contact with *awl, veneer, gimlet,* and *keyhole saw.*

The more activities you engage in, the larger your vocabulary. The more you read, the more you increase your word resources.

Association sometimes helps in answering questions on the SAT, as in the following sentence-completion exercise.

Problem

Before leaving for his favorite painting spot, Mitsui took along brush, canvases, easel, spatula, and _____.

(A) pliers   (D) sweater
(B) dictionary   (E) mask
(C) palette

Strategy. Our painter might conceivably take any one of the items for one reason or another, but in the context of this sentence, the best answer is palette (C), a crucial element in the painter's carrying case.

(C) Before leaving for his favorite painting spot, Mitsui took along brush, canvases, easel, spatula, and palette.

TRIAL TEST

Write the letter for the word in each of the following groups that is *not* ordinarily associated with the others.

(A) cracked
(B) broken
(C) chipped
(D) mended
(E) split

           <u>D</u>

All alternatives suggest a breaking, but *(D)* emphasizes repair and is not as closely associated with the others.

1. (A) song
(B) rhapsody
(C) struggle
(D) hymn
(E) chant

1 ____

2. (A) dwell
(B) lodge
(C) reside
(D) support
(E) occupy

2 ____

3. (A) dye
(B) stain
(C) tint
(D) paint
(E) sketch

3 ____

4. (A) aid
(B) heed
(C) mind
(D) comply
(E) obey

4 ____

5. (A) medley
(B) mixture
(C) hodgepodge
(D) ballad
(E) blend

5 ____

6. (A) impetuous
(B) brash
(C) nervous
(D) bold
(E) impulsive

6 ____

7. (A) root
(B) leaf
(C) stem
(D) bark
(E) violet

7 ____

8. (A) differ
(B) argue
(C) agree
(D) dissent
(E) debate

8 ____

9. (A) majesty
(B) queen
(C) grandeur
(D) greatness
(E) splendor

9 ____

10. (A) flinch
(B) cringe
(C) scratch
(D) recoil
(E) shrink

10 ____

Problem

A sense of the absurd and a keen aware-ness of pretense developed Sharon's skill in satire, caricature, lampoon, and _____.

(A) eulogy
(B) commentary
(C) broadside
(D) dissertation
(E) parody

Strategy. The grouping of *satire, caricature,* and *lampoon* suggests that the answer is probably associated in meaning with all three. All three suggest the sharp humor in revealing human weakness. Like these three, the answer should poke fun for comic effect. (A), high praise, is opposed in meaning to the three. (B) and (D) are neutral. There is a broader, less devious attack in *broadside* (C). Only *parody* (E), a humorous imitation of a writer or composer's skill, fills the slot satisfactorily.

REVIEW

A. Write the letter for the word in each of the groups that is *not* ordinarily associated with the others.

1. (A) plain
(B) ordinary
(C) simple
(D) wealthy
(E) common

1 ____

2. (A) house
(B) apartment
(C) car
(D) cabin
(E) tent

2 ____

3. (A) mystery
   (B) puzzle
   (C) problem
   (D) solution
   (E) riddle

   3 ____

4. (A) championship
   (B) feast
   (C) picnic
   (D) banquet
   (E) party

   4 ____

5. (A) dollar
   (B) finance
   (C) peso
   (D) lira
   (E) franc

   5 ____

6. (A) probable
   (B) likely
   (C) hopeful
   (D) presumable
   (E) amusing

   6 ____

7. (A) song
   (B) ballad
   (C) hymn
   (D) anthem
   (E) story

   7 ____

8. (A) cabinet
   (B) chair
   (C) closet
   (D) cupboard
   (E) pantry

   8 ____

9. (A) beautiful
   (B) gorgeous
   (C) handsome
   (D) pretty
   (E) friendly

   9 ____

10. (A) theater
    (B) stadium
    (C) auditorium
    (D) skyscraper
    (E) arena

    10 ____

B. Write the letter for the word that *best* fits the meaning of the sentence as a whole.

1. Mountain men of the Old West, skilled in the challenges and dangers of the rugged terrain, often acted as _____ for wagon trains through the mountain passes.
   (A) foils   (D) challengers
   (B) pathfinders   (E) comrades
   (C) arbiters

   1 ____

2. Many of the imaginative dreams of the past, decried as being too _____, have proved to be practical solutions for today's problems.
   (A) negative   (D) visionary
   (B) utilitarian   (E) commonplace
   (C) vulgar

   2 ____

3. Kenneth Branagh's bleak and dour version of Shakespeare's Henry V is more _____ than the brighter film of Laurence Olivier.
   (A) popular   (D) placid
   (B) tantalizing   (E) austere
   (C) vital

   3 ____

4. The craggy summit of Mt. Adams can be reached only by a rugged trail passing over _____ rocks.
   (A) jagged   (D) beckoning
   (B) gray   (E) uniform
   (C) delicate

   4 ____

5. When Harris heard the enthusiastic praise for him at his testimonial, he could scarcely believe the _____ was intended for him.

(A) analysis (D) criticism
(B) digression (E) evocation
(C) eulogy

5 ____

SUMMARY

| Word Clue 4: | Associated Words |

1. In general, you learn a cluster of words in a group, not just one word in isolation.

2. If you can associate a group of words on a test question, you can often answer the question correctly even if you are not sure of the *specific* meaning of a word. For example, if you know only that a *parody* is some kind of literary work, you can disregard all word choices that have nothing to do with literature.

3. Rely on free association to recall related words. A group of words somehow associated with a test word will often provide the clues you need. The SAT takes words from every area of life; so, the more words you know, the better you will be able to make word associations.

| Word Clue 5: | **Words Within Words** |

Problem

Despite the separatist movements all around the world, most Americans wish to keep our nation _____.

(A) undisheartened
(B) prosperous
(C) indivisible
(D) modern
(E) unindemnified

Strategy. Longer words may be easy if broken down into their smaller parts. The clue to the best alternative is the mention of separatist movements preceded by the negative *despite*. The answer requires the idea of *not* being separated or divided. *Indivisible* (C) ("not able to be divided") is clearly the answer. Did you remember that the phrase "one nation indivisible" appears in the Pledge of Allegiance to the Flag? Sometimes bits of information come in handy when answering an SAT question.

(C) Despite the separatist movements all around the world, most Americans wish to keep our nation indivisible.

Which is the harder word, *foible* or *incomprehensibility*? *Foible* is harder, even though it's shorter.

Problem
To some readers, the _____ of the essayist's prose was too great a barrier to understanding the message, no matter how significant.
(A) incomprehensibility
(B) triviality
(C) intrepidity
(D) backwardness
(E) inadvertency

Strategy. The key word in the sentence is *understanding*. The answer must mean the opposite. Hidden inside *incomprehensibility* is a common word: *comprehend*. The prefix *in* often means "not." The suffix *ible* means "able." *Incomprehensibility* means "the quality of not being understandable."

(A) To some readers, the incomprehensibility of the essayist's prose was too great a barrier to understanding the message, no matter how significant.

TRIAL TEST

Write the number of each word in column A next to its opposite, or antonym, in column B.

A	B
1. disorganization	___ hope
2. inconclusive	___ clearness
3. disillusionment	___ efficiency
4. unpalatable	___ certain
5. miscalculation	___ normality
6. incoherence	___ tasty
7. improvident	___ understanding
8. commensurate	___ unequal
9. eccentricity	___ criticism
10. endearment	___ thrifty

Problem

Although the candidate's staff urged her to take a strong stand on the housing bill, she remained _____.

(A) obliging (D) staunch
(B) noncommittal (E) entrenched
(C) involved

Strategy. *Although* suggests that the missing word is opposed to *a strong stand.* Inside the larger word *noncommittal* is the common word *commit.* We may commit ourselves to an action or an idea. If we are *noncommittal,* we refuse to commit. *Noncommittal* is the best answer here.

In later sections you will deal with etymology. This is the study of word origins: prefixes, roots, and suffixes. A study of etymology will give you a powerful weapon for analyzing a word and studying its parts. But don't overlook the strategy outlined in this section. It sometimes works when etymology fails. The root of the word *unpalatable,* for example, does not appear in lists of common roots. Yet you might know the word *palate,* meaning *the roof of the mouth.* You might also know that palate has something to do with *taste.* You can guess that *unpalatable* is *not tasty.*

REVIEW

Write the number of each word in column A next to its antonym, or opposite, in column B.

A	B
1. liabilities	___ pliable
2. obstinate	___ kindly
3. inconsequential	___ wealthy
4. incredible	___ conflict
5. malevolent	___ important
6. indolent	___ mature
7. impoverished	___ energetic
8. cooperation	___ assets
9. vendor	___ believable
10. infantile	___ buyer

SUMMARY

Word Clue 5: **Words Within Words**

1. Long words are sometimes easier to define than short ones.

2. Many long words contain within them familiar elements that provide a key to the meaning.

3. Sometimes you may guess at a completely unfamiliar long word by finding the short word within it. For example, within *noncommittal* is the known word *commit*. This word clue will help you to analyze long words that appear on the SAT.

Word Clue 6: Allusions

Problem

Sonny had a(n) _____ appetite; he was known far and wide for his enormous consumption of any food set before him.

(A) mediocre
(B) inconsiderable
(C) sultry
(D) gargantuan
(E) discriminating

Strategy. If you are familiar with the word *gargantuan,* you may stop there. In literature, Gargantua was a giant king noted for his huge size and phenomenal appetite. *Gargantuan* (D) clearly fills the bill. Even if you do not know the allusion to Gargantua, you may still, however, find the answer by elimination. *Mediocre* (A) and *inconsiderable* (B) contradict *enormous. Sultry* (C) is irrelevant. *Discriminating* (E) must be rejected because Sonny ate "any food set before him."

(D) Sonny had a gargantuan appetite; he was known far and wide for his enormous consumption of any food set before him.

An **allusion** is a reference to a literary or historical person, place, or event.

In lifting the fallen tree trunk from the injured boy, the police officer showed *herculean* strength.

Karate is one of the best-known of the Japanese *martial* arts.

If you are unfamiliar with *herculean,* you notice that the sentence suggests that it means "powerful." The lifting achievement is obviously out of the ordinary. *Herculean* comes from *Hercules,* the Greek hero noted for his feats of strength. The concealed allusion, or reference to Hercules, in the word enriches understanding and adds drama to the sentence.

If you know what "karate" means, you can guess that *martial* has to do with discipline, fighting, and war. If you are not sure, however, you have an allusion concealed within *martial:* the word *Mars. Mars* is the name of the fourth planet of the solar system and also of the god of war. Knowing the origin of *martial* enriches the meaning and makes it easier to remember.

Types of Allusions

CONCEALED ALLUSIONS: *Spartan* attitude, *stentorian* voice, *pasteurized* milk, *cashmere* sweater, *iridescent* colors, *mercurial* disposition—all have allusions concealed within them.

Spartans were noted for discipline, courage, moderation, and thrift. A *spartan* attitude is characterized by discipline and bravery.

Stentor was a Greek herald during the Trojan War. His voice was as loud as that of fifty men all shouting together. *Stentorian* means "very loud."

Louis Pasteur, a French scientist, pioneered in the study of microbes and the harm they can do. *Pasteurizing* is a method of killing harmful microbes by heat. (It doesn't have anything to do with a "pasture.")

Cashmere comes from Kashmir, a district of India noted for the fine wool made from Kashmir goats.

Iris was the goddess of the rainbow. *Iridescent* colors are brilliant, shifting like the colors of the rainbow.

Mercury, messenger of the gods and god of speed and travel, moved about rapidly. *Mercurial* suggests changeability, fickleness.

WORDS FROM NAMES: Some words have come from names without change; for example, *boycott, derrick, diesel, macadam, ohm, volt, watt,* and *maverick.*

Boycott arises from Captain Charles Boycott, an English agent in Ireland. The Irish peasants, under Charles Parnell's leadership, refused to work for Boycott or do any business with him. Thus the word *boycott* came to mean a refusal to buy, sell, or have anything to do with a person, a company, or a product. Ironically, Boycott was the victim of the strategy, not its organizer!

Derrick is named for Thomas Derrick, a London hangman. A derrick, an apparatus for lifting heavy objects, looked like a gallows to the first persons using the name.

A *diesel* motor or vehicle is named for the German engineer who invented this kind of engine, Rudolph Diesel.

Macadam is named for John Loudon McAdam. Even as a child, McAdam constructed miniature road systems in his backyard. He pioneered the type of pavement that even today is common around the world.

Ohm, volt, and *watt* are all named for pioneers in the field of electricity and mechanics: Georg Simon Ohm, Alessandro Volta, and James Watt.

Maverick was named for Samuel August Maverick, a fiery Texas rancher who did not brand his cattle. *Maverick* has the primary meaning of "an unbranded calf" and the secondary meaning of a "fiery independent person." *Maverick* cattle do not stay with their group. *Mavericks* in politics can't be tied down to a rigid doctrine or party line.

Now see how you can use allusions to figure out definitions in trial test items.

TRIAL TEST

Select the alternative that best defines the word in capital letters. The explanation of the allusion appears in parentheses.

BLARNEY:
   (A) clever flattery
   (B) skin disease
   (C) plea for funds
   (D) down-to-earth reporting
   (E) repetition

                                    A

(Blarney Castle in Ireland has a famous stone. The person who kisses it is supposed to gain great skill in giving compliments and charming people.) Great skill in giving compliments is allied to clever flattery. The answer is *(A)*.

1. BEDLAM:
   (A) noise and confusion
   (B) calm and serenity
   (C) thoughtfulness and reflection
   (D) joy and contentment
   (E) time and tide

                                    1 ____

(Bedlam was the name of a London hospital for the insane. The full name of the hospital was once *St. Mary of Bethlehem.*)

2. MARTINET:
   (A) small bird
   (B) musical instrument
   (C) strict disciplinarian
   (D) long poem
   (E) piece of furniture

                                    2 ____

(Jean Martinet was a French general during the reign of Louis XIV. Martinet built the first modern army in Europe.)

3. MACHIAVELLIAN:
   (A) forthright
   (B) reliable
   (C) vital
   (D) sound
   (E) crafty

   3 ____

(Niccolò Machiavelli was an Italian writer who believed a ruler should use any means, honorable or deceitful, to maintain a strong government.)

4. QUIXOTIC:
   (A) grave
   (B) fearful
   (C) slow
   (D) contemptible
   (E) impractical

   4 ____

(Don Quixote, hero of Cervantes' novel, was a foolish dreamer who resolved to remake the world by impossible knightly feats.)

5. ACHILLES' HEEL:
   (A) funny bone
   (B) source of weakness
   (C) article of clothing
   (D) unpleasant person
   (E) ailment

   5 ____

(In Greek mythology, the mother of the hero Achilles dipped him, while a baby, into the River Styx to render him safe from injury. She held him by his heel, which was thus not protected.)

6. BERSERK:
   (A) speaking thoughtfully
   (B) sleeping restlessly
   (C) running evenly
   (D) planning craftily
   (E) raging violently

   6 ____

(Berserkers were wild warriors, who in battle howled, growled, bit their shields, and foamed at the mouth.)

7. HOBSON'S CHOICE:
   (A) dilemma
   (B) no alternative
   (C) cream of the crop
   (D) strong preference
   (E) argument

   7 ____

(Thomas Hobson, stablekeeper, let out his horses in strict rotation, not by rider's choice.)

8. MEANDER:
   (A) talk rapidly
   (B) shout loudly
   (C) wander aimlessly
   (D) walk steadily
   (E) run competitively

   8 ____

(The Meander was a river in Asia Minor noted for its twists and turns.)

9. MESMERISM:
   (A) philosophical disagreement
   (B) hypnotic fascination
   (C) dull repetition
   (D) commonplace wisdom
   (E) unchecked evil

   9 ____

(Franz Anton Mesmer was an Austrian physician who believed that his hands had miraculous healing powers, "animal magnetism.")

10. PROTEAN:
    (A) violently cruel
    (B) very nutritious
    (C) carefully selected
    (D) extremely changeable
    (E) attractive and appealing

    10 ____

(Proteus was a sea god, who was able to change his shape at will.)

Problem

Among the staid and sober employees of Grissom's law firm, Jared's erratic behavior seemed more and more _____.

(A) slothful   (D) preprogramed
(B) quixotic   (E) congenial
(C) somber

Strategy. If you recognize *quixotic* as deriving from the comical, unpredictable figure of Don Quixote, you have found the answer, (B). Again, even if you don't recognize the allusion, you can find the answer by eliminating the wrong answers. Mention of *staid* and *sober* is meant to contrast with *erratic* and the blank. The answer cannot be *slothful* (A), *preprogramed* (D), or *congenial* (E). Similarly, *somber* (C) is too close to *staid* and *sober*.

(B)   Among the staid and sober employees of Grissom's law firm, Jared's erratic behavior seemed more and more quixotic.

REVIEW

Write the letter of the alternative that best defines the word in capital letters.

1. BANTAM:
   (A) small, combative person
   (B) sports referee
   (C) reluctant scholar
   (D) volunteer soldier
   (E) welcoming host

   1 ____

2. BIGOT:
   (A) ambidextrous athlete
   (B) intolerant person
   (C) obvious pretender
   (D) marriage broker
   (E) charitable giver

   2 ____

3. CABAL:
   (A) oriental vegetable
   (B) term used in cricket
   (C) unintentional deception
   (D) Scottish folk dance
   (E) secret group

   3 ____

4. CHAUVINISM:
   (A) petty thievery
   (B) attitude of superiority
   (C) nonterminal disease
   (D) English political party
   (E) excessive meekness

   4 ____

5. CUPIDITY:
   (A) curiosity
   (B) amiability
   (C) rage
   (D) greed
   (E) loveliness

   5 ____

6. EXODUS:
   (A) departure
   (B) sermon
   (C) preacher
   (D) assault
   (E) moving stairway

   6 ____

7. GIBBERISH:
   (A) exotic spice
   (B) high-flown idea
   (C) instability
   (D) meaningless language
   (E) term used in sailing

   7 ____

8. HOCUS-POCUS:
   (A) disease resembling influenza
   (B) Austrian card game
   (C) popular song
   (D) art of composing limericks
   (E) sleight of hand

   8 ____

9. JOVIAL:
   (A) loud
   (B) well-intentioned
   (C) good-humored
   (D) complimentary
   (E) reserved in manner

   9 ____

10. LILLIPUTIAN:
   (A) rugged individualist
   (B) cult member
   (C) tiny person
   (D) skilled athlete
   (E) environmentalist

   10 ____

SUMMARY
Word Clue 6: Allusions

1. Some words are taken with little change from names of actual people: *cardigan, mackintosh, raglan, silhouette, zeppelin.*

2. Others use names of actual people, but with some change in form: *dunce, galvanize, nicotine, philippic, saxophone, teddy bear.*

3. Still others use words based on characters in legends and myths: *aurora, cereal, janitor, jovial, saturnine, titanic, vulcanize.*

4. Some words are taken from place names: *china, currant, italic type, morocco leather, peach, sardonic, spruce.*

5. Many words have interesting stories to tell: *blarney, Cassandra, donnybrook, Frankenstein, hector, Job's comforter, Pandora's box, pooh-bah, utopian.*

You may wish to refer to the following books to help you with allusions:

Robert Hendrickson, *Human Words*
Nancy Caldwell Sorel, *Word People*
Willard Espy, *O Thou Improper, Thou Uncommon Noun*
Robert Hendrickson, *Encyclopedia of Word and Phrase Origins*
Ivor H. Evans (ed.), *Brewer's Dictionary of Phrase and Fable*
Laurence Urdang, *Names and Nicknames of Places and Things*

Word Clues: | Review Test

The sentences that follow provide clues to meanings. Write the letter of the word that makes best sense in each sentence.

1. The _____ of the sandy soil caused the beachside buildings to be unsafe.
   (A) beauty
   (B) instability
   (C) height
   (D) age
   (E) length

   1 ____

2. Because of his _____ disposition, you can never predict what he will do.
   (A) sound
   (B) spartan
   (C) stentorian
   (D) mercurial
   (E) herculean

   2 ____

3. Use Renewo shampoo to give your hair its natural _____.
   (A) shininess
   (B) lustre
   (C) reflection
   (D) color
   (E) strength

   3 ____

4. The clever politician was as _____ as an eel.
   (A) quick
   (B) sharp
   (C) shiny
   (D) slippery
   (E) smart

   4 ____

5. The reason for the special traffic lights and turning lanes is to _____ traffic flow, not impede it.
   (A) facilitate
   (B) decrease
   (C) hinder
   (D) delay
   (E) hamper

   5 ____

6. The winner's eyes were _____ with excitement.
   (A) reflecting
   (B) sparkling
   (C) fiery
   (D) charged
   (E) transparent

   6 ____

7. The government's _____ in enforcing the new law encourages lawlessness.
   (A) promptness
   (B) cruelty
   (C) kindness
   (D) prudence
   (E) carelessness

   7 ____

8. The religious service ended with a _____ of praise and joy.
   (A) tune
   (B) melody
   (C) book
   (D) ballad
   (E) hymn

   8 ____

9. It is natural and _____ for a cat to keep itself clean.
   (A) internal
   (B) external
   (C) instinctive
   (D) learned
   (E) accepted

   9 ____

10. The hand-rubbed finish on the custom-built furniture was as _____ as satin.
    (A) slippery
    (B) slick
    (C) shiny
    (D) smooth
    (E) soft

    10 ____

Word Clues: Summary

Review these word clues from time to time. If you understand how word clues help you learn new words, you will do better on the vocabulary and reading sections of the SAT.

Clue 1   **Connotation and Denotation**
Connotation is the tone and meaning acquired by use. Denotation is the dictionary definition.

Father and *Daddy* illustrate the difference between connotation and denotation. Both words have a similar denotation: *male parent*, but the emotional associations with *Daddy* set it apart from the more staid *Father*.

Clue 2   **Figurative Language**
Simile: comparing by using *like* or *as*
    The clean sheets looked *as white as snow.*

Metaphor: implying a comparison of two different things without using *like* or *as*
    The lazy person could not *hold down a job.*

Personification: representing an object or idea as a person
    The *truth cries* out for justice.

Metonymy: using a word for another closely associated word
    She prepared a new *dish* for dinner.

Synecdoche: using the part for the whole, or the reverse
    The show featured fifty *dancing feet.*

Hyperbole: exaggerating for effect
    I was *scared to death.*

Understatement: emphasizing by saying less than is meant
    After the marathon I was a *little tired.*

Irony: saying one thing and implying the opposite
    I love this as much as *going to the dentist.*

Clue 3   **Synonyms:** discriminating between words of similar meaning
    The unpleasant boss was *haughty* and *overbearing.*

Clue 4   **Associated Words:** using related words you already know
    For my term paper I read ballads, sonnets, and many haiku.

Clue 5   **Words Within Words:** looking for the familiar smaller words in larger words
    She tried hard, but her efforts were *ineffectual* (effect).

Clue 6   **Allusions:** using a reference to a literary or historical person, place, or event.
    Martial (Mars) law is sometimes imposed in times of crisis.

Section III: Clues From Etymology

Etymology Clue 1: Latin Prefixes

Problem
Although the oak is a _____ tree, losing its leaves every year, some dead leaves persist through the winter, awaiting the impulses of spring to set them free.
(A) statuesque   (D) deciduous
(B) regressive   (E) provocative
(C) monochromatic

Strategy. Some familiarity with Latin prefixes, suffixes, and stems can help in questions like this. As the sentence states, deciduous trees lose their leaves every year. The root *cid* (from *cad)* means "fall." The prefix *de* means "down." Thus *deciduous* means "falling down." If you don't know the Latin elements, try the elimination process. *Statuesque* (A) has nothing to do with losing leaves. *Monochromatic* (C), "of one color," is equally off the topic. *Regressive* (B) and *provocative* (E) are not ordinarily applied to trees. Mastering the important Latin and Greek root words can pay dividends on tests and in reading comprehension.

(D) Although the oak is a deciduous tree, losing its leaves every year, some dead leaves persist through the winter, awaiting the impulses of spring to set them free.

Would you like the key to thousands of words? According to Dr. James I. Brown of the University of Minnesota, the following 14 words will help you master 100,000 words.

aspect	intermittent	oversufficient
detain	mistranscribe	precept
epilogue	monograph	reproduction
indisposed	nonextended	uncomplicated
insist	offer	

Epilogue and *monograph* are of Greek origin and will be treated in Etymology Clue 4, page 122. All the others contain basic Latin prefixes and roots, which will be treated here in clues 1-3. Several of the prefixes are Anglo-Saxon.

How is it possible for so few words to provide clues to the meanings of so many other words? English, like many other languages, builds words by putting elements together. We call these elements *prefixes, roots,* and *suffixes.* Here are some examples.

PREFIX: beginning word part
              *dis*like *re*port *de*part

ROOT: main word part
              dis*like* re*port* de*part*

SUFFIX: ending word part
              dislik*ing* report*er* depart*ure*

Some words, like *aspect* and *insist,* contain prefixes and roots. Other words, like *victor* and *nutrition,* contain roots and suffixes. Some words contain prefixes, roots, and suffixes; for example, *reproduction* and *uncomplicated.* Some words contain only roots, such as *course* and *pose.*

Where Our Words Come From

In the richness of its resources, English is different from most languages. There are four major streams in English: Greek, Latin, French (ultimately derived from Latin), and Anglo-Saxon. All four provide thousands of words for us to choose from. Synonyms abound in many possibilities. See how some synonyms of *mark,* all from a different source, enrich our language.

mark—from Anglo-Saxon. *Mark* is a general word suggesting a token, impression, feature.

signature—from Latin (modified). *Signature* is the special *mark,* usually handwritten, to identify a person.

imprimatur—from Latin (unchanged). *Imprimatur* is a *mark* of approval signifying that a book has been accepted for publication.

criterion—from Greek. *Criterion* suggests a *mark*, a test, a standard for judging.

vestige—from French (and ultimately Latin). *Vestige* suggests a small *mark,* a remnant of something that has disappeared.

graffiti—from Italian (and ultimately from Latin and Greek). *Graffiti* is a plural word designating *marks* that appear where they don't belong; for example, scribbling on public walls.

An average synonym dictionary suggests other synonyms for *mark;* for example, *badge, blemish, blot, boundary, brand, characteristic, disfigurement.* These words have diverse origins. All contribute to the English treasure house and make distinctions finer and more subtle in English.

You have noticed that a number of words above, listed from other languages, ultimately come from Latin or Greek. *Vestige* and *graffiti,* for example, come through French and Italian, but their ultimate source is Latin. French, however, is a far richer source than Italian.

We have labeled French as one of the four great sources of English, even though it is basically derived from Latin. When William the Conqueror settled in England after the Battle of Hastings in 1066, he brought Norman (French) customs, settlers, and language with him. We thus have pairs like *house* (Anglo-Saxon) and *mansion* (French) to enrich our language.

Many SAT questions rely on such words and word pairs for their answer choices.

Get the Dictionary Habit

To increase your vocabulary, get the dictionary habit. Look up words to find their derivations. Notice how the following excerpt from *Webster's New World Dictionary* tells the fascinating story of *volume*. Why should a word meaning *roll* be used to describe a flat book today? The meaning is there. *Volumes* were originally scrolls—rolled-up papers.

> **vol·ume** (väl′yōōm, -yəm) *n.* ⟦ME < MFr < L *volumen*, a roll, scroll, hence a book written on a parchment < *volutus*, pp. of *volvere*, to roll: see WALK ⟧ **1** orig., a roll of parchment, a scroll, etc. **2** *a*) a collection of written, typewritten, or printed sheets bound together; book *b*) any of the separate books making up a matched set or a complete work **3** a set of the issues of a periodical over a fixed period of time, usually a year **4** the amount of space occupied in three dimensions; cubic contents or cubic magnitude **5** *a*) a quantity, bulk, mass, or amount *b*) a large quantity **6** the degree, strength, or loudness of sound **7** *Music* fullness of tone —*SYN.* BULK¹ —**speak volumes** to be very expressive or meaningful —**vol′-umed** *adj.* *

Following a trail through the dictionary is like playing a video game. The quest can be fascinating and the rewards great. If you get the dictionary habit now, you'll have a lifetime of fun and growth. If, for example, you find *scroll* associated with *volume,* look up *scroll.* You'll find that *scroll* is related to the English *roll.* The dictionary suggests that you look up *escrow,* another related word. *Escrow* introduces you to another expression: *in escrow,* a phrase you should know in adult life. And so it goes if you use your dictionary often.

It has been estimated that 65% of the words in the dictionary come from Latin or Greek. Learning the basic Latin and Greek prefixes and roots is an excellent way to extend your vocabulary.

Common Latin Prefixes

In the following lists, the first column gives the prefix. The second column gives the basic meaning of the prefix. The third column gives a word or words showing the use of the prefix in a word. The fourth column explains

* With permission. From *Webster's New World Dictionary,* Third College Edition. Copyright © 1988 by Simon & Schuster, Inc.

how the prefix keeps some of its original meaning, even though the word may have come a long way from its introduction into English. This explanation often serves as a definition of the word, as well, though its major purpose is to show how a word acquires meanings.

Prefix	Meaning	Example	Explanation
a, ab	away, from	**a**vert	turn *away*
		abnormal	deviating *from* normal
ac, ad, a	to, toward	**ac**cess	coming *toward*
		advance	move *toward*
ambi	both	**ambi**dextrous	skilled with *both* hands
ante	before	**ante**cedent	coming *before*
circum	around	**circum**navigate	sail *around*
com, con	with	**com**pare	make equal *with*, regard as similar
contra	against	**contra**dict	say *against*
de	down, from, away	**de**pose	put *down*
dis, di	apart, from, not	**dis**enfranchise	*not* allow to vote
		digress	move *apart*
e, ex	out of	**e**vict	cast *out*
		exit	go *out*
extra	beyond, additional	**extra**ordinary	*beyond* the ordinary
in	into	**in**sert	put *into*
in	not	**in**imical	*not* friendly
inter	between	**inter**vene	come *between*
intra	within	**intra**mural	*within* a school
intro	in, into	**intro**duction	*into* a book
medi	middle	**medi**eval	pertaining to the *Middle* Ages
non	not	**non**productive	*not* productive
ob	against, toward	**ob**struct	build *against*, hinder
pen	almost	**pen**insula	*almost* an island
per	through, thoroughly	**per**nicious	*thoroughly* evil
		pervade	move *through*
post	after	**post**pone	put *after*
pre	before	**pre**arrange	arrange *before*
prim, prin	first	**prin**cipal	*first* teacher, leader
pro	forward, before	**pro**ceed	go *forward*
re	back, again	**re**mit	send *back*
		reread	read *again*
retro	back, backward	**retro**grade	*backward* motion
se	aside, apart	**se**cede	pull *apart*
sub	under	**sub**marine	*under* the sea
super, supr	above, beyond	**super**human	*beyond* the human
		supreme	*above* all others
trans	across	**trans**migrate	move *across*
ultra	beyond, extremely	**ultra**modern	*beyond* the modern
vice	in place of	**vice** president	*in place of* the president

A few prefixes change the last letter to match the first letter of the root word. Thus **ad** becomes **af** *(affect),* **ag** *(aggression),* **al** *(alliteration),* **an** *(annex),* **ap** *(apply),* **ar** *(arrest),* and **at** *(attend).* **Sub** becomes **suc** *(succumb),* **suf** *(suffer),* **sug** *(suggest),* and **sup** *(supplant).* **In** becomes **il** *(illegal),* **im** *(immature),* and **ir** *(irregular).*

A word of caution about roots, prefixes, and word meanings: words change in use. Word meanings sometimes depart from the original strict meanings. *Extravagant,* for example, according to its root and prefix means "wandering beyond." The word has, however, acquired a wider, more figurative sense. *Extravagant* purchases, for example, "wander beyond" the normal and wise. *Extravagant* yarns "wander beyond" the reasonable. Once you know the roots, you will find these extended meanings interesting.

Try to use your new information in answering the following sentence-completion item.

Problem
Driving with a valid driver's license is _____ for operating a motor vehicle, but boating regulations are too lenient. (A) suggested   (D) frequent (B) archaic   (E) mandatory (C) debated

Strategy. Since states demand the issuance of a driver's license, the answer should contain the thought of requirement. Only *mandatory* carries the idea of "command," from the root *mand.*

   (E) Driving with a valid driver's license is mandatory for operating a motor vehicle, but boating regulations are too lenient.

TRIAL TEST

Take the following trial test for practice in using Latin prefixes. Fill in the blank in each sentence by writing a Latin prefix from the list on page 95. The word in italics is a clue to the needed prefix. The number in parentheses tells the number of letters needed to complete each word.

As I went *back* in imagination to my childhood home, the old cottage seemed huge in **retro**spect. (5)	The italicized word *back* tells you the prefix **retro** should be inserted. *Retrospect* means "looking backward."

1. Most of the words in the description are _____fluous, for they go far *beyond* what is needed to make an effective picture. (5)

2. I feel _____valent toward Jennifer, for I find her *both* charming and annoying at times. (4)

3. A(n) _____mortem is an examination made *after* death to determine the cause of death. (4)

4. Doug gave his _____ry opinion and spoke vehemently *against* the proposal. (6)

5. Because he could *not* function in the game, the fullback was put on the _____abled list. (3)

6. A(n) _____patriate is a person who goes *out* of his country to settle elsewhere. (2)

7. The artist gave a(n) _____spective show and enabled her fans to look *back* at her illustrious past. (5)

8. Marie Antoinette had a(n) _____cluded villa, *apart* from the bustle of the palace. (2)

9. A(n) _____errant social group is one that deviates *from* the normal. (2)

10. That _____diluvian idea of yours must have originated *before* the flood! (4)

Problem

Although the agreement was finally signed in October, under the terms of the pact, payments of lost wages would be _____ to April, the time the original contract _____.

(A) retroactive . . expired
(B) charged . . began
(C) referred . . expanded
(D) conducive . . germinated
(E) applied . . deteriorated

Strategy. The prefix **retro**, meaning "back," provides the key to this answer. *Retroactive* suggests going back into the past, usually to a period before another event. Here the contract was signed in October, but the pact pretended it had been signed in April, with full benefits beginning at that time. The only choice that makes sense is *(A)*. Wages are paid as though the new agreement immediately followed the expiration of the old.

None of the alternatives makes good sense when preceding the words "to April."

Latin Prefixes Denoting Number

Prefix	Meaning	Example	Explanation
bi	two	**bi**ennial	every *two* years
cent	hundred	**cent**imeter	*hundredth* of a meter
dec	ten	**dec**imal	system of *tens*
duo, du	two	**du**et	performance by *two*
duodec	twelve	**duodec**imal	system of *twelves*
mill	thousand	**mill**ennium	a *thousand* years
multi	many	**multi**tude	*many* persons
nona	nine	**nona**genarian	*ninety-year-old*
novem	nine	**Novem**ber	*ninth* month (originally)
oct	eight	**oct**et	group of *eight*
omni	all	**omni**scient	*all-knowing*
quadr	four	**quadr**ilateral	*four-sided*
quinqu, quint	five	**quinqu**ennial	every *five* years
		quintuplets	multiple birth *of five*
semi	half	**semi**circle	*half* a circle
sept	seven	**Sept**ember	*seventh* month (originally)
sex	six	**sex**tet	group of *six*
tri	three	**tri**ple	*three* times
uni	one	**un**animous	of *one* mind

Problem

In an election decided by majority or plurality, the vote need not be _____.

(A) counted   (D) unbiased
(B) total   (E) impartial
(C) unanimous

Strategy. Again, the Latin provides some help. *Uni* means "one" and appears in words like *union, united,* and *unified. Anim* means "mind." *Unanimous* is "of *one* mind . . . one vote." (A) and (B) suggest a faulty procedure. (D) and (E) suggest a misuse of the voting process.

> (C) In an election decided by majority or plurality, the vote need not be unanimous.

TRIAL TEST

Fill in the blank in each sentence by writing a Latin number prefix from the list above. The word in italics is a clue to the needed prefix. The number in parentheses tells the number of letters needed to complete each word.

The setting sun made a perfect **semi**circle, as only *half* was visible on the horizon. (4)

The italicized word *half* tells us the prefix *semi* should be inserted.

1. Some colleges have a(n) _____ mestral organization, dividing the school year into *three* parts. (3)

2. A(n) _____ave is the *eighth* full tone above a given tone, having twice as many vibrations a second. (3)

3. Brock's plans are _____farious, having *many* angles and procedures. (5)

4. In a(n) _____nary system, *two* suns revolve about each other. (2)

5. Our town is celebrating its _____centennial, having been in existence *half* a hundred years. (4)

6. A truly _____que specimen is *one* of a kind. (3)

7. Superman was not _____potent, for he could not overcome *all* obstacles. (4)

8. A(n) _____angle is a *three*-sided figure. (3)

9. In the _____igrade, or Celsius, thermometer, the difference between the boiling point and the freezing point is divided into *100* degrees. (4)

10. A(n) _____ipede may seem to have a *thousand* legs, but the actual number is between 100 and 200. (4)

Problem

Raccoons are survivors because of their flexibility, adaptability, and _____ appetite.

(A) innovative
(B) finicky
(C) omnivorous
(D) ill-proportioned
(E) delicate

Strategy. You may remember *carnivore,* "meat-eating animal," and *herbivore,* "vegetation-eating animal." The prefix *omni,* "all," suggests that an omnivore eats both flesh and vegetation. *Omnivorous* is the preferred word in this context.

REVIEW

Fill in the blank in each sentence by writing the Latin prefix that makes best sense. The word in italics is a clue. The number in parentheses tells the number of letters needed.

---

1. A good _____ator takes a *middle* position, favoring neither one side nor the other. (4)

2. A(n) _____opus is so named because it has *eight* arms. (3)

3. Walt's _____terminable speeches seem *not* to have a purpose or an end. (2)

4. When a seller offers a used car, he is often shocked to learn how much normal _____preciation has brought *down* the price of the car. (2)

5. A group of *five* musicians is called a(n) _____et. (5)

6. An idea that is said to correspond *with* another is _____gruent with that idea. (3)

7. The _____urban bus service ran *between* towns. (5)

8. _____historic events took place *before* the invention of writing. (3)

9. The bottle held only a(n)_____iliter, or *one-tenth* of a liter, of liquid. (3)

10. If you're going *to* Walt Disney World, buy your ticket of _____mission at the main gate. (2)

11. By _____polation Helen went *beyond* present statistics and estimated the probable population of Grimesdale by the year 2010. (5)

12. A(n) _____spect person looks *around* carefully before taking action. (6)

13. A(n) _____el is a formal fight between *two* persons. (2)

14. Our _____genitors, those who came *before* us, have left for us a valuable heritage of art and wisdom. (3)

15. For my taste the Cortland apple is _____lative, far *above* other apples in flavor and texture. (5)

16. The Patriots stated once *again* what they believed in and _____affirmed their allegiance to the cause of freedom. (2)

17. A presidential election is always a(n) _____ennial event, occurring every *four* years. (5)

18. A layer of_____cutaneous fat, *under* the outer layer of skin, provides insulation against the cold. (3)

19. Tiny_____mitters, powered by solar batteries, send messages *across* millions of miles of space. (5)

20. Because the president had been delayed, the _____ president acted *in place of* the president and opened the meeting. (4)

SUMMARY
Etymology Clue 1: Latin Prefixes

1. Etymology, the study of word origins, is extremely helpful in figuring out the meaning of new and unknown words.

2. A great many English words begin with common Latin prefixes and number prefixes. If you know the prefix, you have a good chance of figuring out the whole word.

3. A few prefixes change the last letter to match the first letter of the root word:

    sub—suc (succumb)   **sub**—suf (suffer)

    sub—sug (suggest)   **sub**—sup (supplant)

Etymology Clue 2: | Latin Roots—Verbs

Note how a knowledge of roots helps with a sentence-completion item.

> ### Problem
>
> Pittsburgh is situated at the _____ of two rivers, the Allegheny and the Monongahela, thus forming the Ohio.
>
> (A) confluence
> (B) watershed
> (C) rapids
> (D) cascades
> (E) divergence

Strategy. The sentence suggests that two rivers join at Pittsburgh. *Confluence* (A) means "flowing together." *Flu* means "flow" and appears in words like *fluid, affluent,* and *influenza. Con* is a prefix meaning "together." (B), (C), and (D) do not address the major point of joining. (E) suggests the opposite. *Verg* means "turn" or "bend," but *di* means "away." Thus *divergence* is opposed to *confluence.*

(A) Pittsburgh is situated at the confluence of two rivers, the Allegheny and the Monongahela, thus forming the Ohio.

Now we come to the longest list in our study of word elements: Latin roots. Though the lists seem overwhelmingly long, do not lose heart. You already *know* most of these roots because you see them every day in familiar words. You already know, for example, that *victory* involves *conquering* a person, a group, an obstacle. You may not have put that meaning into so many words before, but your knowledge gives you an advantage in working with the root **vinc-vict**, meaning "conquer." When you meet *invincible,* you know it means "unconquerable."

When you go over the lists that follow, associate a word with each root, preferably a word you already know. Doing so will expand your vocabulary enormously and also help you meet many new words with confidence.

Latin Roots

The lists of Latin roots here are by no means all the roots used in English words, but they include most of the important and helpful ones. Don't forget, even if you meet a word with a root not included in the lists, you can often guess at the meaning of the word by thinking of other words with the same root.

To make the lists more manageable, the words have been arbitrarily divided into two large categories: those derived from Latin nouns and adjectives and those derived from Latin verbs. Some words are borderline. *Labor,* for example, comes from a Latin noun which is related to a Latin verb. The lists 1, 2, and 3 are for convenience, so that you can work with a small number of roots at one time. A trial test follows each list.

Roots From Latin Verbs—1

Root	Meaning	Example	Explanation
ag, act	do, act, drive	**ag**ile	*active*
am, ami	love	**ami**able	good-natured (originally *lov*able)
arbit	judge	**arbit**rate	*judge* between
aud	hear	**aud**ible	able to be *heard*
cad, cas, cid	fall	**cad**ence	*fall* of the voice in speaking
		coin**cid**ence	a *falling* together of events
can, cant, chant	sing	**cant**or	*singer*
cap, capt, cip, cept	take	**cap**ture	*take* by force
ced, cess, cede, ceed	go	pro**ceed**	*go* forward
		re**cede**	*go* back
cern, cert	perceive, separate	dis**cern**	recognize as *separate*, see clearly
cis, cid, caed	kill, cut	sui**cide**	*kill*ing of oneself
		in**cis**ion	*cutting* into
clam, claim	cry out, shout	ex**claim**	*cry* out
		pro**clam**ation	*crying* forth
clud, claus, clus	shut, close	se**clud**ed	*shut* away
cogn	know	re**cogn**ize	*know* by some detail
col, cult	till, inhabit	agri**cult**ure	*till*ing the fields
cred	believe	**cred**ible	*believ*able
cresc, crease	grow	in**crease**	*grow* in size
curr, curs	run	in**curs**ion	*run*ning in, invasion
da, dat, don	give	**don**ation	*gift*
dic, dict	say	**dic**tate	*say* aloud
doc	teach	**doc**trine	*teach*ing
dorm	sleep	**dorm**ant	*sleep*ing, inactive
duc, duct	lead	ab**duct**	*lead* away, kidnap
err	wander	**err**ant	*wander*ing
fac, fec, tic, fy	do, make	magni**fy**	*make* large
		factory	place where things are *made*
fer, lat	carry	re**fer**	*carry* back
		trans**late**	*carry* across
flect, flex	bend	**flex**ible	easily *bent*
flu, flux	flow	**flu**id	something that *flows*
		in**flux**	a *flowing* in
frang, fract, frag, fring	break	**fract**ure	*break*
		fragment	*broken* piece

Root	Meaning	Example	Explanation
fug	flee	**fug**itive	one who *flees*
fund, fus	pour	in**fus**ion	*pour*ing in
gen	cause, bear, produce	con**gen**ital	*born* with
ger, gest	carry	belli**ger**ent	one who *carries* war to another

TRIAL TEST

Fill in the blank in each sentence by writing a Latin root from the preceding list. The word in italics is the clue to the needed root. The number in parentheses tells the number of letters needed.

Mark was too **cred**ulous, *believ*ing everything he heard. (4)

The italicized *believ* tells us the root **cred** should be inserted.

---

1. A(n) _____ent moon soon after sunset tells us the moon is waxing, or *growing*. (5)

2. To prevent someone from *know*ing you, you might travel in_____ito. (4)

3. To *say* in advance is to pre_____. (4)

4. Our play group has a bene_____tor who has *done* many good things for us. (3)

5. He was charged with an in_____ion because he had *broken* the law about parking in restricted areas. (5)

6. Marcia is _____ent in French: her speech *flows* so effortlessly. (3)

7. The _____ry *carried* us across New York Harbor and back. (3)

8. Wally was in_____ed to wear the clown costume and was even *led* to performing a humorous routine. (3)

9. The _____itories could *sleep* a dozen people in a pinch. (4)

10. The sports fans at the airport *shouted* when the plane landed and _____ored for a brief speech by the triumphant coach. (4)

11. When we decided to sell the house, we arranged for a real estate _____ent to *act* for us. (2)

12. When we opened the crowded closet, a pro_____ion of odds and ends *poured* forth. (3)

13. The _____erator *produced* enough current for a small village. (3)

14. Brett *ran* his eye over the manuscript, but his _____ory glance provided no clue to the importance of the contents. (4)

15. If you *go* beyond our budgeted expenditures and ex_____ the amount allotted to costumes, you'll put us in the red before we start. (4)

16. The witch doctor pronounced the in_____ation in a *sing*song voice. (4)

17. Ralph Waldo Emerson preached the _____trine of self-reliance and so *taught* his contemporaries to believe in themselves. (3)

18. Several wealthy _____ors *gave* sufficient funds to build a new rectory. (3)

19. Re_____ees were *fleeing* the city under attack. (3)

20. The *killing* of a brother is called fratri_____e. (3)

Roots From Latin Verbs—2

Root	Meaning	Example	Explanation
grad, gress	walk	prog**ress**	a *walk* forward
hab, hib	hold	**hab**it	something that *holds* us
her, hes	stick	co**here**	*stick* together
		ad**hes**ive	something that *sticks* to something else
it	go	ex**it**	*go* out
jac, ject	throw	re**ject**	*throw* back
jud	judge	pre**jud**ice	a *judg*ing in advance
jung, junct, jug	join	**junct**ion	a *join*ing
jur	swear	**jur**or	one *sworn* to give a just verdict
leg, lect	choose, gather, read	il**leg**ible	not *read*able
		col**lect**	*gather* together
loqu, locut	speak, talk	**loqu**acious	*talk*ative
mand	entrust, command	**mand**ate	a land *entrust*ed to another country
merg, mers	dip, plunge	sub**merge**	*dip* below water
mit, miss	send	trans**mit**	*send* across
mon, monit	warn	ad**mon**ition	mild *warn*ing
mov, mot	move	**mot**or	something that *moves*
mut	change	**mut**able	*change*able
nasc, nat	born	**nat**ive	one *born* in a country
neg	deny	**neg**ative	*deny* truth of
ora	speak, pray	**ora**tor	*speak*er
orn	decorate	ad**orn**	*decorate*
pat, pass	suffer	**pat**ient	one who *suffers,* who receives care
pel, puls	drive	re**pel**	*drive* back
		com**puls**ion	*driv*ing force
pet	seek	centri**pet**al	*seek*ing the center
plac	please	im**plac**able	unable to be *pleas*ed
plaud, plus, plod, plos	clap, strike	ap**plaud**	*clap*
plic, plex, ply	fold	com**plic**ated	involved (*folded* in on itself)
pon, pos	place, put	post**pon**e	*place* after
port	carry	im**port**	*carry* in
prehend, prehens, pris	seize	com**prehend**	*seize* (as an idea)
press	press, print	im**press**ion	something *pressed* or *print*ed on
prob	prove	**prob**ation	a period of test, of *prov*ing someone can perform as expected
pugn	fight	**pugn**acious	ready to *fight*

Root	Meaning	Example	Explanation
quit, ques, quis	seek	in**quis**itive	*seek*ing information
rid, ris	laugh	**rid**iculous	*laugh*able

TRIAL TEST

Fill in the blank in each sentence by writing a Latin root from the preceding list. The word in italics is the clue to the needed root. The number in parentheses tells the number of letters needed.

1. Cheryl *sent* the re_____tance to the power company. (3)

2. In grammar, a con_____ion *joins* two elements together. (5)

3. Who will be chosen to ad_____icate the lawsuit, *judg*ing whether the plaintiff's case will prevail? (3)

4. Pauline in_____ed a few witty remarks, *throw*ing them in casually at intervals. (4)

5. Humans are planti_____e creatures, for they *walk* on the soles of their feet. (4)

6. *Place* this envelope in the de_____it box. (3)

7. A(n) _____tionnaire is designed to *seek* information. (4)

8. Geraldine uses a(n) _____manteau for *carry*ing documents and letters. (4)

9. The minister *read* the Bible verse from the _____ern. (4)

10. Some col_____ial expressions are suitable for *speak*ing but not for writing. (4)

11. The judge re_____ed the prisoner to a detention home, *entrust*ing him to a pair of sheriff's deputies. (4)

12. Sheila im_____ed the dusty jacket in warm soapy water, *dip*ping it again and again until the stains were removed. (4)

13. The governor *changed* his mind and com_____ed the condemned man's sentence to life imprisonment. (3)

14. The re_____ent industrial life of many New England cities proves that a *rebirth* of vigor is not impossible. (4)

15. A(n) _____ligent driver may *deny* others the right to life. (3)

16. The police officers ap_____ed the smuggler and *seized* his cargo. (7)

17. The hero of Cotter's novel is *driven* by unpredictable im_____es. (4)

18. Naturally, Isabelle enjoyed the *clapping* of the audience and the _____its of the critics. (5)

19. A com_____ent person is *pleased* with himself and quite smug. (4)

20. The _____ition *seeks* to bring to the notice of the authorities the dangerous intersection of Fifth and Main streets. (3)

Roots From Latin Verbs—3

Root	Meaning	Example	Explanation
rog	ask	inter**rog**ate	*ask*
rump, rupt	break	**rup**ture	*break*
sal, salt, suit	leap	**sal**ient	*leaping* out
sci	know	con**sci**ous	able to *know*
scrib, script	write	in**scrib**e	*write* in
		in**scrip**tion	*writing* in
seg, sect	cut	bi**sect**	*cut* in two
sed, sess	sit	**sess**ion	a *sitting*
sens, sent	feel	**sens**ation	*feeling*
sequ, secu	follow	**sequ**el	work that *follows* another
solv, solut	loosen	**solv**ent	something that *loosens*
spec, spect	see	**spect**acles	device for *seeing*
spir	breathe	re**spir**atory	pertaining to *breathing*
sta, sist, stit	stand	**sta**ble	able to *stand*
string, strict	bind	**string**ent	*binding*
stru, struct	build	de**struct**ion	opposite of *building*
tang, tact	touch	**tang**ible	able to be *touch*ed
tent, tin, tain	hold	**ten**acious	*holding* on
tend, tens, tent	stretch	ex**tend**	*stretch* out
torqu, tort	twist	dis**tort**ed	*twist*ed
trah, tract	draw	at**tract**ion	something that *draws*
trib	share, pay	**trib**ute	something *paid*
trud, trus	thrust	in**trud**e	*thrust* in
turb	agitate	dis**turb**	*agitate*
vad, vas	go	in**vad**e	*go* in
ven, vent	come	con**ven**e	*come* together
verg	lean, turn	con**verg**e	*turn* together
vert, vers	turn	re**vers**e	*turn* back
vid, vis	see	**vis**ible	able to be *seen*
vinc, vict	conquer	con**vinc**e	*conquer* (in a discussion)
viv, vict	live	re**viv**e	bring back to *life*
voc, vok	call	**voc**ation	*calling*
vol	wish, will	in**vol**untary	against the *will*
volv, volut	turn	re**volv**e	*turn* around

TRIAL TEST

Fill in the blank in each sentence by writing a Latin root from the preceding list. The word in italics is the clue to the needed root. The number in parentheses tells the number of letters needed.

1. The entertainer was able to *twist* his body into the strangest con_____ions. (4)

2. The boa con_____or *binds* and crushes its foe. (6)

3. The car *standing* in the garage will remain _____tionary until you replace the battery. (3)

4. Tele_____ion enables us to *see* events happening far away. (3)

5. The strong armies of Genghis Khan were in_____ible, *conquering* every force in their path. (4)

6. Ancient Egyptian _____es *wrote,* on stone, messages that still survive. (5)

7. _____entary people *sit* too much, avoiding exercise. (3)

8. Although English royalty could not *hold* onto real power, it has re_____ed the pomp and glitter of centuries ago. (4)

9. Fred dreaded dis_____ing the frog in biology class, but after the first *cut* he became fascinated by the complexity of his subject. (4)

10. The cor_____ administration *broke* every moral and legal guideline in running the city. (4)

11. _____ion *stretches* mind and body almost to the breaking point. (4)

12. The purpose of the in_____ion was to *see* if the regulations had been followed. (5)

13. Some of our actions have important con_____ences that *follow* us all our days. (4)

14. The con_____ions of the brain show twists, *turns,* and folds on the surface. (5)

15. The storm *agitated* the formerly calm lake and caused dangerous _____ulence for small boats. (4)

16. Bene_____ent actions arise from feelings of *goodwill* toward others. (3)

17. To re_____e a license is to *call* it back and cancel it. (3)

18. A di_____ent point of view *turns* from the average. (4)

19. To inter_____e in a dispute is to *come* between the two parties in an attempt to settle the argument. (3)

20. The plastic models are formed by ex_____ion, that is, by *thrusting* the plastic through small holes to provide the desired shape. (4)

Problem

Though deceptively smooth in some areas, the Colorado River can become a _____, raging torrent in others.

(A) disagreeable
(B) turbulent
(C) quiescent
(D) distorted
(E) circuitous

Strategy. Though all alternatives may be applied to some river somewhere, only one word fits the sentence: *turbulent.* Turbulent (B) contains the Latin root verb *turb* "agitate." *Turbulent* means "agitated," "stormy," "violent." The pairing with *raging* and the contrast with *smooth* identifies (B) as the answer. (A) is too mild. (C) is opposed in meaning. (D) and (E) are unsuitable adjectives for a raging torrent.

> (B) Though deceptively smooth in some areas, the Colorado River can become a turbulent, raging torrent in others.

REVIEW

Fill in the blank in each sentence by writing a Latin root from the three preceding lists. The word in italics is the clue to the needed root. The number in parentheses tells the number of letters needed.

1. The critic de_____ed the novel's purpose and *laughed* at the intended motivation of the central character. (3)

2. Humane societies protest _____isection, research operations performed on *living* animals. (3)

3. Huge skyscrapers are *built* by specialized con_____ion contractors. (6)

4. Gail is so _____ulous she'll *believe* anything. (4)

5. The _____cle at Delphi *spoke* words that could be taken in many ways. (3)

6. We need an impartial _____er to *judge* the merits of the case. (5)

7. The letter expressed the ap_____ation of the council and *proved* that government was responsible for public needs. (4)

8. Daryl fancies he is omni_____ent, *knowing* everything about everything. (3)

9. The re_____e *shut* himself away from all society. (4)

10. The slightest sound on stage can be *heard* all through the _____itorium. (3)

11. The keynote *speaker* delivered a lengthy _____tion. (3)

12. A manu_____tured article was once, by word origin, *made* by hand. (3)

13. Many elements of Victorian houses were purely _____amental, added for *decoration,* not function. (3)

14. The ex_____it *held* many items of interest to the visitor. (3)

15. Are insects _____ient creatures that *feel* some kind of primitive emotions, like fear? (4)

16. The _____or *drew* the plow through the moist soil. (5)

17. Before the jet aircraft had been perfected, airplanes were *driven* by one or more pro_____lers. (3)

18. The spy inter_____ed the message and *took* it to the enemy contact. (4)

19. The referee ad_____ished the boxer, *warning* him that another foul would cost him the match. (3)

20. Some families are _____ile, *touching* and hugging each other on greetings and farewells. (4)

SUMMARY
Etymology Clue 2: Latin Roots—Verbs

1. Because English contains more words from Latin than from any other language, Latin roots, as well as prefixes, can help you figure out meanings—and SAT answers.

2. Just one root can lead to several words:

   port ("carry")—import, deport, report, portable

Etymology Clue 3: Latin Roots—Nouns and Adjectives

Latin verbs have provided a solid list of roots to help you in attacking new words. Latin nouns and adjectives also supply information you can use to master new and unfamiliar words. Spend time on these lists as you prepare for the SAT.

Roots From Latin Nouns and Adjectives—1

Root	Meaning	Example	Explanation
al, alter, altr	other	**al**ien	person from *another* land
		altruism	concern for *others*
anim	life, mind	**anim**ated	*lively*
		un**anim**ous	of one *mind*
ann, enn	year	**ann**ual	*year*ly
		mill**enn**ium	period of a thousand *years*
apt, ept	suitable, appropriate	**apt**itude	*suitabili*ty for a task
		in**ept**	not *suitable,* unfit
aqu	water	**aqu**eous	*water*y
arm	arm, weapon	**arm**ament	*weapon*ry
art	art, craft, skill	**art**isan	a person skilled in a *craft*
bell	beautiful	em**bell**ish	make *beautiful*
bene, bon	good	**bene**factor	one who does *good*
brev	short	ab**brev**iate	*short*en
cand	white, glowing	in**cand**escent	*glow*ing
capit	head	**capit**al	chief* *(head)* city
centr	center	ec**centr**ic	off *center*
civ, cit	city, citizen	**civ**ic	dealing with problems of the *city*
cor	heart	**cor**dial	sincere, from the *heart*
corp	body	**corp**oreal	*bodi*ly
crux, cruc	cross	**cruc**iform	*cross*-shaped
culp	blame, fault	**culp**able	deserving *blame*

Root	Meaning	Example	Explanation
cur	care	pedi**cur**e	foot *care*
dent	tooth	**dent**al	pertaining to *teeth*
dia, di	day	**di**urnal	*daily*
digit	finger	**digit**al	pertaining to *finger*
dom	house, home	**dom**icile	*house*
domin	master	**domin**ate	rule as a *master*
dur	hard, lasting	**dur**able	*lasting*
ego	I, self	**ego**centric	centered on the *self*
equ	horse	**equ**ine	pertaining to the *horse*
equ	equal	in**equ**ality	condition of being *unequal*
ev	age, time	co**ev**al	of the same *age*
felic	happy	**felic**ity	*happiness*
ferv	boil, bubble	**ferv**ent	*boil*ing, ardent
fid	faith	**fid**elity	*faith*fulness
fil	son	**fil**ial	pertaining to a *son*

*Here's another example of the incredible richness of English. *Chief,* meaning head, comes to us through the French; the French word itself comes from the Latin *capit.* When English borrows the same word twice, the borrowings are called *doublets.* See pages 136, 163.

TRIAL TEST

Fill the blank in each sentence by writing a Latin root from the previous list. The word in italics is the clue to the needed root. The number in parentheses tells the number of letters needed.

The **cur**ator of a museum is a person who takes *care* of the exhibits.

The italicized word *care* tells you to use the root **cur**. The *curator* takes care of the museum.

1. The presti_____ator was a superb magician, as he demonstrated trick after trick with nimble *fingers*. (5)

2. _____ity in writing suggests that the writer take the *shortest* path to his goal, avoiding all unnecessary words. (4)

3. Objects without *life* are in_____ate. (4)

4. A name *other* than your own is a(n) _____ias. (2)

5. The important testimony of the key witness ex_____ated the defendant, removing any *blame* from his actions. (4)

6. A(n) _____uity is an amount of money paid every *year*. (3)

7. A substance _____eficial to the health is *good* for you. (3)

8. A(n) _____ifrice is a powder for cleaning *teeth*. (4)

9. A(n) _____tist uses the pronoun *I* almost exclusively. (3)

10. At the horse show riders demonstrated _____estrian skills. (3)

11. A con_____ant is a close friend, someone we put *faith* in. (3)

12. A(n) _____ilian is a *citizen* not in the armed forces. (3)

13. Dis_____d, or disagreement, is a metaphor suggesting that two *hearts* are not beating together. (3)

14. A(n) _____ulent, obese person has a large *body*. (4)

15. A per _____a distribution is literally according to each *head,* that is, equally to each individual. (5)

16. _____ifugal force flees the *center*. (5)

17. A(n) _____ry is meant to be kept faithfully, every *day*. (3)

18. An ef_____escent liquid *bubbles* and *boils*. (4)

19. A(n) _____ivalent payment is *equal* in value. (3)

20. Scrooge was a(n) _____eering boss, seeking to show himself the *master* in every situation involving his employees. (5)

21. Perkins has a medi_____al attitude toward labor, a point of view lifted straight out of the Middle *Ages*. (2)

22. A(n) _____arium is a *watery* wonderland, with fish as the principal inhabitants. (3)

23. The _____ator of a museum is a person who takes *care* of the exhibits. (3)

24. The victors dis_____ed the losers, taking away all *weapons* and tools of war. (3)

25. A *cross-shaped* object is _____iform. (4)

Problem

Without thought of personal gain, Irene Russell proved to be _____ as she put her personal fortune at risk to help stem the financial panic.

(A) altruistic   (D) egocentric
(B) felicitous   (E) durable
(C) culpable

Strategy. The key to the answer is the pair of opening phrases. Irene Russell had nothing to gain personally from her actions, so they had to be *unselfish,* devoted to others. *Altruistic* (A) from the Latin, *alter* "other," satisfies the requirement. *Altruistic* means "unselfish," "concerned for others." *Felicitous* (B), "pleasant," "suitable," makes little sense. Equally inappropriate are *culpable* (C), "blameworthy," and *durable* (E), "lasting." *Egocentric* (D), "self-centeredness," actually runs counter to the sense of the sentence and must be rejected.

(A) Without thought of personal gain, Irene Russell proved to be altruistic as she put her personal fortune at risk to help stem the financial panic.

Roots From Latin Nouns and Adjectives—2

Root	Meaning	Example	Explanation
fin	end	**fin**ally	at the *end*
firm	strong	in**firm**	not *strong*
flor	flower	**flor**al	pertaining to *flowers*
foli	leaf	**foli**age	*leaves*
form	form, shape	de**form**ation	change in *form* (for the worse)
fort	strong	**fort**ify	make *strong*
fum	smoke	**fum**es	*smoke*
grat	free, thankful, pleased	**grat**itude	expression of *thanks*
grav	heavy	ag**grav**ate	make worse, *heavier*
greg	flock	con**greg**ation	*flock*ing together
herb	grass	**herb**ivorous	*grass*-eating
ign	fire	**ign**ite	set on *fire*
labor	work	**labor**atory	place to *work* in
leg	law	**leg**al	pertaining to *law*
lev	light	al**lev**iate	*light*en
liber	free	**liber**ate	*free*
libr	book	**libr**ary	storehouse of *books*
liter	letter	al**liter**ation	beginning with same *letter*
loc	place	**loc**ation	*place*
lud, lus	play, game	pre**lud**e	before the *game*, introduction
		col**lus**ion	conspiracy (a *play*ing together)
magn	great	**magn**ify	make *great*
mal	evil	**mal**efactor	one who does *evil*
man	hand	**man**ual	by *hand*
mar	sea	sub**mar**ine	beneath the *sea*
mater, matr	mother	**matr**iarch	rule by *mother*
maxim	largest	**maxim**ize	make *largest*
ment	mind	**ment**al	pertaining to *mind*
min	less, little, small	**min**imum	*least* amount
miser	wretched	**miser**able	*wretched*
mor	custom	**mor**es	*customs*
mort	death	im**mort**al	*death*less
nav, naut	ship, sail	**nav**al	pertaining to *ships*

TRIAL TEST

Fill in the blank in each sentence by writing a Latin root from the previous list. The word in italics is the clue to the needed root. The number in parentheses tells the number of letters needed to complete the word.

1. An unfortunate person not in his right *mind* is de_____ed. (4)

2. The famous Rodgers and Hammerstein col_____ated on many musicals, *working* together as an effective team. (5)

3. _____eous rock had its origins in *fire* in the earth's early history. (3)

4. _____islators make *laws;* judges test them. (3)

5. Serious debates can be *lightened* by a touch of _____ity. (3)

6. _____itime regulations have developed from the unwritten laws of the *sea.* (3)

7. _____animity is a *greatness* of spirit reflected in good and generous actions. (4)

8. A(n) _____icure is care of the *hands;* pedicure, of the feet. (3)

9. It is hard for a human mind to conceive of in_____ity, space without *end.* (3)

10. One's *strong* point is called his _____e. (4)

11. A dis_____ated bone is out of its proper *place.* (3)

12. To _____ign someone is to say *evil* things about him. (3)

13. The female stickleback doesn't have _____nal instincts; the male fish acts as *mother* and father. (5)

14. In the battle off Cape Trafalgar, Admiral Nelson received a(n) _____al wound, but he won victory even in *death.* (4)

15. The strict laws were _____alized, *freeing* the citizens from many unnecessary regulations. (5)

16. _____ity on the moon is so much less than on earth that we'd feel much less *heavy.* (4)

17. People who like to *flock* together are _____arious. (4)

18. Keep that _____icide away from the *grass* or you'll kill it. (4)

19. Vince _____imized his injury, making it seem *less* than it really was. (3)

20. To interpret the law too _____ally may emphasize the *letter* of the law at the expense of its spirit. (5)

21. On the _____ly rations allotted them, the serfs lived a *wretched* life. (5)

22. The exterminators used a deadly *smoke* in _____igating the house and ridding it of pests. (3)

23. Because his speech was excellent, the speaker was given a _____uity to express the *thanks* of the audience. (4)

24. The _____ist sold a beautiful bouquet of *flowers* for Mother's Day. (4)

25. Some chemicals de_____ate trees, stripping them of *leaves* and often killing the trees. (4)

Problem

Acid rain may have helped cause the trees on Mt. Mitchell to be _____, gaunt skeletons in midsummer.

(A) herbaceous   (D) cohesive
(B) succulent   (E) defoliated
(C) incinerated

Strategy. If trees are "gaunt skeletons in midsummer," they must have lost their leaves unnaturally. The Latin root *foli,* "leaf," is firmly embedded in (E) *defoliated,* "stripped of leaves." When you meet this kind of sentence, you'll find clues but you'll still need to know the meaning of the key word. Having some knowledge of basic Latin and Greek roots is always helpful.

(E) Acid rain may have helped cause the trees on Mt. Mitchell to be defoliated, gaunt skeletons in midsummer.

Roots From Latin Nouns and Adjectives—3

Root	Meaning	Example	Explanation
noc, nox	night	**noc**turnal	pertaining to *night*
norm	rule, standard	ab**norm**al	away from the *standard*
nov	new	**nov**elty	*new*ness
numer	number	e**numer**ate	list by *number*
ocul	eye	bin**ocul**ars	field glasses for two *eyes*
oper	work	co**oper**ate	*work* together
optim	best	**optim**al	*best*
pac	peace	**pac**ify	make *peaceful*
par	equal	**par**ity	*equality*
pater, patr	father	**pater**nal	pertaining to *father*
ped	foot	**ped**estal	*foot* of a column
plus, plur	more	**plur**ality	*more* than any other candidate
popul	people	**popul**ation	*people* of a country
prim, prin	first	**prim**ary	*first*
reg, rig	rule, straight, right	**reg**ent	*ruler* for another
salut	health	**salut**ary	*health*y
sanct	holy	**sanct**uary	*holy* place
sign	sign	**sign**al	*sign* giving warning
sol	alone	**sol**itary	*alone*
somn	sleep	in**somn**ia	*sleep*lessness
son	sound	re**son**ance	reinforcement of a *sound*
temp	time	**temp**orary	for the *time* being
tenu	thin	at**tenu**ate	*thin* out

Root	Meaning	Example	Explanation
term, termin	end, limit	**term**inal	*end* of a bus or train line
terr	earth	**terr**estrial	pertaining to *earth*
test	witness	**test**ify	bear *witness*
umbr	shade	**umbr**ella	screen to provide *shade*
urb	city	**urb**an	pertaining to *city*
vac	empty	**vac**uum	*empty* space
ver	true	**ver**acious	*truth*ful
verb	word	**verb**al	in *words*
via	way	**via**	by *way* of
voc, vok	call	con**voke**	*call* together
vulg	common	**vulg**arity	*common*ness

TRIAL TEST

Fill in the blank in each sentence with a Latin root from the preceding list. Use the word in italics as a clue. The number in parentheses tells the number of letters needed.

1. Patrick was filled with *new* ideas, but not all his in_____ations proved practical. (3)

2. The equi_____es are the two periods each year when days and *nights* are equally long. (3)

3. Cervantes was a con_____orary of Shakespeare, living at the same *time* though in a different country. (4)

4. Perry's feet are e_____ous, requiring shoes far beyond the *standard* sizes. (4)

5. The government de_____ated the cities, forcing the *people* to go out into the countryside and face death by starvation. (5)

6. The new _____ime *ruled* with heartless disregard of human rights. (3)

7. The _____a donna is the *first* lady of the opera. (4)

8. The driver's license was *called* back and re_____ed for a year. (3)

9. To dis_____age someone is to make him lower in rank, not *equal*. (3)

10. A grain sur_____ means we have *more* than we need for domestic consumption. (4)

11. *Foot*paths over bridges usually delight _____estrians, but many bridges provide only for motor traffic. (3)

12. Vera refused the chance to sing _____o, for she dreaded standing *alone* before a crowded auditorium. (3)

13. On a very clear night the stars seem in_____able, but the *number* of visible stars is tiny compared with the number of stars beyond the range of sight. (5)

14. _____ambulists may walk in their *sleep,* but they usually get back to bed safely. (4)

15. Some modern composers combine *sounds* in harsh and unusual ways, seeking creative dis_____ance rather than harmony. (3)

16. A(n) _____ist considers this the *best* of all possible worlds. (5)

17. A city in the Australian Outback is sub_____anean, below the surface of the *earth* with its scorching heat. (4)

18. During the eclipse of the moon, the moon passed first into the pen_____a, the area of partial *shadow* caused by the earth's position between the sun and moon. (4)

19. _____anity, supposedly a quality of sophisticated *city* dwellers, is no longer a local quality. (3)

20. The Webers _____ated the house, *emptying* it of all their possessions. (3)

21. The star _____ated her contract with the studio, *ending* all contacts with one stroke of the pen. (6)

22. Many *holy* places are _____ified by the unselfish deeds of men and women in the past. (5)

23. A mon_____ar is a telescope with a single *eyepiece*. (4)

24. The officer _____ified the witness's account and found he had given a *true* report. (3)

25. There's too much _____iage in your composition. Cut out half those *words*. (4)

REVIEW

Fill the blank in each sentence by supplying a Latin root from one of the three preceding lists. The word in italics is the clue to the needed root. The number in parentheses tells the number of letters needed.

1. The St. Louis team was _____ly coached by Dick Vermeil, who provided *suitable* leadership all the way to the Super Bowl. (3)

2. When a smaller organization af_____iates itself with a larger one, the result is almost a parent-*son* relationship. (3)

3. The card _____itated the pair on their marriage and wished *happiness* for many years to come. (5)

4. _____estic skills are especially helpful for the running of a *home*. (3)

5. Though times were *hard,* the citizens of London en_____ed the terrors of the London blitz. (3)

6. Because of her *beauty,* Scarlett O'Hara was the _____e of the ball. (4)

7. The _____ifacts of a lost civilization reveal the *crafts* and skills of those who lived before us. (3)

8. The filament of an in_____escent bulb *glows*. (4)

9. _____ality encourages following the right *customs* and behavior of a group. (3)

10. The con_____ation of a building suggests the arrangement of the *forms* and shapes that make up the structure. (4)

11. Even after the crew sighted land, the *ship* had to sail many _____ical miles before reaching the dock. (4)

12. An optical il_____ion is a trick of the eye, a *game* of perception. (3)

13. To con_____ an agreement is to make a *strong* commitment to carry it out. (4)

14. The _____um score was achieved by the candidate who had the *greatest* interest in words and vocabulary building. (5)

15. A(n) _____arism is an expression that is frowned upon as *common* and substandard. (4)

16. Before you can properly _____ate a motor vehicle, you must learn how to *work* the brakes. (4)

17. A person's _____ature is a distinctive *sign* to distinguish the writer from others. (4)

18. A(n) _____duct is a span carrying a road*way* across a valley or a highway. (3)

19. Though named the _____ific, or *"peaceful"* ocean, this largest of all seas can be turbulent and remorseless. (3)

20. By derivation, a(n) _____ation was originally an expression of good will and good *health.* (5)

Which Word Parts Are Most Important?

Return for a moment to the 14 key words on page 92 at the beginning of this section. Which Latin prefixes and roots does Dr. Brown consider most important?

LATIN PREFIXES

ad, a	to	**a**spect
con, com	together	un**com**plicated
de	from	**de**tain
dis	apart from	in**dis**posed
ex	out of	non**ex**tended
in	not	**in**disposed
in	into	**in**sist
inter	between	**inter**mittent
non	not	**non**extended
ob, of	against, towards	**of**fer
pre	before	**pre**cept
pro	forward	re**pro**duction
sub, suf	under	over**suf**ficient*
re	back, again	**re**production
trans	across	mis**trans**cribe

Oversufficient is a good example of how words change through the years. "How," you may ask, "is it possible for a prefix meaning 'over' and a prefix meaning 'under' (**sub**) to appear in the same word?" *Sufficient* originally derived from **sub** and **fac**. How has it reached its present meaning? If you have *sufficient* funds, you have built a foundation *under* your position ("do under"). Thus *sufficient* has come to mean "as much as is needed." *Oversufficient* provides *more* than is necessary. The Anglo-Saxon prefix **over** has retained its common meaning, but the Latin prefix **sub** has lost its literal meaning and become part of a total concept. A word like *oversufficient* that uses elements from two different sources is sometimes called a *hybrid word.*

LATIN ROOTS

cept	take	pre**cept**
duct	lead	repro**duct**ion
fer	carry	of**fer**
fic	do, make	oversuf**fic**ient
mit	send	inter**mit**tent
plic	fold	uncom**plic**ated
pos	place, put	indis**pos**ed
scrib	write	mistran**scrib**e
sist	stand	in**sist**
spec	see	a**spec**t
tain	hold	de**tain**
tend	stretch	nonex**tend**ed

The remaining elements will be treated in the next two chapters, but for completeness they are included here also.

ANGLO-SAXON PREFIXES

mis	bad, badly	**mis**transcribe
over	above, too much	**over**sufficient
un	not	**un**complicated

GREEK PREFIXES

| epi | on, after | **epi**logue |
| mono | one | **mono**graph |

GREEK ROOTS

| graph | write | mono**graph** |
| log | word | epi**log**ue |

Although some of the words have moved away from their original meanings, the core of meaning in each word is still apparent. *Aspect* has something to do with *seeing*. *Detain* has something to do with *holding*. *Epilogue* has something to do with *words*. And so on through the remaining words. The elements of these words lead to thousands of others.

Problem

What makes the modern period in art _____ is that this time, in most categories, the older _____ has not been replaced by something equally substantial, accessible, and satisfying.

(A) exacting . . efficiency
(B) ideal . . illusiveness
(C) unique . . ignorance
(D) unprecedented . . reality
(E) worthless . . depravity

Strategy. This is a difficult question, but if you have been building power for the SAT, you have several ways to attack it.

1. Some students prefer to try out all the alternatives as a first step to see which "sound right" or "possible." This tactic sometimes allows you to reject one or more alternatives immediately. Usually you'll need to go on to the next step.

2. In sentence-completion activities always look for context clues. You know that smaller key words like *not, thus, like,* and *though* are always important, but there are longer key words, too. In this question the word "replaced" obviously carries a lot of weight. If the "older . . . has not been replaced by something satisfying," then you may assume that there is something unusual on the art scene this time.

3. Are there any words that suggest that this situation is unusual? *Exacting (A), ideal (B),* and *worthless (E)* don't seem to fit. *Unique (C)* is a possibility. What of *unprecedented (D)?*

4. Our familiarity with prefixes and roots comes in handy here. We recognize **un** ("not"), **pre** ("before"), and **ced** ("go"). If something is *unprecedented,* nothing like it has gone before. *Unprecedented* is clearly a possibility.

5. Check the second half of the *(C)* and *(D)* pairs. The word paired with *unique* is *ignorance. Ignorance* would not be *substantial* or *satisfying. Ignorance* is clearly incorrect, so we can discard *(C)* as an answer. The word paired with *unprecedented* is *reality.* This fits. The correct answer is *(D).* This is how the completed sentence looks.

What makes the modern period in art **unprecedented** is that this time, in most categories, the older **reality** has not been replaced by something equally substantial, accessible, and satisfying.

This detailed analysis reviews some of the skills you have been acquiring. As you become more and more familiar with this type of question, however, you will speed up your work. You will find your own shortcuts and draw upon your own special strengths.

REVIEW

A. Use context and etymology to figure out the answers. Write the letter for the word or word pair that best completes the meaning.

1. The fox's raid on the chicken coop was like a _____ _____ into an unprotected harbor.
   (A) lion's . . rush
   (B) sailor's . . navigation
   (C) pirate's . . foray
   (D) rower's . . sally
   (E) pilot's . . approach

   1 ____

2. June's bursts of energy are _____;
   she is actually an expert in _____.
   (A) sporadic . . placidity
   (B) overpowering . . relaxation
   (C) unexpected . . karate
   (D) infrequent . . motivation
   (E) illuminating . . electronics

   2 ____

3. That error is fortunately not _____;
   it can be corrected if we retrace our
   steps and follow correct procedures.
   (A) relevant
   (B) irremediable
   (C) hopeful
   (D) advertised
   (E) compromising

   3 ____

4. The departing guest thanked her host
   _____; still the cautious host
   _____ avoided extending a second
   invitation.
   (A) reservedly . . somehow
   (B) reflectively . . angrily
   (C) engagingly . . unconsciously
   (D) tactlessly . . righteously
   (E) effusively . . pointedly

   4 ____

5. Although Timothy much preferred to
   _____ during the summer months,
   his father insisted _____ that Tim-
   othy get a job.
   (A) work . . tentatively
   (B) vegetate . . vehemently
   (C) travel . . vaguely
   (D) compete . . unintentionally
   (E) read . . carelessly

   5 ____

6. The purpose of the roller coaster is to
   provide _____ thrills, to stimulate a
   sense of extreme _____, yet frighten
   people safely.
   (A) vicarious . . vertigo
   (B) inhuman . . illness
   (C) casual . . indifference
   (D) humdrum . . enthusiasm
   (E) unimaginative . . terror

   6 ____

7. Seeking to magnify their own glories at
   the expense of earlier rulers, later pha-
   raohs _____ from tombs and monu-
   ments the names of their illustrious
   _____.
   (A) humiliated . . contemporaries
   (B) deciphered . . progeny
   (C) obliterated . . predecessors
   (D) plagiarized . . scribes
   (E) reconnoitered . . generals

   7 ____

8. According to many therapists, the true
   function of a(n) _____ is to
   _____ energies and revive the spirit.
   (A) chore . . humble
   (B) anecdote . . dramatize
   (C) avocation . . regenerate
   (D) diatribe . . shrivel
   (E) confrontation . . dissipate

   8 ____

9. Despite his reputation for hard-
   heartedness, the sergeant showed
   _____ to the injured recruit, binding
   his injury and speaking encouraging
   words to the young soldier.
   (A) merit
   (B) compassion
   (C) casualness
   (D) indignation
   (E) firmness

   9 ____

10. Some economists feel that a(n)
    _____ distribution of all wealth
    would find great _____ in actual
    holdings less than a year later.
    (A) average . . equalization
    (B) scheduled . . disappointment
    (C) circumspect . . felicity
    (D) equitable . . discrepancies
    (E) unanticipated . . diminution

    10 ____

B. Build your own vocabulary. Put together words of your own by taking prefixes from column A and combining them with roots from the two B columns.

___

A (PREFIXES)	B (ROOTS)	
a, ab	act	pel
ad, ac, af, ag, al, am, at	cede	pone
ante	claim	port
com, cof, col, con	credit	pose
contra	cur	prehend
de	date	rupt
dis, di	dict	scribe
ex, e	duct	sect
extra	fect	sense
in	fer	solve
inter	flux	spect
non	form	strict
ob, o, oc	gress	sult
per	ject	tain
post	junct	tract
pre	late	vene
pro	mand	verge
sub, suc, suf, sup, sus	merge	vert
super	mit	vise
trans	mute	volve

___

___

___

___

___

SUMMARY

Etymology Clue 3: | **Latin Roots—Nouns and Adjectives**

1. English contains more words from Latin than from any other language.

2. Words are often built block by block. If you know what each block (word part) originally meant, you can probably figure out today's meaning—the one used in SAT questions.

3. The best strategy is to know the root and prefix. The second best strategy is to think of other words having the same elements.

Etymology Clue 4: Greek Prefixes and Roots

Though words derived from Greek prefixes and roots often look difficult, their meanings are sometimes easier to guess than words from other sources. First, the commonly used Greek roots are fewer in number than those from Latin. Secondly, the building blocks are often easier to see. A word like Dr. Brown's *monograph* (page 92), for example, is delightfully simple, once you know the elements **mono** and **graph**. Both elements have so many word-cousins, from *monotone* to *monotheism,* from *telegraph* to *biography*. The prefix **mono** means "one" in those *mono* words. The root **graph** means "write" in those *graph* words. A monograph is an article written about one special subject.

Words from Greek and Latin differ from each other in another way, too. Words from Latin usually have *one* root and one or more prefixes, but Greek often combines *two* roots. *Biography,* for example, combines two roots: **bio** and **graph**. We'll have more to say about this kind of combination later.

Before you begin studying lists of Greek prefixes and roots, try an experiment. You probably know more about word origins than you think you do. Take the following test and prove to yourself that you can often derive the meanings of prefixes and roots on your own.

TRIAL TEST

In each of the following ten groups, one root is common to all four words. You already know at least three of the four words in every group. Think of the meanings of the words you know, and try to determine the meaning of the root. You will find the answer among the words following the root. Write the letter for the meaning of the word.

telegraph, autograph, biography, graphic
GRAPH:
    (A) distance   (C) friendship
    (B) writing   (D) pictures
                              B

Since the words all have to do with writing, the correct answer is *(B)*. The meaning of the root **graph** is *writing*.

1. phonograph, telephone, radiophone, euphony
PHON:
    (A) light   (C) sound
    (B) heat   (D) water
               1 ____

2. automatic, autograph, automobile, autocrat
AUTO:
    (A) ruler   (C) only
    (B) self   (D) written
               2 ____

3. monotone, monopoly, monarchy, monogram
MONO:
    (A) busy   (C) two
    (B) loud   (D) one
               3 ____

4. democrat, aristocrat, autocrat, bureau-
crat
CRAT:
(A) person   (C) wealth
(B) rule   (D) nature
                   4 ____

5. synonym, antonym, homonym, patro-
nymic
ONYM:
(A) name   (C) father
(B) opposite   (D) same
                   5 ____

6. bicycle, cyclone, cycle, encyclopedia
CYCL:
(A) storm   (C) play
(B) circle   (D) two
                   6 ____

7. centimeter, meter, metric, perimeter
METER:
(A) coin   (C) 100
(B) instrument (D) measure
                   7 ____

8. biology, biography, autobiography, am-
phibian
BIO:
(A) book   (C) science
(B) life   (D) water
                   8 ____

9. antislavery, antitoxin, antidote, antip-
athy
ANTI:
(A) related   (C) against
(B) before   (D) afterward
                   9 ____

10. microscope, microphotograph, mi-
crobe, microcosm
MICRO:
(A) small   (C) germ
(B) picture   (D) telescope
                   10 ____

Greek Prefixes

Root	Meaning	Example	Explanation
a, an	no, not	**a**typical	*not* typical
		anarchy	condition of *no* government
amphi	around, both	**amphi**bian	on *both* land and sea
ana	up, again, back	**ana**lysis	examination of details (a loosening *up*)
anti	against	**anti**septic	*against* infection
apo	away from, off	**apo**stle	messenger sent *from* one place to another
auto	self	**auto**matic	running by *itself*
cata	down	**cata**clysm	a washing *down,* a flood
dys	bad, badly	**dys**pepsia	*bad* digestion
dia	across, through	**dia**meter	a measure *across* a circle
ec, ex	out of	**ex**odus	a going *out*
en	in, into	**en**gender	bring *into* being, cause
endo	inside	**endo**lithic	living *inside* stony substances
epi	upon, after	**epi**taph	inscription placed *upon* a tomb
eu	well, good, pleasant	**eu**logy	a speaking *well,* praise

hyper	above, beyond	**hyper**bole	speech *beyond* truth, exaggeration
hypo	under, below	**hypo**glycemia	*low* blood sugar
iso	equal	**iso**therm	line to show *equal* heat
mega, megal	great	**mega**lomania	personality disorder of assumed *greatness*
meta	after, beyond, over	**meta**morphosis	change*over* into another form
micro	small	micrometer	tool for making *small* measurements
mis	hatred of	misanthropic	*hating* mankind
neo	new	**neo**logism	*new* word
pan, panto	all	**pan**chromatic	sensitive to light of *all* colors
para	beside	**para**phrase	a speaking *beside,* a rewording
peri	around	**peri**meter	measure *around*
poly	many	**poly**syllabic	having *many* syllables
pro	before	**pro**phet	one who predicts the future (speaks *before*hand)
pseudo	false	**pseudo**science	*false* science
sym, syn	together	**sym**phony	a sounding *together*
		synagogue	a place for bringing people *together*

We have already called your attention to the fact that words sometimes travel far from their origins. Words introduced into the language long ago often have figurative meanings, but usually the basic meaning is still there. Ordinarily the more recently a word has come into the language, the closer the word is to its basic elements. The recent word *astrophysics,* for example, deals with the nature (**physi**) of the stars (**astro**).

Even though they seem simple, Greek prefixes are a little more difficult than Greek roots, because the prefixes have more meanings than the roots. A prefix like **meta**, for example, has many meanings ("along with," "after," "between," "among," "beyond," "over").

The word *metaphysics* has an interesting history. *Physics,* with its root **physi**, means "nature," "natural." When Aristotle was gathering his thoughts about nature and life, he came to those dealing with things *beyond* science, things that cannot be explained by experiment. He called these ideas *metaphysics* because they came *after* or beyond the *physics.*

TRIAL TEST

Fill the blank in each sentence by writing a Greek prefix from the preceding list. The word in italics is a clue to the needed prefix. The number in parentheses tells the number of letters needed.

> When two organisms live *together* with mutual benefit, this unique arrangement is called _____biosis. (3)
>
> The italicized word *together* tells you the prefix **sym** should be inserted.

1. Although at times Pierce pretended to be a *hater* of women, he was not really a(n) _____ogynist. (3)

2. By definition, the two legs of a(n) _____sceles triangle are *equal*. (3)

3. Bert used a(n) _____phone and *greatly* increased the range of his voice. (4)

4. A(n) _____lyst may speed up or slow *down* the rate of a chemical reaction. (4)

5. A(n) _____cracy is a government in which one person, by *himself*, holds absolute power. (4)

6. The critics of astrology call it a(n) _____science, *falsely* assuming the mantle of a true science. (6)

7. Bennett was a true _____glot, writing and speaking *many* languages fluently. (4)

8. The _____eroid barometer, unlike the mercury barometer, uses *no* liquid. (2)

9. A(n) _____biotic works *against* the growth of harmful bacteria. (4)

10. _____trophy is the growth of an organ far *beyond* its normal size. (5)

11. Most colleges and universities now use many _____professionals to work *beside* fully licensed teachers and help with many education projects. (4)

12. A(n) _____scope enables a viewer to look *around* a corner. (4)

13. Despite its *small* size, _____film can store pages of material in a single frame. (5)

14. The _____phytes, all *new* members of the church, came to the altar in a group. (3)

15. Old-time medicine men used to offer their concoctions as _____aceas, guaranteed to cure *all* ailments from headache to pneumonia. (3)

16. In _____grams words are mixed *up* and then put *back* into different forms. (3)

17. In the Greek _____theater the seats curled *around* the stage. (5)

18. Pruitt _____chronized his watch with Helen's, making sure his time agreed *with* hers. (3)

19. _____thermia is a dangerous condition in which the body temperature falls far *below* normal. (4)

20. It is human nature to use _____phemisms, expressions that make unpleasant subjects sound neutral or *pleasant*. (2)

<table>
<tr><th colspan="2">Problem</th></tr>
</table>

John Dickson Carr chose the _____ *Carter Dickson* at the publisher's request, so that there'd not be too many mystery novels with the same author's name.

(A) symbiosis   (D) pseudonym
(B) paradigm   (E) fabrication
(C) counterfeit

Strategy. *Pseudo,* "false," combines with *nym,* "name," to suggest a "false name," in this sentence a pen name. *Counterfeit and fabrication* have negative connotations and may be rejected. *Symbiosis* and *paradigm* are unrelated and unsuitable.

Greek Number Prefixes

Prefix	Meaning	Example	Explanation
hemi	half	**hemi**sphere	*half* a sphere
mono	one	**mono**tone	*one* tone
proto	first	**proto**type	*first* kind
di	two	**di**lemma	*two* choices (both bad!)
tri	three	**tri**cycle	*three-wheeler*
tetra	four	**tetra**meter	having *four* poetic feet
penta	five	**penta**gon	*five*-sided figure
hexa	six	**hexa**gonal	having *six* sides
hepta	seven	**hepta**meter	having *seven* poetic feet
octa	eight	**octa**ve	*eighth* tone above a given tone
deca	ten	**deca**logue	the *Ten* Commandments
hect	hundred	**hect**ograph	machine for making a *hundred* (many) copies
kilo	thousand	**kilo**gram	a *thousand* grams

Greek number prefixes occur in a great many English words. The field of mathematics, for example, relies heavily upon Greek prefixes (as in *trigonometry* or *pentagon),* but these little elements appear in other English words, as well, such as *protozoan* and *monologue.* If you know the number prefix, you can usually figure out the right SAT answer.

Note how efficiently English borrows from both Latin and Greek. The Latin prefix for *thousand,* **mille,** appears in *millimeter* (a *thousandth* of a meter). The Greek prefix for *thousand,* **kilo,** appears in *kilometer* (a *thousand* meters). Neither prefix is wasted. Scientists keep drawing upon Greek for new words to express new ideas. A **milli**second, for example, is a *thou-*

sandth of a second. But suppose you want a word to express a billionth of a second? The Greek word for "dwarf" is **nano**. A billionth of a second is a **nano**second (a very small second!).

TRIAL TEST

Fill the blank in each sentence with a Greek number prefix from the list. The word in italics is a clue to the needed prefix. The number in parentheses tells the number of letters needed.

A small child needs the *three* wheels on a **tri**cycle to provide balance. (3)

The italicized word *three* tells you that *tri* is the correct Greek number prefix.

---

1. A(n) _____meter, which is *1000* meters, is approximately five-eighths of a mile. (4)

2. In the _____thlon each contestant takes part in *five* events. (5)

3. Jim spoke in _____syllables, allowing himself only *one* syllable at a time. (4)

4. _____gonometry, literally the measure of *three* angles, deals with the relationships of triangles. (3)

5. A(n) _____hedron is a solid figure with *four* triangular faces. (5)

6. _____zoans, one-celled animals, may resemble the *first* form of life on earth. (5)

7. In linguistics, a(n) _____phthong, combines *two* vowel sounds into one continuous sound. (2)

8. To win the _____thlon, a contestant need not win all *ten* events; he must, however, have the highest average over all. (4)

9. The great epics of Greece and Rome were written in dactylic _____meter, with *six* beats to every line. (4)

10. The unusual old building has a(n) _____gonal shape, with *eight* equal sides. (4)

Problem

Hester foolishly put a red filter over the lens and found that all her slides were _____, though she had used a good color film.

(A) endomorphic
(B) monochromatic
(C) prototypical
(D) hyperbolic
(E) foreshortened

Strategy. A red filter with color film will result in all-red slides, slides of *one color.* The Greek root *mono,* "one," assures us that *monochromatic* (B) means "of *one* color." The other alternatives may distract if you don't know the root *mono.*

(B) Hester foolishly put a red filter over the lens and found that all her slides were monochromatic, though she had used a good color film.

REVIEW

Fill the blank in each sentence with a Greek prefix from the two preceding lists. The word in italics is a clue to the needed prefix. The number in parentheses tells the number of letters needed.

---

1. Pain on *half* the head or body carries the medical name of _____algia. (4).

   The root *alg* (pain) appears in *neuralgia, nostalgia, analgesic,* and similar words.

2. A(n) _____ergetic person puts much exertion *into* work or play. (2)

3. A slanting straight line *across* a square is called a(n) _____gonal. (3)

4. _____crine glands are nestled *inside* the body and produce secretions carried in the bloodstream. (4)

5. In _____phor, meaning is conveyed indirectly, *beyond* the literal meaning. (4)

6. In 1880, the _____ograph was invented to provide copies, a *hundred* or even more. (4)

7. Utopia is an imaginary place where life is perfect; the word "_____topia" was invented in 1950 to suggest a place where the opposite is true, where good has been replaced by *bad.* (3)

8. A(n) _____gram is prepared *before a* play or concert. (3)

9. Because the Roman emperor Julian fell *away* from the Christian religion, he is known in history as "Julian the _____state." (3)

10. The _____logue of a book or play appears *after* the main presentation. (3)

Greek Roots—1

Now we come to one of the most helpful word groups in the study of etymology—Greek roots. Many of these are different from Latin roots because they may appear anywhere in a word—at the beginning, middle, or end. **Lith**, meaning "stone," may appear at the beginning in *lithography* and at the end in *monolith.* In some ways, Greek roots are more fun to combine because they combine so freely and in so many ways. **Meter**, meaning "measure," appears first in *metronome* and last in *diameter.* It also appears in the middle in *symmetrical.*

All the Greek roots are important and worth studying, but if you wish to concentrate upon some basic ones, study the starred (*) items first. These will be especially helpful as you prepare for the SAT. These Greek roots are also divided into two lists for your convenience.

Root	Meaning	Example	Explanation
alg	pain	neur**alg**ia	nerve *pain*
anthrop, andr	man	**anthrop**ology	study of *man*kind
		android	robot like a *man*
arch	chief, rule	**arch**bishop	*chief* bishop
		mon**archy**	*rule* of one person
bar	weight, pressure	**bar**ometer	measure of *pressure*
bibli	book	**bibli**ophile	one who loves *books*
chiro	hand	**chiro**podist	*hand* and foot specialist
chrom	color	**chrom**atic	highly *color*ed
*chron	time	ana**chron**istic	out of proper *time*
cosm	universe	micro**cosm**	*universe* in little
crat, crac	rule	demo**crac**y	*rule* by the people
crypt	hidden	**crypt**ic	having *hidden* meaning
*cycl	circle	**cycl**one	storm that whirls in a *circle*
*dem	people	**dem**agogue	a rabble-rousing leader of *people*
derm	skin	hypo**derm**ic	beneath the *skin*
dos, dot	give	anti**dote**	something *given* to counteract a poison
dyn, dynam	energy, power	**dynam**ite	*power*ful explosive
erg, urg	work	metall**urg**y	metal *work*ing
gam	marriage	poly**gam**y	many *marriages*
*ge, geo	earth	**geo**physics	dealing with the physics of the *earth*
gen	birth, cause, kind, race, origin	homo**gen**ize	make uniform, of the same *kind*
*gram, graph	writing	autobio**graph**y	*writing about one's own life*
		mono**graph**	*writing* about a particular subject
heli	sun	**heli**otrope	flower that turns toward the *sun*
hem	blood	**hem**orrhage	unchecked flow of *blood*
*hetero	different, other	**hetero**geneous	of a *different* kind
*homo	same	**homo**geneous	of the *same* kind
hydr	water	de**hydr**ation	loss of *water*
iatr	healing	psych**iatr**ist	one who *heals* the mind
lith	stone	mono**lith**	single large block of *stone*
*log	word, study	geo**log**y	*study* of the earth

TRIAL TEST

Fill the blank in each sentence with a Greek root from the preceding list. The word in italics is a clue to the needed root. The number in parentheses tells the number of letters needed.

> A bi**gam**ist has two *marriages* in force at the same time. (3)
>
> The italicized word *marriage* tells you the Greek root **gam** should be used. One who has two marriages in force at the same time is a *bigamist*.

1. _____olysis is a chemical reaction in which a compound reacts with the ions of *water*. (4)

2. Copernicus upset the _____centric theory of the earth, pointing out that the *earth* is not the center of the universe. (3)

3. _____atitis is an inflammation of the *skin*. (4)

4. Ronny has _____ophobia; he has a morbid fear of *work!* (3)

5. An olig_____y is the *rule* of a few people. (4)

6. On a weather map iso_____s are lines of equal *pressure*. (3)

7. Eva is a(n) _____o of *energy*. (5)

8. The presence of _____um on the *sun* was first discovered during a solar eclipse in 1868, and the name reflects its origin. (4)

9. A(n) _____orama is a series of connected pictures in a *circular* room, often showing a landscape. (4)

10. Have you listed in your _____ography all *books* referred to? (5)

11. A basic treatment in _____practic is manipulation of the spine by the trained *hands* of the doctor. (5)

12. The *pain* of being separated from his friends and family gave the college student an acute case of nost_____ia. (3)

13. _____oid apes are so called because of their *manlike* appearance and mannerisms. (7)

14. Ted usually adopts _____dox positions, *different* from those of his peers. (6)

15. At first _____ography used flat *stones* to reproduce a design on paper; later metal plates were introduced. (4)

16. People send *written* messages over distances via the tele_____. (5)

17. A(n) _____nym has the *same* pronunciation as another word but different meaning. (4)

18. _____atic aberration in a lens causes a margin of *colors* to appear around the edges of the image. (5)

19. An epi_____ic is a disease afflicting vast numbers of *people*. (3)

20. Ger_____ics deals with the *healing* of old people's ailments. (4)

21. A(n) _____ic ailment keeps coming back *time* and time again. (5)

22. A pluto_____ seeks the power to *rule* because of his wealth. (4)

23. In a(n) _____ogram the meaning is *hidden,* concealed in code or cipher. (5)

24. A bi_____ist has two *marriages* still in force at the same time. (3)

25. _____oglobin is the red coloring in the *blood*. (3)

Problem
_____ are spelled the same but have different meanings and pronunciations. (A) Antonyms   (D) Heteronyms (B) Synonyms   (E) Aphorisms (C) Epigrams

Strategy. You probably already know *antonyms* and *synonyms* but must look elsewhere for the answer. The word *different* provides the clue that the answer must emphasize difference. The Greek root *hetero,* "different," points to the answer *heteronyms.*

Greek Roots—2

As before, study the starred (*) items first.

Root	Meaning	Example	Explanation
*meter, metr	measure	baro**meter**	*measure* of air pressure
morph	form, shape	a**morph**ous	*form*less
neur	nerve	**neur**itis	inflammation of *nerves*
nom, nomy	law, order, custom	astro**nom**er	one who studies the *order* of the stars
onym, onoma	name	an**onym**ous	*name*less
ortho	straight	**ortho**dontia	teeth *straight*ening
path	suffering, feeling	a**path**y	lack of *feeling*
phan, phen	show, appear	**phen**omenon	something *apparent* to the senses
*phil	love	**phil**anthropist	*lover* of mankind
phor, pher	carry, bear	sema**phor**	apparatus for signaling, for *bear*ing messages
*phos, phot	light	**phot**ography	producing images by use of *light*
pod	foot	**pod**iatrist	*foot* doctor
poli	city	metro**poli**s	main *city*
psych	mind	**psych**ology	study of the *mind*
pyr	fire	**pyr**otechnics	*fire*works
scop	see	tele**scop**e	device for *see*ing at a distance
soph	wise	**soph**isticated	worldly-*wise*
tax, tac	arrangement	**tac**tics	*arrang*ing forces in battle
techn	art, skill	**techn**ique	method of using *skills*
*tele	from afar	**tele**metry	measuring *from afar*
the, theo	god	**the**ist	believer in *God*
therm	heat	**therm**ostat	device for regulating *heat*

thes, thet	place, put	anti**thes**is	a *placing* against, contrast of thought
tom	cut	a**tom**	substance that cannot be *cut* or split (now proved wrong)
top	place	**top**ography	description of a *place*
trop	turn	**trop**ism	tendency to *turn* in response to a stimulus
typ	model, impression	**typ**ical	like a *model*
zo	animal	**zo**ology	study of *animals*

More About Greek Roots

A root like **therm** is easy to find in English words. It always means "heat." Some roots, however, travel a little farther afield. Like Latin roots, they sometimes have figurative meanings. The extremely useful root **graph,** for example, appears in a great many words. You notice the meaning of *writing* instantly in a word like *graphology,* the study of handwriting. But notice the figurative meanings in *phonograph* and *photograph. Photography,* by derivation, is "light written down." *Phonograph* is "sound written down." Here the concept of *writing* is much broader than usual. There's a poetic image in "written sound."

Fortunately, the words with figurative meanings have been in the language a long time. You certainly know *phonograph* and *photograph* anyway. But if you meet a new word like *thermograph,* you can reasonably guess it's a device for recording heat, or temperature. Even though the meanings are sometimes figurative, the core of meaning is usually clear.

TRIAL TEST

Fill the blank in each sentence with a root from the preceding list of Greek roots. The word in italics is a clue to the needed root. The number in parentheses tells the number of letters needed.

1. In a syn_____is ideas are *put* together to form a whole. (4)

2. Maurya is a pan_____ist and believes that *God* is manifest in everything, everywhere. (3)

3. The _____diac was so named because it was considered the zone of the *animals:* the ram, the lion, the bull, and others. (2)

4. In a tonsillec_____y the surgeon removes the tonsils by deft *cutting.* (3)

5. The _____on is the structural and functional unit of the *nervous* system. (4)

6. Meta_____ic rock has been changed in *form* by heat, pressure, or chemical action. (5)

7. An acr_____ is a *name* formed by using the first letters of a series of words; for example, NATO for North Atlantic Treaty Organization. (4)

8. _____pedics is a branch of surgery whose goal is the *straightening* of deformed parts of the body, especially in children. (5)

9. According to legend, Dido prepared a(n) _____e for herself, planning to cast herself upon the *fire* as the ships of Aeneas disappeared in the distance. (3)

10. _____ology is a *love* of learning. (4)

11. _____istry is a misleading but clever argument that gives the impression of being *wise*. (4)

12. A kaleido_____e is a specially designed tube for *seeing* beautiful forms and shapes. (4)

13. _____onomy is the science of the *arrangement* of animals and plants in orders, families, genera, and other groupings. (3)

14. A gastro_____ is a mollusk that has one large *foot* associated with its stomach. (3)

15. _____pathy, communication at a *distance* without using the normal sensory channels, is an attractive, if unproven, possibility. (4)

16. That plant is photo_____ic, *turning* to any light source for energy. (4)

17. The arche_____e is the original *model* from which all others of the same kind are made. (3)

18. Through the dia_____ous curtain on the stage, two shadowy figures suddenly *appeared*. (4)

19. Em_____y is the ability to share another's *feelings* by putting oneself in the other's place. (4)

20. An am_____ *measures* the strength of an electric current in amperes. (5)

REVIEW

Fill the blank in each sentence with a Greek prefix or root. The word in italics is a clue to the needed prefix or root. The number in parentheses tells the number of letters needed.

1. Study of the nature, origin, and structure of the *universe* is known as _____ology. (4)

2. The _____esis of an idea suggests the *origin*, or *birth*, of the concept. (3)

3. Paleonto_____y is the *study* of fossils and the life forms of previous ages. (3)

4. By derivation, an anec_____e was originally not *given* out, not published. It has lost that specialized meaning. (3)

5. By derivation, eco_____ics is the *ordering* and organization of a household. (3)

6. _____iatry is the science that attempts to treat disorders of the *mind*. (5)

7. _____ology is a scientific application of *arts* and *skills* to achieve practical purposes. (5)

8. On the weather map, lines of equal *heat* are called iso_____s. (5)

9. _____ology is the study of a particular *place* or region. (3)

10. Since *city*-states were equivalent to nations in ancient Greece, the art or science of government was called "_____tics." (4)

11. In many seas, _____phorescence, caused by swarms of small organisms, produces flashes of silvery *light* in the water. (4)

12. By derivation, eco_____y means *study* of the home—an appropriate word, for all the earth is our home. (3)

13. Thermo_____ics deals with the *power* of heat. (5)

14. The _____ic of Cancer is the imaginary line on the earth's surface where the sun seems to *turn* southward at the solstice. (4)

15. A mono_____atic painting consists of one *color* or hue. (5)

16. Students who read very *badly* may be suffering from _____lexia. (3)

17. Maureen loved to _____gnosticate events, suggesting their outline *before* they happened. (3)

18. A(n) _____phyte lives *upon* another plant but does not deprive the host plant of food. (3)

19. Sharon is a(n) _____lectic designer, picking *out* what she likes from many different periods and still making a harmonious total design. (2)

20. At _____gee the moon is farthest *away* from the earth. (3)

Greek prefixes and roots play a role in the following sentence-completion item.

Problem

The latest edition of the dictionary defines several thousand _____ and refines the definitions of some older words.

(A) synonyms   (D) homophones
(B) antonyms   (E) polymorphs
(C) neologisms

Strategy. The second half of the sentence contrasts *older* with something else, probably *newer.* If we insert new words into the slot, we make sense, but *new words* is not provided. A substitute is. A knowledge of the Greek prefix *neo,* "new," and the Greek root *log,* "word," provides a ready-made answer. A *neologism* is a "new word."

(C) The latest edition of the dictionary defines several thousand neologisms and refines the definitions of some older words.

REVIEW

Build your own vocabulary. Put together words of your own by taking elements from column A and combining them with elements from column B. You may use any element more than once.

A	B	
auto	algia	_____
chiro	cracy	_____
cosmo	graph(y)	_____
demo	logy	_____
geo	meter	_____
micro	nomic	_____
neur	phone	_____
photo	podist	_____
tele	politan	_____
theo	scope	_____

SUMMARY
Etymology Clue 4:   Greek Prefixes and Roots

1. The Greek language is an important source of English words.

2. When scientists create new words for new concepts and substances, they borrow freely from Greek. You are not likely to meet some of these technical creations, like *microencapsulate* and *neuroendocrinology,* but you will meet a great many others, like *psychedelic* and *Xerox.*

3. Though words change in use, even words with figurative meanings can be guessed at by figuring out their basic elements. *Hydraulic* is derived from **hydr**, the root for *water*. The word has been expanded to mean other liquids: *hydraulic* brakes use *oil*. But if you know **hydr**, you can guess at the meaning of related words like *hydraulic* and *hydrometer.*

4. Some coinages, like *polyunsaturates* and *megavitamins,* borrow from both Latin and Greek.

Etymology Clue 5: | *Anglo-Saxon Prefixes and Roots

You will feel at home with this section. You use Anglo-Saxon prefixes and roots in everyday English words you already know. As we have already seen, William the Conqueror overran England in 1066. He brought his own French language with him, but French did *not* replace the native English, or Anglo-Saxon. Instead of fighting English, it joined with it.

The French nobility lorded it over the Anglo-Saxon peasantry. Some words from French show this master-servant relationship: *dame, peer, prince, treasurer, minister, mayor, baron,* and *noble.* The French upper classes enjoyed the fruits of Anglo-Saxon labor. The Anglo-Saxon *calf* was *veal (veau)* to the French nobility. And so we have both words, one for the living animal and one for the meat of the animal. *Bull* and *beef, sheep* and *mutton, pig* and *pork* all show this relationship.

French enriched the language with new words from the law: *plaintiff, jury, attorney, indictment, felon, bail, decree,* and *prison.* French provided religious words like *sermon, sacrament, prayer, parson, friar,* and *chaplain.* French provided words for clothing: *apparel, gown, embroidery, cape, cloak, frock.* French provided words for medicine: *surgeon, remedy, ointment, jaundice, pulse.* These are topics and words that often come up in SAT questions, especially the sentence-completion type.

We use some of these French words every day. Others, like *hauberk, barbican,* and *portcullis,* are fairly specialized and rarely used. This borrowing from French is, of course, also a borrowing from Latin secondhand. The double borrowing has enriched our language with doublets (page 163).

Anglo-Saxon Is Alive and Well

Despite the power of the new French language, Anglo-Saxon stubbornly held its own. A word count of conversation today would show that we use Anglo-Saxon words most of the time. Here's a typical brief dialogue of greeting:

"How are you, John? I haven't seen you in months. How's everything?"

"Great! Did you hear the news? Joan and I are getting married next week. We're planning to live here, in the city."

This is the language of our everyday life. The Anglo-Saxon words have never given up. In this dialogue there are a few words of French origin: *news, married,* and *city.* All the rest are Anglo-Saxon.

Occasionally, as time went on, a French word replaced the Anglo-Saxon. The briefer *news,* for example, has replaced the lengthier Anglo-Saxon *tidings.* When both words have survived and are frequently used, they

* *Anglo-Saxon* is also included in *Old English,* a label often used in dictionary etymologies.

usually take on somewhat different meanings. *Marriage* (from French) usually refers to the *state* of being married. *Wedding* (from Anglo-Saxon) usually refers to the *ceremony*. In general, however, the nuts-and-bolts words of English—the pronouns, the being verbs, the basic words for things around us—are Anglo-Saxon.

The first words we learn as children are mostly Anglo-Saxon words; for example, *mother, father, sister, dog, cat, love, like, good, see, home, house,* etc. Consequently, because they are associated with things we knew as children, they tend to arouse emotional responses in us.

At the end of Charles Dickens' A *Tale of Two Cities,* Sidney Carton muses on his way to the guillotine. His last thoughts are dramatic and famous:

"It is a far, far better thing I do, than I have ever done; it is a far, far better rest I go to than I have ever known."

Under the stress of great emotion—of happiness, grief, or anger—we tend to use Anglo-Saxon words, which remain the backbone of English.

Scandinavian Words

Before the Normans took over, Viking raiders invaded again and again. They brought many Scandinavian words into the mainstream of English; for example, *sky, skin, skill,* and *whisk.* The *sk* sound is typically Scandinavian and so we have both *shirt* (Anglo-Saxon) and *skirt* (Scandinavian).

TRIAL TEST

In the following sentences the boldfaced words are all of Scandinavian origin. In each sentence write the letter for the word that is closest in meaning to the boldfaced word.

1. Suddenly there was a **rift** in the clouds.
(A) crack
(B) trap
(C) storm
(D) bright spot
(E) drift

1 ____

2. He found the **snare** where he'd left it.
(A) tuba
(B) trap
(C) rope
(D) knife
(E) bite of food

2 ____

3. Imitation **down** is made from milk-weed.
(A) seed
(B) feathers
(C) mats
(D) flour
(E) milky beverage

3 ____

4. He was large in **girth.**
(A) stature
(B) heart
(C) circumference
(D) size of hand
(E) head

4 ____

5. The Spartans were **rugged** people.
   (A) sea-going
   (B) sickly
   (C) curious
   (D) hardy
   (E) unusual

   5 _____

6. The ruthless dictator's followers were recruited from the **dregs** of society.
   (A) worthless part
   (B) wealthiest people
   (C) pillars
   (D) businessmen
   (E) farmers

   6 _____

7. The day was **muggy**.
   (A) hot and dry
   (B) cold and dry
   (C) cold and moist
   (D) warm and moist
   (E) warm and dry

   7 _____

8. Hasn't he an unusual **gait**?
   (A) way of walking
   (B) door
   (C) manner of speaking
   (D) half-door
   (E) reading ability

   8 _____

9. Ichabod despised the **swains** who sought the hand of Katrina Van Tassel.
   (A) old men
   (B) young suitors
   (C) wealthy landowners
   (D) members of the nobility
   (E) rivals

   9 _____

10. They **ransacked** the house.
    (A) burnt
    (B) sold
    (C) plundered
    (D) bought at a sale
    (E) painted

    10 _____

The Scandinavian words were thoroughly absorbed into English at the time of the Norman Conquest. For our purposes no further distinctions need be made between Scandinavian and Anglo-Saxon.

Anglo-Saxon Prefixes

Prefix	Meaning	Example	Explanation
be	completely	**be**draggled	*completely* soiled
by	near	**by**stander	one who stands *near*
for	not	**for**bid	*not* allow
fore	before, front	**fore**going	going *before*
mis	bad, badly, wrong, wrongly	**mis**take	take *wrongly*
in	in	**in**come	money that comes *in*
off	off, from	**off**set	set *off*
out	beyond	**out**law	*beyond* the law
on	on	**on**looker	one who looks *on*
over	too much, over	**over**pay	pay *too much*
		oversee	watch *over*
un	not	**un**happy	*not* happy
under	below, against	**under**pay	pay *below* reasonable amount
up	up	**up**heaval	a heaving *up*
with	against	**with**stand	stand *against*

Some words from Anglo-Saxon, like words from other sources, have acquired figurative meanings in use. *Understand,* for example, by derivation means "stand under." Now it means "get the meaning of." We can only guess how the current meaning came into being. Fortunately, the word has been used in the current sense for so long a time, it is an easy word. Ordinarily, the more figurative the meaning, the longer the word has been in the language and the more likely you are to know and use it.

Some Anglo-Saxon words almost exactly translate words of French or Latin derivation. *Dejected,* for example, is exactly parallel to the Anglo-Saxon *downcast.* Both *dejected* and *downcast* have evolved figurative meanings. *Downcast* does not require physical action; we don't throw or cast anything down. The word, like *dejected,* has become purely figurative.

Anglo-Saxon roots and prefixes rarely cause difficulty, but occasionally knowledge of a prefix can help, as in this sentence-completion item.

Problem

With all the charts and graphs provided, it is difficult to _____ the aims and goals of the new legislation.

(A) comprehend   (D) espouse
(B) misconceive   (E) paraphrase
(C) negotiate

Strategy. Sometimes a seemingly simple challenge is deceptive. In one context or another, each of the preceding alternatives would be acceptable. Again, you must ask, "Which is the *best* alternative in the limited context provided?" *Charts* and *graphs* are provided for clarification. Thus, the word *difficult* suggests an opposing idea. That idea is contained in *misconceive* (B), "fail to understand." The Anglo-Saxon prefix *mis,* "wrongly," reverses the meaning of *conceive,* as it does in the more familiar word *misunderstand.*

(B) With all the charts and graphs provided it is difficult to misconceive the aims and goals of the new legislation.

TRIAL TEST

Fill the blank in each sentence by writing an Anglo-Saxon prefix from the previous list. The word in italics is a clue to the needed prefix. The number in parentheses tells the number of letters.

The director's choice was *wrong.* Denny is **mis**cast as the lead in the school play. (3)

The italicized word *wrong* tells us to insert the prefix **mis.**

1. When Yvonne is _____mused, she is so *completely* plunged in thought, she doesn't see or hear anything. (2)

2. We've cooked the chicken *too much;* it's _____done. (4)

3. That _____landish costume goes *beyond* any reasonable one I've ever seen! (3)

4. Looking back is easy; looking at the years in *front* of us is hard. Hindsight is 20-20, but _____sight is not so certain! (4)

5. It takes a wise person to _____bear saying, "I told you so," for it is hard *not* to gloat. (3)

6. Young children are _____inhibited, *not* yet restrained by adult standards of decorum. (2)

7. _____beat personalities differ *from* normal people in their unusual reactions to ordinary events. (3)

8. Many Americans are still _____nourished, with diets *below* minimum standards for good health. (5)

9. A thousand shoppers descended *on* the store, and the ensuing _____rush was like a riot. (2)

10. When teachers' salaries were _____graded, the average salary went *up* 10%. (2)

No Roots?

At this point you would expect a list of Anglo-Saxon roots, like the ones for Greek and Latin. Such a list would contain a paradox: It would be both too long—and too easy! You already know most Anglo-Saxon roots. They are the word elements you used as a child.

Here's proof. There are two kinds of English verbs: weak verbs and strong verbs. Weak verbs add *ed* for the past tense and the past participle. Examples of weak verbs are *talk, talked,* (have, has, had) *talked* and *help, helped,* (have, etc.) *helped.* Strong verbs change in other ways in the past tense and the past participle. Examples of strong verbs are *go, went,* (have, etc.) *gone* and *sing, sang,* (have, etc.) *sung.* Verbs from French and other languages tend to be weak verbs; for example, *nominate* and *sympathize.* The strong verbs are Anglo-Saxon.

Here's a list of strong verbs in English. *You already know them.* You may have trouble with forms of the tenses, but you know the meaning of every word in the list. There is no need to list the Anglo-Saxon roots.

arise	draw	grind	shine	sting
beat	drink	grow	sink	stride
behold	eat	hold	sit	strike
bind	fall	know	slay	swing
bite	fight	lie	slide	take
blow	find	ring	speak	tear
break	fly	rise	spin	throw
choose	freeze	run	spring	weave
cling	get	see	stand	win
come	give	shake	steal	write

You may meet an Anglo-Saxon word in a sentence-completion test.

Problem

The _____ of all the disagreement was the call for a new election.

(A) undergirding   (D) overreach
(B) foreclosure   (E) upshot
(C) rancor

Strategy. The _upshot_ was once the final shot in an archery match. Thus it came to mean "conclusion." The familiar prefix _up_ and common root _shot_ tell us we have a word of Anglo-Saxon origin here.

REVIEW

A. Write the letter for the antonym of each capitalized word.

1. UNWARRANTED:
   (A) not sold
   (B) garbled
   (C) suitable
   (D) scrutinized
   (E) pressured

   1 ____

2. OFFSPRING:
   (A) cousin
   (B) sibling
   (C) aunt
   (D) sire
   (E) infant

   2 ____

3. MISGIVING:
   (A) assurance
   (B) theft
   (C) reluctance
   (D) gift
   (E) greed

   3 ____

4. FORBEARANCE:
   (A) impatience
   (B) allowance
   (C) leniency
   (D) refusal
   (E) breakdown

   4 ____

5. OUTGROWTH:
   (A) cause
   (B) appendage
   (C) drop in profits
   (D) result
   (E) rock ledge

   5 ____

6. OVERINDULGE:
(A) scan
(B) press
(C) strike
(D) fast
(E) clamor

6 ____

7. WITHDRAWAL:
(A) retreat
(B) deposit
(C) authorization
(D) attainment
(E) decrease

7 ____

8. UNDERTAKE:
(A) give up
(B) pursue
(C) disgrace
(D) carry on
(E) disclose

8 ____

9. BEWITCHMENT:
(A) embarrassment
(B) disenchantment
(C) sorcery
(D) conversion
(E) betrayal

9 ____

10. UPLIFT:
(A) redesign
(B) depart
(C) prevail
(D) discard
(E) debase

10 ____

Compound Words

The Anglo-Saxons loved to build compound words, just as modern German does. (They are related languages.) For our modern word *traveler,* they had *earth-walker.* The *king* was a *ring-giver.* A *successor* was an *after-comer.* A *lamp* was a *light-vessel.* The *sea* was the *whale-road.* *Geometry* was *earth-craft.* A *boat* was *sea-wood.* Many compounds were poetically beautiful, like *day-red* for *dawn.*

Many of the old compounds were dropped. Some, like *ring-finger,* are still with us. Some compounds have been combined to make a single word. *Walrus,* for example, was a *whale-horse.*

Modern English still creates new compound words. Words like *counterculture* and *cost-efficient* are fairly recent additions. A living language never stops changing.

Try your hand at creating compounds from Anglo-Saxon word elements.

B. Match words from column A and words from column B to form present-day compound words. Write the compound words on the lines below.

EXAMPLE:

| *Basket* plus *ball* equals *basketball.* |

	A		**B**
back	rail	ache	mill
dress	saw	band	road
eye	sea	beam	rocket
foot	sky	boat	sickness
gate	snow	book	sight
gold	sun	fish	step
hand	tooth	ground	storm
home	water	less	stroke
life	work	maker	way
moon	wrist	man	works

_____   _____

_____   _____

_____   _____

_____   _____

_____   _____

_____   _____

_____   _____

_____   _____

_____   _____

_____   _____

SUMMARY

Etymology Clue 5: Anglo-Saxon Prefixes and Roots

1. Words from Anglo-Saxon predominate in most writing and nearly all conversation.

2. Words for basic human actions and for commonplace objects tend to be of Anglo-Saxon origin. In times of great emotion, people tend to call upon Anglo-Saxon words.

3. Words long in use often have figurative meanings, but the central meanings of the words tends to be recognizable.

4. Anglo-Saxon words are particularly useful in making compound words.

5. Anglo-Saxon prefixes may combine with roots from other sources: *under-estimate*.

Etymology Clue 6: | Suffixes

Suffixes are crucial little word elements. They make the difference between *hopeful* and *hopeless, journalist and journalese, elective* and *election, thirteen* and *thirty*. They make verbs of adjectives: *short, shorten*. They make adverbs of adjectives: *sweet, sweetly*.

Suffixes provide clues to the part of speech. Typical noun suffixes include **dom, ness, ship, ion**, and **tude**. Typical adjective suffixes include **ish, less, y, esque**, and **ose**. Typical verb suffixes include **fy, ize**, and **ate**.

Although English derives suffixes from Latin, Greek, and Anglo-Saxon, suffixes were not treated in those sections of the book. A major reason is that English tends to make all kinds of combinations, using Latin roots with old Anglo-Saxon suffixes *(gratefully)* and Anglo-Saxon roots with old Latin suffixes *(breakable)*. A word like *hypothetically* has a Greek prefix **hypo** and Greek root **thes**. The Latin suffix **al** combines with the Anglo-Saxon suffix **ly**, and we have a word from three different sources—Greek, Latin, and Anglo-Saxon. When English creates new words, all languages are fair game. There is little practical point in classifying suffixes as of Latin, Greek, or Anglo-Saxon origin.

Suffixes You Already Know

You can instantly recognize many suffixes, like **less** and **able**. You already know the meaning of most suffixes. You can guess, for example, that *happiness* is the "state of being happy" and that **ness** means "state of." You can often identify the meaning of unfamiliar words with suffixes by recalling other words you already know that have the same suffix.

Suppose you come upon the word *quiescent*. You recognize the word *quiet* but what of the suffix, **escent**? Think of other words with the same suffix: *adolescent* and *convalescent*. Both suggest a *state of becoming: becoming* an adult and *becoming* well. The suffix **escent** does mean "becoming." *Quiescent* suggests the process of *becoming* quiet. You would never call the ancient stillness of an Egyptian tomb *quiescent*. It is not *becoming* quiet. It has been quiet for a long time.

If you come upon the word *senescent*, you have something to build upon. You have already decided that the **escent** suffix means "becoming," but what of the root, **sene**? You think of words like *senior, seniority, senile,* and *senility.* These have to do with age. Even *senate* and *senator* originally suggested the older, more experienced, wiser heads in government. You may reasonably decide that *senescent* means "becoming older," "aging." Suffixes help to make fine distinctions.

Some suffixes are so rich and helpful they deserve your special attention. **Fy**, meaning "make," is such a suffix.

Review the meanings of these **fy** words.

amplify	magnify	satisfy
clarify	mortify	simplify
codify	ossify	solidify
deify	pacify	stultify
dignify	petrify	testify
horrify	rectify	unify
identify	revivify	verify
indemnify	sanctify	vilify

The concept of *making* is apparent in all these words, even though in some words the meaning is more figurative than literal. *Mortify,* for example, by derivation means "make dead." Isn't that rather strange? Not at all. Speakers of English are prone to exaggeration. Think of a typical exclamation: "I was so mortified I thought I'd die!"

Suffixes Suggest Meaning

Suffixes go beyond denotation. They may also be clues to connotation. The **ish** suffix, for example, is a popular one. Often it has a negative connotation. Think of *boyish, babyish, childish, mannish, foolish, boorish, kittenish, cleverish,* and *clownish.* Contrast the neutral *childlike* with the negative *childish.* The **ster** suffix also tends to have a negative connotation, as in words like *trickster, mobster, gangster, prankster, gamester, huckster,* and *rhymester.* An occasional **ster** may be an exception. *Punster* may have had a mildly negative tone at one time, but now it seems almost affectionate. *Youngster* is a fairly neutral word, but for some people it seems patronizing. Still, the **ster** suffix is a good clue to negative words.

Some suffixes suggest affection. The suffix **y**, for example, appears in words like *kitty, aunty, Johnny, Elly,* and *sissy* (for sister). Some suffixes suggest science and learning: **ics** in *economics, hydroponics, harmonics, astrophysics,* and *electronics.*

Some suffixes have sudden bursts of popularity. **Ette**, meaning "small," has been widely used in recent years to suggest compactness and charm. Most people would shun a *small kitchen,* but they're proud of a *kitchenette.* Words like *luncheonette, launderette,* and *statuette* are perfectly acceptable. One small grocery store proudly called itself a *superette!* The **ama** suffix, originally from *orama* meaning "to see," started with *cyclorama,* then made its way to *launderama.*

A living language has vitality, vigor, and the capacity for change. Suffixes play a role in that change.

Become familiar with the following lists of suffixes. Knowing suffixes will help you on the SAT. The suffixes here are in two sections for convenience.

Suffixes—1

Suffix	Meaning	Example	Explanation
able, ible	able to	manage**able**	*able to* be managed
		collaps**ible**	*able to* be collapsed
ac, ic	related to	cardi**ac**	*related to* the heart
		dramat**ic**	*related to* drama
acious, scious	having quality of	ver**acious**	*having quality of* truth, true
age	state, quality, act	shrink**age**	*state* of shrinking
al, ical	related to, like	nav**al**	*related to* ships
		crit**ical**	*related to* criticism
an, ian	related to, one who	ur**ban**	*related to* the city
		magic**ian**	*one who* works with magic
ana	information about	Americ**ana**	*information about* America
ance, ence	state, quality	resist**ance**	*state* of resisting
ancy, ency	state, quality	despond**ency**	*state* of being downcast
ant, ent	one who, that which	particip**ant**	*one who* takes part
		tang**ent**	*that which* touches
ar	like, related to, one who	circul**ar**	*like* a circle
		li**ar**	*one who* lies
ary, arium	place where	gran**ary**	*place where* grain is stored
		sanit**arium**	*place where* people go to regain health
ard, art	one who (usually negative)	bragg**art**	*one who* boasts
ate	make, act, one who having quality of	dehyd**rate**	*make* waterless
		advoc**ate**	*one who* pleads another's cause
		moder**ate**	*having quality of* reasonableness
cle	small	parti**cle**	*small* element
craft	skill, practice of	witch**craft**	*practice of* being a witch

Suffix	Meaning	Example	Explanation
dom	state, quality	wis**dom**	*state* of being wise
ee	one who	employ**ee**	*one who* is employed
eer	one who	auction**eer**	*one who* auctions
el, le	little, small	par**cel**	*small* bundle
en	make	hard**en**	*make* hard
	having quality	wood**en**	*having quality* of wood
er, or	one who, that which	sail**or**	*one who* sails
		wash**er**	*that which* washes
ern	related to	east**ern**	*related to* east
ery, erie	place where	hatch**ery**	*place where* fish are hatched
		menag**erie**	*place where* animals are displayed
ery, ry	state of, quality, act of	drudg**ery**	*state of* hard, dull work
		bigot**ry**	*state of* or *act of* prejudice
escent	becoming	obsol**escent**	*becoming* obsolete
ese	like, related to	Chin**ese**	*related to* China
esque	in the manner of	Whitman**esque**	*in the manner of* Whitman
ess*	feminine	act**ress**	*female* actor*
et, ette	little, small	ring**let**	*little* ring
fic, fy	making, make	honori**fic**	*making* or conferring honor
		simpli**fy**	*make* simple
fold	times	ten**fold**	ten *times*
ful	having quality of	care**ful**	*having quality of* care
hood	state of, quality of	child**hood**	*state* of being a child
		false**hood**	*quality of* falseness
ics	science, system	linguist**ics**	*science* of languages
ice	act of, time of	serv**ice**	*act of* serving
id	related to	flu**id**	*related to* a liquid

*This suffix has been under attack as being sexist. Opponents argue that *actor* refers to both sexes. Words like *steward* and *stewardess* have given way to *flight attendant*. The suffix is included here for completeness, but you may wish to think about your own use of it.

TRIAL TEST

Each of the words in column A contains a suffix from the preceding list. Each suffix is in boldface. Write the number for each word from column A next to its meaning in column B. Clues in column B are in *italics*. Note how suffixes can help to sharpen meaning.

A	B
1. avi**ary**	_____ *make* systematic, arrange
2. benefac**tor**	_____ *smallest* speck
3. bliss**ful**	_____ science of production, distribution, and consumption of wealth
4. codi**fy**	_____ *place where* birds are kept
5. incorrig**ible**	_____ *having quality of* happiness
6. econom**ics**	_____ manual *skill*
7. handi**craft**	_____ *related to* light, clear
8. luc**id**	_____ *one who* does good deeds
9. parti**cle**	_____ *in the manner of* a statue
10. sculptur**esque**	_____ not *able to* be reformed

Familiarity with suffixes sometimes helps define a partially familiar word.

Problem

Proof of bad faith may be used as a reason to _____ the agreement.

(A) nullify   (D) temper
(B) celebrate   (E) consider
(C) advertise

Strategy. The context suggests that the agreement is in trouble. *Nullify,* "to make null," satisfies the meaning. You have probably met *null* in the expression *null and void,* meaning "not binding." *Nullify* thus suggests "not binding." Even if you have not heard *null and void,* you have probably heard the word *annul,* meaning "cancel." Or perhaps you've heard the word *annulment,* the "dissolution of a marriage."

The *fy* suffix is one of the most useful, as in words like *magnify, petrify,* and *horrify.*

Suffixes—2

Suffix	Meaning	Example	Explanation
ie, y	small	dogg**ie**	*small* dog
		kit**ty**	*small* kitten
ine	like, related to	fel**ine**	*like* a cat
ion	state, quality, act of	suspic**ion**	*act of* suspecting
ish	like, related to	boor**ish**	*like* a boor
isk	small	aster**isk**	*small* star
ism	state of, quality, act	egot**ism**	*state of* being self-centered
ist	one who	dent**ist**	*one who* works with teeth
ite	one who	favor**ite**	*one who* is favored
itis	inflammation	neur**itis**	*inflammation* of nerves
ity	state, quality, act	nobil**ity**	*quality* of being noble
ize	make, act	tranquil**ize**	*make* quiet
ive	one who, that which	capt**ive**	*one who* has been taken
ive	having power	creat**ive**	*having power* to create
kin	little, small	mani**kin**	*little* man
less	without	home**less**	*without* a home
let	little	book**let**	*little* book
like	like	ape**like**	*like* an ape
ly	having quality of	friend**ly**	*having quality of* a friend
ly	in the manner of (adverb suffix)	hurried**ly**	*in a* hurried *manner*
ment	state of, quality, act	excite**ment**	*state of* being excited
mony	state of, quality, that which	matri**mony**	*state of* being married
or	one who, that which	don**or**	*one who* gives
ory, orium	place where	fact**ory**	*place where* things are made
		audit**orium**	*place where* one can hear
ory	like, having quality of	regulat**ory**	*having quality of* controlling
ose	having quality of	belli**cose**	*having quality of* quarrelsomeness
osis	state, condition, action	hypn**osis**	*state* resembling sleep
	abnormal or diseased condition	tubercul**osis**	*diseased condition* of lungs
ous	having quality of	fam**ous**	*having quality of* fame
ship	state of, quality of	owner**ship**	*state of* being an owner
some	having quality of, full of	worri**some**	*having quality of* worry
ster	one who	prank**ster**	*one who* plays pranks
th	state, quality, that which	tru**th**	*state of* being true
tude	state, quality of, act of	multi**tude**	*state of* being numerous

Suffix	Meaning	Example	Explanation
ty	state of, quality of, that which	safe**ty**	*state of* being safe
ure	state of, quality of, act, that which	rupt**ure**	*state of* being broken
ward, wards	in direction of	home**ward**	*in direction of* home
wise	in the manner of, in a certain direction	clock**wise**	*in the direction* a clock rotates
y	having quality of	hast**y**	*having quality of* haste
	somewhat	yellow**y**	*somewhat* yellow
	tending to	drows**y**	*tending to* drowse
	suggestive of	willow**y**	*suggestive of* a willow, gracefully slender

TRIAL TEST

Each of the words in column A contains a suffix from the preceding list. Each suffix is in boldface. Write the number for each word from column A next to its meaning in column B. Clues in column B are in *italics.* Note how suffixes can help to sharpen meaning.

A	B
1. altru**ism**	_____ *having quality of* being annoying
2. curat**or**	_____ *inflammation* of the stomach
3. cut**let**	_____ *little* slice
4. equ**ine**	_____ *one who* is in charge of a museum or a library
5. eulo**gize**	_____ *make* a speech of praise
6. gastr**itis**	_____ *in the manner of* a greedy person
7. gluttonou**sly**	_____ *place where* people work and experiment
8. laborat**ory**	_____ *like* a horse
9. psych**osis**	_____ *diseased condition* of the mind
10. vexat**ious**	_____ *quality* of unselfishness

Try your skill at another sentence-completion question.

Problem

The _____ of the health-insurance problem can be gauged by the number and variety of plans and solutions offered.

(A) analysis   (D) demographics
(B) amplitude   (E) sturdiness
(C) interest

Strategy. You are familiar with the word *ample,* "generous," "large." The prefix *tude,* "state of," combines with *ample* to produce *amplitude,* the answer best associated with "number and variety."

REVIEW

Write the letter for the word that best fits each sentence

1. The long, _____ speech of the undistinguished candidate put most of the audience to sleep.
   (A) trenchant   (D) confidential
   (B) narrative   (E) consequential
   (C) somnolent

   1 ____

2. Though usually easygoing and tolerant of different viewpoints, the voters in New Jersey showed a strong _____ toward increased taxation without accompanying spending cuts.
   (A) inquiry
   (B) antipathy
   (C) attitude
   (D) approbation
   (E) disenfranchisement

   2 ____

3. At the beginning of his first term, Franklin D. Roosevelt was severely criticized for the introduction of new and revolutionary programs, but he remained _____ throughout.
   (A) imperturbable
   (B) antagonistic
   (C) indeterminate
   (D) unconventional
   (E) undignified

   3 ____

4. Andy Warhol, commenting upon the _____ nature of fame, once said that everyone can be a celebrity for fifteen minutes.
   (A) indomitable   (D) fanatical
   (B) repetitive   (E) transient
   (C) dormant

   4 ____

5. At one time, delivery services required the _____ of every package to sign for acceptance, but nowadays packages are often left at the doorstep.
   (A) dispatcher   (D) owner
   (B) identifier   (E) proprietor
   (C) recipient

   5 ____

6. In an Agatha Christie mystery, Miss Marple early on suspected the identity of the murderer, but her proof was

   _____.
   (A) invulnerable   (D) uninspiring
   (B) inconclusive   (E) unintelligible
   (C) fallacious

   6 ____

7. Carol Burnett won a judgment against a national magazine on the charge of _____ of character.
   (A) disclosure   (D) incongruity
   (B) defamation   (E) restitution
   (C) inflammation

   7 ____

8. Harold is able to hold two divergent points of view at the same time without realizing their _____.
   (A) incomprehensibility
   (B) spontaneity
   (C) variability
   (D) incompatibility
   (E) symmetricality

   8 ____

9. Although I find the sauna _____, Marie enjoys it and can stay inside for ten minutes at a time.
(A) enervating
(B) volatile
(C) propitious
(D) luminous
(E) winsome

9 ____

10. The President's proposals were _____ to the leaders of his own party, and he had to retreat.
(A) tolerable
(B) nurturing
(C) unpalatable
(D) analogous
(E) proliferating

10 ____

SUMMARY
Etymology Clue 6: Suffixes

1. Suffixes provide important clues to the part of speech, word meanings, and word history.

2. English uses suffixes without regard for word origins. Anglo-Saxon and Latin suffixes are often used together.

3. You can find the meaning of most suffixes: think of other words containing the suffix. Then decide what meaning all the words have in common.

4. Suffixes sometimes suggest connotation as well as denotation.

Suffixes can help you with SAT questions, especially when you need to know the part of speech.

Etymology Clue 7: | Foreign Words in English

Think of a typical American **barbecue**. In addition to the meat, there might be baked **potato**, baked **yam**, sliced **tomato**, all served with **lemonade**, **ginger** ale, iced **tea**, or iced **coffee**. Of course the inevitable bottle of **ketchup** would be on hand for the feast. For dessert there might be **orange sherbet**. Some guests might prefer **chocolate** ice cream, made from **cocoa**. In season, **apricots** and **avocados** might be welcome additions. **Bananas** would almost certainly be available.

Notice how much we depend upon foreign borrowings. Every one of the boldfaced words originally came from lands all around the world.

barbecue—American Indian	orange—Persian
potato—American Indian	sherbet—Arabic
yam—African	chocolate—Mexican
tomato—Mexican	cocoa—Mexican
lemon—Persian	apricots—Arabic
ginger—Indian	avocados—Mexican

tea—Chinese
coffee—Arabic
ketchup—Malayan-Chinese

bananas—African
syrup—Arabic
sugar—Arabic

These are just a few of the food words borrowed from other languages. Sometimes the borrowings provide a clue to the special contribution of a particular language. From Hebrew, for example, we get religious terms like **amen, cherub, hallelujah, Jehovah, jubilee, Pharisee, sabbath**, and **shibboleth**.

TRIAL TEST

A. Below are listed groups of words from various other languages. Decide from what language each group of words came and match each group with the proper language from the list below.

---

arcade, balcony, colonnade, corridor, portico

Language: *Italian*

These are all of Italian origin. All have something to do with parts of buildings, so we can safely assume that Italian contributions to architecture have been considerable.

Languages (or places of origin)

African	French
American	German
American Indian	Italian
Arabic	Persian
Dutch	Spanish

1. hominy, maize, pecan, succotash, squash
   Language: _____

2. beret, cambric, chapeau, cretonne
   Language: _____

3. deck, dock, hoist, jib, skipper, sloop
   Language: _____

4. bismuth, cobalt, Fahrenheit, gneiss, quartz, shale, zinc
   Language: _____

5. alchemy, algebra, chemistry, cipher, zenith, zero
   Language: _____

6. adobe, bronco, canyon, corral, lariat
   Language: _____

7. jasmine, lemon, lilac, orange, peach, tulip
   Language: _____

8. andante, aria, opera, piano, soprano
   Language: _____

9. chimpanzee, gnu, gorilla, ibis, quagga
   Language: _____

10. carborundum, cellophane, kodak, listerine, thermos, victrola
    Language: _____

B. The words in column A have all been based upon the names of places in other lands. Look up the origin and the meaning of each word in column A. Then write each word's number next to its country of origin in column *B*.

	A		B
1.	astrachan	_____	China
2.	bayonet	_____	England
3.	calico	_____	England and Scotland
4.	cantaloupe	_____	France
5.	cheviot	_____	Germany
6.	coach	_____	Hungary
7.	damask	_____	India
8.	frankfurter	_____	Italy
9.	muslin	_____	Mesopotamia
10.	oolong	_____	Mexico
11.	peach	_____	Morocco
12.	polka	_____	Persia
13.	tabasco	_____	Poland
14.	tangerine	_____	Russia
15.	worsted	_____	Syria

Word History

Among the ancient Greeks, citizens of Laconia, or Sparta, had the reputation of speaking directly, wasting no words. This characteristic has given us the word **laconic**. **Laconic** means "brief," "to the point." Many qualities or products of various places have given us new words. The American favorite, **hamburger**, is named after the city of Hamburg. **Italic** type originated in Italy. **Copper** took its name from Cyprus, as did **spaniel** from Spain. **China, turkey, cologne**, and **morocco** (leather) are self-explanatory.

Words from sources other than Latin, Greek, or Anglo-Saxon appear occasionally in the word sections of the SAT and the reading sections. The best preparation for this section is also the best preparation for extending your vocabulary in general. Become word curious. When you meet an interesting new word, look up the definition, of course, but also check its history.

Note the interesting history behind the word **bizarre**.

> **bi·zarre** (bi zär′) *adj.* [Fr. < It. *bizarro;* angry, fierce, strange < Sp. *bizarro,* bold, knightly < Basque *bizar,* a beard] 1. odd in manner, appearance, etc.; grotesque; queer; eccentric 2. marked by extreme contrasts and incongruities of color, design, or style 3. unexpected and unbelievable; fantastic [a *bizarre* sequence of events]—**SYN**. see FANTAS-TIC—**bi·zarre′ly** *adv.*—**bi·zarre′ness** *n.**

Bizarre originally came from Basque *bizar,* meaning "beard." The Spaniards borrowed the word as *bizarro* to mean "bold," "knightly." Knights, we may assume, were *bearded.* The Italians then borrowed the word with the same spelling to mean "angry," "fierce." Knightly battles were not gentle struggles! Then English borrowed the same word as **bizarre** to mean "odd," "eccentric." Reading the history makes an impression. (Note that the similar-sounding word, *bazaar,* is completely unrelated. *Bazaar* comes from the Persian *bazar,* meaning "market.")

Karate comes from two Japanese words: *kara* meaning "empty," "open" and *te* meaning "hand." **Karate** literally means "open hand." A demonstration of karate clearly shows how the word originated, as thrusts are made with hands open.

Sometimes a colorful borrowed word appears in a sentence-completion item.

Problem

When contrasted with the staid and sober Charles Darnay, Charles Dickens's Sidney Carton seemed almost _____.

(A) austere   (D) flamboyant
(B) formidable   (E) perspicacious
(C) dour

Strategy. *Contrasted* tells us that the blank must have a word opposed in meaning to *staid* and *sober.* On this basis alone, (A) and (C) fail to qualify. *Formidable* (B) and *perspicacious* (E) are neither synonyms nor antonyms of *staid* and *sober,* thus disqualifying them as answers. *Flamboyant* (D) suggests a "dramatic display," a residue of its French ancestry. We can even discern the word *flame* within it.

(D) When contrasted with the staid and sober Charles Darnay, Charles
      Dickens's Sidney Carton seemed almost flamboyant.

REVIEW

A. After each of the following words, the origin of the word is given, along with its original meaning. Read the clues and write the letter for the answer which most closely explains the test word.

KOWTOW (from the Chinese meaning "knock head"):
- (A) find unexpectedly
- (B) respect excessively
- (C) support enthusiastically
- (D) understand poorly
- (E) reject suddenly

_____B_____

Since the original meaning suggests a person touching his head to the floor in submission, alternative (B), *respect excessively,* is the correct answer.

---

1. CHECKMATE (from the Persian "the king is dead"):
   - (A) delay intentionally
   - (B) replace secretly
   - (C) marry in haste
   - (D) support financially
   - (E) defeat completely

   1 ____

2. PUNDIT (from Hindi "learned person"):
   - (A) authority
   - (B) mayor
   - (C) enthusiast
   - (D) police officer
   - (E) humorist

   2 ____

3. UKASE (from the Russian "to order"):
   - (A) container for bottles
   - (B) kind of instrument
   - (C) voting irregularity
   - (D) official decree
   - (E) all-purpose cement

   3 ____

4. AMOK (from the Malay "fighting furiously"):
   - (A) sympathetic
   - (B) at a standstill
   - (C) in a rage
   - (D) wearily accepting
   - (E) quietly responsible

   4 ____

5. NADIR (from the Arabic "opposite the highest point"):
   - (A) kind of telescope
   - (B) sunspot
   - (C) good fortune
   - (D) tropical fruit
   - (E) time of dejection

   5 ____

6. MOGUL (from Persian "Mongol conqueror"):
   - (A) superb athlete
   - (B) member of endangered species
   - (C) powerful person
   - (D) falsehood
   - (E) bill of sale

   6 ____

7. GARBLE (from Arabic "sieve"):
   - (A) close
   - (B) mix up
   - (C) win at chess
   - (D) wander aimlessly
   - (E) find fault

   7 ____

8. RUCKSACK (from German "back" plus "sack"):
   - (A) potato sack
   - (B) handbag
   - (C) pocketbook
   - (D) hiker's pack
   - (E) wallet

   8 ____

9. ARGOSY (from Italian "vessel from Ragusa"):
   - (A) merchant ship
   - (B) newly published book
   - (C) fan magazine
   - (D) financial wizard
   - (E) tall tale

   9 ____

10. MANDARIN (from Portuguese "minister of state"):
    - (A) skilled chef
    - (B) member of elite group
    - (C) fruit punch
    - (D) stringed instrument
    - (E) mythological monster

    10 ____

B. Words from foreign sources are everywhere in English. They are found in every field of activity, every subject, at every level of difficulty. How many words in the following test are familiar to you? For each item, write the letter for the answer that best defines the test word. If you don't know a word, look it up.

1. WAINSCOT is a
   (A) ceremonial car
   (B) kind of celluloid
   (C) formal dinner
   (D) roofing material
   (E) woodwork

   1 ____

2. QUININE is a
   (A) tropical disease
   (B) medicine
   (C) kind of dance
   (D) paint ingredient
   (E) beef tea

   2 ____

3. A CATAMARAN is a(n)
   (A) tiger-like animal
   (B) insect
   (C) Malayan hut
   (D) kind of boat
   (E) cure for malaria

   3 ____

4. FANFARE involves
   (A) display
   (B) the use of a fan
   (C) charging admission
   (D) baseball
   (E) jealousy

   4 ____

5. CURRY is a
   (A) carriage   (D) seasoning
   (B) harness   (E) comb
   (C) pack animal

   5 ____

6. TURQUOISE is a
   (A) fowl   (D) powder
   (B) plant   (E) French dish
   (C) color

   6 ____

7. FAHRENHEIT and CELSIUS are words dealing with
   (A) severity of earthquakes
   (B) degrees of heat
   (C) electronic calculations
   (D) atmospheric pressure
   (E) relative humidity

   7 ____

8. A SHIBBOLETH is a
   (A) monster   (D) flower
   (B) password   (E) game
   (C) proclamation

   8 ____

9. A SERAPH is a(n)
   (A) kind of print   (D) angel
   (B) old woman   (E) mounted soldier
   (C) medicine

   9 ____

10. A FEZ is a kind of
    (A) fish
    (B) mythical animal
    (C) cap
    (D) coat
    (E) worship

    10 ____

11. A TABOO is a
    (A) mark   (D) narrative
    (B) prince   (E) permit
    (C) restriction

    11 ____

12. AZIMUTH is a term used in
    (A) painting
    (B) music
    (C) navigation
    (D) handicraft
    (E) the study of minerals

    12 ____

13. A MAZURKA is a kind of
    (A) broiled chicken (D) herb
    (B) dance   (E) building
    (C) vehicle
                                    13 ____

14. A FREEBOOTER is a
    (A) football player
    (B) member of a soccer team
    (C) fighter for freedom
    (D) pirate
    (E) weaver
                                    14 ____

15. A JUGGERNAUT is something that
    (A) plays a tune
    (B) crushes
    (C) works automatically
    (D) takes care of gardens
    (E) can perform acrobatic stunts
                                    15 ____

16. An ALPACA is a(n)
    (A) ballad
    (B) artificial fabric
    (C) light jacket
    (D) animal
    (E) special kind of stew
                                    16 ____

17. A JAGUAR is a(n)
    (A) medicinal root (D) injury
    (B) animal   (E) knife
    (C) bird
                                    17 ____

18. A BAZAAR is a
    (A) cloak
    (B) strange tale
    (C) protest
    (D) musical instrument
    (E) fair
                                    18 ____

19. The ZENITH is
    (A) on the horizon
    (B) below one's feet
    (C) at a 45-degree angle
    (D) above one's head
    (E) at the equator
                                    19 ____

20. A PARIAH is a(n)
    (A) staunch friend
    (B) outcast
    (C) religious fanatic
    (D) singer
    (E) weak-willed person
                                    20 ____

SUMMARY
Etymology Clue 7: Foreign Words in English

1. English has borrowed extensively from almost every language and culture it has come in contact with.

2. Borrowing has enriched the language by providing words for new objects and new ideas.

3. Finding the stories in foreign loan words enriches the study of vocabulary and impresses new words on the memory.

4. The borrowing goes both ways. English words also appear in almost every language in the original or changed form.

Studying foreign words in English and word histories will help you to prepare for the SAT.

Etymology Clue 8: The Growth of English

Think of expressions like *space shuttle, launch window, computer chip,* and *video game.* A few years ago these expressions did not exist because the things they name did not exist. We need new words and expressions to name new processes and substances. Unfortunately, as our problems increase, we need new expressions for these, too: *hazardous waste, endangered species, acid rain,* and *ethnic cleansing.*

Sometimes, as in the examples above, new expressions merely combine older words to create wholly new concepts. Sometimes, however, we need a wholly new word. When inflation strained the resources of a stagnant economy, we coined the new word *stagflation.* Words like *microprocessing* and *transistorize* show that we still have the ability to create new words from old roots.

The best way to learn new words is to listen carefully and read widely. Current newspapers and magazines are filled with new words and expressions. The computer alone has generated an entirely new vocabulary, words like *E-mail, Internet, download, Web browser, boot up,* and *search engine.* Political campaigns have given us *sound bite.*

Because words enter the language at so rapid a rate, it is impossible to prepare an up-to-date book on new words, or *neologisms,* as they are called. Dictionaries of new words are out of date before publication day. If there is a knowledge explosion, there is also a language explosion. New words will not play a key role in the SAT, but it is always a good idea to keep up to date.

When you work with roots, be aware of the tendency of language to change. The root of *common* suggests "shared by all." But the word has acquired a negative connotation of "inferiority," even "coarseness." Similarly, *vulgar* once meant "general," "popular," "belonging to the great mass of people." Now a certain snobbishness in language has sent the word downhill to mean "coarse," "crude," "boorish."

Uphill in Meaning

Words can go up the social scale, too. A *knight* was once a "servant." A *marshal* was a "groom," a "horse servant." A *constable* was the "chief groom." A *chamberlain,* now a high official, was once just a "servant." A *steward* was the "guardian of the sty." *Chivalry* was just another word for "cavalry." Even *fame* once meant only "something spoken about someone." Now it suggests "a good reputation."

Narrower in Meaning

While some words are going up or down the social scale, others are changing in different ways. Specialization has changed *meat* from "any solid food" to the "flesh of animals." A *ballad* was once just a "song." Now it's a rather special kind of song. *Corn* was once any "grain." Now in America it refers to the plant the Indians called "maize." *Ghost* once meant just "spirit." Now it is usually applied to an "apparition" said to haunt houses. In fact, *apparition* itself once meant just "appearance."

Downhill in Meaning

Enormity suggests one way in which words change—for the worse. Once it meant merely "something unusual." Now it suggests "unusual in evil." Similarly, *boor* once meant merely "farmer." *Knave* meant just "boy." *Homely* meant "simple," and *sullen* meant "alone." A *villain* was a "farm servant," and a *hussy* was just a "housewife." *Servile* meant "not free." Now it suggests "cringing," "unnecessarily submissive." A *busybody* was just a "busy person," and a *hypocrite* was just an "actor."

Broader in Meaning

English often extends word meanings. A *journey* was originally a "trip of one day's duration." Now it means a "trip of any length." *Front* once meant merely "forehead." *Paper* was a substance made from "papyrus." Now paper can be made from many substances. A *scene* was once just "part of a theater stage." We still use it in that sense, but think of all the broader uses of the term, as in *the modern scene. Hazard* was once a "game of dice." Now it means a "chance occurrence" and, by extension, a "risk," a "danger."

Figurative in Meaning

One of the most common changes in English is figurative use of a word. *Deliberate* literally means "put on the scales." *Dilapidate* means "throw stones." A *pedigree* literally means a "crane's foot." If you look at a pedigree, or family tree (another figurative expression), you can see that foot! Pages 66–71 have already considered the importance of figurative language. The sections on roots have urged you to look for figurative meanings in many common words.

However, language grows and changes in other ways, too. If you know about these changes, you will have a better background for handling some of the questions on the SAT.

Sometimes deceptive changes in meaning can prove puzzling on sentence-completion items.

Problem

The extent of the evil and the _____ of Joseph Stalin's actions became generally known in Russia during the Nikita Khrushchev era.

(A) beneficence   (D) enormity
(B) quality   (E) minimization
(C) revelation

Strategy. *Enormity* (D) once meant "something out of the normal." Then it became associated with evil, as in the sentence above. Through possible misuse or misunderstanding, the word is acquiring the sense of *large size,* of *enormousness.* Whichever definition is chosen, (D) is the correct choice here. Both (A) and (E) run counter to the meaning of the sentence as suggested in "the extent of the evil." (B) is too neutral. (Remember always to choose the *best* answer.) (C) is redundant: "the revelation . . . became known."

(D) The extent of the evil and the enormity of Joseph Stalin's actions became generally known in Russia during the Nikita Khrushchev era.

TRIAL TEST

In each sentence, write the word in parentheses that most suitably completes the meaning of the sentence.

The ending of the musical *Carousel* is so (poignant, pungent), it often brings a tear to every eye in the audience.

In this sentence *poignant* means "emotionally touching," "evoking pity." *Pungent* would be too strong. *Pungent* may be piercing to the mind; *poignant* to the emotions. *Pungent* can apply to taste. *Poignant* cannot.

1. An (abbreviated, abridged) dictionary keeps the most important words and omits infrequently used words.

1 _____

2. Jim's speech was interesting, but his ideas were too (tenuous, thin) for a practical program.

2 _____

3. When Caroline brought out the Ping-Pong balls, the kittens became unusually (fresh, frisky) in playing with them.

3 _____

4. After a morning in the garden. Don's complexion became (florid, flowery) from the heat.

4 _____

5. Because of a disagreement, the two families (separated, severed) all ties that had once joined them.

5 _____

6. Though Billy Dawn in *Born Yesterday* at first seemed (naive, native), she gradually developed a shrewd awareness of Brock's dishonesty.

6 _____

7. From an early age, Teddy showed an (aptitude, attitude) for things mechanical.

7 _____

8. Once Patty becomes interested in a subject, she (jealously, zealously) learns all she can about it.

8 _____

9. By three, Jennifer could already (compute, count) from 1 to 10.

9 _____

10. Pollen granules are (born, borne) on the wind.

10 _____

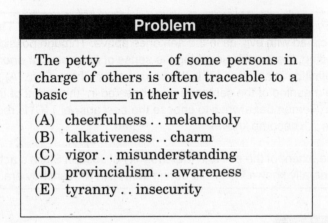

Problem

The petty _____ of some persons in charge of others is often traceable to a basic _____ in their lives.

(A) cheerfulness . . melancholy
(B) talkativeness . . charm
(C) vigor . . misunderstanding
(D) provincialism . . awareness
(E) tyranny . . insecurity

Strategy. Analyze the possibilities. (A) contains a contradiction. *Cheerfulness* cannot logically be traced to *melancholy*. Although it might be argued that such an answer is not impossible, you are not asked to choose just a possible answer. You must choose the best answer. If a clue word like *although* had been included, things might be different. Notice the difference the following wording makes.

> Although some persons in charge of others display *cheerfulness,* they may be concealing a basic *melancholy* in their lives.

Talkativeness and *charm* are negatively related, if at all. We can reject (B). *Vigor* and *misunderstanding* are not related. Misunderstanding would not logically lead to vigor. Reject (C). (D) also contains a contradiction. People who are *open and aware* are not likely to be *provincial.*

A process of elimination leaves you with (E). Do these answers fit? Yes, tyranny can arise from a feeling of insecurity. Those who feel insecure may try to generate security by being oppressive to others. (E) is correct.

Tyranny is a word that has gone downhill. A *tyrant* was once just a "ruler" in ancient Greece. Then, since rulers often abuse their powers, the word *tyrant* came to mean an "unjust, oppressive ruler." For the purpose of this question it is not necessary to know that *tyranny* has gone downhill, as long as you know its present meaning. But knowing a little about the history of a word makes it much easier to remember. Now that you know something about the origin of *tyranny,* you are unlikely to forget it.

Doublets

One of the most fruitful sources of the growth of English is borrowing. As we have already noted, English may borrow the same word twice or even more. This multiple borrowing enriches our language, increases the number of synonyms, and makes for finer discriminations in speaking and writing.

Both **potion** and **poison** come from the Latin word meaning "drink." These doublets have acquired different meanings. A **poison** is a deadly **potion**. **Loyal** and **legal** both come from the Latin *lex* meaning "law." **Loyal**, which reached English through French, has acquired a different meaning from **legal**. Similarly, **frail** has acquired a meaning slightly different from its doublet **fragile**. An ill person may become **frail** but not **fragile**.

Doublets may come from different languages. Here's a sampling.

Anglo-Saxon and Latin	eatable, edible
Anglo-Saxon and French	bench, bank
Anglo-Saxon and Scandinavian	shriek, screech
Anglo-Saxon and Dutch	slide, sled
Latin and French	concept, conceit
French and Italian	study, studio
French and Spanish	army, armada
Greek and French	cathedral, chair

Doublets may come from the same language, though at different periods.

Earlier and later French	castle, chateau
Earlier and later Latin	camp, campus

Doublets may come from various changes within English itself.

Loss of a syllable	despite, spite
Change of vowel	cloths, clothes
Change of consonant	stitch, stick
Word shortening	van, caravan
Spelling variation	flour, flower

Words borrowed three times are called *triplets*.

French, Italian, Spanish	place, piazza, plaza

Some words have been borrowed four times and now appear in four different forms, each with a different meaning: **stack, stake, steak, stock**. Some words have been borrowed five times and appear in five different forms: **discus, disk, dish, desk, dais.**

Why are doublets important in a vocabulary-building program? They provide associated words and synonyms. When you take a test, you must be able to discriminate meanings.

REVIEW

In each of the following sentences, doublets appear in parentheses. Write the word that most suitably completes the meaning of the sentence.

1. As a storyteller Maud is without a (pair, peer) in our club.

   1 _____

2. What seems like (concept, conceit) in Rod is really shyness.

   2 _____

3. With her new hairdo, Fran looks like a (spirit, sprite) from elfdom.

   3 _____

4. When Henry Ford started, his friends were critical of the risky (adventure, venture) he was engaged in.

   4 _____

5. Until Cynthia becomes 18, her uncle remains her legal (guardian, warden).

   5 _____

6. The sign in the window said, "We buy old furniture; we sell (antics, antiques)."

   6 _____

7. You'll need a(n) (example, sample) of your wallpaper if you want to buy a matching bedspread.

   7 _____

8. Making sure all five kittens had a good home was a (human, humane) action.

   8 _____

9. Mr. Hathaway (dealt, doled) out his son's allowance as if he were mortgaging the family homestead for the money.

   9 _____

10. Despite his advanced age, George Bernard Shaw remained surprisingly (hale, whole) and vigorous.

    10 _____

11. Because of her rigorous diet, Madge has become too (tenuous, thin).

    11 _____

12. Mr. Mackenzie has a rugged, (florid, flowery) complexion.

    12 _____

13. How did our ancestors (thrash, thresh) grain in generations past?

    13 _____

14. *Etc.* is an (abbreviation, abridgment) of *et cetera*.

    14 _____

15. When do (male, masculine) chickens begin to develop the characteristic comb?

    15 _____

16. When asked to explain his absence, Mark gave a (feeble, foible) excuse.

    16 _____

17. In certain groups, shunning encourages members to (snob, snub) other members who have strayed from the fold.

    17 _____

18. If the Forty-Niners win Sunday, they'll (clench, clinch) the division title.

    18 _____

19. When the linebacker tackled the quarterback later, there was a (scuffle, shuffle) on the field.

    19 _____

20. (Calibers, Calipers) are adjustable measuring instruments.

    20 _____

SUMMARY
Etymology Clue 8: The Growth of English

1. As a living language, English adds new words constantly.

2. Some words are needed for technological advances and setbacks. Others are needed for new customs, fashions, and lifestyles.

3. Some new expressions merely combine old words in new ways, but some actually create new words.

4. Most new words are constructed by putting together the building blocks of prefixes, roots, and suffixes.

5. Not only are new words created; words change. Some words go downhill; some, up. Some words become narrower in meaning; some, broader. Figurative use of existing words extends the possibilities of English.

6. Some words are borrowed twice, three times, or even more. These multiple borrowings enrich English with new synonyms and new concepts.

If you know how the language grows and changes, you will have a better background for verbal SAT questions.

Clues From Etymology: Review Test

Write the letter for the pair of words that best completes the meaning of the sentence as a whole.

1. Television's _____ appetite for novelty _____ material at an ever-increasing rate.
   (A) insatiable . . devours
   (B) devious . . expands
   (C) indiscriminate . . creates
   (D) well-known . . resolves
   (E) amiable . . displays

   1 ____

2. Thor Heyerdahl, on the *Ra* papyrus boat, discovered floating _____ of oil in the mid-Atlantic, pointing to the continuing _____ of the seas.
   (A) cans . . commerce
   (B) mounds . . beautification
   (C) globs . . pollution
   (D) glimpses . . mining
   (E) tankers . . revival

   2 ____

3. Alice Neel is an artist whose art and life are _____, one feeding the other to the mutual _____ of both.
   (A) exceptional . . surprise
   (B) intertwined . . enrichment
   (C) old-fashioned . . depiction
   (D) separated . . benefit
   (E) contemporary . . appeal

   3 ____

4. For a true _____, democracy encourages _____ opinions as well as those that support the existing state of affairs.
   (A) inference . . complementary
   (B) mandate . . conforming
   (C) elimination . . haphazard
   (D) juxtaposition . . straightforward
   (E) consensus . . heterodox

   4 ____

5. Nature films on television frequently inject a powerful plea for regulations limiting the _____ of natural areas and the inevitable _____ of wildlife.
(A) closure . . hunting
(B) opening . . improvement
(C) depiction . . expansion
(D) exploitation . . destruction
(E) mapping . . census

5 ____

6. Settlers from the Northeast sometimes find it difficult to _____ themselves to the low humidity and _____ beauty of the American Southwest.
(A) transport . . luxurious
(B) invite . . unexpected
(C) adjust . . dank
(D) will . . contrary
(E) acclimate . . austere

6 ____

7. Mike McElroy, eminent scientist and _____ professor of chemistry at Harvard, has _____ interests that carry him from the atmosphere of planets to the origins of life.
(A) dapper . . planetary
(B) prestigious . . wide-ranging
(C) retiring . . enjoyable
(D) emaciated . . biased
(E) susceptible . . meager

7 ____

8. Charles made a _____ bid to mend the broken relationship, but Laura _____ refused to open his letter.
(A) hopeless . . cheerfully
(B) tentative . . disdainfully
(C) lighthearted . . resentfully
(D) fanatical . . casually
(E) pointless . . modestly

8 ____

9. A Washington group teaches children how to _____ with handicapped children by working with puppets that show various kinds of physical _____.
(A) converse . . activities
(B) compete . . variations
(C) walk . . characteristics
(D) win . . aids
(E) interact . . disability

9 ____

10. As video games become more and more _____, the players become more _____ in their search for new challenges.
(A) sophisticated . . discriminating
(B) garish . . alert
(C) metallic . . vigorous
(D) alike . . idiotic
(E) timely . . defiant

10 ____

Clues From Etymology: | Summary

Review these clues from etymology from time to time. If you understand how etymology helps you learn new words, you'll do better on the SAT vocabulary test.

Clue 1   **Latin Prefixes**
Many English words begin with common Latin prefixes and number prefixes. Study these examples.

advance, **ex**it, **prin**cipal, **dec**imal, **tri**ple

Clue 2   **Latin Roots—Verbs**
English has more words from Latin than from any other language. One root can appear in several words.

re**fer**, con**fer**ence, trans**fer**, in**fer**red

Clue 3   **Latin Roots—Nouns and Adjectives**
If you know the root and prefix, you can figure out the meaning. If not, think of other words with the same elements. Then make a good guess.

bene**fac**tor, **ben**ediction, **fac**tory

Clue 4   **Greek Prefixes and Roots**
As with Latin, you can figure out words with Greek origins if you know the prefixes and roots. If not, think of similar words and make a guess.

autocratic, **auto**biography, demo**crat**ic

Clue 5   **Anglo-Saxon Prefixes and Roots**
Anglo-Saxon words are the everyday words. You already know the prefixes and roots because you use them all the time.

Clue 6   **Suffixes**
Suffixes are the third building block (after prefixes and roots). They give important clues to a word's part of speech, its meaning, and its history.

ampli**fy**, manage**able**, moder**ate**

Clue 7   **Foreign Words in English**
English is a great borrower. Find the stories in borrowed words to learn and remember them.

coach, tangerine, muslin, polka

Clue 8   **The Growth of English**
English keeps making new words, usually by putting together prefixes, roots, and suffixes. Words keep changing in meaning— uphill and down, broader and narrower.

Vocabulary Diagnostic Tests

Now you have an opportunity to practice the vocabulary skills and strategies you have been using. First take Test A. Allow yourself 15 minutes. Refer to the "Answers and Analysis" section on pages 524–527. Check your answers and go over the analysis for each of the 15 items. Note your incorrect answers. In the "Answers and Analysis" section you will find the page numbers in this book for additional help and strategy review.

Vocabulary Diagnostic Test A

Each sentence below has one or two blanks, each blank indicating that something has been omitted. Beneath the sentence are five lettered words or sets of words labeled A through E. Choose the word or set of words that *best* fits the meaning of the sentence as a whole.

EXAMPLE

Although its publicity has been _____, the film itself is intelligent, well-acted, handsomely produced, and altogether _____.
(A) tasteless . . respectable
(B) extensive . . moderate
(C) sophisticated . . spectacular
(D) risqué . . crude
(E) perfect . . spectacular

● Ⓑ Ⓒ Ⓓ Ⓔ

---

1. A three-day blizzard seriously _____ the climbers, only a thousand feet from the summit of Mt. Everest.
(A) motivated
(B) embittered
(C) impeded
(D) impaired
(E) revolted

1 ____

2. When the sculptor picked up the clay, it was a(n) _____ mass, but under his _____ fingers, a statuette began to take shape.
(A) sodden . . stubby
(B) incredible . . tapering
(C) manageable . . clumsy
(D) shapely . . skilled
(E) amorphous . . dextrous

2 ____

3. Throughout the world there are Hitler and Mussolini _____ who would sweep democracy away and impose _____ rule on the people.
   (A) clones .. authoritarian
   (B) namesakes .. unified
   (C) associates .. constitutional
   (D) descendants .. popular
   (E) ancestors .. monastic

   3 ____

4. During the debate, the presidential candidate proposed to "guarantee to every American _____ health benefits that could never be taken away."
   (A) inexpensive   (D) comprehensive
   (B) helpful   (E) underfinanced
   (C) superlative

   4 ____

5. Tiger Woods optimistically declared that a windless day would _____ the difficulties of playing the treacherous Pebble Beach course.
   (A) exacerbate   (D) subjugate
   (B) alleviate   (E) innovate
   (C) promulgate

   5 ____

6. When it is time to return home after achieving _____ in medicine, some students from Third World countries _____.
   (A) miracles .. boast
   (B) prominence .. experiment
   (C) control .. question
   (D) competence .. balk
   (E) serenity .. quarrel

   6 ____

7. By the merest _____ Denning attempts to _____ the impressive philosophical structure outlined by his rival.
   (A) quibble .. topple
   (B) insinuation .. tout
   (C) flattery .. rationalize
   (D) hesitation .. justify
   (E) exposition .. deplete

   7 ____

8. Like many modern athletes, _____ athletes in ancient Greek Olympic games _____ their success.
   (A) harried .. envied
   (B) triumphant .. exploited
   (C) participating .. contemplated
   (D) canny .. squandered
   (E) lackluster .. belittled

   8 ____

9. For 240 challenging days a year, Japanese children have a much more _____ schooling than do their American _____.
   (A) diluted .. colleagues
   (B) imaginative .. correspondents
   (C) imitative .. associates
   (D) spontaneous .. adherents
   (E) intensive .. counterparts

   9 ____

10. _____ communication with a pet dog or cat is often excellent _____.
    (A) Casual .. strategy
    (B) Tactile .. therapy
    (C) Verbal .. psychology
    (D) Repetitive .. mimicry
    (E) Intuitive .. discipline

    10 ____

11. Despite the director's _____ after the disastrous dress rehearsal, the opening night performance was a total success, with many curtain calls at its conclusion.
    (A) excitement   (D) vigor
    (B) smugness   (E) foreboding
    (C) apathy

    11 ____

12. Hattie Caraway was the first woman elected to the Senate, an inspiration for those who would _____ her.
    (A) emulate   (D) lionize
    (B) encourage   (E) discuss
    (C) interpret

    12 ____

13. Sequoyah, in a(n) _____ feat of scholarship, created for the Cherokee nation a written language consisting of 86 characters.
(A) comparable   (D) unfettered
(B) singular   (E) dispassionate
(C) imitative

13 _____

14. Although Mandy _____ responsibility for the accident, the jury decided it was a clear case of _____ on her part.
(A) denied . . attentiveness
(B) disclaimed . . negligence
(C) accepted . . boredom
(D) assigned . . dexterity
(E) misinterpreted . . clairvoyance

14 _____

15. Unlike de Kooning, who _____ the perils of modern living, his artist _____, Gorky, Smith, and Pollock, died tragic deaths.
(A) belittled . . henchmen
(B) delineated . . characters
(C) survived . . peers
(D) accepted . . namesakes
(E) attacked . . kinsmen

15 _____

Vocabulary Diagnostic Test B

Each sentence below has one or two blanks, each blank indicating that something has been omitted. Beneath the sentence are five lettered words or sets of words labeled A through E. Choose the word or set of words that best fits the meaning of the sentence as a whole.

> EXAMPLE
>
> Although its publicity has been _____, the film itself is intelligent, well-acted, handsomely produced, and altogether _____.
> (A) tasteless . . respectable
> (B) extensive . . moderate
> (C) sophisticated . . amateur
> (D) risqué . . crude
> (E) perfect . . spectacular
>
> ● Ⓑ Ⓒ Ⓓ Ⓔ

1. During the initial stages of his first term, President Lyndon Johnson, in a search for party harmony, gently _____ the Kennedy aides, while demonstrating his own personal style.
(A) disregarded   (D) cajoled
(B) intimidated   (E) distracted
(C) irritated

1 _____

2. In discussing the shuttle's flight, the director of NASA said that "all the _____ leading to takeoff—two months' delay to be exact—paid off at the end."
(A) tribulations   (D) experimentation
(B) jubilation   (E) achievements
(C) sabotage

2 _____

3. Quilting expert Georgia Bonesteel
_____ lap quilting as _____ mod-
ern American lifestyles.
(A) debunks . . related to
(B) downplays . . in keeping with
(C) studies . . opposed to
(D) describes . . contrary to
(E) espouses . . compatible with

3 _____

4. _____, some of the passengers killed
in the crash had chosen train travel
because of a fear of flying.
(A) Wistfully   (D) Realistically
(B) Ironically   (E) Contradictorily
(C) Prematurely

4 _____

5. The first ten Amendments, known as
the Bill of Rights, were added to the
Constitution because many of the
Founding Fathers felt that the rights
had not been made _____ enough in
the Constitution itself.
(A) responsible
(B) contemporary
(C) explicit
(D) suggestive
(E) uncomplicated

5 _____

6. Americans have been accused of being
_____, wasteful of their _____ re-
sources.
(A) indigent . . plentiful
(B) unconventional . . natural
(C) disillusioned . . subterranean
(D) profligate . . irreplaceable
(E) uncooperative . . aquatic

6 _____

7. Though *abnormality* is a frightening
word, some _____ from normal are
_____, not harmful.
(A) quotations . . curious
(B) abstractions . . medicinal
(C) deviations . . benign
(D) condensations . . concise
(E) fluctuations . . provocative

7 _____

8. Nowhere else in the United States,
during the next decade, are as many
_____ species facing possible
_____ as in the Hawaiian Islands.
(A) exotic . . misinterpretation
(B) desert . . scrutiny
(C) poisonous . . mismanagement
(D) alpine . . stabilization
(E) native . . extinction

8 _____

9. The radio signals were _____, with
_____ static that scrambled the
message.
(A) intermittent . . disruptive
(B) melodic . . harmonious
(C) unanticipated . . frivolous
(D) clear . . isolated
(E) unbroken . . raucous

9 _____

10. _____ changes in the basic swim-
ming strokes have created new world
records and made _____ many pre-
vious swimming techniques.
(A) Unexpected . . ridiculous
(B) Subtle . . obsolete
(C) Extreme . . significant
(D) Mechanical . . dramatic
(E) Trivial . . valuable

10 _____

11. Jean Henri Fabre shifted the _____
of science from dead laboratory speci-
mens to _____, living creatures in
the field.
(A) emphasis . . stodgy
(B) scrutiny . . vibrant
(C) mediocrity . . nameless
(D) nomenclature . . unobserved
(E) carelessness . . active

11 _____

12. The exhibit of American flower paint-
ing shows an _____ diversity from
the _____ realism of Severin Roesen
to the abstract design of Georgia
O'Keeffe.
(A) expected . . shoddy
(B) unpretentious . . breezy
(C) unbroken . . critical
(D) exalted . . unattractive
(E) incredible . . literal

                          12 ____

13. Although the chance of discovering
_____ intelligence may be slim, the
SETI program continues to _____
sounds from outer space.
(A) superior . . transfer
(B) extraterrestrial . . monitor
(C) UFO . . disregard
(D) galactic . . broadcast
(E) inhuman . . clarify

                          13 ____

14. In light of the almost _____ possibil-
ities available, simple coincidence is
neither mysterious nor _____.
(A) incomprehensible . . ridiculous
(B) demonstrable . . expected
(C) inconsequential . . purposeful
(D) limitless . . miraculous
(E) invariable . . substantial

                          14 ____

15. Like a meteor on an August night, the
rock star _____ across stages
throughout the land and then _____
into oblivion.
(A) blazed . . faded
(B) ran . . dashed
(C) flew . . collapsed
(D) marched . . hobbled
(E) promenaded . . fell

                          15 ____

Division B

Reading
Comprehension

A Strategy for the Reading Tests

- Now that you have mastered many of the skills of vocabulary building, you will find yourself ready for the reading tests. Begin to read each selection with calm confidence, for that is half the battle. If you consider each selection as a puzzle and as fun, you'll be more relaxed.

- After you have read a selection, first look for the main idea. The test questions actually help you here, for they always provide five possibilities, one of which is the best. If you use the suggestions given in the text, you'll usually be able to spot the best answer.

- Test questions usually fit into one of three broad categories: language, details, and inference. Even finding the title requires drawing inferences.

- "Language in Action" builds directly on Part A and should be, for you, an extension of the work you've already been doing in this text.

- "Finding Details" is fairly cut and dried. The answers are right there, in the passages themselves, and can be identified.

- "Drawing Inferences" is a broad and challenging skill. It requires you to read between the lines as you draw inferences, predict what happens next, provide applications, and infer tones and attitudes. Though this kind of question is challenging, it can be more fun than merely picking out details. It leads to a disciplined approach that eliminates guesswork.

- Review pages xi–xii.

Section I: Drawing Generalizations and Finding the Main Idea

1. Drawing Generalizations

One of the most important skills tested in the SAT is the ability to generalize. Questions of this type come in a variety of forms, but the essential task in each is to draw a conclusion from ideas or incidents presented in the passage. The most common type of generalization is finding the main idea or supplying a title—covered in subsequent pages. But sometimes you are asked to generalize from a segment of the passage. Here is a sample of such question forms.

1. The author apparently feels that . . .

2. With which statement would the author probably agree?

3. Which of the following terms would the author use to describe . . . ?

TRIAL TEST

Read the passage. Choose the answer to the question that follows it.

In Colin Wilson's science-fiction novel, *The Mind Parasites*, aliens have burrowed into human brains and are living there. To keep human beings from learning the truth, the aliens keep us functioning at about 5% of our mental capacity. That we are all underachievers is not a new idea. William James once wrote, "There seems to be no doubt that we are each and all of us to some extent victims of habit neurosis . . . We live subject to arrest by degrees of fatigue which we have come only from habit to obey. Most of us can learn to push the barrier further off, and to live in perfect comfort on much higher levels of power." Wilson agrees. He is keenly interested in why we are *not* fully alive and alert all the time, why we cannot achieve all we are capable of achieving.

With which of the following statements would the author probably agree? Insert your answer, A, B, C, D, or E, on the line below.

(A) Colin Wilson is unduly critical of William James.

(B) *The Mind Parasites,* though science fiction, is a frightening glimpse of the future.

(C) The human mind ordinarily operates at a fraction of its capacity.

(D) Fatigue is a stimulus to achievement rather than a barrier.

(E) Wilson's point of view is a creative breakthrough, novel and ingenious.

———————

Study a reading question and then analyze the possible answers.

Problem

If people are asked to name dangerous animals, they suggest tigers, rhinos, wolves, leopards, and bears. Yet a far more dangerous creature is the insignificant
5 mosquito, carrier of discomfort, disease, and sometimes death. Most people know about malaria-carrying mosquitoes, but few realize that some mosquitoes in the United States carry the dreaded encephalitis. This
10 disease, usually associated with the tropics, is found even in cold areas of the country, like LaCrosse, Wisconsin. It is transmitted by a nasty little fellow called the "tree-hole mosquito." This woodland dweller tends to
15 bite in the late afternoon rather than the evening hours. But whenever it bites, the results can be painful, even deadly. It's just one representative of a dangerous family.

Throughout the world the lowly mosquito is
20 a vicious enemy of human beings.

With which of the following statements would the author probably agree?

(A) Tigers are more dangerous than leopards, wolves, or bears.
(B) Most disease-bearing mosquitoes are found in Wisconsin.
(C) In classifying our natural enemies, we must realize that size is not proportional to the danger involved.
(D) Mosquito-control efforts are a waste of time, but public moneys are nevertheless spent in the quest.
(E) Encephalitis is almost always fatal, but malaria has several cures.

Strategy. No judgment is made about the relative threat posed by leopards, wolves, or bears. *(A)* is incorrect. The passage admits that mosquitoes are found in Wisconsin but says nothing about comparative percentages of disease-bearing mosquitoes found in Wisconsin and elsewhere. *(B)* is incorrect. There is no mention of mosquito-control efforts and their relative effectiveness. *(D)* is incorrect. Encephalitis is called *dreaded* but not labeled "almost always fatal." *(E)* is incorrect. That leaves *(C)*. The major clue to this answer is the word *insignificant* (line 4 of the passage). This tiny creature is called "far more dangerous" than the larger mammals. The conclusion to be drawn is clear: size is not proportional to danger in classifying dangerous beasts. *(C)* is correct.

REVIEW

Try your skill. The passage below is followed by questions based on its content. Use the preceding example to help you find the answers.

Arts and crafts fairs of recent years have displayed many unfamiliar skills, from the artistic arrangement of found objects and "junk" to the almost-forgotten handicrafts
5 of colonial America. One increasingly common newcomer is the Japanese bonsai, the miniature tree.

The bonsai combines the skill of artist and gardener, of sculptor and architect.
10 Potted in a shallow dish, the young tree or shrub may be carefully shaped to resemble an ancient tree on a windswept mountain. For the creator of a bonsai garden, patience is the essential ingredient. The miniature
15 trees are trained, not tortured. Though in the wild, the effects of nature may weather and dwarf trees naturally, in a cultivated plant, the artist must duplicate the effects of nature.

20 Essential procedures include pruning, repotting, and wiring. Roots, trunk, branches, and foliage are all shaped in the process. Pruning is essential to keep the plant from outgrowing its root system. 25 Repotting is necessary to trim the roots and to provide new soil. Copper wiring is needed to shape the plant in desired forms.

Bonsai artists say their major purpose is to evoke the spirit of nature. Through "con- 30 stant yet relaxed attention" they create a microcosm of serenity. If they are success- ful, they create a masterpiece that is a joy to behold. Their major goal is to achieve, through much direction and intelligent ef- 35 fort, a feeling of spontaneity, of natural beauty. Bob Kataoka, bonsai master, says, "Viewing bonsai is restful, a brief contact with nature's calmness."

1. The author of the selection apparently feels that _____.
   (A) learning to create bonsai requires little experience
   (B) repotting the bonsai is an aes- thetic rather than a practical ne- cessity
   (C) bonsai have long been popular in American craft shows
   (D) bonsai trees are younger than they look
   (E) the best bonsai appear carefully planned

   1 ____

2. *Microcosm* in line 31 refers to a _____.
   (A) painting   (D) replica
   (B) herb garden   (E) model
   (C) bonsai

   2 ____

3. Which of the following terms would the author probably use to describe Bob Kataoka?
   (A) artisan   (D) nurseryman
   (B) landscaper   (E) forester
   (C) artist

   3 ____

SUMMARY
1. Drawing Generalizations

When drawing generalizations, first reread the passage carefully. Then get the feel of the passage as a whole.

Ordinarily the generalization grows out of that total evaluation. With that awareness of the total message, you can readily draw the generalization that is called for.

2. Finding the Main Idea

A common device for testing the ability to generalize is asking you to find the main idea. This kind of question focuses on the entire selection, not a section of it. If there are several ideas developed, you must weigh them all and determine the *main* idea. Here is a sample of question forms.

1. The major subject of the passage is . . .
2. The chief focus of the passage is on which of the following?
3. The main point of the passage is to . . .
4. The author apparently feels that . . .
5. Which of the following best describes the main idea of the passage?

TRIAL TEST

Take the following trial test to evaluate your skill. Read the passage and choose the answer to the question that follows it. Write the letter for your answer.

One man's meat is another man's poison. Tadpoles thrive in situations that would be impossible for other species. Spring ponds that thrive for only a few months of the year
5 before drying up are ideal habitats for tadpoles. Even puddles formed by a heavy spring rain bring forth a batch of tadpoles struggling for survival. Most other species quickly perish in such circumstances, but
10 not the tadpoles.

Like busy Americans, the tadpoles are lovers of fast food. Called "highly efficient, specialized feeding machines," tadpoles eat constantly in almost any aquatic habitat. In
15 some species newly swallowed food may account for 50% of their body weight. They eat and eat—and grow and grow. They thrive on uncertainty and instability. Their life cycles are tied to rapid changes in their
20 environment.

Would tadpoles succeed in larger bodies of water that provide some stability? Oddly enough, the answer is *no*. The young creatures would probably succeed in their eat-
25 ing goals, though they'd be competing with other species for the organic food on which they depend. The real problem would be hungry fish, which would soon gobble up the defenseless tadpoles. In fact, tadpoles
30 and fish rarely occur together. Thus, what

seems like a happy, serene, nurturing environment is, for the tadpoles, a source of greatest danger.

When they grow in inhospitable condi-
35 tions like the temporary pond or puddle, the tadpoles have the opportunity to eat constantly in relative safety. These "safe" conditions are not guaranteed, however. If a pond or a puddle dries up too quickly, the
40 tadpoles may starve to death or die from desiccation.

The tadpoles are creatures of insecurity, taking advantage of short periods and apparently impossible living conditions. They
45 are creatures of the seasons, appearing suddenly, feeding on the chance organic matter in a spring puddle, and then metamorphosing into frogs—if they are lucky.

Which of the following best describes the main idea of the passage?

(A) The life cycle of the tadpole resembles that of the fish.
(B) Tadpoles flourish in spring puddles.
(C) If a spring pond dries up, tadpoles perish.
(D) Tadpoles survive under conditions that seem unlikely and inhospitable.
(E) Tadpoles in large ponds or lakes have an excellent chance of survival.

Problem

Hungarians are sometimes considered a sad and serious people, but the Hungarian sense of humor is delightful and unexpected. Hungarians say, "Disaster is a nat-
5 ural state in Hungary. Every situation there is hopeless—but not serious."

The Hungarian playwright Ferenc Mol-

nar was once asked, "What was the first sentence you learned in English?"
10 Molnar replied. "Separate checks, please."

Hungarians love their great twin city, Budapest. They say the Danube is the bluest there, the sunshine brighter and more

15 pervasive than anywhere else in Hungary. It's like the traveling kazoo band that advertised itself as "the largest quartet in the world." It had five members. Budapest has two million people and all of Hungary ten
20 million. But all Hungarians insist they were born in Budapest.

The spice paprika is the national treasure. Someone asked, "Why do Arabs have oil and Hungarians paprika?" The reply:
25 "When God gave out the goodies, the Hungarians were pushier."

Which of the following best expresses the main idea of the passage?

(A) Hungarians are a sad and serious people.
(B) Ferenc Molnar is both witty and perceptive.
(C) To a true Hungarian, paprika is more valuable than oil.
(D) The Hungarian sense of humor is keen and enjoyable.
(E) Hungarians are unusually proud of their capital city, Budapest.

Strategy. Though all five answers have at least partial validity in one sense or another, only one expresses the *main* idea. The comment that Hungarians are sad and serious *(A)* is listed as a common idea, albeit a partial misconception. At best it is a detail and therefore unacceptable. Ferenc Molnar's wit *(B)* is suggested, but again the point is a small detail. The tongue-in-cheek comment about paprika and oil *(C)* is used to bolster the main point. It is not the main point. Hungarians are very proud of Budapest *(E),* but their pride is used as a humorous illustration of their sense of humor. All points reinforce the central point: Hungarians have a good sense of humor *(D).*

REVIEW

Try your skill. The passage below is followed by questions based on its content. Use the preceding example to help you find the correct answers.

Dangerous drivers account for a disproportionately large number of traffic fatalities. Some drivers are multiple offenders. Keeping such drivers off the
5 roads is a desirable goal, but there are difficulties in enforcing such a plan. Up till now it has been possible for a driver with a suspended or revoked license in one state to get a license in another state. Some of these
10 licensees had been involved in several tragic accidents. The National Driver Register, which attempts to keep a nationwide, up-to-date file on drivers, has not, until recently, been especially prompt or effective
15 in providing essential information to states requesting information. Now a bill passed by Congress provides more funds and puts more clout into the entire program. A California study has shown that license sanc-
20 tions are the most effective means of reducing accidents caused by problem drivers. This device is at least 30% more effective than jail terms, fines, driver-improvement classes, or alcohol-treatment
25 centers. Proponents of the Register feel certain that cooperation by the states and greater efficiency at the national level will reduce traffic deaths on tomorrow's highways.

1. Which of the following expresses the main idea of the passage?
- (A) Most dangerous drivers are multiple offenders.
- (B) The National Driver Register will help states to screen prospective applicants for a license.
- (C) Curbing the dangers posed by problem drivers is a problem disregarded by Congress.
- (D) Denying or limiting the issuance of drivers' licenses is a more effective means of driver control than jail terms or fines.
- (E) A loophole of past procedures is the ability of a problem driver to get a license in a state that does not know his or her record.

1 _____

2. With which statement would the author probably agree?
- (A) More active law enforcement is needed to protect the lives of innocent drivers.
- (B) The principle of the "second chance" should be a major consideration in handling the licenses of drivers who have had accidents.
- (C) Drivers who are at fault in serious accident cases should be jailed.
- (D) Though desirable, the National Driver Register presents a possible infringement on the rights of sovereign states.
- (E) Congress should play a purely advisory role in considering the problem driver.

2 _____

SUMMARY

2. Finding the Main Idea

There is a common expression, "You can't see the forest for the trees." To find the main idea, you must see the forest *as well as* the trees. You must be able to see larger issues (the forest) concealed in smaller ones (the trees) and get to the heart of a reading passage.

3. Providing a Title

A variation of stating the main idea is choosing the best title for the selection. Like the preceding type of question, this focuses on the entire selection. The major difference is that choices are not put into statement form but into headline form. Here is a common question requiring you to provide a good title:

Which of the following titles best summarizes the content of the passage?

TRIAL TEST

Take the following trial test to evaluate your skill. Read the passage and choose the answer for the question that follows it.

Before 1883, local communities had their own time. Each town figured noon when the sun was at the zenith. Clocks in New York City, for example, were 10 minutes and 27
5 seconds ahead of those in Baltimore. Railroad schedules were a nightmare. Then, an unsung hero, William F. Allen, suggested that the country be divided into four time zones, eliminating those hundreds of differ-
10 ent local times. November 18, 1883, was called "The Day of Two Noons," for on that day Washington, D.C., gained four minutes as "local noon" was replaced by "standard noon." Some major cities resisted change.
15 Cincinnati held out for seven years, but gradually the entire country went on Eastern, Central, Mountain, or Pacific Time. This idea, so obviously good and so universally accepted today, was an idea
20 whose time had come, but the coming did not come easily.

Which of the following titles best summarizes the content of the passage?

(A) William F. Allen: A Man for All Seasons
(B) A History of the Calendar
(C) A Day to Remember in Washington
(D) The Introduction of Standard Time
(E) How Time Was Determined Before 1883

_____

Look at a question and then analyze the possible answers.

Problem

Are you taking part in the Birkie this year? This cryptic question would be no mystery to most active cross-country skiers. The Birkie, or *Birkebeiner* as it is correctly
5 called, is North America's largest cross-country ski race. Held every February 25 in Cable, Wisconsin, it brings 10,000 skiers to a sleepy town of several hundred people. The race itself covers the 34 miles from
10 Hayward, Wisconsin, to Cable. During the week before the race, Cable has ice-sculpture contests, skydivers, hot-air balloons, dancing, dozens of bands, ski clinics, a parade of nations and states, and good old
15 Scandinavian smorgasbords. Incredible traffic jams develop. Housing facilities are stretched to the utmost. A thousand racers, for example, sleep in sleeping bags at the Hayward Middle School. The race must
20 accommodate all these eager skiers. The starting area is a quarter-mile wide. Since top long-distance racers from around the world compete, the finishing time of the winning skier may be four hours ahead of
25 the last skier. Yet all have a good time. Finishing the race is in itself a victory.

Which of the following titles best summarizes the content of the passage?

(A) America's Greatest Cross-Country Ski Race
(B) Fun in the Snow
(C) From Hayward to Cable, the Trip of a Lifetime
(D) The Comforts and Discomforts of Cross-Country Skiing
(E) The Race: A Victory Over Self

_____

Strategy. There are several pitfalls in choosing titles.

1. Do not choose a title that is too broad. In this question *(B)* is much too broad. It says nothing about skiing. It could apply equally well to a great many other activities.

2. Do not choose a title that is too narrow. *(C)* focuses on an element of the selection, the start and finish.

3. Do not choose a title that sounds profound but is really off the topic. *(E)* sounds good, but there is nothing in the passage to suggest the philosophical implications in *(E)*.

4. Do not choose a title just because it strikes a responsive chord in your memory. *(D)* looks like the kind of title you'd expect in a passage about skiing. If you did not read the paragraph carefully, you might choose *(D)*.

5. Choose a title that fits, that is neither too broad nor too narrow, that is on the topic and generalizes about the entire passage. *(A)* is such a title. It encompasses the race and all the activities associated with the race. In any consideration about the race, the planners would have to take into account all the subsidiary activities, as well as the housing problems and traffic jams. *(A)* covers the entire passage effectively. The other alternatives do not.

REVIEW

Try your skill. The passage below is followed by questions based on its content. Use the preceding example to help you find the right answers.

The paradox of Gilbert and Sullivan continues to amaze music lovers. The two men, utterly different in temperament and personality, somehow managed to collaborate
5 on more than a dozen operettas of enduring charm. Both men were told they were wasting their talents on the inconsequential Gilbert and Sullivan operettas, but somehow they stayed together, through stormy years
10 and occasional unpleasant sessions, to create immortal songs like "Tell Me, Pretty Maiden" from *Patience*—songs that were a fortuitous blend of lyric and melody.

William Schwenck Gilbert, who wrote the
15 lyrics and generally determined the plot and direction of the operettas, was a rather stern Victorian, intolerant of laziness, indifference, or lack of talent. His guiding hand in the actual production guaranteed the
20 quality of the production and the integrity of the performances. His witty, often satirical, lyrics punctured Victorian pomposity and inefficiency and, it is said, even ruffled the feathers of Queen Victoria.

25 Arthur Sullivan, who composed the lovely music for Gilbert's words, was a contrast to Gilbert. Sullivan was a rather gentle person, aristocratic, fond of the good life, often melancholy. Awed by titles, he loved
30 to hobnob with the great. Seldom robustly healthy, he created some of the most beautiful music while racked with pain.

On many occasions, Sullivan said, "I don't want to do another operetta," but after each
35 refusal, Gilbert would tempt Sullivan with plots, snatches of dialog, production ideas. In the background, Richard D'Oyly Carte

acted as impresario and referee, bringing the two men back together again and again, despite the apparent refusal of Sullivan to
40 go on. Somehow, despite altercations, disagreements, and misunderstandings, the two men created 14 operettas, 11 of which are still frequently played.

1. Which of the following titles best summarizes the content of the passage?
    (A) Operettas of Victorian England
    (B) The Preeminence of Gilbert in the Gilbert and Sullivan Operettas
    (C) A Happy Collaboration
    (D) The Many Sides of Genius
    (E) Gilbert and Sullivan: A Study in Contrasts

                                        1 ____

2. With which statement would the author probably agree?
    (A) Richard D'Oyly Carte was an incompetent go-between, irritating both men.
    (B) Of the two men, Gilbert and Sullivan, Sullivan seemed more easygoing.
    (C) William Schwenck Gilbert was basically warm and forgiving.
    (D) *Patience* is probably the most popular of all Gilbert and Sullivan operettas.
    (E) If Gilbert and Sullivan had channeled their energies into other areas, their achievements would have been greater.

                                        2 ____

SUMMARY

3. Providing a Title

Choosing a title is very similar to finding the main idea. The major difference lies in the way the alternatives are phrased.

4. Providing a Summary

This is another variation of finding the main idea, but the phrasing is somewhat different. Note the following sample question:

> The passage as a whole is best described as . . .

TRIAL TEST

Take the trial test to evaluate your skill.
Read the passage and choose the answer for the question that follows it.

"Because it is there!" George Mallory's explanation of why he kept trying to scale Mt. Everest is not a satisfying answer to a nonclimber. But a true climber under-
5 stands. In an exciting report on his mountain adventures, *Savage Arena,* Joe Tasker attempts to add his explanation to Mallory's. Tasker endured terrible hardships on the Eigerwand in Switzerland, K2
10 in Kashmir, Dunagiri in India, and Everest in Nepal-Tibet. With fellow climbers he experienced hope and despair in a desperate

ascent after an avalanche had covered their tents. In a climb on the West Face of K2 he
15 lost Nich Estcourt, a beloved comrade. Yet he always went back—at last to his death in May 1982 not far from the summit of Everest itself, the ultimate challenge. In the book written shortly before his death,
20 he confessed, "In some ways, going to the mountains is incomprehensible to many people and inexplicable to those who go. The reasons are difficult to unearth and only

with those who are similarly drawn is there no need to try to explain."

The passage as a whole principally deals with _____.

(A) the mysterious appeal of mountain climbing
(B) the heroism of Joe Tasker
(C) the highest peaks in Europe and Asia
(D) the dangers of rock climbing
(E) the waste of life in mountain climbing

_____

Problem

The migration of the monarch butterfly is one of nature's profoundest mysteries and most incredible stories. Each fall the monarchs set forth on the dangerous trip to
5 their winter homes—principally in California and Mexico. They come from diverse areas, fly different routes, and bivouac along the way, often with tens of thousands of their fellows. They are buffeted by winds,
10 threatened by long stretches of water, and soaked by downpours. Yet somehow or other they make their way to "butterfly trees" on the Monterey Peninsula, in the mountains near Mexico City, and in other
15 less-well-known sites. Each spring they mate and head north. Most of the original migrants die on the return journey. Their offspring somehow pick up the journey and fly to areas they have never seen before, only to

20 repeat the process in the fall. No other insects migrate so predictably, very much like birds. The monarch migration has been called "one of the world's great natural events, comparable to the immense mam-
25 mal movements on Africa's Serengeti Plain."

The passage as a whole is best described as a _____.

(A) plea for protection of the monarch's nesting sites
(B) comparison of monarch migration with the migration of other insects
(C) description of a beautiful and mysterious natural phenomenon
(D) testament of courage
(E) scientific evaluation of an event known to everyone

_____

Strategy. Which alternative should you choose? Note that this question asks you to find the main idea, but instead of expressing the idea in statement form, it provides a label (plea, comparison, etc.) with qualifying phrases. Remember that you are seeking the main idea. You are dealing with "the passage as a whole." *(A)* might well be a follow-up to the ideas expressed in the paragraph, but it is not the expressed *main* idea. *(B)* is too narrow. There is a brief comparison with the migration of other insects, but this is a detail. *(D)* is too broad. Then, too, whether to call the instinctive reaction of the monarch "courage" is debatable. It is certainly so in human terms but not necessarily in scientific terms. *(E)* could fit a myriad of other paragraphs. It's too broad. *(C)* is accurate. The paragraph is devoted to the migration (the mysterious phenomenon) and each sentence emphasizes its mystery.

REVIEW

The following selections test your ability to draw conclusions in a variety of formats.

1. How large a part will solar energy play in the future? When will the non-replaceable petroleum begin to run out? How large a role will coal play in the
5 energy program of the future? Is nuclear energy a feasible alternative? Can we depend upon minihydroelectric systems to produce electricity in small but economical chunks? Questions like these are bandied
10 back and forth in television discussions, news reports, and newspaper articles. There is, however, another possibility, little considered but strategically important. We can create tiny habitats that conserve
15 energy.
  Experts estimate that energy-minded landscaping can cut home energy needs by 30%. Early societies knew the value of creative plantings to help people keep cool
20 in summer and warm in winter. Much of today's architecture, however, overlooks creative possibilities for energy conservation, wasting precious resources through inefficient planning. Trees, shrubs, vines,
25 and ground cover can be planted to protect against the summer's blazing sun. These plants are living air conditioners, evaporating water and cooling the air. Planting windbreaks can help keep out wintry
30 blasts. Even small windbreaks around a foundation reduce heat loss by providing a wall of insulating air around the house. Winter and summer, living plants can work for us and save us energy dollars.

The passage as a whole is best described as a _____.
(A) warning against the depletion of coal resources
(B) comparison of today's architecture with that of another day
(C) suggestion for handling the cold of winter
(D) call for a partnership with nature in energy conservation
(E) criticism of nuclear energy as a solution to current energy problems

---

2. Would you like to grow your own vegetables without cultivation, weeding, or soil preparation? Would you like to avoid problems of ground insects, moles, rabbits, or
5 other animals? You may find hydroponic gardening your solution. This branch of gardening uses no soil. Vegetables grow in a nutrient solution in any place convenient to the gardener. Large tracts of land are not re-
10 quired, for plants grow rather close together in perfect harmony. Joe Corso of Altamonte Springs, Florida, hasn't bought a vegetable in 15 years. He grows several varieties of lettuce, tomatoes, cucumbers, green peppers,
15 zucchini, broccoli, basil, scallions, and escarole. He insists a complete garden can be set up for $20–$35 as a one-time cost. The nutrients will cost $15–$20 a year for a complete garden. Soilless gardening has many possi-
20 bilities. Principles of hydroponic gardening, for example, are used for desert gardens where sand contains little or no natural nutrients.

Which of the following titles best summarizes the content of the passage?
(A) Growing Vegetables the Easy Way: Without Soil
(B) A Florida Experiment That Paid Off
(C) Desert Gardens: Using the World's Barren Lands
(D) A New Product for Attacking World Hunger
(E) A Backyard Garden with a Different Approach

———

3. Until relatively recently the exploitation of the vast Amazon Basin was minimal. Extensive clearing of forests and overfishing of rivers were unknown. The primitive
5 dwellers in the region harvested the resources conservatively and thus preserved, until recently, the tremendous natural wealth of the entire area. A restraining influence, not altogether lost on the little
10 farmers and hunters of today, was a belief in supernatural game wardens and forest demons. These creatures, the forest dwellers believed, punish those who abuse nature's generosity. Some of these spirits
15 watch over game. Others harass those who venture too far into the jungle. These deterrents averted the greedy, mindless destruction that has characterized man's treatment of nature in other parts of the
20 world. Though the rise in population and new economic pressures are now threatening the entire basin, there are still signs of primitive beliefs held by the rural population of Amazonia.

Which of the following expresses the main idea of the passage?
(A) A belief in supernatural game wardens and forest demons is a sign of ignorance.
(B) Too often man has exploited the natural resources around him.
(C) A tremendous population explosion has upset the balance of nature in Amazonia.
(D) Primitive dwellers are in reality more sophisticated than urban residents.
(E) A belief in spirits kept men from exploiting the Amazon basin.

———

SUMMARY

4. Providing a Summary

The ability to summarize the essential point of a paragraph is closely related to the ability to choose the correct title and express the main idea. Be sure you are not sidetracked by details, or by generalizations broad enough to cover an article, not a reading passage.

Section I Summary: Drawing Generalizations and Finding the Main Idea

The ability to generalize takes many forms. You may be asked to generalize about a portion of the reading passage: a paragraph or even an important sentence. Or you may have to find the central point of the paragraph in a variety of question formats. The ability to extract main ideas is a crucial skill in note-taking and in study.

The strategies for drawing generalizations and finding the main idea will help you prepare for the SAT.

PART 1. Drawing Generalizations (pp. 176–178)

A. Read the question carefully so that you are sure about the generalization asked for.
B. Find and reread the portion of the passage that has the information for making the generalization.
C. Draw the generalization asked for. Base it on the portion you reread.

PART 2. Finding the Main Idea (pp. 178–181)

A. Reread the entire passage.
B. Get a feel for the *whole passage,* not just a part of it.
C. If several ideas are developed, weigh them all. Then decide on the main idea.

PART 3. Providing a Title (pp. 181–184)

Choosing a title is similar to finding the main idea.

A. Get a feel for the whole passage, not just a part of it.
B. Notice that the title choices are in headline form, not sentence form.
C. Choose the "headline" that best covers the whole "story."

PART 4. Providing a Summary (pp. 184–187)

Choosing a summary is similar to finding the main idea and choosing a title.

A. Keep the whole passage in mind; reread it if you are unsure.
B. Don't be sidetracked by details; on the other hand, don't go beyond the limits of the passage.
C. Choose the statement that sums up the whole passage and that does not go beyond it.

Section II: Drawing Inferences

1. Identifying Inferences

"Sue just sneezed. She must have a cold."

These two statements that sound alike are quite different. The first is a factual observation. The second is an inference. The first is based on a verifiable observation. The second is a judgment that may or may not accord with the facts. Sue may have an allergy. The room may be dusty.

There is nothing wrong with drawing inferences. We often run our lives on the basis of inference. We see people bundled up outside our window and prepare for a cold day. The danger arises when we take an inference for a fact. If we understand the difference between fact and inference, we manage our lives intelligently.

There are good, reasonable inferences; there are poor, irrational ones. When we hear the teakettle whistling, we reasonably infer the water is boiling. When a friend fails to appear for a meeting, we should not infer he or she is rejecting us. There may be dozens of good reasons for his or her failure to come.

Inference plays an important role in SAT reading questions. The following words and phrases are often used to test your ability to draw inferences.

assume	presume	apparently believes
convey	presuppose	can be inferred
emphasize	refer	can best be described as
exemplify	serve to	judging by
hint	suggest	may be interpreted
imply	supported by	used to illustrate
indicate	suppose	

TRIAL TEST

Select the best inference for the following test question.

The barometric pressure dropped rapidly. The wind, formerly at calm, suddenly began to whip up. The harbor flag, which had been flapping listlessly, stood out with the force of the wind. Owners of boats in the marina dashed about, fastening boat covers securely and checking all mooring ropes. A few drops of rain splattered the pavement.

The sun had already disappeared, and the world was dark.

The part of the storm being described is

_____.

(A) the warning
(B) the beginning
(C) the height
(D) the end
(E) the aftermath

_____

Problem

There is one creature perfectly adapted and temperamentally suited to some of the most inhospitable areas of the world: the camel. In the ecology of the Sahara Desert,
5 the nomad and the camel live in a mutually satisfactory dependence on each other. The nomad provides the camel with water and food. The camel provides the nomad with milk, wool, transportation, and meat.
10 Above all, the camel provides work and gives meaning to the lives of the tribes that crisscross the Sahara. The camel provides the only means by which human beings can constructively utilize the desert. Camel
15 herding, combined with nomadism to take advantage of seasonal rains and recurrent scattered vegetation, is the only feasible solution to surviving in the desert. The camel is at the heart of all efforts to live in
20 harmony with the desert.

1. The passage implies that _____.
   (A) human beings should give up the challenge of living in the desert
   (B) no other creature can replace the camel
   (C) nomads unfairly exploit their camels
   (D) the Sahara Desert is less hospitable than any other desert
   (E) camels are less satisfactory than cattle in many ways

   1 ____

2. The essential point made about nomads is that they are _____.
   (A) kindly toward their camels
   (B) essentially traders and merchants
   (C) experts on camel wool
   (D) wanderers
   (E) poets in harmony with life

   2 ____

Strategy. 1. Nowhere does the writer suggest that human beings should give up the challenge of living in the desert. Instead, the author commends survival under difficult conditions. *(A)* is incorrect. The first sentence, on the other hand, does suggest that the camel is one of a kind. The rest of the paragraph supports that suggestion. *(B)* sounds right. There is no mention of unfair treatment of camels. Reject *(C)*. There is no comparison of the Sahara with other deserts. Reject *(D)*. Cattle are nowhere mentioned or implied. Reject *(E)*.

2. There are two clues to *(D)* as the correct answer: crisscrossing the Sahara and movement to take advantage of rains and scattered vegetation. *(A)*, *(B)*, and *(C)* are nowhere suggested. *(E)* is much too grandiose, out of keeping with the straightforward, serious tone of the passage. Note that this question is allied to "drawing generalizations," as outlined in Section I (pages 176–178). The *essential* point is a kind of generalization.

REVIEW

Try your skill. Use the preceding example to help you find the right answers.

The scar wasn't very deep. You could only see it if you were really close to her face. Like if you were going to give her a kiss on the cheek, then you could see it, but only if
5 her hair was pulled back. If you drew a line from her earlobe to her neck, you would see where the scar started. It ended somewhere past her shoulder. The knife was probably dull and that was why the scar wasn't
10 deeper. Hard to tell. She said it was nothing. And when you questioned her more she got angry. Said it had to do with love gone bad. You tried to comfort her, but she would only stiffen. Forget the sympathy, she'd say.
15 Didn't need it. Didn't want it. Then last night, when she thought you were asleep, she left your side and quietly made her way down to the kitchen. You waited for her to return. You waited. You waited. Your stom-
20 ach began to churn. You got up, put on your robe and tiptoed toward the kitchen. The light was on. There wasn't a sound. You hesitated, but got up the nerve to look around the corner. There she was . . . as
25 beautiful as ever. She had her hair pulled back and was putting lotion on her scar and singing gently to herself. She touched her scar like it was some kind of special orchid or fragile piece of cut glass. She looked
30 radiant. You turned around, went back to the bedroom, packed your bags, and left.

1. It may be inferred that _____.
   (A) the woman is being dishonest with the narrator
   (B) the narrator is insensitive
   (C) the two fought constantly
   (D) the woman has forgotten who gave her the scar
   (E) the woman confided in the narrator

   1 ____

2. The passage implies that _____.
   (A) the woman is an untidy partner
   (B) the narrator had never noticed the scar before
   (C) the woman minimized the first lover's cruelty
   (D) the woman's radiance was occasioned by love of the narrator
   (E) the woman and the narrator will reconcile

   2 ____

SUMMARY

1. Identifying Inferences

An inference differs from a factual statement, but a good inference is an educated guess that is closely tied to the facts.

For an SAT answer, read between the lines and make your inference a reasonable one.

2. Supplying an Interpretation

"Joe said he won't play football this Sunday under any circumstances."

"What he really meant was that he wouldn't play unless he could start as quarterback."

Life is filled with situations in which one person interprets the words of another. Doing so requires drawing inferences. SAT questions sometimes ask for interpretations using wording like this.

TRIAL TEST

Read the following and choose the answer for the question that follows it.

Most people are aware that ammonia, bleach, and household cleaners are poison, but few people realize that cosmetics, sham-poos, shaving creams, and lipstick can be
5 deadly if swallowed by small children. The list of dangerous substances is surprisingly large, including hair spray, toothpaste, nail polish and nail polish remover, makeup, and deodorants. Of course, these substances are
10 used by adults only in small quantities and are not swallowed. Thus, many parents fail to realize that since small children put al-most anything into their mouths, they may swallow dangerous amounts of what are
15 usually considered "perfectly safe" sub-stances. Eternal vigilance is the price of safety as well as liberty.

Which of the following best expresses the meaning of the sentence, "Eternal vigilance is the price of safety as well as liberty"?

(A) Parents should probably keep hair spray out of the house.
(B) Young children should never be left unsupervised.
(C) Children should assume a share of re-sponsibility for dangerous substances.
(D) Safety and liberty always go together.
(E) Parents need to be constantly aware of dangers in the home.

Problem

"Prairie fire!" The words struck terror into the hearts of many settlers. Dry grass burns rapidly. Out of control, a prairie fire can be an awesome sight. Yet today con-
5 trolled fires are set to help the grasslands survive. Without occasional fire, undesir-able intruders like red cedar begin to take over the land. Unwelcome smaller plants, like Kentucky bluegrass, soon replace na-
10 tive grasses and change the character of prairie islands preserved as examples of the American natural heritage. Litter on the prairie floor also changes the ecology of an area and permits aggressive exotic plants
15 to move in. Fire removes litter and provides the opportunity for native grasslands to be preserved for generations to come. But the fires must be set only after extensive study and analysis of wind, wind speed, relative
20 humidity, temperature, and the physical factors of the vegetation to be burned.

1. Which of the following best expresses the meaning of the phrase "changes the ecology of an area and permits aggressive exotic plants to move in"?
   (A) upsets the natural balance in favor of nonnative species
   (B) evaluates natural conditions and restrains newcomers
   (C) introduces nonproductive changes and starts fires
   (D) accelerates proper soil management by allowing diversification
   (E) expresses admiration for the forces of nature and survival of the fittest

   1 ____

2. A "controlled fire" is set _____.
   (A) when the native grasses need burning
   (B) after a summer storm
   (C) as soon as a red cedar appears on the grassland
   (D) when environmental factors are right
   (E) on a consistent and regular basis

   2 ____

Strategy. 1. On first reading *(A)* seems to be the best answer, but let's check the others just to be sure. Litter changes the ecology but doesn't evaluate it. *(B)* is incorrect. Litter may permit nonproductive changes, but of itself it does not start fires. *(C)* is incorrect. *(D)* has the wrong meaning altogether. The selection speaks against diversification with exotic plants. *(E)* is also contrary to the idea of the passage. The passage is concerned with the survival of native plants, not necessarily with the survival of the fittest.

2. We may infer that a "controlled fire," by definition, is set when conditions can be controlled. *(D)* provides the right suggestion. The fire is not set when native grasses need burning *(A),* but when total conditions suggest the need for a fire. A summer storm *(B)* might provide one of the safety conditions for the fire, but it is not the determining factor. The removal of a single red cedar *(C)* does not require a fire. There is no indication anywhere that fires are set *(E)* on a regular basis. *(D)* is indeed the correct answer.

REVIEW

Try your skill. The passage below is followed by four questions based on its content. Use the preceding example to help you find the right answers.

Patan is the oldest of the "Three cities of the ancient Kathmandu Valley," whose origins are lost in the mists of history. Visitors to Nepal can take a taxi from the capital,
5 Kathmandu, and find themselves transported to a mystical past, where shrines of Hindu and Buddhist deities rub elbows. On the facades of ancient temples are ornate carvings with religious and historical sig-
10 nificance. Most of these temples have been built in a superb architectural style.

Durbar Square, in the center of the city, is a colorful blend of architectural inspirations and historical associations. Along the
15 cobble-lined streets are the houses of skilled craftsmen, whose arts, processes, and designs have been passed from father to son. Here three generations of a family sit side by side, creating art of exquisite beauty.

20 The imposing Krishna Mandir, temple of the Lord Krishna, dominates the picturesque square, which is always vibrant with life.

1. Which of the following best expresses the meaning of the phrase "a colorful blend of architectural inspirations and historical associations"?
   (A) a subtle attempt to sway the religious beliefs of observers
   (B) a center for folk art and the treasures of another day
   (C) a picturesque mixture of modern and historical arts and crafts
   (D) brilliantly conceived architecture with historical significance
   (E) a number of functional buildings created for long-forgotten deities
   1 ____

2. Which word best summarizes the work of Nepalese craftsmen?
   (A) fatigue   (D) indifference
   (B) continuity   (E) rigidity
   (C) improvisation
   2 ____

3. Which of the following titles best summarizes the content of the passage?
   (A) Durbar Square: Heart of Patan
   (B) From Kathmandu to Patan: A Royal Road
   (C) Nepalese Temples: History in Stone
   (D) Patan: A Many-Splendored City
   (E) Architecture in Nepal
   3 ____

4. An excellent adjective to describe Patan is _____.
   (A) huge   (D) sparkling
   (B) financially sound (E) grim
   (C) unvaried
   4 ____

SUMMARY
2. Supplying an Interpretation

An interpretation calls for drawing inferences about actions, statements, or events. Watch for interpretation questions on the SAT. You will be asked to supply another way of saying something. If you restate the phrase or sentence in your own words, you can then find the answer closest to your own.

3. Providing a Paraphrase

Sometimes you will be asked to provide an interpretation slightly longer than that called for in the previous part. Such an extended interpretation is a **paraphrase**. You might tend to consider such a lengthy interpretation a summary, as in Section I, Part 4, page 184. There is, however, a great difference between a summary and a paraphrase. A summary condenses, provides the gist of a selection in far fewer words. A paraphrase, on the other hand, gives the sense of a given segment in different words, but roughly in the same number of words. A good paraphrase calls for comprehension and the drawing of sound inferences. On the SAT you may meet a question with wording like the following.

Which of the following is the best interpretation of lines _____?

TRIAL TEST

Choose the best answer for the question at the end of the selection.

The Information Explosion adds knowledge at an incredible rate. Some say that knowledge has been doubling every ten years. Others agree and add that the rate is
5 increasing. The new industries spawned by computers alone are increasing at a phenomenal rate. What is behind this breathtaking growth? What spurs people on to new inventions and broader applications of
10 existing technology? Ralph Hinton, an American anthropologist, had an unusual answer: "The human capacity for being bored, rather than man's social or natural needs, lies at the root of man's cultural
15 advance."

Which is the best interpretation of the quotation by Ralph Hinton?

(A) A man's reach should always exceed his grasp.
(B) The Information Explosion is not necessarily a desirable thing.
(C) Man's restless spirit, not his needs, brings advances.
(D) Boredom takes time away from caring for people's needs.
(E) To be bored is to be creative; to be happy is to be lazy.

_____

Problem

"I like my football players agile, mobile, and hostile." Coach Tom Burrows' successful philosophy was summed up in that favorite statement. Not an exponent of trick
5 plays, strange formations, and razzle-dazzle, Burrows concentrated upon fundamentals: clean, hard tackling; crisp, sure blocking; thorough preparation; and a methodical, consistent game plan. He didn't
10 depend upon surprise. If his opponents knew his next play was a plunge off right tackle, Burrows didn't care. He depended upon complete cooperation of all his players, superb execution, split-second timing,
15 and the will to win. Burrows would have agreed with Austin O'Malley, who said, "In dealing with a foolish or stubborn adversary, remember your own mood constitutes half the force opposing you." Other coaches
20 belittled Burrows' coaching philosophy and mentally put him back in the Dark Ages, but they could not fault his incredible string of victories.

1. Which is the best interpretation of the quotation by Austin O'Malley?

(A) In a close game your opponent may foolishly or stubbornly refuse to play your game.
(B) In any sport emotion is as important an ingredient as thought and preparation.
(C) Your opponent may defeat you by doubling his efforts while you halve yours.
(D) In a hard game you may be your own worst enemy.
(E) If your players do not play hard, emotions may help your opponents win.

1 ____

2. The attitude of other coaches toward Burrows might be considered _____.

(A) condescending but respectful
(B) baffled but cheerful
(C) inconsistent and terrified
(D) hostile and uncooperative
(E) curious and imitative

2 ____

3. Burrows probably did not rely on trick
plays because _____.
(A) he preferred razzle-dazzle
(B) he thought they weren't necessary
(C) other coaches liked them
(D) they made his players careless
(E) they need too much planning

3 ____

Strategy. 1. The answer which best paraphrases the quotation is *(D)*. The quotation says that "your own mood constitutes half the force opposing you." If that mood is negative, you help to defeat yourself. *(A)* is off the topic. Nothing is said about the opponents' game. For the same reason *(C)* is incorrect. *(B)* is too broad. *(E)* seems plausible, but there is no suggestion about whether or not the players play hard.

2. The final sentence is the clue to this answer: *(A)*. "Belittled" suggests condescension, but the victories suggest respect.

3. The selection says that Burrows concentrated on fundamentals instead of relying on trick plays. The answer is *(B)*.

REVIEW

Try your skill. The passage below is followed by questions based on its content. Use the preceding example to help you find the right answers.

Grandpa was a monument to sanity in a crazy world. He never set the world on fire or put his name up in lights. He had a modest job at the post office all his working
5 life and retired to hobbies, crafts, and volunteer work. It was his personality that endeared him to all who knew him. It was his philosophy of life that enriched the lives of his friends and relatives. He embodied
10 Reinhold Niebuhr's prayer never to worry about what could not be changed and to concentrate only on what could be changed. He lived today and let those two impostors, yesterday and tomorrow, worry about
15 themselves. He was bright, sunny, jovial, optimistic, and a joy to be with. He often quoted a common quotation to sum up his own beliefs: "Inch by inch, life is a cinch. Yard by yard, life is hard."

1. Which is the best interpretation of the quotation in the selection?
(A) Life can be measured in inches or in yards.
(B) Life is tragic if we stop to think about it too much.
(C) Life is easy or hard depending on your point of view.
(D) To avoid worry and stress, take life a small step at a time.
(E) If you don't plan for the future, you won't have one.

1 ____

2. The best word to describe Grandpa is _____.

(A) skilled
(B) cautious
(C) sensible
(D) anxious
(E) ambitious

2 ____

3. Yesterday and tomorrow are called "impostors" because _____.
(A) the future is uncertain and the past is gone
(B) worry is always destructive
(C) fortune-tellers take advantage of gullible people
(D) we truly live in thinking about the future
(E) they contradict Reinhold Niebuhr's prayer

3 ____

SUMMARY
3. Providing a Paraphrase

A paraphrase is a restatement of a sentence or a selection, not a summary. A paraphrase presents the essential point in other words. It parallels the material; it doesn't condense it.

4. Making a Comparison

Inferences come in many forms. Sometimes on the SAT you will be asked to compare two ideas, persons, expressions, or arguments. Comparisons like these require you to draw several inferences. One SAT question used this phrasing:

In the second paragraph, the author's chief distinction is between which of the following?

TRIAL TEST

Read the following. Then choose the answer to the question at the end.

Stamp collectors sometimes have to make a key decision: whether to concentrate on stamps that have been postally used or to collect only clean, pure, unused stamps,
5 often direct from the printing presses. Postally used stamps are not as pretty as mint stamps. Portions of their designs have been obliterated by cancellation marks. Mint stamps, on the other hand, are sparkling
10 and clear, with every design detail clearly visible. But used stamps have something extra: actual use in the mails. Often their cancellations provide information about date and place of use. They often demon-
15 strate the romance of the mails. Collectors of only used stamps call stamps *mere labels* until they perform their function in the mails. Postally used stamps may conveniently be put into an album with stamp
20 hinges, without any concern about a loss in value. On the other hand, mint stamps that have been hinged lose part of their value in the marketplace. They must thus be encased in transparent envelopes and pockets
25 that show the stamps without sticking hinges to them. Mounting mint stamps thus takes more time, energy, and money. There is something to be said for both decisions, and some collectors collect both kinds of

30 stamps. But usually a collector has a secret preference.

In this selection the author's chief distinction is between which of the following?
(A) used stamps and mint stamps
(B) the arguments for collecting two types of stamps
(C) good stamps and worthless stamps
(D) the market values of two different types of stamps
(E) the aesthetic value of a used stamp as contrasted with that of a mint stamp

_____

Now look at a question and analyze the possible answers.

Problem

Distinguishing between the speaker and his argument is difficult but essential. We tend to accept the statements of those we like and reject the statements of those we 5 dislike. Yet our friends may be speaking nonsense and our enemies, the truth. An obnoxious person may have something valuable to say. A major task is focusing attention on what is said and not on who is 10 saying it. There are four possible reactions. We may accept the speaker and accept his argument. We may reject the speaker and reject his argument. We may accept the speaker and reject his argument. We may 15 reject the speaker and accept his argument. The first two are easy. A person with a closed mind finds no problem here. The person with an open mind must, however, be able to have all four reactions. To focus 20 on the argument and not be swayed unduly by the personality of the speaker is true maturity.

In this selection the writer's chief distinction is between which of the following?

(A) personality and maturity
(B) speakers and their points of view
(C) acceptance and rejection
(D) inductive and deductive reasoning
(E) the open mind and the closed mind

_____

Strategy. Personality *(A)* is mentioned as an influence on reaction to an argument. It is not contrasted with maturity. Speakers *(B)* do have different points of view, but the major point deals with listeners' reactions to speakers' arguments. As an answer, *acceptance* and *rejection (C)* is much too broad for this paragraph. Inductive and deductive reasoning *(D)* are neither mentioned nor implied. The basic contrast is between the open mind, which accepts all four possibilities, and the closed mind, which accepts only the first two. *(E)* is correct.

REVIEW

Try your skill. The passage below is followed by four questions based on its content. Use the preceding example to help you find the right answers.

"The left hand is the dreamer; the right hand is the doer."

Scientists often discover wisdom in folk sayings. There has been much recent spec-
5 ulation about the hemispheres of the brain and their various functions. The right hemi-sphere of the brain controls the left side of the body. The left hemisphere controls the right side. But there is more to the division.
10 In most people language and language-re-lated abilities are located in the left hemi-sphere. Because language is so closely related to thinking and reasoning, the left hemisphere is concerned with conscious
15 thought processes and problem solving. It was once considered the major hemisphere. But recent investigations have shown that the right hemisphere also plays an import-ant role in the total functioning of the per-
20 sonality. This hemisphere provides nonverbal skills and a different mode of thinking. Whereas the left hemisphere tends to be verbal and analytic, the right hemisphere tends to be nonverbal and
25 global. The right hemisphere is not inferior to the left. It processes information differ-ently, often providing creative leaps and sudden insights not available to the left hemisphere. The left hand, controlled by
30 the right hemisphere, is "the dreamer," but the label should not suggest inferiority or incapacity. Both hemispheres play an equivalent, though different, role in the functioning of the personality.

1. Which of the following titles best sum-marizes the content of the passage?
   (A) Creativity and the Human Brain
   (B) Poetry: A Left-Brain Function
   (C) The Brain: A Two-Part Mecha-nism
   (D) Personality Types
   (E) Language and the Human Brain

   1 ____

2. The article suggests that _____.
   (A) the left brain controls left-hand-edness
   (B) the left brain is the major hemi-sphere
   (C) a left-handed person is at a disad-vantage in a right-handed world
   (D) both hemispheres are important for a complete personality
   (E) scientists have discredited the theory that there are two hemi-spheres

   2 ____

3. Of the following skills, which would probably belong to the right hemi-sphere?
   (A) writing a summary
   (B) creating music
   (C) classifying objects
   (D) translating an article
   (E) criticizing a movie

   3 ____

4. In this selection the writer's chief dis-tinction is between which of the follow-ing?
   (A) the left hand and the right hand
   (B) dreamers and doers
   (C) the functions of two brain hemi-spheres
   (D) nonverbal skills and analytic abil-ities
   (E) applied science and folk wisdom

   4 ____

SUMMARY

4. Making a Comparison

When asked to evaluate comparisons, be sure to isolate the two important things being compared. Don't hit upon a minor comparison. Alternative *4A,* page 199, singles out a minor illustration though the question calls for the *chief distinction.*

Section II Summary: Drawing Inferences

An inference is an educated guess. Though it is based on facts, it goes beyond facts. It reads between the lines and makes a judgment. Often many inferences can be drawn from a single statement or situation. Always choose the most reasonable one, the one most consistent with the facts.

Review the strategies for drawing inferences often as you prepare for the SAT.

PART 1. Identifying Inferences (pp. 189–191)
A. Recognize an inference question. Look for such words as: *imply, assume, suggest, apparently believes.*
B. Look for the facts related to the inference question.
C. Base your inference (your "educated guess") on the facts.
D. Remember, a fact is an observation you can prove. An inference is a guess or a judgment. Don't confuse the two.

PART 2. Supplying an Interpretation (pp. 192–194)
A. Recognize an interpretation question, asking you to say something in another way. Look for such wording as:
   Which best expresses the meaning of . . .
   An excellent adjective to describe _____ is . . .
B. Find the word or phrase in question.
C. Use your own word or phrase to say the same thing.
D. Choose the answer that corresponds most closely to what you have said in your own words.

PART 3. Providing a Paraphrase (pp. 194–197)
A. A paraphrase question asks for a restatement (or "interpretation") of an entire sentence or paragraph or more.
B. Find the material to be paraphrased.
C. Put it in your own words; be sure you are saying the same thing. Restate; don't summarize.
D. Choose the answer that corresponds most closely to what you have said in your own words.

PART 4. Making a Comparison (pp. 197–200)
A. A comparison question asks you to compare two ideas, persons, expressions, or arguments.
B. Look for comparison words such as *difference between* or *distinction between*.
C. Be sure you know what is being compared.
D. Focus on the *important* things being compared.

Section III: Finding Details

1. Spotting Details in the Text

In reading tests, you must be able to find more than generalizations. You'll need to pick out details, specific items in the text. These test items occur in a variety of forms. Here's a skeleton sample.

1. The author refers to . . . as an example of . . .
2. The author bases the answer to the question . . . on . . .
3. According to the passage what happens to . . . ?
4. Sousa's work is "practical" in the sense that it is . . .
5. According to the passage, one of the cultural lessons taught by African art is that art should be . . .
6. The author mentions fluorescent lamps and transistors as examples of . . .
7. According to the passage a cohort study is one that . . .
8. The author cites . . . for their . . .
9. The author mentions which of the following as experiences common to . . . ?
10. According to the passage, a true work of art can be the product of all the following EXCEPT . . .

Again, despite the variety of formats, the essential task is straightforward. With these questions you must comb the selection for *specific* phrases and sentences being asked for.

TRIAL TEST

For the following test questions write the letter for the best answer.

The long association of Joseph Duveen and Henry E. Huntington resulted in an art collection of unquestioned excellence. Like many other wealthy men of his time, Huntington distrusted his own judgment, relying instead upon the impeccable taste of an art dealer who had the knack of matching millionaire and painting. It was Joseph Duveen who bought for Huntington and his wife Arabella the two famous paintings often paired in the eyes of the public: Gainsborough's *The Blue Boy* and Lawrence's *Pinkie*. Without prodding from Duveen, Huntington would never have bought Turner's *The Grand Canal*. Over the protest of Arabella Huntington, Duveen persuaded Huntington to buy Reynolds' masterpiece, *Sarah Siddons as the Tragic Muse*. Arabella had at first objected to having a picture of an actress in her home. Another Reynolds gem, *Georgiana, Duchess of Devonshire*, was added to the Huntington collection. One painting that Arabella Huntington bought, with Duveen's help, is

25 the priceless painting, Rogier van der Weyden's *The Virgin and Christ Child*. Visitors to the Huntington Gallery in San Marino, California, owe a debt to Henry E. Huntington, who accumulated the art now
30 available to the public. But it was Joseph Duveen who made it all possible.

1. The painting Arabella was reluctant to buy was _____.
   (A) *The Grand Canal*
   (B) *Georgiana, Duchess of Devonshire*
   (C) *Sarah Siddons as the Tragic Muse*
   (D) *The Blue Boy*
   (E) *The Virgin and Christ Child*

   1 ____

2. Two paintings often paired by the public are _____.
   (A) *The Grand Canal* and *Pinkie*
   (B) *Sarah Siddons as the Tragic Muse* and *Pinkie*
   (C) *The Virgin and Christ Child* and *The Blue Boy*
   (D) *Pinkie* and *The Blue Boy*
   (E) *Georgiana, Duchess of Devonshire* and *Sarah Siddons as the Tragic Muse*

   2 ____

Problem

In June, 1981, Jay Johnson started out on an incredible journey—a self-propelled trip around the United States. At no time did Johnson rely on any motorized transporta-
5 tion, though he used a variety of methods. He started in northern Maine and backpacked south along the Appalachian Trail to Georgia. Still on foot, he reached Montgomery, Alabama. He picked up a 15-foot
10 dory in Montgomery and rowed down the wild Alabama River to the Gulf of Mexico. Rowing 1200 miles along the Gulf coast, he reached Brownsville, Texas. Then he chose a bicycle for his 3000 mile trip through the
15 Southwest. He gave up the bicycle in southern California and backpacked north on the Pacific Coast Trail all the way to British Columbia, arriving in late September, 1982. His trip had lasted 16 months and covered
20 nearly 10,000 miles. To help him along his unusual journey, he estimated his needs in advance and then used the Postal Service for delivery of supplies to prearranged points. He plotted his journey like a mili-
25 tary campaign, with a thorough evaluation of his abilities and needs. This was a magical experience, but there was no magic behind its success.

1. The bicycle portion of the journey took place _____.
   (A) in Montgomery, Alabama
   (B) at the very end
   (C) in British Columbia
   (D) before the arrival in Brownsville
   (E) in the Southwest

   1 ____

2. As used in the selection "self-propelled" means _____.
   (A) highly motivated
   (B) carrying a backpack
   (C) without motorized help
   (D) well planned
   (E) using the Postal Service

   2 ____

3. Jay Johnson used each of the following methods EXCEPT _____.
   (A) bicycle   (D) mule
   (B) dory   (E) rowing
   (C) backpack

   3 ____

Strategy. This is a fairly easy selection to get you started and help you see various strategies used in testing for details.

1. Often the answer is found in a single sentence: "Then he chose a bicycle for his 3000 mile trip through the Southwest." Go no further. *(E)* is correct.

2. All five answers relate to the passage, but only *(C)* is responsive to the question. Sentence 2, following immediately after Sentence 1, provides a ready definition of "self-propelled." *(C)* is correct.

3. This type of question is sometimes confusing because of *except*. Under stress and in haste, sometimes candidates fail to read carefully. They see *bicycle* and say, "He used a bicycle." But the *except*, of course, excludes *bicycle, backpack,* and *dory*. Note, too, that *rowing* and *dory* are essentially the same. There is no mention of using a mule. Therefore *(D)* is correct.

REVIEW

Try your skill. The passage below is followed by questions based on its content. Use the preceding example to help you find the right answers.

In the opinion of some critics, 1999 was a watershed year for films. A new generation of directors turned out films that broke with tradition. Even the innovations of the 70s
5 and 80s were superseded.

Film buffs live in a fortunate age. Television and videotape have given enthusiasts an opportunity to watch the great movies of the past. An informal history of
10 film can be absorbed in a single day; the classic silents like *The Gold Rush*; the color-drenched spectaculars, culminating in *Gone With the Wind* and *The Wizard of Oz*; the somber film noir of the 40s and
15 50s, like *The Big Sleep*; the computer exploits of *Jurassic Park* and *Toy Story*; and now the hyperkinetic films of the new millennium.

What distinguishes these innovative
20 films? The first and most obvious development is the rapid-fire succession of images, some of them almost subliminal, often presented at speeds that tax the eye and mind. If an average movie has 600 images, the
25 new breed may present 2,000. *The Blair Witch Project*, a $60,000 horror movie created by unknown young filmmakers, had no stars, no expensive camera work, none of the trappings of extravagant movies; yet it
30 became a financial blockbuster. Young amateur filmmakers, working with their own camcorders, could relate to this "murky, herky-jerky" film.

Another change is the lack of a straight
35 narrative plot line. A traditional movie runs from A to Z through the alphabet. The iconoclastic movies overlook such niceties. In *Run Lola Run*, Lola is shot through the heart in the first half hour, but she contin-
40 ues running throughout the rest of the film. When she encounters a bystander, a succession of images shows the rest of that bystander's life. When the "game is over," Lola starts running again. Does this sound
45 familiar, like a computer game?

Young people are used to such an experience. In a computer game, the player can always start over, to restart the fleeting images. Even the habit of television chan-
50 nel-surfing provides a kaleidoscope of images: disconnected, jarring, unpleasing to older eyes, but natural to the young. The

computer generation is at home in cyberspace.

55 An explosion of these new-wave films marked the end of the old millennium: *Being John Malkovich*, *The Matrix*, *The Sixth Sense*, *The Limey*, and *Magnolia*, to name a few. More traditional movies contin-
60 ued to be made, like *Random Hearts* and *Runaway Bride*. There is no question, though, that new techniques and philosophies of filmmaking are invading the mainstream with unpredictable results.

1. The best title for this selection is
   _____.
   (A) *The Blair Witch Project*
   (B) The Superiority of Traditional Films
   (C) A Year to Remember
   (D) The Computer Influence
   (E) A Revolution in Show Business

   1 ____

2. Each of the following is presented as a new-wave film except _____.
   (A) *Random Hearts*
   (B) *Being John Malkovich*
   (C) *Run Lola Run*
   (D) *Toy Story*
   (E) *The Matrix*

   2 ____

3. A help in studying the history of films is _____.
   (A) the computer   (D) the Internet
   (B) computer games   (E) videotape
   (C) channel surfing

   3 ____

4. A "color-drenched spectacular" is _____.
   (A) *Jurassic Park*
   (B) *The Wizard of Oz*
   (C) *The Gold Rush*
   (D) *Toy Story*
   (E) *Magnolia*

   4 ____

5. Young people are especially familiar with _____.
   (A) film noir
   (B) the work of John Malkovich
   (C) older directors, like Scorsese
   (D) cyberspace
   (E) film history

   5 ____

6. The new wave seems likely to _____.
   (A) separate young and old viewers
   (B) go out in a burst of glory
   (C) completely eliminate traditional movies
   (D) irritate film critics
   (E) appeal more to women than men

   6 ____

7. From the context, it is clear that "hyperkinetic" (line 17) means _____.
   (A) pleasingly colorful
   (B) challenging
   (C) traditional
   (D) extremely active
   (E) counterproductive

   7 ____

SUMMARY

1. Spotting Details in the Text

When checking for details in a reading passage, look for specific phrases and sentences to support your choice. If more than one answer applies to the passage, be sure you choose the answer that is responsive to the question.

2. Finding Details in Combination

Sometimes the test question will call for a combination of possibilities. Your answer must include all details called for and no details not in the selection.

TRIAL TEST

For the following test question select the best answer.

Oats, wheat, rye, and other grains are well known and often used in America. Barley, however, has been neglected. As Raymond Sokolov has observed, "In this
5 country, today, few people cook barley at all. Most of us taste it rarely and almost exclusively in soup." Though known from Biblical days, barley is "the all-but-forgotten grain, orphan among staples." It deserves to be
10 better known and more often used.

Barley is a superbly hardy grass, growing everywhere from Egypt to Norway and Tibet. It thrives in climates too cold for wheat. It is a versatile grain. Bread made
15 from barley is dark and tasty. It keeps well and is still pleasantly edible when dry. Barley can be used for cakes, breads, pancakes. It is a subtle flavoring when used in combination with other grains. Why, then, has
20 barley done so poorly in modern America?

Wheat is the culprit in the story of barley's retreat. Though less sturdy than barley, wheat can, with modern methods, be transported and preserved more easily
25 than in the past. Wheat has more gluten, thus allowing bread from wheat to rise. Barley bread, by contrast, is flat. Barley cannot replace wheat, but it has a niche to fill.

30 How can we take advantage of this neglected grain? We can combine barley with wheat for a tasty, nutritious bread. We can, of course, use it in soup, where its delicate flavor is a plus. We can eat barley as a side
35 dish with most main courses. We can bake it with mushrooms in a pie crust. We can, like the Koreans, serve it with rice. We can also brew a tea from roasted barley, as the Japanese do. However we use it, we ought
40 to rescue this overlooked grain from its undeserved oblivion.

Which of the following statements may be accurately derived from the selection?

I. Barley makes a bread superior to wheat bread.
II. Barley has an adaptability unsuspected by most Americans.
III. Barley is a member of the grass family.
IV. Barley combines with other grains for tasty foods.
V. Oats and wheat grow in Tibet.

(A) I only
(B) IV only
(C) II, III, and IV
(D) I, III, and V
(E) I and IV

Problem

The Mayan Empire once stretched from the Yucatan to western Honduras. Its power and extent are constantly being restudied as new discoveries rescue import-
5 ant Mayan sites from the jungle. Sites like Uxmal and Chichen-Itza in Yucatan, Tikal in Guatemala, and Copan in Honduras reveal the awesome achievements of the civilization that flourished many centuries ago.
10 The latter two, discovered in the 1840s,

"rank in archaeological importance with the pyramids of Egypt."

A more recent discovery is causing a complete reappraisal of the Mayan influence
15 and the duration of the Mayan Empire. It had previously been thought that the Mayan civilization did not mature before A.D. 300. Then in 1978 Bruce Dahlin uncovered bits of pottery dating from 400 B.C.
20 There, in the lost city called El Mirador, not far from Tikal, a civilization flourished centuries before the date usually assigned to its arrival.

The architecture at El Mirador reveals
25 the sophistication of its artisans: master builders, stonecutters, and sculptors. The various structures also suggest a high level of social organization. Here, too, are beautiful carvings with hieroglyphics as yet un-
30 deciphered. This graphic style of writing provided much of the communication upon which a civilization ultimately rests.

The new discoveries suggest that the Mayan Empire lasted not 500 or so years
35 but 1500 years or more. John Graham of

Berkeley flatly states, "Mayan civilization represents the longest sustained civilization in the New World." Further explorations at El Mirador suggest that we have
40 just scratched the surface of our knowledge about the Maya.

Which of the following statements may be accurately derived from the selection?
I.   Writing is crucial to the success of a civilization.
II. Mayan sites are predominantly in Yucatan.
III. The duration of Mayan civilization is under reappraisal and revision.
IV. The buildings at El Mirador are contemporary with the pyramids of Egypt.
V.   Hieroglyphics are associated with, and restricted to, Egypt.

(A) III only   (D) II and IV
(B) IV only   (E) I and III
(C) I and V

Strategy. Statements II, IV, and V are false. Therefore any answer containing one of these statements is wrong; that is, *(B)*, *(C)*, and *(D)*. Statement III is true, but *(A)* is wrong because it suggests that only III applies. The correct answer, *(E)*, lists both correct statements: I and III.

REVIEW

Try your skill. The passage below is followed by questions based on its content. Use the preceding example to help you find the right answers.

American folklore is filled with tales of hoboes, wanderers who rode the rails and traveled the country as uninvited guests of the railroads. But there is another group of
5 rail-riders, whose presence is never felt by the train but whose journey is made possible by the Iron Horse: weeds! These courageous adventurers establish themselves on

sites that look forbidding, even deadly, to
10 living things. The cinders along the railbed and the borders seem an impossible nursery for any living organism. Yet many plants survive in the hostile environment.

Seeds are carried by trains and dispersed
15 along the right of way. Queen Anne's lace, ragweed, and wild parsnip flourish where a railroad intersects with a road. Clovers, horseweed, and wood sorrels do well at railroad crossings in farm country. Some plants
20 seem to thrive especially well along the

forbidding tracks. Dwarf snapdragon, for example, grows more abundantly along railroad tracks than anywhere else.

It's hard to think of a more inhospitable
25 environment than the land along the railroad tracks. The cinders contain little if any humus. The area is dry, sunbaked, and often sprayed with weed killers. Speeding trains lop off the heads of taller species.
30 Even smaller plants are subjected to the air stresses created by passing trains. Yet persistent plant life struggles and often perpetuates its kind, despite the odds against survival. The track area may not be a luxu-
35 rious garden, but it nurtures many trainborne weeds.

1. Which of the following statements may be accurately derived from the selection?
   I. A railbed is a better place to grow plants than a city garden.
   II. Different plants thrive in different conditions.
   III. The dwarf snapdragon thrives especially well along a railroad line.
   IV. Ragweed and Queen Anne's lace seem to grow well in similar environments.
   V. American folklore features the vitality and dispersion of native weeds.

   (A) II only   (D) III and V
   (B) V only   (E) I, II, and III
   (C) II, III, and IV

   1 ____

2. The "courageous adventurers" referred to in lines 7–8 are _____.
   (A) hoboes   (D) smaller plants
   (B) trains   (E) weeds
   (C) dwarf snapdragons

   2 ____

3. Which two are compared in the selection?
   (A) hoboes and weed killers
   (B) a luxurious garden and a railbed
   (C) the Iron Horse and the tracks
   (D) impossible nursery and hostile environment
   (E) railroads and automobiles

   3 ____

4. Which of the following titles best summarizes the content of the passage?
   (A) Weeds and Their Ways
   (B) Railroads: Preservers of American Wildlife
   (C) Those Unlikely Railroad "Gardens"
   (D) Endangered Species: Railroad Weeds
   (E) Weeds: The Railroads' Persistent Problem

   4 ____

5. It is reasonable to infer that _____.
   (A) some weeds can store moisture for survival
   (B) the wood sorrel is more adaptable than the dwarf snapdragon
   (C) hoboes paid a small railroad fare
   (D) cinders have hidden pockets of soil
   (E) the wild parsnip is sturdier than the ragweed

   5 ____

SUMMARY

2. Finding Details in Combination

When checking for a combination of details in a reading passage, be complete. Include only those details actually included—but don't leave any out.

3. Combining Skills

The reading skills tested are rarely pure examples of only one skill. Frequently two or more skills are needed to ferret out an answer.

An inference, for example, is frequently built upon a key detail in the selection, even though it is not, itself, a detail. You have to do two things: find the detail and make the inference. A title is frequently based on a conclusion that balances various inferences. You have to do three things: make the inferences, form a conclusion, and choose a title.

Some SAT questions require you to figure out details and then make judgments about the details. Note that the wording of the following SAT-type question does more than call for identification of details. It also calls for an inference based on details.

1. In which of the following lines is an appeal made to curiosity?

(A)	1–5	(D)	16–20
(B)	6–10	(E)	21–25
(C)	11–15		

Here's a combination in which you are not expected to state the main idea but to identify the lines in the passage which contain the main idea.

The same skills may be tested in different forms.

2. During which ten-year period was there the greatest unrest in the United States?

(A)	1896–1905	(D)	1945–1954
(B)	1905–1914	(E)	1962–1971
(C)	1920–1929		

3. The central thought of the passage is most clearly expressed in which of the following lines?

(A)	1–5	(D)	16–20
(B)	6–10	(E)	21–25
(C)	11–15		

TRIAL TEST

Select the best answer for the following test question.

You can have your own drugstore right on your windowsill. The aloe vera plant, which is often grown as a houseplant, has some remarkable medicinal properties. The fresh
5 leaf juice of the plant contains the drug aloin, which has many soothing properties when it is used externally.

The roster of the skin problems helped by aloe is impressive. The juice has healing
10 properties for insect bites, minor burns, poison ivy, and athlete's foot. It can also relieve summer sunburn and dry skin.

For minor burns, victims may break off the largest leaf of the aloe plant and squeeze
15 it gently, like a tube of toothpaste or ointment. The sticky clear gel is applied directly to the burn.

Aloe is not a recent newcomer to medication. The ancient Greeks and Egyptians
20 knew of its medicinal properties. Cleopatra
used aloe as part of her beauty treatments
and medications.

The plant itself is inexpensive. It makes
a beautiful pot plant. Because it is a succu-
25 lent, it requires little watering. It does, however, need good drainage and lots of sun.
Some people may have a mild allergy to aloe
vera, but for most people, the plant can be
a multipurpose medicine shelf—and a com-
30 pact, decorative one besides.

In which of the following paragraphs is a
possible drawback to the use of aloe mentioned?

(A) 1   (D)   4
(B) 2   (E)   5
(C) 3

Problems

Accidents will happen but many needn't.
Among the most common type of automobile accidents are rear-end collisions. In a
ranking of types of automobile road acci-
5 dents, these collisions rank second. Over 3
1/2 million drivers are involved each year in
this particular road hazard. Yet much can
be done to cut down the number of such
accidents.
10   The best way to reduce rear-end collisions
is to improve visibility. One experimental
device was the installation of a third brake
light on the back of cars. In an experimental
study this minor addition resulted in a drop
15 of 50% in the number of rear-end collisions.
Placing the new light centrally on the
trunk, just below the rear window, provides
certain new advantages. It is not used as a
directional signal, nor is it used to illumin-
20 ate the back of the car at night. It stays dark
until the driver brakes. This is a clear signal
that the car is slowing or stopping. Because
it is about at eye level of the driver in the
car behind, it is easily visible.
25   Though the installation of the third
light was experimental, its acknowledged
success led to its inclusion on all new cars.

Once again, a minor and inexpensive improvement has become an important safety
30 feature.
    The second method for avoiding rear-end
collisions is to drive a light-colored car.
When visibility is poor, accidents often
occur because a driver doesn't see the other
35 vehicle until it's too late. According to safety
tests, drivers can see light, bright cars from
a distance of up to four times farther away
than they can see cars in darker tones. A
white car is the most visible of all.

1. The advantage of placing the third
   light just below the rear window is
   mentioned in which of the following
   lines?
   (A) 1–6   (D) 25–30
   (B) 7–15   (E) 35–38
   (C) 20–24

                                    1 ____

2. The central thought of the passage is
   most clearly expressed in which of the
   following lines?
   (A) 1–5   (D) 25–30
   (B) 10–14   (E) 31–35
   (C) 22–24

                                    2 ____

Strategy. 1. The advantage of placing the light just below the rear window is mentioned in lines 10–15. Since answer *(B)* includes lines 10–15, *(B)* is the correct answer. The rest of the selection does not deal with that particular detail.

2. The central idea of the entire selection is stated in lines 10–11.

"The best way to reduce rear-end collisions is to improve visibility." The entire passage is devoted to the question of visibility, with the third light discussed at length and the color of the car discussed in the last paragraph. Since line 10 is in 10–14, *(B)* is the correct answer.

REVIEW

Try your skill. The passage below is followed by questions based on its content. Use the preceding example to help you find the right answers.

"Why bother saving wild and endangered species? It is the fate of species to become extinct someday anyway. Why bother with snail darters and wild grains? Let's spend
5 more time on more important problems."

These arguments have a specious reasonableness, but they couldn't be more wrong. We have a selfish interest in wild species. We need to protect them for our own sur-
10 vival.

As Norman Myers has pointed out, "We use hundreds of products each day that owe their existence to plants and animals. The ways in which wild species support our
15 daily welfare fall under three main headings: agriculture, medicine, and industry."

In agriculture, for example, we need a constant infusion of new genetic material from wild plants. Plant geneticists have
20 done more to improve crop yields than artificial additives like fertilizers and pesticides. Natural immunities to pests and extremes of climates are bred into native plants with the help of wild stock. Blight-
25 resistant genes from a wild Mexican plant helped preserve the threatened American corn crop. A wild wheat strain from Turkey is resistant to several diseases afflicting domestic grain. Its introduction saved the
30 farm industry millions of dollars worth of crops each year.

The same situation is true in medicine. Wild organisms continue to contribute remedies for many of our ills. A child suffering
35 from leukemia once had only a 20% chance of remission. With the help of rosy periwinkle, a tropical forest plant, the child now has an 80% chance. Other anticancer drugs may well be found in the vast jungles of the
40 Amazon basin.

The seas provide other medicinal materials. A Caribbean sponge may be an important antiviral agent. Menhaden, a marine fish, provides an oil that may help
45 in treating atherosclerosis. Sea snakes can yield an anticoagulant. Extracts from the toxin of the octopus may be used as an anesthetic in modern surgery. Potential anticancer drugs may come from corals,
50 sea anemones, mollusks, sponges, sea squirts, and even clams.

Industry also depends upon wild species for many products. Seaweeds, for example, contribute to hundreds of products, includ-
55 ing waxes, detergents, soaps, shampoos, paints, lubricants, and dyes. Land plants like the jojoba play a large part in industrial production. The liquid wax from the jojoba is a brilliantly efficient lubricant. The ex-
60 pansion of the chemical industry suggests that we'll need many more supplies of organic industrial chemicals. As yet untapped

or undiscovered species can make major contributions to industry.

65   The wild species of the world are not merely decorative at best or essentially useless at worst. They are a storehouse of genetic material and products that can help us improve our lives—even survive. An investment in

70 the survival of wild species is an investment in the survival of another species—our own.

1. Genetic experimentation with plants is discussed in which of the following lines?
   (A) 1–10   (D) 32–40
   (B) 11–16   (E) 41–51
   (C) 17–31

   1 ____

2. From the selection, it may be inferred that _____.
   (A) wild plants are always superior to domestic plants
   (B) a cure for cancer will come from the blight-resistant Mexican wheat
   (C) domestic plants often have limited resistance to ills
   (D) we need not be concerned about the extinction of wild species
   (E) industry is blindly reluctant to accept the products derived from wild species

   2 ____

3. A wild species that contributes hundreds of products is _____.
   (A) jojoba   (D) octopus
   (B) rosy periwinkle
   (C) seaweed   (E) sea snake

   3 ____

4. The central thought of the passage is most clearly expressed in which of the following statements?
   (A) In agriculture, for example, we need a constant infusion of new genetic material from wild plants.
   (B) It is the fate of species to become extinct someday anyway.
   (C) The seas provide other medicinal materials.
   (D) As yet untapped or undiscovered species can make major contributions to industry.
   (E) An investment in the survival of wild species is an investment in the survival of another species— our own.

   4 ____

5. To save wild species we must _____.
   (A) preserve their natural habitats
   (B) cultivate them in our gardens
   (C) carefully monitor climate
   (D) stop using their genetic material
   (E) experiment with changing their genetic structure

   5 ____

6. Which of the following pairs is correctly matched?
   (A) seaweed-anticancer
   (B) jojoba-anesthetic
   (C) sea snake-detergent
   (D) mollusk-leukemia
   (E) menhaden-atherosclerosis

   6 ____

SUMMARY

3. Combining Skills

Some questions test a combination of skills. First read the question carefully. Then, to double check your answer, carefully rule out the incorrect alternatives.

Section III Summary: Finding Details

Although you cannot ordinarily point specifically to a sentence or section in the text to prove an inferred answer, you can usually find in the text itself the answer to a question turning upon a detail in the selection.

Review the strategies for finding details as you prepare for the SAT.

PART 1. Spotting Details in the Text (pp. 202–205)
A. Look for specific phrases and sentences with the details you want.
B. When you find details for *more than one* answer, do the following:
    1. Reread the question to be sure you understand it.
    2. Choose the answer with the details that specifically answer the question.

PART 2. Finding Details in Combination (pp. 206–208)

When a question calls for two or more details together:
A. Read the passage carefully.
B. Choose the answer with *only* the details that you have read.
C. Be sure you don't leave out any of the details.

PART 3. Combining Skills (pp. 209–212)

When a question asks you to combine skills, usually making an inference or judgment based on details:
A. Find the details you need.
B. Use the details to make the inference or judgment called for.
C. Make any more choices as needed (such as choosing a title or a central idea) based on what you have found and decided.

Section IV: Understanding the Author's Role

1. Evaluating the Author's Tone

When we speak, we indicate the tone of the message by our tone of voice. When we write, we indicate tone in other ways. SAT questions frequently ask you to describe the tone of a passage. The following are some typical adjectives and nouns to describe tone.

"TONE" ADJECTIVES

aggressive and dogmatic	indifferent
argumentative	inquisitive
conciliatory and apologetic	inspirational
honest and straightforward	instructional and explanatory
humble	ironic
objective	scholarly
reflective	sensational and melodramatic

"TONE" NOUNS

apprehension	hope	resignation
deference	indifference	reverence
despair	irrationality	sarcasm
disdain	mistrust	self-pity
enthusiasm	relief	urgency

To answer questions about tone, you must get the "feel" of the passage. You must "read between the lines" and determine what mood is suggested.

TRIAL TEST

The morning dawned cold and gray. The freezing winter rain had stripped all but a few tenacious oak leaves from the trees outside the study window. The colors were
5 muted, with shades of gray and brown predominating in a Rembrandtesque landscape. The autumn distractions of brilliant color were gone, and the tree trunks stood stark and austere a few feet from the win-
10 dow. The corrugations of the bark were clear and distinct. The tiny patches of moss and lichen here and there accentuated the grooves rather than diminished them. Through the tree silhouettes could be dis-
15 cerned the olive-green needles of young Southern pine, struggling for survival in the oak forest. The ground was littered with brown oak leaves, whose otherwise monochromatic appearance was challenged by
20 their curl and twist on the forest floor. Here

and there, fallen gray twigs punctuated the rust mattress, adding a pleasant break in the superficial uniformity. This was a subtle scene, a scene demanding close observa-
25 tion to find the beauty of color and form that was everywhere.

The tone of the passage can best be described as _____.

(A) self-satisfied   (D)   argumentative
(B) conciliatory   (E)   apprehensive
(C) reflective

_____

Problem

OLD IRONSIDES

Ay, tear her tattered ensign down!
  Long has it waved on high,
And many an eye has danced to see
  That banner in the sky;
5 Beneath it rung the battle shout,
  And burst the cannon's roar;—
The meteor of the ocean air
  Shall sweep the clouds no more.
Her deck, once red with heroes' blood,
10 Where knelt the vanquished foe,
When winds were hurrying o'er the floods,
  And waves were white below,
No more shall feel the victor's tread,
  Or know the conquered knee;—
15 The harpies of the shore shall pluck
  The eagle of the sea!

Oh, better that her shattered hulk
  Should sink beneath the wave;
Her thunders shook the mighty deep,
20   And there should be her grave;
Nail to the mast her holy flag,
  Set every threadbare sail,
And give her to the god of storms,
  The lightning and the gale!

1. The tone of the poem as a whole can best be described as _____.
(A) amiable   (D) indifferent
(B) doubtful   (E) angry
(C) acquiescent

1 ____

2. Lines 3–4 convey a sense of _____
(A) humor   (D) delight
(B) pride   (E) worry
(C) uncertainty

2 ____

3. Which of the following lines can best be described as *sarcastic?*
(A) 1   (D) 19
(B) 9–10   (E) 21
(C) 12–13

3 ____

4. The "harpies of the shore" (line 15) are treated with _____.
(A) suspicion   (D) anticipation
(B) contempt   (E) resignation
(C) fear

4 ____

Strategy. 1. The poet resents the fact that the historic ship is going to be scrapped ("tear her tattered ensign down"). This attack is angry, as other lines confirm. The answer is *(E), angry.*

2. If an eye "dances" to see the banner in the sky, the emotion described is pride: *(B).*

3. From the rest of the passage, it is clear that the poet does not want the "tattered ensign" torn down. Quite the opposite. Since sarcasm seems to say one thing while

clearly implying the other, the answer is *(A)*. The other alternatives are straightforward and positive.

4. Contrasting the "harpies of the shore" with "the eagle of the sea" clearly suggests the poet's venomous attitude toward the harpies. Contempt, *(B)*, is an accurate word to suggest the tone of the lines.

REVIEW

Try your skill. The passage below is followed by questions based on its content. Use the preceding example to help you find the right answers.

"Who Cares Who Killed Roger Ackroyd?" The title of Edmund Wilson's 1945 essay clearly indicates the writer's bias. Wilson called detective stories "wasteful of time
5 and degrading to the intellect." Since that time other critics have sneered, condescended, and scorned the whodunit, but its popularity has rarely faltered. The detective story and related types like the spy
10 story, the horror tale, and the Dashiell Hammett type of thriller are often lumped under the general heading *Mystery* and earn a special shelf in most libraries. The mystery shelf is one of the most popular in
15 every library. Novels by old favorite writers like John Dickson Carr vie with current favorites like those by Ruth Rendell, P.D. James, Elizabeth George, and Tony Hillerman. Why do mysteries, and especially de-
20 tective stories, often outlast their critics?

In an era when much modern fiction is plotless and loosely structured, the detective story, with its solid plot, tells a story that appeals to the child in everyone. The
25 detective story begins somewhere and ends somewhere. In between, readers are treated to twists of plot, surprises in characterization, and challenging puzzles.

Detective stories and other mysteries,
30 though often maligned, have influenced other current fiction. Even "literary" fiction has been affected by the mystery and its close relatives. Paul Theroux's *Family Ar-*

senal, Robert Stone's *A Flag for Sunrise,*
35 and Margaret Atwood's *Bodily Harm* all use the conventions of the thriller.

Some writers have gone further. Michiko Kakutani has pointed out that some prestigious writers "have used the conventions of
40 the mystery to make philosophical points about the nature of storytelling itself." Joyce Carol Oates in *Mysteries of Winterthurn,* Alain Robbe-Grillet in *The Erasers,* and Jorge Luis Borges in *Death*
45 *and the Compass* have added a dimension to the possibilities inherent in the mystery form.

1. The tone of the selection as a whole can best be described as _____.
   (A) instructional and explanatory
   (B) inquisitive and investigatory
   (C) sensational and dogmatic
   (D) biased and poorly represented
   (E) careless and unconcerned

   1 ____

2. The tone of the title "Who Cares Who Killed Roger Ackroyd?" is intended to be _____.
   (A) sympathetic and curious
   (B) wittily negative
   (C) brutally callous
   (D) straightforwardly informative
   (E) earnest and prudent

   2 ____

3. We may reasonably infer that Roger Ackroyd is _____.
   (A) a mystery writer
   (B) a book reviewer
   (C) a real-life crime victim
   (D) a character in a famous mystery
   (E) an imaginary name invented by Robert Stone

   3 ____

4. It may be assumed that the writer of this selection considers Paul Theroux's *Family Arsenal* as _____.
   (A) a true detective story
   (B) a philosophical novel
   (C) "literary" fiction
   (D) a book to be grouped with *The Erasers*
   (E) a book for the mystery shelf

   4 ____

5. The main point of the passage is to _____.
   (A) give the mystery its rightful due in current fiction
   (B) explain why Dashiell Hammett's novels have had ups and downs
   (C) present Michiko Kakutani's point of view about spy stories
   (D) answer the critics of John Dickson Carr and Ruth Rendell
   (E) explore the origins of the whodunit

   5 ____

6. As a category name, *mystery* can be best labeled _____.
   (A) inaccurate
   (B) humorous
   (C) broad
   (D) worthless
   (E) noteworthy

   6 ____

7. The major strength of the detective story is its _____.
   (A) philosophical content
   (B) sense of direction
   (C) imitation of the best writing of Joyce Carol Oates
   (D) conventional characterization
   (E) use of exotic settings

   7 ____

8. The sentence "Why do mysteries, and especially detective stories, often outlast their critics?" can be interpreted as _____.
   (A) an unanswerable question
   (B) a petty swipe at mysteries
   (C) a baffling comment on "literary" fiction
   (D) an apologetic defense of literary critics
   (E) a commendation of the detective story

   8 ____

9. The word "literary" in " 'literary' fiction" is in quotation marks because _____.
   (A) it is quoted from a novel by Paul Theroux
   (B) it exposes a critical snobbish attitude
   (C) here it means exactly the opposite of its usual meaning
   (D) it suggests that the novels mentioned are largely biographical
   (E) mystery writers lack true narrative gifts

   9 ____

SUMMARY
1. Evaluating the Author's Tone

The tone of a passage cannot be found in a detail of the selection. It can "be found only in the overall impression created by the combination of descriptive and connotative words." (See connotation and denotation, pages 60–65.) Most SAT selections tend to have a fairly neutral tone, with emphasis upon the presentation of information. Others, like "Old Ironsides," crackle with a special life of their own, a mood that colors the piece.

2. Evaluating the Author's Attitude

Closely related to the tone of a reading passage is the attitude displayed or suggested. A typical SAT question requires you to discover the author's attitude toward someone or something. The following are examples of questions of this type.

1.   Which of the following best expressed the author's attitude toward . . . ?
2.   The attitude toward . . . is one of . . .
3.   It can be inferred from the passage that the author's attitude toward the . . . is one of . . .
4.   The author's attitude toward . . . is primarily one of . . .
5.   The attitude toward . . . conveyed by the author's use of the words . . . is best described as one of . . .
6.   The author's attitude toward the . . . mentioned in lines 1–20 is best described as . . .

Here is a brief cross-section of typical attitudes tested.

admiration	disdain
ambivalence	exasperation
anxiety	nostalgia
apathy	puzzlement
disbelief	skepticism

Sometimes the attitudes are more narrowly and specifically labeled.

delighted amazement	clear distaste
growing anger	apologetic embarrassment
reluctant approval	cold objectivity
mild condescension	admiring support
veiled disdain	detached sympathy

Other questions display a slightly different phraseology, which requires a different type of answer.

The author's attitude toward . . . is that of a . . .

A correctly completed statement might look something like this:

> The author's attitude toward the absentee employees is that of a parent correcting a misbehaving child.

Note that all these questions are quite different from those for tone. Questions about tone are usually general. Questions about attitude are more specific. In these questions you must uncover the author's attitude *toward someone or something*. Though the phraseology varies from question to question, the essential requirement is the same.

There is no substitute for trying your hand at a typical question.

TRIAL TEST

Take the following trial test to evaluate your skill.

Those who see professional football on television are missing half the fun and half the show: the fans. Though the television cameraman occasionally provides tantaliz-
5 ing shots of oddball enthusiasts, the glimpses are not enough. Through the years there have been colorful characters on the field with picturesque names like "Crazylegs," "The Toe," "the Refrigerator,"
10 and even "Sweetness" for the beloved Walter Payton. But the real characters are in the stands.

In subzero weather on the "frozen tundra" of the Green Bay stadium, some fans
15 appear bare-chested, often decorated with creative body paint. At games involving the Tampa Bay Buccaneers, some fans appear in pirate costume. Viking helmets, pig snouts, and ram's horns add to the festivi-
20 ties. Entire sections join in the fun, waving orange banners or white handkerchiefs. Some groups even have their own songs. There's *active* fun in the stands, too. Stadium hijinks at halftime include passing
25 play footballs in the stands to the roaring approval of the crowd. There is much to see and hear at a football game—and much of that is not on the field.

The author's attitude toward football fans is one of _____.
(A) righteous indignation
(B) concealed intolerance
(C) vigorous denunciation
(D) amused affection
(E) calculated indifference

Problem

"The redwing blackbirds are back!" This cry in February or March reassures a winter-weary land that spring will come again. Migrating birds bring song, color, and joy
5 into our lives. Their migrations have been cheered, observed, and analyzed for many years, but the mysteries remain.

Most birds apparently migrate to follow the food chain. When insects start to be-
10 come abundant in northern meadows, migrating insect-eaters return. The appearance of flowers entices the hummingbirds. Food requirements of all species are relatively specialized and keyed to the environ-
15 ment.

There are many hazards, however, in migration. Storms may blow birds far off course over open water, an often fatal acci-

dent. Flying at night, birds crash into tow-
20 ers and tall buildings. They may arrive at
their usual destination only to find a shopping center where their territories once
were.

Birds make these incredible journeys
25 each year, but the how and the why are
often obscure. Why does the Arctic tern
spend eight months each year migrating
from the Arctic to the Antarctic and back
again? How can this tiny creature success-
30 fully navigate vast areas of open seas?
Though migration has been studied since
the time of Aristotle, we are still in the dark.
We can, however, make a contribution by
protecting breeding habitats and protecting
35 the way stations the long-distance travelers
frequent on their hazardous trips.

1. The author's attitude toward migrat-
ing birds is one of _____.
   (A) satisfied curiosity
   (B) cautious skepticism
   (C) mild irritation
   (D) affectionate respect
   (E) unfeeling analysis

   1 ____

2. The author's attitude toward the flight
of the Arctic tern can best be charac-
terized by the word _____.
   (A) wonder
   (B) disbelief
   (C) approval
   (D) indifference
   (E) anxiety

   2 ____

Strategy. 1. Eliminate some of the alternatives and see what is left. Curiosity
about bird migration has not been satisfied; (A) is incorrect. *Skepticism* is not the
word needed. Skepticism implies doubt about the truth or falsity of a statement or
belief. Uncertainty does not generate skepticism; dogma does. (B) is incorrect.
There is no hint of irritation; (C), mild irritation, is incorrect. The author is emotionally
but positively involved. *Unfeeling* tells us (E) is wrong. That leaves (D), affectionate
respect, clearly the attitude of the author.

2. The author takes no direct stand about the flight of the tern (C), but he or she is
not indifferent (D). There is no question of disbelief (B). That leaves us with (A) and
(E). The use of *incredible* (line 24) and the sentences following tell us the correct
answer is wonder, (A).

REVIEW

Try your skill. The passage below is
followed by questions based on its content.
Use the preceding example to help you find
the right answers.

Though often taught as merely a pretty
decoration in poetry, metaphor is in reality
a basic element in language, transcending
mere ornamentation. Simply defined as "an
5 implied comparison between unlike objects," metaphor is really a flash of insight,
a leap of imagination, a poetic explosion.

When the poet Alfred Noyes in "The Highwayman" calls the road "a ribbon of moon-
10 light," he is superficially comparing a road
and a ribbon, but he is really going farther.
He is investing the road with the emotional,
imaginative qualities associated with
moonlight. He is pouring into that solid,
15 substantial road all the ethereal qualities of
moonlight.

Our entire language is metaphorical.
Many of our commonest expressions are
overlooked metaphors. Think, for a mo-

ment, of the actual images concealed in "run
20 out of patience," "a cutting remark," "drop
the subject," "fly into a rage," "pull strings,"
"turn down a suggestion," and "pick up the
threads of a story."

25 Metaphor enlarges language. It takes
commonplace building blocks and by combining them creates new and beautiful
meanings. Shakespeare says, "Life's but a
walking shadow, a poor player that struts
30 and frets his hour upon the stage and then
is heard no more." The individual words are
common, but the extended comparison—of
life and an actor—is uncommon.

Metaphor is concealed in many common
35 words. By derivation, a *coherent* story
"sticks together." A *subliminal* impulse lies
"below the threshold" of consciousness. A
chrysanthemum is "a flower of gold." *Planets* are "wanderers." Most words travel far
40 from their original, narrow, literal meanings. In the process they acquire metaphorical meanings.

Metaphor is everywhere—in sports tele-
casts, on the editorial pages, on the stage,
45 in our everyday speaking and writing. Even
the word *metaphor* contains a hidden metaphor—from the Greek words to "carry beyond." Metaphor indeed *carries* meaning
beyond the narrow and literal.

1. The author's attitude toward the sub-
ject of metaphor is one of _____.
(A) amused boredom
(B) scholarly debate
(C) mandatory approbation
(D) excessive enthusiasm
(E) alert interest

1 ____

2. The author's attitude toward Shakes-
peare is _____.
(A) flattering   (D) uncritical
(B) appreciative   (E) contradictory
(C) curious

2 ____

3. We may reasonably infer that "The
Highwayman" is a(n) _____.
(A) essay   (D) novel
(B) article   (E) poem
(C) historical memoir

3 ____

4. The quotation from Shakespeare is
called an "extended comparison" because _____.
(A) it contains several images
(B) it compares life and an actor
(C) it is more literal than metaphorical
(D) Shakespeare rarely created simple metaphors
(E) it is a better image than that created by Noyes

4 ____

5. Two words that are intentionally
paired and opposed are _____.
(A) road and moonlight
(B) struts and frets
(C) substantial and ethereal
(D) chrysanthemum and planets
(E) life and actor

5 ____

6. According to the selection a concealed
metaphor is contained in the word
_____.
(A) comparison
(B) literal
(C) coherent
(D) derivation
(E) beautiful

6 ____

7. The writer would probably classify the
expression "leap of imagination" as
a(n) _____.
(A) ribbon of moonlight
(B) metaphor
(C) decoration
(D) poem
(E) extended comparison

7 ____

8. The paragraph devoted exclusively to the physical imagery of the metaphor is _____.
   (A) 1
   (B) 2
   (C) 3
   (D) 4
   (E) 5

   8 ____

9. Using clues from the selection, we might guess that the original meaning of *eliminate* was _____.
   (A) cast over the threshold
   (B) discard abruptly
   (C) wander from the truth
   (D) carry beyond
   (E) strut upon the stage

   9 ____

10. The main point of the passage is to _____.
   (A) extol the art of poetry
   (B) compare Noyes and Shakespeare as poets
   (C) encourage the more extensive use of metaphor
   (D) give metaphor its due as a crucial element in language
   (E) provide an implied comparison of metaphor and simile

   10 ____

SUMMARY
2. Evaluating the Author's Attitude

Searching out the author's attitude requires rereading of the selection as a whole. If you read the selection quietly to yourself, you will begin to sense the author's feeling toward her or his material. Individual words may provide clues, but you must get a feeling for the selection in its entirety. Think of the author as speaking to you. What feeling is he or she trying to convey?

3. Evaluating the Author's Purpose

As we have seen, in a reading passage the author's attitude and the tone of the selection are often linked closely together. A third ingredient, the author's purpose, also influences a reading selection. SAT questions frequently challenge you to decide just what the author is trying to achieve.

The following are examples of questions designed to uncover and probe the author's purpose:

1. Which of the following best describes the purpose of the passage?
2. The primary purpose of the passage appears to be to . . .
3. The author includes statistical information specifically to . . .
4. The author's primary purpose in this passage is to . . .
5. The author quotes . . . in order to . . .

TRIAL TEST

Take this trial test to evaluate your skill.

"You smash and slapdash the idea while it's red hot with you. Get it down on paper." This advice by Bergen Evans should be en-graved in every writer's memory. Every au-
5 thor experiences writer's block at some time or other. Just looking at an empty paper waiting to be filled is enough to paralyze the will and freeze determination. But Evans' advice can help break down the barriers.
10   When you have a writing assignment of any kind, don't sit numbly waiting for the perfect outline to suggest itself. Try brain-storming. Jot down everything on a topic that occurs to you. Don't be critical at this
15 stage. Capitalize on those free associations, those creative if unformed ideas, those many images that float to the surface. Don't be inhibited. Don't say, "Oh, that won't work." *Put it down.* Later, after you have
20 poured forth all those ideas, organize your jottings. Decide what belongs and what doesn't. Form the related ideas into a help-ful outline.

Letting your mind roam freely is excel-
25 lent procedure for any creative project. It is especially useful in writing.

The author's primary purpose in this pas-sage is to _____ .
(A) extol the critical faculties in writing
(B) introduce Bergen Evans as a useful guide
(C) stress that writer's block is a trivial problem
(D) suggest a sound prewriting technique
(E) recommend self-criticism in prepar-ing to write

Problem

The explosive growth of racquetball as a sport is traceable in part to an increased interest in physical fitness. Instead of en-gaging in sedentary pursuits, many people
5 have learned to enjoy the demanding activ-ity of jogging, body-building, and other fit-ness sports. While it is true that racquetball enthusiasts have been lured away from ten-nis, handball, squash, and other related
10 activities, the racquetball ranks have also been swelled by newcomers to strenuous physical activity.

What is the appeal of this relatively new sport? The key word is *action*. Racquetball
15 is played inside a box, an enclosed court with six playing surfaces: the four walls, the floor, and the ceiling. A close relative to squash or four-wall handball, racquetball is a flurry of incredibly swift action. Even be-
20 ginners soon learn to hit the ball at speeds exceeding 80 miles an hour. Split-second decisions require reflexes that astound spectators. The ball ricochets off all sur-faces with apparently little rhyme or rea-
25 son, but competent players swoop balls out of corners, hit balls falling to within a few inches off the floor, and "kill" a smash with-out possibility of return. Quickness of re-sponse is the heart of the game.
30   Why has racquetball won converts from other sports? It requires little equipment: a sturdy racquet, a ball, and, desirably, pro-tective eye covering. It requires relatively little time for a thorough workout. Busy
35 people can squeeze in an exciting match during a lunch hour. It requires only one opponent for a rousing game. Racquetball seems to be an idea whose time has come.

The primary purpose of the passage appears to be _____.

(A) a comparison of squash and racquetball

(B) an explanation of racquetball's recent popularity

(C) a plea for physical fitness

(D) promotion of racquetball as a spectator sport

(E) condemnation of sedentary pursuits

_____

Strategy. The key to this question is the word *primary*. While it is true, for example, that the selection contains an implied plea for physical fitness, this thrust is not the primary purpose of the passage. We can eliminate *(C)*. We can also eliminate *(E)*, for though the author apparently approves of physical activity as opposed to sedentary pursuits, this point is by no means the primary purpose. Squash and racquetball come into comparison slightly, since some squash players have turned to racquetball, but this is a minor detail. Similarly, the appeal of racquetball to spectators takes up a sentence. We can thus reject *(A)* and *(D)*. The remaining possibility, *(B)*, is clearly the answer. The expression *explosive growth* in the opening sentence is a clue to the emphasis in the selection. This question might have been rephrased as one testing generalization.

A good title for this selection is . . . Racquetball: A Popular New Sport.

REVIEW

Try your skill. The passage below is followed by questions based on its content. Use the preceding example to help you find the right answers.

In too many performances of *Hamlet*, Polonius is depicted as a doddering old man, tottering shakily on the edge of senility. In productions like these, Polonius is often
5 played strictly for laughs. His advice to Laertes, though not out of keeping for a typical courtier, is ridiculed by the player's exaggerated infirmity of speech and decrepitude of action. His advice to Ophelia,
10 though reasonable in the context of the times, is made to seem arbitrarily absurd. His admitted garrulity is overemphasized, and his interference in the action is made the work of a clown.
15 Unfortunately for Polonius, there is some justification for laughing at his expense now and then. Hamlet derides Polonius at every opportunity, drawing a laugh from the courtier's eagerness to please at any
20 cost. The King often wishes Polonius would get to the point in breaking important news or giving advice on matters concerning Hamlet. Even the generally kindly Queen says at one time, "More matter with less
25 art." Yet these points are not decisive in any full appraisal of Polonius.

Despite the audience's occasional laughter at Polonius's expense, certain facts remain indisputably true. Till his death
30 Polonius remains a respected member of the court. Throughout the play he has been assigned positions of respect. The King seems to value Polonius's judgment and advice. Though Polonius's advice has
35 proved faulty, the King does not object when Polonius volunteers to spy on Hamlet and his mother. Then in her room, the Queen takes Polonius's ill-fated advice to "be round" with Hamlet. That proves to be
40 the wrong tack.

Polonius meets his fate on an errand he interprets as serving his king, and his death precipitates the final tragedy. Polonius is

not a nonentity, not a character provided for
45 comic relief. He is not a pitiful dotard. He
supplies some of the humor, to be sure, but
a sound case can be made for playing him
as a reasonably typical courtier—not a
mental or spiritual giant, but at least a
50 respectable and generally honored member
of the court at Elsinore.

1. The author's primary purpose in this
   passage is to _____.
   (A) suggest Hamlet's unfairness to-
       ward Polonius
   (B) criticize a little-tried interpreta-
       tion of the part of Polonius
   (C) recommend playing Polonius with
       respect
   (D) suggest Shakespeare's uncer-
       tainty about the characterization
       of Polonius
   (E) recommend playing Polonius with
       relieved seriousness
                                1 ____

2. The purpose of paragraph 2 is to
   _____.
   (A) concede that Polonius can be
       laughed at
   (B) criticize the Queen's hypocrisy to-
       ward Polonius
   (C) suggest that a courtier should oc-
       casionally disagree with the King
   (D) present some of Polonius's strong-
       est character traits
   (E) imply that Polonius is second to
       Hamlet in importance
                                2 ____

3. According to the selection, which of the
   following adjectives may reasonably be
   applied to Polonius?
   I.   cruel   IV. loyal
   II. long-winded V. brilliant
   III. senile

   (A) II only   (D) I, II, and V
   (B) III only   (E) II and IV
   (C) V only
                                3 ____

4. The author points out typical errors in
   the portrayal of Polonius in lines
   _____.
   (A) 1–5   (D) 42–44
   (B) 29–34   (E) 45–51
   (C) 34–37
                                4 ____

5. The death of Polonius is _____.
   (A) not explained in the selection
   (B) well merited
   (C) by order of the King
   (D) sometimes played for laughs
   (E) not expected
                                5 ____

6. Which of the following titles best sum-
   marizes the content of the passage?
   (A) Hamlet and Polonius: A Study in
       Contrasts
   (B) Polonius: An Often-Misunder-
       stood Character
   (C) The Dangers of Meddling
   (D) The Courtier's Role in *Hamlet*
   (E) Minor Characters with Major Im-
       pacts
                                6 ____

7. The meaning of the quotation "More
   matter with less art" can probably be
   expressed as _____.
   (A) "Come to the point."
   (B) "Start from the beginning."
   (C) "Speak more slowly."
   (D) "Repeat your last sentence."
   (E) "Don't breathe a word of this to
       anyone."
                                7 ____

8. The advice to "be round" with Hamlet
   proved to be _____.
   (A) generally sound
   (B) thoughtlessly blunt
   (C) ill-advised
   (D) well-planned
   (E) immediately disregarded
                                8 ____

9. The author's attitude toward Polonius is generally _____.

   (A) bitter   (D) unpredictable
   (B) puzzled   (E) indifferent
   (C) favorable

9 _____

SUMMARY
3. Evaluating the Author's Purpose

Determining the author's purpose calls for a special kind of inference. Some questions require you to discover the purpose of the passage as a whole. Others require you to identify the purpose of a portion of the selection, perhaps a single sentence. When in doubt, use the process of elimination to isolate the correct answer.

4. Evaluating the Author's Style

The author's purpose influences the tone of a passage. His or her attitude affects the purpose. All three are interrelated: purpose, tone, attitude. A fourth element belongs with this group: the author's style. SAT questions sometimes ask you to evaluate an author's style. Questions about style may be general or specific.

Note the difference in phraseology between the following two question types:

1. The style of the passage can best be described as . . .
    This general question can be followed by single-adjective alternatives like *light, argumentative,* or *wordy.*
2. Which of the following best describes the author's technique in this passage?
    This more specific question can be followed by more extended phrases like *trying to justify the use of force in certain circumstances.*

Since an author's technique is an ingredient in his or her special style, both questions ask you to appraise the author's effectiveness and the special flavor of the writing.

TRIAL TEST

Take the following trial test to evaluate your skill.

When a forest is ravaged by fire, cut down to make way for a parking lot, or harvested for timber, there is the esthetic loss of something beautiful. A complete ecosystem is [5] destroyed, and the habitats of forest creatures are laid waste. There is an even more serious long-range problem, however: the effect upon the balance of oxygen and carbon dioxide in the atmosphere. On the one [10] hand, the ever-expanding use of fossil fuels

has liberated into the atmosphere tremendous quantities of carbon dioxide. On the other hand, deforestation has reduced the vegetation needed to recycle the carbon di-
15 oxide, store the carbon, and release essential oxygen for the world's living things. Too much release of stored carbon can also potentially raise the temperature of the atmosphere through the "greenhouse effect."
20 Forest vegetation stores 90% of the carbon held in terrestrial ecosystems. In eastern North America there has been some improvement in recent years through reforestation. But gains in the temperate zone
25 have been offset by losses in the tropics.

Wholesale destruction of tropical forests is the greatest single threat, since most of the world's arboreal vegetation is found in the vast forest of the Amazon and other tropical
30 areas. Global awareness of the problem is needed to provide a basis for sound management of forests, the crucial agents in the carbon cycle.

The style of this passage can best be described as _____.
(A) self-conscious   (D) repetitious
(B) lyrical   (E) frivolous
(C) expository

_____

Problem

Saving money takes odd forms. Comparison shoppers visit half a dozen supermarkets, save a total of $1.73, and spend $1.48 for gasoline. Anglers spend a fortune on
5 fishing gear, bait, boat charges—and catch three small flounders. Writers save odd pieces of string, worn rubber bands, rusty paper clips—and then throw out the lot at one time. Coupon clippers save 30¢ by buy-
10 ing a product when an equally good competing product can be bought for 50¢ less without a coupon. Amateur carpenters buy cheap nuts, bolts, and screws and find them stripping under pressure. Is all this econo-
15 mizing foolish? Not at all.

The comparison shopper has enjoyed the challenge and the pursuit. The angler has had a day on the water getting sunburned and happy. The writer has eased his soul,
20 cleaned the slate, and stimulated his genius to start again. The coupon clipper has had the satisfaction of getting "something for nothing." As for the amateur carpenter— well, eventually he is going to call in a pro-
25 fessional anyway. For his sake and the sake of his homestead, the sooner the better.

1. The style of this passage can best be described as _____.
   (A) serious but astute
   (B) light and cheerful
   (C) perceptive and rhetorical
   (D) critical and unfavorable
   (E) argumentative but good-natured
                                                    1 ____

2. The sentence "For his sake and the sake of his homestead, the sooner the better" can best be described as _____.
   (A) humorous   (D) coarse
   (B) bitter   (E) rigid
   (C) calculated
                                                    2 ____

3. "Something for nothing" is put in quotation marks because _____.
   (A) it suggests the purchaser's buying fantasies
   (B) these are the actual words used in the advertising
   (C) this is an actual quotation by the purchaser
   (D) the quotation is literally true
   (E) the writer believes the purchase is a bargain
                                                    3 ____

Strategy. 1. The topic, "saving money," is not taken seriously. The examples are lighthearted. The mock-serious explanation in paragraph 2 provides another clue to the answer. An expression like "getting sunburned and happy" suggests the writer is not really dealing with a subject seriously. Since the selection is not serious, *(A)* is incorrect. There is no real argument here: the purpose is to provide a chuckle. *(E)* is incorrect. *Rhetorical* eliminates *(C)*. *Unfavorable* eliminates *(D)*. *(B)*, the remaining answer, is an accurate description.

2. The author looks upon the amateur carpenter with amused affection, but doesn't have much faith in his ability. The suggestion to call in a professional "for his sake and the sake of his homestead" is not serious. *(A)* is the answer.

3. There is no indication that anyone or anything is being quoted specifically. *(B)* and *(C)* are incorrect. If the saying were literally true, business would go out of business! *(D)* is incorrect. The writer's revelation that another product just as good could be bought for less proves he or she does not consider this purchase a bargain. The quotation marks suggest the buyer's dream is to get the best bargain for the money. The ultimate bargain is "something for nothing," a will-o'-the-wisp. *(A)* is the answer.

REVIEW

Try your skill. The passage below is followed by questions based on its content. Use the preceding example to help you find the right answers.

Our language is a magnificent achievement, but there are pitfalls built into it—snares that catch the unwary. One of the trickiest problems arises from the fact that
5 the structure of the language does not distinguish between *fact* and *opinion*. "Peyton Manning is a member of the Indianapolis Colts" is a factual statement. "Peyton Manning is the best rookie quarterback of all
10 time" is a statement of opinion. Both sentences *look* the same. Both sentences have the same grammatical structure: *subject, being verb, predicate nominative*. But the difference between the two statements is
15 astronomical. Many of the world's problems could be averted if all people—and especially those in positions of power—could recognize the difference and employ the difference honestly in their speeches.
20 There is an essential difference between a statement of fact and a statement of opinion. "This room is 20 × 24" is a factual statement. We can take out a ruler and check the dimensions. We cannot check the
25 statement "This room is cozy (dreary, small, large, impressive, depressing)."

What's wrong? We all have opinions and express them. There's nothing wrong with having and stating opinions. The danger
30 lies in confusing opinions with facts. If we make opinionated pronouncements and believe they are factual, we are muddying our thought processes and confusing our messages. If we read someone else's opinionated
35 pronouncements and believe they are factual, we are clogging our brains with error.

Statements in factual form may be inaccurate, but at least they can be checked. That room may actually be only 20 × 22.
40 Statements in opinion form are neither *wrong* nor *right* in any test of truth. They are merely expressions of a point of view—interesting, perhaps, but not to be taken as Truth. Statements of opinion tend to tell us

45 more about the speaker or writer than about the subject matter of the statement.

Learning to distinguish between fact and opinion is a test of linguistic sophistication and emotional maturity.

1. The author's style can best be described as _____.
   (A) impassive
   (B) sportive
   (C) ironic
   (D) persuasive
   (E) formal

   1 ____

2. Which of the following best describes the author's technique in this passage?
   (A) Emphasizing the essential weakness of the English language
   (B) Deriding the use of opinion to make any statement
   (C) Presenting a viewpoint without recommending any action
   (D) Using examples to make an important point
   (E) Minimizing the crucial difference between fact and opinion

   2 ____

3. Which of the following sentences best expresses the central idea of the selection?
   (A) "The danger lies in confusing opinions with facts."
   (B) "The difference between the two statements is astronomical."
   (C) "If we read someone else's opinionated pronouncements and believe they are factual, we are clogging our brains with error."
   (D) "The former can be checked."
   (E) "Both sentences have the same grammatical structure: *subject, being verb, predicate nominative*."

   3 ____

4. From the selection we may infer that _____.
   (A) it is worse to state an opinion than to make a factual statement, no matter how erroneous the latter may be
   (B) to call a 20 × 24 room "large" is to make a factual statement
   (C) most speakers intentionally use statements of opinion to mislead
   (D) statements of fact and of opinion are sometimes difficult to tell apart
   (E) a knowledge of grammar will guarantee the ability to distinguish between fact and opinion

   4 ____

5. The writer obviously believes that _____.
   (A) Peyton Manning is the best rookie quarterback
   (B) the same room may be classified as *large* and *small*
   (C) a ruler can settle all arguments of fact
   (D) most people do indeed distinguish sharply between fact and opinion
   (E) a viewpoint is different from an opinion

   5 ____

6. From the passage it may be inferred that _____.
   (A) statements of fact cannot tell us anything about the speaker or writer
   (B) emotions play a larger role in expressions of opinion than in statements of fact
   (C) speakers who avoid statements of opinion are the most respected debaters
   (D) having a point of view is risky
   (E) people in positions of power tend to rely heavily on factual arguments

   6 ____

7. *Truth* is capitalized in line 44 because it represents _____.
(A) substantiated opinion
(B) verifiable fact
(C) fundamental reality
(D) modified skepticism
(E) idiosyncratic viewpoint

7 ____

8. The author's purpose in the last paragraph is to _____.
(A) provide another example of his or her basic thesis
(B) urge readers to be on guard
(C) recommend further studies in semantic evaluation
(D) suggest overtly contesting the opinion of others
(E) reveal hitherto unsuspected similarities between fact and opinion

8 ____

SUMMARY

4. Evaluating the Author's Style

If a person's style expresses who he or she is, then writers put themselves into every page they write. When evaluating the author's style for an SAT question, read the passage through to get the flavor of it. If you are uncertain, read it again. Be on the lookout for certain clues: humorous contradictions, angry pronouncements, subtle suggestions.

Section IV Summary: Understanding the Author's Role

The author's role reveals itself throughout an entire passage.

The *tone* and *attitude* can "be found in the overall impression created by the combination of descriptive and connotative words."

The *purpose* can be discovered by drawing an inference based upon the whole passage (unless, of course, a smaller portion is asked for).

The *style* reveals itself throughout the passage—in humorous touches, angry comments, criticisms, compliments, informal remarks, or formal statements.

The *tone, attitude, purpose,* and *style* are all ingredients calling for an examination of the flavor of the passage, the total impact.

PART 1. Evaluating the Author's Tone (pp. 214–218)

A. Questions that ask about the author's tone provide answer choices of adjectives (*argumentative, ironic, reflective,* etc.) or sometimes nouns (*despair, indifference, sarcasm,* etc.).

B. Get an overall impression of the *whole* passage. Don't worry about details.

C. Think of words that describe its tone. Then choose the answer that best agrees with your description.
D. Most SAT passages are neutral in tone, but a few are not. If a question asks about the tone, it is probably *not* neutral.

PART 2. Evaluating the Author's Attitude (pp. 218–222)
A. Questions ask for such attitudes as admiration, disdain, nostalgia, apathy, and skepticism.
B. Questions about attitude are often quite specific. They ask about the author's attitude *toward someone or something.*
C. Read the question and be sure you understand exactly whom or what it asks about.
D. Look for the persons or things asked for.
E. If you are unsure about specifics, reread the whole passage. Get a sense of the author's feeling toward the entire subject.

PART 3. Evaluating the Author's Purpose (pp. 222–226)
A. Because the author's purpose usually is not stated, you must draw an inference based on the information, tone, and attitude in the passage.
B. Some questions ask about the purpose of the whole passage; others ask about a portion or a detail.
C. Read the question carefully. Be sure you understand what it asks about.
D. Reread what is asked about—the whole passage or a portion—to draw your inference about the purpose.

PART 4. Evaluating the Author's Style (pp. 226–230)
A. Some questions about style are general; they ask for overall judgments of style, offering such word choices as *ironic, persuasive,* and *formal.*
B. Some questions about style are more specific; they ask for certain judgments of technique, offering detailed phrase choices such as *deriding the use of opinion to make any statement.*
C. Read the whole passage to get the flavor of it, the total impact. If you are unsure, reread it.
D. Look for evidence of humor, anger, cleverness, formality, persuasiveness, etc., to form your judgment.

Section V: Understanding Language in Action

1. Evaluating the Author's Diction

SAT questions occasionally ask you to evaluate the use of an author's diction: its aptness or effectiveness. Words acquire special meanings in various contexts. A word's connotation (pages 60-65) is often determined by its neighbors on the printed page. We cannot tell what most words "mean" until they are used. *Old* means one thing when it applies to a joke and quite another when it applies to a person.

This aspect of words is tested in questions like these:

> The word . . . as used in line . . . means . . .
> The narrator suggests that . . . speaks of her husband as if he were . . .
> The word . . . is meant to suggest . . .

Note that the skill being tested is basically the same skill tested in "Context Clues," pages ■4–59. If you have mastered the material on those pages, you should do well with questions of meaning.

TRIAL TEST

Take the trial test to review your skill.

A perplexing mystery disturbs scientists and environmentalists the world over. What has been happening to amphibians? Frogs, toads, and salamanders are disap-
5 pearing from their former habitats. Amphibians, those hardy links between land and water, have survived and flourished for 75 million years . . . until recently. Because they can live in two environments, land and
10 water, they are vulnerable to assault in either medium. They can breathe through their skin, absorbing oxygen under water or above it. They also have humanlike lungs on land. Their permeable skins can absorb
15 toxins from land or water. Some explanations for the disappearances have been offered: acid rain, pesticide runoff, loss of habitat through grazing, logging, land de-velopment, or other human activities. Per-
20 haps a natural danger like an occasional drought may play a role. No explanation offers a completely satisfactory explanation. Amphibian numbers are decreasing even in protected national parks and for-
25 ests, on pristine mountaintops far from man's depredations. From the inhospitable Australian interior to the lush tropical hills of Costa Rica, the puzzle persists.

The word *pristine* as used in line 25 means _____.
(A) towering   (D) rugged
(B) heavily forested   (E) protected
(C) unspoiled

From the contexts, can you guess at the meanings of *perplexing, vulnerable,* and *depredations*?

Problem

The annals of our time are filled with horror stories, of beautiful rivers converted to sewers, of lakes destroyed by acid rain, of forests ruthlessly and thoughtlessly laid waste. There are, fortunately, a growing number of success stories also, tales of people who rolled up their sleeves and refused to be defeated.

For some blasé city dwellers, there is nothing novel under the sun, but New Yorkers have something new to cheer about. In the very backyard of New York City, in the shadow of skyscrapers and right next to busy Kennedy airport, a miracle has taken place. Jamaica Bay Wildlife Refuge, covering 13,000 acres of marsh and woodland, is now a naturalist's paradise. It is home to more than 300 species of birds— nesting not far from the heart of the city.

The refuge did not come into existence overnight. Between World Wars I and II, Jamaica Bay became a disaster area, a dumping ground for sewage and industrial waste. It was an ecologist's nightmare. After World War II the city took steps to clean up the mess. Dikes were built to create two freshwater ponds. Then, in 1953, Herbert Johnson, who was appointed superintendent of the new refuge, planned the gathering and planting of the shrubs, trees, and grasses that make the area a haven for wildlife—for rare birds like the white pelican, the cinnamon teal, and the red-wing thrush.

Now a part of Gateway National Recreation Area, Jamaica Bay Wildlife Refuge has become a mecca for bird-watchers, an idyllic retreat for citizens overwhelmed by city tensions, and a model for other cities to emulate. It is unique. It is probably the "world's only wildlife sanctuary reachable by subway."

1. The word *blasé* in the second paragraph is meant to suggest _____.
 (A) charm   (D) indifference
 (B) enthusiasm   (E) commitment
 (C) anger

1 ____

2. The word *idyllic* in the last paragraph means _____.
 (A) happy and peaceful
 (B) elusive and uncertain
 (C) calm but taut
 (D) spiritual and religious
 (E) slow and unchallenging

2 ____

3. The word *emulate* in the last paragraph adds to imitation the suggestion of _____.
 (A) failing   (D) planning
 (B) striving   (E) envying
 (C) studying

3 ____

Strategy. 1. The phrase *nothing much new under the sun* suggests boredom. If *blasé* means "bored," then it suggests *indifference, (D)*.

2. The contrast of the refuge with city noises and tensions provides the clue: *happy and peaceful, (A)*.

3. The use of the word *model* suggests that other cities might try *(strive)* to imitate the refuge. *(B)* is correct.

REVIEW

Try your skill. The passage below is followed by questions based on its content. Use the preceding example to help you find the right answers.

"Nothing is the way we thought it was, and whatever we think we understand today will be changed to something else when looked at more closely tomorrow."

5 As we look outward from our island in the solar system, space probes and improved technology have changed our view of the cosmos we inhabit. As we direct our study inward, toward the very small, experimen-
10 tation in subatomic physics is changing our understanding of the microcosm. Now Lewis Thomas, author of the quotation above, suggests that biologists also are crossing a new threshold in their study of life forms. Until
15 recently, experts have held some hard-and-fast opinions about the conditions needed for life. Those opinions have now been turned upside down. We have discovered a set of creatures that violate all the rules about life
20 and life-support systems.

At the bottom of certain oceanic abysses, there are, from interior sources, chimneys that heat the sea water to temperatures exceeding 660 degrees Fahrenheit. We
25 know that water turns into steam at 212 degrees at sea level. At 660 degrees water remains a liquid only because it is under enormous pressure. Everything we thought we knew suggested that life could not sur-
30 vive in this superheated water under 265 atmospheres of pressure. But it does.

When John Baross and some fellow oceanographers scooped up water from a depth of 2,600 meters, they discovered liv-
35 ing bacteria flourishing in the superheated liquid. Later, Baross and Jody Deming of Johns Hopkins University proceeded to du-plicate these extreme conditions and grow these incredible life forms. They were
40 amazed to discover that at 482 degrees Fahrenheit the bacteria increased a thou-

sandfold in six hours. If "chilled" just below boiling, the bacteria would not grow at all.

Their joint discovery has opened up vast
45 new vistas. These bacteria produce meth-ane, hydrogen, and carbon monoxide. There is a possibility these tiny creatures might play a role in long-range geologic change. They might become a valuable source of a
50 new natural gas industry. Their enzymes might be useful in industrial processes that involve high temperatures and pressures.

When we think we have closed a door on one corridor of science, another door swings
55 wide open. Fixed ideas and closed minds have no place in science. The world is truly the home of miracles.

1. The word *microcosm* in line 11 means
   _____.
   (A) little world
   (B) scientific method
   (C) galaxy
   (D) scientific instrument
   (E) exploration

   1 ____

2. The word *abysses* in line 21 is meant to suggest _____.
   (A) extreme heat
   (B) submarine peaks
   (C) underwater vegetation
   (D) great depths
   (E) submerged continents

   2 ____

3. The word *chilled* in line 42 is enclosed in quotation marks because _____.
   (A) it is taken directly from Lewis Thomas' article
   (B) the writer intended to use a bet-ter word
   (C) the water was hot
   (D) Lewis Thomas disagrees with John Baross
   (E) the experiment was essentially in-exact

   3 ____

4. The author's purpose is to _____.
  (A) amuse and entertain while enlightening the reader
  (B) suggest a sense of wonder at recent discoveries
  (C) engage in a subtle debate over the value of "pure research"
  (D) discredit any experimentation that cannot be repeated
  (E) criticize biologists of the past

  4 ____

5. The bacteria grew a thousandfold at temperatures of _____.
  (A) 212 degrees   (D) 600 degrees
  (B) 265 degrees   (E) 2,650 degrees
  (C) 482 degrees

  5 ____

6. Which of the following best expresses the main idea of the selection?
  (A) Bacteria are remarkably adaptable organisms.
  (B) Baross and Deming are pioneers in an unexplored area.
  (C) Scientists must be ready to accept and explore new ideas.
  (D) The oceans may solve most of our problems.
  (E) Life can survive in inhospitable environments.

  6 ____

7. The passage suggests that _____.
  (A) we have barely scratched the surface of knowledge
  (B) oceanographers, as a group, are superior to physicists
  (C) life is certain to be found on the moon
  (D) there are no miracles in science
  (E) the various ice ages are attributable to the deep-sea bacteria

  7 ____

8. One effect of putting water under great pressure is to _____.
  (A) prevent instruments from probing it
  (B) kill all life forms
  (C) change its subatomic structure
  (D) release enzymes useful for industry
  (E) prevent heated water from turning into steam

  8 ____

SUMMARY

1. Evaluating the Author's Diction

Questions about diction on the SAT rely heavily upon context (page 24). When you answer such questions, carefully study the surrounding words. Use the various clues—contrast, pairing, signal words, direct explanation—to help you identify the correct alternative. All the words in a reading selection directly or indirectly affect the total context. Identifying one element in the fabric often requires understanding of the whole.

2. Understanding Figurative Language

Your ability to interpret a figurative expression may be tested on the SAT. You will most likely be asked to identify the hidden comparison in a metaphor, but other figures of speech may also be tested.

This aspect of words is tested in a question like this:

> The author uses the phrase *towering battlements* to describe . . .

In that particular question the *towering battlements* are skyscrapers. In another context they might apply to cliffs, tall trees, or castles.

Note that the skill being tested is basically the same skill tested in "Figurative Language," pages 66–71. If you have mastered that material, you should do well with questions involving figurative language.

TRIAL TEST

Take the trial test to review your skills.

The victim explained from his hospital bed, "I had the right-of-way at the intersection."

Nearly half of all accidents occur at inter-
5 sections, especially intersections with traffic lights. Good preventive driving practice
requires caution at all times. "Expect the
worst" is one expert's advice. Writing in the
AAA magazine, Deborah Allen says, "Even
10 if you think you have the right-of-way, don't
assume that cross-traffic is going to stop for
you. Check both ways to make sure the
intersection is clear of both vehicles and
pedestrians before you move out into it. If
15 you're approaching an intersection as the
light turns green, take your foot off the gas
pedal and be prepared to brake if necessary.
Look first to the left and then to the right—
then to the left again—to make sure the
20 intersection is clear." Whether you brake or
accelerate depends upon the traffic pattern.
If a lumbering juggernaut heads for you,
accelerating and proper steering, rather
than braking, may avert an accident. If you
25 expect the worst, you'll be prepared.

The author uses the phrase "lumbering juggernaut" to mean a _____.
(A) heavy vehicle
(B) speeding ambulance
(C) school bus
(D) construction truck
(E) trailer

Problem

We left our houseboat and stepped into
a shikara, that all-purpose floating store,
post office, florist shop, supply vessel,
water taxi, and suburban bus. Not unlike
5 a Venetian gondola, the shikara is easily
and effectively maneuverable by one person, sometimes poling, sometimes pad-
dling. Because power boats would pollute
beautiful Dal Lake, the jewel of the Vale
10 of Kashmir, the shikara reigns supreme,
darting back and forth across the surface
with charm and grace.

Soon we left the open charms of Dal Lake
for a tributary of the River Jhelum. A hand-

15 operated lock regulates the water level of the lake and prevents river pollutants from flowing back into the lake. Through narrow passageways lined with houseboats in every stage of repair and disrepair, we
20 floated noiselessly along, observing the everyday life of the Kashmiri, waving to happy children and nodding gravely to older members of the river community. Here was poverty but not ugliness. Beauti-
25 ful pewter implements graced the shelves of even the poorest houseboat. Washed clothes hung to dry from every home, no matter how modest.

After 45 minutes and another lock, we
30 were carried into the broad expanse of the River Jhelum. Instead of simple houseboats, tall multiple dwellings lined the river on both sides. A five-story apartment house, at a Pisa-like angle, clung to the hillside
35 with Kashmiri tenacity. Old and decrepit, this aged skeleton still housed families glad for some shelter in a crowded land. By contrast, the crumbling palace of a former maharajah, a ghostly sepulcher, showed no
40 signs of life.

The vitality of the Kashmiri, their will to survive, is epitomized in the river and the vitality along the river banks. If life is a river, each Kashmiri has a shikara to carry
45 him along.

1. The "suburban bus" in the first sentence is _____.
   (A) a front-wheel-drive vehicle
   (B) an official car
   (C) a boat
   (D) a tractor
   (E) a houseboat

   1 ____

2. The "skeleton" referred to in the third paragraph is _____.
   (A) a former palace
   (B) a sinking houseboat
   (C) a condominium
   (D) a temple
   (E) an apartment house

   2 ____

3. The phrase "ghostly sepulcher" in the third paragraph suggests _____.
   (A) lifelessness
   (B) a supernatural tale
   (C) plague
   (D) limited vitality
   (E) a legend

   3 ____

4. The expression "Pisa-like angle" suggests that the house _____.
   (A) has collapsed
   (B) is basically sound
   (C) has a holy aura
   (D) is leaning
   (E) is being rebuilt

   4 ____

5. The shikara in the last sentence is _____.
   (A) a gondola
   (B) a native ferry
   (C) a canoe
   (D) a government steamship
   (E) not a boat

   5 ____

Strategy. 1. Like the five other functions, *suburban* bus is a function of the shikara. *(C)* is the correct answer.

2. The context tells us this "aged skeleton" still housed families. It is clearly the apartment house, *(E)*.

3. *Ghostly sepulcher* is contrasted with the lively apartment house, with all its people and vitality. It does not have even limited vitality, *(D)*. *(A), lifelessness,* is correct.

4. One of Pisa's claims to fame is the Leaning Tower. If the angle is Pisa-like, the building *is leaning, (D).*

5. The meaning of boat and river shifts here. Life is compared with a river. Then shikara must refer to the strength each Kashmiri has to carry him along that difficult river. In any event, shikara does not mean a boat here. *(E), not a boat,* is correct.

REVIEW

Try your skill. The passage below is followed by questions based on its content. Use the preceding examples to help you find the right answers.

The Extraordinary is easy. And the more extraordinary the Extraordinary is, the easier it is: "easy" in the sense that we can almost always recognize it. . . . The Ex-
5 traordinary does not let you shrug your shoulders and walk away.

But the Ordinary is a much harder case. In the first place, by making itself so notice-able—it is around us all the time—the Or-
10 dinary has got itself in a bad fix with us: we hardly ever notice it. The Ordinary, simply by *being* so ordinary, tends to make us ig-norant or neglectful; when something does not insist on being noticed, when we aren't
15 grabbed by the collar or struck on the skull by a presence or an event, we take for granted the very things that most deserve our gratitude.

And this is the chief vein and deepest
20 point concerning the Ordinary: that it *does* deserve our gratitude. The Ordinary lets us live out our humanity; it doesn't scare us, it doesn't excite us, it doesn't distract us. . . . Ordinariness can be defined as a breathing-
25 space: the breathing-space between getting born and dying, perhaps, or else the breath-ing-space between rapture and rapture; or, more usually, the breathing-space between one disaster and the next. Ordinariness is
30 sometimes the *status quo,* sometimes the

slow, unseen movement of a subtle but in-eluctable cycle, like a ride on the hour hand of the clock; in any case the Ordinary is above all *what is expected.*

35 And what is expected is not often thought of as a gift.

1. The author uses the phrase "struck on the skull" in line 15 to mean _____.
   (A) seriously injured
   (B) mildly irritated
   (C) overwhelmed
   (D) physically confronted
   (E) overlooked

   1 ____

2. A "breathing-space between rapture and rapture" in lines 26–27 could be described as _____.
   (A) an uneventful period
   (B) a preparation for excitement
   (C) a reliving of an exciting past
   (D) an unsuspected tension
   (E) a crucial training regimen

   2 ____

3. The important characteristic of "a ride on the hour hand of the clock" in lines 32–33 is that it is _____.
   (A) slow and boring
   (B) depressingly time-consuming
   (C) subtle but unavoidable
   (D) characterized by staccato leaps
   (E) not always welcome

   3 ____

4. Ordinariness may be _____.
(A) cyclical or unchanging
(B) cyclical and unexpected
(C) cyclical and upsetting
(D) unchanging or revolutionary
(E) unexpected or rapturous

4 ____

5. The author implies that you can shrug your shoulders and walk away from _____.
(A) the Extraordinary
(B) the rapturous
(C) the unexpected
(D) the Ordinary
(E) the neglectful

5 ____

6. This selection is basically _____.
(A) a snide comment on pretense
(B) an attack on boredom
(C) a praise of the predictable
(D) an exposé of the "average"
(E) a paean to excitement

6 ____

7. The author thinks that we take too much for granted those things that are _____.
(A) noticeable   (D) cyclical
(B) ordinary   (E) unexpected
(C) critical

7 ____

SUMMARY

2. Understanding Figurative Language

Someone once said of figurative language "it is what it isn't." Figurative expressions always mean more than they seem to say. Get behind the author's literal language and see if the author is making a subtle comparison. Figurative language is a kind of poetry. You need to use your imagination for best results.

3. Evaluating Degree and Exclusion

Sometimes the phraseology of SAT questions requires a reversal of familiar techniques. Questions of this type are usually phrased as follows:

1. With which of the following statements would the author be LEAST likely to agree?
2. In the passage, the author exhibits all of the following attitudes toward the surroundings EXCEPT . . .
3. It can be inferred from the passage that all of the following might explain why the author describes the EARTH as "presumably lifeless" EXCEPT . . .

These questions are the reverse of most questions. Ordinarily you are asked to choose the main idea or the most likely statement. In question 1 you do the opposite. You choose the *least* likely statement. Similarly, questions like 2 or 3 list a majority of items that are included and ask you to choose the one that is *not* included. These test many skills already touched upon, even though the phraseology is different.

TRIAL TEST

Take the trial test to evaluate your skill.

When an insect army marches on trees, the old warriors are not without their own defenses. Scientists once thought that insect populations were controlled only by the
5 weather and by natural predators, like birds. New findings, however, show that trees and other plants are not passive victims. They fight back with an arsenal of deadly chemicals to thwart the insect
10 hordes. What is even more amazing is that trees under siege may warn their neighbors to get ready to fight!

Apparently when insects begin to ravage a tree, the tree sends poisonous chemicals
15 into its leaves to discourage or kill the invader. What is more, the tree sets off a silent alarm. An airborne chemical from the infested tree is carried to neighboring trees. Forewarned, the neighboring trees increase
20 the concentration of chemicals in *their* leaves to protect themselves from the rampaging horde.

Different plants create different chemicals. A short-lived wildflower often has ex-
25 tremely powerful toxins ready to repel any insect invader before it strikes. Since it has little time to grow and reproduce, it cannot waste any time. Long-lived trees, on the other hand, have a more elaborate strategy.
30 Some of their chemicals merely interfere with an insect's digestion. Others are more deadly. In the continuing battle between insect and plant life, the stationary, exposed plants are not entirely defenseless,
35 even without man's intervention.

1. With which of the following statements would the author be LEAST likely to agree?
   (A) Without man's help, the great forests of the Northeast would be almost entirely denuded.
   (B) Insects avoid plants with toxic chemicals as their first line of defense.
   (C) In some way or other, trees transmit crucial messages to other trees.
   (D) Insect populations are not entirely controlled by birds and weather.
   (E) Plants vary in their ability to fight infestation.

   1 ____

2. In the struggle against insect infestations, the author mentions all of the following defenses EXCEPT _____.
   (A) chemicals that interfere with digestion
   (B) powerful toxins
   (C) messages from one tree to another
   (D) other insects
   (E) concentration of chemicals

   2 ____

Problem

There is nothing more alone in the universe than man. He is alone because he has the intellectual capacity to know that he is separated by a vast gulf of social memory
5 and experiment from the lives of his animal associates. He has entered into the strange world of history, of social and intellectual change, while his brothers of the field and forest remain subject to the invisible laws
10 of biological evolution. Animals are molded by natural forces they do not comprehend. To their minds there is no past and no future. There is only the everlasting present of a single generation—its trails in the
15 forest, its hidden pathways of the air and in the sea.

Man, by contrast, is alone with the knowledge of his history until the day of his death. When we were children we wanted to talk to animals and struggled to understand why this was impossible. Slowly we gave up the attempt as we grew into the solitary world of human adulthood; the rabbit was left on the lawn, the dog was relegated to his kennel. Only in acts of inarticulate compassion, in rare and hidden moments of communion with nature, does man briefly escape his solitary destiny. Frequently in science fiction he dreams of worlds with creatures whose communicative power is the equivalent of his own.

1. With which of the following statements would the author be LEAST likely to agree?
   (A) In reality, children would like a closer communion with animals.

(B) Man's solitary destiny is sometimes escaped, but only for brief moments.
(C) Animals intuitively understand more than does man.
(D) Social and intellectual change has molded man.
(E) Science fiction may be a kind of wish fulfillment.

                                    1 ____

2. All the following are mentioned as characteristic of man EXCEPT _____.
   (A) social memory
   (B) living completely in the present
   (C) knowledge of history
   (D) hidden moments of communion
   (E) acts of compassion

                                    2 ____

Strategy. 1. Man's peculiar and unique destiny is awareness—of past and future. The first sentence in the second paragraph specifically says that man is *alone.* The animals cannot share his experience. *(C),* which gives animals a greater awareness, is in contradiction to the sense of the passage. *(C)* is correct.

2. Animals, rather than man, are able to live in *the everlasting present of a single generation. (B)* is correct.

REVIEW

Try your skill. The passage below is followed by questions based on its content.

Few manifestations of natural forces are as terrifying as the tsunami, the tidal wave that begins as a disturbance in the sea because of an earthquake and ends as a devastating wall of water inundating an unprotected shore. As the tsunami strikes the shore, it may exceed 100 feet in height. Its power and destructiveness are awesome. A tsunami arising from the explosion of the volcano Krakatoa, west of Java, killed more than 36,000 people 100 years ago. In 1896, on the northeast coast of Honshu in Japan, a tsunami killed more than 27,000 people. Modern detection and warning systems have greatly reduced the loss of life from these deadly waves, but as recently as 1983 a tsunami raised havoc on the northwest coast of Honshu. Human error delayed the warning and many children lost their lives.

Some readers picture tsunamis as towers of water, rushing across the surface of the ocean, causing ships to rise and fall a hundred feet in a few seconds. Nothing could be further from the truth. Storm waves may indeed rise to mountainous heights at sea and toss ships about like corks. Not tsuna-

mis. If a tsunami passes beneath a boat in the open ocean, the passengers may be un-
30 aware of the gentle rise and fall of water, so slight does it seem. These mild swells become deadly as the tsunami approaches land. The ocean becomes shallower. Friction builds up. The sea bottom near shore is
35 exposed as the tsunami seems to draw in its breath before striking. Fish and other sea creatures flop about on the hitherto unexposed sea bottom. Then the tsunami strikes with devastating effect, crushing buildings
40 near shore, tossing about ships in the harbor, washing out to sea any curious, unlucky bystanders.

The basic difference between a tsunami and other sea waves is in the length of the
45 wave, between crest and crest. Tsunamis, generated by a displacement in the land beneath the sea, have extraordinarily long wavelengths. William Van Dorn of the Scripps Institution of Oceanography in La
50 Jolla, California, says, "A big wave is generated when you move a big piece of real estate perhaps the size of Indiana a couple of meters." This tremendous displacement causes a huge bulge on the water that races
55 out in all directions. These waves may move out with jet-plane speeds—as high as 600 m.p.h. Since the Pacific area is marked by geologic instability, most tsunamis occur in that area, with Japan particularly vulnera-
60 ble to their deadly arrival.

These seismic sea waves appropriately have the Japanese name, *tsunami;* Japan, located on the Ring of Fire, is frequently hit. The Pacific is encircled by a zone of earth-
65 quake and volcanic activity. Seismic activities anywhere in the vast area may have consequences thousands of miles away.

There have been destructive tsunamis in other areas, however. About 1450 B.C. the
70 volcano on the island of Thera in the Aegean Sea exploded. The resulting tsunami seriously crippled the Minoan civilization. More than 3000 years later, a catastrophic earthquake struck Lisbon on November 1,
75 1755. The resulting waves and aftershocks killed 60,000 people.

The Pacific Tsunami Warning Center in Hawaii monitors potential tsunami activity and sends out warnings of the impending
80 arrival of a tsunami, along with its strength and probable arrival time. These warnings do not prevent destruction of property but they do save lives.

1. With which of the following statements would the author be LEAST likely to agree?
   (A) The tsunami can have severe economic and social effects.
   (B) A tsunami is immediately recognizable at the point of origin because of the great height of water generated above it.
   (C) The excitement of watching a tsunami approach a shore outweighs any slight danger attendant upon the observation.
   (D) Tsunamis are quite different from storm waves, both in origin and in appearances.
   (E) An area with much volcanic activity is more likely to generate a tsunami than a more stable area.

   1 ____

2. All of the following are characteristic of the tsunami EXCEPT _____.
   (A) tie-in with earthquakes
   (B) great height at the shore
   (C) slow speed of dispersal
   (D) shallow height at sea
   (E) prevalence in the Pacific area

   2 ____

3. If faced by an approaching tsunami on the open sea, the best procedure for a ship's captain to protect the ship is to _____.
   (A) turn the prow of the ship into the wave
   (B) steam in the same direction as the tsunami
   (C) alert all passengers to stand by for lifeboat drill
   (D) radio for help as a precautionary measure
   (E) take no unusual steps

   3 _____

4. The author uses the phrase "draw in its breath" to mean _____.
   (A) pull water away from the shore
   (B) send jets of water forward
   (C) completely squander its strength
   (D) generate a strong wind
   (E) meet resistance on the beach

   4 _____

5. The author uses the phrase "seismic activities" to indicate _____.
   (A) waves
   (B) wavelengths
   (C) friction
   (D) detection
   (E) earthquakes

   5 _____

6. In the grip of a storm, ships are compared with _____.
   (A) walls
   (B) sea creatures
   (C) corks
   (D) crushed buildings
   (E) mild swells

   6 _____

7. The best example of figurative language is the expression _____.
   (A) earthquake zone
   (B) deadly waves
   (C) Ring of Fire
   (D) warning systems
   (E) unprotected shore

   7 _____

8. Which of the following titles best summarizes the content of this passage?
   (A) Earthquakes: The Unexpected Enemy
   (B) The Ring of Fire
   (C) The Killer Waves
   (D) Detecting Tsunamis
   (E) Nature at Its Deadliest

   8 _____

SUMMARY

3. Evaluating Degree and Exclusion

Least and *except* questions are merely variations of questions already discussed and tested. A *least* question calls for the opposite of a main idea. An *except* question asks you to identify a missing item. The key to success with these questions is reading the directions carefully.

Section V Summary: Understanding Language in Action

How the author uses language is a legitimate testing area for the SAT. When asked to supply a meaning for a word in a reading passage, examine the context carefully. The question will not ordinarily ask for a strict dictionary definition. It will ask you to consider how the word is being used in the text selection (Connotation and Denotation, pages 60–65). It may also ask you to consider whether or not there are figurative meanings concealed in the text (pages 66–71). When reading LEAST and EXCEPT questions, be especially careful.

Review these strategies for understanding language in action as you prepare for the SAT.

PART 1. Evaluating the Author's Diction (pp. 232–235)

A. Questions on diction ask about the meaning and usage of specific words in the context of a passage.

B. Deciding on a word's meaning is the same skill as using context clues.

C. Read at least the whole sentence to decide on a word meaning.

D. Use your "Context Clues" (pages 24–59): the entire sentence, pairing, direct explanation, comparison, contrast, sequence, signal words.

PART 2. Understanding Figurative Language (pp. 236–239)

A. Giving the meaning for a figurative expression is the same skill explained in "Figurative Language" (pages 66–71).

B. Most such questions ask for the meaning of a metaphor, such as *lumbering juggernaut* for a *heavy vehicle*.

C. Find the expression and read at least the whole sentence in which it occurs. Then decide on the meaning.

D. Use your knowledge of "Figurative Language": metaphor, simile, personification, metonymy, synecdoche, hyperbole, understatement, irony.

PART 3. Evaluating Degree and Exclusion (pp. 239–243)

A. "Least" and "except" questions are the reverse of most SAT questions.

B. A "least" question asks for a statement with which the author would be *least* likely to agree.

C. An "except" question presents information or statements, all of which the author would agree with *except* one.

D. Read "least" or "except" questions *very* carefully. Remember, they are the reverse of most questions.

E. Check back through the passage for information as needed.

Section VI: Looking Beyond the Passage

1. Predicting Outcomes

SAT questions occasionally ask you to take a step beyond the selection, to predict what will happen next. The required skill is an extension of drawing an inference—with one difference. Instead of inferring something about an idea or event in the selection, you must decide what the future consequences of an idea or event will be.

Questions of this type may be phrased as follows:

1. The final statement in the passage suggests which of the following outcomes?
2. Which of the following is likely to happen next?

Though the answer is not spelled out in the reading selection, there are clues to help you. If an anxious lawyer candidate receives notice he or she has passed the bar exam, his or her likely reaction is exuberance. Read between the lines and take one step further. Though other answers may be possible, the most probable answer is the one to choose.

TRIAL TEST

Take the trial test to evaluate your skill.

Ted glanced across the net at his opponent, Frank Gilbert, number one seed in the tournament. Coolly waiting for Ted to serve, Frank danced lightly on his toes and
5 smiled. Through dogged determination, Ted had stayed close in this final match and had kept the score respectable. But having lost the first set, 6–3, and dropped behind, 5–1, in the second set, Ted knew that the
10 match was nearly over.

Frank was living up to his reputation as a hard hitter with control and finesse. With a backhand as good as his forehand, Frank moved to either side easily to return the ball
15 with grace and authority. In desperation Ted had tried lobbing over the head of his opponent, but Frank reached up and showed an overhead shot as strong as his forehand. Ted searched his memory for ad-
20 vice from friends and coaches. "When in trouble, change your game. Whatever you've been doing—drop it. Do something different. Instead of angling your shots, hit back toward your opponent's belt buckle.
25 What have you got to lose?"

Ted served. Frank returned the ball with apparent ease. The rally continued. Then Ted tried a drop shot from midcourt. It was a beauty, falling two feet from the net.
30 Frank rushed in, scooped it up and gently lobbed the ball over Ted's head. The first point went to Frank. Ted served to Frank's backhand. The ball came back to Ted's forehand. "I've got to change," thought Ted as
35 he moved toward the ball.

1. The final statement in the passage suggests which of the following outcomes?
   (A) Ted hits a smashing drive to Frank's backhand.
   (B) Ted tries a deep lob over Frank's head.
   (C) Frank unexpectedly rushes the net.
   (D) Ted hits the ball directly at Frank.
   (E) Ted glances up into the stands and gets a secret signal from his coach.

   1 ____

2. Which of the following suggests the most probable outcome of the match?
   (A) Ted turns the match around and wins in three sets.
   (B) After Frank has won in two sets, the two boys shake hands.
   (C) After losing in two sets, Ted refuses to shake hands with Frank.
   (D) Ted wins the second set, but Frank comes back to win the third.
   (E) In exasperation, Ted walks off the court and defaults.

   2 ____

Problem

On a quiet St. Valentine's Day in 1981, 12-year-old Todd Domboski ran across his grandmother's yard in Centralia, Pennsylvania. Suddenly a 100-foot pit opened beneath his feet and he tumbled in. Fortunately a tree root broke his fall, and his cousin was able to pull him safely to the surface. This frightening episode symbolizes the troubles of Centralia, a once-prosperous mining town in the heart of some of the richest anthracite regions in the world. Centralia has a devastating problem. Beneath the streets and houses of this community, a coal-fire has been burning for decades. No one knows just how long. Each year increases the danger as the fire spreads through rich coal seams and old mine tunnels.

Many efforts have been made to drown, smother, or in some other way contain the blaze, but every effort has failed. There is just not enough water for drowning it. There are too many natural vents to smother it. The fire could take a hundred years to burn out—or a thousand. It could spread to an additional 3,500 acres with potential for even greater havoc.

What have been the results of the fire thus far? Carbon monoxide seeps into houses, posing serious threats to health and life. Basement walls crack. Lawns sink several feet into the ground. Steam vents make the area seem like the thermal display of Yellowstone National Park.

Some residents have already left. Many are reluctant to leave their homesteads, hoping against hope that the fire will burn itself out. Most, however, have reached the conclusion that the situation is hopeless and are asking the federal government for financial assistance in relocating. The financial burden would be enormous, and officials are seeking solutions that would not harm the residents.

In Calamity Hollow, Pennsylvania, a smaller mine fire turned out to be a blessing. A new technique called *controlled burning* did not attack the fire, attempting fruitlessly to put it out. Instead this innovation used the underground fire to produce natural energy in this huge natural furnace. Controlled burning can actually produce heat and electricity at a profit.

There are two additional advantages to controlled burning. First, it utilizes coal that would otherwise be wasted. Even an abandoned mine retains at least half its coal. Secondly, by fanning the flames this method could end mine fires much sooner than they would die out on their own.

The history of humankind is filled with disasters that turned out to have many

beneficial results. War, the ultimate horror, has accelerated medical and surgical im-
65 provements. Citywide fires have encouraged inhabitants to re-build—and improve. To be sure, no one recommends encouraging disasters so that we might be tested and thus make far-reaching discoveries. But
70 sometimes misfortunes may open doors to new achievements.

1. Which of the following suggests the most probable outcome of the Centralia problem?
   (A) Most former inhabitants will be encouraged to return.
   (B) Profit from controlled burning will finance the relocation of Centralians.

(C) Controlled burning will be found to be impractical for Centralia.
(D) The government will make one last concerted attempt to put the underground fire out.
(E) The Centralia fire will influence the price of coal on the open market.

1 ____

2. The future of controlled burning as a solution to underground fires can best be described as _____.
   (A) dubious   (D) uneconomical
   (B) hopeless   (E) unpopular
   (C) encouraging

2 ____

Strategy. 1. Since all efforts at putting out the fire have failed miserably, it is unlikely the government will try again. *(D)* is incorrect. For the same reasons, it is unlikely that most inhabitants will return. *(A)* is incorrect. There is no indication that this fire in a small area of the United States could influence the price of coal. *(E)* is incorrect. There is no suggestion that the controlled burnout technique would not be successful in Centralia. Its inclusion in this excerpt clearly suggests it is a likely solution for the Centralia problem. *(C)* is incorrect. Since the selection mentions the profit from controlled burning, *(B)* is the most likely answer.

2. The excerpt is clearly enthusiastic about the future of controlled burning. The two advantages listed are specific clues. *(C)* is the most likely answer.

REVIEW

Try your skill. The passage below is followed by questions based on its content. Use the preceding example to help you find the right answer.

Half a billion books have been published since Gutenberg printed his first Bible. Publication has reached flood proportions, with many, many thousands published
5 each year. And each year about the same number go out of print. What happens to this abundance of out-of-print books?

Most books disappear from public notice within a few years. They are stored in dusty
10 attics, damp basements, and back rooms. They are discarded in paper drives. They find their way to church fairs, old bookstores, and library book sales. The bright promise of their publication fades, and they
15 land in ignominious heaps on the tables of discount dealers, sold at a fraction of their publication price.

Many are physically destroyed. Fire and flood take a heavy toll. The deterioration of

20 cheap paper consigns many to the dustheap prematurely. A great many titles disappear utterly.

Despite the hazards of existence, many titles do survive in odd and unusual places.
25 There are some clever book detectives who make their living hunting up wanted out-of-print books and selling them at a high enough markup to provide a living. These bookfinders are ingenious, resourceful, per-
30 sistent, and often lucky!

Donald Dryfoos is a successful book detective. As he describes his business, "One, you find the people who want to find books; two, you find the books." Both steps require time
35 and effort.

Dryfoos has built up a list of regular customers. Some are individuals. Some are publishers. Some are other booksellers. When he is given a title to find, he checks
40 his own stock and then goes hunting elsewhere. He makes no charge for the search, but the price he gets for the book must cover his expenses. Profits from individual sale are not tremendous, but the thrill of the
45 search keeps Dryfoos ever on the trail.

What kind of people send out lists of books they want to find? Dryfoos calls them *uncategorizable.* They're all different. They all want different books. A bookstore spe-
50 cializing in bestsellers sells hundreds of copies of the same book. "To me that would be boring," insists Dryfoos.

Although customers vary, there are a few discernible trends. One group seeks books
55 with happy childhood associations. These people want their children or grandchildren to share their remembered joys. Another group specializes in medicine, science, music, or another field. These people want
60 to build up a specialized library, sometimes to provide a bibliography for a doctoral degree. Still another group has discovered an author, like Doris Miles Disney, whose works strike a responsive chord. These peo-
65 ple will buy anything by the favorite author.

Dryfoos has extensive sources beyond his own stock. Like all bookfinders, he frequents book fairs, hastily checking the books donated by retirees, house
70 redesigners, people moving out of state, legatees who don't want to be bothered with the impedimenta of an uncle's life. The competition between bookfinders is keen, and the pace is swift.

75 He has frequented the stores of all his competitors and knows where many titles can be found. He confesses, "I can't remember what I had for breakfast, but I remember the location of those books." As he says,
80 it's a lot of fun just to meander through bookstores, even though it cannot provide a reasonable financial result for time spent.

Dryfoos has also built up contacts with many book suppliers throughout the coun-
85 try—bookstores and private libraries. Dealers who specialize in a particular field send him their catalogs. The magazine *AB Bookman's Weekly* provides advertising space for dealers on the prowl for certain
90 titles.

How successful is the search? "We find very close to exactly 50 percent of the books we look for," says Dryfoos. If the book is to be found, it will probably be located within
95 six weeks. As time goes on, hope dims, though occasionally a book will unexpectedly turn up late in the search.

A true book detective is a lover of books. The same amount of skill, intelligence, and
100 persistence when applied in another field might bring more lucrative results. But a true book lover picks up a book with affection and anticipation. Every book is a key to a world beyond its pages.

1. If Donald Dryfoos found a book requested by one of his clients, he would probably _____.
   (A) send it out immediately to the customer
   (B) send the customer a description of the book's condition, together with its price
   (C) arrange to have the book cleaned up and rebound if it were discovered in imperfect condition
   (D) keep it temporarily for himself and the next customer, while looking for another copy of the book
   (E) contact another customer to set up a competitive bidding situation

   1 ____

2. The word *ignominious* in line 15 is meant to suggest the _____.
   (A) author's crushed hope
   (B) publisher's anger
   (C) bookfinder's irritation
   (D) editor's embarrassment
   (E) advertiser's loss of revenue

   2 ____

3. The primary purpose of the passage appears to be to _____.
   (A) explain   (D) irritate
   (B) amuse   (E) challenge
   (C) persuade

   3 ____

4. The word *uncategorizable* in line 48 is applied to _____.
   (A) remaindered books
   (B) professional magazines
   (C) buyers of used books
   (D) bookfinders
   (E) book fair sponsors

   4 ____

5. The legatees in lines 70-71 may best be characterized as _____.
   (A) prudent   (D) disloyal
   (B) cruel   (E) impatient
   (C) antagonistic

   5 ____

6. All the following are mentioned as book-finding methods EXCEPT _____.
   (A) attending book fairs
   (B) tapping competitors' stocks
   (C) advertising in a magazine
   (D) getting in touch with private libraries
   (E) dealing directly with the original publishers

   6 ____

7. Which of the following best expresses the main idea of the passage?
   (A) Publishers are missing out on a profitable sideline.
   (B) Finding specific old books is an almost hopeless task.
   (C) Book detectives, on average, are wealthy individuals.
   (D) Looking for out-of-print books can be an exciting search.
   (E) Library book fairs are excellent sources for wanted books.

   7 ____

8. Doris Miles Disney is mentioned as an author _____.
   (A) of children's books
   (B) of professional books
   (C) in demand
   (D) for candidates of doctoral degrees
   (E) who is never remaindered

   8 ____

9. From this selection we may infer that
_____.

(A) more books are published in science than in literature
(B) book dealers never cooperate with each other
(C) Dryfoos stays in his business primarily for monetary reasons
(D) many books in recent years have been printed on rapidly deteriorating paper
(E) there are no original Gutenberg Bibles in existence

9 ____

SUMMARY

1. Predicting Outcomes

When asked to predict outcomes, read the passage carefully for clues that point the way to future activity. Your answer should be consistent with the elements in the passage. It should reasonably be inferred from the salient points in the selection itself. Keep in mind that though all suggested answers may be possible, you will be asked to choose the most probable.

2. Providing an Application

Another skill that takes you beyond the passage itself is providing applications of ideas in the reading passage. Like predicting outcomes, this skill requires that you carefully analyze the content of the passage and then take a step beyond. From a general principle in the passage, you might be asked to make a specific application. If, for example, the selection discussed the advantages of speed reading as a general skill, you might be asked to decide whether a light novel, an editorial, a math textbook, an article on quantum physics, or a legal contract should be read rapidly.

Here, for example, are two application questions taken directly from the SAT.

1. According to the information in the passage, an artist inspired by the basic principles of African art would most likely have produced which of the following?
2. The author believes that an "ordinary" person (lines 17 and 31) would be most likely to agree with which of the following statements about art?

TRIAL TEST

Take the trial test to evaluate your skill.

Logical reasoning is usually classified as one of two kinds: inductive and deductive.

People use both types often without knowing their names. Inductive reasoning pro-
5 ceeds from the particular to the general.

Deductive reasoning proceeds from the general to the particular.

Children begin using a kind of inductive reasoning at an early age. A child may touch
10 a hot radiator on a number of occasions and conclude that all radiators are hot. He has reasoned from the particular experiences— touching radiators—to the generalization—all radiators are hot. Though the
15 conclusion may be faulty because of insufficient and uncharacteristic examples, the process is still inductive.

Deductive reasoning proceeds in reverse. A child may be told by a parent not to touch
20 radiators because radiators are hot. Then he may test the generalization by touching a radiator. If the generalization is sound, the specific examples should follow. In this example, the generalization is unsound be-
25 cause it is incomplete. Radiators are hot only at certain times. The example demonstrates the method, however.

Inductive reasoning is commonly used in science. On the basis of observation and
30 experiment, general principles or laws may be derived. These conclusions are subject to review as additional information becomes available, but they serve as useful guides in the meantime.

35 Deductive reasoning is commonly used in argumentation and persuasion. From a presumably accepted generalization, debaters derive arguments in favor of their positions. If the statement that smoking is harmful to
40 health is accepted, an editorial writer can plead for more restrictions on smoking in public places. Deductive arguments can often be put in the form of syllogisms, with major and minor premises and conclusions.

45 Both forms of reasoning are useful. Once their limitations are understood, they provide useful tools for handling the problems of everyday living.

According to the information in the passage, which of the following would be an example of deductive reasoning?

(A) A visitor to Mexico tastes several dishes with jalapeño peppers and decides that such dishes are too hot for his taste.

(B) On Saturday afternoon in a small city on his route, a traveler looks in vain for an open hardware store. He concludes stores in this city close Saturday afternoons.

(C) A chocolate enthusiast finds that he gets a headache after every bout of chocolate indulgence. He decides to give up chocolate because he may be allergic to it.

(D) Because Labrador retrievers have the reputation of being good with children, a father buys one for his young family.

(E) After finding a dozen strawberries in the basket utterly tasteless despite their luscious appearance, a cook throws away the rest of the box.

Problem

If wheels are the most efficient form of land transport ever invented by human beings, why did nature not develop creatures with some kind of wheels instead of feet, pad-
5 dles, or flippers? The question is not so frivolous as it sounds. Nature anticipated the invention of the submarine, glider, airplane, and jet-propelled vehicles. Why not wheels?

Some animals use their whole bodies as
10 wheels. The pangolin of Southeast Asia curls into a ball and rolls down steep hills to avoid predators. Rolling spiders and somersaulting shrimps use the principle of the wheel. Even rolling plants, like the
15 western tumbleweed, demonstrate the

wheel in action. But none of these has wheels in place of appendages.

Some writers conjecture that the joint problem proved an insuperable obstacle for the development of a living wheel. A rotating joint of living tissue might be a biological impossibility. Other writers dispute this explanation, pointing out that nature has devised unbelievably sophisticated solutions to all kinds of problems. These scientists believe nature did not provide wheeled animals for sound reasons of survival.

Michael LaBarbera of the University of Chicago has suggested three reasons why animals are better off without wheels. As a preface, he pointed out that human beings use wheels only under special conditions, for longer rather than shorter trips.

First, wheels are efficient only on hard surfaces. The heavier the wheeled vehicle, the more difficult it is to move on a soft surface. The use of oversized tires reduces the problem but does not eliminate it.

Secondly, wheels are not too useful when confronted with vertical obstructions. A wheeled vehicle with a rigid chassis cannot climb a curb higher than half the wheel radius.

Finally, wheels do not permit quick turning in a space cluttered with obstacles. Nor can wheeled vehicles turn efficiently in a small space. The switchbacks on mountain roads, for example, test the limits of the maneuverability of wheeled vehicles.

The efficiency of the wheel under certain conditions is more than offset by its inefficiency under other conditions. Certainly, under suitable conditions the wheel is incredibly more efficient than walking or running. In the Boston Marathon a wheelchair athlete finished the course 22 minutes faster than the best runner. The bicycle, a common example of a wheeled vehicle, is 15 times as efficient as a running dog.

When conditions are right, the wheel is indeed unexcelled for quick, clean, efficient locomotion. But since conditions are rarely "right" in the animal's natural domain, "wheeled animals" are an unlikely development in the scheme of things.

1. According to the point of view of the passage, which of the following statements is most likely true?
   (A) If the earth's surface were relatively flat and hard, creatures with wheels might have evolved.
   (B) The form of the wheel does not appear anywhere in natural design.
   (C) The adaptability of living tissue is severely limited.
   (D) Wheels would be particularly useful in woodlands.
   (E) The principle of jet propulsion in animals is quite different from the principle of jet propulsion in aviation.

   1 ____

2. With which of the following statements would the writer of this passage agree?
   (A) Wheeled prey animals would more easily escape their predators than four-footed ones.
   (B) Camels are more efficient in deserts than bicycles.
   (C) Any speculation about wheeled animals is a ridiculous waste of time.
   (D) Roller skates will eventually be used almost universally to save time and energy during shopping.
   (E) It is difficult to understand why animals have not developed wheels for locomotion.

   2 ____

Strategy. 1. Since the passage emphasizes the adaptability of animals, it suggests three reasons why wheels were not developed. A surface relatively flat and hard would have removed the three obstacles. Theoretically, then, wheeled animals might have developed. *(A)* is correct. The passage says the form of the wheel appears in ways other than as appendages. Therefore, *(B)* is incorrect. The passage emphasizes the adaptability of living tissue. *(C)* is incorrect. Since woodland surfaces are not flat and hard, *(D)* is incorrect. Though the fuels are different, animals and man both use the same principle of jet propulsion. *(E)* is incorrect.

2. Since soft surfaces are difficult for wheeled vehicles, *(B)* is correct. Since prey animals do not live in conditions suitable for wheels, *(A)* is incorrect. The entire passage is devoted to speculation about wheeled animals. *(C)* is incorrect. There is no indication that roller skates will take over for legs during short walking trips. The passage emphasizes the value of wheels for longer trips, not shorter ones. *(D)* is incorrect. Since the passage gives three reasons why animals have not developed wheels, *(E)* is incorrect.

REVIEW

Try your skill. The passage below is followed by questions based on its content.

Jules Verne is credited with anticipating many technological and scientific achievements of the 20th century, but 400 years earlier another prophet foresaw the world
5 of the future with even more uncanny accuracy. Verne embodied his prophecies in a series of enchanting science-fiction novels. Leonardo da Vinci sketched his prophetic visions in great detail. His sketches are so
10 clear and informative that working models have been constructed. A traveling IBM exhibit encourages young people to turn cranks, pull levers, and push buttons to demonstrate mechanically how brilliant
15 were the conceptions of this artist-scientist-inventor.

Leonardo's notebooks contain the fruits of his fertile imagination. Written in tiny but accurate left-handed mirror writing,
20 the notebooks are filled with sketches of innovations, creative ideas, inventions, and improvements of already existing devices. Designs for air conditioners, two-level highways for pedestrians and vehicles, para-
25 chutes, and rotating hoists poured from his inventive brain.

Leonardo devised an airplane that mod-

ern engineers say is technically sound. He defined a key aerodynamic principle 200
30 years before Newton. He foresaw the helicopter and devised an aerial screw to lift it. His analysis of gears anticipated their use in modern-day machines. He even designed the first mechanical car.

35 He was a truly scientific mapmaker, devising an instrument for measuring the radius of the earth accurately to within a few miles—all of this while Columbus was making his voyage of discovery to the New
40 World. He invented a printing press that could be run by one man, a vast improvement over the more cumbersome Gutenberg press. He devised a tank for warfare centuries before the British unveiled the
45 first tank on the Western Front in World War I.

What kept all his inventions from revolutionizing world technology? He was too soon. His genius outstripped the facilities of
50 his time. He needed a compact power unit and a metal hard enough for his needs. Though these were far in the future, his free-ranging mind had an impact on progress to come.

55 His studies in other branches of science were far-ranging and perceptive. He described ring patterns of trees as a key to

their growth. He systematically and individually pursued scientific studies of anat-
60 omy—of plants and the human body. He
became interested in the laws of optics. He
studied meteorology and geology.

The breadth and the depth of Leonardo's
genius are emphasized by his success in non-
65 scientific areas. He was an artist of renown,
painter of the "Mona Lisa," "The Last Supper," "Virgin and Child with St. Anne," and
other masterpieces. He had a powerful impact on the young Raphael and Michelan-
70 gelo. Sometimes his paintings suggest the
fusion of his scientific and artistic interests.

This restless genius, turning from one
field to another and interpreting the world
with unimpaired vision, is the prototype of
75 that many-faceted personality sometimes
called "Renaissance Man."

1. Which of the following persons most
   closely approaches the "Renaissance
   Man" qualities of Leonardo as outlined
   in the passage?
   (A) H. G. Wells, who wrote science fic-
       tion dealing with time machines
       and interplanetary travel
   (B) Emily Dickinson, who wrote
       poems of outstanding sensitivity
       from her self-imposed isolation
   (C) Samuel F. B. Morse, who was a
       painter of great renown before pi-
       oneering work in electric telegra-
       phy
   (D) Ludwig van Beethoven, whose
       musical achievements were a tri-
       umph over deafness
   (E) Claude Monet, whose paintings
       helped to launch the Impression-
       ist movement in art

   1 ____

2. The word *cumbersome* (line 42) sug-
   gests _____.
   (A) inefficiency
   (B) speed
   (C) plodding effectiveness
   (D) compactness
   (E) streamlining

   2 ____

3. In the fourth paragraph Columbus is
   mentioned for which of the following
   reasons?
   (A) Leonardo measured the size of
       the earth, while some people
       (though not Columbus) still be-
       lieved in the flat-earth theory.
   (B) Columbus as an active adven-
       turer, physically exploring, is con-
       trasted favorably with Leonardo
       as an armchair scientist.
   (C) Columbus probably had worked
       closely with Leonardo in deter-
       mining his strategy for exploring
       the New World.
   (D) Neither Columbus nor Leonardo
       could possibly anticipate the pro-
       found results of the opening up of
       the New World.
   (E) Columbus and Leonardo were
       both Italians, citizens of regions
       in social and political ferment.

   3 ____

4. All the following inventions of
   Leonardo are mentioned in the selec-
   tion EXCEPT _____.
   (A) parachute
   (B) two-level highway
   (C) mechanical car
   (D) machine gun
   (E) printing press

   4 ____

5. The author's attitude toward Leonardo
   is one of _____.
   (A) skepticism   (D) awe
   (B) envy   (E) acceptance
   (C) disbelief

   5 ____

6. From this passage we may infer that

_____.

(A) Leonardo at first accepted the idea of a flat earth but later rejected it.

(B) Leonardo provided Columbus with a map for his first voyage to the New World.

(C) working models can teach mechanical principles more effectively than can mere sketches.

(D) Jules Verne consulted the notebooks of Leonardo before beginning a novel.

(E) Leonardo's airplane could not have flown, even with modern energy sources and materials.

6 ____

7. For which of the following reasons does the writer mention Jules Verne?

(A) Jules Verne is the best prophet of the future in all of history.

(B) The popular mind associates Jules Verne with prophecy, but Leonardo is more deserving of the reputation.

(C) Jules Verne and Leonardo were essentially alike as personalities.

(D) Both Jules Verne and Leonardo were painters as well as prophets.

(E) Leonardo's time machine anticipated Jules Verne's by four centuries.

7 ____

8. Which of the following titles best summarizes the content of the passage?

(A) Science in the 15th Century

(B) Jules Verne and Leonardo da Vinci: A Study in Contrasts

(C) Leonardo as a Key Renaissance Painter

(D) Leonardo da Vinci: Renaissance Man

(E) Unrecognized Genius: A Study in Failure

8 ____

SUMMARY

2. Providing an Application

Though providing applications requires you to go beyond the facts and statements in the passage, you will find in the passage sufficient hints and clues to guide you in your selection. The extraordinary virtuosity of Leonardo in the preceding passage provides clues for the application question, as well as for other questions.

Section VI Summary: Looking Beyond the Passage

Predicting outcomes and providing applications are further extensions of one major skill: _drawing inferences._

The inferences analyzed in this section are more specialized and often more challenging because they ask you to bring experience to bear on the answers. In one form or another, you have been predicting outcomes and providing applications all your life. In this section you will put those experiences and skills to work.

Review these strategies for looking beyond the passage when you are preparing for the SAT.

PART 1. Predicting Outcomes (pp. 245–250)

A. Predicting an outcome is drawing an inference about a *probable* event based on information in the selection.
B. Look for clues that suggest what may happen in the future. (Sometimes you must "read between the lines.")
C. Many answers may be *possible*. Choose the most *probable* one.
D. Remember, information *in the passage* (not information you already know) should lead you to your answer.

PART 2. Providing an Application (pp. 250–255)

A. Providing an application is predicting a specific outcome. It is another special kind of inference.
B. Look for clues in the passage that can suggest the application.
C. Choose the most probable (not just possible) application.
D. Although you must move beyond the passage for the application, the reasons for it are in the passage itself.

1. Characterization

Narrative depends upon the depiction of characters in challenging situations. The characters may be human beings, aliens, robots, inanimate objects, or cartoon characters. The many Disney films suggest the range of possibilities. All narrative characters have traits that may be identified by defining labels.

A SAMPLE OF DESCRIPTIVE ADJECTIVES

even-tempered	callous
exuberant	cantankerous
friendly	domineering
fun loving	flighty
generous	melancholy
humorous	overbearing
kindly	pugnacious
likable	self-indulgent
reliable	smug
upright	stingy
vivacious	temperamental
witty	vindictive

TRIAL TEST

The following brief passage from *Look Homeward, Angel,* by Thomas Wolfe, suggests the essence of a colorful character. Your decision about Gant's character will be based on his actions, his dialogue, and how others react to him.

Seated before a roast or a fowl, Gant began a heavy clangor on his steel and carving knife, distributing thereafter Gargantuan portions to each plate. Eugene feasted from
5 a high chair by his father's side, filled his distending belly until it was drumtight, and was permitted to stop eating by his watchful sire only when his stomach was impregnable to the heavy prod of Gant's big finger.

10 "There's a soft place there," he would roar, and he would cover the scoured plate of his infant son with another heavy slab of beef. That their machinery withstood this hammerhanded treatment was a tribute to
15 their vitality and Eliza's cookery.

Gant ate ravenously and without caution. He was immoderately fond of fish, and he invariably choked upon a bone while eating it. This happened hundreds of times, but
20 each time he would look up suddenly with a howl of agony and terror, groaning and crying out strongly while a half-dozen hands pounded violently on his back.

"Merciful God!" he would gasp finally, "I
25 thought I was done for that time."

"I'll vow, Mr. Gant," Eliza was vexed. "Why on earth don't you watch what you're doing? If you didn't eat so fast you wouldn't always get choked."

30 The children, staring, but relieved, settled slowly back in their places.

1. The chief focus of the passage is on which of the following?
   (A) Describing a typical meal in a middle-class family
   (B) Portraying the character of Gant
   (C) Sermonizing on the dangers of eating rapidly
   (D) Praising moderation in all things
   (E) Suggesting that a roast is a better meal than fish

   1 ____

2. Of Gant it might reasonably be said that _____.
   (A) he was a devoted father and husband
   (B) he believed in moderation in all things
   (C) he was cruel to Eliza
   (D) he didn't learn from experience
   (E) he was careful not to make the children nervous

   2 ____

3. The author's attitude toward Gant's table behavior is one of _____.
   (A) awe   (D) envy
   (B) endorsement (E) disapproval
   (C) fury

   3 ____

4. Gant prodded Eugene's belly to _____.
   (A) make sure Eugene was completely stuffed
   (B) keep the baby awake
   (C) irritate Eliza
   (D) keep the children in line
   (E) show his favoritism for the youngest child

   4 ____

5. As used in this selection, *Gargantuan* (line 3) means _____.
   (A) modest   (D) tasty
   (B) thrifty (E) rationed
   (C) huge

   5 ____

Look at a typical question and analyze the possible answers. In this selection, Prince Florizel is ready for more adventures.

Problem

During his residence in London, the accomplished Prince Florizel of Bohemia gained the affection of all classes by the seduction of his manner and by a well-consid-
5 ered generosity. He was a remarkable man even by what was known of him; and that was but a small part of what he actually did. Although of a placid temper in ordinary circumstances, and accustomed to take the
10 world with as much philosophy as any ploughman, the Prince of Bohemia was not without a taste for ways of life more adventurous and eccentric than that to which he was destined by his birth. Now and then,
15 when he fell into a low humour, when there was no laughable play to witness in any of the London theatres, and when the season of the year was unsuitable to those field sports in which he excelled all competitors,
20 he would summon his confidant and Master of the Horse, Colonel Geraldine, and bid him prepare himself against an evening ramble. The Master of the Horse was a young officer of a brave and even temerarious disposition.
25 He greeted the news with delight, and hastened to make ready. Long practice and a

varied acquaintance of life had given him a singular faculty in disguise; he could adapt not only his face and bearing, but his voice
30 and almost his thoughts, to those of any rank, character, or nation; and in this way he diverted attention from the Prince, and sometimes gained admission for the pair into strange societies. The civil authorities
35 were never taken into the secret of these adventures; the imperturbable courage of the men and the ready invention and chivalrous devotion to each other had brought them through a score of dangerous passes; and
40 they grew in confidence as time went on.

One evening in March they were driven by a sharp fall of sleet into an Oyster Bar in the immediate neighborhood of Leicester Square. Colonel Geraldine was dressed and
45 painted to represent a person connected with the Press in reduced circumstances; while the Prince had, as usual, travestied his appearance by the addition of false whiskers and a pair of large adhesive eye-
50 brows. These lent him a shaggy and weather-beaten air, which, for one of his urbanity, formed the most impenetrable disguise. Thus equipped, the commander and his satellite sipped their brandy and
55 soda in security.

1. The context suggests that *temerarious* (line 24) probably means _____.
   (A) rash and daring
   (B) impatient and nasty
   (C) reserved and thoughtful
   (D) proud but shy
   (E) rebellious and cruel

   1 ____

2. Lines 8–14 suggest that the Prince's personality is _____.
   (A) essentially agreeable and loving
   (B) complex and somewhat contradictory
   (C) unruffled and consistent

   (D) predictable but interesting
   (E) unpleasant if superficially charming

   2 ____

3. Which of the following best describes the main idea of the selection?
   (A) Prince Florizel is well liked by his friends and associates.
   (B) Disguise is a deceitful, disagreeable device with little justification for its use.
   (C) The Prince of Bohemia is basically an industrious, hardworking individual.
   (D) The Prince and the Colonel seek new adventures and unusual experiences.
   (E) Colonel Geraldine is the motivator of the disguised friends.

   3 ____

4. Which of the following is likely to happen next?
   (A) The Colonel is greeted by an old, forgotten friend.
   (B) The Prince tires of the masquerade and returns home.
   (C) The Prince and the Colonel have an unusual adventure.
   (D) The disguised pair are unmasked by the press.
   (E) The storm gets worse, and the men find lodgings.

   4 ____

5. As used in the selection, *in reduced circumstances* (line 46) means _____.
   (A) on a restricted assignment
   (B) in a state of uncertainty
   (C) attached to a newspaper
   (D) in a shabby suit
   (E) somewhat low in money

   5 ____

Strategy. 1. The word *brave* suggests courage, and the word *even* implies that *temerarious* is *brave* to a greater degree. "Rash and daring" (A) suggest an extension of *brave*. The other alternatives are either obviously incorrect, like (E), or not covered, like (C).

2. The Prince has a "placid temper" and takes life as it comes, but he has a "taste for ways of life more adventurous and eccentric." He is "complex" in his interests and "contradictory" in his mood swings (B).

3. Though statement (A) is true, it does not represent the *main* idea. It is an important detail. (B) is nowhere implied. (C) suggests boredom and avoidance of adventure. (E) is obviously false. Only (D) accurately describes the attitudes and personalities of the two men.

4. The stage is set for something unusual to happen. The men are disguised. The weather is bad. The adventurers are in a strange place. There's certainly an adventure to come (C).

5. "In reduced circumstances" (line 46) suggests a shortage of money (E).

REVIEW

In the following excerpt, Rosemary picks up a street person and brings her home to tea.

"Rosemary, may I come in?" It was Philip. "Of course."

He came in. "Oh, I'm sorry," he said, and stopped and stared.

5 "It's quite all right," said Rosemary smiling. "This is my friend, Miss—"

"Smith, madam," said the languid figure, who was strangely still and unafraid.

"Smith," said Rosemary. "We are going to 10 have a little talk."

"Oh, yes," said Philip. "Quite." And his eye caught sight of the coat and hat on the floor. He came over to the fire and turned his back to it. "It's a beastly afternoon," he 15 said curiously, still looking at that listless figure, looking at its hands and boots, and then at Rosemary again.

"Yes, isn't it?" said Rosemary enthusiastically. "Vile."

20 Philip smiled his charming smile. "As a matter of fact," said he, "I wanted you to come into the library for a moment. Would you? Will Miss Smith excuse us?"

The big eyes were raised to him but Rose-25 mary answered for her. "Of course she will." And they went out of the room together. "I say," said Philip, when they were alone. "Explain. Who is she? What does it all mean?"

Rosemary, laughing, leaned against the 30 door and said: "I picked her up in Curzon Street. Really. She's a real pick-up. She asked me for the price of a cup of tea, and I brought her home with me."

"But what on earth are you going to do 35 with her?" cried Philip.

"Be nice to her," said Rosemary quickly. "Be frightfully nice to her. Look after her. I don't know how. We haven't talked yet. But show her—treat her—make her feel—"

40 "My darling girl," said Philip, "You're quite mad, you know. It simply can't be done."

"I knew you'd say that," retorted Rosemary. "Why not? I want to. Isn't that a 45 reason? and besides, one's always reading about these things. I decided—"

"But," said Philip slowly, and he cut the end of a cigar, "she's so astonishingly pretty."

50 "Pretty?" Rosemary was so surprised that she blushed. "Do you think so? I—I hadn't thought about it."

"Good Lord!" Philip struck a match. "She's absolutely lovely. Look again, my 55 child. I was bowled over when I came into your room just now. However . . . I think you're making a ghastly mistake. Sorry, darling, if I'm crude and all that. But let me

60 know if Miss Smith is going to dine with us
in time for me to look up *The Milliner's
Gazette.*"

"You absurd creature!" said Rosemary,
and she went out of the library, but not back
65 to her bedroom. She went to her writing-
room and sat down at her desk. Pretty!
Absolutely lovely! Bowled over! Her heart
beat like a heavy bell. Pretty! Lovely! She
drew her cheque book towards her. But no,
70 cheques would be no use, of course. She
opened a drawer and took out five pound
notes, looked at them, put two back, and
holding the three squeezed in her hand, she
went back to her bedroom.

1. The author's primary purpose in this
   passage is to _____.
   (A) expose Philip as a cruel cynic
   (B) analyze, through conversation
       alone, the character of Rosemary
   (C) suggest some of the dangers in
       old relationships
   (D) reveal aspects of a bitter class
       struggle
   (E) show how some people recognize
       beauty where others are blind

   1 ____

2. Rosemary's purpose in bringing the
   stranger home was to _____.
   (A) make a friend of Miss Smith
   (B) provide a dinner guest
   (C) indulge a whim
   (D) hire her as a personal maid
   (E) make amends for a previous slight

   2 ____

3. The word *languid* in line 7 is meant to
   suggest _____.
   (A) Miss Smith's fatigue
   (B) Rosemary's lack of perception
   (C) Philip's curiosity
   (D) Philip and Rosemary's essential
       malice
   (E) repressed anger

   3 ____

4. Although she speaks only two words,
   Miss Smith maintains a certain
   _____.
   (A) irritation   (D) amiability
   (B) composure   (E) anxiety
   (C) coquettishness

   4 ____

5. Rosemary's answering for Miss
   Smith (line 25) suggests Rosemary's
   _____.
   (A) real interest in Miss Smith's wel-
       fare
   (B) repressed dislike for Philip
   (C) unselfish generosity
   (D) curiosity about Miss Smith's back-
       ground
   (E) snobbishness

   5 ____

6. "One's always reading about these
   things . . ." (lines 45–46) suggests that
   (A) Rosemary is a keen student of
       human motivation
   (B) Miss Smith is responsible for her
       own plight
   (C) Rosemary is playing out a fantasy
   (D) Philip is an unkind husband
   (E) money isn't everything

   6 ____

7. The sentence "Her heart beat like a
   heavy bell" suggests that Rosemary
   _____.
   (A) has a physical weakness
   (B) finds she is running low on funds
   (C) is about to scream at Miss Smith
   (D) is jealous
   (E) realizes some money has been
       stolen

   7 ____

8. The turning point of the episode comes
   with which quotation?
   (A) "Be nice to her."
   (B) "Will Miss Smith excuse us?"
   (C) "She's a real pick-up."
   (D) "It's a beastly afternoon."
   (E) "But she's so astonishingly
       pretty."

   8 ____

9. The most significant key to Rosemary's character is found in the word(s) _____.

(A) "Vile" (line 19)
(B) "laughing" (line 29)
(C) "nice" (line 36)
(D) "frightfully" (line 37)
(E) "haven't talked yet" (line 38)

9 ____

10. It might reasonably be said that Philip _____.

(A) has fallen in love with Miss Smith
(B) is surprisingly cruel in his attitude toward Miss Smith
(C) understands his wife better than she knows
(D) really hopes that Miss Smith will stay on
(E) is ready to indulge his wife's every impulse

10 ____

11. Which of the following is likely to happen next?
(A) Philip leaves in an angry mood.
(B) Miss Smith speaks at length with Philip.
(C) Philip and Rosemary take Miss Smith to dinner.
(D) Philip and Rosemary argue about Miss Smith's presence.
(E) Rosemary sends Miss Smith away promptly.

11 ____

12. A word that might reasonably be applied to Rosemary is _____.
(A) insightful
(B) nasty
(C) secure
(D) unfashionable
(E) pampered

12 ____

13. The end of the episode _____.
(A) was planned and anticipated by Philip
(B) came as a surprise to Philip
(C) showed Rosemary's deep concern for Miss Smith
(D) ran counter to Rosemary's real wishes
(E) showed Miss Smith's ability to forecast events

13 ____

SUMMARY

1. Characterization

Characterization is a major element in narration. Characters most frequently are human, but nonhuman, even inanimate, characters can arouse emotional responses in readers or listeners. Characters usually exhibit specific traits, which are revealed in challenging situations.

2. Plot

"What happened next?" If you have ever asked this question, you have been interested in plot, in what happened. Plot is the essence of storytelling. Some plots are relatively simple—a succession of incidents without much conflict. Confrontation, however, is an important element of a good story.

The skeleton of a typical plot is found in the simplest plot outline of all.

1. Boy meets girl. The opening situation sets the stage for later events.
2. Boy loses girl. There is conflict, opposition, a stirring up of the earlier serene waters.
3. Boy wins girl. Despite the problems, there is a resolution.

This spare outline, though oversimplified, is not entirely out of place in a good story. There is almost always a static situation which is destroyed by conflict. The final solution ties threads together. Though not always happy, the usual story ending wraps up the plot elements.

Some stories are open-ended, with conclusions that are not neatly wrapped up. Perhaps the most famous of this type is "The Lady or the Tiger?" which leaves the ending entirely to the reader. Still, it does contain other plot elements like conflict. Character, of course, plays a major role in plot. Character affects plot; plot affects character.

Another influence on plot and character is setting. Characters are tested by harsh environments. Challenging environments help shape what happens. Robert Louis Stevenson wrote, "Some places speak distinctly. Certain dank gardens cry out for a murder; certain old houses demand to be haunted; certain coasts are set apart for shipwreck."

The following passage from *The Great Railway Bazaar* by Paul Theroux suggests, in a brief excerpt, the elements of a longer literary selection. It contains conflict, an essential ingredient in plot. The conflict shows how character and plot can be interrelated. In this excerpt the conflict reveals character, and character influences incident. Setting is an all-important element in the story.

TRIAL TEST

At Trieste, Molesworth discovered that the Italian conductor had mistakenly torn out all the tickets from his Cook's wallet. The Italian conductor was in Venice, leaving Molesworth no ticket for Istanbul, or, for that matter, Yugoslavia. But Molesworth stayed calm. He said his strategy in such a situation was to say he had no money and knew only English: "That puts the ball in their court."

But the new conductor was persistent. He hung by the door of Molesworth's compartment. He said, "You no ticket." Molesworth didn't reply. He poured himself a glass of wine and sipped it. "You no ticket."

"Your mistake, George."

"You," said the conductor. He waved a ticket at Molesworth. "You *no* ticket."

"Sorry, George," said Molesworth, still drinking. "You'll have to phone Cook's."

"You no ticket. You pay."

"I no pay. No money." Molesworth frowned and said to me, "I do wish he'd go away.

"You cannot go."

"I go."

"No ticket! No go!"

"Good God," said Molesworth. This argument went on for some time. Molesworth was persuaded to go into Trieste Station. The conductor began to perspire. He explained the situation to the stationmaster, who stood up and left his office; he did not return. Another official was found. "Look at the uniform," said Molesworth. "Absolutely wretched." That official tried to phone Venice. He rattled the pins with a stumpy finger and said, *"Pronto! Pronto!"* But the phone was out of order.

40 Finally Molesworth said, "I give up. Here—here's some money." He flourished a handful of 10,000 lire notes. "I buy a new ticket."

The conductor reached for the money. 45 Molesworth withdrew it as the conductor snatched.

"Now look, George," said Molesworth. "You get me a ticket, but before you do that, you sit down and write me an endorsement 50 so I can get my money back. Is that clear?" But all Molesworth said when we were again under way was, "I think they're all very naughty."

1. Which of the following statements can reasonably be made?
   (A) Molesworth's ticket was in Venice, but he was in Trieste.
   (B) The conductor was acting vindictively in asking for a ticket.
   (C) Molesworth stuck to his guns and never paid for a ticket.
   (D) The telephone call proved that Molesworth was right.
   (E) The narrator of the story was embarrassed by Molesworth's actions.

   1 ____

2. Molesworth's strategy can best be described by the word _____.
   (A) sympathetic
   (B) indifferent
   (C) stonewalling
   (D) responsive
   (E) humorous

   2 ____

3. The essential conflict in this excerpt is between _____.
   (A) Yugoslavs and Italians
   (B) official regulations and human error
   (C) Molesworth and the narrator
   (D) Istanbul and Trieste
   (E) the laws of one country and the laws of another

   3 ____

4. Molesworth's attitude toward the conductor is revealed by his _____.
   (A) sympathetic understanding of the conductor's plight
   (B) willingness to speak the conductor's language
   (C) payment of a handful of 10,000 lira notes
   (D) use of the name *George*
   (E) acceptance of local train procedures

   4 ____

5. The conductor's attitude toward Molesworth can best be described as one of _____.
   (A) murderous rage
   (B) sweet reasonableness
   (C) patience
   (D) soothing persuasion
   (E) exasperation

   5 ____

Problem

I was on the point of slinking off, to think how I had best proceed, when there came out of the house a lady with a handkerchief tied over her cap, and a pair of gardening 5 gloves on her hands, wearing a gardening-pocket like a toll-man's apron, and carrying a great knife. I knew her immediately to be Miss Betsey, for she came stalking out of the house exactly as my poor mother had so

10 often described her stalking up our garden at Blunderstone Rookery.

"Go away!" said Miss Betsey, shaking her head, and making a distant chop in the air with her knife. "Go along! No boys here!"

15 I watched her, with my heart at my lips, as she marched to a corner of her garden, and stopped to dig up some little root there. Then, without a scrap of courage, but with a great deal of desperation, I went softly in

20 and stood beside her, touching her with my finger.

"If you please, ma'am," I began.

She started and looked up.

"If you please, aunt."

25 "Eh?" exclaimed Miss Betsey, in a tone of amazement I had never heard approached.

"If you please, aunt, I am your nephew."

"Oh, Lord!" said my aunt. And sat flat down in the garden path.

30 "I am David Copperfield, of Blunderstone, in Suffolk—where you came, on the night when I was born, and saw my dear mamma. I have been very unhappy since she died. I have been slighted, and taught nothing,

35 and thrown upon myself, and put to work not fit for me. It made me run away to you. I was robbed at first setting out, and have walked all the way, and have never slept in a bed since I began the journey." Here my

40 self support gave way all at once; and with a movement of my hands intended to show her my ragged state, and call it to witness that I had suffered something, I broke into a passion of crying, which I suppose had

45 been pent up within me all the week.

My aunt, with every sort of expression but wonder discharged from her countenance, sat on the gravel staring at me, until I began to cry; when she got up in a great

50 hurry, collared me, and took me into the parlour. Her first proceeding there was to unlock a tall press, bring out several bottles, and pour some of the contents of each into my mouth. I think they must have been

55 taken out at random, for I am sure I tasted aniseed water, anchovy sauce, and salad dressing. When she had administered these restoratives, as I was still quite hysterical, and unable to control my sobs, she put me

60 on the sofa, with a shawl under my head, and the handkerchief from her own head under my feet, lest I should sully the cover; and then, sitting herself down behind the green fan or screen I have already men-

65 tioned, so that I could not see her face, cried out at intervals, "Mercy on us!" letting those exclamations off like minute-guns.

1. Complication as a typical element in plot development is here demonstrated by _____.
   (A) David's beginning uncertainty
   (B) the appearance of Miss Betsey
   (C) the shyness of David Copperfield
   (D) David's identifying himself
   (E) David's crying spell

   1 ____

2. The word that quickly got Miss Betsey's attention was _____.
   (A) "please"   (D) "Suffolk"
   (B) "ma'am"   (E) "robbed"
   (C) "aunt"

   2 ____

3. The author's mention of "aniseed water, anchovy sauce, and salad dressing" is intended to _____.
   (A) suggest Miss Betsey's basic indifference
   (B) add a touch of humor
   (C) reveal the manners and mores of the time
   (D) show how David would react to an unusual drink
   (E) display a mastery of prose rhythms

   3 ____

4. In line 58 *restoratives* most nearly means _____.
   (A) "health aids"
   (B) "bitter pills"
   (C) "vegetable oils"
   (D) "sound foods"
   (E) "helpful suggestions"

   4 ____

5. The expression "Mercy on us" is meant to suggest Miss Betsey's _____.
(A) sense of humor
(B) deeply religious nature
(C) control of the unexpected situation
(D) love for her newly arrived nephew
(E) agitation

5 ____

6. The passage implies that _____.
(A) David is a cruel boy, about to take advantage of a relative
(B) Miss Betsey is, at best, an inefficient gardener
(C) Miss Betsey is not really disturbed by David's arrival
(D) Miss Betsey has a prejudice against boys
(E) David's hysteria is feigned

6 ____

7. From her actions we may infer that Miss Betsey _____.
(A) despised David immediately and intensely
(B) felt a house should be lived in, not preserved as a museum piece
(C) was gruff but not unkind
(D) kept in close communication with David's mother
(E) welcomed the newcomer without reservations

7 ____

8. At the close of the passage, Miss Betsey probably _____.
(A) disclaimed all responsibility for David
(B) called the local welfare office
(C) fell into a deep faint
(D) helped David
(E) wrote a letter to Blunderstone

8 ____

9. Which of the following titles best summarizes the content of the passage?
(A) David Meets Miss Betsey
(B) A Sad Story
(C) How I Traveled from Blunderstone to Miss Betsey's
(D) The Practical Uses of Hysteria
(E) A Frightened Little Boy

9 ____

Strategy. 1. Miss Betsey seems quite self-sufficient by her initial appearance and actions, but then her calm is shaken by David's revelation of his relationship to her. His arrival (D) introduces a complication.

2. When David uses the word *aunt,* (C), Miss Betsey reacts "in a tone of amazement I had never heard approached." The other words produce no emotional response.

3. Since the subjects mentioned are ill-assorted and not medicinal, we may assume that they have been introduced for a touch of humor (B).

4. The restoratives have been administered to David so that he will recover his composure. We may assume they are health aids (A). The basic word *restore* provides an additional clue.

5. The previous context suggests that Miss Betsey has been upset by David's arrival. The emotional exclamation, "Mercy on us," suggests agitation (E). Miss Betsy has not demonstrated a sense of humor (A). The context suggests that the exclamation is not religious (B). Miss Betsey has not yet exhibited control over the

situation (C). It is much too soon for Miss Betsey to have developed love for her nephew (D).

6. When Miss Betsey tells David, "Go away! No boys here!" we may assume she has a prejudice against boys (D). She doesn't say, "No children here," suggesting that boys may be a particularly unwelcome sight. David is pathetic, not cruel (A). Miss Betsey's actions with gloves and gardening knife suggest that she is an efficient gardener (B). Her agitation reveals her disturbance at David's arrival (C). David reveals that his crying is uncontrolled, not feigned (E).

7. Miss Betsey's immediate attempts to help David in his impassioned crying suggest that she has a good heart. Her actions have shown her to be gruff, but she doesn't turn David away heartlessly. She is gruff but not unkind (C).

8. Since Miss Betsey has apparently assumed some responsibility for David because she is his aunt, we may assume that she helped David (D). Her hasty efforts at restoratives show that she has his welfare at heart.

9. A process of elimination helps to determine the title. (B) is much too general. It could apply to many passages. (C), by contrast, is too specific. Besides, it omits mention of the meeting between David and Miss Betsey. (D) is quite off the subject. There is nothing to suggest that David tried to manipulate his aunt by crying. (E) presumes to say more than is implied. Perhaps later events will prove the truth of this statement, but there is not enough in the passage itself to justify the broad comment. The simple title, (A), is a good title for the passage.

REVIEW

In this excerpt from a short story, Elaine, a divorced mother, has charge of her two sons for a brief time. At the time of the divorce, nine-year-old Jesse and eleven-year-old Matthew had both chosen to live with their father, Peter, who was as surprised as Elaine by the boys' decision. Elaine and her children are staying at her parents' condominium in Florida.

Ignoring her mother's warning and her father's dire predictions, Elaine took the boys everywhere they wanted to go: Monkey Jungle, Parrot Jungle, and the Seaquar-
5 ium. The boys seemed excited and happy, though often they would run ahead of her, too impatient to stay by her side. Once, from a distance, Elaine saw Jesse casually rest his arm on his brother's shoulder as the two
10 of them stood watching a pair of orangutans groom each other; she kept waiting for Matthew to shake Jesse off, but it never happened. Two nights in a row, they went to see the movie *Airplane!* A couple of nights, they
15 played miniature golf. At the end of each day, Jesse and Matthew told Elaine they had had "the best time." She supposed that this meant the trip was a success, that they would have nothing to complain about to
20 their father when they went back home. She had kept them entertained, which was all they seemed to have wanted from her. She might have been anyone—a camp counsellor, a teacher leading them on class trips, a
25 friend of the family put in charge while their parents were on vacation. There was plenty of time to talk, and they told her a lot—long, involved stories about the fight Jesse had recently had with his best friend,
30 the rock concert Matthew had gone to with

two thirteen-year-olds, the pair of Siamese fighting fish with beautiful flowing fins they'd bought for the new fish tank in their bedroom—all about the things that had
35 happened to them in the four months they had been out of touch. But she still didn't know if they were really all right, if they loved their father, loved her. You couldn't ask questions like that. When, several years
40 ago, her brother had started seeing a shrink, he'd complained that his parents were always asking him if he was happy. It's none of their business, the shrink told him—if you don't feel you want to give them
45 an answer, don't. As simple as that.

It was nearly midnight; the boys had just gone to bed. Elaine went into her parents' room, where her mother and father were sitting up in their king-size bed watching
50 *Columbo* on a small color TV. Dick Van Dyke was tying his wife to a chair. He took two Polaroid pictures of her and then he picked up a gun. His wife insisted he was never going to get away with it; he aimed
55 the gun at her and pulled the trigger.

"Wait a minute," Elaine's mother said. "Is this the one where Columbo tricks him into identifying his camera at the—"

"Thanks a lot," her father said. "You
60 know how I love Peter Falk."

"Who knows, maybe I'm wrong."

"You're not," Elaine said. "I saw this one, too."

"Well, it's nice to be right about some-
65 thing."

Elaine lay down on her stomach at the foot of the bed, facing the TV set. She yawned and said, "Excuse me."

"All that running around," her mother
70 said. "Who wouldn't be tired?"

"It's not necessary to run like that all day long," her father said. "Didn't those two kids ever hear of sleeping around the pool, or picking up a book or a newspaper? Maybe
75 they're hyperactive or something."

"They're kids on vacation. What do they want to read the newspaper for?" her mother said.

Elaine sat up and swung her legs over the
80 side of the bed. "It's my fault," she said. "I couldn't bring myself to say no to them about anything."

"Did you accomplish anything all those hours you were running?" her mother
85 asked. "Do you feel like you made any head-way?"

Elaine was watching an overweight woman on TV dance the cha-cha with her cat along a shining kitchen floor. "What?"
90 she said.

"Of course, if they really are just fine there with Peter and his sleep-over girlfriends, that's another story," her father said.

95 "Quiet," her mother said. "Look who's here."

Jesse stood in the doorway, blinking his eyes. "There's a funny noise in my ears that keeps waking me up," he said. He sat down
100 on the floor next to the bed and put his head in Elaine's lap. "You know," he said, "like someone's whistling in there."

Elaine hesitated, then kissed each ear. "Better?"

105 "A little."

"More kisses?"

Jesse shook his head.

"Let me take you back to bed." Elaine walked him to the little den at the other end
110 of the apartment, where Matthew was asleep on his side of the convertible couch. Jesse got onto the bed. On his knees, he sat up and looked out the window. "I can't go to sleep right now," he said quietly. Beneath
115 them the water was black; above, the palest of moons appeared to drift by. There were clouds everywhere, and just a few dim stars.

"Did you want to tell me something?" Elaine waited; she focused on the sign lit up
120 on top of the Holiday Inn across the Water-way.

"We're getting a new car. A silver BMW," Jesse said dreamily. "We saw it in the show-room." He moved away from the window
125 and slipped down on the bed. "We might drive it over to Fort Lee and come and see

you. And when Matthew has his license, the two of us will pick you up every day and take you anywhere you want to go."

130 Elaine still faced the window; she did not turn around. "To the moon," she said. "Will you do that for me?"

Jesse didn't answer for a long time. "We can do that," he said finally, and when she 135 turned to look at him he was asleep.

1. Tension is an important element in plot complication. Part of Elaine's tension is generated by her desire to _____.
   (A) help her parents' marriage
   (B) belittle the boys' father
   (C) make the boys' visit as perfect as possible
   (D) play one son against the other
   (E) find out from the boys what went wrong

   1 ____

2. The probable follow-up to the passage is _____.
   (A) the boys' changed decision to live with their mother
   (B) a bitter exchange of letters between Peter and Elaine
   (C) a decision by Elaine to remain with her parents
   (D) a bold action by Elaine's father to keep the children
   (E) a return to the situation as before

   2 ____

3. The author introduces lines 7–13 to show that _____.
   (A) Jesse is more mature than Matthew
   (B) the boys have been deeply disturbed by the divorce
   (C) the boys have bonded together
   (D) the boys are unhappy in Elaine's presence
   (E) the boys have no love for either parent

   3 ____

4. A sentence that captures Elaine's essential heartbreak is _____.
   (A) "At the end of each day, Jesse and Matthew told Elaine they had had 'the best time.' "
   (B) "She might have been anyone—a camp counsellor, a teacher leading them on class trips, a friend of the family put in charge while their parents were on vacation."
   (C) "I couldn't bring myself to say no to them about anything."
   (D) " 'It's not necessary to run like that all day long,' her father said."
   (E) "Elaine walked him to the little den on the other side of the apartment, where Jesse was asleep on the convertible couch."

   4 ____

5. The experience of Elaine's brother suggests that _____.
   (A) his childhood may have been unhappy
   (B) he'd probably have made a poor husband
   (C) Elaine's parents were excellent role models
   (D) he and Elaine never got along well
   (E) he understood Jesse and Matthew very well

   5 ____

6. The author introduces the *Columbo* episode (lines 47–63) to _____.
   (A) explore the parents' addiction to television
   (B) bring Elaine and her parents closer together
   (C) show the father's enjoyment of Peter Falk
   (D) paint a pleasant picture of a family evening
   (E) point up a flaw in the parents' relationship with each other

   6 ____

7. The "headway" Elaine's mother refers to in lines 84–85 is _____.
   (A) physical stamina for the excursions
   (B) an effort to win back the children
   (C) an improvement in Elaine's financial situation
   (D) a desire to learn more about Peter's current lifestyle
   (E) an attempt to establish Elaine's Florida residency

   7 ____

8. The author mentions the woman doing the cha-cha with the cat (lines 87–89) to _____.
   (A) introduce an ironic trivial note in a tense situation
   (B) show the diversity of television's offerings
   (C) make a negative comment about the mother's taste
   (D) distract the reader momentarily
   (E) suggest that Elaine was not really concerned about her sons

   8 ____

9. The father's comments in lines 91–94 are an example of _____.
   (A) compassion
   (B) broad-mindedness
   (C) acceptance
   (D) sarcasm
   (E) deception

   9 ____

10. When, at the end, Elaine asks, "Did you want to tell me something?" she probably hopes that Jesse will _____.
    (A) mention again the good time they had all had
    (B) tell her about the new car
    (C) fall asleep before answering
    (D) tell her how much he liked Florida
    (E) express his love and need for her

    10 ____

11. Elaine's answer, "To the moon" (line 131) expresses her _____.
    (A) jubilation   (D) curiosity
    (B) sadness   (E) hatred
    (C) indifference

    11 ____

12. Elaine can take some comfort in the knowledge that _____.
    (A) her ex-husband is having his problems, too
    (B) Matthew has been relatively indifferent to her
    (C) her parents deeply understand her feelings
    (D) Jesse shows signs of missing his mother
    (E) the children will soon return to their father

    12 ____

13. An essential truth demonstrated in this passage is that _____.
    (A) divorce is easier on wives than on husbands
    (B) older people cannot relate successfully to the young
    (C) material things are obstacles to happiness
    (D) innermost thoughts are hard to verbalize
    (E) children are intentionally cruel

    13 ____

14. The author seems to be saying that in unfortunate divorce situations, _____.
    (A) the husband is to blame
    (B) unfeeling children may bring about the split
    (C) there may be no villains
    (D) mothers-in-law may play negative roles
    (E) the wife is an unfit mother

    14 ____

15. The setting plays a role in the story because _____.
- (A) the heat makes the boys inactive
- (B) it suggests that Elaine's parents are poor
- (C) the children and their father cannot get in touch with each other
- (D) the apartment accommodations throw the characters closely together
- (E) there are relatively few things for the boys to do in the area

15 ____

SUMMARY
2. Plot

The ancient art of storytelling is alive and well. The thread of the narrative, *plot,* is a crucial element in most fiction. As in life, character, incident, and setting interact. Character may influence plot or be influenced by setting. All three tend to play a role in narrative.

Section VII Summary: Understanding Narrative

Most people find narrative easy to read, but appreciation of a good story is heightened by an awareness of the ingredients, especially plot, character, and setting.

PART 1. Characterization (pp. 257–262)

A. When you read a story, think about the characters. What special traits do they display? How do they interact with each other?

B. Get a general impression of each character. Are the actions consistent? Are the characters self-aware or do they act blindly?

C. As a person outside the action, how do you picture each character? Do you identify with one of the characters?

PART 2. Plot (pp. 262–271)

A. As you read, note the opening situation. Get an impression of each character as the plot is set in motion.

B. Note how some kind of conflict or confrontation sets the wheels rolling.

C. Follow the conflict to its conclusion. Is the ending satisfactory? Does it grow reasonably out of the previous events?

D. What role does characterization play in the resolution? Do the characters change the direction of the plot? How? How do the incidents impact upon the characters, influencing their actions?

E. What role does setting play? Could the events have taken place in a quite different setting? Why or why not?

Section VIII: Studying the Longer Passage

1. The Single Selection

In an earlier revision of the SAT, the College Board introduced a critical reading section with longer and more challenging selections than before. All the skills you have been developing in this book will stand you in good stead when you meet a difficult longer passage. This section will provide some additional practice, using examples of the type you will face on the test itself.

Because the new reading passages run much longer than those used in the past, each selection can test a great many skills. A *single* selection can test a majority of such skills as these:

> Generalizations and Main Ideas
> The Author's Purpose, Style, Method, and Tone
> Vocabulary and the Interpretation of Phrases
> Figurative Language
> Inferences
> Outcomes and Applications
> Sequence
> Awareness of Skills Being Used

The new reading passages signal a shift in emphasis from the literal understanding of text information, like finding details. The College Board notes that the new passages measure "students' ability to make inferences; to relate parts of the text to each other or to the whole; to follow the logic of an argument; to synthesize meaning; to identify the author's purpose, attitude, or tone, etc."

TRIAL TEST

The following passage, written during the Bosnian-Serb conflict in the last decade of the twentieth century, discusses a disturbing trend with dangerous implications for the future.

When George Orwell published his provocative novel *1984,* in 1948, the world seemed to be going in one inevitable direction. As Orwell looked 36 years into the future, he projected then-current trends and envisioned a world of three superpowers: Oceania, Eurasia, and Eastasia. Each dominated completely its own people and spheres of influence, using technology for complete mind manipulation. Rulers of the three superpowers maintained power by waging perpetual limited warfare, not for the usual territorial or political reasons but principally for internal social control. How accurate was the prophecy of the division of the world into three monolithic geographical areas?

Thirty years earlier, another prophecy had been made. During World War I, President Woodrow Wilson argued for the self-determination of all peoples, but his own Secretary of State, Robert Lansing, was worried by the sweeping declaration. He wrote, "Will it not breed discontent, disorder, and rebellion? The phrase is simply loaded with dynamite. It will raise hopes which can never be realized. It will, I fear, cost thousands of lives.

"What a calamity that the phrase was ever uttered! What misery it will cause!"

After 1984 rolled around, there were significant indications that Lansing, rather than Orwell, was in one way the better prophet. The concept of the superpower was being eroded. The most significant events in this trend were the fall of the Berlin Wall, the end of the Cold War, and the disintegration of the Soviet empire. As states broke away from that union, other areas picked up the battle cry of self-determination.

Self-determination is a worthy ideal. Reasonable persons uphold the principle. It often works well. Some "new" nations, like the Baltic republics—Latvia, Lithuania, and Estonia—had already demonstrated a capacity for nationhood in the years between World Wars I and II. But other new nations suffered violent disruptions at their birth, with serious continuing problems.

The roots of the problem lie in history, in the invasions and suppressions in the long, unhappy tale of war and conquest. The collapse of the Yugoslavian Republic in the late twentieth century and the consequent troubles provided a sense of déjà vu. It had all happened before. Sarajevo, scene of bitter fighting in the Bosnian-Serb conflict, was the city where the assassination of Archduke Ferdinand provided the spark that ignited World War I. When the Austro-Hungarian and Ottoman empires dissolved early in the twentieth century, the nationalistic components of these empires had their sights set on independence, but there were conflicting claims. At the Treaty of Versailles, an attempt was made to integrate smaller groups into larger units, like Czechoslovakia and Yugoslavia, but those experiments were ultimately doomed.

Upon what bases are claims for national sovereignty made? Religious, ethnic, racial, and political differences fuel sectional fires. The problem is aggravated by the simple reality that the groups are often intermingled, as with Muslim enclaves in largely orthodox communities and ethnic minorities inside ethnic majorities. Differences in language and culture play a role, too. Adolf Hitler annexed the Czechoslovakian Sudetenland in 1938 with the excuse that the peoples of that area were largely of German origin, language, and culture.

By 1919, the word *Balkanize* had appeared: "to break up a region into smaller, ineffectual, and often hostile units." By 1990, the word had taken on new and dangerous applications. The process was being demonstrated, not only in a corner of Europe, the Balkans; it had applications around the world.

During the Bosnian-Serb crisis, the *New York Times* printed a map of the world, identifying actual and potential trouble spots. Europe, Asia, and Africa showed the most danger signals, but even traditional paradises like Indonesia, Fiji, and Papua New Guinea were not exempt from the violence. Nearly all dissident groups called for the creation of new states composed of disaffected minorities.

New states are not always born in violence. Czechs and Slovaks, for example, agreed to go their separate ways, and the Republic of Czechoslovakia disappeared in 1993, without bloodshed. Elsewhere the transitions were not so peaceful. Bloody civil war in the former Yugoslavia pointed up the hazards of creating new states by

carving them out of the bodies of former
110 larger nations.

The creation of new states often encourages further splintering, as dissidents within these new nations attempt to break away into still smaller units. The eastern
115 region of Moldova, for example, declared independence in 1990, but western Moldova sought closer ties with Romania. Other former Soviet republics, like Georgia and Azerbaijan, slipped into near anarchy.
120 Chechnya has been a battleground.

The principle of self-determination, long a tenet of the United States, was incorporated into the charter of the United Nations. Sometimes good principles clash. The
125 principle of human rights is *also* a cornerstone of U.N. policy. Unfortunately, when new nations are formed, human rights are often trampled upon. When minorities become majorities, they sometimes persecute
130 new minorities.

In the *Times* article, the list of trouble spots was long: Northern Ireland, Romania, and Spain in Europe; Iraq, Turkey, and the Sudan in the Middle East and North Africa;
135 Liberia, Togo, Angola, Kenya, and Senegal in Africa; Afghanistan, Pakistan, India, and Sri Lanka in Asia; Guatemala, Colombia, Peru, and Brazil in South America. The list goes on and on. And the article didn't even
140 mention less dangerous but troublesome problems like the Quebec separatist movement in Canada.

Even when peace is tentatively restored in turbulent areas, problems remain. The
145 difficulties faced by the multinational peacekeeping forces in Kosovo underline the difficulties of restraining ethnic hatreds that have festered through the ages. Serbs and Albanians, who lived in peace for long
150 periods, were stirred by ancient bitterness.

The world has been presented with problems that have deep roots and far-reaching consequences. No one can predict the future.

1. The author believes that George Orwell and Robert Lansing _____.
   (A) were clear-sighted prophets with uncanny ability to foresee the future
   (B) gained their expertise through actually being involved in the running of government
   (C) looked at the world around them and developed somewhat different views about future events
   (D) were contemporaries who had arrived at similar, but incorrect, conclusions based on current trends
   (E) both played a role in the development of the novel *1984*

   1 ____

2. In line 16, the word *monolithic* most nearly means _____.
   (A) permanently nonsectarian
   (B) unexpectedly heterogeneous
   (C) narrowly defined
   (D) rigidly uniform
   (E) carelessly created

   2 ____

3. At the moment of writing, the author of the passage felt that _____.
   (A) there was danger that the Cold War would reappear on the world scene
   (B) the disintegration of the Soviet Union had few dangerous results
   (C) the Baltic republics had a promising future
   (D) the coming years would bring a significant reduction in the number of danger spots
   (E) the Czechs and Slovaks would eventually reunite

   3 ____

4. Orwell probably intended to show that waging "perpetual limited warfare" (line 12) helped to maintain internal social control by _____.
   (A) increasing farm production for military purposes
   (B) supplying an "enemy" against which all citizens could rally
   (C) training low-level citizen leaders in the armies of the superpowers
   (D) demonstrating the legitimacy of the cause for which each superpower fought
   (E) encouraging freedom of thought and expression

   4 ____

5. The meaning of "déjà vu" in line 55 can best be captured by the expression _____.
   (A) "I've seen it all before."
   (B) "Let sleeping dogs lie."
   (C) "Don't trouble trouble or trouble will trouble you."
   (D) "Birds of a feather stick together."
   (E) "Nothing happens the same way twice."

   5 ____

6. The author's attitude toward the principle of self-determination is one of _____.
   (A) undiluted support
   (B) approval with some concerns
   (C) disagreement with Lansing but not Orwell
   (D) unreserved disapproval
   (E) objection to its being included in the U.N. charter

   6 ____

7. The "larger units" mentioned in line 67 were doomed because of _____.
   (A) disputes over the wording of the Treaty of Versailles
   (B) the powerful and negative influence of the Soviet Union

(C) the conflicting positions of the Austro-Hungarian and Ottoman empires
(D) positive models of independence provided by the United States
(E) reviving nationalist ambitions

   7 ____

8. In line 75, the word "enclaves" means _____.
   (A) distinct units enclosed within larger units
   (B) restless and potentially dangerous groups
   (C) cultural majorities
   (D) democratically elected local governments
   (E) peaceful areas in the midst of violence

   8 ____

9. The author probably mentions Hitler's annexation of the Sudetenland to show that _____.
   (A) World War II would not have started if Hitler had not entered Czechoslovakia
   (B) irresponsibly exploited self-determination can have tragic consequences
   (C) language and culture are stronger unifying elements than religion
   (D) the Western Allies were inattentive to the just needs of a people
   (E) Hitler was more concerned with the well-being of Sudeten Germans than of his own people

   9 ____

10. A sharp contrast is pointed up in the author's comparison of _____.
    (A) Estonia and Czechoslovakia
    (B) Georgia and Yugoslavia
    (C) India and Turkey
    (D) Yugoslavia and Czechoslovakia
    (E) Liberia and Senegal

   10 ____

11. The basic problem for the U.N. is the conflict between two good principles: _____.

(A) economic security and political independence
(B) education and self-determination
(C) self-determination and human rights
(D) human rights and economic security
(E) political independence and education

11 ____

12. With which of the following statements would the author probably agree?

(A) Once Yugoslavia is quiet, the rest of the world will also quickly quiet down.
(B) The world would be better off with 1,500 nations in the U.N. than with 150.
(C) The United States should send troops to all the world's trouble spots.
(D) Force is the only way to settle problems of self-determination.
(E) The future will see additional demands for the creation of new nations.

12 ____

Problem

The following longer selection will provide practice in critical reading. Take the test before reading "Strategy," the analysis of the questions (pages 280–282). Try to uncover any weak areas in your reading. Then review helpful sections of the text itself.

How healthy is dieting? The following passage addresses some of the questions raised by dieters.

Among the topics of table conversation in the United States, diet holds an important place. So many people are future dieters, current dieters, or backsliders that nearly
5 everyone has something to say about dieting. On the surface, the problem is simple. *Eat less and lose weight.* While this statement is partly true, its simplicity is deceptive. As the title of one article states,
10 "Weight regulation may start in our cells, not psyches."

Some weight loss is always possible. Diets like those proposed by Weight Watchers have an understandable rationale, allowing
15 for reasonably nutritious and balanced meals throughout the dieting process. Others may be fad diets that recommend excessive consumption of single foods like bananas or grapefruit, good in themselves but
20 likely to result in a neglect of some important food groups. Since the number of diet books is astronomical, the number of persons trying diets must be surprisingly large.
25 The body is a self-repairing, self-perpetuating machine. All diets must fight the body's natural desire to protect itself, to retain the status quo. If there is a deviation, the body begins to fight against the change.
30 In general, if the body feels it is being starved, it takes protective measures that make continuing weight loss difficult—and often agonizing. This defensive strategy of the body explains the high failure rate of
35 dieters, most of whom relapse after a strenuous effort to lose weight and thus to become fashionably slim. The percentage of recidivists, those who relapse and regain their former weight, is estimated at two
40 thirds. For those who are far above their ideal weights, the failure rate is higher. The body's tendency to retain a state of equilibrium is called *homeostasis*—"staying the same."
45 Diets begin with enthusiasm. Initial suc-

cess disguises the difficulties ahead. Losing weight is only part of the problem. Maintaining the weight loss is the major hurdle. Many persons go on and off diets, the so-
50 called yo-yo effect. These persons are chagrined to discover that it's harder to lose weight on the second time around than on the first time. The situation gets worse on the third, fourth, and fifth attempts.

55 Recent studies have overturned some favorite explanations of obesity. Though it was once thought that emotional disorders cause obesity by overeating, a research group at the University of Pennsylvania
60 thinks that obesity causes emotional disorders. In societies that accept, even admire, obesity, the overweight person does not feel guilt, envy, or rejection. Being excessively overweight does present some health haz-
65 ards, but the condition is not helped by acute anxiety and self-condemnation.

Extreme concern for trendy slenderness, especially in young women, may result in bulimia or anorexia. With bulimia, defined
70 as "an abnormally voracious appetite," victims overeat and then purge themselves. With anorexia, defined as "a pathological fear of weight gain," victims starve themselves until malnutrition causes severe
75 health damage, even death. Their gaunt appearance is anything but attractive.

In their constant depiction of the so-called "ideal woman," the media saturate the minds of young women with images of
80 extremely slender models and actresses. As a result, the self-esteem of young girls is eroded. In one study, 60% of elementary-school girls said, "I'm happy the way I am." By high school, only 29% of the girls made
85 the same statement. There is much less uneasiness reported for boys than for girls. Part of the upset can be traceable to the glandular turbulence of adolescence. But a major part of the damage can be laid at the
90 door of faddish appearance. Healthy, lovely girls starve themselves, seek cosmetic surgery, attempt to emulate the models whose genetic makeup is largely responsible for

that thin, sometimes gaunt, appearance.
95 The girls' efforts may be in a losing struggle. The genetic component cannot be underestimated. Thin people tend to come from "thin families."

At Rockefeller University, three obesity
100 researchers have come to the conclusion that one's weight has something to do with the fat cells in the body. A major problem is how large these fat cells become. Generally the fat cells tend to stay constant in size in
105 animals and even in human beings. There is a subtle regulation in effect. When this regulation is disturbed, the fat cells may increase in size. When scientists destroyed the part of a rat's brain that regulates its
110 eating behavior, the rat became grossly obese. Fat cells grew to four or five times their normal size. Probably, in obese people, the signals that regulate fat-cell size may be somehow disturbed.

115 What about the problem with human beings? Two of the researchers selected a group of women and one man, all of whom belonged to Overeaters Anonymous. These people are formerly obese people. They are now of nor-
120 mal weight, but their body chemistries have been disturbed. They have tiny fat cells, but the dieters look gaunt and starved. They have low blood pressure and below-normal pulse rates. They are always cold. They con-
125 stantly think about food because they survive on a very low-calorie diet.

Would people of normal weight have similar biochemical changes if they lost weight? The researchers studied a volunteer for a
130 year and concluded that the body constantly fights to adjust its metabolism to retain its ideal weight. They also found that people have problem fat cells in specific areas. Women tend to have such fat cells on
135 their hips and thighs. Different people have different distributions of fat cells. One man complained, "Everything I eat goes to waist." Dieters sometimes find that weight loss is uneven. A desirable loss of 20 pounds
140 may come not from the paunch but from elsewhere.

There is much research to be done before any hard-and-fast conclusions can be drawn. What, then, is an overweight person 145 to do? The first bit of advice is to make only small changes in the lifestyle, at least at first. A drastic change is often self-defeating. This realization leads to the second bit of advice: don't be a yo-yo dieter. Your body 150 will work against you. Finally, monitor your eating by restricting calories in a reasonable way. Don't seek to become someone you were never, by nature, intended to be. Exercise more. Above all, don't develop a habit 155 of self-recrimination. Accept yourself. Realize that the problem is difficult and pervasive. You are not alone. Work on the attainable—and eliminate that anxiety.

1. The author's general attitude toward dieting can best be characterized as _____.
   (A) strongly approving
   (B) fervently dogmatic
   (C) unalterably opposed
   (D) somewhat skeptical
   (E) generally recommended

   1 ____

2. The author thinks that the "simple problem" (line 6) is _____.
   (A) best disregarded
   (B) poorly stated
   (C) tried and true
   (D) not accepted by most dieters
   (E) quite complex

   2 ____

3. "Weight regulation may start in our cells, not psyches" (lines 10–11), can best be matched with which statement from the passage?
   (A) "Emotional disorders cause obesity by overeating." (lines 57–58)
   (B) "Make only small changes in the lifestyle." (lines 145–146)
   (C) "The number of persons trying diets must be surprisingly large." (lines 22–24)
   (D) "Exercise more." (lines 153–154)

(E) "If the body feels it is being starved, it takes protective measures." (lines 30–31)

3 ____

4. As used in line 11, "psyches" means _____.
   (A) minds
   (B) genes
   (C) cultural backgrounds
   (D) early training
   (E) good intentions

   4 ____

5. As used in line 14, "rationale" means _____.
   (A) underlying reason
   (B) weak excuse
   (C) graphic chart
   (D) alternative plan
   (E) rallying cry

   5 ____

6. As used in line 22, the word "astronomical" is an example of _____.
   (A) simile
   (B) hyperbole
   (C) personification
   (D) alliteration
   (E) innovation

   6 ____

7. Yo-yo dieting can best be characterized as _____.
   (A) ultimately rewarding
   (B) entertaining
   (C) self-defeating
   (D) constantly encouraging
   (E) often fatal

   7 ____

8. All the following are mentioned as eating problems EXCEPT _____.
   (A) anorexia
   (B) yo-yo dieting
   (C) bulimia
   (D) fad diets
   (E) cholesterol

   8 ____

9. In answering question 8, which of the following skills would you use?
   (A) determining the author's purpose
   (B) looking for significant generalizations
   (C) intensive rereading of the selection
   (D) skimming for words mentioned
   (E) drawing inferences

   9 ____

10. The quotation marks around the expression following the word *homeostasis* in lines 43–44 suggest that the expression _____.
    (A) is a quotation from one of the research articles
    (B) is an interesting, though somewhat inaccurate, statement
    (C) provides the etymological definition
    (D) is too far-fetched for acceptance
    (E) provides an alternative interpretation of homeostasis

    10 ____

11. A major problem leading to diets, with their consequent failure, is _____.
    (A) a person's self-image
    (B) business disagreements
    (C) anorexia
    (D) eating more than 1,000 calories daily
    (E) broken engagements

    11 ____

12. The power of the media is probably best reflected in the word _____.
    (A) "exercise" (lines 153–154)
    (B) "trendy" (line 67)
    (C) "backsliders" (line 4)
    (D) "turbulence" (line 88)
    (E) "relapse" (line 35)

    12 ____

13. In line 92, "emulate" means _____.
    (A) outdo
    (B) analyze
    (C) report
    (D) imitate
    (E) photograph

    13 ____

14. That anorexic persons starve themselves to look better is an example of _____.
    (A) indifference
    (B) common sense
    (C) metaphor
    (D) irony
    (E) good health

    14 ____

15. In line 93, "genetic" means _____.
    (A) unclassifiable
    (B) irrational
    (C) manageable
    (D) nonspecific
    (E) inherited

    15 ____

16. From current research, it seems apparent that _____.
    (A) the body may actually encourage obesity
    (B) fat cells increase in size and number entirely on their own
    (C) some persons have no fat cells
    (D) definitive answers about curing obesity have now been found
    (E) obesity results from eating too much of one kind of food

    16 ____

17. "Everything I eat goes to waist" (lines 137–138) is intended to be _____.
    (A) gritty
    (B) self-pitying
    (C) untrue
    (D) humorous
    (E) solemn

    17 ____

18. In lines 156–157, *pervasive* means
_____.
(A) discouraging
(B) widespread
(C) pessimistic
(D) trivial
(E) time-consuming

18 ____

19. The last paragraph in the passage is intended to _____.
(A) reassure as well as inform
(B) say the last word about dieting
(C) condemn all attempts at losing weight
(D) frighten the reader
(E) provide a humorous summary

19 ____

20. The following outline of the structure of the passage is scrambled. Choose the sequence that best suggests the order of treatment.
    a. Challenges to Conventional Thinking About Diet
    b. Popularity of Dieting
    c. Advice to Dieters
    d. Dangers of Dieting
    e. Problems of Dieting
    f. The Part Played by Fat Cells

(A) a, d, c, b, e, f
(B) d, a, f, b, e, c
(C) b, e, a, d, f, c
(D) e, f, d, c, b, a
(E) c, d, f, b, a, e

20 ____

21. The tone and style of the author can best be characterized as _____.
(A) strongly reproachful
(B) quietly informative
(C) characteristically bitter
(D) pungently witty
(E) consistently argumentative

21 ____

22. The author's attitude toward crash diets is basically _____.
(A) disapproving
(B) apathetic
(C) accepting under controlled situations
(D) unequivocally favorable
(E) not implied in the passage

22 ____

23. Young women are especially vulnerable to anorexia because _____.
(A) they are more likely to have the spirit of adventure than young men
(B) there are inherited tendencies toward the disease
(C) they are more likely to catch an infection from friends
(D) they are subject to more pressure than men to look slender
(E) many movie stars have exhibited signs of the disease

23 ____

24. After reading this passage, a reader is likely to feel _____.
(A) impelled to disagree strongly with the author
(B) a little more secure about himself or herself
(C) free to eat anything and everything formerly considered harmful
(D) that nothing works in weight control
(E) motivated to enter a weight-loss contest

24 ____

Strategy. 1. The *general* tone of the passage is skeptical about diets, but lines 142–144 *specifically* indicate reserved judgment. The answer is (D) somewhat skeptical.

2. The passage repeatedly discusses the complexities of diet. The answer is (E) quite complex.

3. Taking protective measures (lines 30–31) is equivalent to regulating weight. Therefore (E) is the best answer.

4. The wording of the sentences suggests that the answer is contrasted with *cells.* Genes are part of cells, so this answer (B) may be eliminated. Only (A) suggests a reasonable contrast: *cells* not *minds.*

5. Context provides the answer, not only in the whole sentence but also in the use of *reasonably* and *balanced* in line 15. The answer is (A) underlying reason.

6. Astronomy deals with billions and multibillions. The number of diet books, though large in comparison with books on other topics, is tiny when compared with the immensities of space. This is exaggeration or (B) hyperbole.

7. After the author mentions yo-yo dieting in line 50, he tells how dieters usually cannot keep their weight down, suggesting that the yo-yo diet is (C) self-defeating.

8. The answer to this question requires skimming. A process of elimination reveals that cholesterol has nowhere been mentioned (E).

9. See question 8. The answer is (D).

10. The pairing of the word and the quoted expression following suggests that the author is defining an unfamiliar word for the reader (C). The other possibilities are irrelevant.

11. Lines 90–93 deal specifically with self-image and its effect on eating habits. Unrealistic goals bring unrealistic diets and unhealthy bodies. The answer is (A) a person's self-image.

12. Lines 77–80 detail the power of the media in shaping the images and goals of young women. Line 90 introduces the word faddish, a clue to the answer (B) trendy.

13. The girls are trying to be like the models, suggesting that the answer is (D) imitate.

14. Irony (D) is a contrast of opposites. Anorexic persons hope to look better, but they actually have a "gaunt appearance" (lines 75–76). The intended purpose is beauty, but the result is its opposite.

15. In lines 97–98, the author writes that "thin people tend to come from 'thin families.' " Thus the answer is (E) inherited.

16. By fighting against weight loss and by striving to maintain the status quo, the body may actually encourage (A) obesity. The other answers are in no way suggested.

17. The pun on *waist* and *waste* suggests that the statement is intended to be (D) humorous.

18. If "you are not alone," the problem is (B) widespread.

19. After all the discouraging statements, the final paragraph provides a brief blueprint for effective action. An overweight person *can* do something, even if only in a modest way. The author is thus reassuring as well as informing the reader (A).

20. The opening paragraph immediately comments about the popularity of dieting. Thus (C) jumps out at once as having the best opening topic. For purposes of answering this question, this recognition is all that is needed, but further check will reveal that the sequence of topics is popularity, problems, challenges, dangers, fat cells, and advice. (C) is the confirmed answer.

21. Though (B) seems obvious, it is sometimes prudent to eliminate the other possibilities. The author is nowhere reproachful (A). He is positive, rather than bitter (C). There is one small pun, not enough to characterize the passage as a whole (D). The author is modest, balanced, and understated, if anything, not argumentative (E).

22. The author suggests his disapproval (A) throughout the passage. He talks about the body's protective measures, the high percentage of dieters who relapse, the dangers of yo-yo dieting, the threat of anorexia, and other problems of dieting.

23. In line 68, the author uses the expression *especially in young women, a* clue to (D).

24. The passage is upbeat about the possibilities for modest success in dieting. It also disapproves the media's efforts to make all women clones of a few unusual types. It shows the futility of yo-yo dieting. It says, "Work on the attainable—and eliminate that anxiety." This is a reassuring message that should make readers feel more secure (B)

REVIEW

The authorship of Shakespeare's plays is a perennial source of controversy, as this passage points out.

Who wrote the plays of Shakespeare? Nearly all scholars logically and reasonably answer, "William Shakespeare," but for the past 200 years, there have been attempts to
5 "prove" that someone else wrote the plays. Sir Francis Bacon, English philosopher and statesman, was the first to be considered seriously. He was a slightly older contemporary of Shakespeare and had a busy but
10 not-altogether-successful career in politics.
Bacon, however, was only the first of many candidates. Some others proposed for the honor include the Earl of Essex, John Donne, Ben Jonson, Sir Walter Raleigh, the
15 Earl of Southampton, and even Cardinal Wolsey. There is no limit to the absurdities. Among the proposed creators were Mary, Queen of Scots; Queen Elizabeth; and an Irish nun.
20 Why did all these candidates gain any credence at all? One argument is heard over and over. How could a simple country boy become so brilliant, so knowledgeable, so sophisticated, so wise in the ways of the
25 world? The answer, like that to the opening question, is obvious. Shakespeare was not a "simple country boy."
There is little doubt that Shakespeare had a good education. The fact that there is
30 no record of his schooling is irrelevant.

There is no record of the schooling of most of Shakespeare's contemporaries. School records are generally not permanent documents. Indeed, there are even such gaps in
35 the biographies of recent writers. Shakespeare's knowledge of history and the classics may well have come from the commonly used schoolbooks of the time. Since his father was a prominent town official, it
40 is likely that Shakespeare was given a suitable education. In *The Merry Wives of Windsor,* Shakespeare parodies a typical Latin lesson of the kind he was probably subjected to.

45 There are other equally baseless objections to Shakespeare's claim to authorship of the plays, but one calm and measured voice relies on a very subtle reading of the plays themselves. More than half a century
50 ago, Caroline Spurgeon published a study that forever settled the matter of Shakespeare's authorship, at least to the satisfaction of most scholars. *Shakespeare's Imagery* is a seminal book of great insight
55 and impressive erudition. Shakespeare's use of figurative language, the author claims, is idiosyncratic, unique to the playwright. His use of various images reflects his personality and provides insight into his
60 mind.

In *Orlando,* the novelist Virginia Woolf writes, "Every secret of a writer's soul, every experience of his life, every quality of his mind, is written large in his works, yet
65 we require critics to explain the one and biographers to expound the other."

Since no two persons have exactly the same experiences, personalities inevitably vary. People develop individual ways of
70 speaking, of expressing an idea, of using figurative language. The specialized experiences of childhood and adulthood inevitably determine the images we use. The moon has been variously called a "ghostly gal-
75 leon," a "feather," a "silver pinhead," an "arrant thief," an "orbed maiden with white fire laden," the "hostess of the sky," even the "sweet surprise of heaven." At this very

moment, perhaps, a lover is writing a love
80 poem with still another image for the journeying moon.

Shakespeare's imagery, the author points out, is quite different from that of Francis Bacon or any other contemporary.
85 More significantly, a great many of Shakespeare's images can be traced to specific incidents and experiences in his life. As a boy, Shakespeare undoubtedly dreamed on the Stratford bridge as he watched the
90 current beneath. The peculiar ebb and flow of the River Avon at that point appears in an image in a play.

Images often arise unbidden from the unconscious; yet Shakespeare channels
95 these bursting images and furthers the dramatic qualities of his plays by their use. The images almost explode. In *Troilus and Cressida,* Ulysses tries to lure Achilles back into the fight against the Trojans. In a
100 speech of 36 lines, Shakespeare pours forth more than 25 images, tumbling and cascading over each other, showing Achilles that fame and honor are, at best, transient and must be attended to constantly.

105 Spurgeon has analyzed plays individually to show how a specific constellation of images dominates certain plays. *Othello,* for example, has many sea images. Images of sickness in *Hamlet* reinforce the thought
110 that something is "rotten in Denmark." *The Tempest* abounds in sound imagery. *As You Like It* includes a great many country images. Sleep and the lack of it have a prominent place in *Macbeth.* And so it goes. The
115 number is astounding—for example, 204 images in *Romeo and Juliet* and 279 in *Hamlet.*

Spurgeon does more than analyze Shakespeare's plays. She also studies the
120 writing of his contemporaries, especially those who have been put forth as claimants to the authorship of the plays. She finds vast differences, for example, between the images of Shakespeare and those of Chris-
125 topher Marlowe. Marlowe's imagery is bookish, chiefly classical. Animals and na-

ture come second, with most nature images confined to celestial bodies. With Shakespeare, nature and animals lead. Learning
130 is in fourth place. Marlowe's images tend to be imaginative, chiefly personifications. Shakespeare's nature images are drawn from daily life.

There is one last rebuttal to the argu-
135 ments that Shakespeare did not, could not write the plays. Shakespeare's contemporaries—fellow actors and playwrights alike—respected him enough to preserve his plays. By contrast, most of the vast play
140 production of his fellow playwrights has been lost forever. When all is said and done, Shakespeare is really Shakespeare!

Wearying of the fruitless controversy, a scholar once wrote, "William Shakespeare
145 didn't write the plays. It was another person of the same name."

1. The use of quotation marks around the word *prove* in line 5 suggests _____.
   (A) that an authority is being quoted
   (B) the author's skepticism
   (C) a conviction that Shakespeare was not the author of the plays
   (D) a subtle tribute to Sir Francis Bacon
   (E) a linkage with the later discussion of *Shakespeare's Imagery*

   1 ____

2. The use of *even* in line 15 suggests that the author considers Cardinal Wolsey _____.
   (A) a more likely candidate than the Earl of Essex
   (B) a possible associate of the Irish nun
   (C) the leading contender for the title of Shakespearean author
   (D) a most unlikely candidate
   (E) a secret author

   2 ____

3. In line 21, *credence* means _____.
   (A) unreliable report
   (B) criticism
   (C) advantages
   (D) misfortune
   (E) believability

   3 ____

4. The author dismisses the no-education argument because _____.
   (A) school records confirm Shakespeare's attendance at a common school
   (B) Shakespeare probably attended Oxford or Cambridge University
   (C) school records are ordinarily not preserved
   (D) Francis Bacon attested to Shakespeare's education
   (E) all records were probably destroyed in the great London fire

   4 ____

5. In line 30, *irrelevant* means _____.
   (A) impossible
   (B) immaterial
   (C) irreproachable
   (D) irremediable
   (E) inexplicable

   5 ____

6. Shakespeare's knowledge of history, unlike his knowledge of nature, probably came from _____.
   (A) his early experiences in and around Stratford
   (B) his school textbooks
   (C) his father's prominence as a local dignitary
   (D) a special course in the classics
   (E) his friendly association with Ben Jonson and the Earl of Southampton

   6 ____

7. The gaps in the biographies of recent authors suggest that _____.
   (A) we should cease to worry about Shakespeare's attendance at a Stratford school
   (B) keepers of records are incredibly remiss and worthy of reproach
   (C) those authors probably had some skeletons in their closets
   (D) modern record keeping is probably worse than that of Shakespeare's time
   (E) biographies are inherently more difficult to write than novels

   7 ____

8. The "calm and measured voice" mentioned in lines 47–48 belongs to _____.

   (A) Caroline Spurgeon
   (B) Virginia Woolf
   (C) a critic of *Shakespeare's Imagery*
   (D) an unnamed scholar
   (E) Shakespeare himself

   8 ____

9. In line 55, *erudition* means _____.
   (A) conjecture
   (B) length
   (C) credentials
   (D) writing style
   (E) scholarship

   9 ____

10. In line 57, *idiosyncratic* means _____.

    (A) overwhelming
    (B) individualistic
    (C) unexpected
    (D) untamed
    (E) unwise

    10 ____

11. In line 64, *yet* suggests that Virginia Woolf _____.
    (A) concludes that Shakespeare wrote the plays
    (B) considers most critics biased and unreliable
    (C) has a surprising unfamiliarity with the writing of biography

    (D) deplores the excessive use of imagery in a writer's work
    (E) thinks the writer's secrets should be clear to all readers

    11 ____

12. The labels attached to the moon (lines 74–78) are all _____.
    (A) in poor taste
    (B) images
    (C) examples of personification
    (D) used by young poets writing to their lovers
    (E) similes

    12 ____

13. In lines 80–81, *the journeying moon* is an example of _____.
    (A) simile
    (B) irony
    (C) exaggeration
    (D) metaphor
    (E) understatement

    13 ____

14. If a specific image relating to the River Avon appears in a Shakespeare play, we may assume that _____.
    (A) Shakespeare probably wrote that play
    (B) a great many other writers saw the same ebb and flow
    (C) Francis Bacon could never have used a nature image
    (D) Shakespeare probably lived within sight of the bridge
    (E) he probably used the same image over and over

    14 ____

15. In line 94, *channels* suggests _____.
    (A) ineptness
    (B) exploitation
    (C) destruction
    (D) control
    (E) repression

    15 ____

16. In lines 101–102, *cascading* suggests comparison with _____.
    (A) water
    (B) fireworks
    (C) volcanic ash
    (D) athletics
    (E) storms

    16 ____

17. The author obviously considers Ulysses' speech in *Troilus and Cressida* _____.
    (A) an ineffective argument to present to Achilles
    (B) a digression from the dramatic action
    (C) an amazing achievement
    (D) an excessive use of simile
    (E) an indication that Shakespeare probably did not write the play

    17 ____

18. In line 103, *transient* means _____.
    (A) fleeting
    (B) confusing
    (C) contradictory
    (D) useless
    (E) common

    18 ____

19. In line 106, *constellation* suggests a _____.
    (A) burst of creativity
    (B) predominance of astronomical images
    (C) study
    (D) slight scattering
    (E) special grouping

    19 ____

20. In the discussion of images, the author mentions all the following plays EXCEPT _____.
    (A) *Hamlet*
    (B) *Macbeth*
    (C) *The Tempest*
    (D) *The Merry Wives of Windsor*
    (E) *As You Like It*

    20 ____

21. In lines 124–125, the name of Christopher Marlowe _____.
    (A) bolsters the claims of other candidates
    (B) is put forth for the first time in the passage
    (C) suggests a preeminent master of nature images
    (D) is brought in almost as an afterthought
    (E) has often been linked to *As You Like It*

    21 ____

22. The comparison of Marlowe and Shakespeare suggests that _____.
    (A) Marlowe, at least in his early years, was probably superior to Shakespeare
    (B) Marlowe drew more on personal experience than Shakespeare did
    (C) Marlowe probably had more formal education than Shakespeare
    (D) the two men probably disliked each other intensely
    (E) Spurgeon may have actually liked Marlowe's plays better than Shakespeare's

    22 ____

23. The last paragraph is an attempt at _____.
    (A) mild humor
    (B) scholarly pretense
    (C) self-glorification
    (D) bitter anger
    (E) timid uncertainty

    23 ____

REVIEW

Like the preceding passage, this dialogue is a longer exercise to challenge your critical reading abilities. It tests a variety of skills, but your experiences with previous chapters will help you meet the challenge.

When is a screwdriver not a screwdriver? The following passage presents some surprising answers.

I was putting up storm windows. My neighbor, Alfred Nansen, loves to supervise a job, any job.

5 "Hey! Need any help?"

Knowing the quality of the "help" he was offering, I declined graciously, but Al came over anyway. Besides being a nondoer of any physical work, Al is a homespun philos-
10 opher. No, he never worked as a stevedore, but his work as a bridge tender on the Mathers Bridge gives him plenty of time to read—and think.

I was having trouble. "This window is
15 sticking. I need to chisel a small section off the corner, but I can't find my wood chisel. Got one?"

"No. Use your screwdriver," he suggested. He handed it to me, and I nicked just
20 enough off the frame to ease the window back into place.

"You know," he said, "if you understand the screwdriver, you can understand what language is all about."

25 "What's to understand? A screwdriver is a screwdriver."

"Ah, but there you're wrong. *You* say a screwdriver is a screwdriver. I say it breaks through those simple boundaries. A screw-
30 driver can be a chisel, a scriber, a wedge, a lever for prying open can tops, a knife, a letter opener, a . . ."

"Whoa," I interrupted. "A screwdriver was designed for a specific purpose. Why
35 burden it with other chores?"

"Why not? It can be the core of a puppet,

a doorstop, a hammer, a post in croquet, a boundary marker, a plumb bob, a splint, the gnomon of a sundial, a . . .

"But what's the point?" I again inter-
40 rupted a bit peevishly. "What is this catalogue of yours proving? What's so great about using a screwdriver as a hammer? Why not get a hammer?"

"Ah, but suppose you don't have a ham-
45 mer handy? Also, suppose you need a tool that hasn't been invented yet, like a skrillion. How can you get a skrillion if there isn't any to be had?"

"What's a skrillion?" I asked a bit testily.

50 "I don't know," Al replied, "but you certainly could use one. A skrillion would be useful for retrieving items that have fallen beneath heavy objects like stoves and refrigerators. I know. I've used a screwdriver
55 for the job, but a skrillion would have been better. But if it hasn't been invented yet, what can you do?"

"Well," I said, getting into the spirit of things, "maybe you don't need a skrillion.
60 Besides the screwdriver you could use a dowel, a piece of lath, a poker, a marshmallow fork, a coat hanger, a cane, a walking stick, a sword, a javelin, a sickle, a boomerang, a . . ."

65 "*Now* you're getting it," Al chuckled.

"But you said I'd understand what language is all about. How does that screwdriver provide such magnificent enlightenment? You've convinced me I can use a
70 screwdriver for many different things. So what?"

"So what!" Al echoed. "Don't you see what we've just been doing?"

"Yes, we've been talking about different
75 uses of tools for different jobs. I don't get any special enlightenment from that information."

"We have been crossing boundaries and breaking boxes. Like most people," Al told
80 me, "you live in boxes. No, I'm not insulting

the shape of your lovely house. I'm talking about the boxes you can't see."

"What are these mysterious boxes?" I asked. "Four-dimensional boxes? Tesser-
85 acts?"

"No, no, no. These are the boxes of language, the names we give things, the classifications we make, the generalizations we derive every day of our lives."

90 "What's wrong?" I protested. "We need names and classifications. How could we communicate if we didn't agree on various word meanings and classifications? Language is the greatest achievement of hu-
95 mankind, and you're criticizing it."

"Not at all. Language is indeed a miracle, but miracles are dynamite. We have to know what we're dealing with. We have to set up these boxes to live in society, but we
100 must not be overwhelmed by them. The boxes were made for us; we were not made for the boxes."

"What's all this got to do with screwdrivers?" I asked mischievously.

105 "Everything! If you say a screwdriver is a screwdriver, period, you are being controlled by your boxes. A screwdriver isn't really anything until it is used. When you use it to attach a fixture to the wall, you are
110 indeed using it as a screwdriver. But when you use it to open a can of paint, you are breaking out of a box. The screwdriver is now a 'can opener.'"

"It's still a screwdriver to me!" I insisted.

115 "OK, if it makes you feel better, just as long as you know you can break out of that box. Breaking out of the box once frees you for other little victories. I had trouble opening a jar of wheat germ, which is vacuum-
120 packed. I couldn't turn the cover. I didn't have a jar clamp. What to do? Aha, my 'screwdriver.' I gently placed the blade under the cover and twisted. Success! The vacuum was broken. My screwdriver was
125 now a 'jar opener.'"

"Very clever," I noted grudgingly, "but I'm still a little unsure of your point about boxes."

"In a nutshell this is it: we have to have
130 boxes but we have to understand their limitations. We have to create boxes and then we must break out of them."

"Why is breaking out so important?"

"Because we are straitjacketed by the
135 boxes. The major characteristic of the creative person is a willingness to break out of the boxes, an ability to go beyond the classifications. The artist creates patterns that open our eyes to new ways of seeing. The
140 poet links unlikely words to create unique combinations and 'new boxes.' The inventor looks at a need and creates a clothespin, a safety pin, a zipper. After the invention, everything looks simple. But how many
145 people stayed in the boxes before the geniuses broke through?"

"Hmmm," I mused. "But aren't some boxes fixed? Aren't some classifications tied so close to nature they can't be attacked or
150 shifted? How about the classification for *dog*? Isn't there something out there that always and forever matches our word *dog*?"

"*All* our classifications are made by us. A dog doesn't know it's a dog. We have decided
155 to lump all of a certain type of animal in a box we label *dog*. But the label is ours. We could have used other bases of classification. Even the word *dog* becomes a little fuzzy when wolves breed with dogs. There's
160 a huge something we label 'reality.' To handle this huge whatever, we slice it up into convenient pieces. This piece we'll label 'dog.' That piece we'll label 'tree' and so on. But the slices are our own! All ours!"

165 "Those slices are helpful," I interposed.

"No, not just helpful; they're essential."

"Agreed," Al said. "A marvelous achievement all right. But it sometimes gives us the feeling we know more than we know. Real-
170 ity is unknowable. The mystery of life is beyond us. Like Newton, we are playing with pebbles on the shores of knowledge. I often think of a quotation attributed to Ralph Sockman: 'The larger the island of
175 knowledge, the longer the shoreline of wonder.' But in everyday life we must play with

those pebbles and build roads with them. Language certainly helps."

Al had me thinking. I picked up the
180 screwdriver and looked at it thoughtfully. Finally, I said to Al, "You know what I'm going to do? I'm going out and invent a skrillion."

1. The selection is essentially about
   _____.
   (A) the handyman's approach to tasks
   (B) the many uses of a screwdriver
   (C) the genius vs. the common man
   (D) language at work
   (E) the meaning of friendship

   1 ____

2. Skrillion is introduced as _____.
   (A) a practical solution to a problem
   (B) a new tool
   (C) an alternative to a screwdriver
   (D) a power tool as opposed to a manual tool
   (E) an example

   2 ____

3. "We are straitjacketed by boxes" suggests that _____.
   (A) we are limited by language
   (B) our lives are cluttered by material things
   (C) creative people are especially confined
   (D) the accumulation of goods is self-defeating
   (E) we are trapped, without escape

   3 ____

4. The writer is using narrative essentially to _____.
   (A) depict two interesting friends
   (B) make a point
   (C) demonstrate an ability to write dialogue
   (D) entertain
   (E) mislead the reader

   4 ____

5. Of the following quotations from the article, the most important is _____.
   (A) "I need to chisel a small section off the corner, but I can't find my wood chisel."
   (B) "What's to understand? A screwdriver is a screwdriver."
   (C) "A screwdriver isn't really anything until it is used."
   (D) "A screwdriver was designed for a specific purpose."
   (E) "What's so great about using a screwdriver as a hammer?"

   5 ____

6. The boxes mentioned throughout the article are _____.
   (A) in the mind only
   (B) easily understood and easily handled
   (C) essentially areas where tools are kept
   (D) animal pens, especially for dogs
   (E) labels for social position

   6 ____

7. Which of the following comments by baseball umpires accurately reflects the point of view of Al Nansen?
   (A) "Some are strikes and some are balls, and I try my best to call them."
   (B) "Some are strikes and some are balls, but I occasionally miss a call."
   (C) "Some are strikes and some are balls, and I call them as they are."
   (D) "Some are strikes and some are balls, and I call them as I see them."
   (E) "Some are strikes and some are balls, but they aren't anything till I call them."

   7 ____

8. Of the two neighbors, we may say that
   _____.
   (A) Al is a better carpenter
   (B) the writer is a more astute student
   (C) Al is a good teacher
   (D) there is considerable animosity between them
   (E) Al is less sympathetic
                                    8 ____

9. The writer uses conversation to
   _____.
   (A) make abstract ideas concrete
   (B) reveal Al's superficiality
   (C) dramatize the battle of wits between the neighbors
   (D) make the appearance of the page more interesting
   (E) compare a box of cereal with a toolbox
                                    9 ____

10. In his attitude toward the screwdriver, Al is _____.
    (A) dogmatic and limited
    (B) unconsciously funny
    (C) free and unrestricted
    (D) grossly in error
    (E) incongruously reverent
                                    10 ____

11. Al Nansen would probably be most critical of _____.
    (A) directions for assembling a kite
    (B) a television sitcom
    (C) the weather report
    (D) campaign speeches
    (E) lovers' conversations
                                    11 ____

12. The expression "pebbles on the shores of knowledge" is an example of
    _____.
    (A) simile
    (B) irony
    (C) exaggeration
    (D) a literal statement
    (E) metaphor
                                    12 ____

13. The style of the dialogue is _____.
    (A) interesting but ponderous
    (B) dull and argumentative
    (C) repetitious and self-conscious
    (D) light and breezy
    (E) deceptively unpleasant
                                    13 ____

14. A tesseract (lines 83–84) is probably
    _____.
    (A) a screwdriver
    (B) a box with more than six sides
    (C) a fourth-dimension concept
    (D) another name for *skrillion*
    (E) something Al made up
                                    14 ____

15. At the conclusion of the dialogue, the author probably _____.
    (A) invented a skrillion
    (B) invited Al in for a three-dimensional tea
    (C) understood language a little better
    (D) found a chisel in his toolbox
    (E) thought things over and disagreed with Al
                                    15 ____

SUMMARY

1. Studying the Longer Passage

The SAT now includes longer and more challenging critical reading selections. Each selection tests a greater variety of skills than is possible with shorter selections. Readers have to hold on to a point of view for a longer period. The skills tested, however, are those developed working with shorter passages. For greater teaching effectiveness, the preceding chapters in this book isolate the reading skills being reviewed. Longer passages provide the opportunity for readers to flex their critical muscles, to call upon their skills to handle new and more complex combinations.

----

2. Studying Paired Passages

The test also includes paired passages. The passages may agree with each other, disagree, or complement each other, thereby enriching the point of view presented. The College Board notes, "Some of the questions on the paired passages will assess students' ability to compare or contrast the two passages, to use information from one to interpret information in the other, and to identify assumptions they share or pivotal differences between them." Paired passages provide greater challenges but also arouse greater interest in the subject matter. Readers welcome different viewpoints on the same or similar topics. The paired passages provide those viewpoints.

TRIAL TEST

The following two passages talk about a common tendency that may have deeper implications than we realize.

Passage 1

In my previous talk, "On a Certain Blindness," I tried to make you feel how soaked and shot-through life is with values and meanings which we fail to realize because
5 of our external and insensible point of view. The meanings are there for the others, but they are not there for us. There lies more than a mere interest of curious speculation in understanding this. It has the most tre-
10 mendous practical importance. I wish that I could convince you of it as I feel it myself. It is the basis of all our tolerance, social, religious, and political. The forgetting of it lies at the root of every stupid and sangui-
15 nary mistake that rulers over subject-peoples make. The first thing to learn in intercourse with others is noninterference with their own peculiar ways of being happy, provided those ways do not assume
20 to interfere by violence with ours. No one has insight into all the ideals. No one should presume to judge them offhand. The preten-

sion to dogmatize about them in each other is the root of most human injustices and
25 cruelties, and the trait in human character most likely to make the angels weep.

Passage 2

She was, moreover, one of those few persons—for they are very few—who are contented to go on with their existence without
30 making themselves the center of any special outward circle. To the ordinary run of minds it is impossible not to do this. A man's own dinner is to himself so important that he cannot bring himself to believe that it is
35 a matter utterly indifferent to everyone else. A lady's collection of baby clothes, in early years, and of house linen and curtain fringes in later life, is so very interesting to her own eyes that she cannot believe but
40 that other people will rejoice to behold it. I would not, however, be held as regarding this tendency as evil. It leads to conversation of some sort among people, and perhaps to a kind of sympathy. Mrs. Jones will look
45 at Mrs. White's linen chest, hoping that Mrs. White may be induced to look at hers.

One can only pour out of a jug that which is in it. For the most of us, if we do not talk of ourselves, or at any rate of the individual
50 circles of which we are the centers, we can talk of nothing.

1. A common proverb that sums up the philosophy of the author of Passage 1 is _____.
   (A) "Never leave till tomorrow what you can do today."
   (B) "Live and let live."
   (C) "A good name is rather to be chosen than great riches."
   (D) "A soft answer turneth away wrath."
   (E) "Look before you leap."

   1 ____

2. The author feels that "a mere interest of curious speculation" _____.
   (A) may fail to realize the deeper significance
   (B) may lead to rigidity and inflexibility
   (C) interferes with the rights of others
   (D) inevitably leads to deeper awareness
   (E) is a waste of time

   2 ____

3. The rights we take for granted are _____.
   (A) seldom appreciated
   (B) gained at the expense of others
   (C) given up too easily to authority figures
   (D) basically deceptive and unreal
   (E) limited by the rights of others

   3 ____

4. When the author says, "No one has insight into all the ideals," he is calling for _____.
   (A) his own particular insights and ideas
   (B) strong leaders
   (C) reviewers who judge film through their own special insights
   (D) higher education
   (E) an open mind

   4 ____

5. In line 23, the word *dogmatize* most nearly means _____.
   (A) express a rigid opinion
   (B) talk sympathetically
   (C) research extensively
   (D) speak loudly
   (E) seek revenge

   5 ____

6. Throughout, the author's approach is one of _____.
   (A) anxious pleading
   (B) measured reasonableness
   (C) strong denunciation
   (D) feigned indifference
   (E) subtle humor

   6 ____

7. Both Passage 1 and Passage 2 deal with _____.
   (A) personal ill will
   (B) self-centeredness
   (C) deep-seated prejudice
   (D) human injustices and cruelties
   (E) attempts to convert others politically

   7 ____

8. In comparison with the basic premise of Passage 1, Passage 2 is more concerned with _____.
   (A) the evils brought on by monopolizing conversations
   (B) generally unselfish behavior
   (C) the pointlessness of human communication
   (D) harmless human weaknesses
   (E) the dangers of misleading others

   8 ____

9. The author suggests that many speakers _____.
   (A) have uninterested listeners
   (B) seek to dominate their listeners
   (C) would rather listen to others than speak
   (D) have much of interest to speak about
   (E) are rather shy with strangers

   9 ____

10. One way of suggesting the central idea of Passage 2 is the expression _____.

(A) Talk is the lubricant of friendship.
(B) Dinner conversation makes dining pleasant.
(C) Talking about the experiences of childhood may not be interesting to others.
(D) Excellent conversationalists are born, not made.
(E) Every person is the hero of his/her own life.

10 ____

11. The author introduces the jug metaphor (lines 47–48) to suggest the _____.

(A) dangers of alcoholism
(B) limitations of human conversation
(C) techniques of interpersonal relationships
(D) need for communication
(E) source of conversational ideas

11 ____

Let's analyze together another paired selection.

Problem

When social scientists talk about the future of the world and population growth, they tend to divide into two groups, popularly called the Cassandras and the Pollyannas. Authorities in the former group take a negative position, foretelling global disaster. They tend to be biologists. Authorities in the latter group take a positive position, suggesting that the world will somehow solve its problems. They tend to be economists. The first passage below takes the Cassandra position; the second passage, the Pollyanna.

Passage 1

Concern about the dangers of over-population is not new. In 1589, Giovanni Botero, an Italian scholar, warned of the dangerous maladjustment of population
5 and resources. These two, he said, were on a collision course. Two centuries later, in 1798, Robert Thomas Malthus warned, in his "Essay on Population," that the world faced a terrible problem. He wrote, "The
10 power of population is indefinitely greater than the power in the earth to provide subsistence for man." Population grows faster than the means to feed all the new mouths.

Although Malthus did not know or use
15 the term *ecology*, modern scientists point out the environmental catastrophes created by unchecked population growth. There are ecological limits beyond which land cannot support life. Nature is ruthless. When wild
20 creatures expand beyond the carrying capacity of their habitat, disaster occurs, whether they be deer in Michigan or lemmings in Norway.

Every year, the earth is adding a hundred
25 million people. At current rates, by the year 2100, the earth will have to support 10 to 12 billion people. They will not only have to be fed. They'll have to be provided living space, jobs, cars, recreation, material goods and
30 services. How can the global economy provide all the necessary elements? The traffic of life will be in perpetual gridlock.

In sub-Saharan Africa, overpopulation has led to desertification, the destruction of
35 land. Overgrazing, deforestation, and erosion make the land less habitable, but meanwhile the population soars. In the Himalayas, the destruction of mountain forests has led to soil erosion and subsequent
40 floods in the populous cities of India. Today's firewood is used at the expense of

tomorrow's flood control. Again, population pressures result in ecological nightmares.

In some instances, population tensions 45 have led to civil strife and famine, as in Somalia in the last decade of the twentieth century. Even when food is available, civil repression often prevents its distribution. Laboratory rats kept in too close confine-50 ment exhibit serious personality disorders. Perhaps people do, too.

Overpopulation is felt in many related ways. To feed growing populations, fishing fleets exhaust fisheries. Tropical rain for-55 ests are destroyed to provide farmlands, often abandoned because of infertile soil. The ozone layer becomes more and more punctured, opening the world's populations to new dangers. Some authorities believe 60 the greenhouse effect, the result of the combustion of fossil fuels, may cause a rise in the world's temperatures, with some significant negative results all too possible.

Some writers emphasize a decline in the 65 quality of life as population increases so rapidly. The demands upon health organizations become more difficult to meet. Overcrowding leads to frazzled tempers, ill health, and civil explosions. In the United 70 States, three states—Florida, Texas, and California—will feel the brunt of the pressure most keenly. All three states already have problems. California has a perennial water problem. Texas, the giant among 75 states, has an "unsteady economy," as the writer Charles C. Mann has pointed out. Florida's fragile ecosystem has had too many demands upon it. Greed and indifference have irreparably damaged many areas.

80 Rich countries can ameliorate many of the growing problems. Americans have forced petroleum companies to phase out leaded gas. Twenty-three industrialized countries have drastically reduced the rate 85 of release of the most dangerous compounds that destroy the ozone. But poorer countries, caught in the vicious cycle of ever-increasing population, cannot do the same. All human beings want a piece of the pie, 90 but the future may find the pie divided into shreds.

Somehow the world's governments must devise ways to check the disastrous growth of population. At this writing, the future 95 looks bleak.

Passage 2

The "authorities" have been predicting catastrophes for 400 years. So far, none have arrived. The world has had its share of troubles, of course, but the horrible apoc-100 alypse so often predicted has not materialized. No one denies the dangers of unchecked population growth. Nature's incredible fertility has led many wild creatures to starvation, as resources dwindle. 105 But nature also institutes a system of balances. When the arctic hare diminishes in numbers, the arctic fox has fewer offspring.

Of course, humankind has no such system. Wars, famines, and plagues have kept 110 populations in check in the past. To some extent they still do, with war, starvation, and diseases like AIDS checking to some slight degree the increases in population. The word is *slight,* for despite these terrible 115 checks, population continues to grow.

There is, of course, a major difference between human beings and gypsy moths. People have shown an amazing resiliency and flexibility in dealing with seemingly 120 insuperable problems. Malthus was right. Given the productivity of the world's farmlands at his time, we'd already be starving now. But even though population has grown, food is still plentiful. Tons of food 125 were shipped to Somalia to pull the inhabitants back from the brink of starvation. These tons of food represent food surpluses elsewhere in the world. The ability to increase food production has been phenome-130 nal. Ansley Coale of Princeton says, "If you had asked someone in 1890 about today's population, he'd say, 'There's no way the United States can support two hundred and fifty million people. Where are they going to 135 pasture all their horses?' "

In 1949, Paul Ehrlich wrote *The Population Bomb,* a depressing scenario for the future. As Mann writes, "Twenty-five years ago 3.4 billion people lived on earth. Now
140 the United Nations estimates that 5.3 billion do—the biggest, fastest increase in history. But food production increased faster still. The per capita food production rose more than 10% from 1968 to 1990. The
145 number of chronically malnourished people fell by more than 16 percent." Though some authorities declare that the good days are ending, others insist that by using modern agricultural methods, Third World coun-
150 tries could keep that favorable trend going.

Pessimists overlook the fact that trends can be reversed. Many former forests were cut down for farms only to return to forests when the farms were abandoned. In 1875,
155 six counties in the lower Hudson Valley contained 573,003 acres of forest. In 1980, the forests covered an area three times as large. American forests as a whole are bigger and healthier now than they were at the
160 turn of the century. Salmon are returning to American rivers. White-tailed deer, once hunted to the point of near-extinction, are now more numerous than ever. Wild turkeys now enjoy a greater range than they
165 did 300 years ago. All these happy events occurred while the population was growing.

Some think that the problem we are concerned with is less population growth than political incompetence and corruption.
170 Pressures upon governmental agencies increase as population grows, but foresight and intelligent management can often minimize the resulting problems and even take advantage of new conditions. Increases in
175 local populations, for example, can open the way to better health facilities, more varied shopping possibilities, and improved educational opportunities.

No one denies that population growth
180 brings with it new challenges and new dangers, but many of the threats repeated by the doomsayers are overstated and inaccurate projections, or excuses for gloomy apathy. One reliable survey has pointed out
185 that fertility in poor countries actually dropped 30 percent in the period between 1965–1970 and 1980–1985. The problem is admittedly complex, but the peoples of the world have the potential of meeting the
190 challenge of population growth while avoiding the wholesale collapse of civilization sometimes prophesied.

1. The author of Passage 1 mentions Botero and Malthus to _____.
   (A) contrast their respective positions
   (B) quote their statistics on the modern growth of population
   (C) show that population concerns are not new
   (D) make use of their studies of explosive growth in wild populations
   (E) suggest that they may have overstated their case

   1 ____

2. A word that graphically suggests the meaning of *gridlock* (line 32) is _____.
   (A) disappointment
   (B) anger
   (C) mobility
   (D) strangulation
   (E) indifference

   2 ____

3. The author suggests that tropical rain forests _____.
   (A) have relatively infertile soil
   (B) play a minor role in the world's ecology
   (C) can be explored for lifesaving new drugs
   (D) will return in a generation after wholesale timbering
   (E) can provide a home for some of the world's excess population

   3 ____

4. The author's attitude toward tree cutting by Himalayan peoples is one of _____.
   (A) unrestrained rejection
   (B) sympathetic disapproval
   (C) limited admiration
   (D) studied indifference
   (E) complete bafflement

   4 _____

5. In lines 44–51, the author _____.
   (A) deplores the actions of callous researchers
   (B) suggests that Somali fighters are motivated by survival
   (C) indicates that rats in the wild do not have the same personality disorders as laboratory rats
   (D) approves of laboratory research with animals
   (E) compares the world to a laboratory

   5 _____

6. Throughout, the author uses figurative language to make a point. All the following are examples of figurative language EXCEPT _____.
   (A) the traffic of life will be in perpetual gridlock
   (B) again, population pressures result in ecological nightmares
   (C) the ozone layer becomes more and more punctured
   (D) every year, the earth is adding a hundred million people
   (E) the future may find the pie divided into shreds

   6 _____

7. In line 80, *ameliorate* most nearly means _____.
   (A) overlook
   (B) relieve
   (C) explore
   (D) uncover
   (E) deplore

   7 _____

8. The opening sentence of Passage 2 conveys a sense of _____.
   (A) wry humor
   (B) perverse hostility
   (C) sympathetic agreement
   (D) puzzled research
   (E) understated disagreement

   8 _____

9. Though *apocalypse* has several meanings, the synonym closest in meaning in lines 99–100 is _____.
   (A) prophecy
   (B) mismanagement
   (C) devastation
   (D) war
   (E) drought

   9 _____

10. The author of Passage 2 places his hopes for human survival on _____.
    (A) zero population growth
    (B) research into social forces that encourage increases
    (C) persuading the Cassandras to accept his blueprint for the future
    (D) studying closely the natural cycles of Norwegian lemmings
    (E) human ingenuity and flexibility

    10 _____

11. The same author says, "Malthus was right" in his _____.
    (A) essentially hopeless picture of the world's future
    (B) estimates of the world's potential for growing enough food
    (C) warning about deforestation and the dangers of desertification
    (D) projections into the future based on then-current situations
    (E) friendly disagreement with the previous prophet, Giovanni Botero

    11 _____

12. Ansley Coale says, "Where are they going to pasture all their horses?" to show how _____.
    (A) changing conditions modify the truth or falsity of prophecies
    (B) an agrarian economy can effectively handle population growth
    (C) the horse has become superfluous in today's world
    (D) the prediction was incorrect in details but essentially correct in general
    (E) people were stupid in 1890

    12 ____

13. Salmon, turkeys, and deer are mentioned as examples of _____.
    (A) endangered species
    (B) food sources for the future
    (C) trend reversal
    (D) game animals
    (E) successful adjustment to urban life

    13 ____

14. The mythical Cassandra was probably noted for _____.
    (A) cheerful evaluations that were usually incorrect
    (B) steadfastness and loyalty toward those she admired

(C) superficial skepticism tinged with basic optimism
(D) gloomy prophecies that no one believed
(E) a willingness to accept varying points of view

    14 ____

15. Both authors are similar in their _____.
    (A) long-term projections of population growth
    (B) desire to limit the number of children in a family
    (C) acceptance of the views of Malthus
    (D) emphasis upon trend reversal as a possible solution
    (E) acceptance of the point that population growth *is* a problem

    15 ____

16. When confronted with negative news about drought, famine, and war, the author of Passage 2 would probably use which of the following well-known quotations?
    (A) "Figures don't lie, but liars figure."
    (B) "We shall overcome."
    (C) "Every dog will have his day."
    (D) "The times are out of joint."
    (E) "This is a day of infamy."

    16 ____

Strategy. 1. The author of Passage 1 introduces his arguments by pointing out that population problems were predicted centuries ago. Since Botero and Malthus essentially agree, (A) is wrong. The two men generalize about the future but do not provide statistics (B). Wild populations are not mentioned by the writers (D). Since the author generally agrees with Botero and Malthus, (E) is wrong. The author of Passage 1 is generally in agreement with the two writers' position. The answer is (C).

2. The strain placed on all elements of life as population grows will cause breakdowns. The global economy will fail to provide needed elements. The author uses figurative language—traffic, gridlock—to suggest that life will be poorer in the years to come. Gridlock is to traffic as strangulation is to the normal flow. (D) is the answer.

3. Line 56 mentions the infertile soil of rain forests. (A) is the answer.

4. Tree cutting for firewood is an understandable human need, but short-term gains result in long-term disasters. (A) is too strong. The author cannot admire the destruction of forests (C). The author's concern rules out (D). The author isn't baffled (E). He understands why trees are cut but deplores the actions. The answer is (B) sympathetic disapproval.

5. The author compares the personality disorders of laboratory rats kept in close confinement with similar manifestations of violence among humans in too close contact. The answer is (E).

6. (D) is a straightforward, literal statement. The figurative expressions include *traffic* and *gridlock* (A), *pressures* and *nightmares* (B), *punctured* (C), and *pie* and *shreds* (E).

7. In lines 80–86, the author provides two examples of environmental improvement through the efforts of rich countries. The context suggests that (B) is the answer.

8. The author puts quotation marks around "authorities" to suggest that the authorities are not good prophets. His dig at authorities is intended to be ironic. The answer is (A).

9. The context clearly links "catastrophes" in line 97 with "apocalypse" in lines 99–100. Prophecy (A) is irrelevant. Mismanagement (B) is too mild. War (D) is too specific, as is drought (E). The answer is (C) devastation.

10. Lines 187–192 clearly state the author's faith in human ingenuity and flexibility (E).

11. The clue to the answer is "then-current." Lines 121–124 note that the productivity of Malthus's time would be inadequate now. Productivity has soared. Malthus's projections were adequate for his time but inadequate now. The answer is (D).

12. In 1890 horses were a mainstay of commerce, transportation, agriculture, and recreation. A hundred years later in the United States, the number of horses has greatly diminished even though the population has greatly increased. Worrying about pasturing horses has become a minor problem. The answer is (A).

13. Lines 160–166 point out that species once endangered have now become numerous, even though population has grown. The answer is (C).

14. The contrast between Cassandras and Pollyannas in the introduction stresses that Cassandras take a negative view. "Cheerful" eliminates (A). "Optimism" rules out (C). Cassandra's open-mindedness or lack thereof is nowhere mentioned or implied. (E) is wrong. There is no indication about Cassandra's steadfastness and loyalty, eliminating (B). "Gloomy prophecies" accords with the adjective *negative* applied to the pessimists. (D) is correct.

15. The projections of population growth are specific and alarming in Passage 1. They are less specific and alarming in Passage 2. Thus (A) is wrong. (B) isn't mentioned. The two authors look upon Malthus differently. The author of Passage 1 believes that Malthus's predictions are more likely to happen than not. The author of Passage 2 is more optimistic. (C) is wrong. Although Passage 2 suggests trend reversal as a possible solution, Passage 1 doesn't rely upon it. Elimination of the others leaves (E). Passage 1 is devoted almost entirely to the dangers of population growth. Passage 2 agrees that population growth is a serious problem (lines 179–181), but it takes a more optimistic view of the world's prospects.

16. The concluding lines, 187–192, state the author's belief that the peoples of the world can successfully meet the challenges and dangers that lie ahead. The answer is (B).

REVIEW

Will robots ever be able to act and think like human beings? What limits exist? The following two excerpts by philosophers, one American and one French, discuss the differences between living things and nonliving things. William James (Passage 1) published The Principles of Psychology *in 1890. René Descartes (Passage 2) published* Discourse on Method *250 years earlier, in 1637. Yet both philosophers address a problem very much in current science news. The debate about artificial intelligence continues.*

Passage 1

If some iron filings be sprinkled on a table and a magnet brought near them, they will fly through the air for a certain distance and stick to its surface. A savage seeing the

5 phenomenon explains it as the result of an attraction or love between the magnet and the filings. But let a card cover the poles of the magnet, and the filings will press forever against its surface without its ever

10 occurring to them to pass around its sides and thus come into more direct contact with the object of their love. Blow bubbles through a tube into the bottom of a pail of water, they will rise to the surface and

15 mingle with the air. Their action may again be poetically interpreted as due to a longing to recombine with the mother-atmosphere

above the surface. But if you invert a jar full of water over the pail, they will rise and

20 remain lodged beneath its bottom, shut in from the outer air, although a slight deflection from their course at the outset, or a re-descent towards the rim of the jar when they found their upward course impeded,

25 would easily have set them free.

If now we pass from such actions as these to those of living things, we notice a striking difference. Romeo wants Juliet as the filings want the magnet; and if no obstacles

30 intervene, he moves toward her by as straight a line as they. But Romeo and Juliet, if a wall be built between them, do not remain idiotically pressing their faces against its opposite sides like the magnet

35 and the filings with the card. Romeo soon finds a circuitous way, by scaling the wall or otherwise, of touching Juliet's lips directly. With the filings the path is fixed; whether it reaches the end depends on ac-

40 cidents. With the lover it is the end which is fixed; the path may be modified indefinitely.

Passage 2

If there were machines which bore a resemblance to our body and imitated our

45 actions as far as it was morally possible to do so, we should always have two very cer-

tain tests by which to recognize that, for all
that, they were not real men. The first is,
that they could never use speech or other
50 signs as we do when placing our thoughts
on record for the benefit of others. For we
can easily understand a machine's being
constituted so that it can utter words, and
even emit some responses to action on it of
55 a corporeal kind, which brings about a
change in its organs; for instance, if it is
touched in a particular part it may ask what
we wish to say to it; if in another part it may
exclaim that it is being hurt, and so on. But
60 it never happens that it arranges its speech
in various ways, in order to reply appropriately to everything that may be said in its
presence, as even the lowest type of man can
do. And the second difference is, that al-
65 though machines can perform certain
things as well as or perhaps better than any
of us can do, they infallibly fall short in
others, by which means we may discover
that they did not act from knowledge, but
70 only from the disposition of their organs.
For while reason is a universal instrument
which can serve for all contingencies, these
organs have need of some special adapta-
tion for every particular action. From this
75 it follows that it is morally impossible that
there should be sufficient diversity in any
machine to allow it to act in all the events
of life in the same way as our reason causes
us to act.

1. The author of Passage 1 uses "its ever
occurring to them . . ." in lines 9–10 to
suggest _____.
   (A) the flexibility of magnetic attraction
   (B) the limitations of nonliving things
   (C) that bubbles act differently from
   iron filings
   (D) the way a savage interprets natural events
   (E) the poetic union of filings and
   magnet

   1 ____

2. The word *phenomenon* in line 5 means
_____.
   (A) unexpected surprise
   (B) colorful demonstration
   (C) source of confusion
   (D) observable fact
   (E) apparent contradiction

   2 ____

3. In line 10, the pronoun *them* refers to
_____.
   (A) savages
   (B) magnets
   (C) cards
   (D) objects
   (E) filings

   3 ____

4. It may be inferred that the bubble example is used to _____.
   (A) reinforce the point of the magnet
   example
   (B) contrast the way in which nonliving things act
   (C) compare it with the following example of Romeo and Juliet
   (D) demonstrate the illogicality of all
   three examples
   (E) demonstrate the force of hydraulic pressure

   4 ____

5. In line 17, mother-atmosphere is an
example of _____.
   (A) simile
   (B) understatement
   (C) literal language
   (D) metaphor
   (E) exaggeration

   5 ____

6. The word *impeded* in line 24 means
_____.
   (A) facilitated
   (B) hindered
   (C) demonstrated
   (D) misdirected
   (E) uncovered

   6 ____

7. In line 36, *circuitous* means _____.
   (A) effective
   (B) surprising
   (C) roundabout
   (D) inferior
   (E) mechanical

   7 ____

8. The author uses the example of Romeo and Juliet to _____.
   (A) pay a special tribute to William Shakespeare
   (B) emphasize the unpredictability of life
   (C) show differences between living and nonliving things
   (D) suggest the importance of romance in life
   (E) add a note of sadness at their ultimate tragedy

   8 ____

9. The word *want* in line 29 _____.
   (A) strikes a note of subtle humor
   (B) is a literal representation of the filings' desires
   (C) is meant to irritate the reader
   (D) suggests that inanimate objects may have feelings
   (E) is so extreme as to be confusing

   9 ____

10. The word *idiotically* in line 33 suggests _____.
   (A) the impetuosity of Romeo
   (B) the imprudence of the romance
   (C) the power of a wall
   (D) the inflexibility of nonliving things
   (E) the rule of natural law

   10 ____

11. *The end* in line 39 refers to _____.
   (A) a meeting of lovers
   (B) an inevitable tragedy
   (C) union with the magnet
   (D) the means
   (E) the lovers' final breakup

   11 ____

12. In Passage 2, the two "certain tests" mentioned in lines 46–47 are _____.
   (A) hesitant speech and limited mobility
   (B) organic composition and brisk responsiveness
   (C) steadfast reliability and flawless speech
   (D) responsive speech and reasoning ability
   (E) self-repair and alert awareness

   12 ____

13. The word *infallibly* in line 67 means _____.
   (A) infrequently
   (B) certainly
   (C) unwittingly
   (D) flawlessly
   (E) disappointingly

   13 ____

14. In line 72, the word *contingencies* means _____.
   (A) failures
   (B) successes
   (C) organic requirements
   (D) personal contracts
   (E) possibilities

   14 ____

15. The word *morally* in line 75 suggests that machines _____.
   (A) cannot reason from knowledge
   (B) are superior to human beings in certain essentials
   (C) are incapable of making mistakes
   (D) have a weakly developed moral sense
   (E) might induce weak human beings to act immorally

   15 ____

16. In line 76, *diversity* means _____.
   (A) compatibility
   (B) intelligence
   (C) comprehensiveness
   (D) variety
   (E) resilience

   16 ____

17. If the author of Passage 2 were confronted with a current computer that asks and answers questions, his response would probably be one of _____.
(A) relief
(B) fatigue
(C) boredom
(D) disbelief
(E) irritation

17 ____

18. Passages 1 and 2 are alike in their _____.
(A) emphasis upon a machine's capabilities
(B) use of magnet and filings as illustrations
(C) tribute to human reason
(D) use of a literary example
(E) chatty, colloquial style

18 ____

19. Passage 2 differs from Passage 1 in its _____.
(A) emphasis on machines rather than natural processes
(B) downplaying the role of human knowledge
(C) disdain for uncomplicated procedures
(D) rejection of any mechanical capabilities
(E) suggestion that machines might someday replace human beings

19 ____

20. Compared to the tone of Passage 2, the tone of Passage 1 is more _____.
(A) argumentative
(B) humble
(C) inspirational
(D) humorous
(E) scholarly

20 ____

21. Which assumption does the author of Passage 2 make?
(A) Machines could be made to speak as humans do.
(B) Machines could be made to act as flexibly as humans do.
(C) Machines could never perform tasks better than humans do.
(D) Machines could never be made with the infinite responsiveness of humans.
(E) Machines could be made that could not be distinguished from humans.

21 ____

22. In lines 31–42, to make his point, the author uses _____.
(A) obvious humor
(B) balanced contrast
(C) dull repetition
(D) subtle understatement
(E) exaggerated explanation

22 ____

SUMMARY

2. Studying Paired Passages

Paired passages add a dimension to critical reading. The reader must not only understand the two passages but must also be aware of relationships between them. The relationships may be complementary or contrasting. They may be overt or susceptible only to sound inference.

Passages may start out with basic agreements—for example, in the population passages (pages 293–299), both writers agree that the population explosion is a serious challenge. But they may differ in projections, interpretations, and emphases. In paired passages, the same details used to buttress one argument may be used to support another. A critical reader must be aware of persuasion techniques. Studying paired passages is an especially effective way to study how language works, how a writer supports a point of view by selection of details favorable to the position taken, and how selective omission, as well as carefully chosen details, provides a clue to the writer's general philosophy.

Section VIII Summary: Studying the Longer Passage

The longer passage provides unique challenges, possible only with a more complex selection or paired selection.

PART 1. The Single Selection (p. 272)

A. Read the passage carefully. Before answering any questions, determine the author's general point of view. What position does he or she take with respect to the topic discussed?

B. Take the sample test before analyzing the answers.

C. Check your answers against those given in the text.

D. If your answer disagrees with one given in the text, carefully go back over the passage. Try a process of elimination to see whether this procedure provides the accepted answer. If not, look again. In a test situation, if a choice must be made between two possible answers, you must select the BEST. Do you feel you have as acceptable an answer as the one provided? If possible, talk things over with classmates. Although not common, an alternative possibility will sometimes slip by the test constructors. The important part of the test is your close evaluation, your reasons for deciding on an answer. The book provides acceptable reasons. Does your answer do so?

E. The ultimate purpose of test taking is sharpening critical perceptions, not just writing letters on a test answer sheet. Take advantage of Problem and Strategy to fine-tune your own reading skills.

PART 2. Studying Paired Passages (p. 305)

A. Everything said about the single selection above holds especially strongly for this section. Review A–E.

B. The paired selections add an extra challenge: critically reading two somewhat related passages and trying to ferret out the relationships. This challenge invites more rereading than does the single selection.

C. The test usually includes questions about the first passage, questions about the second, and then questions relating to the two passages. These combining questions send you back to both selections.

D. Keep in mind that the paired passages have been chosen for a reason. When you discover the reason (agreement, disagreement, comparison, contrast, enrichment), you will find the questions easier to answer.

Section IX: Studying the Discrete Passage

In its 2005 revision of the SAT, the College Board introduced shorter critical reading passages, concentrated, discrete paragraphs about 100 words long, as well as paired paragraphs about 200 words long. Again, all the skills you have been developing in this book will stand you in good stead when you meet a difficult paragraph. This section will provide some additional practice, using examples of the type you will face on the test.

TRIAL TEST

The following paragraph strikes a responsive chord in everyone's life. Answers are on page 531.

Inanimate objects are out to get us. What happened to that missing gray sock? Why does a piece of toast with jelly fall to the floor and land jelly-side down? Why does plastic
5   wrap curl in your hands as you try to wrap something? Why do you need a plumber on a Sunday, when no plumber's available? Why do you stub your toe on a sneaky projection of a table leg? Why does the phone
10 ring while you're sitting down to dinner, only to find no one on the line? Things can be mean. At least, there is a word for the malevolence of those lifeless objects: *resistentialism*—defined in the *Shorter Ox-*
15 *ford English Distionary* as "a mock philosophy maintaining that inanimate objects are hostile to humans or seek to thwart human endeavors." That just about sums it up!

1. The basic tone of the selection is _____
   (A) aggressive
   (B) whimsical
   (C) complacent
   (D) contradictory
   (E) didactic

Let's analyze another discrete passage.

Aeschylus, Sophocles, and Euripides—Greek writers of tragedy—wrote 2,500 years ago but speak to modern audiences. In any given year, a play by one of these—
5   especially the latter two—is probably mounted on Broadway or another prestigious stage around the world. Though the settings are exotic for us, the plots, characterizations, and human touches are all too
10 familiar. Aeschylus was the pioneer of the two, introducing innovative elements of stagecraft and design. Sophocles was most like William Shakespeare, a dispassionate observer of the human condition and a su-
15 perb playwright. He relied on human strengths and weaknesses, not the gods. Euripides, less popular in his own day, has been a favorite in Elizabethan times and in our own day. Marianne McDonald has "lo-
20 cated fifty operas based on or including the myth of *Medea*." This total does not include stage versions or adaptations. Even the Japanese produced *Medea* in Kabuki style.

2. Which of the following statements may be accurately derived from the selection?

I. The plays of Aeschylus, Sophocles, and Euripides are played equally often nowadays.

II. The organization of the paragraph suggests that *Medea* was written by Euripides.

III. Operas based on the plays of Sophocles are perennial favorites.

IV. The last of the great Greek tragic writers was Aeschylus.

V. Aeschylus and Euripides used the gods more often than Sophocles in the unraveling of their plots.

(A) I and II
(B) III and IV
(C) III and V

(D) II and V
(E) I and IV

Studying Paired Passages

Problem

The following passages come to grips with one of the major problems facing America: the preservation of liberty and the protection against terrorist attacks.

Passage 1
Ever since 9/11, terrorism has constituted the greatest threat to American stability and security. This overwhelming danger has changed the way government
5 operates. It has spawned new agencies and merged existing entities, all with the praiseworthy goal of reducing the terrorist threat, anticipating hostile action, and preserving democracy in an unstable world.
10 The effort brings with it new challenges, some loss of privacy and an occasional encroachment on civil liberties. Our traditions are strong enough to preserve the principles of the Constitution, with its built-in safe-
15 guards. We can both protect and preserve.

Passage 2
The preservation of our liberties depends upon holding fast in difficult times. The shock waves generated by the 9/11 attacks threatened more than the physical well-
5 being of Americans. There is always the possibility that self-evident liberties will be eroded in the commendable attempts to secure our safety. The very real threats must be balanced against the basic principles of
10 our society as laid down in the Constitution. How far can we tolerate the invasion of privacy and the suspension of due process in the desire to keep us safe? Some think that the greater threat may be internal.
15 Eternal vigilance is the price of liberty.

1. It may be said that the authors of Passages 1 and 2 _____.
   (A) would give unlimited powers to the President in all matters judged by him to involve national security.
   (B) support detaining suspected terrorists without bail

   (C) are both concerned for the good of the country
   (D) would accept martial law by decree of the Secretary of Defense
   (E) would applaud the extradition of suspected terrorists without trial

   1 ____

2. Passage 1 _____.
   (A) puts essential trust in good leadership
   (B) shows little respect for the Constitution
   (C) considers public opinion unimportant
   (D) would reject wiretapping in any situation
   (E) would support the writ of habeas corpus in all arrests

   2 _____

3. Passage 2 suggests _____.
   (A) finding the reasons for the intelligence breakdown prior to 9/11
   (B) seeking out possible subversives in Homeland Security
   (C) improving liaison between the legislative and executive branches
   (D) weeding out all those with social ties to terrorist sympathizers
   (E) being aware of the fine line between prudent safeguards and abridgment of civil rights

   3 _____

4. In Passage 2, *vigilance* suggests _____.
   (A) monitoring on a daily basis the financial activities of large corporations
   (B) forming neighborhood surveillance groups
   (C) merging the CIA and FBI into one cohesive unit
   (D) resisting infringement of Constitutional guarantees
   (E) forming citizen groups to surf the Internet for signs of terrorist activity

   4 _____

Strategy. 1. Although the writers disagree, they are both concerned for the good of the country (C). The writer of Passage 2 would not accept the other alternatives.

2. The writer of Passage 1 emphasizes traditions and the principles of the Constitution. (B) contradicts those beliefs. Only (A) could be applied to that writer.

3. In a concern for civil liberties, the writer of Passage 2 emphasizes the dangers in (E). The other alternatives are nowhere considered.

4. (D) continues the emphasis on guarding against loss of liberties. The other alternatives are opposed or irrelevant.

REVIEW

Sometimes a word or two will capture the tone of the passage. The following passage considers the incredible good fortune and combination of circumstances that gave the young country the heartland of what was to become the current United States.

   The Louisiana Purchase, that incredible bargain at four cents an acre, was the result of several fortuitous events. New Orleans, essential for controlling traffic on the Mis-
5 sissippi river, was a crucial element. When France reacquired the territory from Spain in 1800, Americans worried that France might close the port. Happily, Napoleon had lost interest in the area. He was planning
10 further confrontations with the British and needed money. Helping the new nation might also provide a counterweight to British power and influence. And so the United States nearly doubled its territory, without
15 war, for $15,000,000.

5. Two words that best establish the tone of the paragraph are _____.
(A) *fortuitous* and *happily*
(B) *confrontations* and *war*
(C) *power* and *influence*
(D) *planning* and *needed*
(E) *essential* and *crucial*

5 _____

SUMMARY
Studying the Discrete Passage

Review the suggestions for Section IX, on pages 304–307. The shorter passage often provides a bit more conciseness than the longer selection, but the skills used in all reading challenges are the same. The paired passages require an understanding of relationships between them. They have obviously been paired for a reason.

Practice Tests

How well have you developed skill in extracting the meaning from reading passages? Take the following practice tests for additional drill.

A

The following selection answers the question: "Does a leap year come every four years?" The answer may surprise you.

The solar year is 365.2422 days long, not a convenient 365. The Julian calendar rounded out the number to 365.25 days and added a leap year every four years to com-
5 pensate for the difference. That arrangement broke down in time: it brought about a growing discrepancy between solar time and calendar time. By the 16th century, the vernal equinox came on March 11. To bring
10 the calendar back in line with the seasons, Pope Gregory dropped ten days from the calendar and decreed that henceforth years ending in hundreds would not be leap years unless divisible by 400. This provides a year
15 of 365.245 days, closer to solar time and usable for many years to come.

The following are all true EXCEPT ____.
(A) adding ten days brought the vernal equinox back to March 21
(B) the Julian calendar assumed that
   solar time was longer than it was
(C) ten calendar days actually disappeared
(D) the Julian calendar was closer to
   solar time than was the Gregorian
(E) the year 1900 was not a leap
   year, but the year 2000 was

____

B

Modern science talks about change and chaos. This thought is not new, as this passage suggests.

"You can't step into the same river twice." Twenty-five hundred years ago the Greek philosopher Heraclitus emphasized the in-evitability of change and its implications for
5 human beings. The world shifts before our eyes: unchanging stability is an illusion. Embracing change, accepting and adjusting to it are therapeutic. Resisting change is not only futile but psychologically harmful. Be-
10 cause human beings are participants as well as observers, they affect change and contribute to it.

The main idea of the selection can best be expressed by the saying:
(A) Change is progress.
(B) Change enriches the mind.
(C) Change brings fortune to some,
   misfortune to others.
(D) Change is underrated by
   Heraclitus.
(E) Change is the only constant.

____

C

This passage discusses the mystery of Easter Island, that lonely speck in the Pacific Ocean.

Massive stone statues stand in rows, staring silently at the sea. These recognizable monuments conjure up a tiny island, only 64 square miles in area, isolated in the
5 Pacific, 2,355 miles from Chile, its administering country. Easter Island, so called because of its discovery by a Dutch admiral on Easter Sunday 1722, has become a source of worldwide interest. How did the settlers
10 reach this lonely outpost, known locally as Rapa Nui? Where did they come from? How did they raise these haunting sculptures, some forty feet high and weighing more than 50 tons? Many seek answers.

The paragraph implies that _____.
(A) the mysteries of Easter Island will soon be solved
(B) the islanders will seek a break with Chile
(C) the current name, Easter Island, will be changed to Rapa Nui
(D) scientists will keep coming to the island for explanations
(E) the Dutch may reassert their right to the island

_____

D

As pet owners know, cats, dogs, and even hamsters have personalities. The following passage describes one of these.

Bongo was a charming rogue of a dog, a dictator in his household, a self-appointed keeper of the holy flame. His whims, his needs, his aversion to boredom guided the
5 household through a maze of unspoken demands and subtle dissatisfaction with the meager efforts of the harassed master and mistress. His body language told all: a stiff walk from his cajoling mistress, a roll of
10 doggie eyes to express how the master had missed the mark . . . again! For sixteen years in his domain, Bongo had said, "Jump!" and his compliant servants had replied, "How high?"

1. The basic tone of the paragraph is one of _____.
   (A) enthusiasm for the owners' foibles
   (B) sadness at acquiring the dog originally
   (C) a distaste for Bongo's antics
   (D) amused acceptance of the dog's idiosyncrasies
   (E) amazement at the mistress's obsequiousness

1 _____

2. The function of the word *flame* can best be characterized as _____.
   (A) literal
   (B) metaphorical
   (C) intemperate
   (D) ambiguous
   (E) dissonant

2 _____

E

In this segment from a story by Edith Wharton, a woman proposes to her husband that they adopt a baby. The conversation opens.

Lethbury, surveying his wife across the dinner table, found his transient glance arrested by an indefinable change in her appearance.

5 "How smart you look! Is that a new gown?" he asked.

Her answering look seemed to deprecate his charging her with the extravagance of wasting a new gown on him, and he now
10 perceived that the change lay deeper than any accident of dress. At the same time, he noticed that she betrayed her consciousness of it by a delicate, almost frightened blush. It was one of the com-
15 pensations of Mrs. Lethbury's protracted childishness that she still blushed as prettily as at eighteen. Her body had been privileged not to outstrip her mind, and the two, as it seemed to Lethbury, were
20 destined to travel together through an eternity of girlishness.

"I don't know what you mean," she said.

Since she never did, he always wondered at her bringing this out as a fresh grievance
25 against him; but his wonder was unresentful, and he said good-humoredly: "You sparkle so that I thought you had on your diamonds."

She sighed and blushed again.
30 "It must be," he continued, "that you've been to a dressmaker's opening. You're absolutely brimming with illicit enjoyment."

She stared again, this time at the adjective. His adjectives always embarrassed
35 her; their unintelligibleness savored of impropriety.

"In short," he summed up, "you've been doing something that you're thoroughly ashamed of."
40 To his surprise she retorted: "I don't see why I should be ashamed of it!"

Lethbury leaned back with a smile of enjoyment. When there was nothing better going he always liked to listen to her expla-
45 nations.

"Well—?" he said.

She was becoming breathless and emotional. "Of course you'll laugh—you laugh at everything!"

50 "That rather blunts the point of my derision, doesn't it?" he interjected; but she pushed on without noticing.

"It's so easy to laugh at things."

"Ah," murmured Lethbury with relish,
55 "that's Aunt Sophronia's, isn't it?"

Most of his wife's opinions were heirlooms, and he took a quaint pleasure in tracing their descent. She was proud of their age, and saw no reason for discarding
60 them while they were still serviceable. Some, of course, were so fine that she kept them for state occasions, like her great-grandmother's Crown Derby; but from the lady known as Aunt Sophronia she had
65 inherited a stout set of everyday prejudices that were practically as good as new; whereas her husband's, as she noticed, were always having to be replaced. In the early days she had fancied there might be a cer-
70 tain satisfaction in taxing him with the fact; but she had long since been silenced by the reply: "My dear, I'm not a rich man, but I never use an opinion twice if I can help it."

She was reduced, therefore, to dwelling
75 on his moral deficiencies; and one of the most obvious of these was his refusal to take things seriously. On this occasion, however, some ulterior purpose kept her from taking up his taunt.

80 "I'm not in the least ashamed!" she repeated, with the air of shaking a banner to the wind; but the domestic atmosphere being calm, the banner drooped unheroically.

85 "That," said Lethbury judicially, "encourages me to infer that you ought to be, and

that, consequently, you've been giving yourself the unusual pleasure of doing something I shouldn't approve of."

90   She met this with an almost solemn directness.

"No," she said. "You won't approve of it.
I've allowed for that."

"Ah," he exclaimed, setting down his li-
95 queur glass. "You've worked out the whole
problem, eh?"

"I believe so."

"That's uncommonly interesting. And
what is it?"

100   She looked at him quietly. "A baby."

If it was seldom given her to surprise
him, she had attained the distinction for
once.

"A baby?"

105   "Yes."

"A—human baby?"

"Of course!" she cried, with the virtuous
resentment of the woman who has never
allowed dogs in the house.

110   Lethbury's puzzled stare broke into a
fresh smile. "A baby I shan't approve of?
Well, in the abstract I don't think much of
them, I admit. Is this an abstract baby?"

Again she frowned at the adjective, but
115 she had reached a pitch of exaltation at
which such obstacles could not deter her.

"It's the loveliest baby—" she murmured.

"Ah, then it's concrete. It exists. In this
harsh world it draws its breath in pain—"

120   "It's the healthiest child I ever saw!" she
indignantly corrected.

"You've seen it, then?"

Again the accusing blush suffused her.
"Yes—I've seen it."

125   "And to whom does this paragon belong?"

And here indeed she confounded him. "To
me—I hope," she declared.

He pushed his chair back with an articulate murmur. "To you—?"

130   "To *us*," she corrected.

"Good Lord!" he said. If there had been
the least hint of hallucination in her transparent gaze—but no; it was as clear, as
shallow, as easily fathomable as when he

135 had first suffered the sharp surprise of
striking bottom in it.

It occurred to him that perhaps she was
trying to be funny: he knew that there is
nothing more cryptic than the humor of the
140 unhumorous.

"Is it a joke?" he faltered.

"Oh, I hope not. I want it so much to be a
reality—"

He paused to smile at the limitations of a
145 world in which jokes were not realities, and
continued gently: "But since it is one already—"

"To us, I mean: to you and me. I want—"
her voice wavered, and her eyes with it. "I
150 have always wanted so dreadfully . . . it has
been such a disappointment . . . not to . . ."

"I see," said Lethbury slowly.

But he had not seen before. It seemed
curious now that he had never thought of
155 her taking it in that way, had never surmised any hidden depths beneath her out-
spread obviousness. He felt as though he
had touched a secret spring in her mind.

There was a moment's silence, moist and
160 tremulous on her part, awkward and
slightly irritated on his.

"You've been lonely, I suppose?" he began.
It was odd, having suddenly to reckon with
the stranger who gazed at him out of her
165 trivial eyes.

"At times," she said.

"I'm sorry."

"It was not your fault. A man has so many
occupations; and women who are clever—or
170 very handsome—I suppose that's an occu-
pation too. Sometimes I've felt that when
dinner was ordered I had nothing to do till
the next day."

"Oh," he groaned.

175   "It wasn't your fault," she insisted. "I
never told you—but when I chose that rose-
bud paper for the front room upstairs, I
always thought—"

"Well—?"

180   "It would be such a pretty paper—for a
baby—to wake up in. That was years ago,
of course; but it was rather an expensive

paper . . . and it hasn't faded in the least . . ."
she broke off incoherently.

185 "It hasn't faded?"

"No—and so I thought . . . as we don't use
the room for anything . . . now that Aunt
Sophronia is dead . . . I thought I might . . .
you might . . . oh, Julian, if you could only
190 have seen it just waking up in its crib!"

"Seen what—where? You haven't got a
baby upstairs?"

"Oh, no—not *yet*," she said, with her rare
laugh—the girlish bubbling of merriment
195 that had seemed one of her chief graces in
the early days. It occurred to him that he
had not given her enough things to laugh
about lately. But then she needed such very
elementary things: she was as difficult to
200 amuse as a savage. He concluded that he
was not sufficiently simple.

"Alice," he said almost solemnly, "what *do*
you mean?"

She hesitated a moment: he saw her
205 gather her courage for a supreme effort.
Then she said slowly, gravely, as though she
were pronouncing a sacramental phrase:

"I'm so lonely without a little child—and I
thought perhaps you'd let me adopt one. . . .
210 It's at the hospital . . . its mother is dead . . .
and I could . . . pet it, and dress it, and do
things for it . . . and it's such a good baby
. . . you can ask any of the nurses . . . it
would never, *never* bother you by crying. . . ."

1. In line 7, *deprecate* means _____.
   (A) misunderstand (D) encourage
   (B) belittle   (E) reinforce
   (C) emphasize

   1 ____

2. The best word to apply to Lethbury's
   treatment of his wife at the beginning
   of the passage is _____.
   (A) cruel   (D) patronizing
   (B) understanding (E) intolerant
   (C) violent

   2 ____

3. In essence, the sentence "Her body . . .
   girlishness" (lines 16–20) means that
   _____.
   (A) maturity characterized the wife's
       appearance and behavior
   (B) the wife's travels had not broad-
       ened her mind
   (C) the wife's appearance gave a
       more mature impression than her
       mind
   (D) though the wife's body had not
       matured, her mind had
   (E) immaturity characterized the
       wife's appearance and behavior

   3 ____

4. Lethbury probably spoke as he did to
   his wife to _____.
   (A) keep asserting his own sense of
       superiority
   (B) remember constantly her beloved
       Aunt Sophronia
   (C) remind her of their early married
       years
   (D) enjoy conversation with his intel-
       lectual equal
   (E) complain about her spendthrift
       ways

   4 ____

5. Which of the following pairs is incor-
   rectly matched?
   (A) (line 15) protracted—drawn out
   (B) (line 32) illicit—improper
   (C) (lines 35–36) impropriety—
       unkindness
   (D) (line 40) retorted—replied
   (E) (lines 50–51) derision—ridicule

   5 ____

6. The "heirlooms" mentioned in lines 56–
   57 were _____.
   (A) of considerable monetary value
   (B) jewels
   (C) convictions
   (D) her great-grandmother's
   (E) frequently changed

   6 ____

7. In comparison with his wife, Lethbury might be said to be less _____.
   (A) skilled in give-and-take
   (B) prejudiced
   (C) self-satisfied
   (D) intelligent
   (E) attractive in appearance
                                    7 ____

8. Lethbury's intent in the reply, "My dear . . . help it" (lines 72–73), can be characterized as _____.
   (A) wry humor
   (B) cruel deception
   (C) agreement with his wife
   (D) prejudice
   (E) confession of evil thoughts
                                    8 ____

9. In the wife's eyes, one of Lethbury's most grievous faults was his _____.
   (A) wife abuse
   (B) careless attire
   (C) unfaithfulness
   (D) quick temper
   (E) taunting humor
                                    9 ____

10. Which of the following pairs is incorrectly matched?
   (A) (line 78) ulterior—hidden
   (B) (line 79) taunt—mockery
   (C) (line 85) judicially—repetitively
   (D) (line 123) suffused—spread over
   (E) (line 125) paragon—standard of excellence
                                    10 ____

11. In lines 83–84, the "banner drooped unheroically" because _____.
   (A) the storm had abated
   (B) the wife stumbled as she walked
   (C) Lethbury decided to change the subject
   (D) the wife raised her voice
   (E) there was no loud argument
                                    11 ____

12. What will probably happen next is that Mrs. Lethbury will _____.
   (A) win over Lethbury immediately
   (B) come to her senses and give up the idea of adoption
   (C) be judged incompetent and not be given the baby
   (D) stick to her guns and get the baby
   (E) ask a friend to adopt the child for her
                                    12 ____

13. In line 116, *deter* means _____.
   (A) restrain   (D) reveal
   (B) inform   (E) insult
   (C) distract
                                    13 ____

14. "The virtuous resentment of the woman who has never allowed dogs in the house" (lines 107–109) suggests _____.
   (A) an animal hater
   (B) an orderly housekeeper
   (C) an ill-tempered hag
   (D) a relaxed servant
   (E) a frustrated veterinarian
                                    14 ____

15. In line 126, *confounded* means _____.
   (A) soothed
   (B) provoked
   (C) ridiculed
   (E) humored
   (D) baffled
                                    15 ____

F

The following article discusses two challenging concepts: irony and paradox. It seeks to explain both.

"I was boxed in and didn't know where to turn."

The box appears in everyday speech as a metaphor for restraint. What is not always
5 apparent is that boxes are not just convenient metaphors. They are built into the structure of the language. Boxing, or classification, is at the very heart of language. It enables us to function. Without classifica-
10 tion, most communication would be impossible. Words are neat pigeonholes into which we fit our ideas.

Classification is a remarkable achievement, but it is deceptive. It cannot capture
15 reality. The "real world" out there has nothing to do with classification. The lion doesn't know that it is a "lion." Analyzing the classification practice clarifies two devices, seemingly disparate, but all related to the
20 "boxing" habit: irony and paradox.

Irony is usually defined as a confrontation of opposites. John Glenn returns safely from a hazardous trip through space to injure himself in a bathroom fall. The irony
25 involves the confrontation of what *is* and what *appears to be,* between reality (whatever that is) and appearance. The appearance assigned "danger" to space and "safety" to home. The reality proved quite
30 the opposite.

Irony implies an observer who can see the contradiction. Unless there is someone to evaluate appearance and reality, there is no irony. In *Oedipus Tyrannus* the audience
35 knows the reality and notes the discrepancy between Oedipus's misevaluation of the situation and the situation itself. It is the observer who sees the difference between appearance and reality. He makes the clas-
40 sifications. Otherwise there is no irony. In "reality" the bathroom was a more dangerous place than space, at least for John Glenn in the context he found himself in.

The irony, then, consists in our setting up
45 categories which produce the contradictions.

Since we act on assumptions and extrapolations, many of our actions in retrospect seem to us "ironic" because they contrast
50 the reality (what actually happened) with the appearances or expectations (what we assume would happen). The irony, however, is linguistic in origin. It depends upon putting things into mutually exclusive boxes
55 (appearance and reality—or something and its opposite). Reality, which is unconcerned with linguistic classification, has nothing to do with irony.

Like irony, paradox involves contradic-
60 tions, but the contradictions are more readily apparent. "I lie all the time." This paradoxical statement seems to set up irreconcilable contradictions. If in reality I lie all the time, then the verbalization must be
65 a lie. But if the verbalization is a lie, then I cannot in reality lie all the time. This paradox, like irony, involves classification, putting things into boxes. Here we are actually setting up two boxes: one we might label
70 "those who lie all the time" and one we might label "those who don't lie all the time." The speaker linguistically cannot fit into both boxes. The paradox is clarified when the classification is cleared up. If "I lie
75 all the time," I set up a linguistic box that excludes the possibility of telling the truth. But there are really two different boxes: (1) "lying all the time" and (2) "lying some of the time." Obviously the statement is an
80 indication that the second box is the one we might use here.

Paradox is a favorite literary device. Authors sometimes employ it to illuminate a truth by suggesting the apparent but super-
85 ficial absurdity of the statement. The works of G. K. Chesterton abound in paradox.

1. The closest metaphor to the images in the second paragraph suggests that the mind is a kind of _____.
   (A) desktop computer
   (B) seamless quilt
   (C) filing cabinet
   (D) steam turbine
   (E) rainbow

   1 ____

2. In line 15, the author put "real world" in quotation marks because he or she _____.
   (A) is quoting from another article
   (B) thinks that no one knows what reality is
   (C) believes that reality yields to concentration
   (D) considers them the most important words in the sentence
   (E) feels that so doing improves the rhythm of the sentence

   2 ____

3. The author suggests that irony _____.
   (A) exists in the mind of an observer
   (B) is another word for metaphor
   (C) is the same as paradox
   (D) destroys a person's faith in ultimate goodness
   (E) is always associated with bad luck

   3 ____

4. The word which does NOT belong with the others is _____.
   (A) bags
   (B) classifications
   (C) categories
   (D) appearances
   (E) boxes

   4 ____

5. In lines 47–48, the word *extrapolations* most closely suggests _____.
   (A) thoughts and ideas that surface during discussions
   (B) classifications based on previous positive experiences
   (C) projections into the future based on current information
   (D) dream states that promote positive actions
   (E) vigorous denunciations of counterproductive activities

   5 ____

6. Using the paragraph beginning on line 59 as a guide, decide which of the following may be considered a paradox.
   (A) Toby is a friend of mine. She is also a good friend of Annette's.
   (B) Terry lies all the time.
   (C) An irresistible force met an immovable object.
   (D) A friend in need is a friend indeed.
   (E) April showers bring May flowers.

   6 ____

7. "All generalizations are untrue, including this one." This is an example of paradox because _____.
   (A) generalizations are usually true
   (B) the statement is itself a generalization
   (C) the author is trying to be funny
   (D) the author successfully avoids generalizations
   (E) it is also ironic

   7 ____

8. The author probably believes that _____.

(A) classifications should be avoided in everyday conversation
(B) the less frequently irony is used, the better
(C) G. K. Chesterton weakened his writing by using paradox
(D) classifications are necessary, but we must be wary when setting them up
(E) irony and paradox are interchangeable terms

8 ____

9. *Oedipus Tyrannus* is introduced into the passage to _____.

(A) provide an illustration of irony
(B) arouse the readers' sense of pity
(C) show how insensitive some theatergoers can become
(D) approve of the punishment received by Oedipus
(E) demonstrate a basic difference between John Glenn and Oedipus

9 ____

10. All the following are correctly paired EXCEPT _____.

(A) (lines 84–85) superficial—shallow
(B) (lines 62–63) irreconcilable—incompatible
(C) (line 35) discrepancy—inconsistency
(D) (line 48) retrospect—a look back
(E) (line 19) disparate—anxious

10 ____

11. The author apparently believes that _____.

(A) irony is essential to provide color to every kind of writing
(B) Greek tragedies, though relevant for their own time, have little to say to us today
(C) most people are aware of the many boxes and classifications they set up
(D) figures don't lie, but liars figure
(E) to a great extent, language controls our actions

11 ____

12. With which of the following quotations would the author probably agree?

(A) "He who does not know the force of words cannot know men." Confucius
(B) "Women are always on the defensive." John C. Collins
(C) "I often quote myself. It adds spice to my conversation." George Bernard Shaw
(D) "It is certain that more people speak English correctly in the United States than in Britain." Ralph Waldo Emerson
(E) "Words are feminine; deeds are masculine." Baltasar Gracian

12 ____

G

Below are two excerpts from books by English philosophers of the past. Both passages deal with education: its advantages and purposes. Passage 1, by Adam Smith, appeared in 1776, the year of the Declaration of Independence. Passage 2, by John Locke, appeared almost a century earlier, in 1690. Both address themselves to the issue of education and its place in life.

Passage 1

A man without the proper use of the intellectual faculties of a man, is, if possible, more contemptible than even a coward, and
5 seems to be mutilated and deformed in a still more essential part of the character of human nature. Though the state was to derive no advantage from the instruction of

the inferior ranks of people, it would still deserve its attention that they should not
10 be altogether uninstructed. The state, however, derives no inconsiderable advantage from their instruction. The more they are instructed the less liable they are to the delusions of enthusiasm and superstition,
15 which, among ignorant nations, frequently occasion the most dreadful disorders. An instructed and intelligent people, besides, are always more decent and orderly than an ignorant and stupid one. They feel them-
20 selves, each individually, more respectable and more likely to obtain the respect of their lawful superiors, and they are therefore more disposed to respect those superiors. They are more disposed to examine, and
25 more capable of seeing through, the interested complaints of faction and sedition, and they are, upon that account, less apt to be misled into any wanton or unnecessary opposition to the measures of government.
30 In free countries, where the safety of government depends very much upon the favourable judgment which the people may form of its conduct, it must surely be of the highest importance that they should not be
35 disposed to judge rashly or capriciously concerning it.

Passage 2

A sound mind in a sound body is a short but full description of a happy state in this world. He that has these two has little more
40 to wish for; and he that wants either of them will be but little the better for anything else. Men's happiness or misery is for the most part of their own making. He whose mind directs not wisely will never take the right
45 way; and he whose body is crazy and feeble will never be able to advance in it. I confess there are some men's constitutions of body and mind so vigorous and well framed by nature that they need not much assistance
50 from others; but by the strength of their natural genius they are from their cradles carried towards what is excellent; and by the privilege of their happy constitutions

are able to do wonders. But examples of this
55 kind are but few; and I think I may say that of all the men we meet with, nine parts of ten are what they are, good or evil, useful or not, by their education. 'Tis that which makes the great difference in mankind.

1. The word *even* (line 3) suggests that Adam Smith uses "coward" to _____.

   (A) label the coward the most frightened of all persons
   (B) deepen the guilt of a person who lives in constant fear
   (C) absolve a coward of all personal responsibility
   (D) strongly emphasize the importance of using the intellect properly
   (E) comment in passing on the many ways in which talented persons can fail

   1 ____

2. "Should not be altogether uninstructed" (lines 9–10) can be interpreted as _____.
   (A) a plea for universal education
   (B) an aristocratic argument for selective education
   (C) a counterproposal for managing the educational budget
   (D) an exploration of the need for teacher education and selection
   (E) a cool, unemotional appraisal of current educational practices

   2 ____

3. The expression "no inconsiderable advantage" (lines 10–11) suggests that the state will _____.
   (A) be indifferent
   (B) muddle through
   (C) benefit
   (D) object strenuously
   (E) waste resources

   3 ____

4. The word *delusions* in line 14 means _____.
   (A) misconceptions
   (B) instances
   (C) applications
   (D) interpretations
   (E) clarifications

   4 ____

5. Adam Smith feels that education _____.
   (A) helps individuals to accept their place in the social order
   (B) spreads unrest among those most highly trained
   (C) helps every person to reach a level of total equality
   (D) is often wasteful and ineffective
   (E) guarantees every person economic security

   5 ____

6. *Always* in line 18 can best be characterized as a(n) _____.
   (A) misguided falsehood
   (B) oratorical pronouncement
   (C) concerned benevolence
   (D) optimistic generalization
   (E) unvarying truth

   6 ____

7. The word *capriciously* in line 35 means _____.
   (A) venomously
   (B) vigorously
   (C) slyly
   (D) mournfully
   (E) impulsively

   7 ____

8. If we were to put Adam Smith's opinion of education into a metaphor, we might call it _____.
   (A) a gadfly
   (B) a lighted fuse
   (C) an island of serenity
   (D) a safety valve
   (E) a pot of gold

   8 ____

9. The tone of Passage 1 is _____.
   (A) aggressive and dogmatic
   (B) inspirational, though illogical
   (C) measured and reasonable
   (D) bitter and sarcastic
   (E) concerned and uneasy

   9 ____

10. According to Passage 1, a good reason for the state's support of education is _____.
    (A) thought control
    (B) financial solvency
    (C) pure altruism
    (D) military training
    (E) informed citizens

    10 ____

11. Both Passage 1 and Passage 2 are alike in their _____.
    (A) emphasis upon good health as well as intellect
    (B) suggestion that the state benefits little by its educational system
    (C) celebration of the naturally brilliant individual
    (D) tribute to the benefits of education
    (E) fear of popular uprisings

    11 ____

12. Passage 2 differs from Passage 1 in its _____.
    (A) concentration upon the individual rather than the state
    (B) concern for the stability of government
    (C) indifference to the excesses of ignorance
    (D) glorification of parental guidance
    (E) equating terrorism with poverty

    12 ____

13. As contrasted with Passage 2, Passage 1 is more _____.
(A) accepting of class differences
(B) critical of sex differences
(C) interested in child welfare
(D) concerned with health and sanitation
(E) convinced that people determine their own happiness

13 ____

14. "The privilege of their happy constitutions" in line 53 is a reference to _____.
(A) home nurture
(B) specialized educational techniques
(C) genetic advantages
(D) governmental protection by a social contract
(E) inequality before the law

14 ____

15. Which of the following statements may reasonably be made about Passage 2?
(A) A sound mind is more important than a sound body.
(B) A sound body is more important than a sound mind.
(C) Man's misery comes from external sources.
(D) In the nature-nurture controversy, it supports nurture as more important.
(E) Natural geniuses always have excellent constitutions as well as keen minds.

15 ____

16. What irony does the publication date of *Wealth of Nations* suggest?
(A) Rebellion and revolution may come even with education.
(B) Sound reasoning can avert bloodshed.
(C) Violence is always an offshoot of excessive education.
(D) Adam Smith was a leader of the American Revolution.
(E) Luck plays a major role in human affairs.

16 ____

17. The use of the masculine pronoun *he* throughout both passages suggests that _____.
(A) it was a convention to use the masculine pronoun for both men and women
(B) both Smith and Locke were essentially opposed to providing any education for women
(C) men generally make the best educators, though some women achieve extraordinary teaching skill
(D) the apparently greater strength of men is a matter of nurture, not nature
(E) even untutored men are likely to have keen intellects when sufficiently stimulated

17 ____

H

Seeing is a difficult and complicated task, as the author of the following passage makes clear.

I chanced on a wonderful book by Marius von Senden, called *Space and Sight.* When Western surgeons discovered how to perform safe cataract operations, they 5 ranged across Europe and America operating on dozens of men and women of all 10 ages who had been blinded by cataracts since birth. Von Senden collected accounts of such cases; the histories are fascinating. Many doctors had tested their patients' sense perceptions and ideas of space both before and after the operations. The vast majority of patients, of both sexes and all ages, had, in von Senden's opinion, no idea of space whatsoever. Form, distance, and size were so many meaningless syllables. A patient "had no idea of depth, confusing it with roundness." Before the operation a doctor would give a blind patient a cube and a sphere; the patient would tongue it or feel it with his hands, and name it correctly. After the operation the doctor would show the same objects to the patient without letting him touch them; now he had no clue whatsoever what he was seeing. One patient called lemonade "square" because it pricked on his tongue as a square shape pricked on the touch of his hands. Of another postoperative patient, the doctor writes, "I have found in her no notion of size, for example, not even within the narrow limits which she might have encompassed with the aid of touch. Thus when I asked her to show me how big her mother was, she did not stretch out her hands, but set her two index-fingers a few inches apart." Other doctors reported their patients' own statements to similar effect. "The room he was in . . . he knew to be but part of the house, yet he could not conceive that the whole house could look bigger"; "Those who are blind from birth . . . have no real conception of height or distance. A house that is a mile away is thought of as nearby, but requiring the taking of a lot of steps. . . . The elevator that whizzes him up and down gives no more sense of vertical distance than does the train of horizontal."

For the newly sighted, vision is pure sensation unencumbered by meaning: "The girl went through the experience that we all go through and forget, the moment we are born. She saw, but it did not mean anything but a lot of different kinds of brightness." Again, "I asked the patient what he could see; he answered that he saw an extensive field of light, in which everything appeared dull, confused, and in motion. He could not distinguish objects." Another patient saw "nothing but a confusion of forms and colors." When a newly sighted girl saw photographs and paintings, she asked, "Why do they put those dark marks all over them?"

"Those aren't dark marks," her mother explained, "those are shadows. That is one of the ways the eye knows that things have shape. If it were not for shadows many things would look flat."

"Well, that's how things do look," Joan answered. "Everything looks flat with dark patches."

But it is the patients' concepts of space that are most revealing. One patient, according to his doctor, "practiced his vision in a strange fashion; thus he takes off one of his boots, throws it some way off in front of him, and then attempts to gauge the distance at which it lies; he takes a few steps towards the boot and tries to grasp it; on failing to reach it, he moves on a step or two and gropes for the boot until he finally gets hold of it."

"But even at this stage, after three weeks' experience of seeing," von Senden goes on, " 'space,' as he conceives it, ends with visual space, i.e. with color-patches that happen to bound his view. He does not yet have the notion that a larger object (a chair) can mask a smaller one (a dog), or that the latter can still be present even though it is not directly seen."

In general the newly sighted see the world as a dazzle of color-patches. They are pleased by the sensation of color, and learn quickly to name the colors, but the rest of seeing is tormentingly difficult. Soon after his operation a patient "generally bumps into one of these color-patches and observes them to be substantial, since they resist him as tactual objects do. In walking about it also strikes him—or can if he pays attention—that he is continually passing in between the colors he sees, that he can go past a visual object, that a part of it then steadily disappears from view; and that in spite of this, however he

twists and turns—whether entering the
110 room from the door, for example, or returning back to it—he always has a visual

space in front of him. Thus he gradually
comes to realize that there is also a space
behind him, which he does not see."

1. With which of the following statements
   would the author of the passage prob-
   ably agree?
   (A) A suddenly blinded sighted per-
       son would soon be as competent
       in moving about as a person blind
       at birth.
   (B) In their impact, cataract opera-
       tions generally do more harm
       than good.
   (C) Though newly sighted persons
       are puzzled by color, they quickly
       learn to manipulate shapes and
       forms.
   (D) Because of their long years of ex-
       perience, newly sighted older per-
       sons adapt more readily to the
       new sensations.
   (E) Sight is an obvious physical gift,
       but seeing is a process that takes
       a long time to achieve.

                          1 ____

2. Which of the following statements sug-
   gests a parallel with the feelings of
   many newly sighted persons?
   (A) Becoming suddenly sighted im-
       mediately opens a new world of
       familiar objects given an exciting
       new dimension.
   (B) Some hearing impaired persons
       have regretted the insertion of co-
       chlear implants, preferring the
       impairment to the confusion of
       sound.
   (C) The removal of a cataract from a
       sighted person does not have re-
       sults different from those of a per-
       son blind from birth.
   (D) Cataract surgery has experienced
       many improvements in the past

decade, rendering the surgery almost routine.
   (E) The reactions of newly sighted
       persons are quite similar,
       whether the persons be young or
       old, men or women, children or
       adults.

                          2 ____

3. A person's conceptions of space are ap-
   parently _____.
   (A) inborn, part of the genetic
       makeup that determines a
       person's physical characteristics
   (B) learned instantaneously, inas-
       much as the physical world sur-
       rounds a person at birth
   (C) a factor of intelligence, as deter-
       mined by the ability of a person
       to function effectively in a social
       environment
   (D) dependent upon the visual keen-
       ness of both parents
   (E) mastered only after a consider-
       able period of time with many set-
       backs

                          3 ____

4. In line 33, *encompassed* most nearly
   means _____.
   (A) surrounded   (D) expanded
   (B) comprehended (E) appreciated
   (C) surmised

                          4 ____

5. The phrase "pure sensation unencum-
   bered by meaning" (lines 50–51) sug-
   gests _____.
   (A) a significant glow of brilliant light
   (B) a joyous sensory experience
   (C) a confusing blur
   (D) a reference to all five senses
   (E) the most meaningful experience
       of a lifetime

                          5 ____

6. From the passage we may infer that a child at birth _____.
   (A) recognizes his mother's face immediately
   (B) has none of the problems that a newly sighted person experiences
   (C) has more acute sight than hearing
   (D) takes a while to learn to differentiate objects visually
   (E) prefers a brightly lighted room to one less brilliantly lit

   6 ____

7. Lemonade was called "square" by _____.
   (A) a person with limited mental ability
   (B) a writer of humorous essays
   (C) a person dependent upon touch
   (D) Marius von Senden in *Space and Sight*
   (E) a child with no experience of lemonade

   7 ____

8. For spatial problems, blind persons generally depend upon _____.
   (A) the sense of touch
   (B) information picked up by Braille reading
   (C) a kind of sonar, developed through trial and error
   (D) sighted partners who explain problems to them
   (E) the uncertain guidance of other blind persons

   8 ____

9. The author's writing style may be best characterized as _____.
   (A) heavy but informative
   (B) smooth and flowing
   (C) interesting though somewhat disconnected
   (D) breathless and a bit jerky
   (E) plodding and monotonous

   9 ____

10. The author quotes von Senden (lines 85–93) to _____.
    (A) undercut, by providing poorly expressed explanations, his central thesis
    (B) provide a break in sentence structure and rhythm
    (C) suggest the author's incredulity at the astounding cases being reported
    (D) point out that even after three weeks a newly sighted patient has difficulties with space and distance
    (E) provide an insight into the kinds of small-muscle tension that interfere with seeing

    10 ____

11. In line 102, the word *tactual* most nearly means _____.
    (A) in accord with the facts
    (B) verifiable
    (C) showing sensitivity
    (D) pertaining to touch
    (E) obvious to sight

    11 ____

12. As we read the author's description of the experiences of newly sighted persons, we may detect a sense of _____.
    (A) interest coupled with amazement
    (B) fatigue in trying to explain
    (C) dissatisfaction with the reports
    (D) light humor in the guise of scientific reporting
    (E) personal interest in each case history

    12 ____

13. In one example, a patient _____.
  (A) threw a boot in front of him to capitalize on his keen sense of hearing
  (B) equated shadows with dark patches
  (C) correctly judged how big her mother was
  (D) correctly identified a cube and a sphere with purely visual help
  (E) had a keen sense of vertical distance while riding in an elevator

  13 ____

14. We may infer that to a newly sighted person the visual world seems _____.
  (A) a continuing delight because of the new experience
  (B) basically of one color
  (C) a friendly combination of sight and sound
  (D) a familiar and secure place
  (E) two dimensional

  14 ____

I

This first chapter of a classic novel suggests the theme of the novel and introduces interesting characters.

It is a truth universally acknowledged that a single man in possession of a good fortune must be in want of a wife.

However little known the feelings or views
5 of such a man may be on his first entering a neighborhood, this truth is so well fixed in the minds of the surrounding families, that he is considered as the rightful property of some one or other of their daughters.

10 "My dear Mr. Bennet," said his lady to him one day, "have you heard that Netherfield Park is let at last?"

Mr. Bennet replied that he had not.

"But it is," returned she; "for Mrs. Long
15 has just been here, and she told me all about it."

Mr. Bennet made no answer.

"Do not you want to know who has taken it?" cried his wife impatiently.

20 "*You* want to tell me, and I have no objection to hearing it."

This was invitation enough.

"Why, my dear, you must know, Mrs. Long says that Netherfield is taken by a
25 young man of large fortune from the north of England; that he came down on Monday in a chaise and four to see the place and was so much delighted with it that he agreed with Mr. Morris immediately; that he is to
30 take possession before Michaelmas, and some of his servants are to be in the house by the end of next week."

"What is his name?"

"Bingley."

35 "Is he married or single?"

"Oh! single, my dear, to be sure! A single man of large fortune; four or five thousand a year. What a fine thing for our girls !"

"How so? How can it affect them?"

40 "My dear Mr. Bennet," replied his wife, "how can you be so tiresome! You must know that I am thinking of his marrying one of them."

"Is that his design in settling here?"

45 "Design! Nonsense, how can you talk so! But it is very likely that he *may* fall in love with one of them, and therefore you must visit him as soon as he comes."

"I see no occasion for that. You and the
50 girls may go, or you may send them by themselves, which perhaps will be still better, for as you are as handsome as any of them, Mr. Bingley might like you the best of the party."

55 "My dear, you flatter me. I certainly *have* had my share of beauty, but I do not pretend

to be anything extraordinary now. When a woman has five grown-up daughters, she
60 ought to give over thinking of her own beauty."

"In such cases, a woman has not often much beauty to think of.

"But, my dear, you must indeed go and
65 see Mr. Bingley when he comes into the neighborhood."

"It is more than I engage for, I assure you."

"But consider your daughters. Only think
70 what an establishment it would be for one of them. Sir William and Lady Lucas are determined to go, merely on that account, for in general, you know, they visit no new-comers. Indeed you must go, for it will be
75 impossible for *us* to visit him if you do not."

"You are over-scrupulous, surely. I dare say Mr. Bingley will be very glad to see you; and I will send a few lines by you to assure him of my hearty consent to his marrying
80 whichever he chooses of the girls: though I must throw in a good word for my little Lizzy."

"I desire you will do no such thing. Lizzy is not a bit better than the others; and I am
85 sure she is not half so handsome as Jane, nor half so good-humored as Lydia. But you are always giving *her* the preference."

"They have none of them much to rec-ommend them," replied he; "they are all
90 silly and ignorant, like other girls; but Lizzy has something more of quickness than her sisters."

"Mr. Bennet, how can you abuse your own children in such a way? You take delight in
95 vexing me. You have no compassion of my poor nerves."

"You mistake me, my dear. I have a high respect for your nerves. They are my old friends. I have heard you mention them
100 with consideration these twenty years at least."

"Ah! You do not know what I suffer."

"But I hope you will get over it, and live to see many young men of four thousand a
105 year come into the neighborhood."

"It will be no use to us, if twenty such should come, since you will not visit them."

"Depend upon it, my dear, that when there are twenty, I will visit them all."
110 Mr. Bennet was so odd a mixture of quick parts, sarcastic humor, reserve, and ca-price, that the experience of three-and-twenty years had been insufficient to make his wife understand his character. *Her*
115 mind was less difficult to develop. She was a woman of mean understanding, little in-formation, and uncertain temper. When she was discontented, she fancied herself ner-vous. The business of her life was to get her
120 daughters married; its solace was visiting and news.

1. The author's intent in the first sen-tence is to achieve _____.
   (A) sly humor
   (B) profound philosophy
   (C) subtle argument
   (D) economic protest
   (E) deep character analysis

   1 ____

2. Mrs. Bennet's manner of addressing her husband suggests _____.
   (A) an ill-concealed dislike
   (B) a confidence in her ability to con-trol him
   (C) the formality of an earlier time
   (D) a self-assuredness superior to her husband's
   (E) a pixie sense of humor

   2 ____

3. When Mr. Bennet makes no answer (line 17) his reason is _____.
   (A) complete inattention to what his wife has been saying
   (B) anger at her raising the subject of marriage for his daughter
   (C) a slight defect that occasionally impairs his hearing
   (D) his awareness that he'll hear about the matter anyway
   (E) an inner turmoil at the complexi-ties of everyday living

   3 ____

4. Mrs. Bennet considers the new occupant of Netherfield _____.
   (A) somewhat pretentious because of his arrival in a chaise and four
   (B) an interesting young man born in the nearby vicinity
   (C) an insensitive, impetuous aristocrat with several faults
   (D) a person to be manipulated according to her design
   (E) a landowner considerate of his servants and tenant farmers

   4 ____

5. When Mr. Bennet delivers the line, "Is that his design in settling here" (line (44), he is being _____.
   (A) moderately curious
   (B) gently sarcastic
   (C) in full support of his wife
   (D) favorably disposed toward Mr. Bingley
   (E) suitably impressed

   5 ____

6. The dialogue between husband and wife suggests that Mrs. Bennet _____.
   (A) has somewhat of a one-track mind
   (B) is quick thinking and excellent at repartee
   (C) has unselfish motives in making a stranger welcome
   (D) understands her husband only too well
   (E) has a clear favorite among her daughters

   6 ____

7. The coming visit of the Lucases to Mr. Bingley has convinced Mrs. Bennet that _____.
   (A) the Bennets should do more charity work on their own
   (B) the family should visit Bingley as a group
   (C) one can count on friends when times are difficult

   (D) Bingley might be a very good catch
   (E) friends must stick together

   7 ____

8. In talking about his children, Mr. Bennet shows that he _____.
   (A) apparently prefers Jane to Lizzy
   (B) has no inflated ideas of their capabilities
   (C) thinks that his wife has been a cruel mother
   (D) becomes uncharacteristically serious
   (E) would like to get all daughters married quickly

   8 ____

9. The paragraph beginning "You mistake me, my dear" (line 97) suggests that _____.
   (A) Mr. Bennet misses certain old friends
   (B) Mrs. Bennet often forgets old friends
   (C) Mr. Bennet is a bit weary of certain conversations
   (D) Mr. Bennet is here expressing his love in a subtle way
   (E) Mrs. Bennet's worries are principally financial

   9 ____

10. The author's appraisal of Mrs. Bennet is that she is essentially _____.
    (A) relaxed
    (B) inconsiderate
    (C) impolite
    (D) beautiful
    (E) shallow

    10 ____

11. The character of Mr. Bennet, as suggested in the last paragraph, can best be characterized as _____.
    (A) transparent
    (B) vulgar
    (C) complex
    (D) bitter
    (E) unreliable

    11 ____

12. In lines 111–112, the word *caprice* most nearly means _____.
(A) judgment
(B) whim
(C) sincerity
(D) fascination
(E) agreeableness

12 ____

13. In line 120, the word *solace* most nearly means _____.
(A) tiring exercise
(B) vocation
(C) humorous action
(D) revenge
(E) comfort

13 ____

14. The tone of the passage can best be characterized as _____.
(A) pretentious
(B) lighthearted
(C) humorless
(D) disdainful
(E) inspirational

14 ____

15. If we may judge by the conversation, it is reasonable to assume that in later pages _____.
(A) Mrs. Bennet will come to love Lizzy best
(B) Mr. Bennet will leave his family
(C) Mrs. Bennet will change and become less nervous
(D) Mr. Bennet will visit Mr. Bingley
(E) Mr. Bingley won't move to Netherfield

15 ____

J

How does a novel come into being? What impulses and forces drive an author to create a special world of his own? The following passage, part of a long explanation, suggests some of the challenges.

I am not so pretentious as to imagine that it is possible for me to account completely for my own book, *Native Son*. But I am going to try to account for as much of it as I can,
5 the sources of it, the material that went into it, and my own years' long changing attitude toward that material.

In a fundamental sense, an imaginative novel represents the merging of two ex-
10 tremes; it is an intensely intimate expression on the part of a consciousness couched in terms of the most objective and commonly known events. It is at once something private and public by its very nature
15 and texture. Confounding the author who is trying to lay his cards on the table is the dogging knowledge that his imagination is a kind of community medium of exchange: what he has read, felt, thought, seen, and
20 remembered is translated into extensions as impersonal as a worn dollar bill.

The more closely the author thinks of why he wrote, the more he comes to regard his imagination as a kind of self-generating
25 cement which glued his facts together, and his emotions as a kind of dark and obscure designer of those facts. Always there is something that is just beyond the tip of the tongue that could explain it all. Usually, he
30 ends up by discussing something far afield, an act which incites skepticism and suspicion in those anxious for a straight-out explanation.

Yet the author is eager to explain. But the
35 moment he makes the attempt his words falter, for he is confronted and defied by the inexplicable array of his own emotions. Emotions are subjective and he can communicate them only when he clothes them in
40 objective guise; and how can he ever be so arrogant as to know when he is dressing up the right emotion in the right Sunday suit?

He is always left with the uneasy notion that maybe *any* objective drapery is as good
45 as *any* other for any emotion.

And the moment he does dress up an emotion, his mind is confronted with the riddle of that "dressed up" emotion, and he is left peering with eager dismay back into
50 the dim reaches of his own incommunicable life. Reluctantly, he comes to the conclusion that to account for his book is to account for his life, and he knows that that is impossible. Yet, some curious, wayward motive
55 urges him to supply the answer, for there is the feeling that his dignity as a living being is challenged by something within him that is not understood.

So, at the outset, I say frankly that there
60 are phrases of *Native Son* which I shall make no attempt to account for. There are meanings in my book of which I was not aware until they literally spilled out upon the paper. I shall sketch the outline of how
65 I *consciously* came into possession of the materials that went into *Native Son,* but there will be many things I shall omit, not because I want to, but simply because I don't know them.

70 The birth of Bigger Thomas goes back to my childhood, and there was not just one Bigger, but many of them, more than I could count and more than you suspect. But let me start with the first Bigger, whom I shall
75 call Bigger No. 1.

When I was a bareheaded, barefoot kid in Jackson, Mississippi, there was a boy who terrorized me and all of the boys I played with. If we were playing games, he would
80 saunter up and snatch from us our balls, bats, spinning tops, and marbles. We would stand around pouting, sniffling, trying to keep back our tears, begging for our playthings. But Bigger would refuse. We never
85 demanded that he give them back; we were afraid, and Bigger was bad. We had seen him clout boys when he was angry and we did not want to run that risk. We never recovered our toys unless we flattered him
90 and made him feel that he was superior to us. Then, perhaps, if he felt like it, he condescended, threw them at us and then gave each of us a swift kick in the bargain, just to make us feel his utter contempt.

95 That was the way Bigger No. 1 lived. His life was a continuous challenge to others. At all times he *took* his way, right or wrong, and those who contradicted him had him to fight. And never was he happier than when
100 he had someone cornered and at his mercy; it seemed that the deepest meaning of his squalid life was in him at such times.

I don't know what the fate of Bigger No. 1 was. His swaggering personality is swallowed up somewhere in the amnesia of my
105 childhood. But I suspect that his end was violent. Anyway, he left a marked impression upon me; maybe it was because I longed secretly to be like him and was afraid. I don't know.

1. In line 1, *pretentious* suggests _____.

   (A) being bright and alert
   (B) winning without concern for others
   (C) doing things for show
   (D) having a winning manner
   (E) justifying wrong actions

                                    1 _____

2. The writer looks upon the imaginative novel as _____.
   (A) a conflict between the author and the blank page
   (B) a transformation of the subjective into the objective
   (C) the result of many attempts to sample reader opinion
   (D) a cooperative effort involving publisher, editor, author, and, ultimately, reader
   (E) an attempt to avoid laying cards on the table

                                    2 _____

3. The author introduces the example of a dollar bill as _____.
   (A) a subtle attack upon greed as a writer's motivation
   (B) a metaphor for unrecognized creativity in an increasingly indifferent world
   (C) a sad expression of the writer's dependence upon financial success
   (D) a medium through which authors express observations, thoughts, and feelings
   (E) an image emphasizing the impersonality of the actual writing result

   3 ____

4. According to the author, the "community medium of exchange" is _____.
   (A) the ever-present dollar bill
   (B) objectively known events
   (C) the emotions
   (D) the imagination
   (E) the merging of two extremes

   4 ____

5. In his search of the source and origin of his novel, the author _____.
   (A) is not altogether sure about the creative process
   (B) considers emotions "a kind of self-generating cement"
   (C) calls upon literary authorities for an answer
   (D) considers his childhood experiences of little value
   (E) proclaims his opposition to novels without emotion

   5 ____

6. In line 37, the word *inexplicable* _____.
   (A) is opposed to the phrase "eager to explain"
   (B) emphasizes the objectivity of the imaginative novel
   (C) suggests a confrontation between fact and fiction

   (D) has the meaning "unjustified"
   (E) labels the author's creative efforts as futile

   6 ____

7. All the following are examples of figurative language EXCEPT _____.
   (A) "glued his facts together"
   (B) "beyond the tip of the tongue"
   (C) "dressing up the right emotion"
   (D) "he knows that that is impossible"
   (E) "peering with eager dismay"

   7 ____

8. "They literally spilled out upon the paper" is _____.
   (A) an attempt to present an interrupted flow of words
   (B) actually a contradiction between *literal* and *figurative*
   (C) the author's excuse for hasty, slipshod writing
   (D) a reference to notes jotted down by the author over a period of years
   (E) an unsuccessfully repressed attempt at self-concealment

   8 ____

9. In line 54, the word *wayward* most nearly means _____.
   (A) unintentional
   (B) incomprehensible
   (C) vigorous
   (D) pressing
   (E) erratic

   9 ____

10. When the author examines the challenge to "account for the book," his reaction may be paraphrased in the following way: _____
   (A) "I plan to omit long sections as being too private."
   (B) "An outsider could possibly do a better job."
   (C) "I can't really explain but I'll try."
   (D) "I'll explain all emotional impulses as they appear in the book."
   (E) "I regret the experience as being too painful."

   10 ____

11. The passage suggests that a novelist
_____.
    (A) may include meanings he's un-
        aware of
    (B) needs a bitter childhood to suc-
        ceed
    (C) enjoys proofreading his own
        novel, not others
    (D) finds his best material in the
        news media
    (E) is usually a wide and perceptive
        reader
                                11 ____

12. Throughout, the attitude of the author
seems _____.
    (A) reflective but inhibited
    (B) self-satisfied and glib
    (C) intentionally obscure
    (D) open and honest
    (E) weak and hesitant
                                12 ____

13. Bigger Thomas is apparently _____.
    (A) the author of *Native Son*
    (B) based on the author's own physi-
        cal prowess
    (C) a character in *Native Son*
    (D) a particular bully in Jackson, Mis-
        sissippi
    (E) the pen name of the writer
                                13 ____

14. The author in describing his experiences with the bully makes clear that
at the time he _____.
    (A) resolved to use the experience in
        a novel some day
    (B) felt degraded in having to flatter
        the bully
    (C) formed a group with other boys to
        defeat the bully
    (D) felt that the bully would be a suc-
        cess some day
    (E) did not allow the troubles to
        make him depressed
                                14 ____

15. When the bully "condescended," he
_____.
    (A) apologized for his actions but
        then continued
    (B) walked down the stairs to abuse
        the other boys
    (C) yelled horrible names at the boys
    (D) became violent and broke the
        other boys' toys
    (E) dealt with the boys as inferiors
                                15 ____

16. In line 102, the word *squalid* means
_____.
    (A) violent and uproarious
    (B) mean and unclean
    (C) poor but understated
    (D) thoughtless and unfriendly
    (E) depressing and uncertain
                                16 ____

17. "The amnesia of my childhood" is in all
probability _____.
    (A) a disease that the author outgrew
        in maturity
    (B) the sights, sounds, and other sen-
        sations of childhood
    (C) a protective mechanism against
        the early troubles
    (D) an inability to defeat the bully of
        early years
    (E) the uncluttered recollections of
        an observant writer
                                17 ____

18. The last two sentences suggest that the
author _____.
    (A) really had a warm spot in his
        heart for Bigger No. 1
    (B) didn't want to reveal the real
        identity of Bigger No. 1
    (C) is discounting the importance of
        his early childhood
    (D) is being honest in evaluating his
        own motivations
    (E) considered himself a coward for
        not striking Bigger No. 1
                                18 ____

K

The following description captures for the reader a moment in time at the shore.

At noon white wings sailed over the sand dunes and a snowy egret swung down long black legs. The bird alighted at the margin of a pond that lay, half encircled by marsh,
5   between the eastern end of the dunes and the inlet beach. The pond was called Mullet Pond, a name given to it years before when it had been larger and mullet had sometimes come into it from the sea. Every day
10   the small white heron came to fish the pond, seeking the killifish and other minnows that darted in its shallows. Sometimes, too, he found the young of larger fishes, for the highest tides of each month cut through the
15   beach on the ocean side and brought in fish from the sea.

The pond slept in noonday quiet. Against the green of the marsh grass the heron was a snow-white figure on slim black stilts,
20   tense and motionless. Not a ripple nor the shadow of a ripple passed beneath his sharp eyes. Then eight pale minnows swam single file above the muddy bottom, and eight black shadows moved beneath them.

25   With a snakelike contortion of its neck, the heron jabbed violently, but missed the leader of the solemn little parade of fish. The minnows scattered in sudden panic as the clear water was churned to muddy
30   chaos by the feet of the heron, who darted one way and another, skipping and flapping his wings in excitement. In spite of his efforts, he captured only one of the minnows.

The heron had been fishing for an hour
35   and the sanderlings, sandpipers, and plovers had been sleeping for three hours when a boat's bottom grated on the sound beach near the point. Two men jumped out into the water and made ready to drag a haul
40   seine through the shallows on the rising tide. The heron lifted his head and listened. Through the fringe of sea oats on the sound side of the pond he saw a man walking down the beach toward the inlet. Alarmed, he

45   thrust his feet hard against the mud and with a flapping of wings took off over the dunes toward the heron rookery in the cedar thickets a mile away. Some of the shore birds ran twittering across the beach
50   toward the sea. Already the terns were milling about overhead in a noisy cloud, like hundreds of scraps of paper flung to the wind. The sanderlings took flight and crossed the point, wheeling and turning
55   almost as one bird, and passed down the ocean beach about a mile.

The ghost crab, still at his hunting of beach fleas, was alarmed by the turmoil of birds overhead, by the many racing shad-
60   ows that sped over the sand. By now he was far from his own burrow. When he saw the fisherman walking across the beach he dashed into the surf, preferring this refuge to flight. But a large channel bass was lurk-
65   ing nearby, and in a twinkling the crab was seized and eaten. Later in the same day, the bass was attacked by sharks and what was left of it was cast up by the tide onto the sand. There the beach fleas, scavengers of
70   the shore, swarmed over it and devoured it.

1. A recurring contrast in the selection is the difference between _____.
    (A) the cruelty of the heron and the nonaggressiveness of the minnows
    (B) the apparent serenity of the beach scene and the tumultuous events occurring all around
    (C) the wastefulness of the fishermen and the economy of the heron
    (D) the colorful nature of the pond and the dullness of the surrounding sea
    (E) the gentleness of nature and the violence of human beings

1 ____

2. The variety of fish in Mullet Pond depends upon _____.
(A) a temporary inlet
(B) restocking by fishermen
(C) the efforts of herons and other shore birds
(D) patternless weather conditions
(E) dredging by local contractors

2 ____

3. From the passage we may infer that _____.
(A) killifish are not minnows
(B) the name *Mullet Pond* is no longer an accurate description
(C) the heron is rarely disturbed by the arrival of humans
(D) plovers do not rest during the day
(E) the heron perches on tall black posts

3 ____

4. In line 40, *seine* most nearly means a _____.
(A) narrow rowboat
(B) baited line
(C) block and tackle
(D) kind of net
(E) clam rake

4 ____

5. From the selection we may infer that _____.
(A) herons are more at home in deeper water than in shallow
(B) sandpipers are more efficient at fishing than sanderlings
(C) the lack of maneuvering by minnows makes them easy targets
(D) channel bass subsist for the most part on sea oats
(E) herons and plovers have different times for activity

5 ____

6. The author makes an ironic and powerful comment on life by pointing out that _____.
(A) in a sense, beach fleas are at the bottom of the food chain and at the top
(B) the channel bass, though larger than the ghost crab, is also its prey
(C) fishermen are working at the rising tide, perhaps a poor time to fish
(D) though basically nonsocial birds, herons frequently flock with sandpipers
(E) the men are spoiling the beach habitat

6 ____

7. All the following are examples of figurative language EXCEPT _____.
(A) "the pond slept" (line 17)
(B) "figure on slim black stilts" (line 19)
(C) "the minnows scattered" (line 28)
(D) "milling about overhead in a noisy cloud" (lines 50–51)
(E) "hundreds of scraps of paper" (line 52)

7 ____

8. The heron may have been largely unsuccessful in his fishing because of _____.
(A) a lack of concentration on the task at hand
(B) his own efforts that stirred up the water
(C) an individual ineptitude uncharacteristic of herons
(D) too intense competition between the heron and the other shore birds
(E) turbulence caused by tides

8 ____

9. The attitude of the author towards the events described can best be characterized as _____.
   (A) horror at the cruelty displayed
   (B) bored reporting of essentially repetitive actions
   (C) alert interest in the workings of nature
   (D) protest at the wastefulness of natural processes
   (E) sensitivity to the humor beneath the surface

   9 ____

10. The "white wings" mentioned in line 1 belong to a(n) _____.
    (A) tern   (D) sandpiper
    (B) sanderling   (E) egret
    (C) plover

    10 ____

11. The author's purpose in introducing the episode of the ghost crab is to _____.
    (A) deplore the arrival of the fishermen
    (B) demonstrate the courage of this lowly creature
    (C) contrast its behavior with that of the heron
    (D) show how the food chain operates
    (E) underscore the voraciousness of the channel bass

    11 ____

12. The "eight black shadows" (lines 23–24) belong to _____.
    (A) terns
    (B) herons
    (C) egrets
    (D) ghost crabs
    (E) minnows

    12 ____

13. It might be said of scavengers (line 69) that they will _____.
    (A) eat all kinds of food
    (B) survive long after the herons have disappeared
    (C) litter the shore with their carcasses
    (D) provide nourishing food for egrets
    (E) become an endangered species

    13 ____

14. Which of the following quotations is closest in spirit to that of the passage?
    (A) "Nature I loved, and next to nature, art." W. S. Landor
    (B) "Those things are better which are perfected by nature than those which are finished by art." Cicero
    (C) "Nothing which we can imagine about Nature is incredible." Pliny the Elder
    (D) "Nature is visible thought." Heinrich Heine
    (E) "Art quickens nature." Robert Herrick

    14 ____

L

The following passage describes a new method of mining that may bring changes in mining techniques.

The recovery of copper from the drainage water of mines was probably a widespread practice in the Mediterranean basin as early as 1000 B.C. Although such mining operations are difficult to document, it is known that the leaching of copper on a large scale was well established at the Rio Tinto mines in Spain by the 18th century. What none of the miners engaged in this traditional method of mineral extraction realized until about 25 years ago is that bacteria take an active part in the leaching process. They help to convert the copper into a water-soluble form that can be carried off by the leach water. Today bacteria are being deliberately exploited to recover millions of

pounds of copper from billions of tons of
low-grade ore. Copper obtained in this way
accounts for more than 10 percent of the
20 total U.S. production. In recent years bacterial leaching has also been applied to the
recovery of another nonferrous metal: ura-
nium.

Recent progress in the genetic manipula-
25 tion of microorganisms for industrial purposes promises to revitalize not only the
bacterial leaching of metal-bearing ores but
also the microbiological treatment of metal-
contaminated wastewater. The enthusiasm
30 of the microbiologists working on the development of the new "biomining" techniques
is matched by a need in the minerals industry to find alternatives to conventional
methods of mining, ore processing, and
35 wastewater treatment. The need arises
from recent trends in the industry: the continued depletion of high-grade mineral resources, the resulting tendency for mining
to be extended deeper underground, the
40 growing awareness of environmental problems associated with the smelting of sulfide
minerals and the burning of sulfur-rich fossil fuels, and the rising cost of the prodigious amounts of energy required in the
45 conventional recovery methods. The current methods will surely prevail for many
years to come. But biological processes are
generally less energy-intensive and less
polluting than most nonbiological technol-
50 ogy in mining, ore processing, and wastewater treatment and is likely to become
increasingly important.

1. All the following are mentioned as
   stimulating the need for biomining
   EXCEPT _____.
   (A) depletion of high-grade mineral
       resources
   (B) environmental problems
   (C) intensive foreign competition
   (D) need for ever deeper mining
   (E) energy considerations

   1 ____

2. Microorganisms are playing a greater
   role in industrial technology as a result
   of _____.
   (A) presidential decree
   (B) historical study
   (C) genetic manipulation
   (D) innovation by Spanish miners
   (E) underground exploration

   2 ____

3. As used in the passage, "leaching" re-
   fers to _____.
   (A) bleaching discolored elements
   (B) chemically destroying pollutants
   (C) smelting sulfide minerals
   (D) separating components
   (E) depleting high-grade mineral re-
       sources

   3 ____

4. Which of the following best describes
   the main idea of the passage?
   (A) Copper obtained from drainage
       water is superior to that directly
       mined.
   (B) Microbiologists decry the exploita-
       tion of genetics for industrial pur-
       poses.
   (C) The role of biological technology
       in mining and related areas is
       growing.
   (D) Wastewater treatment is under-
       going major changes in technol-
       ogy.
   (E) Biological processes tend to be
       more polluting than nonbiological
       ones.

   4 ____

5. "Biomining" is put in quotation marks
   because _____.
   (A) biomining is an unnatural proce-
       dure
   (B) it should really be *bioleaching*
   (C) it is a newly coined word
   (D) no scientist believes in its efficacy
   (E) the word was first used in the
       18th century and revived

   5 ____

6. The leaching process is apparently most economically feasible with _____.
(A) low-grade ore
(B) sulfide minerals
(C) burning of fossil fuels
(D) rich veins of ore
(E) agriculture

6 ____

7. The recovery of copper from the waste water of mines _____.
(A) began in the Rio Tinto mines of Spain
(B) is an attractive plan but a will-o'-the-wisp in practice
(C) relies basically on sulfur-rich fossil fuels during the processing
(D) probably goes back 3,000 years
(E) accounts for most copper produced in the United States

7 ____

8. The passage admits which of the following are being exploited in the copper-recovery process?
(A) miners
(B) wastewater processors
(C) microbiologists
(D) bacteria
(E) biochemical engineers

8 ____

9. In line 16, *exploited* most nearly means _____.
(A) disregarded
(B) utilized
(C) changed
(D) advertised
(E) transported

9 ____

10. In line 37, the word *depletion* most nearly means _____.
(A) increasing   (D) revitalizing
(B) neglecting   (E) draining
(C) scattering

10 ____

11. The author's attitude toward new methods of mining is one of _____.
(A) skepticism   (D) tolerance
(B) approval   (E) indifference
(C) antagonism

11 ____

M

The following passage discusses the difficulties that computers face when tackling a problem in language. Of the five problem areas, four are analyzed here. Will the computer be able to overcome these semantic obstacles?

Computers stand up well to a grand master when it comes to the logic of chess, but they can't match the skills of a seven-year-old when it comes to language.

5 The reason for the glacial pace of progress in MT (machine translation) over the past four decades can be found in one factor: the intractable ambiguities of natural language. An MT system must peel away at
10 least five layers of ambiguity before it is able to map sentences from one language to another with any degree of accuracy. If you understand how MT copes with these difficulties, you will have a clear idea of just how

15 these systems work and why they do not work better.

Step inside an MT system and see how it handles the following simple sentence: *The heavy-duty truck turned into a driveway.* As
20 you follow this sentence through the system, notice how nearly every other word poses a challenge—and an opportunity for error.

When the system looks in the dictionary
25 for the word *truck,* it immediately encounters ambiguity: The word is encoded in the dictionary as both a noun and a verb. The system's dictionary can tell you only that

truck can take the form of two parts of
30 speech. It can't tell you which form it takes
in this sentence.

To make that determination, you must
move further into the system and view the
word in the context of the sentence. At this
35 point, the system still has no idea what the
sentence means and sees it only as a syntactic string containing elements that have
more than one interpretation.

To operate at the sentence level of the
40 syntactic stage, you must have some kind of
grammar—typically stored as a set of rules.
One of these rules will determine that, in
the given sentence, without violating grammatical rules, *truck* cannot be anything but
45 a noun. So far, so good—although it is not
always going to be that easy.

Now that you know that *heavy-duty truck*
is a noun phrase, a second layer of ambiguity comes to light. The system still sees your
50 noun phrase purely syntactically, as the
string Adj N1 N2. It has no idea, for example, whether the adjective *heavy* modifies
duty or *truck*. The system has to resolve this
ambiguity if it's to get the agreement right.
55 Therefore, you have to go beyond syntax
into lexical semantics.

At this deeper stage, more intelligent
rules come into play and use the semantic
properties that were retrieved for the words
60 earlier in your sentence during the dictionary lookup stage. These semantic-property   codes   are   designed   to   resolve
ambiguities such as that posed by *heavy-
duty truck*. Now you're going to run into
65 some rough going.

The majority of low-end MT systems don't
get into semantics—or they do so only in
trivial ways. These systems generally are
weak, but even high-end systems will have
70 trouble trying to figure out which noun
heavy modifies. The issues are subtle. At
this point, most developers will resort to
brute force by storing the phrase as a unit
in the dictionary.
75 Slightly more tractable examples of this
kind of ambiguity would be *old people and*

children and *smart girls and boys*. If a
smart rule uses a test for semantic symme-
try (or lack thereof) among the noun pairs,
80 it could figure out that the adjective *old*
modifies only *people* and that *smart* modifies both *boys* and *girls*. Clearly, getting a
machine to cope with this challenge isn't
easy.

85 Processing at the lexical semantic stage
introduces its own kind of confusion—the
third layer—having to do with multiple
meanings of words. For example, the verb
turn into has at least two lexical meanings:
90 One is the sense of motion, and the other is
the sense of becoming. To decide which
meaning applies in your sentence, you have
to move to sentence-level semantics, where
the verb *turn into* can be examined in its
95 semantic context.

A semantic rule associated with the
words *turn into* would know that the meaning of this verb is going to be a function of
the verb's direct object. So, in this sentence,
100 the rule has to test only the semantic-property code for *driveway* to determine the
verb's meaning: If *driveway* were given a
semantic-property code signifying a path,
the rule would know to select the verb's
105 motional sense. Such a rule would work
with Cinderella, too, if her carriage turned
into a driveway rather than a pumpkin.

A fourth layer of difficulty has to do with
ambiguities introduced at the sentence
110 level of the semantic stage. Unfortunately
(or fortunately), the sample sentence
doesn't illustrate this kind of complexity.
But to get the idea, consider the meaning of
the preposition *for* in the following senten-
115 ces: Check the newspapers for errors. Check
the newspapers for dates.

In the first sentence, the preposition *for*
signifies *for the presence of,* and in the second sentence, it means *for information*
120 *about*. As used in this example, in a language like Vietnamese, the preposition *for*
would be expressed differently in each case.

Thus, the system has to determine which
case applies if it's to translate the meaning

125 correctly. You can see that the meanings of
the word *for* are a function of the sentence
as a whole; you won't find them in any
dictionary. Also, notice how the sentence as
a whole affects the meaning of the verb
130 *check*. In the first sentence, *check* means to
examine. In the second, *check* means to
consult.

1. In line 8, "intractable ambiguities" sug-
   gests _____.
   (A) a difficulty brought on by falla-
       cies in logic
   (B) the logical organization and struc-
       ture of natural language
   (C) an ornery problem with two or
       more meanings
   (D) a double dose of crystal-clear
       prose
   (E) an inferior example of circular
       reasoning

                                    1 ____

2. The language skills of a seven-year-old
   are superior to those of the finest com-
   puter because _____.
   (A) the child's brain is a superior ma-
       chine for translation
   (B) computer skills in chess are no
       better than those in language
   (C) a computer is an inanimate ob-
       ject without logical skills
   (D) the complexities of even a simple
       sentence baffle the computer
   (E) seven is the age at which chil-
       dren begin to speak standard En-
       glish

                                    2 ____

3. The author implies that the sentence
   "The heavy-duty truck turned into a
   driveway" _____.
   (A) poses only two difficulties for a
       computer
   (B) is simple enough for certain types
       of computers to translate
   (C) is not a good example of English
       sentence structure

(D) would be extremely difficult to
    translate into Vietnamese
(E) would not be a problem for a
    seven-year-old

                                    3 ____

4. When determining whether "truck" is
   a noun or a verb, a person or computer
   would _____.
   (A) have to look at the rest of the sen-
       tence
   (B) check the dictionary or built-in
       word list
   (C) first assume that it is a verb
   (D) instantaneously sift through the
       rules of grammar
   (E) have to make a guess

                                    4 ____

5. From the selection, we may assume
   that semantics deals principally with
   _____.
   (A) word order
   (B) meaning
   (C) spelling
   (D) literature
   (E) metaphor

                                    5 ____

6. In line 89, *lexical* most nearly means
   _____.
   (A) linked to computers
   (B) literate
   (C) open-ended
   (D) pertaining to words
   (E) challenging

                                    6 ____

7. Which of the following methods would
   make it easier for the computer to han-
   dle the "truck" sentence?
   (A) Change "driveway" to "roadway."
   (B) Rearrange the word order of the
       sentence.
   (C) Insert into its dictionary "heavy-
       duty" as one unit.
   (D) Change "into" to "from."
   (E) Anticipate the sentence by put-
       ting it into the system before-
       hand.

                                    7 ____

8. In the two quoted sentences (lines 115–116), the major difficulty is _____.
   (A) similar to a difficulty found in Vietnamese
   (B) deciding on the meaning of the preposition "for"
   (C) determining the part of speech of "for"
   (D) the rather slipshod word order
   (E) determining the motive of the speaker of each sentence

   8 ____

9. In the quoted sentences mentioned in question 8, an added difficulty is _____.
   (A) differences in the meaning of "check"
   (B) a deceptive difference in word order
   (C) use of the imperative rather than the declarative
   (D) the placement of the two prepositional phrases
   (E) the subtle difference between "newspapers" in sentences 1 and 2

   9 ____

10. The author uses a fairly simple English sentence, "The heavy-duty truck turned into the driveway," to _____.
    (A) critically evaluate different types of computers
    (B) show, step by step, how a computer successfully manages the difficulties of translation
    (C) demonstrate his own complete mastery of English sentence structure
    (D) contrast the sentence with "Check the newspaper for errors"
    (E) point out some of the critical difficulties in translating even a simple sentence

    10 ____

11. All the following are examples of figurative language EXCEPT _____.
    (A) "peel away" (line 9)
    (B) "some kind of grammar" (lines 40–41)
    (C) "system still sees" (line 49)
    (D) "run into some rough going" (lines 64–65)
    (E) "brute force" (line 73)

    11 ____

12. The author's style may best be described as _____.
    (A) flowery
    (B) halting
    (C) methodical
    (D) pompous
    (E) flamboyant

    12 ____

13. The author intends the opening sentence _____.
    (A) as a shocker to get the reader's attention
    (B) to belittle the much-vaunted powers of computers
    (C) to glorify humanity at the expense of the inanimate computer
    (D) to emphasize that the days of human superiority in chess are dying
    (E) as an indication that both chess and language are to be discussed in the passage

    13 ____

Reading Diagnostic Tests

First take Test A, below, and Test B on page 342. Referring to pages 531–533, check your answers, and go over the analysis. In the analysis you will find the page numbers where to turn in this book for additional help and strategy.

Find your weaknesses well in advance of the SAT testing date so that you will have ample time to work on the types of test items that you find most difficult. Remember you are building your personal power to take the SAT with confidence.

Reading Diagnostic Test A

Each passage below is followed by questions based on its content. Answer all questions following a passage on the basis of what is stated or implied in that passage.

Understanding ancient languages is a continuing challenge. The mystery of hieroglyphics was eliminated with help from the Rosetta Stone. Linear B, the script of the
5 Cretan Minoan civilization, was deciphered in fairly recent times. However, there are other challenging inscriptions awaiting clarification by inspired amateur cryptographers. These tantalizing scripts
10 include Etruscan, Iberian, and the Bronze Age seals of the Indus civilization. Why bother? Understanding a language provides a key that unlocks a culture and a civilization available in no other way.

1. The paragraph implies that _____.
   (A) certain languages, like Iberian, will never be deciphered
   (B) cryptanalysis can help in translating an obscure script
   (C) the Minoan and Etruscan are scripts from the Bronze Age
   (D) Linear B and hieroglyphics were based on identical principles
   (E) without the Rosetta stone, hieroglyphics would still be a mystery

   1 _____

The character of the prince who now ascended the throne of England and became lord of Normandy, Anjou, Touraine, and Maine, claimant to Brittany and heir to
5 Queen Eleanor's Aquitaine, was already well known. Richard had embodied the virtues which men admire in the lion, but there is no animal in nature that combines the contradictory qualities of John. He
10 united the ruthlessness of a hardened warrior with the craft and subtlety of a Machiavelli. Although from time to time he gave way to furious rages, in which "his eyes darted fire and his countenance became
15 livid," his cruelties were conceived and executed with a cold, inhuman intelligence. Monkish chroniclers have emphasized his violence, greed, malice, treachery, and lust. But other records show that he was often
20 judicious, always extremely capable, and on occasions even generous. He possessed an original and inquiring mind, and to the end of his life treasured his library of books. In him the restless energy of the Plantagenet
25 race was raised to a furious pitch of instability. A French writer, it is true, has tried to throw the sombre cloak of madness over his moral deformities, but a study of his actions shows John gifted with a deep and

30 persistent sagacity, of patience and artifice
and with an unshakable resolve, which he
fulfilled, to maintain himself upon the
throne while the breath was in his body.
The difficulties with which he contended,
35 on the whole with remarkable success, deserve cool and attentive study. Moreover,
when the long tally is added it will be seen
that the British nation and the English-
speaking world owe far more to the vices of
40 John than to the labours of virtuous sovereigns; for it was through the union of many
forces against him that the most famous
milestone of our rights and freedom was in
fact set up.

2. The selection focuses its major atten-
   tion upon _____.
   (A) the virtues of Richard
   (B) the progeny of Queen Eleanor
   (C) the energy of the Plantagenets
   (D) the contradictory nature of John
   (E) the deviousness of the Normans

   2 _____

3. Which of the following pairs of adjec-
   tives may be applied to John?
   (A) gentle and mad
   (B) cruel and intelligent
   (C) handsome and ruthless
   (D) patient and weak
   (E) greedy and stupid

   3 _____

4. Monkish chroniclers _____.
   (A) tended to report John's worst
       qualities
   (B) glorified John
   (C) praised him for supporting free-
       dom
   (D) called him a Machiavelli
   (E) commented on his fine library

   4 _____

5. A generalization that may be drawn
   from the passage is that _____.
   (A) you can't tell a book by its cover
   (B) violence begets violence
   (C) evil actions may bring good re-
       sults
   (D) restless energy leads to virtuous
       action
   (E) the concept of kingship is obsolete

   5 _____

Kentucky-born John Stark was fifty-
eight years old when he first heard Joplin
play the piece that was the patrons' favorite
at Sedalia's Maple Leaf Club. Disregarding
5 warnings that no market existed for black
composers' works, Stark agreed to have
Joplin's piece printed and to sell it in his
music store. Published in September 1899,
"Maple Leaf Rag" did not sell well at first.
10 But it gained popularity in the fall of 1900,
boosted by the sudden eruption of a national ragtime craze. Stark and his son
moved to St. Louis, where they printed ten
thousand copies of Joplin's piece on a small
15 hand press and hung up a sign reading
"John Stark and Son, Music Publishers."
Orders for "Maple Leaf Rag" came in from
all over the country. Stark hired a staff,
exchanged his work clothes for a business
20 suit, and prepared to face life as a successful
publisher. Soon he had a fine house in St.
Louis and a thriving business whose principal product was the works of a previously
unknown composer named Scott Joplin.
25   Joplin followed Stark to St. Louis in 1901.
He bought a house there, equipped it with
a piano, and settled down to his chosen
work of serious composing. The composi-
tions that Joplin produced in the next ten
30 years are still remembered as classics of
ragtime. They were appealing pieces with
flowing melodies, intricate syncopations,
and expressive themes. They bore such
names as "The Entertainer," "Peacherine
35 Rag," "The Easy Winners," "Elite Syncopations," and "The Strenuous Life." He also

wrote songs, marches, waltzes, and an elegant tango called "Solace." For several
years, he appeared on vaudeville stages,
40 billed as "King of Ragtime Composers—Author of 'Maple Leaf Rag.'" But his ambitions
transcended the confines of popular dance
and show music. He longed to adapt the
rhythms of ragtime to more ambitious mu-
45 sical forms, to show that characteristic
black syncopation was capable of expressing enduring musical ideas.

6. Which of the following titles best summarizes the content of the passage?
   (A) John Stark, Entrepreneur
   (B) St. Louis, Home of Ragtime
   (C) The Problems of Music Publishing
   (D) Famous Composers of Ragtime
   (E) The King of Ragtime

   6 _____

7. "Maple Leaf Rag" took its name from
   _____.
   (A) a club in Sedalia
   (B) a sign in John Stark's office
   (C) Canada
   (D) a tree in Joplin's garden
   (E) a previous composition

   7 _____

8. All the following types of musical composition are mentioned in the passage
   EXCEPT _____.
   (A) waltz
   (B) tango
   (C) march
   (D) opera
   (E) song

   8 _____

9. Scott Joplin had to earn his living as
   _____.
   (A) an assistant to John Stark
   (B) a dance instructor
   (C) a vaudeville entertainer
   (D) a printer
   (E) a distributor of his own work

   9 _____

On a global basis, it has been estimated
that the annual net loss of soil from cropland is some 23 billion tons in excess of soil
formation. As world population expands,
5 demand for food and fiber expands. Driven
by economic and social pressures, more of
the world's marginal cropland is put to the
plow each year—only to be abandoned as
soils are depleted after a short period of
10 production. Mining of the world's arable
soils is an ongoing and accelerating process,
the inevitable consequences of which must
be obvious to any thinking person. It may
come to pass that sustaining this nation's
15 food- and fiber-producing capacity may become our most potent deterrent to international conflict.

To blame farmers for abandoning well-
known soil-conservation practices is akin to
20 denouncing one who is drowning for futilely
clutching at straws. In far too many cases,
the farmer is fighting for survival; when he
is reduced to choosing between bankruptcy
now or later, his choice is obvious. Long-
25 term conservation practices suffer under
the harsh demands of economic survival.
But there are others who are farming the
subsidy/tax-incentives system for a quick
profit at the expense of family farmers, con-
30 sumers, and taxpayers alike.

10. As used in the selection *marginal* is
    equivalent to _____.
    (A) bordering
    (B) arable
    (C) desert
    (D) terminal
    (E) poor

    10 _____

11. The author uses the phrase "futilely clutching at straws" to suggest _____.
    (A) promising survival strategies
    (B) measures of desperation
    (C) short-term ineffectiveness, long-term success
    (D) taking advantage of the incentives system
    (E) compromises with reality

    11 ____

12. A major deterrent to global war may be America's _____.
    (A) new, improved mining techniques
    (B) food-producing capacity
    (C) intelligent use of tax incentives
    (D) current treatment of farm problems
    (E) arsenal of military might

    12 ____

In 1644, the Manchus, a tribal people on the northeastern frontier of the Ming empire, captured Peking, overthrew the Ming and established the Ch'ing dynasty, which
5 lasted until the founding of the Chinese Republic in 1911. Under the K'ang-hsi emperor (reigned 1662–1722), the early Ch'ing world was one of reconstruction after late Ming fragmentation. Orthodox painters
10 aimed to recapture the former glories of traditional painting by studying and copying ancient models. By infusing old conventions with renewed energy, painters attempted to achieve a true correspondence
15 (ho) to ancient models. On the other hand, some artists scorned the new orthodox conservatism. The so-called individualist masters often painted in a free, emotion-filled calligraphic manner. Because of their loy-
20 alty to the fallen Ming dynasty, they expressed a strong sense of dislocation and alienation in their works. Avoiding the rationalism and methodology of the orthodox painters, the individualists preferred to de-
25 rive their art directly from nature and to express it through more personal artistic means.

13. Which of the following is the best characterization of the K'ang-hsi emperor?
    (A) He was the last of the Ming emperors; with him the Ming dynasty ended.
    (B) He was a painter who mastered the calligraphic style.
    (C) He was the spiritual forerunner of the Chinese republic.
    (D) He was an early emperor of the Ch'ing dynasty.
    (E) He was a master of the emotion-filled calligraphic manner.

    13 ____

14. Those who "preferred to derive their art directly from nature" are described in the selection as _____.
    (A) orthodox painters and new conservatives
    (B) a tribal people on the frontier of the Ming empire
    (C) concentrating on the correspondence (ho) to ancient models
    (D) former warriors forced to become artists in peacetime
    (E) alienated because of loyalty to the Ming empire

    14 ____

15. The primary purpose of the passage appears to be to _____.
    (A) compare the Ch'ing paintings unfavorably with those of the Ming
    (B) explain the failure of the 17th century artists to paint from nature
    (C) explain the two major schools of painting in the Ch'ing period
    (D) show how orthodox painters expressed nature through personal means
    (E) slyly suggest the inferior simplicity of Ming paintings

    15 ____

16. Toward the end of the Ming dynasty the "former glories of traditional painting" were _____.
(A) fragmented
(B) overthrown
(C) despised
(D) forgotten
(E) improved

16 ____

Reading Diagnostic Test B

Each passage below is followed by questions based on its content. Answer all questions following a passage on the basis of what is stated or implied in that passage.

In every work of genius we recognize our own rejected thoughts; they come back to us with a certain alienated majesty. Great words and art have no more affecting lesson for us than this. They teach us to abide by our own spontaneous impression with good-humored inflexibility the most when the whole cry of voices is on the other side.

1. "The whole cry of voices" refers to ____.
(A) inner voices of dissent
(B) those who disagree
(C) genius under stress
(D) rejected thoughts
(E) spontaneous impressions

1 ____

In the following passage, Mark Twain engages a native Egyptian in a strange activity.

The traditional Arab proposed, in the traditional way, to run down Cheops, cross the eighth of a mile of sand intervening between it and the tall pyramid of Cephren,
5 ascend to Cephren's summit and return to us on the top of Cheops—all in nine minutes by the watch, and the whole service to be rendered for a single dollar. In the first flush of irritation, I said let the Arab and
10 his exploits go to the mischief. But stay. The upper third of Cephren was coated with dress marble, smooth as glass. A blessed thought entered my brain. He must infallibly break his neck. Close the contract with
15 dispatch, I said, and let him go. He started. We watched. He went bounding down the vast broadside, spring after spring, like an ibex. He grew smaller and smaller till he became a bobbing pygmy, away down to-
20 ward the bottom—then disappeared. We turned and peered over the other side—forty seconds—eighty seconds—a hundred—happiness, he is dead already?—two minutes—and a quarter—"There he goes!"
25 Too true—it was too true. He was very small, now. Gradually, but surely, he overcame the level ground. He began to spring and climb again. Up, up, up—at last he reached the smooth coating—now for it. But
30 he clung to it with toes and fingers, like a fly. He crawled this way and that—away to the right, slanting upward—away to the left, still slanting upward—and stood at last, a black peg on the summit, and waved
35 his pygmy scarf! Then he crept downward to the raw steps again, then picked up his agile heels and flew. We lost him presently. But presently again we saw him under us, mounting with undiminished energy.
40 Shortly he bounded into our midst with a gallant war-whoop. Time, eight minutes, forty-one seconds. He had won. His bones were intact. I was a failure. I reflected. I said to myself, he is tired, and must grow
45 dizzy. I will risk another dollar on him.
He started again. Made the trip again.

Slipped on the smooth coating—I almost had
him. But an infamous crevice saved him. He
was with us once more—perfectly sound.
50 Time, eight minutes, forty-six seconds.

I said to Dan, "Lend me a dollar—I can
beat this game, yet."

Worse and worse. He won again. Time,
eight minutes, forty-eight seconds. I was
55 out of all patience now. I was desperate.
Money was no longer of any consequence. I
said, "Sirrah, I will give you a hundred
dollars to jump off this pyramid head first.
If you do not like the terms, name your bet.
60 I scorn to stand on expenses now. I will stay
right here and risk money on you as long as
Dan has got a cent."

2. The purpose of the author is to
_____.
   (A) horrify
   (B) enlighten
   (C) entertain
   (D) persuade
   (E) preach

                                              2 ____

3. Dan is probably playing the role of
_____.
   (A) knowledgeable go-between
   (B) skilled interpreter
   (C) angry friend
   (D) weary athlete
   (E) unwilling banker

                                              3 ____

4. What is likely to happen next?
   (A) The climber agrees to jump off
       the pyramid.
   (B) The author grumpily gives up his
       plan to win the bet.
   (C) Dan says he hasn't enjoyed him-
       self so much in years.
   (D) The author is arrested by police
       for encouraging a criminal act.
   (E) The author determines to outdo
       the climber by performing the
       feat himself.

                                              4 ____

5. The "black peg" on the summit is actu-
ally _____.
   (A) the apex of the pyramid
   (B) a pygmy scarf
   (C) an ibex
   (D) the climber
   (E) the author

                                              5 ____

6. The author of the selection can best be
characterized as _____.
   (A) humorously irascible
   (B) benevolently charitable
   (C) single-mindedly serious
   (D) unrelievedly vicious
   (E) unashamedly greedy

                                              6 ____

*The following passage suggests some of the difficulties in using language to interpret the real
world.*

Anyone who has sincerely tried to describe some genuine experience exactly, no
matter how small and insignificant it may
have been, to someone who did not share
5 that experience with some degree of similarity, probably became keenly aware of the
discrepancy between experience and words.
And yet, the problems of knowing and understanding others—and, to some extent,
10 ourselves—centers around the relationship
of language to reality or experience. The
problem with using language to talk about
and represent knowledge of the world is
that the structure of language does not cor-
15 respond to the structure of reality. Although it seems obvious that a word itself
is not the same as the object to which it
refers, this type of structural difference is
commonly forgotten. Such structural differ-
20 ences are simple in themselves, but can be
critically important to each of us in our daily
lives, as well as to the scientist in her or his

pursuit of scientific knowledge. Simple examples of these structural differences include such facts as: 1) there is not one word for each object, 2) the same word refers to many different things, and 3) many words can be used to describe any single aspect of one thing.

Another discrepancy between language and reality centers around the "process nature" of reality. Language, used in a certain way, can give the impression that reality itself is static. While we cannot do without generalizations, classes, categories, and names, we should realize that things change; generalizations are not always dependable or useful; classifications should not become rigid. To different degrees, we are all guilty of identifying the generalization, category, or name with the object it describes and in doing so, we limit our own experiences and decrease our effectiveness in dealing with the real world.

Korzybski uses the analogy of a map's relation to the territory it depicts to describe the relation of language to reality. His point is that the usefulness of a map depends precisely on the degree to which it corresponds to the territory. As differences arise between the map and the territory, we must quickly be able to separate the two of them and recognize that it is the map that needs changing.

7. Which of the following titles best summarizes the content of the passage?
(A) Words, Not Things
(B) Limiting Our Experiences
(C) Problems of Understanding Others
(D) Differences Between Language and Reality
(E) Korzybski: Language Pioneer

7 ____

8. Which of the following pairings is most accurate?
(A) language—territory
(B) map—reality
(C) language—map
(D) map—territory
(E) territory—categories

8 ____

9. The "process nature" of reality can best be characterized as _____.
(A) static
(B) changing
(C) analogous
(D) generalizing
(E) dependable

9 ____

10. A map is valuable if _____.
(A) it corresponds to the territory
(B) its language is creative
(C) it is not static
(D) it is scientifically explainable
(E) it clarifies the discrepancies in language

10 ____

11. The author points out that generalizations _____.
(A) are avoidable
(B) describe reality accurately
(C) are constantly changing
(D) cannot be described in words
(E) are essential

11 ____

The planet itself is a sojourner in airless space, a wet ball flung across nowhere. The few objects in the universe scatter. The coherence of matter dwindles and crumbles toward stillness. I have read, and repeated, that our solar system as a whole is careering through space toward a point east of Hercules. Now I wonder: what could that possibly mean, east of Hercules? Isn't space curved? When we get "there," how will our course change, and why? Will we slide down the universe's inside arc like mud slung at a wall? Or what sort of welcoming shore is this east of Hercules? Surely we don't an-

15 chor there, and disembark, and sweep into dinner with our host. Does someone cry, "Last stop, last stop"? At any rate, east of 20 Hercules, like east of Eden, isn't a place to call home. It is a course without direction; it is "out." And we are cast.

12. The expression "a wet ball flung across nowhere" is meant to suggest _____.
(A) hilarity
(B) condescension
(C) insignificance
(D) purpose
(E) courage

12 ____

13. The author's appraisal of the future of earth is _____.
(A) confident
(B) sad
(C) hopeful
(D) angry
(E) imitative

13 ____

14. As used in the selection, *careering* means _____.
(A) vibrating
(B) speeding
(C) pulsating
(D) sliding
(E) anticipating

14 ____

15. According to the writer of this passage, the earth _____.
(A) has destination and a mission in space
(B) is inextricably linked with every object in the universe
(C) will slide down the universe's inside arc
(D) is a homeless wanderer in space
(E) will come to rest east of Hercules

15 ____

16. The tone of the passage can best be described as _____.
(A) perky and optimistic
(B) coldly logical
(C) assured and happy
(D) vigorously antiscientific
(E) wryly humorous

16 ____

Division C

Mastery Tests/ Critical Reading

A Strategy for the Mastery Tests / Critical Reading

- You have come a long way and are ready for the moment of truth. The tests that follow approximate the SAT you will be taking, but they are practice tests only.

- Review the Introduction, pages ix–xvi.

- Before you begin, be sure you have the appropriate amount of time to spend on the test. Try to approximate test conditions as much as possible.

- Have a watch with you to check your timing. Don't spend too much time on any one question. If you waste time on a question, you may not reach questions that are easy for you. If you have trouble with a question, put a check mark next to it so that you can find it quickly again, and go right on. If you have time later, go back and try again.

- Read the questions carefully. Following directions is an important part of the test.

- If you are unsure of an answer, don't panic. You won't know all the answers, but do the best you can. By now you have discovered that you have unexpected resources if you stay calm and build upon what you already know.

- You will find complete explanations for the correct answers for Mastery Tests 1–3 beginning on page 537. These answers will help you analyze your responses. The page reference before each question tells you where to look in this book for help.

Organization

- The Mastery Tests for Critical Reading are divided into three sections. Sections 1, 2, and 3 are devoted to sentence completions and reading questions.

Directions

- In general, you will find typical SAT directions in the Mastery Tests. However, the format for answering questions is slightly different on the SAT, as explained on page xvi.

A Final Word on the Reading Passages

Keep in mind that a bulletin of the College Board says, "A much smaller number of questions will assess students' literal understanding of significant information in the text." The basic, bread-and-butter skills are still, and always will be, important, for they help with more challenging questions. The SAT assumes that you have these skills.

The bulletin also declares, "Most questions based on the reading selections will be analytical and evaluative, measuring students' ability to make inferences, to relate parts of the text to each other or to the whole; to follow the logic of an argument; to synthesize meaning; to identify the author's purpose, attitude, or tone, etc."

The reading selections will vary. "One type of selection will consist of a *pair* of related passages, the second of which will oppose, support, or in some other way complement the point of view expressed in the first. Some of the questions on the paired passages will assess students' ability to compare or contrast the two passages, to use information from one to interpret information in the other, and to identify assumptions they share or pivotal differences between them."

The test will draw upon general categories: narratives, humanities, natural sciences, and social sciences. All of these categories are well represented in the teaching text (pages 175–345). Each Mastery Test (351–387) contains a passage from each category, at least one of which is a paired passage. There is practice aplenty in the pages that follow.

Mastery Test 1 / Critical Reading

Section I

Directions: For each question in this section, select the best answer from among the choices given.

Each sentence below has one or two blanks, each blank indicating that something has been omitted. Beneath the sentence are five lettered words or sets of words labeled A through E. Choose the word or set of words that *best* fits the meaning of the sentence as a whole.

Example:

Although its publicity has been - - - - - -, the film itself is intelligent, well-acted, handsomely produced, and altogether - - - - - -.

(A) tasteless . . respectable
(B) extensive . . moderate
(C) sophisticated . . spectacular
(D) risqué . . crude
(E) perfect . . spectacular

(pages 47–51)
1. Denny's - - - - - - behavior may lead him from the conventional to the - - - - - - in a few brief moments.

 (A) erratic . . outrageous
 (B) smooth . . uninspired
 (C) snobbish . . orthodox
 (D) atrocious . . solicitous
 (E) consistent . . theatrical

1 _____

(pages 35–39)
2. Some endangered creatures may survive by transfer of populations, - - - - - - species in areas where they no longer occur.

 (A) commemorating (B) reestablishing
 (C) studying (D) uniting (E) popularizing

2 _____

(pages 43–47)
3. The arbitrator remained - - - - - - despite efforts of the press to anticipate his decision.

 (A) sluggish (B) prejudiced (C) irritated
 (D) insensitive (E) noncommittal

3 _____

(pages 24–30)
4. If a patient's hospital room has a window overlooking a scenic stand of trees, - - - - - - tends to be - - - - - -.

 (A) boredom . . manifest
 (B) interest . . dispersed
 (C) convalescence . . inflexible
 (D) recuperation . . accelerated
 (E) mobility . . minimal

4 _____

(pages 35–39)
5. Newborn infants are little Buddhas, observing life with - - - - - - glances and impressive - - - - - -.

 (A) inattentive . . comprehension
 (B) compassionate . . condescension
 (C) penetrating . . equanimity
 (D) competent . . indifference
 (E) stolen . . magnanimity

5 _____

(pages 24–30; 102)
6. The poet Emily Dickinson was such a(n) - - - - - - that she would not meet her guests but speak to them from another room.

 (A) raconteur (B) ogre (C) chatterbox
 (D) recluse (E) observer

6 _____

GO ON TO THE NEXT PAGE

(pages 43–47)

7. After the - - - - - - review of his novel *Jude the Obscure,* Thomas Hardy gave up writing novels and turned to poetry for the rest of his life.

(A) elaborate (B) laudatory (C) mandatory
(D) derogatory (E) illusory

7 _____

(pages 24–27)

8. It is with a sense of - - - - - - that Henry Jekyll began to realize that his evil "twin," Edward Hyde, was beginning to take control of his life.

(A) ennui (B) elation (C) foreboding
(D) approbation (E) recollection

8 _____

(pages 24–30; 112)

9. The chance that a man and his wife may have the same first name is - - - - - -; yet the Marquis de Lafayette and his wife did have the same first name: *Marie.*

(A) minuscule (B) predetermined
(C) irregular (D) trite (E) unpopular

9 _____

Each passage below is followed by questions based on its content. Answer the questions following each passage on the basis of what is *stated* or *implied* in that passage and in any introductory material that may be provided.

The magnificent voices of opera singers come at a price.

Opera singers are vulnerable. Age, stress, fatigue, overuse, poor choice of roles — all take their toll. Nowhere was this more poignant than in an ill-starred performance of *Don Giovanni* in the winter of
5   1966. The voice of the diva Elizabeth Schwarzkopf began to falter. Then other cast members showed vocal problems, among them Cesare Siepi and Jan Peerce, both Mozart veterans. The mutual distress was particularly alarming, but the voices of all great
10   singers gradually lose power and clarity.

(pages 24–30; 304–307)

10. The word *poignant* is meant to suggest the author's

(A) total recall
(B) displeasure
(C) sympathy
(D) sense of his own superiority
(E) apathy

10 _____

A brief story can suggest, in a few lines, a setting, character interrelationships, and a simple plot.

Marge . . . Day's work is an education! Well, I mean workin' in different homes you learn much more than if you was steady in one place. . . . I tell you, it really keeps your mind sharp tryin' to watch
5   for what folks will put over on you.

What? . . . No, Marge, I do not want to help shell no beans, but I'd be more than glad to stay and have supper with you, and I'll wash the dishes after. Is that all right? . . .
10   Who put anything over on who? . . . Oh yes! It's like this. . . . I been working for Mrs. E . . . one day a week for several months and I notice that she has some peculiar ways. Well, there was only one thing that really bothered me and that was her pocketbook habit
15   . . . No, not those little novels. . . . I mean her purse—her handbag.

Marge, she's got a big old pocketbook with two long straps on it . . . and whenever I'd go there, she'd be propped up in a chair with her handbag double
20   wrapped tight around her wrist, and from room to room she'd roam with that purse hugged to her bosom . . . yes, girl! This happens every time! No, there's nobody there but me and her. . . . Marge, I couldn't say nothin' to her! It's her purse, ain't it? She can hold
25   onto it if she wants to!

I held my peace for months, tryin' to figure out how I'd make my point. . . . Well, bless Bess! Today was the day! . . . Please, Marge, keep shellin' the beans so we can eat! I know you're listenin', but you listen with
30   your ears, not your hands. . . . Well, anyway, I was almost ready to go home when she steps in the room hangin' onto her bag as usual and says, "Mildred, will you ask the super to come up and fix the kitchen faucet?" "Yes, Mrs. E . . ." I says, "as soon as I leave."
35   "Oh, no," she says, "he may be gone by then. Please go now." "All right," I says, and out the door I went, still wearin' my Hoover apron.

I just went down the hall and stood there a few minutes . . . and then I rushed back to the door and
40   knocked on it as hard and frantic as I could. She flung

GO ON TO THE NEXT PAGE →

open the door sayin', "What's the matter? Did you see the super?" . . . "No," I says, gaspin' hard for breath, "I was almost downstairs when I remembered . . . I left my pocketbook!"

45   With that I dashed in, grabbed my purse and then went down to get the super! Later, when I was leavin' she says real timid-like, "Mildred, I hope that you don't think I distrust you because . . ." I cut her off real quick. . . . "That's all right, Mrs. E . . . , I under-

50   stand, 'cause if I paid anybody as little as you pay me, I'd hold my pocketbook too!"

Marge, you fool . . . lookout! . . . You gonna drop the beans on the floor!

(pages 189–191)
11. The "pocketbook habit" (lines 14–15) bothered the narrator because it demonstrated - - - - - -.

(A) mean-spirited cruelty
(B) a sick sense of humor
(C) potential senility
(D) bitter anger
(E) a lack of trust

11 ____

(pages 239–243)
12. Marge probably asked all the following questions EXCEPT - - - - - -.

(A) "Would you shell the beans?"
(B) "Would you have supper with me?"
(C) "Does she read a lot?"
(D) "Are you fond of her?"
(E) "Is there anyone else there besides you?"

12 ____

(pages 189–191)
13. When the narrator said, "You listen with your ears, not your hands," she - - - - - -.

(A) probably broke into a loud laugh
(B) was telling Marge to keep working
(C) suggested Marge's laziness
(D) paused for a minute to gather her thoughts
(E) was referring directly to Mrs. E

13 ____

(pages 192–194)
14. The narrator's final comment to Mrs. E is an example of - - - - - -.

(A) unjustified cruelty
(B) an expression of despair
(C) an undignified plea
(D) a bitter lament
(E) an appropriate retort

14 ____

(pages 257–262)
15. Throughout, the author stresses Mildred's - - - - - -.

(A) deep-seated anger
(B) sense of dignity
(C) love of her job
(D) fondness for food
(E) lack of understanding

15 ____

(pages 262–271)
16. When the narrator talks about knocking "hard and frantic," - - - - -.

(A) it reveals an inner upset
(B) she's putting on an act
(C) she hopes to catch Mrs. E before she leaves
(D) she hopes to get the super's attention
(E) she's afraid she'll be too late for the super

16 ____

As children, we soon discover how things work. Fire burns. A well-hit tennis ball zips across the net. In winter, the days are shorter and colder than in the summer. But of all these perceptions we form a picture of the world, a paradigm as the philosopher Thomas Kuhn has said. If we discovered that our paradigm didn't work, we'd be upset. In the following selection, a brilliant scientist, Lynn Margulis, challenges familiar scientific paradigms.

Despite her success, Margulis' work remains controversial. Hers is not the kind of work with which the scientific community can simply agree to disagree. "It's a question of changing your religion," she

5   says. Academia rewards its brightest stars with a specially funded teaching position called a named chair. A few years ago, Margulis was on the verge of being appointed to a named chair at a major university but was not offered the position, though the

10   possibility still remains. The antagonism stems, in part, from Margulis' collaboration with British chemist James Lovelock on Gaia, the hypothesis that the Earth acts as a self-regulating, self-maintaining system *(Phenomena,* May 1988). Gaia's most vocal sup-

15   porters are ecoactivists, church groups, and science-fiction writers. To some establishment scientists, these countercultural associations make the ideas behind Gaia suspect. Ironically, Margulis is hard on Gaia's popular supporters. "Lynn is ferocious

20   about going after mysticism," says Stewart Brand, founder of the *Whole Earth Catalog.* "New Age types are drawn to her and then she busts them high, low, and center for being softheaded."

In a sense, Margulis challenges the American

25   myth of the rugged individual—alone, self-contained and able to survive. "Our concept of the individual is

GO ON TO THE NEXT PAGE ▷

totally warped," she says. "All of us are walking communities of microbes. Plants are sedentary communities. Every plant and animal on Earth today is
30 a symbiont, living in close contact with others."

Consider one species of desert termite. Living in its hindgut are millions of single-celled, lemon-shaped organisms called *Trichonympha ampla*. Attached to the surface of one *T. ampla* live thousands
35 of whiplike bacteria known as spirochetes. Inside live still other kinds of bacteria. If not for these microbial symbionts (in some wood-eating insects, the symbionts are too numerous to count), the termite, unable to digest wood, would starve.

40 But, the termite itself is only one element in a planetary set of interlocking, mutual interactions—which Lovelock's neighbor, novelist William Golding, dubbed Gaia, for the Greek goddess of the Earth. After digesting wood, the termite expels the gas
45 methane into the air. (In fact, the world's species of termites, cows, elephants and other animals harboring methane-producing bacteria account for a significant portion of Earth's atmospheric methane.) Methane performs the vital task of regulating the
50 amount of oxygen in Earth's atmosphere. If there were too much oxygen, fires would burn continuously; too little, and animals, plants and many other live beings would suffocate. Earth's atmospheric oxygen is maintained, altered and regulated by the breathing
55 activities of living creatures, such as those of the methane-makers in the micro-cosmos. Life does not passively "adapt." Rather, it actively, though "unknowingly," modifies its own environment.

When NASA sponsored a search for life on Mars,
60 in the early 1970s, Lovelock looked for ways that life might have modified the Martian atmosphere. Finding no particular modification attributable to microbes or any other form of life, he and Margulis predicted that the Viking probe would find a dead
65 Mars. They turned out to be right. "Gaia is more a point of view than a theory," says Margulis. "It is a manifestation of the organization of the planet."

That organization resembles those hollow Russian dolls that nest one inside another. "For example,
70 some bacteria in the hindgut of a termite cannot survive outside that microbial community," explains Gail Fleischaker, Boston University philosopher of science and a former graduate student of Margulis'. "The community of termites, in turn, requires a
75 larger ecological nest. And so it expands. You will never find life in isolation. Life, if it exists at all, is globe-covering."

Although Margulis provided the "biological ammunition" for Gaia and remains its staunch advocate,
80 she does little work on it directly. "I've concentrated all my life on the cell," she says. The ideas that she has championed were once "too fantastic for mention in polite biological society," as one scientific observer described them in the 1920s. As recently as 20 years
85 ago, these ideas were so much at odds with the established point of view that, according to another observer, they "could not be discussed at respectable scientific meetings." Although aspects of the symbiotic theory of cell evolution still provoke hostility, the
90 theory is now taught to high school students. "This quiet revolution in microbiological thought is primarily due to the insight and enthusiasm of Lynn Margulis," states Yale ecologist G. Evelyn Hutchinson. "Hers is one of the most constructively specula-
95 tive minds, immensely learned, highly imaginative, and occasionally a little naughty."

(pages 202–205)

17. The author believes that Lynn Margulis - - - - - -.

(A) has some good ideas and many wrong ones
(B) is opposed to the views of James Lovelock
(C) was wrong about life on Mars
(D) spends too much time on the microcosm
(E) was not treated fairly by a university

17 _____

(pages 35–39; 122–135)

18. In line 30, "symbiont" means - - - - - -.

(A) a consumer of methane
(B) an interdependent organism
(C) an organism that can live without oxygen
(D) a self-contained organism
(E) a microbiologist

18 _____

(pages 176–178)

19. According to Margulis, life has survived on earth because of - - - - - -.

(A) the survival of the fittest
(B) modified competition
(C) adaptations to climate
(D) interlocking associations
(E) pure chance

19 _____

(pages 184–187)

20. A way of expressing Margulis's viewpoint is - - - - -.

(A) "We're all in this together."
(B) "Self-interest is the highest good."
(C) "Throughout nature, the female is the stronger sex."
(D) "Fair-weather friends are not true friends."
(E) "Every species has a chance to become dominant."

20 _____

GO ON TO THE NEXT PAGE

(pages 189–191)

21. Margulis's attitude toward "New Age types" is one of - - - - - -.

(A) warm enthusiasm
(B) complete indifference
(C) strong disapproval
(D) friendly assistance
(E) genuine rapport

21 ____

(pages 239–243)

22. "The American myth of the rugged individual" - - - - - -.

(A) has been blasted by Hollywood
(B) is the major tenet of Margulis's philosophy
(C) is counter to the views of Lynn Margulis
(D) has sparked Margulis's career
(E) is a helpful guide to living

22 ____

(pages 202–205)

23. The quotation "You will never find life in isolation" was made by - - - - - -.

(A) James Lovelock
(B) William Golding
(C) Lynn Margulis
(D) Gail Fleischaker
(E) G. Evelyn Hutchinson

23 ____

(pages 202–205)

24. To find the answer to question 23, the best technique is to - - - - - -.

(A) carefully reread each paragraph
(B) skim for the quotation
(C) stop for each name mentioned and check for the quotation
(D) try to think which person would have been likely to use the quotation
(E) check just the topic sentence of each paragraph

24 ____

(pages 184–187)

25. The author of the article makes the point that - - - - - -.

(A) James Lovelock is wrong, even though Margulis works with him
(B) scientific research into the cell is a tedious process
(C) methane plays a minor role in the health of the planet
(D) the rejected theory of yesterday may be accepted today
(E) true genius is recognized almost immediately

25 ____

Section 2

Directions: For each question in this section, select the best answer from among the choices given.

Each sentence below has one or two blanks, each blank indicating that something has been omitted. Beneath the sentence are five lettered words or sets of words labeled A through E. Choose the word or set of words that *best* fits the meaning of the sentence as a whole.

Example:

Although its publicity has been - - - - -, the film itself is intelligent, well-acted, handsomely produced, and altogether - - - - -.

(A) tasteless . . respectable
(B) extensive . . moderate
(C) sophisticated . . amateur
(D) risqué . . crude
(E) perfect . . spectacular

● Ⓑ Ⓒ Ⓓ Ⓔ

(pages 43–47)

1. In his autobiography Simenon does not spare himself, recounting his - - - - - - failures as well as his many - - - - successes.

(A) incredible . . undeserved
(B) tolerable . . conspicuous
(C) ludicrous . . peevish
(D) personal . . professional
(E) cinematic . . ecclesiastical

1 ____

GO ON TO THE NEXT PAGE ⇒

(pages 47–51)
2. As the favorable election results poured from the television screen, the candidate went from quiet ------ to expressive ------.

   (A) uneasiness . . contentment
   (B) curiosity . . concern
   (C) statement . . exaggeration
   (D) confusion . . preeminence
   (E) pleasure . . jubilation

              2 ____

(pages 24–30)
3. In the ------ view of some critics, the only ------ goal of television is not to inform or even entertain but to sell goods.

   (A) positive . . overlooked
   (B) jaundiced . . unrealized
   (C) cynical . . serious
   (D) tiresome . . illusory
   (E) blatant . . unacknowledged

              3 ____

(pages 43–47)
4. Although some ecosystems are ------ and able to adjust, others are too ------ to survive much tampering.

   (A) dependable . . accommodating
   (B) resilient . . fragile
   (C) prodigal . . incompetent
   (D) inflammable . . arid
   (E) inexhaustible . . self-contained

              4 ____

(pages 24–30)
5. Formerly accepted ------ of the proper roles of men and women have ------ the fate of the mastodon and the saber-toothed tiger.

   (A) stereotypes . . experienced
   (B) assignments . . retold
   (C) depictions . . broadcast
   (D) critiques . . elucidated
   (E) reprimands . . analyzed

              5 ____

(pages 35–39; 159)
6. The word *chortle* was devised by Lewis Carroll, ------ the two words "chuckle" and "snort."

   (A) destroying (B) accepting
   (C) transporting (D) dissecting
   (E) telescoping

              6 ____

(pages 35–39)
7. The Tower of London has had a(n) ------ career, for it has served as a mint, a prison, the royal palace, an observatory, and the home of the British Crown jewels.

   (A) humdrum (B) irksome (C) prosaic
   (D) checkered (E) prophetic

              7 ____

(pages 24–30)
8. An inspirational book about the ------ of Marco Polo accompanied Christopher Columbus on his first voyage to the New World.

   (A) eccentricities (B) dogma (C) spleen
   (D) odyssey (E) proficiency

              8 ____

(pages 30–34)
9. *Charlotte Temple,* by America's first best-selling woman novelist Susanna Rowson, may have had wooden characters and a(n) ------ plot, but it went through 200 editions.

   (A) superlative (B) original (C) hackneyed
   (D) scintillating (E) coherent

              9 ____

(pages 24–30)
10. In 1844, New York policemen staged a strike against the wearing of blue uniforms, considered by the men to be a symbol of ------.

   (A) perturbation (B) squalor (C) servitude
   (D) ambiguity (E) decorum

              10 ____

GO ON TO THE NEXT PAGE

Directions: For each question in this section, select the best answer from among the choices given.

The two passages below are followed by questions based on their content and on the relationship between the two passages. Answer the questions on the basis of what is *stated* or *implied* in the passages and in any introductory material that may be provided.

Someone once said that cat lovers and dog lovers live in separate worlds. The following two passages briefly explore the differences between cats and dogs.

Passage 1

It has been said that a dog provides the only love that money can buy. For undivided loyalty and unswerving affection and happy companionship, no pet can top the dog. From his doggie past in the wolf strain,
5   dogs have been used to packs and rule of the alpha male or female. To a dog, his master or mistress is the alpha leader, to whom proper respect and fidelity are due. From the Arctic to the tropics, tales of canine devotion are commonplace. To mushers in Alaska, dogs
10 are their lifeline. To detectives on the trail of a criminal, dogs are indispensable. Even that little Norwich terrier dozing by the fireplace has the genes of greatness.

Passage 2

Cats are ideal pets. To be graciously accepted by a cat as a friend or even a companion is a joyous
15 moment in a cat lover's life. Unlike dogs, cats do not spread their affection around freely. They are discriminating, dispassionate, and reserved. They accept the obedience due them with amused satisfaction. Cloaked in their feline self-assurance,
20 they keenly observe the world around them. If there is a remnant of the pack in some distant past, the cat is the alpha leader. Having been domesticated more recently than the dog, the cat retains a sense of untamed wildness, an elegant aloofness, an expecta-
25 tion of being served … and there's the charm.

(pages 305–307)
11. The two passages agree in their ------.
(A) admiration of the pets
(B) disdain for other viewpoints
(C) acceptance of the superiority of cats
(D) consideration of identical qualities
(E) tribute to working pets

11 ____

(pages 189–191)
12. The best inference to be drawn from the two passages is that the length of time since the domestication of animals may affect their ------.
(A) gene pools
(B) current behavior
(C) intelligence
(D) furry coats
(E) indifference to noise

12 ____

(pages 197–200)
13. The opening sentence of Passage 1 is related to the saying ------
(A) "the love of money is the root of all evil."
(B) "all things are possible with love."
(C) "love isn't love until you give it away."
(D) "money is a good servant but a bad master."
(E) "true love is not for sale."

13 ____

(pages 189–191)
14. According to Passage 2, the relationship of owner to the pet cat is one of ------.
(A) master .. master
(B) servant .. servant
(C) servant .. master
(D) master .. servant
(E) apathy

14 ____

The following passage talks about a special aspect of language, the use of is and other linking verbs. It suggests a more disciplined approach to communication.

In 1923, the philosopher George Santayana wrote, "The little word *is* has its tragedies. It names and identifies different things with the greatest innocence; and yet no two are ever identical, and if therein
5   lies the charm of wedding them and calling them one, therein, too, lies the danger."

Surprisingly, Santayana uses the word *are* in the passage above, even as he decried the use of such linking verbs!
10 Philosophers have been concerned with *is* since the 17th century. Why? Why denounce this most useful word, a common element in serious essays as well as in everyday conversation? How can anyone object to its use?
15 Words like *is* suggest deceptive couplings. A moment's consideration can detect the vast difference between "Inez is a student" and "Inez is insufferably conceited." Both use the same verb, but the second doesn't express the same relationship as the first.
20 Irresponsible use of *is* can damage friendships, mislead correspondents, and cause havoc with communication.

GO ON TO THE NEXT PAGE ⇒

Students of general semantics concern themselves with language in action. Language attempts to inter-
25 pret the "real world," but reality resists easy capture in words. Calling Inez *conceited* does an injustice to her, for it conceals the fact that someone's subjective judgment masquerades as objective truth.

The preceding two examples of the use of *is* barely
30 scratch the surface. Many such statements defy reasoning while assuming the mask of reason. An expression like "As is well known" assumes a dubious truth. The word *is* makes everything neat and orderly, but the real world resists such tidiness.

35 In recent years, semanticists have concerned themselves with a new and challenging idea. In the late 1940s, D. David Bourland, Jr., decided to eliminate all forms of *is* in his own writing. He called his writing system "E-Prime." From that time on, he
40 wrote everything in E-Prime, but for a while no one noticed. In 1965, he went public with his idea in an article written for *General Semantics Bulletin*. Since then, other semanticists have supported the cause.

Complete agreement about the use of E-Prime has
45 eluded language philosophers. Some writers take a strict position. They eliminate *is* and its relatives in all forms. They even try to eliminate absolute words like *always* and *never*. Others take a more lenient position, allowing the *is* of existence, helping verbs in
50 passives and *ises* of identity, like "Iron is a mineral."

E-Prime tends to make writing more objective, though not entirely so. E-Prime reflects a subjective judgment in "Juliana sang poorly," but it avoids subjective judgments like "Juliana is a busybody."

55 Does a listener or reader recognize E-Prime as something strange and exotic? Does the elimination of verbs like *is, was,* and *seem* create a noticeable gap? Perhaps E-Prime doesn't call attention to itself. It retains normal rhythm and expressions. It does re-
60 quire a great deal of discipline, particularly for those trying it for the first time. Despite the appeal, however, E-Prime has a formidable adversary: Convenience. It will probably not eliminate linking verbs from the language. But occasionally trying to write
65 and speak in E-Prime sharpens perceptions and gives users additional awareness of the ways in which language can mislead us.

Except for quoted examples, this passage provides an example of E-Prime. Did you notice?

(pages 43–47)
15. In line 8, *decried* means - - - - - -.

(A) explained
(B) promoted
(C) evaluated
(D) condemned
(E) uncovered

15 ____

(pages 222–226)
16. The author quotes Santayana to - - - - - -.

(A) express the basic problem attacked by E-Prime
(B) present a point of view later discredited
(C) provide a sample of a paragraph written in E-Prime
(D) point out that Santayana would disagree with Bourland
(E) discredit the widespread practice of E-Prime

16 ____

(pages 60–65)
17. The phrase *cause havoc with communication* suggests - - - - -.

(A) sabotage
(B) deception
(C) explanation
(D) hatred
(E) vitality

17 ____

(pages 239–243)
18. All the following sentences are written in E-Prime EXCEPT - - - - - -.

(A) Some semanticists have reservations about E-Prime.
(B) E-Prime had its beginnings in the 1940s.
(C) George Santayana possibly used a linking verb unconsciously.
(D) E-Prime is an excellent new technique for writing clearly.
(E) General semantics concentrates on language in action.

18 ____

(pages 189–191)
19. In line 25, "real world" is put in quotation marks because - - - - - -.

(A) George Santayana referred to it in his paragraph
(B) the author is poking gentle fun at semanticists
(C) no one is sure just what the real world is
(D) semanticists are self-promoting in their description of reality
(E) E-Prime is further from reality than is traditional communication

19 ____

GO ON TO THE NEXT PAGE

(pages 245–250)

20. E-Prime doesn't call attention to itself because - - - - - -.

(A) listeners don't pay attention
(B) Bourland has always been modest about his creation
(C) the majority of speakers intentionally use E-Prime for greater clarity
(D) the sentence structure of E-Prime is that of traditional communication
(E) most television shows are boring and forgettable

20 _____

(pages 30–34)

21. In line 65, *perceptions* means - - - - - -.

(A) insights
(B) prejudices
(C) language skills
(D) conversations
(E) sympathies

21 _____

(pages 226–230)

22. The author's style may best be characterized as - - - - - -.

(A) self-conscious and artificial
(B) light and informative
(C) humorous and frivolous
(D) critical and unfavorable
(E) dull and repetitious

22 _____

(pages 239–243)

23. To a student of E-Prime, the LEAST objectionable of the following sentences would probably be: - - - - - -:

(A) Juanita is self-sufficient and intelligent
(B) Juanita seems modest
(C) Juanita is captain of the field-hockey team
(D) Juanita was irritable yesterday
(E) Juanita is a poor leader but a good player

23 _____

(pages 66–71)

24. The strict interpretation of E-Prime would eliminate a metaphor like - - - - - -.

(A) In his sly maneuvering, Elliot resembles a snake
(B) Margot was president of the junior class last year
(C) On the basketball court, Maria is a tiger
(D) Dogs give love without expecting anything in return
(E) The Super Bowl is always a lavish spectacle

24 _____

(pages 189–191)

25. Some users of E-Prime avoid using words like *always* and *never* because - - - - - -.

(A) these words inevitably destroy sentence rhythms
(B) life is open-ended and the next moment may provide exceptions
(C) they want to show how clever they can be
(D) Santayana implies that these words are dangerous
(E) meanings of the two words cancel each other out

25 _____

(pages 60–65)

26. Which is an example of a subjective statement?

(A) Jennifer completed her first marathon last spring
(B) E-Prime was introduced by D. David Bourland, Jr.
(C) In winter, the United States imports fresh fruits from Chile
(D) Chad spoke boringly about his prowess on the football field
(E) Hurricane Andrew struck Homestead, just south of Miami

26 _____

(pages 60–65)

27. An example of the *is* of identity is contained in - - - - - -.

(A) Toby is often indiscreet.
(B) Despite her all-knowing air, Marcia was wrong.
(C) Samuel Adams and Thomas Jefferson were signatories of the Declaration of Independence.
(D) Has Dick been his usual obnoxious self?
(E) Essays and poems are less interesting than fiction.

27 _____

GO ON TO THE NEXT PAGE ▷

Section 3

The passages below are followed by questions based on their content. Answer the questions on the basis of what is *stated* or *implied* in the passage and in any introductory material that may be provided.

What helped Shakespeare create his great characters?

Nowadays casting directors have a large pool of talent to draw from. By contrast, Shakespeare had a limited number. The eight sharers in the acting company took the major roles. Boy aprentices played
5 women and young boys, often in scenes dominated by the masters. Hired men filled in where needed. When Shakespeare wrote a play, he needed a good comic actor, or clown, for the humorous interludes and a powerful actor for the great tragedies. Without Rich-
10 ard Burbage, there might not have been a *Hamlet*.

(pages 239–243; 304–307)
1. The most significant phrase in the paragraph is
------.

    (A) By contrast
    (B) the eight sharers
    (C) Boy apprentices
    (D) humorous interludes
    (E) Without Richard Burbage

                              1 ____

The following passages celebrate two brilliant historical periods centuries apart. The two periods share many resemblances.

Passage 1
There have been times in human history when the earth seems suddenly to have grown warmer or more radioactive . . . I don't put that forward as a scientific proposition, but the fact remains that three or four
5 times in history, humans have made a leap forward that would have been unthinkable under ordinary evolutionary conditions. One such time was about the year 3000 B.C., when quite suddenly civilization appeared, not only in Egypt and Mesopotamia but in the
10 Indus valley; another was in the late sixth century B.C., when there was not only the miracle of Ionia and Greece—philosophy, science, art, poetry, all reaching a point that wasn't reached again for 2000 years—but also in India a spiritual enlightenment that has per-
15 haps never been equaled. Another was round about the year 1100. It seems to have affected the whole world; but its strongest and most dramatic effect was in Western Europe—where it was most needed. It was like a Russian spring. In every branch of life—
20 action, philosophy, organization, technology—there

was an extraordinary outpouring of energy, an intensification of existence. Popes, emperors, kings, bishops, saints, scholars, philosophers were all larger than life, and the incidents of history—Henry II at
25 Canossa, Pope Urban announcing the First Crusade, Heloise and Abelard, the martyrdom of St. Thomas à Becket—are great heroic dramas, or symbolic acts, that still stir our hearts.

The evidence of this heroic energy, this confidence,
30 this strength of will and intellect, is still visible to us. In spite of all our mechanical aids and the inflated scale of modern materialism, Durham Cathedral remains a formidable construction, and the east end of Canterbury still looks very large and very complex.
35 And these great orderly mountains of stone at first rose out of a small cluster of wooden houses; everyone with the least historical imagination has thought of that. But what people don't always realize is that it all happened quite suddenly—in a single lifetime. An even
40 more astonishing change took place in sculpture. Tournus is one of the very few churches of any size to have survived from before the dreaded year 1000, and the architecture is rather grand in a primitive way. But its sculpture is miserably crude, without even the
45 vitality of barbarism. Only fifty years later sculpture has the style and rhythmic assurance of the greatest epochs of art. The skill and dramatic invention that had been confined to small portable objects—goldsmith work or ivory carving—suddenly appear on a
50 monumental scale.

Passage 2
The men who had made Florence the richest city in Europe, the bankers and wool-merchants, the pious realists, lived in grim defensive houses strong enough to withstand party feuds and popular riots.
55 They don't foreshadow in any way the extraordinary episode in the history of civilization known as the Renaissance. There seems to be no reason why suddenly out of the dark, narrow streets there arose these light, sunny arcades with their round arches
60 "running races in their mirth" under their straight cornices. By their rhythms and proportions and their open, welcoming character they totally contradict the dark Gothic style that preceded, and, to some extent, still surrounds them. What has happened? The an-
65 swer is contained in one sentence by the Greek phi-

GO ON TO THE NEXT PAGE

losopher Protagoras, "Man is the measure of all
things." The Pazzi Chapel, built by the great Florentine Brunelleschi in about 1430, is in a style that has
been called the architecture of humanism. His friend
70 and fellow-architect, Leon Battista Alberti, ad-
dressed man in these words: "To you is given a body
more graceful than other animals, to you power of apt
and various movements, to you most sharp and delicate senses, to you wit, reason, memory like an im-
75 mortal god." Well, it is certainly incorrect to say that
we are more graceful than other animals, and we
don't feel much like immortal gods at the moment.
But in 1400 the Florentines did. There is no better
instance of how a burst of civilization depends on
80 confidence than the Florentine state of mind in the
early fifteenth century. For thirty years the fortunes
of the republic, which in a material sense had declined, were directed by a group of the most intelligent individuals who have ever been elected to power
85 by a democratic government. From Salutati onwards
the Florentine chancellors were scholars, believers in
the *studia humanitatis,* in which learning could be
used to achieve a happy life, believers in the application of free intelligence to public affairs, and believ-
90 ers, above all, in Florence.

(pages 176–178)
2. When the author of Passage 1 contemplates
the year 1100, he is - - - - - -.

(A) convinced that a moderation in climate
had produced a sensational change
(B) overcome by awe at the unexpected
achievements of the period
(C) certain that perhaps only half a dozen
great leaders brought on the surprising
upheavals
(D) more impressed by the achievements in
drama than in architecture
(E) convinced that such a spectacular experience happens only once a century

2 _____

(pages 202–205)
3. The author makes the point that these
remarkable leaps forward were - - - - - -.

(A) cyclical in nature
(B) anticipated by outstanding philosophers
(C) more widespread than local
(D) strong in philosophy, weak in art
(E) criticized by large clusters of the
population

3 _____

(pages 197–200)
4. The birth date of Buddha is estimated to be
about 563 B.C. The birth date of Lao-tzu is
estimated to be about 604 B.C. The author
would agree that these are - - - - - -.

(A) linked with "the miracle of Ionia and
Greece"
(B) almost supernatural coincidences
(C) not uncommon in the history of humankind
(D) sources of the civilization that arose in
the Indus Valley
(E) dates with little significance for the major
point of the passage

4 _____

(pages 176–181)
5. To call historical personages "larger than life"
is to - - - - - -.

(A) suggest, through irony, their essential
weaknesses
(B) wonder at the secret of their incredible
longevity
(C) highlight the spiritual nature of their
achievements
(D) be amazed that persons of average ability
were raised to such heights
(E) emphasize the dramatic nature of their
lives and achievements

5 _____

(pages 202–205)
6. Durham Cathedral and the east end of Canterbury are singled out as - - - - - -.

(A) prime examples of the flourishing of art
that took place in a brief period
(B) cathedrals of great architectural skill but
poor sculpture
(C) mirror images of the church at Tournus
(D) cathedrals that stack up poorly against
the churches that preceded them
(E) cathedrals from which Pope Urban
announced the First Crusade

6 _____

(pages 189–191)
7. We may assume that fine goldsmith work and
ivory carving were - - - - - -.

(A) neglected after 1100
(B) considered during the Middle Ages to be
more important than architecture
(C) practiced before 1100
(D) not essentially products of "skill and
dramatic invention"
(E) artworks dominated by vitality of barbarism

7 _____

GO ON TO THE NEXT PAGE

(pages 43–47)

8. In line 50, *monumental* most nearly means
- - - - - -.

   (A) made of stone
   (B) surprising and unexpected
   (C) continuing on a smaller scale
   (D) religious and spiritual
   (E) massive and enduring

   8 _____

(pages 197–200)

9. In Passage 2, the "dark Gothic style" of architecture is - - - - - -.

   (A) essentially the architecture of the Italian Renaissance
   (B) criticized as ugly and ever debasing
   (C) the style of architecture used in the Pazzi Chapel
   (D) contrasted with the architecture that followed it
   (E) the crowning achievement of Leon Battista Alberti

   9 _____

(pages 189–191)

10. According to the Florentines, the happy life could be achieved through - - - - - -.

   (A) access to power
   (B) a reasonable amount of wealth
   (C) art, especially architecture
   (D) learning
   (E) luck

   10 _____

pages 197–200)

11. The events described in Passage 2 are different from those in Passage 1 in that - - - - - -.

   (A) no great leaders are mentioned
   (B) a discerning person could have predicted them
   (C) architecture is not mentioned
   (D) no important work of art is mentioned
   (E) they are more localized

   11 _____

(pages 197–200)

12. Passage 2 is similar to Passage 1 in its - - - - - -.

   (A) emphasis upon sudden bursts of glory
   (B) main idea that architecture reflects material, not spiritual, goals
   (C) stress on the importance of democratic leadership
   (D) exaltation of modern technology over older inferior skills
   (E) assertion that the cycles of history make predictions relatively routine

   12 _____

(pages 250–255)

13. To find out more about the subject of the second passage, a student should find a book on - - - - - -.

   (A) Gothic architecture in Florence
   (B) the beginnings of the Renaissance
   (C) Italian history
   (D) the life of Leon Battista Alberti
   (E) a history of democracy

   13 _____

STOP

Mastery Test 2 / Critical Reading

Section I

> **Directions:** For each question in this section, select the best answer from among the choices given.

Each sentence below has one or two blanks, each blank indicating that something has been omitted. Beneath the sentence are five lettered words or sets of words labeled A through E. Choose the word or set of words that *best* fits the meaning of the sentence as a whole.

Example:

Although its publicity has been - - - - - -, the film itself is intelligent, well-acted, handsomely produced, and altogether - - - - - -.

(A) tasteless . . respectable
(B) extensive . . moderate
(C) sophisticated . . spectacular
(D) risqué . . crude
(E) perfect . . spectacular

(pages 52–57)
1. The dependence of public television upon public contributions for - - - - - - is a sad but - - - - - - fact of life.

(A) expansion . . harrowing
(B) survival . . inescapable
(C) news . . humdrum
(D) ratings . . captivating
(E) audiences . . general

1 ____

(pages 30–34)
2. The great horned owl, one of the most efficient and - - - - - - of all - - - - - -, occasionally kills more prey than it can eat.

(A) docile . . birds
(B) casual . . fliers
(C) inept . . hunters
(D) ruthless . . predators
(E) amusing . . parents

2 ____

(pages 30–34; 35–39)
3. The - - - - - - celebration of the Metropolitan Opera recalled a hundred years of great artists, innovative directors, and - - - - - - designers.

(A) centennial . . creative
(B) showy . . headstrong
(C) recent . . inept
(D) halfhearted . . indifferent
(E) biennial . . avant-garde

3 ____

(pages 47–51)
4. As the day wore on, New Delhi, at first uncomfortably warm, became - - - - - - hot and - - - - - -.

(A) somewhat . . annoying
(B) cloudlessly . . quiet
(C) unbearably . . stifling
(D) unexpectedly . . torrential
(E) sleepily . . cheery

4 ____

(pages 24–30)
5. First - - - - - - in 1865 by a group of French Republicans, Liberty was finally unveiled in New York Harbor in 1886.

(A) advertised
(B) completed
(C) photographed
(D) engineered
(E) conceived

5 ____

GO ON TO THE NEXT PAGE

(pages 43–47)

6. Because of the tremendous potential for good or ill, recent progress in the field of genetic engineering has raised both - - - - - - and - - - - - - for the future.

(A) hopes . . fears
(B) challenges . . disappointments
(C) energy . . concern
(D) faith . . disbelief
(E) concerns . . anxieties

6 ____

(pages 47–51)

7. At the antique car rally an ancient Franklin began slowly and - - - - - -, then accelerated and - - - - - - by the judges' stand, to the delight of all spectators.

(A) grotesquely . . wheezed
(B) steadily . . inched
(C) noisily . . crept
(D) uncertainly . . whizzed
(E) sadly . . went

7 ____

(pages 24–30)

8. After the - - - - - - reception of his early paintings, Picasso sometimes kept warm by burning his drawings.

(A) frenzied
(B) diminutive
(C) insatiable
(D) long-delayed
(E) lackluster

8 ____

(pages 43–47)

9. Although a bottom quark has a lifetime of only 1.5 trillionths of a second, this period is much - - - - - - than scientists had anticipated.

(A) shorter
(B) longer
(C) more dramatic
(D) less important
(E) more informative

9 ____

Each passage below is followed by questions based on its content. Answer the questions following each passage on the basis of what is *stated* or *implied* in that passage and in any introductory material that may be provided.

Joan Miro, like Pablo Picasso and Henri Matisse, influenced the direction of modern art. Though noted primarily for his abstract paintings, Miro later ventured into other areas to express his "celebration of
5 life," as Mario Pei once put it. A recent exhibit of his sculptures shows an impish whimsy and a sometimes outrageous sense of humor. Miro looked everywhere for his inspiration. He created sculptures from odd-shaped stones and discarded junk, like an old tortoise
10 shell. At 81, Miro told his fellow artist Alexander Calder, "I am an established painter but a young sculptor."

(pages 206–208; 304–307)

10. Which of the following statements may be accurately derived from the selection?

I. Miro eclipsed the achievements of Henri Matisse.
II. Miro's sense of humor may well have offended some.
III. Miro considered his abstract paintings superior to his sculpture.
IV. Both Mario Pei and Alexander Calder are quoted.
V. The expression "found art" may be applied to Miro's sculptures.

(A) I and V
(B) II and III
(C) I and IV
(D) II and V
(E) III and IV

10 ____

GO ON TO THE NEXT PAGE ⇨

Has humankind progressed beyond the Age of Superstition? The following passage presents a challenging point of view.

Those who speak of the various "ages" of man, such as the Age of Belief, the Age of Discovery, the Age of Reason, the Atomic Age, and so forth, may be responsible for the nonsensical belief, widely held today,
5   that humankind has become sophisticated, that we are less superstitious than the species used to be, less susceptible to hoaxes and irrational fears; that our minds, in short, are far from the primitive.

Perhaps the matter can never be fully resolved,
10 since a scientific poll cannot be taken of the human beings of other ages to learn just how superstitious they were. Certainly some of their superstitions have been exploded by modern science, and certainly there are hundreds of thousands of people today, able to
15 read, who can be aware of such exposés. But we accept new superstitions as we discard old ones; intellectual development does not necessarily reform our mental behavior and habits even when we know better. A scientist may develop a most complicated computer, and
20 still toss some salt over his left shoulder if he spills it at the table, or walk around a black cat, or refuse the third light on a match, or whatever it is he harbors in the way of superstitious hangover. For, no matter how far advanced our intellectual development, we still
25 have no control over the autonomic nervous system: we cannot prevent the hair from "standing on end" when we are suddenly frightened in the dark.

So, while we have every right to point out the nonsense which humankind accepts, and indeed by which
30 we direct our lives, we would do well to temper our merriment with the realization that at bottom our own thinking is just as solidly based upon the primitive mentality as was that of the serf, the ancient Roman, or the tribesman in awe of the Umbundu chant. As the
35 French philosopher Lévy-Bruhl put it: *"Dans tout esprit humain, quel qu'en soît le développement intellectuel, subsiste un fond indéracinable de mentalité primitive."* (In all humankind, whatever its intellectual attainments, an ineradicable basis exists of prim-
40 itive mentality.) And Nilsson said: "Primitive mentality is a fairly good description of the mental behavior of most people today except in their technical or consciously intellectual activities."

(pages 178–181)
11. Which of the following best describes the main idea of the passage?

(A) The mind of modern man is far from the primitive.
(B) The Atomic Age is the latest in a list of famous "ages."
(C) The autonomic nervous system sometimes makes our hair stand on end.

(D) For all their sophistication, people today have their primitive superstitions.
(E) Lévy-Bruhl and Nilsson share a particular point of view.
                                              11 ____

(pages 239–243)
12. All the following are mentioned as examples of superstition or primitive mentality EXCEPT
- - - - - -.

(A) walking around a black cat
(B) being in awe of the Umbundu chant
(C) refusing the third light on a match
(D) throwing salt over the left shoulder
(E) breaking a mirror and worrying about bad luck
                                              12 ____

(pages 218–222)
13. The author believes that mental behavior and habits - - - - - -.

(A) often run counter to intellectual development
(B) are directly correlated with the degree of sophistication
(C) are usually life-enhancing
(D) block the impact of irrational thought
(E) are fairly similar in persons of similar intellectual development
                                              13 ____

(pages 43–47)
14. In line 30, *temper* most nearly means - - - - - -.

(A) increase
(B) understand
(C) reduce
(D) moderate
(E) advertise
                                              14 ____

(pages 250–255)
15. Which of the following proverbs best expresses a point of view in the passage?

(A) "A rolling stone gathers no moss."
(B) "People in glass houses shouldn't throw stones."
(C) "A stitch in time saves nine."
(D) "He who hesitates is lost."
(E) "A friend in need is a friend indeed."
                                              15 ____

GO ON TO THE NEXT PAGE ▷

(pages 81–84)

16. In line 39, *ineradicable* most nearly

means "not able to be - - - - - -."
- (A) comprehended
- (B) uprooted
- (C) matched or equaled
- (D) taught
- (E) repeated

16 ____

The following excerpt from a short story suggests the impact of a new family's arrival in a neighborhood.

"It certainly feels good to sit down," Mrs. Harris said. She sighed. "Sometimes I feel that moving is the most terrible thing I have to do."

"You were lucky to get that house," Mrs. Tylor said, and Mrs. Harris nodded. "We'll be glad to get nice neighbors," Mrs. Tylor went on. "There's something so nice about congenial people right next door. I'll be running over to borrow cups of sugar," she finished roguishly.

"I certainly hope you will," Mrs. Harris said. "We had such disagreeable people next door to us in our old house. Small things, you know, and they do irritate you so." Mrs. Tylor sighed sympathetically. "The radio, for instance," Mrs. Harris continued, "all day long, and so *loud*."

Mrs. Tylor caught her breath for a minute. "You must be sure and tell us if ours is ever too loud."

"Mr. Harris cannot bear the radio," Mrs. Harris said. "We do not own one, of course."

"Of course," Mrs. Tylor said. "No radio."

Mrs. Harris looked at her and laughed uncomfortably. "You'll be thinking my husband is crazy."

"Of course not," Mrs. Tylor said. "After all, lots of people don't like radios; my oldest nephew, now, he's just the *other* way—"

"Well," Mrs. Harris said, "newspapers, too."

Mrs. Tylor recognized finally the faint nervous feeling that was tagging her; it was the way she felt when she was irrevocably connected with something dangerously out of control: her car, for instance, on an icy street, or the time on Virginia's roller skates.... Mrs. Harris was staring absent-mindedly at the movers going in and out, and she was saying, "It isn't as though we hadn't ever *seen* a newspaper, not like the movies at all; Mr. Harris just feels that the newspapers are a mass degradation of taste. You really never *need* to read a newspaper, you know," she said, looking around anxiously at Mrs. Tylor.

"I never read anything but the—"

"And we took *The New Republic* for a *number* of years," Mrs. Harris said. "When we were first married, of course. Before James was born."

"What is your husband's business?" Mrs. Tylor asked timidly.

Mrs. Harris lifted her head proudly. "He's a scholar," she said. "He writes monographs."

Mrs. Tylor opened her mouth to speak, but Mrs. Harris leaned over and put her hand out and said, "It's *terribly* hard for people to understand the desire for a really peaceful life."

"What," Mrs. Tylor said, "what does your husband do for relaxation?"

"He reads plays," Mrs. Harris said. She looked doubtfully over at James. "Pre-Elizabethan, of course."

"Of course," Mrs. Tylor said, and looked nervously at James, who was shoveling sand into a pail.

"People are really very unkind," Mrs. Harris said. "Those people I was telling you about, next door. It wasn't only the radio, you see. Three times they *deliberately* left their *New York Times* on our doorstep. Once James nearly got it."

"Good Lord," Mrs. Tylor said. She stood up. "Carol," she called emphatically, "don't go away. It's nearly time for lunch, dear."

"Well," Mrs. Harris said. "I must go and see if the movers have done anything right."

Feeling as though she had been rude, Mrs. Tylor said, "Where is Mr. Harris now?"

"At his mother's," Mrs. Harris said. "He always stays there when we move."

"Of course," Mrs. Tylor said, feeling as though she had been saying nothing else all morning.

"They don't turn the radio on while he's there," Mrs. Harris explained.

"Of course," Mrs. Tylor said.

Mrs. Harris held out her hand and Mrs. Tylor took it. "I do so hope we'll be friends," Mrs. Harris said. "As you said, it means such a lot to have really thoughtful neighbors. And we've been so unlucky."

"Of course," Mrs. Tylor said, and then came back to herself abruptly. "Perhaps one evening soon we can get together for a game of bridge?" She saw Mrs. Harris's face and said, "No. Well, anyway, we must all get together some evening soon." They both laughed.

"It does sound silly, doesn't it," Mrs. Harris said. "Thanks so much for all your kindness this morning."

"Anything we can do," Mrs. Tylor said. "If you want to send James over this afternoon."

"Perhaps I shall," Mrs. Harris said. "If you really don't mind."

"Of course," Mrs. Tylor said. "Carol, dear."

With her arm around Carol she walked out to the front of the house and stood watching Mrs. Harris and James go into their house. They both stopped in the doorway and waved, and Mrs. Tylor and Carol waved back.

"Can't I go to the movies," Carol said, *"please,* Mother?"

"I'll go with you, dear," Mrs. Tylor said.

GO ON TO THE NEXT PAGE ⇨

(pages 68–69)

17. Mrs. Tylor's comment, "We'll be glad to get nice neighbors," turns out to be ironic because ------.

(A) the two families will fight bitterly
(B) the Harrises will probably stay only a month or two
(C) the children will never speak to each other
(D) the new neighbors are not "nice" in the usual way Mrs. Tylor expects
(E) Mrs. Harris is an evil person

17 _____

(pages 257–262)

18. When Mrs. Tylor "sighed sympathetically" (line 13), she

(A) tried to catch Mrs. Harris off guard
(B) had no idea what was coming
(C) already had the radio on too loud
(D) suggested her puzzlement
(E) revealed her basic cunning

18 _____

(pages 81–84; 95, 106)

19. In line 29, *irrevocably* suggests ------.

(A) no possibility of escape
(B) excitement
(C) many possibilities of action
(D) a not unpleasant depression
(E) a host of alternatives

19 _____

(pages 176–178)

20. The most appropriate word to apply to Mr. Harris is ------.

(A) brutish
(B) agreeable
(C) antisocial
(D) extroverted
(E) companionable

20 _____

(pages 192–194)

21. In the paragraph beginning line 27, Mrs. Harris is saying that ------.

(A) the movers aren't doing a good job
(B) most newspapers are bad, though not all
(C) she herself thinks that newspapers are necessary
(D) the Harrises never go to the movies
(E) she really agrees with Mrs. Tylor's statements thus far

21 _____

(pages 257–262)

22. The repetition of the phrase "of course" suggests ------.

(A) Mrs. Tylor's inability to have two consecutive coherent thoughts
(B) Mrs. Tylor's growing desperation at the way the conversation is going
(C) an author's device for making short, readable paragraphs
(D) Mrs. Tylor's complete agreement with everything that Mrs. Harris has said
(E) unfriendliness on the part of Mrs. Tylor

22 _____

(pages 81–84; 257–262)

23. In line 36, *degradation* most nearly means

(A) elevation
(B) corruption
(C) advertisement
(D) expansion
(E) exclusion

23 _____

(pages 189–191)

24. Mrs. Harris classifies the leaving of a *New York Times* on the doorstep as a(n) ------.

(A) cruel deed
(B) act of kindness
(C) mistake
(D) attempt to upset James
(E) insane action

24 _____

(pages 245–250)

25. Mrs. Tylor decides to go to the movies because ------.

(A) she feels she hasn't been paying enough attention to Carol
(B) by providing an example, she may help Mrs. Harris out of her isolation
(C) she wants to shake off the depressing conversation she has been having
(D) she is a movie enthusiast and is looking forward to a favorite star
(E) she wants to demonstrate to Mrs. Harris that she is a modern, up-to-date person

25 _____

GO ON TO THE NEXT PAGE

Section 2

Directions: For each question in this section, select the best answer from among the choices given.

Each sentence below has one or two blanks, each blank indicating that something has been omitted. Beneath the sentence are five lettered words or sets of words labeled A through E. Choose the word or set of words that *best* fits the meaning of the sentence as a whole.

Example:

Although its publicity has been ------, the film itself is intelligent, well-acted, handsomely produced, and altogether ------.

(A) tasteless . . respectable
(B) extensive . . moderate
(C) sophisticated . . .spectacular
(D) risqué . . crude
(E) perfect . . spectacular

(pages 43–47)

1. The more the insect tried to disentangle itself from the spider's web, the more ------ it became.

   (A) wary (B) formidable (C) careless
   (D) angry (E) enmeshed

1 ____

(pages 43–47)

2. Although most people consider cities ------ wildlife, birds and even mammals ----- in even the most unlikely urban areas.

(A) favorable toward . . thrive
(B) devoid of . . deteriorate
(C) receptive toward . . appear
(D) alien to . . abound
(E) unconcerned with . . dart

2 ____

(pages 24–30)

3. The book *The Evening Stars* presents a history of television's evening news programs, with ------ those news anchors who came to ------ the news.

(A) disregard for . . lead
(B) minor attention to . . enjoy
(C) description of . . study
(D) emphasis upon . . dominate
(E) affection for . . represent

3 ____

(pages 47–51)

4. Plentiful and crystal-clear at its source, the Arkansas River becomes less and less ------ as it flows east, finally disappearing on the ------ Kansas plains.

(A)   abundant . . dry
(B)   powerful . . fruitful
(C)   beautiful . . moisture-laden
(D)   polluted . . unplowed
(E)   available . . hilly

4 ____

(pages 39–43)

5. Initial reserve soon disappeared, and the gathering of bird-watchers soon became as ------ as a congregation of first-graders on the school playground.

   (A) dignified (B) exuberant
   (C) mischievous (D) subtle (E) impressive

5 ____

(pages 47–51)

6. In 1789, George Washington urged Congress to use its "best endeavors to improve the education and manners of a people to accelerate the progress of art and science; to ------ works of genius, to confer rewards for inventions of utility and to cherish institutions favorable to humanity."

   (A) support (B) advertise (C) admire
   (D) confirm (E) study

6 ____

GO ON TO THE NEXT PAGE ⟩

(pages 43–47)

7. Vincent van Gogh, whose - - - - - - reputation has helped sell his works for millions of dollars, is known to have sold only one painting during his lifetime.

(A) fanciful (B) posthumous (C) erratic
(D) stolid (E) faded

7 ____

(pages 43–47)

8. In an attempt to become an upwardly mobile English gentleman, the teenage Gandhi spent hours practicing how to arrange his tie and hair, a far cry from the - - - - - - tendencies of his maturity.

(A) ascetic (B) egotistical (C) bashful
(D) antagonistic (E) acquiescent

8 ____

(pages 24–30)

9. Though blind, Bill Irwin walked the 2100-mile Appalachian Trail, - - - - - - by his faithful dog Orient.

(A) followed (B) revitalized (C) driven
(D) encumbered (E) accompanied

9 ____

(pages 24–30)

10. When Juanita, after much searching, discovered the elusive Mouse King for her nutcracker collection, she was in a state of - - - - - - for days.

(A) lethargy (B) elasticity
(C) consternation (D) euphoria
(E) disgruntlement

10 ____

Directions: For each question in this section, select the best answer from among the choices given.

The two passages below are followed by questions based on their content and on the relationship between the two passages. Answer the questions on the basis of what is *stated* or *implied* in the passages and in any introductory material that may be provided.

The Challenger *and* Columbia *tragedies stirred up an old debate: Are we really prepared to send human beings into space right now? The following passages take opposing positions.*

Passage 1

The mission of the *Star Trek Enterprise* was to go where no one had gone before. This is a noble goal, but an unrealistic one in the context of modern space exploration. The unpalatable truth is that it is unwise
5 to send human beings into space given the current state of the art. For all essential projects, unmanned space probes will suffice. The incredible successes of the *Voyager* and later probes have demonstrated the possibilities without risking a single human life.
10 With current technology, keeping human beings alive in space is expensive . . . and dangerous. Robots are a lot cheaper . . . and expendable.

Passage 2

If *Apollo 13* had been manned by robots, the space-craft would probably be hurtling somewhere beyond
15 the solar system. The resourcefulness and determination of astronauts Lovell, Haise, and Swigert brought the crippled spacecraft back to earth. Of course, there *is* a risk in space flight. There is a risk in driving on an Interstate! Columbus knew the risks,
20 and Magellan paid with his life. The argument is pointless: men (and women) will not be satisfied to remain bystanders. The number of successful shuttle missions puts the failures into perspective. Of course, unmanned probes play a role, but ultimately we need
25 "human beings" out there as well as robots.

(pages 305–307)

11. Both writers would probably agree with which of the following statements?

(A) If carefully planned, manned space flights are desirable now.
(B) The space station must be maintained and expanded.
(C) The human thirst for knowledge propels space exploration.
(D) The *Voyager* probes had limited success.
(E) Despite the losses, the *Columbia* tragedy was ultimately positive in its results.

11 ____

GO ON TO THE NEXT PAGE

(pages 197–200)
12. In the context of these passages, Lovell and Magellan may be paired for their - - - - - -.

    (A) uncommon valor
    (B) scientific curiosity
    (C) willingness to compromise
    (D) unfortunate deaths
    (E) knowledge of seamanship

                       12 ____

(pages 68–71; 197–200)
13. The author in Passage 2 mentions the Interstate for a touch of - - - - - -.

    (A) realistic appraisal
    (B) sly humor
    (C) political commentary
    (D) resignation
    (E) despair

                       13 ____

(pages 202–205)
14. Passage 1 objects to manned space travel because of the risk and the - - - - - -.

    (A) human ineptitude
    (B) astronauts' motivation
    (C) ceaseless competition
    (D) unrealistic projects
    (E) unnecessary expense

                       14 ____

Passage 1 is the opening section of the Constitution of the United States. Passage 2 is the opening section of the Charter of the United Nations.

Passage 1
We the People of the United States, in Order to form a more perfect Union, establish Justice, insure domestic Tranquillity, provide for the common defence, promote the general Welfare, and secure the
5 Blessings of Liberty to ourselves and our Posterity, do ordain and establish this Constitution for the United States of America.

ARTICLE I
SECTION 1. All legislative Powers herein granted shall be vested in a Congress of the United States,
10 which shall consist of a Senate and House of Representatives.
SECTION 2. The House of Representatives shall be composed of Members chosen every second Year by the People of the several States, and the Electors in
15 each State shall have the Qualifications requisite for Electors of the most numerous Branch of the State Legislature.
No Person shall be a Representative who shall not have attained to the age of twenty five Years, and
20 been seven Years a Citizen of the United States, and who shall not, when elected, be an Inhabitant of that State in which he shall be chosen.

Representatives and direct Taxes shall be apportioned among the several States which may be in-
25 cluded within this Union, according to their respective Numbers, which shall be determined by adding to the whole Number of free Persons, including those bound to Service for a Term of Years, and excluding Indians not taxed, three fifths of all other Persons. The actual
30 Enumeration shall be made within three Years after the first Meeting of the Congress of the United States, and within every subsequent Term of ten Years, in such Manner as they shall by Law direct. The Number of Representatives shall not exceed one for every thirty
35 Thousand, but each State shall have at Least one Representative; and until such enumeration shall be made, the State of New Hampshire shall be entitled to choose three, Massachusetts eight, Rhode-Island and Providence Plantations one, Connecticut five, New-
40 York six, New Jersey four, Pennsylvania eight, Delaware one, Maryland six, Virginia ten, North Carolina five, South Carolina five, and Georgia three.
When vacancies happen in the Representation from any State, the Executive Authority thereof shall
45 issue Writs of Election to fill such Vacancies.
The House of Representatives shall choose their Speaker and other Officers; and shall have the sole Power of Impeachment.

Passage 2
We the peoples of the United Nations deter-
50 **mined**

to save succeeding generations from the scourge of war which twice in our lifetime has brought untold sorrow to mankind, and

to reaffirm faith in fundamental human rights, in the
55 dignity and worth of the human person, in the equal rights of men and women and of nations large and small, and

to establish conditions under which justice and respect for the obligations arising from treaties and
60 other sources of international law can be maintained, and

to promote social progress and better standards of life in larger freedom.

and for these ends

65 to practice tolerance and live together in peace with one another as good neighbors, and

to unite our strength to maintain international peace and security, and

to ensure, by the acceptance of principles and the
70 institution of methods, that armed force shall not be used, save in the common interest, and

to employ international machinery for the promotion of the economic and social advancement of all peoples,

GO ON TO THE NEXT PAGE ⟩

have resolved to combine our efforts to accom-
75 **plish these aims**.

Accordingly, our respective Governments, through representatives assembled in the city of San Francisco, who have exhibited their full powers found to be in good and due form, have agreed to the present
80 Charter of the United Nations and do hereby establish an international organization to be known as the United Nations.

CHAPTER I

Purposes and Principles

Article 1

The Purposes of the United Nations are:

1. To maintain international peace and security,
85 and to that end: to take effective collective measures for the prevention and removal of threats to the peace, and for the suppression of acts of aggression or other breaches of the peace, and to bring about by peaceful means, and in conformity with the principles
90 of justice and international law, adjustment or settlement of international disputes or situations which might lead to a breach of the peace;

2. To develop friendly relations among nations based on respect for the principle of equal rights and
95 self-determination of peoples, and to take other appropriate measures to strengthen universal peace;

3. To achieve international cooperation in solving international problems of an economic, social, cultural, or humanitarian character, and in promoting
100 and encouraging respect for human rights and for fundamental freedoms for all without distinction as to race, sex, language, or religion; and

4. To be a center for harmonizing the actions of nations in the attainment of these common ends.

(pages 202–205)

15. This section of the Constitution is concerned principally with - - - - - -.

   (A) the election of the president
   (B) impeachment procedures for the removal of a federal officer
   (C) determining the number of representatives
   (D) eligibility rules for presidential candidates
   (E) electing members of the Senate

15 _____

(pages 24–30)

16. In line 15, *requisite* most nearly means - - - - - -.

   (A) essential
   (B) voted upon
   (C) suggested
   (D) developed
   (E) discovered

16 _____

(pages 24–30)

17. The expression "bound to Service" in lines 27–28 probably refers to - - - - - -.

   (A) the perennially unemployed
   (B) slaves
   (C) members of the new Congress
   (D) indentured servants
   (E) newly elected Representatives

17 _____

(pages 189–191)

18. In Section 2, the suggested numbers of representatives are based on - - - - - -.

   (A) the first national census
   (B) statistics supplied by the new Senate
   (C) the states' contributions to the American Revolution
   (D) the number of delegates to the convention
   (E) temporary estimates

18 _____

(pages 189–191)

19. By a process of elimination, we may infer that the three-fifths figure refers to - - - - - -.

   (A) civil servants
   (B) native Americans
   (C) slaves
   (D) electors in each state
   (E) senators

19 _____

(pages 202–205)

20. *Providence Plantations* is obviously linked with - - - - - -.

   (A) Connecticut
   (B) New Jersey
   (C) New York
   (D) Rhode Island
   (E) Massachusetts

20 _____

GO ON TO THE NEXT PAGE

(pages 35–39)

21. In line 51, *scourge* most nearly means - - - - - -.

(A) occurrence
(B) affliction
(C) challenge
(D) threat
(E) unexpectedness

21 _____

(pages 197–200)

22. The similarity between the opening words of the Constitution and the United Nations Charter is probably - - - - - -.

(A) coincidental
(B) a cause of present difficulties in the U.N.
(C) intentional
(D) accidental
(E) an indication of unfair domination by the U.S.

22 _____

(pages 197–200)

23. The U.N. Charter is different from the Constitution in its emphasis upon - - - - - -.

(A) proper representation
(B) monetary agreements between nations
(C) the election of delegates
(D) the creation of larger national units
(E) international peace

23 _____

(pages 197–200)

24. The Charter and the Constitution resemble each other in their emphasis on - - - - - -.

(A) securing freedom and liberty
(B) concern for the elimination of world tensions

(C) the role of the executive
(D) the importance of economics
(E) social and cultural differences between peoples

24 _____

(pages 239–243)

25. The Charter does NOT - - - - - -.

(A) eliminate the possible use of force
(B) concern itself with both self-determination and human rights
(C) support equal rights for women
(D) approve the signing of new treaties between nations
(E) mention universal law

25 _____

(pages 176–178)

26. If a single word were chosen to express the essential spirit of the Charter, the word would be - - - - - -.

(A) culture
(B) cooperation
(C) principles
(D) sadness
(E) joy

26 _____

(pages 202–205)

27. As stated in Article 1, a major purpose of the census is - - - - - -.

(A) setting an economic base for financial planning
(B) emphasizing the superiority of Virginia in constitutional matters
(C) establishing senatorial precedents
(D) determining congressional representation
(E) suggesting areas that need increased population

27 _____

GO ON TO THE NEXT PAGE

Section 3

Directions: For each question in this section, select the best answer from among the choices given.

The two passages below are followed by questions based on their content. Answer the questions on the basis of what is *stated* or *implied* in the passage and in any introductory material that may be provided.

In a hundred years, America has certainly changed. But how?

Within a hundred years, America has been completely transformed. A century ago in the United States, the average wage was 22 cents an hour, sugar cost 4 cents a pound, and eggs 14 cents a dozen. There
5 were 114 miles of paved roads and only 8,000 cars to enjoy them. More than 95% of all physicians never went to college but attended medical schools of often substandard quality. Perhaps that is one reason why the average life expectancy was only 47.

(pages 189–191; 304–307)

1. The passage clearly implies a causal relationship between - - - - - -.

   (A) wages and life expectancy
   (B) the price of eggs and the price of sugar
   (C) physicians' training and mortality rates
   (D) the average wage and the number of cars
   (E) the number of paved roads and the number of physicians

                                        1 ____

In the perennial battle against insect pests, certain names stand out. The following selection discusses the work of an outstanding African scientist.

A famous cartoon shows a dinosaur stepping on a cockroach. The dinosaur says, "That's the end of the cockroach!" The dinosaurs have long since disappeared, but the hardy cockroach, now 300 million
5 years old as a species, is still with us. Insects have survived and flourished, sometimes for the benefit of human beings, but often to their detriment. An estimated 30 million different species inhabit the planet, but only a million have been discovered. Insects out-
10 weigh the human population at least 12 times and account for about 85% of all animal life.
In Africa, insects have dominated human life. Termites and ants outweigh elephants, rhinos, and all other mammals put together. Two insects especially
15 have influenced how and where human beings live: the mosquito and the tsetse fly. The mosquito carries malaria and yellow fever; the tsetse fly, sleeping sickness.

These two insects did put a limit on colonial settlements, but they have also devastated the Africans
20 themselves.
Thomas Odhiambo, a Kenyan entomologist, vowed to do something about the insect depredations. In the early seventies he founded ICIPE in a Nairobi garage. The International Center of Insect Physiology and
25 Ecology has grown into a major research center with many world-class scientists, graduate students, and postdoctoral students at work.
The tsetse fly's deadly bite has spread sleeping sickness across a vast area, larger than that of the
30 United States. Another deadly disease, malaria, carried by mosquitoes, kills great numbers of children every year. But the diseases of Africa are not limited to those that make a direct assault on human beings. The farmer's livelihood and the people's food are
35 threatened by crop pests and cattle infestations. Weevils, mites, and stem-borers destroy crops. Diseases carried by ticks destroy cattle. Though ticks and mites are technically arachnids, not insects, ICIPE is concerned with all threats. It attempts to attack all
40 of them.
Thomas Risley Odhiambo is a tireless visionary. Called "the smartest man in East Africa," he is a dynamo of energy and planning. Ralph Waldo Emerson said, "An institution is the lengthened shadow of
45 one man." ICIPE is the lengthened shadow of Thomas Odhiambo.
In the control of insects, poisonous chemicals have been shown to have limitations. There is always the threat to pets, livestock, birds, and human beings.
50 More serious, though, is the insects' ability to overcome pesticides. If a few insects are naturally immune to the pesticide, they will survive and breed other immune insects.
Odhiambo believes that we can find more ways to
55 use insects positively. "There are obvious cases, like honey from bees. But did you know that termites make excellent chicken food? It seems sensible to incorporate insects into our livestock-production systems." To a chicken in a farmyard, eating insects is
60 nothing new, but large-scale use of insects as food may provide two benefits at once.

GO ON TO THE NEXT PAGE >

Odhiambo earned his graduate degrees at Cambridge University. On returning to Africa, he established the entomology department at the University
65 of Nairobi. He began organizing "centers of excellence" in Africa. He attracted many outstanding research scientists. With help from American scientific academies, he set up an international center. Other nations, the World Bank, and OPEC also
70 contributed.

Odhiambo faces powerful and pitiless adversaries. Among these terrifying enemies, the tsetse fly has been especially dangerous. The fly may give a painful bite, but the serious damage is done by a blood para-
75 site transmitted by the bite. If the fly is infected, the victim of the bite develops sleeping sickness, so called because the victim sinks into a lethal doze. On the shores of Lake Victoria alone, 200,000 people died after being bitten by an infected fly. The disease has
80 also spread to animals, reducing Africa's cattle crop by 85%.

Many methods, including a drastic scorched-earth policy, have temporarily halted the spread of the fly, or even, in a few instances, caused a retreat. But the
85 victories have always been temporary. Odhiambo's plan is more strategically sound: to "make sure the blood parasite and the tsetse are not in the same place at the same time." New and better traps have been introduced and have reduced the tsetse population by
90 half over a 62-square-mile area.

While experimentation is concerned with the tsetse fly, research into other insect pests goes on apace. Stem-boring moths, other biting flies, mosquitoes, even seemingly innocuous sandflies—host to a
95 deadly parasite—are being studied by some of the best minds in entomological research. In a *Smithsonian* magazine article for August, 1988, Thomas Bass examines in some detail many of the projects under the general direction of Thomas Risley Odhiambo,
100 entomologist extraordinary.

(pages 68, 71)
2. "That's the end of the cockroach" is introduced as an example of - - - - - -.

(A) metaphor
(B) irony
(C) literal language
(D) euphemism
(E) hyperbole

2 ____

(pages 176–178)
3. From the various contexts, we may infer that entomology is the study of - - - - - -.

(A) the higher mammals
(B) African geology
(C) insects
(D) word origins
(E) human behavior

3 ____

(pages 202–205)
4. Honey is mentioned as a - - - - - -.

(A) medicine used in fighting sleeping sickness
(B) major ingredient in Odhiambo's experimentation
(C) carrier of dangerous parasites
(D) positive contribution of insects
(E) major West African crop

4 ____

(pages 192–194)
5. Ralph Waldo Emerson is quoted - - - - - -.

(A) as an amateur authority on insects
(B) to pay tribute to Odhiambo
(C) to add sophistication to the passage
(D) for his courageous stand on the environment
(E) because he is Odhiambo's favorite author

5 ____

(pages 43–47)
6. In line 94, *innocuous* means - - - - - -.

(A) gaudily colored
(B) poisonous
(C) tiny
(D) unpredictable
(E) harmless

6 ____

(pages 176–178)
7. The scorched-earth policy may be evaluated as - - - - - -.

(A) helpful in the long run
(B) creatively designed
(C) ultimately unsuccessful
(D) the answer to one insect only
(E) a mistake by Odhiambo

7 ____

GO ON TO THE NEXT PAGE

(pages 239–243)

8. All the following insects have been mentioned EXCEPT - - - - - -.

(A) sandflies
(B) moths
(C) tsetse flies
(D) mosquitoes
(E) butterflies

8 ____

(pages 24–30)

9. *Depredations* in line 22 means - - - - - -.

(A) savage attacks
(B) peaceful interactions
(C) strengths and weaknesses
(D) manifestations
(E) retreats

9 ____

(pages 218–222)

10. The writer's attitude toward Odhiambo and his work is one of - - - - - -.

(A) watchful waiting
(B) excessive amazement
(C) idle curiosity
(D) sincere admiration
(E) professional jealousy

10 ____

(pages 189–191)

11. Odhiambo's attack on the insect problem may best be characterized as - - - - - -.

(A) enthusiastic but doomed
(B) all-embracing
(C) tediously slow
(D) ill-balanced
(E) based on intuition, not research

11 ____

(pages 202–205)

12. A method mentioned as having good results is - - - - - -.

(A) pesticides
(B) sending out infertile males
(C) genetic engineering
(D) trapping
(E) scorched-earth

12 ____

(pages 214–218)

13. The tone of the passage may be characterized as - - - - - -.

(A) quietly informational
(B) breathlessly enthusiastic
(C) vigorously critical
(D) lukewarm
(E) somewhat indifferent

13 ____

STOP

Mastery Test 3 / Critical Reading

Section I

Directions: For each question in this section, select the best answer from among the choices given.

Each sentence below has one or two blanks, each blank indicating that something has been omitted. Beneath the sentence are five lettered words or sets of words labeled A through E. Choose the word or set of words that *best* fits the meaning of the sentence as a whole.

Example:

Although its publicity has been - - - - - -, the film itself is intelligent, well-acted, handsomely produced, and altogether - - - - - -.

(A) tasteless . . respectable
(B) extensive . . moderate
(C) sophisticated . . spectacular
(D) risqué . . crude
(E) perfect . . spectacular

Ⓐ Ⓑ Ⓒ Ⓓ Ⓔ

(pages 39–43)
1. Like an airplane in a steep power dive, the falcon - - - - - - down upon the - - - - - - sparrows and captured a terrified victim.

(A) swooped . . scattering
(B) lunged . . assembled
(C) flew . . disinterested
(D) looked . . sluggish
(E) circled . . courageous

1 ____

(pages 43–47)
2. Though playwrights can usually manage a good first act, by the middle of the last act, - - - - - - often replaces - - - - - -.

(A) consternation . . contemplation
(B) desperation . . inspiration
(C) deliberation . . commendation
(D) cancellation . . alteration
(E) stagnation . . disorganization

2 ____

(pages 24–30)
3. The - - - - - - of many coastal plains and moors for housing and other development has - - - - - - many fine ecological habitats.

(A) inaccessibility . . uncovered
(B) analysis . . displayed
(C) suitability . . doomed
(D) advertisement . . enhanced
(E) exclusion . . emphasized

3 ____

(pages 43–47)
4. On our Spaceship Earth, recycling is not a - - - - - - to be - - - - - - but a necessity to guide our actions.

(A) concept . . followed
(B) plant . . adapted
(C) dream . . fantasized
(D) luxury . . indulged
(E) discipline . . fostered

4 ____

(pages 43–47)
5. The - - - - - - heat at midday was briefly relieved by a thunderstorm, but a short time later the temperatures again began to climb.

(A) anticipated
(B) moderate
(C) timely
(D) dappled
(E) oppressive

5 ____

(pages 24–30)
6. The name *United Nations,* suggested by Winston Churchill from a poem by Lord Byron, - - - - - - the original name: *Associated Powers.*

(A) refurbished
(B) galvanized
(C) acknowledged
(D) divulged
(E) supplanted

6 ____

GO ON TO THE NEXT PAGE ▷

(pages 24–30; 85)

7. To be ready for the ballet tryouts, Marie followed a(n) - - - - - - diet for several months.

(A) copious
(B) Spartan
(C) carnivorous
(D) condiment
(E) alternative

7 ____

(pages 24–30; 124)

8. Because of their continuing search for perfection, experts are likely to be - - - - - - in judging the work done in their special area.

(A) lackadaisical
(B) generous
(C) therapeutic
(D) hypercritical
(E) fretful

8 ____

(pages 30–34)

9. Indiana Jones seemed to have a - - - - - - love of danger, inherited, no doubt, from some swashbuckling adventurer in Francis Drake's navy.

(A) tiresome
(B) negative
(C) congenital
(D) grisly
(E) rational

9 ____

Great inventors, like Thomas Edison, are well known, but one of the most important, John Harrison, has been largely forgotten. His contribution was a clock that could function accurately on a pitching
5 vessel at sea. Why is such a clock important? It helps determine longitude. With simple instruments, a navigator can determine latitude, but for longitude, astronomical observations are inadequate. During the great age of exploration, only an accurate, func-
10 tioning clock could have provided longitudinally correct information. Now the older methods have been supplanted by the GPS (Global Positioning Service), which provides exact information by satellite.

(pages 189–191; 304–307)

10. The selection implies that - - - - - -.

(A) functioning clocks had been in use before John Harrison
(B) longitude can also be determined by accurate solar and lunar observation
(C) latitude and longitude were confused at times.
(D) John Harrison was a greater inventor than Thomas Edison.
(E) GPS information is available with a simple radio.

10 ____

The two passages below are followed by questions based on their content and on the relationship between the two passages. Answer the questions on the basis of what is *stated* or *implied* in the passages and in any introductory material that may be provided.

What dangers do nations face? How can a democracy be destroyed? The following two passages, both written many years ago, discuss the dangers and offer warnings to a free people.

Passage 1

Democracy's Danger

To turn a republican government into a despotism the basest and most brutal, it is not necessary formally to change its constitution or abandon popular elections. It was centuries after Caesar before the
5 absolute master of the Roman world pretended to rule other than by authority of a Senate that trembled before him.

But forms are nothing when substance is gone, and the forms of popular government are those from
10 which the substance of freedom may most easily go. Extremes meet, and a government of universal suffrage and theoretical equality may, under conditions which impel the change, most readily become a despotism. For there despotism advances in the name
15 and with the might of the people. The single source of power once secured, everything is secured. There is no unfranchised class to whom appeal may be made, no privileged orders who in defending their rights may defend those of all. No bulwark remains
20 to stay the flood, no eminence to rise above it. They were belted barons led by a mitered archbishop who curbed the Plantagenet with Magna Charta; it was the middle classes who broke the pride of the Stuarts; but a mere aristocracy of wealth will never struggle
25 while it can hope to bribe a tyrant.

And when the disparity of condition increases, so does universal suffrage make it easy to seize the source of power. . . . Given a community with republican institutions, in which one class is too rich
30 to be shorn of its luxuries, no matter how public affairs are administered, and another so poor that

---

GO ON TO THE NEXT PAGE ▷

a few dollars on election day will seem more than
any abstract consideration; in which the few roll in
wealth and the many seethe with discontent as a
35 condition of things they know not how to remedy,
and power must pass into the hands of jobbers who
will buy and sell it as the Praetorians sold the
Roman purple, or into the hands of demagogues
who will seize and wield it for a time, only to be
40 displaced by worse demagogues.

Passage 2

The Deadliest Enemies of Nations

The deadliest enemies of nations are not their foreign foes; they always dwell within their own borders.
And from these internal enemies civilization is always
in need of being saved. The nation blest above all na-
45 tions is she in whom the civic genius of the people does
the saving day by day, by acts without external pictur-
esqueness; by speaking, writing, voting reasonably; by
smiting corruption swiftly; by good temper between
parties; by the people knowing true men when they see
50 them, and preferring them as leaders to rabid parti-
sans or empty quacks. Such nations have no need of
wars to save them. Their accounts with righteousness
are always even; and God's judgments do not have to
overtake them fitfully in bloody spasms and convul-
55 sions of the race.

(pages 176–178)
11. According to the author of Passage 1, having
popular elections - - - - - -.

(A) insures that freedom may not be lost
(B) provides a check against corruption
(C) tends to equalize the distribution of
wealth
(D) tends to take care of the poorest citizens
(E) may still lead to despotism

11 ____

(pages 202–205)
12. For centuries after Caesar, the Roman
emperors - - - - - -.

(A) consulted the Senate on all important
decisions
(B) acted as model rulers during their early
years
(C) were intimidated by the Roman Senate
(D) concealed the source of true authority
(E) were lawful descendants of the preceding
emperors

12 ____

(pages 189–191)
13. In the discussion of form and substance,
substance is represented by - - - - - -.

(A) a constitution
(B) the privilege of voting
(C) freedom
(D) popular elections
(E) republican institutions

13 ____

(pages 24–30)
14. In line 19, the word *bulwark* most nearly
means - - - - - -.

(A) strong leader
(B) constitutional restraint
(C) diversion
(D) creative idea
(E) barrier

14 ____

(pages 176–178)
15. The author of Passage 2 suggests that nations
are most vulnerable to - - - - - -.

(A) foreign aggressors
(B) mercenary ideals
(C) depletion of natural resources
(D) incompetent military leaders
(E) internal weakness

15 ____

(pages 250–255)
16. The authors of both passages would most
probably subscribe to which of the following
quotations?

(A) "It is my certain conviction that no man
loses his freedom except through his own
weakness." Gandhi
(B) "Nothing is so weak and unstable as a
reputation for power not based on force."
Tacitus
(C) "A shortcut to riches is to subtract from
our desires." Petrarch
(D) "There is no worse torture than the torture of laws." Francis Bacon
(E) "Honour sinks where commerce long pre-
vails." Oliver Goldsmith

16 ____

GO ON TO THE NEXT PAGE

The passage below is followed by questions based on its content. Answer the questions on the basis of what is *stated* or *implied* in the passage and in any introductory material that may be provided.

This introduction to the stories of Edith Wharton evaluates her work and personality.

Edith Wharton's autobiography, *A Backward Glance*, is a brilliant exercise in both worldliness and concealment. Both of these qualities are completely authentic: no cover-up is intended. For she was both
5 the great lady she so pleasingly describes and that secret inward-looking creature to whom she only briefly alludes. The writing of fiction—and she was tirelessly prolific, combining her work with an extensive social life—proceeds from the hidden self, a self
10 which exists only on the borders of consciousness. Edith Wharton's outer life was spent in the public gaze. She was *mondaine* in every sense of the word, born into a rigidly stratified society of accepted families, married young to a suitable husband, owner of
15 many beautiful houses, and tirelessly available to a host of friends. She was also a great traveller, a great expatriate, and a great worker: indeed her efforts in the First World War earned her a Légion d'Honneur from the French government. As she tells the story,
20 there would not seem to be either the time or the place for a writer of fiction to emerge and to blossom. Indeed the world in which she grew up saw her literary activity as a sort of aberration or solecism, and only one of her numerous relations ever read her
25 books. Her easy sophistication enables her to dismiss this as she seems to have dismissed every other obstacle in her path.

And yet she was that awkward thing, a born writer. When she was a very small child, before she
30 could read or write, she was subject to compulsive episodes of "making up." When one of these came upon her she would seize a book, walk up and down, and chant stories of her own invention, turning the pages at intervals which an adult reader might ob-
35 serve. She was even known to abandon a children's tea party when visited by a sudden desire to "make up." Perhaps this is not surprising in a child, but then few children go on to write forty books. The same magic impulse that went into the making-up episodes
40 seems to have stayed with her throughout her career, for, as she tells it, she never had to search for a theme or a subject, and even the names of her characters arrived of their own accord, sometimes long in advance of the characters themselves.

45 Those who seek for a sober explanation for these phenomena would no doubt point to the excellence of her education, the sort of education not enjoyed by anyone today. The young Edith Wharton was allowed to read only the finest works in any language. As she
50 spoke French, German, and Italian from an early age she grew up acquainted with the masterpieces of four

languages. At the same time she was introduced to the pleasures of Europe, which was to become her second home, in an age when such pleasures had to
55 be pursued over unmade roads and in occasionally dubious hotels. Although she never went to school, she seems to have had the best and kindest of governesses. And of course agreeable company was assured from the start, the society of old New York reinforcing
60 what her own extensive family habitually provided.

This brilliant education had excellent results. A gracious manner and an inspired way with friends might be qualities one would expect from such an upbringing, but in addition to these qualities Edith
65 Wharton had a characteristic which can only be described as zest. She was zestful in the decoration of her houses, zestful in her long and audacious travels, zestful in the delight and enthusiasm which she felt for her work. She seems not to have known fear or
70 discouragement or everyday depression, but perhaps her innate moral and social code forbade her ever to refer to such moods.

That she was aware of the tensions and restrictions of life lived among others is evident in her
75 writing, particularly in her masterpieces, *The House of Mirth, The Custom of the Country, The Reef,* and *The Age of Innocence.* These novels have to do with the doomed attempts to challenge the social code, but at the same time they establish the
80 very real validity of the Dionysiac impulse at work in the challenger. Lily Bart and Undine Spragg are far stronger than those among whom they attempt to establish themselves, just as the exquisite Anna Leath is weaker than the coarse beings to whom it
85 is her lot to be superior. Yet if society wins every time, it is a society of vaguely disappointed and disappointing people, idle, rigid, without ambition. Although not as nerveless as the heroes of her great friend Henry James, Edith Wharton's men are no
90 match for her women.

(pages 189–191)
17. In reporting the two sides of her personality, Edith Wharton - - - - - -.

(A) concentrates on her innermost thoughts and feelings
(B) tells how her childhood experiences had no effect on her fiction
(C) reveals a life plagued by unhappiness and self-disgust
(D) underplays her innermost feelings
(E) presents a woman almost completely withdrawn from the world

17 _____

GO ON TO THE NEXT PAGE

(pages 239–243)

18. All the following are correctly paired EXCEPT - - - - - -.

(A) (line 7) alludes—refers
(B) (line 8) prolific—productive
(C) (line 13) stratified—layered
(D) (line 17) expatriate—former political leader
(E) (line 67) audacious—bold

18 ____

(pages 176–178)

19. Edith Wharton's behavior in childhood might be characterized as - - - - - -.

(A) unhappy
(B) traditional
(C) disrupted by family
(D) aimless
(E) unusual

19 ____

(pages 30–34)

20. In line 23, the context suggests that a "solecism" is - - - - - -.

(A) an excess of overweening pride
(B) a revelation of basic uncertainty
(C) a departure from the normal
(D) an indication of inner turmoil
(E) an intolerant attack on the establishment

20 ____

(pages 189–191)

21. When Edith Wharton realized that only one of her relations read her books, she was

(A) saddened
(B) furious
(C) vengeful
(D) indifferent
(E) amused

21 ____

(pages 189–191)

22. A thread running throughout the four novels mentioned in lines 75–77 is - - - - - -.

(A) the loss of innocence in a sophisticated society
(B) the inevitable victory of culture
(C) a rebellion against society
(D) the greater happiness of the upper crust
(E) the foolish impetuosity of youth

22 ____

(pages 24–30)

23. In line 80, *validity* most nearly means - - - - - -.

(A) soundness
(B) strangeness
(C) contradiction
(D) explanation
(E) wonder

23 ____

(pages 66–71; 239–243)

24. Each of the following is an example of figurative language EXCEPT - - - - -.

(A) "no cover-up is intended" (line 4)
(B) "the borders of consciousness" (line 10)
(C) "fiction to emerge and blossom" (line 21)
(D) "a very small child" (line 29)
(E) "visited by a sudden desire" (line 36)

24 ____

(pages 250–255)

25. The author would probably maintain that Edith Wharton is suitable for modern readers. One reason might be that - - - - -.

(A) her characters are two-dimensional but the plots are artfully conceived
(B) her picture of her own childhood can present models of parenting
(C) she presents women characters who are modern in their attitude toward men and society
(D) her experiences during the war have a modern ring when placed alongside modern war stories
(E) the picture of her contemporary society, though essentially untrue, does provide some colorful hints of life many years ago

25 ____

GO ON TO THE NEXT PAGE ⟩

Section 2

> **Directions:** For each question in this section, select the best answer from among the choices given.

Each sentence below has one or two blanks, each blank indicating that something has been omitted. Beneath the sentence are five lettered words or sets of words labeled A through E. Choose the word or set of words that *best* fits the meaning of the sentence as a whole.

Example:

Although its publicity has been ------, the film itself is intelligent, well-acted, handsomely produced, and altogether ------.

(A) tasteless . . respectable
(B) extensive . . moderate
(C) sophisticated . . spectacular
(D) risqué . . crude
(E) perfect . . spectacular

(pages 43–47)
1. Events in the Olympics are not ------, for many events once popular have been dropped and, ------, many new events have been added.

(A) dull . . certainly
(B) controlled . . surprisingly
(C) changeable . . similarly
(D) unvarying . . conversely
(E) historical . . advantageously

1 ____

(pages 24–30)
2. In an attempt to stop the ------ filibuster, some senators mapped strategy to ------ the cloture rule.

(A) interminable . . enforce
(B) amusing . . dramatize
(C) unexpected . . discuss
(D) simple . . research
(E) enlightening . . evaluate

2 ____

(pages 24–30)
3. Tour groups in the South Pacific ------ seem to find that explorer Captain James Cook ------ them, whether the scene is Hawaii, Tahiti, or New Caledonia.

(A) doggedly . . outdid
(B) inevitably . . preceded
(C) breathlessly . . foresaw
(D) irritably . . missed
(E) complacently . . avoided

3 ____

(pages 43–47)
4. Though perpetual motion has long been classified as an impossible dream, ------ inventors still try to patent machines that are supposed to run forever.

(A) informed (B) callous (C) biased
(D) candid (E) undaunted

4 ____

(pages 24–30)
5. The ranger explained, to our ------, that there is no typical "sled dog," that many breeds have proved suitable for the ------ demands of exertion in temperatures below zero.

(A) consternation . . delicate
(B) horror . . occasional
(C) surprise . . rigorous
(D) amusement . . unfair
(E) satisfaction . . expected

5 ____

(pages 30–34)
6. Many tennis experts suggest that the difference between the greats in tennis and the nearly greats is more a matter of ------ and single-mindedness of purpose rather than raw ability.

(A) talent (B) dexterity (C) egotism
(D) concentration (E) guile

6 ____

GO ON TO THE NEXT PAGE

(pages 43–47)

7. The All-Star game is a(n) - - - - - affair, offering the opportunity of making a great play and becoming a hero or committing a serious error and becoming an object of - - - - - -.

  (A) breathless . . wonderment
  (B) typical . . scorn
  (C) one-shot . . criticism
  (D) well-publicized . . analysis
  (E) nightmare . . approval

  7 _____

(pages 43–47)

8. - - - - - gas furnaces may run at 65 percent efficiency or less, but a - - - - - breakthrough now offers furnaces with efficiency ratings of 96 percent or more.

  (A) Conventional . . technological
  (B) Rejected . . former
  (C) Natural . . modest
  (D) Ancient . . well-documented
  (E) Unpopular . . costly

  8 _____

(pages 52–57)

9. The vice-presidency is widely considered a do-nothing office with little or no - - - - - -; yet there is never a shortage of applicants for that - - - - - - lowly position.

  (A) money . . truly
  (B) regrets . . apparently
  (C) clout . . disgracefully
  (D) reward . . historically
  (E) prestige . . supposedly

  9 _____

(pages 24–30)

10. Looking like something out of - - - - - -, a new X-ray machine can explore the body from every angle without putting a scalpel to the patient and making - - - - - -.

  (A) mystery stories . . an enquiry
  (B) science fiction . . an incision
  (C) motion pictures . . a fuss
  (D) westerns . . a diagnosis
  (E) fantasy . . a disturbance

  10 _____

Directions: For each question in this section, select the best answer from among the choices given.

The two passages below are followed by questions based on their content. Answer the questions on the basis of what is *stated* or *implied* in the passage and in any introductory material that may be provided.

What role does time play in attitudes toward established ideas, customs, and opinions? The following passages emphasize the power of change.

Passage 1

Men's ideas are like cards and other games. Ideas which I remember to have seen regarded as dangerous and over-bold have since become commonplace and almost trite, and have descended to men little
5 worthy of them. So it is that some of the ideas which today we call audacious will be considered feeble and conventional by our descendants.

Passage 2

Often in early youth an opinion or custom seems absurd to us, which, with advancing years, we dis-
10 cover has some justification and so appears less absurd. Ought we to conclude from this that certain customs are not so ridiculous as others: One might sometimes be tempted to think that they were established by people who had read the book of life
15 through, and that they are judged by those who, despite their intelligence, have only glanced at a few pages.

(pages 197–200; 304–307)

11. Which of the following is a common element in Passages 1 and 2?

  (A) the impact of time upon ideas and customs
  (B) an abiding respect for ideas of an earlier day
  (C) a consideration of changing attitudes towards ideas and customs
  (D) an evaluation of ideas
  (E) an acceptance of change

  11 _____

(pages 189–191)

12. Passage 1 implies that - - - - - -.

  (A) ideas are imperishable
  (B) our descendants will treasure our ideas
  (C) card games provide answers to life's most perplexing questions
  (D) supposedly imperishable ideas go out of fashion in time
  (E) spite and envy destroy old, trusted ideas

  12 _____

GO ON TO THE NEXT PAGE ▷

(pages 197–200)

13. A comparison of Passage 1 and 2 suggests that - - - - -.

    (A) Passage 2 has a more positive conclusion
    (B) old ideas fare better in Passage 1
    (C) Passage 1 pays more tribute to those who have gone before
    (D) both passages suggest the futility of striving
    (E) a good reputation favors the action heroes

                           13 ____

(pages 189–191)

14. According to Passage 2, - - - - -.

    (A) intelligence rightly determines the appeal of customs
    (B) it's wise and adventurous to give up an established custom
    (C) some old customs were established by people who had lived a long, thoughtful life
    (D) youth is essentially wiser than age
    (E) we lose good judgment with advancing years

                           14 ____

The following selection analyzes causes of severe floods and suggests possible preventive measures.

"For too long, we've been trying to adjust rivers to human needs, and then we wonder why our rivers are messed up and why we continue to get flooded; it's not a mystery." Larry Larson, director of the Associ-
5 ation of State Floodplain Managers, then went on to say, "We need to adjust human behavior to river systems."

The Midwest floods of 1993 were the worst since records were first kept. For some experts, the disaster
10 was not a surprise. In the previous twenty years, there had been four serious floods. The new situation was a catastrophe just waiting to happen. Property and crop damage ran into the billions of dollars, not millions. The cost in human suffering was incalcula-
15 ble, with many deaths directly attributable to the raging waters.

The questions asked by many victims were "Why? Why didn't our flood-control measures protect us? Could we have foreseen the breaks in the levees? Are
20 we at the mercy of a capricious weather system wholly beyond our control?"

Flood experts agree that weather is unpredictable, that excessive rainfall and drought alternate in unanticipated ways. But before people arrived
25 on the scene, nature had ways of handling such extremes. Natural floodplains were safety valves that let off pressure, reducing the quantity and intensity of flow downstream. Many of these natu-

ral balances yielded to commercial, industrial, and
30 residential developments.

People like to build near the seashore. The views are magnificent; the air is cool and clear; the living is pleasurable. But recent northeasters, tropical storms, and hurricanes have shown how tenuous is
35 our grip upon the seashore. Houses are washed away. Beaches are eroded. The sea covers tennis courts, swimming pools, hotel sites. Living at dune line is chancy at best. Attempts to protect the shore—by building barrier jetties, for example—often exacer-
40 bate the problem.

Rivers present similar dangers. It's pleasant to live on the shore of a lovely river, even within walking distance. There is a risk, however. Unsuspecting residents are sometimes washed away by a stream that
45 held a trickle of water the day before. In like manner but on a grander scale, the areas bordering the Missouri-Ohio-Mississippi basin are also at risk.

In an attempt to tame the wild rivers, engineers have prevented the floodplain from performing its
50 basic natural function: flood control. The plain stores and slows flood waters, reducing the force and height of the water. The situation has a parallel in a common household experience. When a nozzle isn't available, a gardener can partially block with fingers the end of
55 the hose, increasing its force and reach. The levee system squeezes the river water in the same way, increasing the force of the water. Such water is concentrated, not allowed to dissipate its strength and volume in a floodplain. When the levees fail to hold,
60 as so often happens, the water rushes through with ferocious intensity and forms a floodplain not always convenient for those who live in the flooded areas.

"Cooperate with nature; don't fight it." The new approach to flood control doesn't try to subdue natu-
65 ral forces but to work with them. It tries to restore natural ecosystems, permitting natural flood-control systems to work.

New methods are being devised. Communities are acquiring wetlands to serve as natural flood basins.
70 Throughout the plain, they are creating natural detention areas for flood waters. Stretches of natural floodplain are being used as parks, ball fields, and green belts. When these are flooded the problem is temporary. Many communities are discouraging de-
75 velopment of areas that are prime targets for flooding. Soldiers Grove in Wisconsin has moved the entire business district to higher ground. Littleton, Colorado, has established a 625-acre park in its floodplain to relieve the flood pressures of the South Platte
80 River.

"We can't pick Des Moines up and put it on a hill," an army engineer, Harry Fitch, declared. Existing cities in the floodplain present continuing difficulties. Long-range planning, combining some structural
85 methods along with natural ones, holds some hope for

GO ON TO THE NEXT PAGE →

the future. One thing is certain. Sometime in the future, the rains in the great river watershed will again be excessive. Rampaging waters will roar down the narrow river corridors. Will the people again be
90 subjected to communities without water, power, or sewage? Will they watch the waters rise to the top floors of their houses? How quickly and effectively can we take measures that take the sting out of abnormal weather conditions?
95   Mankind continues to learn, at its peril, that tampering with natural ecosystems can be fatal.

(pages 178–181)

15. The overriding message of the selection is that
- - - - - -.

    (A) the 1993 floods were the worst in history
    (B) some communities are making progress in flood control
    (C) floods are a continuing nightmare for people of the Midwest
    (D) cooperation with nature makes more sense than fighting it
    (E) floodplains are safety valves

    15 ____

(pages 35–39)

16. In line 20, *capricious* most nearly means
- - - - - -.

    (A) cruel
    (B) overloaded with moisture
    (C) erratic
    (D) regularly cyclical
    (E) nourishing

    16 ____

(pages 189–191)

17. The author asks two questions in lines 19–21: "Could... control?" His two answers would be
- - - - - -.

    (A) No. Yes.
    (B) No. No.
    (C) No. Not entirely.
    (D) Yes. Not entirely.
    (E) Yes. Yes.

    17 ____

(pages 197–200)

18. The author brings in the seashore example to
- - - - - -.

    (A) contrast the problems of seashore dwellers with those who live near rivers
    (B) provide an example of how well people have coped with problems at the shore
    (C) provide a light change of pace in the development of his idea
    (D) show how a floodplain also exists at the shore
    (E) compare two areas with somewhat similar problems

    18 ____

(pages 197–200)

19. The two items that are most similar in intended function are - - - - - -.

    (A) levees and town parks
    (B) jetties and levees
    (C) jetties and floodplains
    (D) levees and floodplains
    (E) jetties and green belts

    19 ____

(pages 24–30)

20. In line 33, *tenuous* most nearly means - - - - - -.

    (A) recent
    (B) sharp
    (C) slight
    (D) firm
    (E) well-intended

    20 ____

(pages 66–71; 239–243)

21. All the following are examples of figurative language EXCEPT - - - - - -.

    (A) "there had been four serious floods" (11)
    (B) "catastrophe just waiting to happen" (12)
    (C) "floodplains were safety valves" (26)
    (D) "waters will roar" (88)
    (E) "measures that take the sting out" (93)

    21 ____

(pages 43–47)

22. In line 58, *dissipate* most nearly means - - - - - -.

    (A) intensify
    (B) scatter
    (C) pollute
    (D) gather
    (E) discover

    22 ____

GO ON TO THE NEXT PAGE ⟩

(pages 239-243)

23. The following are all mentioned as remedies for flood control EXCEPT - - - - -.

(A) acquiring wetlands
(B) using parks
(C) discouraging development
(D) moving to higher ground
(E) reinforcing levees

23 ____

(pages 218–222)

24. Which of the following quotations best expresses the viewpoint of the author?

(A) "Let us permit nature to have her way: she understands her business better than we do." Montaigne
(B) "Nature, like us, is sometimes caught without her diadem." Emily Dickinson
(C) "Nature, red in tooth and claw." Tennyson
(D) "In nature's infinite book of secrecy / A little I can read." Shakespeare
(E) "Nature is visible thought." Heinrich Heine

24 ____

(pages 202–205)

25. The most serious difficulty in controlling the floods is - - - - -.

(A) trying to guess when the next bad weather will occur
(B) stated by Harry Fitch
(C) overlooked by citizens of Soldiers Grove
(D) overlooked by Larry Larson
(E) obvious to all riverside dwellers

25 ____

(pages 176–178)

26. The key problem in flood control is - - - - -.

(A) the lack of neighborliness among townspeople
(B) insufficient levees
(C) unawareness of solutions by any engineer
(D) failure to warn areas of impending floods
(E) shortsightedness

26 ____

(pages 176–178)

27. The best example of an effective ecosystem is - - - - -.

(A) household management
(B) the stock market
(C) a virgin forest
(D) social security and medicare
(E) a cabin by a tranquil lake

27 ____

Section 3

Directions: For each question in this section, select the best answer from among the choices given.

The two passages below are followed by questions based on their content. Answer the questions on the basis of what is *stated* or *implied* in the passage and in any introductory material that may be provided.

One of the most fascinating survival mechanisms is hibernation.

Learning the secrets of hibernation may help solve human health problems. Studying how a hibernating black bear loses only 20% of its muscle strength in a six-month dormancy period may help bedridden pa-
5   tients attack muscle degeneration during that inactivity. It may also be noted parenthetically that a human "couch potato" in that same period may lose 90% of muscle tone! The achievement of the black bear is matched by that of the Arctic ground squirrel,
10 which can lower its body temperatures below freezing during subzero temperatures. Unlocking these se-
crets may help make people more resistant to stroke and other ailments.

(pages 189–191; 304-307)

1. The exclamation point (!) after muscle tone suggests - - - - -.

(A) a sense of amazement at the information
(B) foreshadowing the incredible information about the squirrel
(C) an apology for a biting comparison
(D) a recognition that *couch potato* is informal
(E) the writer's tendency to exaggerate

1 ____

GO ON TO THE NEXT PAGE ⇨

In this excerpt from a detective novel set in the American Southwest, two Navajo police officers are at odds over the place of witchcraft in the Navajo culture. A bone bead begins the confrontation.

Still, Leaphorn had kept the bone bead.

"I'll see about it," he'd said. "Send it to the lab. Find out if it is bone, and what kind of bone." He'd torn a page from his notebook, wrapped the bead in it, and
5 placed it in the coin compartment of his billfold. Then he'd looked at Chee for a moment in silence. "Any idea how it got in here?"

"Sounds strange," Chee had said. "But you know you could pry out the end of a shotgun shell and pull
10 out the wadding and stick a bead like this in with the pellets."

Leaphorn's expression became almost a smile. Was it contempt? "Like a witch shooting in the bone?" he asked. "They're supposed to do that through a little
15 tube." He made a puffing shape with his lips.

Chee had nodded, flushing just a little.

Now, remembering it, he was angry again. Well, to hell with Leaphorn. Let him believe whatever he wanted to believe. The origin story of the Navajos
20 explained witchcraft clearly enough, and it was a logical part of the philosophy on which the Dinee had founded their culture. If there was good, and harmony, and beauty on the east side of reality, then there must be evil, chaos, and ugliness to the west.
25 Like a nonfundamentalist Christian, Chee believed in the poetic metaphor of the Navajo story of human genesis. Without believing in the specific Adam's rib, or the size of the reed through which the Holy People emerged to the Earth Surface World, he believed in
30 the lessons such imagery was intended to teach. To hell with Leaphorn and what he didn't believe. Chee started the engine and jolted back down the slope to the road. He wanted to get to Badwater Wash before noon.

35 But he couldn't quite get Leaphorn out of his mind. Leaphorn posed a problem. "One more thing," the lieutenant had said. "We've got a complaint about you." And he'd told Chee what the doctor at the Badwater Clinic had said about him.
40 "Yellowhorse claims you've been interfering with his practice of his religion," Leaphorn said. And while the lieutenant's expression said he didn't take the complaint as anything critically important, the very fact that he'd mentioned it implied that Chee
45 should desist.

"I have been telling people that Yellowhorse is a fake," Chee said stiffly. "I have told people every chance I get that the doctor pretends to be a crystal gazer just to get them into his clinic."
50 "I hope you're not doing that on company time," Leaphorn said. "Not while you're on duty."

"I probably have," Chee said. "Why not?"

"Because it violates regulations," Leaphorn said, his expression no longer even mildly amused.
55 "How?"

"I think you can see how," Leaphorn had said. "We don't have any way to license our shamans, no more than the federal government can license preachers. If Yellowhorse says he's a medicine man, or a hand
60 trembler, or a road chief of the Native American Church, or the Pope, it is no business of the Navajo Tribal Police. No rule against it. No law."

"I'm a Navajo," Chee said. "I see somebody cynically using our religion . . . somebody who doesn't
65 believe in our religion using it in that cynical way. . . ."

"What harm is he doing?" Leaphorn asked. "The way I understand it, he recommends they go to a *yataalii* if they need a ceremonial sing. And he
70 points them at the white man's hospital only if they have a white man's problem. Diabetes, for example."

Chee had made no response to that. If Leaphorn couldn't see the problem, the sacrilege involved, then
75 Leaphorn was blind. But that wasn't the trouble. Leaphorn was as cynical as Yellowhorse.

"You, yourself, have declared yourself to be a *yataalii,* I hear," Leaphorn said. "I heard you performed a Blessing Way."
80 Chee had nodded. He said nothing.

Leaphorn had looked at him a moment, and sighed. "I'll talk to Largo about it," he said.

And that meant that one of these days Chee would have an argument with the captain about it and if he
85 wasn't lucky, Largo would give him a flat, unequivocal order to say nothing more about Yellowhorse as shaman. When that happened, he would cope as best he could. Now the road to Badwater had changed from bad to worse. Chee concentrated on driving.

(pages 189–191)

2. The officers are apparently concerned with the bone bead because it is some kind of - - - - - -.

 (A) ornamentation
 (B) shotgun shell
 (C) writing
 (D) evidence
 (E) food

2 ____

(pages 257–262)

3. When Leaphorn says, "They're supposed to do that through a little tube," he is being - - - - - -.

 (A) cruel
 (B) witty
 (C) sarcastic
 (D) sympathetic
 (E) alarmed

3 ____

GO ON TO THE NEXT PAGE

(pages 189–191; 257–262)

4. The relationship between Chee and Leaphorn can best be described as - - - - - -.

(A) comradely
(B) prickly
(C) indifferent
(D) satisfying
(E) dangerous

4 ____

(pages 189–191)

5. We might infer that Chee's attitude toward his religion is basically - - - - - -.

(A) reverent
(D) negative
(B) confused
(E) depressing
(C) belligerent

5 ____

(pages 192–194)

6. The best description of Yellowhorse is that he - - - - - -.

(A) is a Navajo doctor who scorns Western medicine
(B) is an undercover member of the Navajo Tribal Police
(C) has set himself up as some kind of medicine man
(D) once did Leaphorn a favor and is now protected by him
(E) proposes to cure all diseases himself

6 ____

(pages 24–30)

7. In line 74, *sacrilege* suggests - - - - - -.

(A) a disrespect for sacred things
(B) a religious rite performed by a priest
(C) unintentional humor
(D) active participation in religion
(E) a sacred activity

7 ____

(pages 202–205)

8. Yellowhorse's practices cannot be stopped because - - - - - -.

(A) he is a member of another Native American tribe
(B) he has somehow bribed persons in high authority
(C) he is doing a wonderful job
(D) there is no law against his activities
(E) his intentions are honorable

8 ____

(pages 202–205)

9. Largo is identified as - - - - - -.

(A) Leaphorn's subordinate
(B) Chee's detective partner
(C) a doctor supplied by the federal government
(D) a Tribal Police captain
(E) a relative of Yellowhorse's

9 ____

(pages 92–109)

10. In lines 85–86, the word *unequivocal* most nearly means - - - - - -.

(A) unique
(B) confusing
(C) double-barreled
(D) clear
(E) improper

10 ____

(pages 202–205)

11. The best way to find the answer to question 9 is to - - - - -.

(A) reread the first sentence of each paragraph for topic-sentence clues
(B) skim through rapidly, looking for the word *Largo*
(C) read the entire article carefully
(D) search your memory for possible recall
(E) examine carefully the first two paragraphs for early clues

11 ____

(pages 257–262)

12. Lieutenant Leaphorn may best be characterized as - - - - - -.

(A) a world-weary man of keen intelligence
(B) a rather gullible believer in the status quo
(C) a hot-headed irrational bully
(D) an enthusiastic newcomer to tribal matters
(E) a person willing to scrap the rules for a cause

12 ____

(pages 222–226)

13. The central character of the story seems to be Chee, but Leaphorn is introduced by the author to provide essential - - - - - -.

(A) local color
(B) humorous episodes
(C) conflict and give-and-take
(D) tragic overtones
(E) suspects for the mystery

13 ____

STOP

Division D

Writing

Take the following test for an advance look at what this part of the SAT test looks like. Find out which areas you are strong in. These areas won't require much work in the weeks ahead. Also find out which areas are most difficult for you. **Page numbers in parentheses refer you to specific areas of this book that explain and illustrate the testing point of each question.**

Complete Diagnostic Test for Writing

Section 1 — Identifying Sentence Errors

The following sentences test your knowledge of grammar, usage, diction (choice of words), and idiom. Some sentences are correct. No sentence contains more than one error. You will find that the error, if there is one, is underlined and lettered. Elements of the sentence that are not underlined will not be changed. In choosing answers, follow the requirements of standard written English. If there is an error, select the one underlined part that must be changed to make the sentence correct. If there is no error, choose answer E.

EXAMPLE

If the size of the brain is positively correlated with intelligence, the giant stegosaurus, with a brain the size
A   B
of a walnut, must of had difficulty fending off the voracious carnivores of the Jurassic period. No error
         C   D   E

C

1. Neither one of the twins were able to pass the qualifying examination even though they had prepared
                          A   B   C
   as thoroughly and diligently as possible. No error
                              D   E

1 ___

2. Current spacecraft travel is much too slow to make exploration outside the solar system practical.
                              A   B   C   D
   No error
   E

2 ___

3. In giving advice to her younger sister, Eileen flatly declared, "When you go to a dance, always go
   A   B
   home with the one who brung you." No error
                    C   D   E

3 ___

4. After a lengthy name-calling session, the beleaguered committee decided to award the prize to
                    A   B
   whomever showed the most flexibility and resiliency. No error.
   C   D   E

4 ___

5. Despite the ravages of time, we have fortunately preserved more of Shakespeare's plays than those
   $\underset{A}{}$ $\underset{B}{}$ $\underset{C}{}$

   of any Elizabethan dramatist. No error.
   $\underset{D}{}$ $\underset{E}{}$

   5 ____

6. Geraldine and myself decided to prepare a collaborative report on a new study suggesting that
   $\underset{A}{}$ $\underset{B}{}$ $\underset{C}{}$

   laughter is a social tool as well as an expression of personal well-being. No error
   $\underset{D}{}$ $\underset{E}{}$

   6 ____

7. According to mainline criticism, each of Shakespeare's major tragic heroes has a character flaw
   $\underset{A}{}$ $\underset{B}{}$ $\underset{C}{}$

   which causes his downfall. No error
   $\underset{D}{}$ $\underset{E}{}$

   7 ____

8. In going through the picture book, Jason suddenly pointed out, "That aardvark's snout looks like
   $\underset{A}{}$ $\underset{B}{}$ $\underset{C}{}$

   a pig!" No error
   $\underset{D}{}$ $\underset{E}{}$

   8 ____

9. In the popular stereotype, on television and in the movies, mother-in-laws are caricatures, making
   $\underset{A}{}$ $\underset{B}{}$ $\underset{C}{}$

   life miserable for their children and their spouses. No error
   $\underset{D}{}$ $\underset{E}{}$

   9 ____

10. That selection of H.L. Mencken's essays are especially helpful in my study of the American
    $\underset{A}{}$ $\underset{B}{}$ $\underset{C}{}$ $\underset{D}{}$

    language. No error
    $\underset{E}{}$

    10 ____

11. Being that a bird doesn't have stereo vision, when after a worm, it cocks its head and looks with
    $\underset{A}{}$ $\underset{B}{}$ $\underset{C}{}$ $\underset{D}{}$

    one eye for a telltale movement in the soil. No error
    $\underset{E}{}$

    11 ____

12. If you are interested in those kind of tennis shoes, you can find them at the store in the
    $\underset{A}{}$ $\underset{B}{}$ $\underset{C}{}$ $\underset{D}{}$

    mall. No error
    $\underset{E}{}$

    12 ____

Section 2   Improving Sentences

In each of the following items, select the best version of the underlined part of the sentence. Choice (A) is the same as the underlined portion of the original sentence. If you think the original sentence is best, choose answer (A).

EXAMPLE

In its search for extraterrestrial intelligence, SETI patiently <u>listens for whomever may be transmitting out there, hoping</u> a meaningful signal will some day come through.

    (A) listens for whomever may be transmitting out there, hoping

    (B) listens for whoever may be transmitting out there, and they hope

    (C) listens for whoever may be transmitting out there, hoping

    (D) is listening for whomever may be transmitting out there, hoping

    (E) listens for whomever might be transmitting out there and hope

                                                                C

13. The meteorologist <u>declared, "The first of a string of clear, crisp days are coming</u> our way."

    (A) declared "The first of a string of clear, crisp days are coming

    (B) declared, "The first of a string of clear, crisp days is coming

    (C) predicted, "The first of a string of clear, crisp days are coming

    (D) declared, "The first of a string of clear, crisp days are coming

    (E) declared, that the first of a string of clear, crisp days is coming.

                                                     13 ____

14. The oldest trees still alive at Mount Vernon are probably the pecans <u>which were planted by George Washington in 1786 from nuts that had been sent</u> to him as a gift by Thomas Jefferson.

    (A) which were planted by George Washington in 1786 from nuts that had been sent

    (B) planted by George Washington in 1786 from nuts sent

    (C) planted by George Washington in 1786 from nuts that had been sent

    (D) which had been planted by George Washington in 1786 from nuts sent

    (E) which had been planted by George Washington in 1786 from nuts that are sent

                                                     14 ____

Section 3   Improving Paragraphs

The following passage is an early draft of an essay. Some parts of the passage need to be rewritten. Read the passage and select the best answers for the questions that follow. Some questions are about particular sentences or parts of sentences and ask you to improve sentence structure and word choice. Other questions refer to parts of the essay or the entire essay and ask you to consider organization and development. In making your decisions, follow the conventions of standard written English.

(1) It was long believed that life could exist only within certain narrow limits of temperature and air quality, and there are living organisms that challenge common sense and astound scientists every year with new discoveries. (2) The bacteria are so numerous that in a single gram of fertile soil may contain as many as 100-million bacteria. (3) As separate individuals, other organisms are outnumbered by bacteria. (4) They exist everywhere: in the bodies of all living creatures, inside Antarctic rocks, in all parts of the ocean, even the stratosphere. (5) Sulfur-loving bacteria provides a life-enhancing function in the ecosystem huddled around volcanic vents in the ocean, where sunlight never reaches and temperatures exceed the boiling point of water.

(5) Bacteria are paradoxical: they keep us alive ... and sometimes try to kill us. (6) The words *bacterial infection* reminds us that there are harmful bacteria that can seriously impact the quality of life. (7) The human body is fortunately equipped to counteract bacterial infections with antibodies, but the immune system cannot handle all infections by itself. (8) Antibiotics and other approaches like vaccination and tetanus shots they can help for a while, but in the course of natural selection, mutations arise that prove immune to the weapons.

(9) Though the very word *bacteria* frightens people, the vast majority of bacteria either are harmless or even beneficial to mankind. (10) Bacteria assist in decomposition of organic matter, in soil enrichment, pickling, fermentation, cheese making, and other specialized processes. (11) On balance, bacteria are life-enhancing.

15. Which revision is most needed in sentence 1?

(A) Change *life* to *life forms*.

(B) Reverse *exist only* to *only exist*.

(C) Replace *and* with *but* to begin the second clause.

(D) Change *there* to *their*.

(E) Change *challenge* to *confirm*.

15 _____

16. Which revision is most needed in sentence 2?

(A) Replace *the bacteria* with *those*.

(B) Replace *so* with *quite*.

(C) Omit *in*.

(D) Change *may* to *will*.

(E) Omit the hyphen in *100-million*.

16 _____

17. Which revised sentence is an improved version of sentence 3?

    (A) As separate individuals, the number of bacteria surpasses that for other organisms.

    (B) Other organisms, as separate individuals are outnumbered by bacteria.

    (C) As separate individuals, bacteria outnumber any other type of organism.

    (D) As separate individuals, there are more bacteria than any other type of organism.

    (E) Bacteria have been studied as individuals, and they outnumber other organisms.

    17 _____

18. Which revision is most needed in sentence 4?

    (A) Change *everywhere* to *everywheres*.

    (B) Replace the colon with a comma.

    (C) Change *bodies* to *body*.

    (D) Insert *of* after *inside*.

    (E) Insert *in* after *even*.

    18 _____

19. Which revision is most needed in sentence 8?

    (A) Replace the first *and* with *as well as*.

    (B) Omit *they* after *shots*.

    (C) Change *but* to *so*.

    (D) Change *course of natural selection* to *natural course of selection*.

    (E) Insert *and* after *arise*.

    19 _____

20. Which revision is most needed in sentence 9?

    (A) Replace *though* with *as*.

    (B) Change *very* to *terrifying*.

    (C) Replace *majority* with *plurality*.

    (D) Reverse *either are* to *are either*.

    (E) Replace *even* with *astoundingly*.

    20 _____

Section 4   Writing the Essay

Consider carefully the following excerpt and the assignment following it. Then plan and write an essay that explains your ideas as persuasively as possible. Keep in mind that the support you provide—both reasons and examples—will help make your view convincing to the reader.

To waste, to destroy, our natural resources, to skin and exhaust the land instead of using it so as to increase its usefulness, will result in undermining in the days of our children the very prosperity which we ought by right to hand down to them amplified and developed.

Theodore Roosevelt in a Message to Congress, December 3, 1907.

Assignment: It has been about a century since Roosevelt's stirring message. How has America done? Is government taking enough steps to preserve the environment? What role should the public play? In an essay, present your appraisal of governmental failures or successes. Provide suggestions and specific examples.

Part One   Review of Writing Skills

Section I: Writing Skills—
The Single Sentence

The French writer Anatol France once wrote, "Caress your sentence tenderly; it will end up smiling at you."

All writing begins with the sentence; yet the sentence is often ignored, left to watch out for itself. This section will direct your attention to the sentence. It will ask you to judge between good and bad sentences. It will encourage you to write some good sentences.

TRIAL TEST

Which sentence in each pair do you consider better? Tell why.

(Answers to this and other Trial Tests begin on page 551, included with answers to Writing Exercises and Reviews.)

1. (A) We went on the roller coaster and then we went on the flume ride and then we went on the monorail.
   (B) We went on the roller coaster, the flume ride, and the monorail.

   _____

   _____

2. (A) At the library, I picked up a Sherlock Holmes detective story and a book about photography.
   (B) I went to the library and I picked up a detective story about Sherlock Holmes and a book that tells all about photography.

   _____

   _____

Characteristics of Good Sentences

Sentences are of many types, varied in style and subject matter. Yet good sentences have certain qualities in common.

1. Good sentences don't waste words. They use only enough words to carry the thought. They don't wander. They make their point . . . and stop (pages 401–405).

WORDY:	The difficulties we cause in this all-too-brief life of ours are often those that we bring upon ourselves, even if unintentionally.
ECONOMICAL:	Most of the shadows of this life are caused by our standing in our own sunshine. (Ralph Waldo Emerson)

2. Good sentences are clear. They express a thought clearly and directly (pages 406–410).

MUDDLED:	Gil got up to bat and sent it into the right-field stands.
CLEAR:	Gil got up to bat and sent the ball into the right-field stands.

3. Good sentences have unity. They stick to one general topic in a sentence (pages 416–420).

LACKING IN UNITY:	Good tennis players don't have to work very hard, but golfers sometimes seem to enjoy the game more.
UNIFIED:	If you see a tennis player who looks as if he is working very hard, then that means he isn't very good. (Helen Wills Moody)

4. Good sentences are coherent, using accurate connectives (pages 407–409).

LACKING COHERENCE:	Because Sue was our best pitcher, she didn't get a chance to pitch in the playoffs.
COHERENT:	Although Sue was our best pitcher, she didn't get a chance to pitch in the playoffs.

5. Good sentences are varied in structure. They do not always follow a set pattern (pages 410–416).

MONOTONOUS:	Edgar is handsome and rich. He is also a fine artist. I envy him.
VARIED:	Edgar is not only handsome and rich, but also a fine artist. How I envy him!

6. Good sentences call upon strong, specific nouns and vivid verbs to carry the thought. They use adjectives and adverbs sparingly but effectively (pages 445–449).

DULL:	The duck landed on the ice unsuccessfully and finally came to a stop after a long slide along the ice on the pond.
VIVID:	The mallard landed uncertainly on the ice, skidded and flopped along for twenty feet, and then scrambled to its feet with dignity.

7. Good sentences are pleasing to read, usually an enjoyable part of a larger whole (pages 421–432).

8. Good sentences are complete, neither fragments (pages 438–443) nor run-ons (pages 443–444).

9. Good sentences are technically correct, using correct usage (pages 433–473) and correct spelling (pages 474–477).

Problem

Which sentence in each of the following pairs do you consider better?

1. (A) Although we sometimes seem overwhelmed by the common housefly, actually a single individual lives only two weeks.

   (B) We sometimes seem overwhelmed by the common housefly, because a single individual lives only two weeks.

2. (A) The letter *m* is commonly used to begin a word, like the word for *mother*, as is demonstrated in most of the world's languages.

   (B) In the vast majority of the world's languages, the word for *mother* begins with the letter *m*.

Strategy. The best English sentence makes its point economically and efficiently. (1A) accurately expresses the relationship between being overwhelmed and the short life of the housefly. *Because*, in (1B), suggests incorrectly that our being overwhelmed occurs because the housefly has a short life. The shorter sentence isn't necessarily the better, though in (2B), brevity expresses the central point. (2A) is unnecessarily wordy.

Writing Exercise 1   Proverbs

From the proverbs listed below, select two. For each, write a one-sentence restatement. Try to capture the same meaning. Because proverbs are by nature concise, rephrasing is a challenge.

> A burnt child dreads the fire.
>
> Actions speak louder than words.
>
> Soft words don't scratch the tongue.
>
> Always have two strings to your bow.
>
> Every man is his brother's keeper.
>
> Man shall not live by bread alone.
>
> Expect to be treated as you have treated others.
>
> Don't saw off the branch you're sitting on.
>
> If you want to lead, you must be able to follow.
>
> The bigger they are, the harder they fall.

EXAMPLE

Original: You never miss the water till the well runs dry.

Restated: You often fail to appreciate things until you lose them.

_____

_____

Writing Exercise 2   Eliminating Jargon

Restate each of the following jumbled sentences in clear English

ORIGINAL: If one studies snowfall on an annual basis, one will find that Salt Lake City experiences more snowfall on average than does Fairbanks, Alaska.

RESTATED: On the average, Salt Lake City gets more snowfall annually than Fairbanks, Alaska.

1. My father rendered a negative decision on the subject of my solicitation to use the family car Saturday night.

2. It is requested that all pedestrians refrain from walking across those areas that have been planted in grass.

_____

_____

_____

_____

Writing Exercise 3   Completing Sentences

Select two of the following. Complete each to make a good sentence.

Medicating a cat is …   That summer job …

My experiences on the Internet are …   My opinion of action movies …

Taking a test …   When I got behind the wheel …

My pet peeve is …

_____

_____

_____

_____

_____

REVIEW

Which sentence in each pair do you consider better? Tell why.

1. (A) Macbeth informed Lady Macbeth that she would be most favorably impressed by a deed which he was contemplating though he did not wish her to achieve the status of actual complicity in the action.

   (B) Macbeth hinted to Lady Macbeth of a deed that she would approve, though he wished her innocent of the action.

2. (A) Being able to say goodbye quickly and gracefully is an art unmastered by some visitors.

   (B) Some visitors can't say goodbye quickly and gracefully and they stand and they keep talking on and on.

3. (A) Poison oak and poison ivy are enemies of gardeners and hikers, and they are surprisingly related to those much-loved cashews.

   (B) Poison oak and poison ivy, enemies of gardeners and hikers, are related to those much-loved cashews.

SUMMARY
The Single Sentence

Writing a single sentence is the basic achievement of all writing. Deceptively simple, a good sentence challenges slovenliness of expression, undisciplined construction, wordiness, and muddled thinking. The old political slogan KISS is often appropriate here: "Keep it simple, stupid."

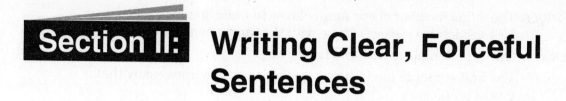

Section II: Writing Clear, Forceful Sentences

Good writing has four major characteristics: economy, clarity, variety, and unity.

Economy

Never make a thought more complicated than it really is. If you can express yourself simply and directly, do so. Here are some errors to avoid.

Useless Words

Eliminate all useless words.

WORDY: At the soccer match, Joel met up with two friends from elementary school.
CONCISE: At the soccer match, Joel met two friends from elementary school.

Duplication

Avoid saying the same thing twice, even though in different words.

WORDY: The football Giants flew to Buffalo by air, but had to return by bus because of a lake-effect blizzard.
CONCISE: The football Giants flew to Buffalo, but returned by bus because of a lake-effect blizzard.

Wordy Construction

Don't use too many words to express an idea. Condense a phrase (see page 438) to a word, a clause to a phrase or even a word. Be a *which* hunter and eliminate all unnecessary *whiches*.

WORDY: The newscast which was televised this morning on a local station described a suspicious car which had a license plate from the state of North Dakota.
CONCISE: This morning's local television newscast described a suspicious car with a North Dakota license plate.

Pretentious Language

Unless you are being humorous, don't use a longer word if a simpler word will do the job. Save the longer word for a context in which the simpler word is not as meaningful.

PRETENTIOUS: The feline member of our family loves to frolic, gambol, and cavort
for considerable periods of time with the canine member of our family ménage.

SIMPLER: Our cat often plays with the family dog.

NOTE: The first sentence might be acceptable in a humorous essay that
mocks pretension.

Piled-up Modifiers

Don't pile adjective upon adjective, adverb upon adverb. Where possible, use specific
nouns and verbs to reduce the number of modifiers.

WORDY: The young, immature baby of but a year walked unsteadily and shakily
across the floor into the outstretched, waiting arms of her waiting mother.

CONCISE: The one-year-old tottered across the floor into her mother's outstretched arms.

The No-No Group

Some expressions, like weeds, should be eradicated and replaced.

Avoid	**Say and Write**
at all times	always
at the present time	now
due to the fact that, for the reason that, in view of the fact that	as, because, since
inasmuch as	since
in order to, with a view to	to
in the amount of	for
in the case of, in the event that, in the event of	if
in the meantime	meanwhile
in the near future	soon
in the neighborhood of	nearly, about, around
in this place	here
previous to, prior to	before
there can be no doubt that	doubtless
with reference to, with regard to	about

The Duplicators

These common expressions include unnecessary words.

cheap ~~in price~~

combined ~~together~~

connect ~~up~~, finish ~~up~~, end ~~up~~, join ~~up~~

~~every~~ once in a while

gray ~~in color~~

I think ~~in my opinion~~

inside ~~of~~

long ~~length of~~ time

meet ~~up with~~

modern colleges ~~of today~~

rarely ~~ever~~

requirements ~~needed~~ for

round ~~in shape~~

small ~~in size~~

the ~~two~~ twins

throughout the ~~whole~~ night

TRIAL TEST

Using the preceding sections as a guide, rewrite the following sentences to make them more concise. Suggested answers are on page 551.

1. It was in 1949 that Molehill, West Virginia, changed its name to *Mountain*.

_____

_____

2. At the Career Conference which was given for seniors this year, students could learn what were the requirements needed for beginners in any or all of ten different fields of endeavor.

_____

_____

3. Inasmuch as I can't use the Braves tickets, I'll give them to my brother.

_____

_____

4. My dream is to own a car along the lines of a Toyota Tercel.

_____

_____

5. When pressed for an answer to the question, the witness hesitantly answered in the affirmative.

_____

_____

6. Taking into consideration the fact that tomorrow is a holiday, I'll take Jennie to the picnic.

_____

_____

7. In the absence of Sylvia, we'll have to put Jennifer at forward.

_____

_____

8. We are writing to tell you that we regret to tell you that we are unable to fill your order as sent.

_____

_____

Problem

Which sentence in each of the following pairs do you consider better?

1. (A) Unlike most fruit trees, an orange tree may bear fruit for more than a hundred years.

   (B) The orange tree does not have the fruiting qualities of most trees, for it may bear fruit for more than 100 years.

2. (A) Though a sheet sounds like a sail, it is actually, in nautical terms at least, a rope or chain.

   (B) In nautical terms, a sheet is a rope or chain, not a sail.

3. (A) Of the equine breed, the Paso Fino is a horse that is relatively small but with a distinctive, appealing gait.

   (B) The Paso Fino is a relatively small horse with a distinctive, appealing gait.

Strategy. Though the same message is conveyed in both (1A) and (1B), (1B) uses more words than necessary to make the point. Duplication of _for_ is a distraction. (2A) uses a complex sentence, beginning with _though_, to provide the same information given in the more concise (2B). (3A) is hopelessly verbose, with the affected _of the equine breed_ and an unnecessary subordinate clause introduced by _that_. (3B) provides the same information simply and economically.

Writing Exercise 1   Writing Concisely

Rewrite the following sentences to make them more concise. Keep in mind the preceding suggestions.

EXAMPLE

PADDED: Anyone who confines his interests to himself and his own affairs is bound, in the end, to amount to very little in life and because of his selfish interests has stunted his chances of self-development.

CONCISE: A man wrapped up in himself makes a very small bundle. (Benjamin Franklin)

1. In the *Matrix* movies, they tell the story of nonhuman robots that have the goal of ruling the world.

_____

_____

2. I'm writing this note in order to tell you that I am very sorry and regret that I'll have to miss the class reunion.

_____

_____

3. There were three Buccaneer linemen and two running backs who were chosen to play a role in the Pro Bowl in Hawaii.

_____

_____

Writing Exercise 2   Identifying Familiar Proverbs

Identify the familiar proverb restated in each of the following sentences.

1. Always look in all directions before you propel yourself into the unknown.

_____

_____

2. Having an overabundance of cooks is likely to have a negative effect on the broth being prepared.

_____

_____

3. The grassy vegetation seems a more attractive shade of green when noticed on the other side of the fence.

_____

_____

Clarity

Write clearly as well as concisely. Here are some errors to avoid.

Unclear Antecedents

Make certain that a pronoun has a clear antecedent (464). Reword the sentences, supply a needed noun, or quote the exact words of the speaker.

CONFUSING:	Use that towel to mop your brow and put it in the clothes hamper. (The brow or the towel?)
CLEAR:	Use that towel to mop your brow and put the towel in the clothes hamper.
CONFUSING:	If papers are left behind by untidy hikers, burn them.
CLEAR:	Any papers left behind by untidy hikers should be burned.
CONFUSING:	Sally told her mother that she had left the lawn sprinklers on. (Is the antecedent of "she" Sally or her mother?)
CLEAR:	Sally told her mother, "I left the lawn sprinklers on."
CLEAR:	Sally told her mother, "You left the lawn sprinklers on."

Dangling Modifiers and Appositives

A modifier dangles if it is placed so that it seems to modify a word it was not intended to modify. Put a modifier close to the word it modifies. Sometimes the word itself must be supplied. Check every appositive at the beginning of a sentence to make sure that it doesn't dangle.

DANGLING:	Turning the corner, the post office was on the left. (The post office was not turning the corner.)
CLEAR:	Turning the corner, I noticed the post office on my left.
CLEAR:	As I turned the corner, I noticed the post office on my left.
CONFUSING:	Terry saw a deer riding her bike through the Hopkins meadow.
CLEAR:	Riding her bike through the Hopkins meadow, Terry saw a deer.
CONFUSING:	At the age of three, Mark's mother remarried.
CLEAR:	When Mark was three, his mother remarried.
CONFUSING:	While working in the library, a new shipment of books arrived.
CLEAR:	While I was working in the library, a new shipment of books arrived.
CONFUSING:	At the party, packages were given to all the children filled with Halloween candy. (The children may be filled later!)
CLEAR:	At the party, packages filled with Halloween candy were given to all the children.
DANGLING:	One of our most popular foods, people once considered the tomato poisonous.
CLEAR:	One of our most popular foods, the tomato was once considered poisonous.

Inaccurate Connectives

Use the connective that expresses your thought accurately.

CONDITION: *If* it rains
TIME: When Dan arrives
CAUSE: *Because* I forgot my lines
CONCESSION: *Although* I have never danced before

And equals *plus*; *but* equals *minus*.

CONFUSING: Emily Dickinson wrote more than 900 poems, and only four were published during her lifetime.

CLEAR: Emily Dickinson wrote more than 900 poems, but only four were published during her lifetime.

CONFUSING: Because the wattage is the same, one 75-watt bulb gives more light than three 25-watt bulbs.

CLEAR: Although the wattage is the same, one 75-watt bulb gives more light than three 25-watt bulbs.

The Inexact Word

Be sure to choose the word that expresses your thought clearly, exactly, and completely.

CONFUSING: The greatest problem of the rescue patrol was good visibility.

CLEAR: The greatest problem of the rescue patrol was poor visibility.

CONFUSING: Our Saturday project is to install all broken windows in the school.

CLEAR: Our Saturday project is to replace all broken windows in the school.

CONFUSING: Don't fail to miss tonight's rerun of *Seinfeld*.

CLEAR: Don't miss tonight's rerun of *Seinfeld*.

CLEAR: Don't fail to see tonight's rerun of *Seinfeld*.

Writing Exercise 3   Choosing Clear Sentences

In each pair of sentences, choose the clearer one and point out why the chosen sentence is preferable.

1. (A) Listening for a cardinal's song, my attention was captured by the cawing of a crow.

   (B) As I was listening for a cardinal's song, my attention was captured by the cawing of a crow.

   _____

   _____

2. (A) Maria told Consuelo, "You've just won the athlete-of-the month award."

   (B) Maria told Consuelo that she had just won the athlete-of-the month award.

_____

_____

3. (A) We thought everyone had accepted Hank's suggestion, and suddenly Jason got up to object strongly.

   (B) We thought everyone had accepted Hank's suggestion, but suddenly Jason got up to object strongly.

_____

_____

4. (A) Regular attendance is a major cause of failure in school.

   (B) Irregular attendance is a major cause of failure in school.

_____

_____

5. (A) I used moist heat for my sore elbow, and it disappeared.

   (B) I used moist heat for my sore elbow, and the soreness disappeared.

_____

_____

Writing Exercise 4   Writing Clearly

Rewrite the following sentences to make them clearer. Before beginning, briefly review the preceding suggestions.

1. Grandma loves to watch passersby sitting in her chair on the porch.

_____

_____

2. Carl told his brother that he had been accepted at Duke University.

_____

_____

3. Because Ellen had been away for the summer vacation, she still was able to return for Sandra's birthday party.

_____

_____

4. Having misplaced my ticket, my chance of seeing the Bulls play the Lakers was slim.

_____

_____

5. The problem of driving to Craggy Gardens on the Blue Ridge Parkway was good visibility.

_____

_____

Vague, General Words

To add clarity and forcefulness to your writing, use specific words.

GENERAL dog, flower, fruit, predator, star

CONCRETE papillon, gladiolus, mango, cheetah, Antares

VAGUE: We walked up a steep peak and rejoiced at the top.

SPECIFIC: We clambered up the cone of Mt. Katahdin and shouted, "We made it!"

VAGUE: On our western trip, we visited three national parks.

SPECIFIC: On our western trip, we visited Rocky Mountain National Park, Grand Canyon, and Bryce Canyon.

VAGUE: We had several different kinds of transportation.

SPECIFIC: We tried horseback riding, canoeing, and helicoptering.

Writing Exercise 5   Using Specific Words

Rewrite the following sentences, using a specific word to replace the italicized general words.

1. In _school_, we studied _a play_.

_____

_____

2. I enjoy *a hobby* especially when I am tired after a *hard* day.

_____

_____

3. I visited the library and took out *a book* and *a magazine*.

_____

_____

Variety

To keep your readers interested, introduce variety into your writing. Don't get into a rut. For maximum effect, vary both the length and type of sentence.

Length of Sentence

Conciseness is always a desirable goal. By avoiding padding and unnecessary words, you can create a concise sentence. Note that the following sentences use words economically, though they vary in length.

SHORT: In fair weather, prepare for foul. (Thomas Fuller)

LONGER: If you think you're tops, you won't do much climbing. (Arnold Glasow)

STILL LONGER: There is only one thing better than making a new friend and that
   is keeping an old one. (Elmer G. Leterman)

Type of Sentence

For variety, use an occasional question, exclamation, or command, but don't overdo.

QUESTION: Where did I leave my tennis racket?

EXCLAMATION: I just remembered—the public courts!

COMMAND: Call the pro shop and say I'm on my way.

POLITE REQUEST: Please let my mother know I'll be late.

Subject-Not-First Sentence

Avoid monotony. Don't begin every sentence with the subject. When a shift in placement is both natural and effective, begin a sentence with a word other than the subject. Again, don't overdo.

ADVERB: Wearily, the home team went onto the field for the fifteenth inning.

ADVERB PHRASE: After much soul-searching, Carla decided to enroll in a premed course.

ADVERB CLAUSE: Although yellow sweet corn is more abundant in our area, Dad and I prefer the white.

THERE: There are still many undiscovered galaxies.

PREPOSITIONAL PHRASE: Contrary to popular belief, a person's hair cannot turn white overnight.

PARTICIPIAL PHRASE: Finding the passage blocked, the cave explorers retraced their steps.

INFINITIVE PHRASE: To melt its way through spring snows, the skunk cabbage runs temperatures higher than its surroundings.

PREPOSITIONAL PHRASE WITH GERUND: Before starting the car, adjust seat belts and rearview mirrors.

APPOSITIVE: A language expert for the United Nations, Georges Schmidt can translate 66 languages.

NOUN CLAUSE: How Indiana Jones could escape his deadly antagonist, no one could have anticipated.

As for all ways to achieve variety, the inverting device can be overdone. In poking fun at one magazine's habit of inverting sentences, Wolcott Gibbs wrote, "Backward run sentences until reeled the mind."

Writing Exercise 6   Writing Subject-Not-First Sentences

Revise each of the sentences by placing a word or words before the subject.

1. The ideograph for "trouble" in the Chinese written language shows two women under one roof.

_____

_____

2. Forbid your kids to do it if you want to get something done.

_____

_____

3. Mosquitoes survive in cold weather, unlike the common housefly.

_____

_____

4. Al Gore, winner of the popular vote, lost the election in 2000 to George W. Bush, winner of the electoral vote.

_____

_____

5. Mozart died at 36 after a life filled with diverse achievements in music.

_____

_____

Appositives

Use appositives to achieve conciseness and vary the sentence structure.

WITHOUT APPOSITIVES: The eagle, which is the U.S. national symbol, won out over the turkey, which was Benjamin Franklin's choice.

WITH APPOSITIVES: The eagle, the U.S. national symbol, won out over the turkey, Benjamin Franklin's choice.

WITHOUT APPOSITIVE: A thick slice of bread that was stale and unappetizing was once used as the dinner plate.

WITH APPOSITIVE: A thick slice of bread, stale and unappetizing, was once used as the dinner plate.

WITHOUT APPOSITIVE: Caligula was a ruthless emperor of Rome, and he got his name from the military boots he wore as a child.

WITH APPOSITIVE: Caligula, a ruthless emperor of Rome, got his name from the military boots he wore as a child.

Writing Exercise 7   Using Appositives

In each of the following, substitute an appositive for a clause or a sentence.

1. Napoleon Bonaparte, who was a military genius, had once been expelled from the army in disgrace.

_____

_____

2. Connemara is a lovely old estate in Flat Rock, North Carolina. It was once the home of the poet Carl Sandburg.

_____

_____

3. Ted Moorhead, who is always happy and upbeat, is a source of inspiration to his friends.

_____

_____

4. Chester Carlson was the inventor of the dry copying process. He had previously had the idea for the ballpoint pen.

_____

_____

Compound Subjects

For variety and conciseness, combine two separate sentences into a single sentence with a compound subject.

Two Sentences: Terriers make excellent pets. Retrievers do also.
Compound Subject: Terriers and retrievers make excellent pets.

Compound Predicates

Avoid the _and I, and we, and they_ habit. Use an occasional compound predicate instead of a compound sentence or two separate sentences.

Compound Sentence: I visited the local library, and I found the latest mystery by P.D. James.
Compound Predicate: I visited the local library and found the latest mystery by P.D. James.
Two Sentences: _Gone with the Wind_ was rejected many times. It was finally published.
Compound Predicate: _Gone with the Wind_ was rejected many times but was finally published.

Writing Exercise 8   Using Compound Subjects and Compound Predicates

Condense each of the following by substituting compound subjects and predicates for pairs of simple sentences or for compound sentences.

1. We visited the Grand Canyon, and then we headed toward the Petrified Forest.

   _____

   _____

2. The Peace Corps helps Third World countries with their problems. It also broadens the lives of the volunteers.

   _____

   _____

3. Charles Babbage thought out the basic principles of modern computers. He didn't have electronic solutions for his challenges.

   _____

   _____

Complex Sentences

Avoid a string of simple or compound sentences. Use complex sentences (page 435) to add variety and show more accurately the connection between ideas. By using complex sentences, you can avoid overusing *and, but,* and *so.*

SIMPLE SENTENCES: Thomas Edison was still in possession of his sight. He found braille preferable to visual reading.

COMPLEX SENTENCE: Though he was still in possession of his sight, Thomas Edison found braille preferable to visual reading.

COMPOUND SENTENCE: The thin atmosphere at 12,000 feet above sea level barely supports fire, and La Paz, Bolivia, is nearly a fireproof city.

COMPLEX SENTENCE: Because the thin atmosphere at 12,000 feet above sea level barely supports fire, La Paz, Bolivia, is nearly a fireproof city.

Writing Exercise 9   Creating Complex Sentences

By using proper connectives (page 407), combine each of the following into a sound complex sentence.

1. The Navajo language is difficult to master, and it was used as a code by the United States in World War II.

   _____

   _____

2. Berengaria, wife of Richard the Lion-Hearted, was queen of England. She never even visited there.

_____

_____

3. Charlotte was weeding the vegetable patch, and Dan was watering the extensive lawn.

_____

_____

4. We must support efforts to save wild plants. They may yet provide cures for presently incurable disease.

_____

_____

5. Harry S. Truman had been expected to lose the election. He won a smashing victory over Thomas E. Dewey.

_____

_____

Using Verbals

For variety, introduce verbals (pages 440–441) into your writing.

WITHOUT PARTICIPLE: I discovered an interest in various kinds of mushrooms. I decided to take a course in botany.

WITH PARTICIPLE: Having discovered an interest in various kinds of mushrooms, I decided to take a course in botany.

WITHOUT GERUND: I met Bette, a feisty Norwich terrier with an attitude, and then I fell victim to her irresistible personality.

WITH GERUND: After meeting Bette, a feisty Norwich terrier with an attitude, I fell victim to her irresistible personality.

WITHOUT INFINITIVE: Lars read *Plutarch's Lives* in order that he might learn more about the Roman emperors.

WITH INFINITIVE: Lars read *Plutarch's Lives* to learn more about the Roman emperors.

Writing Exercise 10   Using Verbals

Improve these sentences by using verbals for some of the verbs.

1. Paul had studied Spanish for three years in high school. He nervously asked directions in Madrid. (use *after*.)

_____

_____

2. Thomas Edison unsuccessfully tried hundreds of filaments for the lightbulb. Then he found the perfect filament.

_____

_____

3. In order that she might be chosen for Guinevere in *Camelot*, Tonya practiced the songs over and over.

_____

_____

4. Hercule Poirot gathered the suspects together and identified the murderer.

_____

_____

5. I discovered a keen interest in flower arrangement and took a course in ikebana, the Japanese art of flower arranging.

_____

_____

Unity

Unity is oneness. Be sure that every part of a sentence is related to one main idea.

Lack of Unity

Correct a lack of unity by breaking a sentence into shorter sentences or by subordinating one part of a sentence to a main part. (See also pages 436–438; 441–442) A sentence may lack unity because a part of a thought has been omitted.

LACKING UNITY: The cockroach is a survivor, and the body can survive for weeks if the head is carefully removed.

HAVING UNITY: The cockroach is a survivor. The body can survive for weeks if the head is carefully removed.

LACKING UNITY: The ancestors of the horse were only a foot tall, and modern Percherons may stand over five feet at the shoulders.

HAVING UNITY: Although the ancestors of the horse were only a foot tall, modern Percherons may stand over five feet at the shoulders.

LACKING UNITY: We seniors weren't able to publish a yearbook, and our graduation is June 3.

HAVING UNITY: We seniors weren't able to publish a yearbook, but we'll console ourselves with graduation on June 3.

Overlapping Construction

Avoid using a series of overlapping *that*, *which*, or *who* clauses. These create a house-that-Jack-built sentence: "This is the dog that chased the cat that killed the rat, that ate the malt that lay in the house that Jack built." Also avoid piling up possessives of possessives.

POOR: My sister's friend's father's lineage can be traced back to the Mayflower

BETTER: My sister has a friend whose father can trace his lineage back to the Mayflower

UNWIELDY: In the 1860s, a New York firm offered a prize which would be given for a satisfactory substitute for ivory which was used in the manufacture of billiard balls which were in demand because of the growing popularity of billiards.

MANAGEABLE: In the 1860s, a New York firm offered a prize for an ivory substitute. Ivory had been used in the manufacture of billiard balls for the increasingly popular game of billiards.

Parallel Structure

Be sure items are parallel. Ordinarily, *and* and *but* connect like grammatical elements—for example, two or more nouns, verbs, adjectives, phrases, or clauses.

NOT PARALLEL: At camp, we most enjoyed swimming, hiking, and how to play volleyball.

PARALLEL: At camp, we most enjoyed swimming, hiking, and playing volleyball.

NOT PARALLEL: Our dog Jolly is tiny, a rich brown coat, and a perky disposition.

PARALLEL: Our dog Jolly is tiny, wears a rich brown coat, and has a perky disposition.

NOT PARALLEL: The atmosphere of the earth filters the sun's rays, and making the sun seem unusually red at sunset.

PARALLEL: The atmosphere of the earth filters the sun's rays and makes the sun seem unusually red at sunset.

Correct Use of Correlatives

Correlative conjunctions are placed just before the words or expressions they connect (pages 407; 460–461).

POOR: Michael Vick not only excels in passing but in his ability to evade tacklers.

IMPROVED: Michael Vick excels not only in passing but in his ability to evade tacklers.

Writing Exercise 11   Achieving Sentence Unity

Make each of the following sentences unified. Follow the suggestions in the preceding pages.

1. The well-rounded tennis player has a good serve, a strong forehand, and he must have a dependable backhand.

_____

_____

2. John F. Kennedy was the first U.S. President to be born in the twentieth century, and he didn't take office until 1961.

_____

_____

3. James Madison was the shortest President, who was only five feet four inches tall and who weighed only a hundred pounds.

_____

_____

4. A professional basketball player should be tall, agile, with a great deal of courage.

_____

_____

5. Four times the Wright brothers flew that first airborne plane which was finally struck by a gust of wind which overturned it and wrecked it.

_____

_____

6. The original *Star Trek* series only had a mild success during its run.

_____

_____

REVIEW

Which choice in each pair do you consider better? Tell why.

1. (A) Paul told his brother Lloyd that he had won the lottery.
    (B) Paul told his brother Lloyd that he, Lloyd had won the lottery.

2. (A) Sea otters are the acrobats of the sea, and they are fascinating to watch.
    (B) Sea otters, the acrobats of the sea, are fascinating to watch.

3. (A) Although Neanderthal man has often been looked down upon as an inferior being, his brain size was actually larger than modern man's.
    (B) Neanderthal man has often been looked down upon as an inferior being. His brain size was actually larger than modern man's.

4. (A) To see the new *Harry Potter* movie, Suellen waited in line all night.
    (B) In order that she might get to see the new *Harry Potter* movie, Suellen waited in line all night.

5. (A) Sandra not only won a modern dictionary in the spelling bee but also a reprint of Noah Webster's *Compendious Dictionary* published in 1806.
    (B) Sandra won not only a modern dictionary in the spelling bee but also a reprint of Noah Webster's *Compendious Dictionary* published in 1806.

SUMMARY

If a thought can be expressed simply and directly, choose that route.

Conciseness. As a general guide, simplicity is the most effective strategy.

Clarity. Avoid unclear antecedents, dangling modifiers, inaccurate connectives, and muddy, general words.

Variety. Vary the length of your sentences but keep in mind the comment about simplicity above. The use of compound predicates, complex sentences, and verbals can achieve variety without falling into one of the traps mentioned above. Be sure your sentences are unified.

Unity. Achieve unity in your sentences by concentrating on one idea.

Section III: Writing the Paragraph

You have been writing single sentences that are complete in themselves. The next step in the art of writing is the paragraph. The ideal paragraph, like each of the single sentences in the preceding two sections, develops one idea.

Paragraphs vary greatly in length, but each one says, in effect, "Here is something new." The first line of a new paragraph is indented to indicate that "something new" is coming.

As a general rule, when you write, begin a new paragraph:

> in a *description*—when you change the mood or the point of view
> in an *explanation*—when you begin to develop a new idea
> in a *story*—when you change the time, the place, or the action
> in a *written conversation*—when you change the speaker

Characteristics of Good Paragraphs

Two closely related types of paragraphs are the paragraph to explain and the paragraph to persuade. The first type, often called the *expository paragraph*, attempts to explain a process, a point of view, or a concept. The paragraph to persuade is similar to the expository paragraph, but its principal purpose is not just to explain, though that may be part of the strategy. It intends to change a point of view, urge a course of action, or win converts.

The following suggestions apply to paragraphs of exposition and persuasion. The sample paragraph provided below includes both types.

1. A good paragraph develops one topic and sticks to that topic. It often provides a ***topic sentence*** to help the reader know what's ahead.
2. A good paragraph supports the topic sentence with examples, details, and comparisons.
3. A good paragraph is arranged in a sensible, easy-to-follow order. It uses connecting words like *this, since, when, and, but,* and *which* to tie parts of the paragraph together.
4. A good paragraph has interest-catching beginnings and forceful endings.
5. A good paragraph uses vivid, exact words.

<u>Every inhabitant of this blue ball in space has a responsibility to preserve our fragile environment especially that thin layer of topsoil.</u> This precious resource is rarely more than a foot or two thick, but this tiny layer supports all the world's agriculture . . . and life on earth. Every farmer in every land depends upon the fertility of this fragile skin. All the cattle and other domesticated animals depend upon it for grazing. All the trees and shrubs need it for their food. Through the vegetation it supports, the topsoil holds precious moisture in reserve, ready for our use. When the soil is abused or lost through erosion, an invaluable resource may be lost forever. <u>Since our lives depend upon this delicate layer, we all should be concerned about its conservation.</u>

1. This paragraph develops one topic: our responsibility in preserving a precious resource, the thin layer of topsoil that makes life possible. It opens with the topic sentence (underlined).

2. This paragraph uses details to support the topic sentence: importance to all agriculture; dependence of farmers, cattle, trees, and shrubs; water retention.

3. The paragraph is easy to follow. It uses connecting words like *but, this, when,* and *since* to tie parts of the paragraph together.

4. It has a good beginning. It also has a forceful ending (underlined).

5. For effect, it uses vivid words like *priceless resource, fragile skin,* and *delicate layer.*

TRIAL TEST

Study this paragraph and be ready to point out how it displays each of the five characteristics mentioned above. Suggested answers are on page 552.

If you are seeking a fascinating hobby, try stamp collecting, rightly called *the hobby of kings* and *the king of hobbies*. Its popularity depends upon certain major appeals. First, stamps are easy to study and store. They take up little space. Second, stamps have many appeals for different people. Some hobbyists collect stamps of one or two countries. Others open their albums to the whole world. Still others collect topics like animals or stamps. Third, stamps are educational. They teach geography, history, economics, art, architecture, current events, and a host of other subjects. Finally, stamps open doors to other nations. Collectors correspond with people in other countries and learn something about how other people live. Start with a simple, inexpensive mixture of world stamps and then enter this fantastic world.

Problem

The following paragraph lacks a topic sentence. After you have read the paragraph, follow the directions below.

In 1987, a child accidentally punched a hole in a wall with a billiard cue. The owners had always assumed the wall was an outside wall, but there was a concealed space within. After the owners had stripped away layers of wallpaper they found a small door. There, beyond the door, was a secret compartment left behind by a family more than a century before. Inside the compartment was a bundle of letters. One of the envelopes had been postmarked in Natal, South Africa, and sent to Birmingham, England. The stamps on the cover exhibited a rare error, a lack of perforation between the upper and lower stamps in a block of four. The discovery was estimated to be worth more than $5,000.

Circle the letter of the best topic sentence.

(A) Stamp collecting can be a fascinating hobby.

(B) It pays to be persistent, for who knows what may result from sticking to a task?

(C) Who knows what treasure may still be found in attics and nooks of old houses?

(D) Correspondence between South Africa and England a century ago included some rare stamps.

Strategy.—Though all the suggested topic sentences bear some relationship to the contents of the paragraph, only one fits snugly (C). There are several weaknesses that topic sentences are prone to: too broad, too narrow, and off the topic. In the example, (A) is too broad, deserving of a book. (B) is too general, not tied directly enough to the paragraph. (D) misses the point of the paragraph, the combination of luck and persistence. (C) accurately introduces the paragraph and whets the reader's appetite to discover how and why.

Writing Exercise 1   Eliminating a Sentence That Does Not Belong

Read the following paragraph and follow the directions at the end.

(A) In the nineteenth century, new post offices in the United States often had colorful names. (B) As long as a proposed new name didn't conflict with an existing one, it was usually approved by the Post Office Department. (C) As a result, new names were unique and colorful. (D) At a Massachusetts town meeting to choose a name, everyone had a different idea beginning with "Why not...." (E) Because there was no agreement, *Why Not* became the official name. (F) A Missouri town submitted a number of names, all of which sounded peculiar. (G) *Peculiar* became the name of the town. (H) The names of products have unusual origins. (I) A California town couldn't agree either, and someone stated it wasn't likely the citizens would ever agree. (J) *Likely* became the accepted name. (K) A list of towns with unusual names, many of them still in existence, includes *Ordinary*, Virginia; *Bowlegs*, Oklahoma; *Truth or Consequences*, New Mexico; *Chosen*, Florida; *Dime Box*, Texas; *Coarsegold*, California; and *Waterproof*, Louisiana. (L) American place names reflect the hopes and experiences of a bygone era.

Circle the letter of the sentence that does not belong in the paragraph and tell why you consider it unnecessary or distracting.

A B C D E F G H I J K L

The Narrative

In the essay you will write for the SAT (pages 425–432), you may incorporate narrative elements to support your argument. Storytelling is one of the most ancient of all arts. It is probably the most popular of the four composition types: narration, exposition, persuasion, and description. These are seldom unmixed, however; all four types overlap at times.

The anecdote is always popular. The following anecdote not only tells a story; it deftly reveals a personality. It brings a chuckle and an appreciative nod toward our 30th President.

President Coolidge was known for two qualities: taciturnity and thrift. A visitor to the White House once asked if he might have one of the President's cigars for a friend who collected cigar bands. Coolidge thought a moment, took a cigar from the box, slipped off the band, and handed it to the surprised visitor.

Writing Exercise 2   Writing an Anecdote

Try your hand at a brief anecdote. One of the following may suggest a subject.

> An incident involving a celebrity or a historical personage
> An embarrassing moment
> A humorous personal experience
> A television blooper

Writing Exercise 3   Writing to Persuade

Choose one of the topic sentences listed below, or another of your choosing, and write a paragraph. Follow the suggestions listed previously.

1. For better health, choose a diet low in saturated fats and high in fiber.
2. If you are looking for an entertaining movie, with believable characters, see ____.
3. For a cleaner, better-managed city, support ____ in the next election.
4. For unmatched beauty, visit us here in New Hampshire (or any other state) in October.
5. For companionship, reliability, and continuing entertainment, choose a ____ as a pet.

Writing Exercise 4   Writing a Paragraph

Here's a challenge that will help prepare you for the SAT. Consider carefully the following excerpt and the assignment below it. Then plan and write a paragraph that explains your ideas as persuasively as possible. Within the limits of a paragraph, you must select only the salient points in your thinking. Keep in mind that the support you provide — both reasons and examples — will help make your view convincing to the reader.

> In a Florida school district, a parent objected to the inclusion of a certain book because it contained an objectionable racial epithet. She requested that the school board remove the book from the course of study. Supporters of the book insisted that the book had been accepted many years as a classic opposed to racism in any form. The epithet was a historical fact that illuminated our past and helped prevent such slurs in the future. A committee of educators had approved the book. The parent insisted that her child's welfare was her responsibility, that the epithet in any context was too sensitive to tolerate.

Assignment: Does a parent have the right to dictate school policy in the interests of the child? Or do a parent's actions come under the heading of unwarranted censorship? Take a position, providing reasons for encouraging the school board to accede to the request, or to reject it.

Section IV: Writing the Essay to Persuade

As the SAT information brochures state, the test checks the student's ability to write on demand. Since the test essay is written in a short period of time, it will not be a finished product, but a rough draft. The bulletin continues by saying the essay "will be persuasive in nature and will ask the student to take a position on an issue and support it with reasons and evidence from his or her reading, experience, or observation. It will elicit an open-ended response, allowing students to support their position in a variety of ways, including exposition and narration."

Since you will be writing a short essay in a 25-minute period, you will benefit by keeping in mind certain basic requirements. Practice and an awareness of standards can make these characteristics second nature in your writing.

Suggestions for Writing the Essay

1. Stick to your topic (pages 421–423).
2. Develop your point of view.
3. Don't waste words. Avoid padding and unnecessary details (pages 401–402).
4. Avoid confusion and ambiguity (pages 406–407; 409).
5. For coherence, use the right connecting words to join parts and correctly express relationships (pages 407–409).
6. Choose effective, specific words to give life to the writing (page 409).
7. Demonstrate sound English structure, without sentence fragments or run-ons (pages 438–444).
8. Avoid errors in grammar, usage, and spelling (pages 433–477).

Scoring Your Essay

Your essay will be rated on a 1–6 scale. The following will give you some idea of how the papers will be scored.

Score of 6
A paper in this category demonstrates clear and consistent competence, though it may have occasional errors. Such a paper:

- effectively and insightfully addresses the writing task

- is well organized and fully developed, using clearly appropriate examples to support ideas

- displays consistent facility in the use of language, demonstrating variety in sentence structure and range of vocabulary

Score of 5

A paper in this category demonstrates reasonably consistent competence, though it will have occasional errors or lapses in quality. Such a paper:

- effectively addresses the writing task

- is generally well organized and well developed, using appropriate examples to support ideas

- displays facility in the use of language, demonstrating some syntactic variety and range of vocabulary

Score of 4

A paper in this category demonstrates adequate competence with occasional errors and lapses in quality. Such a paper:

- addresses the writing task

- is organized and adequately developed, using examples to support ideas

- displays adequate but inconsistent facility in the use of language, presenting some errors in grammar or diction

- presents minimal sentence variety

Score of 3

A paper in this category demonstrates developing competence. Such a paper may contain one or more of the following weaknesses:

- inadequate organization or development

- inappropriate or insufficient details to support ideas

- an accumulation of errors in grammar, diction, or sentence structure

Score of 2

A paper in this category demonstrates some incompetence. Such a paper is flawed by one or more of the following weaknesses:

- poor organization

- thin development

- little or inappropriate detail to support ideas

- frequent errors in grammar, diction, and sentence structure

Score of 1

A paper in this category demonstrates incompetence. Such a paper is seriously flawed by one or more of the following weaknesses:

- very poor organization

- very thin development

- usage and syntactical errors so severe that meaning is somewhat obscured

TRIAL TEST

What is your opinion about the growing number of state lotteries? More and more states are adopting the lottery as a means of supplementing income and balancing budgets. Sometimes those lotteries are linked in the gigantic *Powerball* game, increasing the incentives. Should all remaining states adopt the lottery as a partial solution to continuing budget problems?

Assignment: What is your opinion? Should all states adopt the lottery? Support your point of view by supplying examples, pro or con. For this test, take a point of view and list five arguments you would use in developing your topic. (Answers will vary.)

_____

_____

_____

_____

_____

_____

_____

_____

_____

Problem

The following essay was written on the topic "Drivers should be prohibited from using cellphones while driving." After you have read the essay, identify the four errors listed.

(A) Drivers should be prohibited from using cellphones while a vehicle is moving. (B) Admittedly, cellphones are a wonderful device for helping keep friends in touch. (C) Not attending to the driving at the driver's full capacity has many hazards. (D) At best, the cellphone message itself is distracting. (E) At worst, it may include bad news that negatively affects the driver's judgment and reflexes. (F) Inevitably, although the driver is fumbling with his cellphone, only one hand is on the steering wheel. (G) His attention and performance seriously impaired. (H) If the cellphone malfunctions or the communication dies away, any attempt to restore the connection will take the driver's attention away from the road. (I) The dangers from the use of cellphones in moving cars, however, are probably exaggerated. (J) Driving requires 100% concentration, not the fraction left over while drivers use cellphones.

1. Sentence off the topic _____
2. Sentence fragment _____
3. Incorrect connecting word _____
4. Sentence with an opposing point of view _____

Strategy. Sentence (B) is off the topic. It doesn't support the argument being made elsewhere. Sentence (G) is a fragment. *Impaired* is part of a verb, not a complete predicate. Sentence (F) uses *although*, an incorrect connecting word here. *While* correctly suggests the time relationship. Sentence (I) actually runs counter to the arguments presented. After all those telling arguments, this sentence essentially discounts them.

Developing the Essay

Let's follow, step by step, the creation of an essay as required by the SAT.

Consider carefully the following excerpt and the assignment below it. Then plan and write an essay that explains your ideas as persuasively as possible. Keep in mind that the support you provide—both reasons and examples—will help make your view convincing to the reader.

> School news is not reported adequately in the community. Announcements in school and the school newspaper provide some coverage, but the importance of the school to the community is never realized. The local television station could fill the void by allotting five minutes of the local news telecast to school news, such as announcements of coming school events.

> **Assignment:** What is your view? Is school news adequately reported? Should the local channel devote a five-minute segment to school news?

In an essay, support your position by using arguments that might influence a local TV station manager to put your plan into effect.

As you plan the composition, be sure to:

- Keep in mind that you are trying to persuade the school board, not other students.
- State your opinion clearly.
- Give the school board *two* reasons for your opinion.
- *Explain* each of your two reasons fully.
- Organize what you write.

Test Strategy

The SAT essay is different from a typical school assignment. There is no time for a leisurely development of ideas on the topic. You must plunge right in. Whether or not you jot down a few points before you begin, or take a few moments to consider the approach you will take, you must waste no time in putting pen to paper. The actual writing process often starts the flow.

Items like the following might be jotted down briefly or organized in your mind as you go along:

1. Benefits to both school and station
2. News at a convenient time
3. Students and parents a large segment of the community
4. Limitations of school newspaper
5. Increase in interest and participation
6. Positive news to balance the negative
7. Information about school events, programs, goals

First Steps

State your position clearly at once.

> We have an important resource in our community, station WEXZ, but we are not taking advantage of it. Though it provides information for most groups in the community, it neglects one of the most important: the school. While it is true that the station provides coverage of local sports events, it neglects areas of interest to other groups. There are two reasons for supporting this argument.

What Then?

You have made your point immediately and concisely. Now you must expand your statement with examples, details, anything that reinforces the initial argument. You have mentioned two reasons. Develop each as quickly and concisely as you can.

> Those news reports would benefit the school and its students. The present set-up cannot keep students and parents up to date. The school newspaper appears every two weeks. During that interval, most of the news grows stale. Important announcements about coming events just cannot be kept up to date. A nightly five-minute segment would keep students and their parents informed. It would enrich the lives of present students and give future students a glimpse of what high school is like.

And Also

You have supported reason 1. Don't overlook reason 2.

> Such a news segment would benefit the community and the station as well. Students, their parents, and other citizens interested in school life are a large portion of your listeners. A school tragedy like Columbine makes

national news, but schools are entitled to coverage of all the positive news that doesn't make the headlines or the television news. A daily five-minute segment would balance those accidents, robberies, and murders that dominate the local news.

Wrap It Up

Most problems require complicated solutions, often contradictory and sometimes impossible. The problem of underreported school news is easily solved. That five-minute segment would help cement various groups together and would link the community with the school, in many ways its most precious resource.

Looking Back

You have created a reasonably successful essay. You have begun with a strong statement and concluded with an effective summary.

Writing Exercise 1   Evaluating an Essay to Persuade

Study the following essay by yourself. Be ready to list five arguments that support the writer's point of view.

The twelve-month school year has become increasingly popular. Once considered a far-fetched attack on tradition, it has won converts. Under the plan, the building would be kept open the entire year. Vacation durations would be unchanged, but seasonal vacations would replace the fixed.

Assignment: How do you feel about a twelve-month school year? Write an essay persuading the school board either to initiate the new plan or to reject its adoption. Keep in mind that you are attempting to persuade the school board, not other students. Show how students and school benefit.

The twelve-month school year is an excellent idea, a win-win situation. It is one of those rare suggestions that benefits everyone: both students and schools. I propose to our school board that we adopt the 12-month system for the benefits that arise from such an adoption.

After the first resistance to change, students would realize that they benefit. The length of vacations would not be cut, but they would come at different times of the year. Whether students prefer rest or activity, the different vacation periods would provide variety and a welcome change of pace at a different time each year. Students who love winter sports would enjoy winter vacations, now less available. Summer vacations would still be available, of course, but not as often as before.

Air-conditioned rooms make summertime accessible for learning. The changes in routine would be refreshing.

Schools benefit tremendously. The new plan uses the school building at capacity. The financial gains might actually include eliminating the need to build a new school. Expected economies might also provide enriched educational opportunities.

This is an idea whose time has come. Change can introduce new ideas, new methods, new financial strategies. I hope that you will consider the twelve-month school year.

List five arguments that you consider especially effective that support a twelve-month school year.

_____

_____

_____

_____

_____

_____

_____

_____

_____

_____

Writing Exercise 2   Writing an Essay to Persuade

The Oscar ceremonies, the jewel in the crown, the most prestigious of all award events, are in need of a makeover. The reason for the existence of the Oscars is to honor the achievements of film during the previous year. That lofty ideal has been tainted by the glitz and glamour, the red carpet and the fashion show, the borrowed diamonds hanging from celebrated ears. The ceremony itself, long and fatiguing, needs retooling.

Assignment: What is your evaluation of the Oscar ceremonies? Do you feel that the current procedures are adequate or wanting? In an essay either defend the present Oscar ceremony providing positive examples to support your position, or take the opposing view: that the Oscars are sick and need healing. Provide specific suggestions for improvement.

Writing Exercise 3   Writing an Essay to Persuade

Scarcely a week goes by without an awards ceremony somewhere. The Oscars, the Emmys, and the Tonys are the most famous but there are a host of others. When the air waves are saturated, the importance of each ceremony is diminished.

Many awards are showcases for celebrities who are "famous for being famous," and for B-list actors, who welcome the free exposure. Critics have complained that some awards ceremonies are merely "people thanking and congratulating each other."

Assignment: Are there too many awards ceremonies? Should viewers boycott what some consider senseless proliferation and latent exploitation? Or do you feel that the awards ceremonies hold a special place in American television for the recognition of achievement? Present your point of view with examples and viewer reactions.

Writing Exercise 4   Writing an Essay to Persuade

Consider carefully the following excerpt and the assignment below it. Then plan and write an essay that explains your ideas as persuasively as possible. Keep in mind that the support you provide—both reasons and examples—will help make your view convincing to the reader.

   A winning football or basketball team brings prestige and money to a college. Television, with its eye inevitably turned toward ratings, has made college sports visible and profitable. The student athletes give generously of their energy and time to the cause. Should these young people be held to the same academic standards as their fellow students who have more time for their studies? Are coaches justified in asking a professor to raise a student's grade "for the good of the school"?

Assignment: "Winning is the only thing." This motto, often quoted in sports reporting, motivates alumni to raise their contributions to the school. Since the student athletes pay a price for winning, should college administrators be a bit more lenient in applying the standards to student athletes? In an essay, present your point of view. Use specific examples to support your argument.

PRACTICE: Writing an Essay to Persuade

Consider carefully the following excerpt and the assignment below it. Then plan and write an essay that explains your ideas as persuasively as possible. Keep in mind that the support you provide—both reasons and examples—will help make your view convincing to the reader.

   By a year and a half before a Presidential election, the campaigns have already begun. Prospective candidates declare their intentions and begin the exhausting process of trying to sway the voters, first in the primaries and then in the general election. The grueling campaigns accompany elections at all levels, though none are so expensive, time-consuming, and exhausting as for the Presidency. Why not limit the time period during which campaigning can occur?

Assignment: Should an effort be made to find ways to limit campaigns to a shorter period before elections? Can all the issues be explored as well in a month as in six months, a year, or a year and a half? Take a position, providing reasons why you believe the campaign period should (or should not) be limited in time as well as in finances. Provide illustrations, examples, and precedents to support your presentation.

Part Two   Review of Common Usage Problems

The SAT will test your knowledge of usage and sentence structure in many ways. Obviously, your essay should display some mastery of grammar and usage. But you will also be tested specifically on identifying sentence errors (pages 477–480). In addition, you will be asked to improve sentences (pages 480–482 and paragraphs (pages 482–484). This section provides a quick but inclusive review of usage rules that you probably know but need to revisit. Refreshing your memory will give you more confidence in writing your essay and meeting the other challenges put before you.

Section I: Problems with Sentence Structure

There are three basic kinds of sentences. Their names are less important than your ability to write them correctly. However, knowing their names makes it possible to discuss them clearly.

1. Simple Sentences

In school, you have learned that a sentence must have a **subject** and a verb. The verb is often called a **predicate**. In the following sentences, the subject has one line under it; the verb has two.

> One hundred miles out to sea, a thirsty <u>sailor</u> <u><u>can drink</u></u> the water from the Amazon.
> The <u>Nile</u> <u><u>has frozen</u></u> over twice—in 829 and 1010 C.E.

The preceding examples are simple sentences. Each one contains a subject and a verb. Either the subject or the verb may be compound.

COMPOUND SUBJECT: One hundred miles out to sea a thirsty <u>sailor</u> or a marooned <u>boatman</u> <u><u>can drink</u></u> the water from the Amazon.

COMPOUND VERB: One hundred miles out to sea a thirsty <u>sailor</u> <u><u>can dip</u></u> into the ocean and <u><u>drink</u></u> the water from the Amazon.

COMPOUND SUBJECT AND VERB: One hundred miles out to sea a thirsty <u>sailor</u> or a marooned <u>boatman</u> <u><u>can dip</u></u> into the ocean and <u><u>drink</u></u> the water from the Amazon.

Writing Exercise 1   Simple Sentences with Compound Parts

Each item has two sentences. Combine each pair into one sentence with compound parts, either a compound subject or a compound verb.

1. Keats died young. Shelley also died young.

_____

_____

2. Theodore Roosevelt advocated the strenuous life. He followed his own advice.

_____

_____

3. Sugar is a popular ingredient in food. It lacks nutritional value.

_____

_____

2. Compound Sentences

Two or more simple sentences can be combined to form a compound sentence.

SIMPLE SENTENCE: Medicating a dog is easy.
SIMPLE SENTENCE: Medicating a cat is a disaster.
COMPOUND SENTENCE: Medicating a dog is easy, but medicating a cat is a disaster.

The parts of a compound sentence are often joined together by *and, but, or,* or *nor.* These "joining words" are called ***coordinating conjunctions***.

When two sentences are joined to make a compound sentence, the two main parts are called ***clauses***. Because these two parts can stand by themselves as complete sentences, they are called ***independent clauses***.

COMPOUND SENTENCE: The bells rang, AND students quickly filled the corridors.
COMPOUND SENTENCE: Are you coming to the game, OR have you made other plans?
COMPOUND SENTENCE: Helen doesn't like lima beans, NOR does she care for okra.
    (To identify subject and verb, arrange the sentence in subject-verb order: "she does care for okra.")

Writing Exercise 2   Compound Sentences

Combine each pair of sentences into a compound sentence.

1. You may think of Dobermans as vicious dogs. Many of them are gentle.

_____

_____

2. For the perfect electric bulb filament Thomas Edison experimented over and over. He did not stop even at the 600th try.

_____

_____

3. Lightning struck the tree. The bark peeled off in layers.

_____

_____

4. Pay your credit cards on time. The interest will destroy your financial health.

_____

_____

5. The rain poured down. The sun was shining.

_____

_____

Complex Sentences

3. A *complex sentence* has two or more clauses, too, but at least one of the clauses cannot stand by itself as a sentence. Note the following example.

COMPLEX SENTENCE: If winter comes, can spring be far behind?
FIRST CLAUSE: If winter comes   (subordinate clause)
SECOND CLAUSE: can spring be far behind?   (independent clause)

The *first clause* cannot stand by itself as a sentence. Although it has both a subject and a verb, it needs something to complete its thought. It is a *subordinate clause*. The *second clause* can stand by itself. It is an *independent clause*.

Subordinate Clauses

Many students have difficulty with subordinate clauses in their writing. They sometimes make the mistake of punctuating subordinate clauses as if they were complete sentences.

4. Subordinate clauses begin with connectives, or "joining words," called *subordinating conjunctions*.

after	before	lest	though	whenever
although	but that	provided that	till	where
as	even if	since	unless	whereas
as if	how	so that	until	whether
as though	if	than	when	while
because	in order that	that	whence	why

Adverb Clauses

5. In an ingenious extension of simple language, subordinate clauses may act as different parts of speech: as adverbs, adjectives or nouns. In grammatical terms, the adverb clause may function as an adverb and may modify verbs, adjectives, or other adverbs. The conjunctions listed above usually introduce adverb clauses, though occasionally a word like *that* or *where* may be used for adjective or noun clauses.

In the following sentences, the conjunction is capitalized; the subordinate clauses is circled: and the independent clause is underlined.

AFTER he had failed as a candymaker in four cities, Milton Hershey built his famous factory near dairy farms for his delicious milk chocolate.

Writing Exercise 3   The Adverb Clause

Circle the adverb clause in each sentence.

1. Although he was French, the Marquis de Lafayette is buried in France, in American dirt and in a grave belonging to the United States.
2. When a New York manufacturer of billiard balls offered a $10,000 prize for a substance to replace ivory, John Wesley Hyatt invented the first plastic, celluloid.
3. Many agencies are available for crucial assistance whenever an emergency occurs.

Adjective Clauses

6. Adjective clauses may be introduced in several ways. Frequently the relative pronouns *who, whose, whom, which,* and *that* are used.

According to an article in *American Heritage*, Benjamin Franklin is the Founding Father *who* speaks most directly to modern Americans.

Adjective clauses may be introduced by subordinating conjunctions.

A record-breaking temperature was registered in 2003 in Paris, *where* the temperatures exceeded 100 degrees.

The connecting word in adjective clauses may even be omitted.

The bee and the praying mantis are the insects scientists consider most useful to people. (*That* has been omitted before the word *scientists*.)

Writing Exercise 4   The Adjective Clause

Circle the adjective clause in each sentence.

1. Along the Florida shore I found coquina, a soft limestone that had been formed by the action of the waves on sand, shells, and coral.

2. James Smithson, whose contributions helped found the Smithsonian Institution, was English, not American.

3. Sheila knows a mountain in the Pisgah National Forest where zircons may be found.

Noun Clauses

7. Since a noun clause takes the place of a noun, it may occur wherever a noun may be used.

A number of connecting words are useful in introducing noun clauses: *that, who, which, what, why, how, where, whether,* or by compounds like *whoever* and *whatever*. Sometimes, as in direct quotations, the introductory word is omitted.

Cervantes said, "A proverb is a short sentence based on long experience." (The quotation is a noun clause object of *said*.)

AS SUBJECT OF A VERB: *Whatever the majority decides* is all right with me.

AS OBJECT OF A VERB: I learned *that Charles Dickens aligned his bed from north to south for unsupported scientific reasons*.

AS PREDICATE NOUN: Life is *what you make it*.

AS NOUN IN APPOSITION: We hold these truths to be self evident; *That all men are created equal*. (The adverb clause is in apposition with *truths*.)

Writing Exercise 5   Complex Sentences

Combine each pair of sentences to make one strong complex sentence.

1. A lightning bolt generates temperatures five times hotter than that found on the surface of the sun. I read this.

_____

_____

2. The most numerous of all living things are the insects. They are followed by the mollusks.

_____

_____

3. Jeremiah was eighteen, and he hiked the entire Appalachian Trail.

_____

_____

4. The driest spot on earth is in Chile's Atacama Desert. Not a drop of rain has ever been
seen there.

_____

_____

Sentence Fragments

8. Incomplete sentences, called *sentence fragments*, are often the result of carelessness or
haste. Check each sentence in your essay to make sure that it expresses a complete
thought.

These are common types of sentence fragments:

NO VERB Eskimos using wooden "eyeglasses" with narrow slits for eye protection.

COMPLETE SENTENCE: Eskimos use wooden "eyeglasses" with narrow slits for
eye protection.

NO SUBJECT Read *Pride and Prejudice* and enjoyed it.

COMPLETE SENTENCE: I read *Pride and Prejudice* and enjoyed it.

NO VERB, NO SUBJECT: With some reservations.

COMPLETE SENTENCE: The club finally adopted the new plan, with some reservations.

Prepositions and Prepositional Phrases

9. The preceding example used a prepositional phrase, *with some reservations*, as a complete sentence. A preposition shows the relationship of the noun or pronoun following
it to some other word in the sentence. A *phrase* is a group of connected words that do
not contain a subject or predicate.

PREPOSITIONAL PHRASES: On the floor in a corner of the room near the bookcase.

COMPLETE SENTENCE: I finally found my keys on the floor in a corner of the room near
the bookcase.

Writing Exercise 6   Converting Fragments into Complete Sentences

Rewrite each sentence fragment as a complete sentence. Add words as needed.

1. In the American wing at the Metropolitan Museum of Art.

_____

_____

2. Studied for four hours and aced that test.

_____

_____

3. A new park near the downtown theater district.

_____

_____

Subordinate Clauses as Fragments

10. Subordinate Clauses are not complete sentences.

SUBORDINATE CLAUSE: Automobiles that combine gasoline power and a powerful battery.

COMPLETE SENTENCE: Automobiles that combine gasoline power and an electric battery are the hope of the future.

SUBORDINATE CLAUSE: Which has become a major industry

COMPLETE SENTENCE: Much money comes into Egypt from tourism, which has become a major industry.

SUBORDINATE CLAUSE: When you are completely engaged in something.

COMPLETE SENTENCE: When you are completely engaged in something, you don't hear the clock strike.

SUBORDINATE CLAUSE: That Franklin D. Roosevelt gave the ocean explorer William Beebe the idea for a spherical underwater craft.

COMPLETE SENTENCE: I was amazed to discover that Franklin D. Roosevelt gave the ocean explorer William Beebe the idea for a spherical underwater craft.

Writing Exercise 7   Correcting Sentence Fragments

Rewrite each fragment as a complete sentence. Add words as needed.

1. When the big blackout of 2003 struck the Northeast on August 14, 2003.

_____

_____

2. In the Asheville, North Carolina, house where Thomas Wolfe lived as a child.

_____

_____

3. How the magician David Copperfield creates his incredible illusions.

_____

_____

4. The city where the Liberty Bell is located.

_____

_____

5. John Hancock, whose signature stands out boldly on the Declaration of Independence.

_____

_____

Verbals as Fragments

11. Verbals look like verbs and act like verbs, but they cannot carry a sentence by themselves. Verbals are hybrids: they act simultaneously like verbs and also like other parts of speech. They provide flexibility, conciseness, and variety to communication. There are three kinds of verbals: participles, gerunds, and infinitives. Though these labels may seem forbidding, they merely identify common devices in speaking and writing.

Participles

12. A participle acts as both a verb and an adjective.

> We found Dot *painting* a decoy.
> (*Painting* modifies *Dot*, like an adjective, and takes an object, *decoy*, like a verb.)
> *Exhausted* by the heat, we all jumped into the cool mountain stream.
> (*Exhausted* modifies *we*, like an adjective, and in turn is modified by a prepositional phrase, *by the heat*, like a verb.)
> *Having pitched* a perfect game, Jerry spoke to the reporters.
> (*Having pitched* modifies *Jerry*, like an adjective, and takes an object, *game*, like a verb.)

A participle cannot make a complete sentence without a true verb.

NOT A SENTENCE: Donna jumping up and down with a hornet sting.

SENTENCE: Donna was jumping up and down with a hornet sting. (The helping verb *was* completes the verb.)

SENTENCE: Donna jumped up and down with a hornet sting.

NOT A SENTENCE: Shanti packing a lunch for the picnic.

SENTENCE: Shanti packed a lunch for the picnic.

SENTENCE: Packing a lunch for the picnic, Shanti made sandwiches of tomato, avocado, and cheese.

Participles are sometimes dangling modifiers. To avoid dangling modifiers, review page 406.

Gerunds

13. A gerund acts as both a verb and a noun, and can appear in any slot a noun might fill.

AS SUBJECT: *Driving a car* in modern city traffic requires concentration and no distractions.

AS DIRECT OBJECT: I enjoy *riding my bike* in the cool, early morning hours.

AS OBJECT OF A PREPOSITION: Ellie saved Saturday *for hiking* on the Green River Valley trails.

AS PREDICATE NOMINATIVE: Vince Lombardi's goal was *winning* at any cost.

AS APPOSITIVE: Anne and Dot devised a plan: *surprising Nancy* on her birthday.

Infinitives

14. Participles can act as adjectives. Gerunds can act as nouns. Infinitives can act as adjectives, nouns or adverbs. These versatile modes of thought are indispensable in communication. They are usually introduced by *to*, but sometimes *to* is omitted.

AS NOUN, OBJECT OF A VERB: Susie tried *to find* Nero for her collection of Roman coins.

AS NOUN, SUBJECT OF ADVERB: *To be* young was very heaven.

AS ADJECTIVE: There is no time *to waste*.

AS ADVERB: Originally Beethoven wrote the Eroica Symphony *to honor* Napoleon

OMITTED TO: From the tower on Frying Pan mountain, we watched the smoke *pour* from a fire in the Little River valley.

Like other verbals, infinitives by themselves cannot make a complete sentence without a true verb.

NOT A SENTENCE: To prove Fermat's Last Theorem.

SENTENCE: Mathematicians tried for centuries to prove Fermat's Last Theorem.

NOT A SENTENCE: To gather blackberries for a pie.

SENTENCE: We gathered blackberries for a pie.

Writing Exercise 8   Complete Sentences

Each of the following uses a verbal in place of a verb. Rewrite each to make a complete sentence. Review the suggestions in the preceding pages.

1. Our dog Oliver watching patiently while our cat Noel kept tugging at his tail.

_____

_____

2. To dream the impossible dream, like Don Quixote.

_____

_____

3. The old house standing on the corner of Main and King Streets.

_____

_____

4. Putting my best foot forward in the interview

_____

_____

5. To do the best job possible under difficult conditions.

_____

_____

Run-on Sentences

15. The opposite of the sentence fragment might be the run-on sentence: two or more sentences punctuated as one sentence.

RUN-ON SENTENCE: During World War I, Americans shunned anything German, sauerkraut was actually called "liberty cabbage."

TWO SENTENCES: During World War I, Americans shunned anything German. Sauerkraut was actually called "liberty cabbage."

The preceding example shows the most obvious way of avoiding run-on sentences. Often, the sentences can be improved in one of three other ways: writing a compound sentence; writing a complex sentence; or introducing verbals.

RUN-ON SENTENCE: Many ocean waves are described as "mountain high," they are actually 30–40 feet in height.

COMPOUND SENTENCE: Many ocean waves are described as "mountain high," but they are actually 30–40 feet in height.

COMPLEX SENTENCE: Although many ocean waves are described as "mountain high," they are actually 30–40 feet in height.

SIMPLE SENTENCE WITH VERBAL: Most of the ocean waves described as "mountain high" are actually 30–40 feet in height.

Sometimes run-on sentences can be corrected by eliminating unnecessary words.

RUN-ON SENTENCE: England and Portugal have never been at war with each other, this is a major achievement among nations.

SINGLE SENTENCE: England and Portugal have never been at war with each other, a major achievement among nations.

The following words can lead to run-on sentences: _also, hence, nevertheless, then, therefore_, and _thus_. These words are not conjunctions. They cannot join sentences with only a comma. Sometimes a semicolon is used.

RUN-ON SENTENCE: The driver stopped, then he got out of his car.

SEPARATE SENTENCES (CORRECT): The driver stopped. Then he got out of his car.

RUN-ON SENTENCE: My best subject is science, therefore I took a science elective this year.

WITH SEMICOLON (CORRECT): My best subject is science; therefore, I took a science elective this year.

Writing Exercise 9   Eliminating Run-on Sentences

Eliminate all run-on sentences. For practice, try to use a different method for each corrected sentence.

1. Many would-be inventors have tried to create a perpetual-motion machine, they are all doomed to disappointment.

2. Whales usually bear only one offspring, baby twin whales have been observed.

3. Luther Burbank experimented with thousands of plants, he developed new varieties of apples, plums, and other fruits.

4. I found my keys after a search, I then proceeded to mislay my purse.

5. Robin is in a performance of *Phaedra*, she plays the tormented wife of Theseus.

Section II: Problems with Nouns

There are two main problems with nouns. The first is forming **plurals**. The second is forming **possessives**. When you have to form plural possessives, you are faced with both problems.

Plurals of Nouns

1. **To form the plurals of most nouns, add *s*.**

   apple—apple***s***   friend—friend***s***

   desk—desk***s***   shoe—shoe***s***

   train—train***s***   message—message***s***

2. **To form the plurals of nouns ending in *s, ch, sh, x,* or *z*, add *es*.** (This gives the word an extra syllable and makes it easier to pronounce.)

   address—address***es***   tax—tax***es***

   church—church***es***   waltz—waltz***es***

   dish—dish***es***   lunch—lunch***es***

3. **To form the plurals of nouns ending in *y* preceded by a CONSONANT, change *y* to *i* and add *es*.**

   ally—all***ies***   lady—lad***ies***

   company—compan***ies***   navy—nav***ies***

   country—countr***ies***   secretary—secretar***ies***

   cry—cr***ies***   ferry—ferr***ies***

   The vowels are ***a, e, i, o,*** and ***u*.** The consonants are all the other letters of the alphabet. The letter *y* acts as a vowel in words like *myth* and a consonant in words like *yes*.
   Nouns ending in *y* preceded by a VOWEL add only *s*.

   alley—alley***s***   ray—ray***s***

   valley—valley***s***   holiday—holiday***s***

   alloy—alloy***s***   attorney—attorney***s***

4. **To form the plurals of some nouns ending in *f* or *fe*, add *s*.**

   belief—belief***s***   handkerchief—handkerchief***s***

   fife—fife***s***   roof—roof***s***

   gulf—gulf***s***   safe—safe***s***

   chief—chief***s***   proof—proof***s***

5. **To form the plurals of other nouns ending in *f* or *fe*, change the *f* to *v* and add *es*.**

   calf—cal***ves***   knife—kni***ves***

   leaf—lea***ves***   life—li***ves***

   shelf—shel***ves***   loaf—loa***ves***

   wife—wi***ves***   self—sel***ves***

Nouns ending in *ff* always add *s*.

cliff—cliff**s**   cuff—cuff**s**

Writing Exercise 1   Writing Plurals

Write the plural form of each of the following nouns.

1. baby _____   7. miss _____
2. bunch _____   8. pinch _____
3. crash _____   9. pony _____
4. puff _____   10. stone _____
5. glass _____   11. story _____
6. half _____   12. tank _____

6. **To form the plurals of most nouns ending in *o*, add *s*.**

   alto—alto**s**   piano—piano**s**
   dynamo—dynamo**s**   rodeo—rodeo**s**
   Eskimo—Eskimo**s**   soprano—soprano**s**

   These familiar nouns ending in *o* have plural forms with *es*.

   echo—echo**es**   tomato—tomato**es**
   hero—hero**es**   veto—veto**es**
   potato—potato**es**   torpedo—torpedo**es**

7. **To form the plurals of most compound nouns, add *s*.**

   classroom—classroom**s**   cupful—cupful**s**
   schoolbook—schoolbook**s**   teaspoonful—teaspoonful**s**

8. **A few nouns form their plurals in special ways, without adding *s* or *es*.**

   child—children   mouse—mice
   deer—deer   ox—oxen
   foot—feet   series—series
   goose—geese   tooth—teeth
   man—men   woman—women

9. **In a few compound nouns the first part of the compound is the main word and is made plural:** mothers-in-law, courts-martial, lookers-on, attorneys-general.

   A few words or expressions make both parts plural: women lawyers, men teachers.

10. **Some nouns have the same form in the singular and the plural.**

    cod   moose   salmon
    athletics   headquarters   politics

11. **Some nouns ending in *s* are used only in the plural or have special meanings in the plural.**

ashes	proceeds	tactics
clothes	riches	thanks
gymnastics	scissors	trousers

12. **A few nouns ending in *s* are singular in meaning.**

civics	measles	physics
economics	mumps	the United States
mathematics	news	

13. **Some nouns from foreign languages keep their foreign plurals.**

analysis—analyses	crisis—crises
axis—axes	datum—data
basis—bases	ellipsis—ellipses

(*Data* is commonly and loosely used in the singular, although it is historically plural.)

Writing Exercise 2   Writing Plurals

Write the plural form of each of the following nouns.

1. hero _____

2. foot _____

3. strawberry _____

4. textbook _____

5. family _____

6. mouthful _____

7. cupful _____

8. brother-in-law _____

9. potato _____

Possessives of Nouns

To show ownership or possession, use the possessive form. The possessive singular is easy to form; the possessive plural is trickier.

14. **To form the possessive of a singular noun, just add *'s*. Don't change the word by adding any letter or omitting a letter.**

Carrie + s	Carrie's
friend + s	friend's
sister-in-law + s	sister-in-law's

15. **Some proper names ending in *s* sometimes omit the *s* to show possession, but you'll be correct if you add *'s*.**

Phelps	Phelps' or Phelps's

16. **To form the plural possessive of any noun, take the following two steps, *one at a time*.**

> FIRST: write the plural. (Don't omit this step!)
>
> Notice the last letter in the plural form.

If plural ends in s:	*If plural does not end in s:*
artist—artist*s*	child—childre*n*
astronaut—astronaut*s*	man—me*n*
rocket—rocket*s*	sheep—shee*p*
trainer—trainer*s*	woman—wome*n*

> SECOND: (*a*) If the plural form ends in *s*, add an apostrophe (').
>
> (*b*) If the plural form does not end in *s*, add an apostrophe and an *s* (*'s*).

If plural ends in *s*, *add an apostrophe.*	If plural does not end in *s*, *add an apostrophe and an s.*
artist*s'* easels	children*'s* games
astronaut*s'* training	men*'s* jackets
rocket*s'* red glare	sheep*'s* clothing
trainer*s'* advice	women*'s* movement

> That's all there is to it. If you follow the two steps, you will never go wrong.

Writing Exercise 3   Writing Plural Possessives

Write the plural possessive form of each of the following nouns. *Remember:* First write the plural. Then add an ' or *'s* as needed.

1. athlete _____

2. city _____

3. salesman _____

4. mouse _____

5. month _____

6. parent _____

7. four-year-old _____

8. goose _____

9. house _____

10. search _____

11. tree _____

12. wolf _____

Writing Exercise 4   Writing Possessives

Write the singular possessive, the plural, and the plural possessive of each of the following nouns. When you write the possessive plural, be sure to use the plural form as your guide.

Singular	Singular Possessive	Plural	Plural Possessive
1. book	_____	_____	_____
2. man	_____	_____	_____
3. box	_____	_____	_____
4. lady	_____	_____	_____
5. sheep	_____	_____	_____
6. brush	_____	_____	_____
7. rose	_____	_____	_____
8. punch	_____	_____	_____

Writing Exercise 5   Writing Plurals and Possessives

Write the correct form of the noun in parentheses as required by the sense of the sentence.

1. He left two of his (*book*) _____ on the bus.

2. The (*book*) _____ cover was torn.

3. Bill drove his (*sister*) _____ car.

4. The two (*sister*) _____ bought two (*house*) _____ .

5. The hunter shot three (*goose*) _____

6. The ranger found that many of the (*goose*) _____ wings were broken.

7. Two of Mr. Dixon's (*daughter*) _____ own a computer store.

8. The two (*daughter*) _____ store is on Main Street.

9. Both of my (*brother*) _____ belong to the (*school*) _____ bowling team.

10. Ten of the hotel's (*doorman*) _____ worked on Sunday.

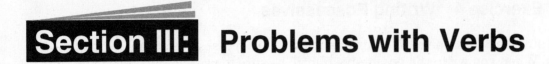

Section III: Problems with Verbs

There are three common problems with verbs: tense, principal parts, and agreement of subject and verb. Here's a quick review.

Using the Correct Tense

1. **Tense means "time." The form of a verb shows the time of the action that the verb expresses.**

PRESENT TENSE: The Cairo Museum contains a room with the mummies of the great pharaohs.

PAST TENSE: Vinegar was the strongest acid known to the ancients.

FUTURE TENSE: Judy will visit us over the Columbus Day weekend.

PRESENT PERFECT TENSE: The Hunzas of northwest Kashmir have always been free of cancer in any of its forms.

PAST PERFECT TENSE: By the age of ten, Mozart had already composed symphonies, sonatas, and arias.

FUTURE PERFECT TENSE: By the end of next year, Marcy will have read all the Sherlock Holmes mysteries.

Keeping to the Same Tense

2. **Don't mix tenses. Choose the appropriate tense and then use it consistently.**

MIXED TENSE: Jenny *entered* her mountain bike in the YMCA competition, (present) and *trains* for the event. (past)

SAME TENSE: Jenny *enters* her mountain bike in the YMCA competition (present) and *trains* for the event. (present)

SAME TENSE: Jenny *entered* her mountain bike in the YMCA competition (past) and *trained* for the event. (past)

Writing Exercise 1   Consistent Tenses

Rewrite the following sentences to make both verbs consistent, either present or past.

1. The 727 circled Greenville Airport and then heads toward Atlanta.

_____

_____

2. The players sneak up behind coach Bill Parcells and dumped a bucket of Gatorade on him.

_____

_____

3. Dad handed the tiller to me and then ducks as the boom swings over.

_____

_____

Principal Parts of Verbs

Regular Verbs

3. Most verbs are regular. They form tenses (express time of an action) in regular, predictable ways.

> Jennifer _enters_ many diving competitions.
> (Expresses an action taking place, or always true.)
> Jennifer _entered_ many diving competitions.
> (Expresses an action gone by.)
> Jennifer _has entered_ many diving competitions.
> (Expresses an action begun in the past and possibly still going on.)

Irregular Verbs

4. Unfortunately, not all verbs are regular. While fewer in number than regular verbs, irregular verbs are among the most commonly used.

> Jason _drives_ a Mustang.   Jason _drove_ a Mustang.
> (Expresses an action taking place.)   (Expresses an action gone by.)
> Jason _has driven_ a Mustang.
> (Expresses an action completed at the time of speaking.)

Principal Parts of Irregular Verbs

5. A relatively small number of irregular verbs cause trouble for speakers and writers. The following list is worth reviewing.

Principal Parts of 40 Irregular Verbs

Present	_Past_	_Past Participle_
am	was	(have) been
become	became	(have) become
begin	began	(have) begun
blow	blew	(have) blown
break	broke	(have) broken
bring	brought	(have) brought

Present	Past	Past Participle
catch	caught	(have) caught
choose	chose	(have) chosen
come	came	(have) come
do	did	(have) done
draw	drew	(have) drawn
drink	drank	(have) drunk
drive	drove	(have) driven
eat	ate	(have) eaten
fall	fell	(have) fallen
find	found	(have) found
freeze	froze	(have) frozen
get	got	(have) gotten *or* got
give	gave	(have) given
go	went	(have) gone
hold	held	(have) held
know	knew	(have) known
leave	left	(have) left
lie	lay	(have) lain
ride	rode	(have) ridden
rise	rose	(have) risen
say	said	(have) said
see	saw	(have) seen
shake	shook	(have) shaken
sit	sat	(have) sat
speak	spoke	(have) spoken
stick	stuck	(have) stuck
swim	swam	(have) swum
take	took	(have) taken
teach	taught	(have) taught
tear	tore	(have) torn
throw	threw	(have) thrown
win	won	(have) won
wind	wound	(have) wound
write	wrote	(have) written

Forms of *have, be,* and *do* are often used as helping verbs.

DON'T SAY: The wind blowed all night.

DO SAY: The wind blew all night.

DON'T SAY: Sandra has chose nursing as her career.

DO SAY: Sandra has chosen nursing as her career.

Writing Exercise 2   Choosing the Correct Principal Part

In each sentence, underline the correct form of the verb.

1. Ellie (swam, swimmed) ten laps in the pool.
2. The backup quarterback (brought, brung) new life to the team.
3. Nathaniel (drawed, drew) a picture of a dinosaur to illustrate his story.
4. I have never (ate, eaten) a more delicious meal than lasagna.
5. Suellen (catched, caught) a five pound bass in the lake.
6. Jonathan (became, become) the first player to win in two sets.
7. The weather at the soccer game turned cold, and we were nearly (froze, frozen).
8. That unopened envelope has (laid, lain) on the desk all week.
9. You completed that difficult project and (did, done) well.
10. Yesterday's storm has (shaken, shook) most of the apples from the tree.

Agreement of Subject and Verbs

6. The third challenge is making sure that a verb agrees with its subject in number and person. Remember that an *s* is added to a verb to make it singular; an *s* is added to a noun to make it plural. *Winds blow, wind blows.*

	Singular	*Plural*
FIRST PERSON:	I enjoy	we enjoy
SECOND PERSON:	you enjoy	you enjoy
THIRD PERSON:	he, she, it enjoys	they enjoy

The verb *to be*, the commonest verb in English, is, alas, irregular. These are the present-tense forms:

	Singular	*Plural*
FIRST PERSON:	I am	we are
SECOND PERSON:	you are	you are
THIRD PERSON:	he, she, it is	they are

These are the past tense forms of *to be:*

I was	we were
you were	you were
he, she, it was	they were

The important verb *to have* is worth a look. These are the present-tense forms:

FIRST PERSON:	I have	we have
SECOND PERSON:	you have	you have
THIRD PERSON:	he, she, it has	they have

These are the past-tense forms:

I had	we had
you had	you had
he, she, it had	they had

Most native speakers of English tend to use the right form in sentences, like the one below, in which the verb follows the subject.

> A *tree* STANDS at the front gate.

In other sentences, not as simple as the above, subject-verb agreement is the cause of some common mistakes. So study these few rules.

7. **A difficulty comes when there are words (those in parentheses below) between the subject and the verb.**

> A *tree* (with green leaves) STANDS at the front gate.

Some people would mistakenly write *stand* in the belief that *leaves* is the subject. It is not.

8. **Expressions like *together with, according to, including, as well as*, and others do not affect subject-verb agreement.**

> The *players*, including the coach, ARE GOING to the game by plane.

In the above sentence, *players* is the subject, not *coach*.

9. **Another common difficulty arises in agreement when the subject is compound. The words *and, or, nor, either … or, neither … nor* signal the presence of a compound subject.**

10. **When two subjects are connected by *and*, the subject is plural and the verb is usually plural.**

> High *seas* AND dense *fog* HAVE SLOWED the rescue operation.

11. **When two singular subjects are joined by *or* or *nor*, the subject is singular and the verb is singular.**

> *Rain* OR *snow* IS the forecast for today.

12. **When two subjects of different number are joined by** *neither . . . nor* **or** *either . . or,* **the verb agrees with the nearer subject.**

    NEITHER *Fran* NOR her *brothers* ARE GOING to the state convention.

    EITHER these telephone *numbers* OR that *address* IS wrong.

13. *You* **always takes a plural verb. "You was" is wrong.**

    You WERE LISTED on today's honor roll.

    WERE *you* EXPECTING the honor?

14. **When the subject comes after the verb, find the subject and make the verb agree with it.**

    (Was, Were) the nominees for Best Actor all present at the Academy Awards ceremony?

    (The subject is *nominees.* Therefore, *were* is correct.)

    There (was, were) three raccoons digging in the rubbish heap.

    (The subject is *raccoons,* not the introductory word *there. Were* is correct. *Here* is a similar introductory word.)

    In a corner of my desk (are, is) the schedules for the Spurs' basketball games and the Bears' football games.

    (The subject is *schedules. Are* is correct.)

15. **Make the verb agree with the positive subject, not with the negative subject or the interrupter.**

    The stark courage of the New York police and firefighters, NOT their tragic losses, is the memory we cherish.

16. **Make a verb agree with its subject, not its predicate noun or pronoun.**

    The greatest literary achievement of Geoffrey Chaucer *was* his insightful portrayals of the Canterbury pilgrims.

    The insightful portrayals of the Canterbury pilgrims *were* the greatest literary achievement of Geoffrey Chaucer.

17. **In an adjective clause with the relative pronoun used as subject, make the verb agree with the antecedent of the relative pronoun.**

    It was Brittany who was to blame for the incorrect meeting time.

    The list of students who were accepted by Dartmouth appears in today's paper.

Writing Exercise 3   Making Verbs Agree with Their Subjects

In each sentence, underline the correct form of the verb.

1. The girl with the pearl earrings (was, were) made immortal in a Vermeer painting.
2. The incumbent, according to the latest polls, (are, is) leading.
3. Neither the president nor the other officers (was, were) present at the election.
4. (Was, Were) you able to complete your science project on time?
5. (Are, Is) there any late registrants for the rollerblade competition?
6. Benjamin Franklin's wisdom, not any personal flaws, (are, is) best remembered.
7. Ogden Nash's supreme achievement (was, were) his outrageous puns and clever rhymes.
8. It is I who (am, is) responsible for the loss, not Frank.
9. Mary Jane (doesn't, don't) know whether or not to apply to the University of Texas.
10. A heavy downpour during the summer months (help, helps) keep down brush fires.

Section IV: Problems with Modifiers

Nouns and verbs are the power words: they carry the content of a sentence. Other kinds of words, called *modifiers*, add exactness and color to writing. Notice the difference they make.

1. Monkeys chattered.
2. A hundred monkeys chattered noisily.

The bare sentence in 1 is considerably enriched by the added modifiers in sentence 2. An **adjective** modifies (tells something about) a noun. An **adverb** modifies (tells something about) a verb. In sentence 2 above, *hundred*, an adjective, modifies the noun *monkeys*. *Noisily*, an adverb, modifies the verb *chattered*.

Caution: In your writing, don't overuse modifiers. A good rule is: if you can say it more simply and more effectively, trim those adjectives and adverbs.

OVERDONE: Quite unexpectedly, dawn came dramatically with a sudden rush.
BETTER: Dawn came with a rush.

Adjectives and Adverbs Confused

1. **Don't use an adjective where an adverb is called for.**

   Lance Armstrong did especially *well* on the mountain portions of the Tour de France. (Not *good*)

Writing Exercise 1   Choosing the Correct Modifier

In each sentence, underline the correct modifier in parentheses.

1. Speak (gentle, gently) to a horse if you seek its trust.
2. Young birds in nests must be fed (regular, regularly).
3. To do (good, well) on the SAT requires a knowledge of test strategy.

Double Negatives

2. **Avoid the double negative. Negative words include *no, not, never, nothing, none, nobody, hardly,* and *scarcely*. Be careful with the half-negatives *hardly, scarcely, barely, only,* and *but* when it means *only*.**

DOUBLE: I don't have no homework assignment for tonight.

ONE: I don't have a homework assignment for tonight.

ONE: I have no homework assignment for tonight.

DOUBLE: The regular party members didn't have nothing to do with the recall election in California.

ONE: The regular party members didn't have anything to do with the recall election in California.

ONE: The regular party members had nothing to do with the recall election in California.

Writing Exercise 2   Avoiding the Double Negative

In each sentence, underline the correct word in parentheses.

1. Pauline doesn't go (anywhere, nowhere) without her pocket calculator.
2. The first submarine wasn't (anything, nothing) but a leather-covered rowboat.
3. We (had, hadn't) barely started when the left front tire blew.

Double-Duty Words

3. **Some words, like *well*, *fast*, and *slow* can be used either as adjectives or as adverbs, but often the context helps you make a decision.**

   I'm feeling good.   (In good spirits)
   I'm feeling well.   (In good health)

Other Common Errors

4. **Don't add *s* to *anyway*, *anywhere*, *everywhere*, *nowhere*, or *somewhere*.**

   My Spanish book must be somewheres around here.

5. **Don't say *this here* or *that there* to describe a noun.**

   This ~~here~~ cake was made without eggs.

6. **Don't use *more* with an *-er* word (*more wiser*) or *most* with an *-est* word (*most prettiest*).**

   Our cat is ~~more~~ smarter than our cocker spaniel.

7. **Don't use *them* as the subject of a verb.**

   Those
   ~~Them~~ are the books I've read for my research paper.

Writing Exercise 3   Choosing the Correct Modifier

1. We hope that we grow (more wiser, wiser) as we grow older.
2. Ponce de Leon thought that the Fountain of Youth was (somewhere, somewheres) in Florida.
3. (Them, Those) are the tastiest cantaloupes I've ever eaten.

Section V: Problems with Joining Words

Though nouns, verbs, adjectives and adverbs provide the content of a sentence, prepositions and conjunctions provide the glue that holds sentences together.

1. **Use *unless* as a conjunction, *without* as a preposition.**

   > UNLESS Dad's refund check comes through, I'll have to wait for that new play station. (*Unless* introduces the subordinate clause.)
   > WITHOUT good directions, traveling is frustrating.
   >   (*Without* is a preposition; its object is *directions.*)

2. **Never use *being* as a conjunction: it is a participle (page 441).**

   > Since the blueberries are ripe on Pine Mountain, I'm taking the afternoon off.
   > (Not *Being that the blueberries are. . .*)

3. **Use prepositions idiomatically.**

   > die *of* a disease (not *from*)
   > identical *with*
   > in search *of*, to search *for*
   > need *of* nourishment
   > comply *with* a request
   > agree *to* a proposal; agree *with* a person; *agree* on a plan

4. **Don't omit a needed preposition.**

   > I like historical novels as well *as* or better than mysteries.

5. **Substitute a prepositional phrase for a misleading noun.**

   > We left *in October* for the Southern Highlands. (Do not omit *in.*)

Writing Exercise 1   Using Correct Connectives

In each sentence, underline the correct word in parentheses.

1. (Unless, Without) Terry joins us at the concert, Karen won't want to go.
2. (Because, Being that) I didn't have fast access to the Internet, I decided to invest in Road Runner.

3. David Copperfield went in search (for, of) his Aunt Betsy Trotwood.

4. The Hughes family left (December, in December) for a cruise to the Falkland Islands and Antarctica.

5. Meredith's solution to the club's financial crisis was as (good, good as), if not better, than Taylor's.

Section VI: Problems with Pronouns

Personal Pronouns

Subjects and Objects

A handful of pronouns cause more trouble than all the rest put together. These **personal pronouns,** as they are called, have different forms when used as subjects and as objects. Here are the troublemakers:

	Singular			Plural	
As subjects:	**I**	**he**	**she**	**we**	**they**
As objects:	**me**	**him**	**her**	**us**	**them**

Notice that these pronouns are paired. Your choice in a sentence would be between *I* and *me*, for example. *I* is the form used for the subject and *me* for the object.

> We watched the Super Bowl together.
>
> > (*We* is subject of the verb *watched*.)
>
> The Adamses had invited us to the get-together.
>
> > (*Us* is object of the verb *had invited*.)

1. **Most pronoun difficulties occur when two pronouns are joined by *and*. When in doubt, say what you would say if each pronoun stood alone.**

> Laura and *she* (not *her*) competed in the spelling bee.
>
> > (*She* is one-half of the compound subject of the verb *competed*.)
> >
> > > Check yourself. Say:
> > >
> > > Laura competed.
> > >
> > > She competed.
> > >
> > > Laura and she (not *her*) competed.
>
> Mr. Foster gave Mollie and *me* (not *I*) a chance to play in the mixed-doubles tournament. (It is courteous to mention the other person first: "Mollie and me," NOT "me and Mollie.")
>
> > (*Me* is one-half of the compound object of the verb *gave*.)
> >
> > > Check yourself:
> > >
> > > Mr. Foster gave Mollie.
> > >
> > > Mr. Foster gave me.
> > >
> > > Mr. Foster gave Mollie and me (not *I*).

Go with Margo and *him* (not *he*) to the flea market.

(*Him* is one-half of the compound object of the preposition *with*.)

Say to yourself:

Go with Margo.

Go with him.

Go with Margo and him (not *he*).

2. **Note this correct form.**

The apples were divided between Tom and me.

(*Me*, like *Tom*, is an object of the preposition *between*.)

3. **Study these additional examples of pronoun difficulties. Don't be fooled by the words *swimmers* and *students* in these two sentences. They do not affect the pronouns to be used.**

We (not *Us*) swimmers are competing in the county championships.

(*We* is a subject of the verb *are competing*.)

Mr. Edmonds took *us* (not *we*) students on a tour of the Edison home in Fort Myers.

(*Us* is an object of the verb *took*.)

4. **Watch out for sentences that leave out a verb because it is understood.**

Gwen is already as tall as *he* (not *him*).

(*He* is the subject of the understood verb *is*. Think of the sentence as reading, "Gwen is already as tall as *he is tall*.")

Writing Exercise 1   Using Correct Pronouns

In each sentence, underline the correct form of the pronoun in parentheses.

1. (We, Us) members of the Virginia Cavaliers marching band leave for Chicago tonight.
2. We found our dog Oliver and (she, her) asleep on the sofa.
3. (Tom and I, Me and Tom) worked on a sculpture project for the Art Festival.
4. When I'm working on my model trains, nobody can be as happy as (I, me).
5. Just between you and (I, me), today's cafeteria lunch was tasteless.

Agreement of a Pronoun with Its Antecedent

5. **A pronoun must agree with its antecedent in number. (The word *antecedent* comes from two Latin words meaning "going before.")**

> A wolf is gentle with *its* young.
>
> *Its* refers to *wolf*. *Wolf* is the antecedent of *its*. *Wolf* is singular. Therefore, *its* is singular. (Notice that the antecedent "goes before" the pronoun.)

> Wolves are gentle with *their* young.
>
> *Their* refers to *wolves*. *Wolves* is the antecedent of *their*. *Wolves* is plural. Therefore *their* is plural.

Look at these additional correct forms.

> The boy from the visiting team left *his* jacket on the bus.
>
> (*Boy* is the subject of the sentence. *Boy* is the antecedent of *his*. Both are singular.)

Writing Exercise 2   Making Pronouns Agree with Their Antecedents

In each sentence, underline the correct word in parentheses.

1. An elephant forms close bonds with (its, their) trainers.
2. Everybody brought (his, their) Harley to the rally.
3. One of the new clarinetists made (her, their) debut.
4. Neither Boris nor Bobby kept (his, their) chess title for long.
5. The backup players on the team (are, is) crucial to (its, their) success.

Indefinite Pronouns

Many problems of agreement arise with the words on the following list. They are called *indefinite pronouns*. A personal pronoun that has one of these words as an antecedent must be singular.

anybody	**either**	**neither**	**one**
anyone	**everybody**	**nobody**	**somebody**
each	**everyone**	**no one**	**someone**

6. **Note the use of the correct forms.**

> Each of the girls must bring *her* track shoes.
>
> (*Each* is singular. *Her* is singular.)

Everybody must report to *his* or *her* adviser.

(*Everybody* is singular. *His ... her* with *or* is singular. Even though *everybody* "sounds" plural, it isn't. The use of *their* with *everybody* (or with any other word on the list) is incorrect in formal English.)

7. **With *either ... or* or *neither ... nor*, use the nearer antecedent when choosing a pronoun.**

Either *Jill* or *Claire* will bring *her* records to the dance.

(*Jill ... Claire* is a compound subject. Since *Jill* is singular and *Claire* is also singular, the singular *her* is used.)

Neither *Norm* nor his *cousins* buy *their* groceries here.

(*Norm* is singular, but *cousins* is plural. Therefore, the plural *their* is used to agree with the nearer antecedent, *cousins*.)

Writing Exercise 3   Making Verbs Agree with Indefinite Pronouns

Underline the correct form of the verb in parentheses.

1. Nobody among all the members (was, were) completely in favor of the proposed new charter.
2. A few in the club (was, were) determined to reject the plan.
3. One of the council members (was, were) disappointed by the vote.
4. Either Paul or she (are, is) sponsoring a new resolution.
5. Neither Grace nor her two brothers (are, is) interested in the trip to Gatlinburg.

8. **Still another error is using a plural verb with one of the singular subjects listed on page 464, the indefinite pronouns. Note these correct forms.**

Everyone at the meeting *has* a stake in the decision.

(*Everyone* is singular. *Has* is singular.)

Each of the members *was* asked to vote.

(*Each* is singular. *Was* is singular.)

Neither the *twins* nor *she wants* to go to camp this summer.

(*Twins* is plural, but *she* is singular. The singular verb, *wants*, agrees with the nearer subject, *she*, which is also singular.)

9. **Some indefinite pronouns usually require a plural verb: *several, many, both, some, few*.**

Some *were* not invited to Yolanda's party.

Many of the apples *are* still green.

Several in the stands *cheer* whenever Buck comes to bat.

10. **Unlike nouns, the possessives of personal pronouns have NO apostrophes. Note the following correct forms.**

> Is this *yours* or *hers*?
>
> Those books are *theirs*, not *ours*.
>
> Where is *its* collar?

Look carefully at the last one. You have seen the word *it's*, with an apostrophe. It is a contraction of *it is*. Whenever you wonder whether *its* needs an apostrophe, simply replace *its* with *it is*. If the sentence does make sense, use an apostrophe. If it doesn't make sense (as in Where is *it is* collar?), *don't* use the apostrophe.

11. **The possessives of *indefinite pronouns*, unlike personal pronouns, DO use apostrophes.**

> *Somebody's* briefcase is on the kitchen table.
>
> *Everyone's* job is *nobody's* job.
>
> *No one's* opinion is more valued than Janet's.

12. **Don't confuse *whose* with *who's*. Note these correct forms.**

> Whose sweater is this?
>
> Who's going to claim it? (Who is)

Writing Exercise 4   Choosing the Correct Pronoun

In each sentence, underline the correct pronoun in parentheses.

1. Everyone on the girls' soccer team had (her, their) name read aloud at the school assembly.
2. Rhonda says that this book of Emily Dickinson's poetry is (hers, her's).
3. Between you and (I, me), I would have preferred to go to Colorado this summer, not Florida.
4. (It's, Its) starting to pour; cover the chairs.
5. (Me and Talbot, Talbot and I) are planning to hike part of the Appalachian Trail this summer.

Section VII: Problems with Punctuation

A complete list of the rules of punctuation would fill a small book. Fortunately, you don't have to learn them all. Mastery of a few basic rules will help you avoid most of the pitfalls in punctuating sentences. The following review covers the main points.

End Punctuation

1. Every sentence ends with a period, a question mark, or an exclamation point.

STATEMENT: A Pekingese has a longer life expectancy than a Saint Bernard.

COMMAND: Read this book about how to repair a faucet.

POLITE REQUEST: May I hear from you soon?

QUESTION: Have you ever visited Acadia National Park?

STRONG FEELING: What a wonderful time we had at Sea World!

2. The period is also used after abbreviations and most initials.

    Dr. R. J. Lowenherz   p.m.   R.S.V.P.

The Comma

The comma has many uses. Three important uses that you should review are commas in a series; commas to show interrupters; and commas in letters, dates, and addresses.

Commas in a Series

3. Use a comma to separate items in a series.

> At camp we hiked, swam, golfed, and played softball.
> My brother collects stamps, coins, and picture postcards.
> Sue looked for the tickets on the desk, in the desk drawer, and on the dresser.

(Some writers omit the comma before the *and*. This can be confusing in some sentences, however. The safest practice is to include the final comma in all such sentences.)

4. When more than one adjective precedes a noun, use a comma for a pause.

> The gloomy, isolated mansion stood at the edge of a cliff. (Pause after *gloomy*.)
> Oliver was a lively young dog. (No pause.)

5. If there is no pause, omit the comma.

> Jalapeño is a red-hot pepper.

Commas to Show Interrupters

6. Use a pair of commas to enclose most interrupting words or expressions.

> Our Mr. Pooch, like most beagles, is a friendly dog.
> Siamese cats, on the other hand, are more reserved.
> Tallahassee, not Miami, is the capital of Florida.
> I'm surprised, Madge, that you believe his story.
> She admitted that, yes, she could see his point of view.
> The route through Evansville is, according to Jack, the best route to Janet's house.
> The old car, rusted and dented, was not worth fixing.

7. When an interrupter comes at the beginning or at the end of a sentence, only one comma is needed.

> Like most beagles, our Mr. Pooch is a friendly dog.
> On the other hand, Siamese cats are more reserved.
> The capital of Florida is Tallahassee, not Miami.
> I'm surprised that you believe his story, Madge.
> Yes, I admit that I can see your point of view.
> Paul disagrees, however.
> Rusted and dented, the old car was not worth fixing.

8. Use a pair of commas to enclose most appositives. An appositive explains the noun or pronoun it follows. It is most commonly a noun.

> Songhay, an African *kingdom* in the late 1400s, was larger than western Europe.
> The Antarctic waters, *fertilizer* for the rest of the world, help support life in the other oceans.

9. Adjectives sometimes appear in the appositive position.

> The old house, *grim* and *foreboding*, lowered over Main Street.
> Spiders, *unpopular* but *essential*, destroy a hundred times their number in insects.

10. Use commas to enclose appositives preceded by *or*.

> The avocado, or *alligator pear*, was first cultivated by the Aztecs.

Writing Exercise 1   Punctuating Correctly

Add all needed punctuation.

1. Our spring garden features snowdrops crocuses aconites, hyacinths and tulips.
2. Are you aware that George Washington first President of the United States served two terms?
3. William Henry Harrison on the other hand served only a month.
4. Two Adamses two Harrisons two Roosevelts and two Bushes have been Presidents of the United States.
5. The sassafras unlike most trees has three different and distinct leaf patterns.

Quotation Marks

11. A direct quotation shows the speaker's exact words. An indirect quotation does not.

DIRECT QUOTATION: Dad said, "You can go to camp this summer." (Quotation marks needed)

INDIRECT QUOTATION: Dad said that I can go to camp this summer. (No quotation marks)

12. Quotation marks always go in pairs. If you have opening quotation marks, you must have closing quotation marks.

> Ellen said, "I'm taking the school bus home."
> "I'm taking the school bus home," Ellen said.
> "When do you leave?" asked Carlos.
> Carlos asked, "When do you leave?"
> "I hope," said Fran, "that you remember to take your science book home."
> "When do we eat?" Billy asked. "I'm hungry."
> Did Billy say, "I'm hungry"? (The entire sentence is a question.)
> "I had never seen a snow leopard before," Maureen said. "Had you?"

Writing Exercise 2   Punctuating Correctly

Add all needed punctuation in these sentences.

1. How did jazz start asked Cynthia.
2. Mark exclaimed excitedly Geraldine won the spelling bee by correctly spelling *syzygy*
3. Work is the best method for killing time said William Feather
4. If you can come camping with me said Tom bring your fishing gear
5. All cruelty wrote the Roman philosopher Seneca springs from weakness

Punctuating Titles

13. **In general, use quotation marks around the titles of short works—a short story, an essay, a song, a magazine article, or the chapter of a book. Underline the titles of longer works—a book, a film, a magazine, or a newspaper. (In printed material, underlined words appear in *italics*.)**

> "I Am Born" is the title of a chapter in *David Copperfield* by Charles Dickens.
>
> "On Running After One's Hat" is a classic essay by G. K. Chesterton.
>
> "Memphis" is my favorite song from the Statler Brothers' album *Funny, Familiar, Forgotten Feelings*.
>
> I've seen the movie *Back to the Future* at least five times.
>
> *TV Guide* is one of the most successful magazines ever published.
>
> The Newark *Star-Ledger* publishes different editions for different counties.

(Be careful to capitalize the exact name of the newspaper. Usually *the* is not capitalized as part of the name, but in *The New York Times* it is. Sometimes the name of the city is part of the name of the paper, as in the *Chicago Sun-Times*, and sometimes it isn't.)

Writing Exercise 3   Punctuating Correctly

Add needed punctuation to the following sentences.

1. The Most Dangerous Game is a short story I have never forgotten.
2. The newspaper Newsday has many readers but not as many as the Times
3. Wagner's music slyly declared humorist Bill Nye is better than it sounds
4. One of the best movies of all time in my opinion is Music Man
5. They that know no evil declared Ben Jonson will suspect none

Section VIII: Problems with Capitalization

The following review summarizes the important rules of capitalization.

1. **Capitalize the first word of a complete sentence, the comments of each new speaker in conversation, and each line of poetry or verse.**

   Sentence:
   A newly sighted person has great difficulty in making sense of the visual images.

   Conversation:
   "**It** is not cold which makes me shiver," said the woman in a low voice.
   "**What,** then?"
   "**It** is fear, Mr. Holmes. It is terror."
   —from Arthur Conan Doyle's "The Adventure of the Speckled Band"

   Poetry:
   The pedigree of honey
   Does not concern the bee;
   A clover, any time, to him
   Is aristocracy.
   —Emily Dickinson

2. **Capitalize proper nouns, their abbreviations, and proper adjectives derived from proper nouns.**

   PROPER NOUN: **New Mexico**
   ABBREVIATION: **N.M.** (or NM, the postal abbreviation)
   PROPER ADJECTIVE: **New Mexican** (as in *New Mexican* art)

3. **Capitalize these specific kinds of proper nouns.**

   Names of particular persons, real or imaginary
   Jacques, Isabella, Sean Connery, Sandra Day O'Connor, James Bond, Harry Potter
   Geographical names
   Afghanistan, Utah, Madison County, Great Smoky Mountains National Park, Broadway

Titles of organizations, companies, and buildings

Habitat for **Humanity, National Audubon Society, General Motors, Eiffel Tower, Cologne Cathedral**

Political parties, nations, religions, government bodies

Democrat, Republican, Spain, Roman Catholic, Protestant, Hebrew, Muslim, Senate, Department of **Defense**

Titles of persons showing office, rank, or profession

President James Monroe, Secretary of **State Colin Powell, Dr. Jonas Salk**

Names of planets, satellites, stars, and constellations

Mars, Ganymede, Aldebaran, Orion

(The words *sun*, *moon*, and *earth* are not usually capitalized.)

Names of days of the week, months, holidays

Saturday, October, Labor Day

(The names of the seasons are not capitalized: autumn, winter.)

Titles

The Lord of the Rings, American Heritage, "The Lottery"

(Articles (a, an, the), prepositions, and conjunctions are not capitalized unless they occur at the beginning or end of a title.)

Brand names

Campbell's soups, **Mueller's** noodles, **Pepperidge Farm** bread

Names referring to God, the Bible, or religions

the **Almighty, Genesis**, the **New Testament**, the **Koran, Buddhism, Hinduism**

4. Note these three kinds of items that require extra thought in capitalizing.

Sections of the country

the **Southeast**, the **Northwest**, the **Southwest**

Do *not* capitalize these words if they are merely compass points:

Philadelphia lies southwest of New York City.

Family relationships

Father, Sis, Cousin, Gene, Aunt Gloria, Grandpa

Do *not* capitalize these family titles unless they are used before a name (**Uncle** Sid) or as a name (Hi, **Mom**):

My sister, cousin, and aunt visited Duke Gardens.

School subjects: languages and numbered courses

English, French, Spanish, German, Mechanical Drawing 2, Social Studies 3, Mathematics 4

Do *not* capitalize the names of unnumbered courses except for languages:

I'm taking mechanical drawing, social studies, mathematics, and **German** in the fall.

5. **Capitalize the first letter of a direct quotation, but when a quotation is interrupted, do not begin the second part with a capital.**

> The philosopher Montesquieu declared, "What the crators want in depth, they give you in length."

> "I would rather sit on a pumpkin and have it all to myself," insisted Henry Thoreau, "than to be crowded on a velvet cushion."

6. **In letters, capitalize the first word of all nouns used in the salutation. Capitalize only the first word in the complimentary close.**

Dear Ms. Hoffman	Your friend
Dear Aunt Betsy	Sincerely yours

Writing Exercise 1   Capitalizing Correctly

Capitalize words as needed.

1. my aunt, colonel andrea langer, has just returned from a tour of duty in iraq.
2. the alamo in the heart of san antonio, texas, is a major tourist attraction.
3. happiness grows at our own firesides declared douglas jerrold and is not to be picked in strangers' gardens.
4. tides along shores bordering the english channel can be dramatically high and low.
5. the department of agriculture has charge of our national forests, and the department of the interior has charge of our national parks.

Section IX: Problems with Spelling

English spelling is the despair of foreign-born speakers, students, and adult correspondents. Because spelling is only partially phonetic, sound is sometimes a poor guide to spelling. Yet, despite the obstacles, there are some spelling guides that can be of some help.

1. First, review these words commonly used in English but frequently mispelled.

Seventy-six Hard/Easy Words

1. **The words in the following list are among the most commonly used in English. Yet they are frequently misspelled. Review them and master them.**

ache	certain	heard	realize
acquaint	character	hospital	really
across	coming	immediately	says
agreeable	committee	instead	scene
all right	cough	knew	since
almost	course	knowledge	speech
always	disappear	library	straight
among	disappoint	meant	studying
another	doctor	minute	success
asked	doesn't	necessary	surely
athletic	dropped	occasion	surprise
beautiful	enough	occurred	though
before	every	often	thought
believe	exception	once	threw
benefit	excitement	piece	together
boundary	experience	pleasant	toward
break	friend	principal[school]	until
built	grammar	privilege	which
captain	having	probably	woman

Words Often Confused

2. **Learn to distinguish between words often confused.**

I'll **accept** every package **except** the one with the torn wrapping.
We looked at old pictures. **Then** Peter was taller **than** Norm.

She's **too** late **to** enter the race.

Because of the trees all around, our house is **quite quiet**.

Your necklace is **loose**. Don't **lose** it.

Whether we go or not depends on the **weather**.

It's time to give the hamster **its** lunch.

You're leading **your** opponent in the election.

They're going **there** with **their** hopes high.

Where can I **wear** this formal gown?

Some Helpful Spelling Rules

Though rules are often broken, you will find the following helpful.

3. **ei, ie. Put *i* before *e* except after *c*, or when sounded like *a* as in *neighbor* and *weigh*.**

i before *e*:	bel*ie*ve, ch*ie*f; n*ie*ce, f*ie*ld, sh*ie*ld
except after *c*:	c*ei*ling, rec*ei*ve, dec*ei*t, conc*ei*t, perc*ei*ve
sounded like *a*:	w*ei*ght, v*ei*l, v*ei*n, r*ei*gn, r*ei*n
Exceptions:	foreigner, leisure, either, neither, height, weird

4. **ly. Keep the original *l* when adding *ly* to a word ending in *l*.**

   actua**ll**y, beautifu**ll**y, cheerfu**ll**y, fina**ll**y, rea**ll**y

5. **Final e Before Vowel. Drop the silent *e* before a suffix beginning with a vowel.**

   Admirable, arguing, largest, enclosing, scarcity

6. **Final e Before Consonant. Keep the final silent *e* before a suffix beginning with a consonant.**

   amazement, atonement, hopeful, fortunately, useful
   Exceptions: acknowledgment, argument, awful, duly, judgment, ninth, truly, wholly

7. **Final y. If a final *y* is preceded by a consonant, change *y* to *i* when you add a suffix.**

   app*ly* + *ed* = appl*ied* (The *y* changed to *i*.)
   friend*ly* + er = friendl*ier*
   nois*y* + est = nois*iest*

But notice the following forms.

apply + ing = applying

(The *y* does not change to *i* if the suffix begins with *i*.)

play + er = player

(The *y* does not change to *i* if *y* is preceded by a vowel.)

8. **Doubling Final Consonant—One-Syllable Words. Note the following correct forms. Each final consonant is preceded by a single vowel.**

bat + er = ba*tt*er

(The final consonant, *t*, is doubled.)

big + est = bi*gg*est

drop + ing = dro*pp*ing

grin + ed = gri*nn*ed

What happens when the final consonant is preceded by more than one vowel?

beat + en = bea*t*en

(The final consonant, *t*, is not doubled.)

sail + ed = sai*l*ed

dream + er = drea*m*er

fool + ish = foo*l*ish

foam + ing = foa*m*ing

9. **Doubling Final Consonant—Words of More Than One Syllable. If a word has more than one syllable and the accent is on the last syllable, the same rule applies as for a one-syllable word.**

commit + ed = commi*tt*ed

(The accent is on the last syllable—*t* is doubled.)

control + ing = contro*ll*ing

equip + ed = equi*pp*ed

propel + er = prope*ll*er

refer + ed = refe*rr*ed

What happens if the word is not accented on the last syllable?

refer + ence = refe*r*ence

(The accent is not on **er**; **r** is not doubled.)

Contractions

10. **A** *contraction* **is a word that has been shortened by omitting one or more letters. Insert an apostrophe where one or more letters are left out in a word. When writing contractions, don't add a letter and don't change the letters around.**

she + is = she's	we + are = we're
he + will = he'll	can + not = can't
they + have = they've	I + would = I'd

Exception: will + not = won't

Don't put an apostrophe in the wrong place:

WRONG:	have'nt	could'nt	do'nt
RIGHT:	haven't	couldn't	don't

Remember: The possessives of personal pronouns do not have apostrophes (page 466).

PRACTICE: Identifying Sentence Errors

The following sentences test your knowledge of grammar, usage, diction (choice of words), and idiom. Some sentences are correct. No sentence contains more than one error. You will find that the error, if there is one, is underlined and lettered. Elements of the sentence that are not underlined will not be changed. In choosing answers, follow the requirements of standard written English. If there is an error, select the one underlined part that must be changed to make the sentence correct. If there is no error, choose answer E.

1. A student who <u>graduates</u> from high school and plans to attend an <u>away-from-home</u> college must be
   A   B
   prepared for <u>adjustments</u> to his or her lifestyle <u>and a flexible</u> attitude in solving problems. <u>No error</u>
   C   D   E

1 ___

2. Although we have a full <u>compliment</u> of senior <u>staff members</u> on our school paper, we can always use
   A   B
   enthusiastic reporters, especially those interested in the <u>offbeat</u> and <u>out-of-the-way</u>. <u>No error</u>
   C   D   E

2 ___

3. When the votes <u>were</u> finally counted, there were <u>less</u> votes in favor of the planned bus ride <u>than</u> we had
   A   B   C
   <u>formerly</u> anticipated. <u>No error</u>
   D   E

3 ___

4. Our Inca guide told us that <u>by the time</u> the Spanish arrived, the Incas <u>already developed</u> an irrigation
   A   B
   system <u>that</u> was <u>remarkably</u> efficient. <u>No error</u>
   C   D   E

4 ___

5. In his historic final speech, the American patriot Nathan Hale regretted <u>that</u> he <u>hadn't</u> <u>but</u> one life
$\qquad$ $\overset{}{\underset{A}{}}$ $\qquad$ $\overset{}{\underset{B}{}}$ $\overset{}{\underset{C}{}}$

$\quad$ <u>to give</u> for his country. <u>No error</u>
$\quad\;\; \overset{}{\underset{D}{}}$ $\qquad\qquad\;\; \overset{}{\underset{E}{}}$

$\hfill$ 5 ____

6. <u>On the whole</u>, Jeremy does pretty <u>good</u> in algebra, but he is <u>unfortunately</u> finding Spanish much more
$\quad\;\overset{}{\underset{A}{}}$ $\qquad\qquad\qquad\;\; \overset{}{\underset{B}{}}$ $\qquad\qquad\quad\; \overset{}{\underset{C}{}}$

$\quad$ <u>of a challenge</u>. <u>No error</u>
$\qquad \overset{}{\underset{D}{}}$ $\quad\;\; \overset{}{\underset{E}{}}$

$\hfill$ 6 ____

7. True Gilbert and Sullivan fans, the devoted Savoyards, <u>used to</u> prefer the productions of the
$\qquad\qquad\qquad\qquad\qquad\qquad\qquad\qquad\quad\;\; \overset{}{\underset{A}{}}$

$\quad$ D'Oyly Carte Company because the <u>group's</u> productions were <u>polished</u>, witty, and
$\qquad\qquad\qquad\qquad\qquad\qquad\;\; \overset{}{\underset{B}{}}$ $\qquad\qquad\quad\; \overset{}{\underset{C}{}}$

$\quad$ <u>showed discipline</u>. <u>No error</u>
$\qquad \overset{}{\underset{D}{}}$ $\qquad\;\; \overset{}{\underset{E}{}}$

$\hfill$ 7 ____

8. I have just finished reading a fascinating article about Lucy Audubon, a courageous young pioneer,

$\quad$ <u>and who</u> <u>braved</u> the wilderness to follow her husband, John James Audubon, <u>principally</u> <u>known</u>
$\quad\;\; \overset{}{\underset{A}{}}$ $\quad \overset{}{\underset{B}{}}$ $\qquad\qquad\qquad\qquad\qquad\qquad\qquad\qquad\quad \overset{}{\underset{C}{}}$ $\qquad \overset{}{\underset{D}{}}$

$\quad$ as a painter of birds. <u>No error</u>
$\qquad\qquad\qquad\quad\;\; \overset{}{\underset{E}{}}$

$\hfill$ 8 ____

9. After <u>flying</u> out three times, Sammy Sosa came to bat in the ninth and sent <u>it flying</u> over the
$\qquad \overset{}{\underset{A}{}}\;\overset{}{\underset{B}{}}$ $\qquad\qquad\qquad\qquad\qquad\qquad\qquad\qquad\qquad\qquad\; \overset{}{\underset{C}{}}$

$\quad$ bleachers in right field. <u>No error</u>
$\qquad \overset{}{\underset{D}{}}$ $\qquad\qquad\quad \overset{}{\underset{E}{}}$

$\hfill$ 9 ____

10. As in Edgar Allan <u>Poe's</u> "The Purloined Letter," the missing wallet had been
$\qquad\qquad\qquad\;\; \overset{}{\underset{A}{}}$

$\quad$ <u>laying</u> in plain <u>sight</u> <u>all along.</u> <u>No error</u>
$\quad\;\; \overset{}{\underset{B}{}}$ $\qquad \overset{}{\underset{C}{}}$ $\quad\; \overset{}{\underset{D}{}}$ $\qquad \overset{}{\underset{E}{}}$

$\hfill$ 10 ____

11. Although Grandpa had never <u>rode</u> in a roller coaster before, he found the trip on the Cyclone
$\qquad\qquad\qquad\qquad\qquad\;\; \overset{}{\underset{A}{}}$

$\quad$ <u>so exciting</u> that he insisted on <u>going</u> again, <u>despite</u> Grandma's protests. <u>No error</u>
$\qquad \overset{}{\underset{B}{}}$ $\qquad\qquad\qquad \overset{}{\underset{C}{}}$ $\qquad \overset{}{\underset{D}{}}$ $\qquad\qquad\qquad\qquad\; \overset{}{\underset{E}{}}$

$\hfill$ 11 ____

12. <u>According to</u> the appliance salesperson, on the average only one in ten of all qualified customers actually
$\quad\;\; \overset{}{\underset{A}{}}$

$\quad$ <u>send</u> in the rebate form, <u>thus</u> providing an attractive <u>but</u> deceptive sale price. <u>No error</u>
$\quad \overset{}{\underset{B}{}}$ $\qquad\qquad\qquad \overset{}{\underset{C}{}}$ $\qquad\qquad\qquad\qquad \overset{}{\underset{D}{}}$ $\qquad\qquad\qquad \overset{}{\underset{E}{}}$

$\hfill$ 12 ____

13. We <u>all</u> remembered that the keys to the garden shed had been <u>lying</u> around for weeks, but when we
     A   B

wanted <u>to get out</u> some tools, the key was <u>nowheres</u> to be found. <u>No error</u>
      C   D   E

13 ____

14. Between you and <u>I</u>, neither Chet nor his brothers <u>are</u> <u>qualified</u> to <u>take over</u> the landscaping for the
              A   B   C   D

Goodman estate, a 300-acre haven of beauty. <u>No error</u>
                                     E

14 ____

15. <u>Here is</u> a selection of <u>misnomers</u> from Tom's research paper: the jackrabbit is a hare, not a rabbit; the
    A   B   C

Jerusalem artichocke is a sunflower, not an artichoke; Arabic numerals are not Arabic. <u>No error</u>
                                    D   E

15 ____

16. Before a tidal <u>wave, or tsunami,</u> reaches shore, the water <u>resedes</u>, so that a person foolish enough
                 A   B

<u>to do so</u> <u>could</u> walk out miles before the wave came crashing ashore. <u>No error</u>
   C   D   E

16 ____

17. Serge Koussevitsky <u>not only</u> was a distinguished conductor <u>of</u> symphony orchestras <u>but also</u> an
                     A   B   C

expert player <u>of</u> the double bass. <u>No error</u>
         D   E

17 ____

18. <u>As</u> I watched Harold Lloyd <u>teetering</u> on the edge of the building, <u>threatening</u> to fall hundreds of feet
  A   B   C

to the pavement below, I was <u>literally</u> scared to death. <u>No error</u>
                     D   E

18 ____

19. Agatha Christie <u>is</u> a master <u>creator</u> of great detective stories and a fascinating detective, Hercule Poirot,
              A   B   C

and <u>has for years.</u> <u>No error</u>
    D   E

19 ____

20. <u>In my opinion,</u> <u>I think</u> that collecting old coins is uniquely satisfying, <u>for</u> holding in my hand a coin
      A   B   C

that Shakespeare might have used is a <u>tangible</u> link with the past. <u>No error</u>
                               D   E

20 ____

21. Krakatoa erupted in the East Indies in 1883 <u>the</u> sound was heard in Bangkok <u>3,000 miles away,</u> <u>and</u>
                                     A   B   C

Londoners <u>could see</u> a thin haze in the sky for the next two years. <u>No error</u>
       D   E

21 ____

22. Ambrose Bierce's "The Horseman in the Sky" is a brilliant example of subtlety in plotting, economy
                                           A   B

    in writing, and perceptive in suggesting emotion. No error
                     C   D   E

    22 ____

23. Karen and Alice are superb basketball players, sinking three pointers regularly, but at the foul line,
                                              A   B   C

    Karen is the more consistent. No error
                 D   E

    23 ____

24. If the size of the brain is positively correlated with intelligence, the giant stegosaurus, with a brain
    A   B

    the size of a walnut, must of had difficulty fending off the voracious carnivores of the Jurassic
                                   C   D

    period. No error
            E

    24 ____

25. Three fourths of the recent federal grant are being assigned to the preservation of the
                                        A   B

    scrub-jay habitat and cleanup of the beach nearby. No error
           C   D   E

    25 ____

PRACTICE: Improving Sentences

In each of the following questions, select the best version of the underlined part of the sentence. Choice (A) is the same as the underlined portion of the original sentence. If you think the original sentence is best, choose answer (A).

1. When his cat ran across the keys of his piano, Chopin was taken with the resulting notes and he incorporated the sounds in "The Cat Waltz."

    (A) was taken with the resulting notes and he incorporated the sounds in "The Cat Waltz."

    (B) was so taken with the resulting notes that he incorporated the sounds in "The Cat Waltz."

    (C) was so taken with the results, incorporating the sounds in "The Cat Waltz."

    (D) being taken by the resulting notes and incorporating the sounds in "The Cat Waltz."

    (E) incorporated the sounds in "The Cat Waltz" because he had been taken by the resulting notes.

    1 ____

2. Because of the late-night finishes, the winner of the Monday night football game <u>will either be reported in Tuesday's paper or in Wednesday's.</u>

   (A) will either be reported in Tuesday's paper or in Wednesday's.

   (B) either will be reported in Tuesday's paper or in Wednesday's.

   (C) will either be reported in Tuesday's paper or in Wednesday.

   (D) will be reported either in Tuesday's paper or in Wednesday's.

   (E) will either be reported in Tuesday paper or in Wednesday's.

                                                               2 ____

3. The lonely island of St. Helena in the south Atlantic had two famous <u>residents, and one of these was Napoleon and the other was the astronomer Edmund Halley, and he mapped the southern skies in 1676.</u>

   (A) residents, and one of these was Napoleon and the other was the astronomer Edmund Halley, and he mapped the southern skies in 1676.

   (B) residents, and one of these was Napoleon, the other being the astronomer Edmund Halley, and he mapped the southern skies in 1676.

   (C) residents, one of whom was Napoleon, the other being the astronomer Edmund Halley, and he mapped the southern skies in 1676.

   (D) residents: Napoleon and the astronomer Edmund Halley, who mapped the southern skies in 1676.

   (E) residents, and one of these was Napoleon, the other being the astronomer Edmund Halley, having mapped the southern skies in 1676.

                                                                3 ____

4. Wondering at the incredible popularity of *The Merry Widow,* <u>created by the bandmaster Franz Lehar, the composer Gustav Mahler and his wife used</u> to sneak in to discover for themselves Lehar's special gifts.

   (A) created by the bandmaster Franz Lehar, the composer Gustav Mahler and his wife used to

   (B) which had been created by the bandmaster Franz Lehar, Gustav Mahler and his wife used to

   (C) created by the bandmaster Franz Lehar, its success enticed the composer Gustav Mahler and his wife to

   (D) a creation of the bandmaster Franz Lehar, the composer Gustav Mahler and his wife use to

   (E) created by the bandmaster Franz Lehar, and motivated by curiosity, the composer Gustav Mahler and his wife discovered the Lehar's special gifts.

                                                                4 ____

5. "If you read the papers, <u>everybody and their mother are bin Laden supporters in Saudi Arabia,</u>" Prince Bandar declared.

    (A) everybody and their mother are bin Laden supporters in Saudi Arabia,"

    (B) in Saudi Arabia, everyone and his mother is a bin Laden supporter,"

    (C) everybody is a bin Laden supporter in Saudi Arabia,"

    (D) Everybody and their mothers are bin Laden supporters in Saudi Arabia,"

    (E) bin Laden supporters and their mother are everywhere in Saudi Arabia

5 ____

PRACTICE: Improving Paragraphs

Directions: The following passage is an early draft of an essay. Some parts of the passage need to be rewritten. Read the passage and select the best answers for the questions that follow. Some questions are about particular sentences or parts of sentences and ask you to improve sentence structure and word choice. Other questions refer to parts of the essay or the entire essay and ask you to consider organization and development. In making your decisions, follow the conventions of standard written English.

(1) Either the sitcom is an invulnerable staple of television or an ultimately doomed fossil. (2) Apart from any specific program, the form itself has its negative detractors and doomsayers: an article in *Newsweek* had called great sitcoms "an endangered species." (3) Many critics agree that the average sitcom, with its frantic jokes has seen better days: 46 programs in 1993 and only 24 a decade later, a significant decline. (4) A further look back brings an appreciative chuckle at the groundbreaking success of sitcoms like *All in the Family* and *I Love Lucy*, followed by hardy survivors like *Cheers, Murphy Brown*, and last but not least *Frasier*. (5) The longevity of *Friends* invites analyses: why so successful?

(6) Ingredients of failure are more easier to identify than are elements of success: disasters including hackneyed dialogue, a succession of uninspired one-liners, lifeless stereotypes, and an irritating laugh track. (7) Character-driven sitcoms seem to do well, with accomplished actors like Dick Van Dyke, Mary Tyler Moore and Jerry Seinfeld, but even these talented comedic professionals wisely surround theirselves with gifted ensembles. (8) Because comedy is a serious business, some sitcom producers should usually always take Hamlet's advice to the Players: don't let the clowns laugh at their own jokes, for that will "set on some barren spectators to laugh, too."

1. How may sentence 1 be improved?

    (A) Move *either* after *is*.

    (B) Change *an invulnerable* to *a perishable*.

    (C) Insert *it is* after *or*.

    (D) Replace *an ultimately* with *a possibly*.

    (E) Replace *fossil* with *experiment*.

1 ____

2. Which revison is most needed in sentence 2?
- (A) Insert *really* after *itself*.
- (B) Eliminate *negative*.
- (C) Change the *colon* to a *semicolon*.
- (D) Insert *magazine* after *Newsweek*.
- (E) Omit the quotation marks around *an endangered species*.

2 ____

3. How may sentence 3 be improved?
- (A) Insert *perverse* after *many*.
- (B) Insert a comma after *jokes*.
- (C) Change *has* to *have*.
- (D) Omit *only*.
- (E) Insert *reflecting* before *a significant decline*.

3 ____

4. How may sentence 4 be improved.
- (A) Change *back* to *backward*.
- (B) Change *brings* to *can bring*.
- (C) Replace *groundbreaking* with *tremendous*.
- (D) Insert *which were* before *followed*.
- (E) Remove *last but not least* before *Frasier*.

4 ____

5. How may sentence 6 be improved?
- (A) Attach to previous sentence and do not begin a new paragraph with this sentence.
- (B) Eliminate *more*.
- (C) Insert *it may be said* after *failure*.
- (D) Replace *and* with *as well as*.
- (E) End the sentence with an exclamation point.

5 ____

6. How may sentence 7 be revised?
- (A) Omit the hyphen between *character* and *driven*.
- (B) Replace *with* with *having*.
- (C) Change *but* to *and*.
- (D) Change *theirselves* to *themselves*.
- (E) Change *ensembles* to *staffs*.

6 ____

7. How may sentence 8 be improved?

    (A) Change *Because* to *although*.

    (B) Omit *usually always*.

    (C) Change *let* to *allow*.

    (D) Change *clowns* to *clown* and *their* to *his*.

    (E) Change *for* to *inasmuch as*.

7 _____

Writing Diagnostic Tests

First take Test A, below, and Test B on page 490. Referring to pages 558–561, check your answers, and go over the analysis. In the analysis you will find the page numbers where to turn in this book for additional help and strategy.

Find your weaknesses well in advance of the SAT testing date so that you will have ample time to work on the types of test items that you find most difficult. Remember, you are building your personal power to take the SAT with confidence.

Writing Diagnostic Test A

Identifying Sentence Errors

The following sentences test your knowledge of grammar, usage, diction (choice of words), and idiom. Some sentences are correct. No sentence contains more than one error. You will find that the error, if there is one, is underlined and lettered. Elements of the sentence that are not underlined will not be changed. In choosing answers, follow the requirements of standard written English. If there is an error, select the one underlined part that must be changed to make the sentence correct. If there is no error, choose answer E.

1. Living on a globe reveals surprising facts; for example, a direct flight from New York to Tokyo would
    A   B   C D

pass over Alaska, and a direct line from San Francisco to Egypt would pass close to the North

Pole. No error
     E

1 _____

2. While we were walking through the woods, Travis casually identified a cardinal, a nuthatch, a
  A   B   C

mourning dove, and etc. No error
       D   E

2 _____

3. On the preliminary vote, nearly every one of the committee members were in favor of the resolution,
                A   B

but that consensus disappeared as the discussions proceeded. No error
      C   D   E

3 _____

4. <u>After</u> disparaging her contributions 50 years ago, James D. Watson, winner of the <u>Nobel Prize</u> for his
   A   B

work on <u>DNA</u>, now thinks that Rosalind Franklin <u>deserved</u> her own Nobel Prize. <u>No error</u>
       C   D   E

4 ____

5. The fullback <u>having found</u> a hole off left tackle, bursting <u>through</u> the secondary and eluding the last
               A   B

tackler <u>on his way</u> to the end zone. <u>No error</u>
     C   D   E

5 ____

6. Plants that depend on the wind for pollination <u>don't need</u> bright flowers, but those <u>that</u> depend upon
                                         A   B

insects <u>they</u> do advertise their availability <u>by displaying</u> attractive colors. <u>No error</u>
       C   D   E

6 ____

7. For Terry, <u>running</u> the marathon <u>three times</u> a year and participating in the <u>iron-man</u> competition
          A   B   C

once <u>is</u> paying off in helping to improve his health and sense of well-being. <u>No error</u>
     D   E

7 ____

8. Throughout its <u>two-century</u> history, the home of the President has been known as the Palace, the
                 A

Executive Mansion, and <u>it was known</u> as the White House after it had to be painted <u>to cover</u> the
                            B   C

damage <u>caused</u> by the British during the War of 1812. <u>No error</u>
      D   E

8 ____

9. Uriah Heep, one of the most detestable characters <u>in all of</u> fiction, proved <u>by</u> all his actions that he
                                           A   B

<u>only</u> had one goal in life: the accumulation of money. <u>No error</u>
 C   D   E

9 ____

10. In many parts of Africa, the rains come too <u>infrequent</u> to <u>restore</u> life <u>after</u> a long and <u>devastating</u>
                                         A   B   C   D

dry season. <u>No error</u>
        E

10 ____

11. The early <u>Presidents</u> demonstrated <u>the long and the short of it</u>, <u>surprisingly</u>, Thomas Jefferson at 6'2"
          A   B   C

was eight inches taller than his <u>one-time</u> Secretary of State, James Madison. <u>No error</u>
                             D   E

11 ____

12. <u>Irregardless</u> of the dangers they faced, the rescue team defied the threat of avalanches in
    A

their <u>desperate</u> search for the skiers, <u>missing</u> since nightfall two <u>days ago</u>. <u>No error</u>
      B   C   D   E

12 ____

13. No matter what the <u>naysayers</u> suggested, Dr. Robert Atkins <u>insisted</u> upon his revolutionary diet
                   A   B

plan <u>emphasizing</u> the important role of fat and proteins in a <u>lose-weight</u> diet. <u>No error</u>
       C   D   E

                                                                          13 _____

14. <u>Talking</u> to a lot of running backs, Warrick Dunn is a runner <u>that</u> can find an opening <u>when</u> the
   A   B   C

defensive line is solid and the tacklers are waiting <u>with open arms</u>. <u>No error</u>.
                                                          D   E

                                                                          14 _____

15. If he <u>were</u> a few inches <u>taller</u>, <u>he'd</u> try out for the basketball team, but as it is, at six <u>feet</u> he's too short!
      A   B   C   D

<u>No error</u>
  E

                                                                          15 _____

Improving Sentences

In each of the following questions, select the best version of the underlined part of the sentence. Choice (A) is the same as the underlined portion of the original sentence. If you think the original sentence is best, choose answer (A).

16. In 1930, the first airline stewardesses went aboard a Boeing San Francisco-Chicago flight, <u>a trip that took 20 hours and made 13 stops.</u>

   (A) flight, a trip that took 20 hours and made 13 stops.

   (B) flight and experienced a trip that took 20 hours and made 13 stops.

   (C) flight, on a long trip if we apply modern schedules.

   (D) flight, enduring a long trip that took as much as 20 hours, with 13 stops.

   (E) flight, experiencing a long trip that lasted 20 hours and made 13 stops.

                                                              16 _____

17. A surprising moment in my research <u>was when I discovered that 90% of all scientists who have ever lived are alive today.</u>

   (A) was when I discovered that 90% of all scientists who have ever lived are alive today.

   (B) was when I discovered that 90% of scientists of all time are alive today.

   (C) was my discovery that 90% of all scientists who have ever lived are alive today.

   (D) was when I discovered that of all scientists who have ever lived, 90% are alive today.

   (E) was my discovery about the predominance of living scientists over those of the past.

                                                            17 _____

18. According to David Hockney, the use of optics, beginning in the 15th Century, enabled artists to capture nature more economically, <u>sketch an outline in seconds, and they found they could record the tiniest details effectively.</u>

    (A) sketch an outline in seconds, and they found they could record the tiniest details effectively.

    (B) quickly sketch an outline and the tiniest details presented effectively in seconds.

    (C) sketch an outline in seconds while the tiniest details were effectively presented.

    (D) sketch an outline in seconds, and record the tiniest details effectively,

    (E) sketch an outline in seconds, and the tiniest details were effectively presented.

18 ____

Improving Paragraphs

The following passage is an early draft of an essay. Some parts of the passage need to be rewritten. Read the passage and select the best answers for the questions that follow. Some questions are about particular sentences or parts of sentences and ask you to improve sentence structure and word choice. Other questions refer to parts of the essay or the entire essay and ask you to consider organization and development. In making your decisions, follow the conventions of standard written English.

(1) Words are magic. (2) Primitive, as well as industrial societies, have played a role throughout history, dazzling speakers and listeners by words. (3) As used in chants, words can cast a psychological spell over listeners. (4) The witches in *Macbeth* use an incantation whose purpose is to call up the spirits of prophecy: "Double, double toil and trouble." (5) In modern society, advertisers and political speakers use words to cast different kind of spells, with "magic words" like *free, new and improved* in advertising; *freedom* and *democracy* in politics.

(6) A fascination with words seems to be part of the human psyche, from infancy, children are delighted by the babble they create, and they find satisfaction in sounds and words. (7) Some wordplay is social, like *Scrabble, anagrams*, or transmitting a message from one person to another at a party to see how the message survives. (8) Other wordplay is individual, like discovering or creating palindromes, words or sentences that can be read backward as well as forward—for example, *eye, refer, kayak*.

(9) The amazing diversity and the surprising flexibility of the English language are often uncovered by wordplay. (10) Here's a tantalizing example: what do the words *bag, ball, last, pack*, and *pat* have in common? (11) There's obviously no semantic relationships, but each word creates other words by replacing *a* with each of the other four vowels: *bag, beg, big, bog*, and *bug*. Similarly, *ball* can generate *bell, bill*, (12) *boll*, and *bull*, and so on.

19. Which of the following is the best revision of sentence 2?

   (A) The speakers and listeners, who have played a role in primitive and industrial societies, have been dazzled by words.

   (B) Throughout history, words have played a major role in primitive and industrial societies, dazzling speakers and listeners.

   (C) In primitive and industrial societies throughout history is the role of how words dazzle speakers and listeners.

   (D) Throughout the history of primitive and industrial societies, the role of words have dazzled speakers and listeners.

   (E) Playing a major role throughout history, in primitive and industrial societies, speakers and listeners have been dazzled by words.

19 ____

20. Which of the following is the best revision of sentence 4?

   (A) The incantation "Double, double toil and trouble" is an incantation that the witches use in *Macbeth* in order to call up the spirits of prophacy.

   (B) "Double, double toil and trouble" is used in *Macbeth* as an incantation for the purpose of calling up the spirits of prophecy by the witches.

   (C) The witches in *Macbeth* use an incantation to call up the spirits of prophecy: "Double, double toil and trouble."

   (D) *Macbeth* uses an incantation by the witches and their calling up the spirits of prophecy, "Double, double toil and trouble."

   (E) The spirits of prophecy are called upon by *Macbeth's* witches in the form of an incantation: "Double, double toil and trouble."

20 ____

21. Which revision is best in sentence 5?

   (A) Replace the first *and* with *as well as*.

   (B) Insert *tend to* after *speakers*.

   (C) Replace *to cast* with *so that they can cast*.

   (D) Replace *kind* with *kinds*.

   (E) Omit quotation marks around *magic words*.

21 ____

22. Which of the following is the best revision of sentence 6?

   (A) A fascination with words seems to be part of the human psyche; from infancy children are delighted by the babble they create and find satisfaction in sounds and words.

   (B) A fascination with words seems to be part of the human psyche, for from infancy, children are delighted by sounds and words. And satisfaction in the babble they create.

(C) A fascination with words seems to be part of the human psyche, for from infancy children are delighted by sounds and words, when they find satisfaction in the babble they create.

(D) A fascination with words seems to be part of the human psyche, but from infancy, children are delighted by sounds and words, to find satisfaction in the
babble they create.

(E) Since a fascination with words seems to be part of the human psyche from infancy, children are delighted by sounds and words and finding satisfaction in
the babble they create.

22 ____

23. Which of the following is the best revision of sentence 9?

(A) The English language shows amazing diversity and flexibility, and wordplay
often uncovers them.

(B) The amazing flexibility and diversity of the English language are two characteristics of the English language that can be uncovered by wordplay.

(C) Through wordplay, the English language often is revealed to have the amazing qualities of diversity and flexibility.

(D) Flexibility and diversity are two characteristics of the English language as revealed by wordplay.

(E) Wordplay often uncovers the amazing diversity and flexibility of the English
language.

23 ____

24. Which revision is best in sentence 11?

(A) Replace *There's* with *There are*.

(B) Change *for* to *but*.

(C) Change *replacing* with *replacement of*.

(D) Replace *each* with *every one*.

(E) Insert *as in* after the colon.

24 ____

Writing the Essay

Consider carefully the following excerpt and the assignment below it. Then plan and
write an essay that explains your ideas as persuasively as possible. Keep in mind that
the support you provide—both reasons and examples—will help make your view convincing to the reader.

A woman who thinks herself well dressed has no suspicion that her costume will one day
come to seem as ludicrous as the headdress of Catherine de Medici. All the fashions we
are taken with will grow old, perhaps before we ourselves.

Luc de Clapiers Vauvenargues.

Assignment. What is your view about changing fashions in clothing, TV programs, or popular music? Do the changes provide excitement and stimulation, or do they often waste time
and money in a fruitless quest to be "with it"? In an essay, support your position by mention-
ing good or bad changes. Use examples that make your argument more effective.

Writing Diagnostic Test B

Identifying Sentence Errors

The following sentences test your knowledge of grammar, usage, diction (choice of words), and idiom. Some sentences are correct. No sentence contains more than one error. You will find that the error, if there is one, is underlined and lettered. Elements of the sentence that are not underlined will not be changed. In choosing answers, follow the requirements of standard written English. If there is an error, select the one underlined part that must be changed to make the sentence correct. If there is no error, choose answer E.

1. A person, standing at the North Pole can choose whatever time he wishes it to be
        A   B   C
   by stepping off a few feet in any direction. No error.
           D   E

   1 ____

2. Salt has always been one of the most valuable of all commodities, even today the
        A   B
   expression "worth his salt" pays tribute to its importance. No error.
             C   D   E

   2 ____

3. Just when it appeared that Len Mattiace might win the tournament easy, he hit a
      A   B   C   D
   disastrous drive into the trees on the 18th hole and subsequently lost the playoff. No error
                                                                  E

   3 ____

4. That tiny bit of dynamite, the humming bird, can easily pull out of a power
                     A   B
   dive, consequently it never hesitates to shoot downwards at high speed. No error
        C   D   E

   4 ____

5. From early childhood, Tom wanted to live in the west, not too far from the ocean;
         A   B   C
   he finally found a home in Jamul, California. No error
                       D   E

   5 ____

6. After weeks of agonizing, Sally was finally accepted by the university of Florida. No error
        A   B   C   D   E

   6 ____

7. In their abundance of courses and wealth of facilities, the modern colleges
                                 A
   of today are a far cry from the more limited schools of even a century ago. No error
     B   C   D   E

   7 ____

8. Commenting upon stylistic improvement, Mark Twain once said wryly, "As to the
   A   B   C D

adjective, when in doubt, strike it out." No error
             E

                             8 ____

9. Working steadily to produce a suitable document, Thomas Jefferson's masterpiece, The Declaration
  A   B   C

of Independence, became the rallying cry for the new nation. No error
         D   E

                             9 ____

10. When Adolf Hitler absorbed the rest of Czechoslovakia in 1938, it was

probably certain that he would not rest until he had overrun Poland. No error
   A   B   C D   E

                           10 ____

11. By studying the music of the Forty-Niners will offer unusual insight into the life
  A   B

and experiences of these colorful Western migrants. No error
           C   D   E

                           11 ____

12. In his never-ending search for unimportant trivia, Ben discovered that the shortest war in history
     A   B

was when the sultan of Zanzibar surrendered to the British after a 38-minute bombardment.
 C   D

No error
E

                           12 ____

13. During our trip to Kashmir, our houseboat was met by buses and taken to a
  A   B   C

colorful hotel near the center of town. No error
       D   E

                           13 ____

14. The mermaid statue in the harbor of Copenhagen, intended to perpetrate the memory
                A   B   C

of Hans Christian Andersen, greets visitors as they approach land. No error
                D   E

                           14 ____

15. When you follow the recipe that I gave you, be sure to put two tablespoons full of
  A   B   C   D

chili sauce into the stew. No error
        E

                           15 ____

Improving Sentences

In each of the following questions, select the best version of the underlined part of the sentence. Choice (A) is the same as the underlined portion of the original sentence. If you think the original sentence is best, choose answer (A).

16. Commenting upon the celebrities' choice of jewelry at the Oscar ceremonies, one <u>designer declared, "The best accessory of these is tasteful and understated."</u>

    (A) designer declared, "The best accessory of these is tasteful and understated."

    (B) designer declared, "The best accessory of these are tasteful and understated."

    (C) designer declared that the best accessory of these were understated.

    (D) "The best accessory of these, "declared the designer, "is understated."

    (E) "The best accessory of these is tasteful and understated," declared the designer.

          16 _____

17. Paradoxically, President Martin Van Buren prevented a proposed invasion of Canada <u>in 1838, but who, a month later, hailed the forcible transfer</u> of the Cherokee Indian tribe to new lands in the West.

    (A) in 1838, but who, a month later, hailed the forcible transfer

    (B) in 1838, but a month later, hailing the forcible transfer

    (C) in 1838, but a month later hailed the forcible transfer

    (D) in 1838, who, a month later, hailed the forcible transfer

    (E) in 1838, and a month later he hailed the forcible transfer

          17 _____

18. During the birthday segment on *Entertainment Tonight*, the announcer <u>asked, "Which star changed their name for</u> a career in the movies."

    (A) asked, "Which star changed their name for

    (B) asked, "Which star changed her name for

    (C) asked, "Which star changed their name to advance

    (D) asked, "Which star changed their name for

    (E) asked, "What star changed her name for

          18 _____

Improving Paragraphs

The following passage is an early draft of an essay. Some parts of the passage need to be rewritten. Read the passage and select the best answers for the questions that follow. Some questions are about particular sentences or parts of sentences and ask you to improve sentence structure and word choice. Other questions refer to parts of the essay or the entire essay and ask you to consider organization and development. In making your decisions, follow the conventions of standard written English.

(1) We can enjoy the plays of Shakespeare, thanks largely to those fellow actors who printed the First Folio after Shakespeare's death, but many plays by contemporaries, even a talented contemporary, has been lost. (2) Examining early films; sometimes considered a transitory art form, films were shown and often discarded. (3) Some of the early classics have been preserved, like the films of D. W. Griffith: *Intolerance* and *Birth of a Nation*; but many others have been lost, carelessly stored, or just oblivion.

(4) In more modern times, multiple prints have guaranteed the survival of even inferior films. (5) Though some of the better old silents have had extended lives on television, video, and DVD, the very poorest films may be stored but seldom shown again after the initial showings. (6) They depart with few mourners to lament their passing, generally forgotten, except by fans of cult films.

(7) What is a cult film? The magazine *Entertainment* declared, "Now they compose our cultural Esperanto, a subliminal vocabulary of vaguely subversive images, ideas, and phrases that we continue to obsess over and dissect around watercoolers, in bars over the blaring banalities of the mainstream media din." (9) They may have been dismal failures critically or so inaccessible that audiences walked out. (10) Somehow they are purchased by science-fiction enthusiasts, lovers of the weird, fans of outrageously exaggerated horror (11) These cult films were generally not mainstream movies, a lack of popularity savored by their fans. (12) Instead of dying a quick, merciful death, these films live on in special theaters, in ordinary theaters at midnight after the mainstream audience has filed out, on late-night television—not for Mr. Average Filmgoer.

(13) Although *Entertainment* listed the fifty "best" cult films, including *The Rocky Horror Picture Show* and the sentimental *Harold and Maude*, readers promptly sent in their own lists. (14) All these films have one thing in common—a surprising charm thanks to the dedicated fans of this unusual genre.

19. Which revision is most needed in sentence 1?

    (A) Insert a comma after *actors*.

    (B) Replace *Shakespeare's* with *Shakespeares'*

    (C) Change *by* to *assigned to*.

    (D) Remove comma after *contemporary*.

    (E) Replace *has* with *have*.

19 ____

20. In sentence 2, *Examining early films* can be expressed more effectively by replacing it with _____.

    (A) *A critical glance at early films*

    (B) *With respect to experiences with early films*

    (C) *So it is with early films*

    (D) *In the matter of early films*

    (E) *Early films have had a checkered history*

20 ____

21. Which revision is most needed in sentence 3?

    (A) Replace *have been* with *are*.

    (B) Replace *like* with *as have*.

    (C) Substitute *and* for *but*.

    (D) Replace *lost* with *mislaid*.

    (E) Change *oblivion* to *discarded*.

21 ____

22. In sentence 10, a more effective replacement for *are purchased by* would be_____.
    (A) fill a niche for
    (B) gain the attention of
    (C) win the approval of
    (D) provide emotional highs for
    (E) spur the interest of

    22 ____

23. Which revision is most needed in sentence 13?
    (A) Replace *Although* with *When*.
    (B) Remove the quotation marks around *best*.
    (C) Replace *including* with *listing*.
    (D) Replace the comma after *Maude* with a semicolon.
    (E) Replace *their* with *there*.

    23 ____

24. In sentence 14, a better word for *charm* would be
    (A) likability
    (B) longevity
    (C) challenge
    (D) interest
    (E) extravagance

    24 ____

Writing the Essay

Consider carefully the following excerpt and the assignment below it. Then plan and write an essay that explains your ideas as persuasively as possible. Keep in mind that the support you provide—both reasons and examples—will help make your view convincing to the reader.

The rush-hour streets of any city are clogged with workers who clocked in between eight and nine and left between four and five. Drivers inch along, consuming gasoline, polluting the air, inwardly fretting—is there any way to minimize the crush? There are two partial solutions: flextime and adjusted work-hours. Flextime allows employees to set their own hours. Adjusting work schedules might bring workers in at seven instead of eight with a similar adjustment at the other end.

Assignment: Do you feel that one or both of these solutions are practicable? Or do you find too many difficulties with either or both? Present your point of view in an essay. Include as many examples as possible within the time requirements of your assignment.

Division E

Mastery Tests / Writing

A Strategy for the Mastery Tests / Writing

- These tests have been prepared to familiarize you with the kind of challenges you'll face in taking the SAT. The tests that follow approximate the SAT you will be taking, but they are practices only.

- Review the Introduction, pages iv–xvi.

- Before you begin, be sure you have the appropriate amount of time to spend on the test. Try to approximate test conditions as much as possible.

- Have a watch with you to check your timing. Don't spend too much time on any one question. If you waste time on a question, you may not reach questions that are easy for you. If you have trouble with a question, put a check mark next to it so that you can find it quickly again, and go right on. If you have time later, go back and try again.

- Read the questions carefully. Following directions is an important part of the test.

- If you are unsure of an answer, don't panic. You won't know all the answers, but do the best you can. By now you have discovered that you have unexpected resources if you stay calm and build upon what you already know.

- You will find complete explanations for the correct answers for Writing Mastery Tests 1–3 beginning on page 562. These answers will help you analyze your responses. The page reference before each question tells you where to look in this book for help.

Directions

- In general, you will find typical SAT directions in the Mastery Tests. However, the format for answering questions is slightly different on the SAT, as explained on page xvi.

Mastery Test 1 / Writing

Directions: For each question, select the best answer from among the choices given and insert the correct answer at the lower right.

IDENTIFYING SENTENCE ERRORS

The following sentences test your knowledge of grammar, usage, diction (choice of words), and idiom. Some sentences are correct. No sentence contains more than one error. You will find that the error, if there is one, is underlined and lettered. Elements of the sentence that are not underlined will not be changed. In choosing answers, follow the requirements of standard written English. If there is an error, select the one underlined part that must be changed to make the sentence correct. If there is no error, choose answer E.

EXAMPLE

If the size of the brain is positively correlated with intelligence, the giant stegosaurus, with a brain the size
A   B
of a walnut, must of had difficulty fending off the voracious carnivores of the Jurassic period. No error
C   D   E

C

1. Marilyn objected strenuously to Jerry taking over the reins of the Shutterbug Club after the
A   B
welcome departure of the lame-duck president. No error
C   D   E

1 ___

2. The dolphin, an intelligent animal , is also a strong swimmer equipped with superb eyesight.
A B   C   D
No error
E

2 ___

3. Ellen told me that *The Spoon River Anthology* it's a collection of frequently sardonic epitaphs
A   B   C   D
supposedly written by the occupants of a graveyard. No error
E

3 ___

4. Our driving instructor recommended that when the front wheels of a car start skidding that it is
A   B   C
usually best to pump the brakes gently and let the car roll. No error
D   E

4 ___

5. Because Anderson seldom ever fumbles, his crucial error in Saturday's game was all the more
A   B   C   D
unexpected. No error
E

5 ___

GO ON TO THE NEXT PAGE >

6. Each committee that had been set up by the executive council presented their own report assessing

                                                                                              A   B

the feasibility of the projected road bypass around the city itself. No error

       C   D   E

6 ___

7. Adolf Hitler's suicidal invasion of Soviet Russia in 1942 demonstrated that he could care less for the

                      A   B   C

contrary recommendations of senior staff members. No errors

   D   E

7 ___

8. My brother promised that he would get home for my parents' Golden Wedding Anniversary , and he

                                A   B   C

kept it. No error

  D   E

8 ___

9. Max told Oliver that he ought to attend the crucial meeting to forestall efforts by the minority opposition

                      A   B   C   D

to destroy the program. No error

                          E

9 ___

10. Wobbling ungracefully on land, the penguin's grace and skill are demonstrated in the icy water of

    A   B   C

the Antarctic Ocean. No error

       D   E

10 ___

11. After a heated disagreement in the opening session, the committee cannily suggested that the

                                                        A   B   C

moderator limit debate of the question to one hour. No error

          D   E

11 ___

IMPROVING SENTENCES

> **Directions:** In each of the following questions, select the best version of the underlined part of the sentence. Choice (A) is the same as the underlined portion of the original sentence. If you think the original sentence is best, choose answer (A).

EXAMPLE

In its search for extraterrestrial intelligence, SETI patiently listen's for whomever may be transmitting out there, hoping a meaningful signal will some day come through.

(A) listen's for whomever may be transmitting out there, hoping

(B) listens for whomever may be transmitting out there, and they hope

(C) listens for whoever may be transmitting out there, hoping

(D) is listening for whomever may be transmitting out there, hoping

(E) listens for whomever might be transmitting out there, and hope

C

GO ON TO THE NEXT PAGE ⇨

12. Marla couldn't decide whether <u>she should study computer programing or to become a financial analyst.</u>

    (A) she should study computer programing or to become a financial analyst.

    (B) she should study computer programing or become a financial analyst.

    (C) she should study computer programing or she could become a financial analyst.

    (D) it should be computer programing or will it be financial analysis?

    (E) to study computer programing or become a financial analyst.

12 ____

13. <u>If a vote were to be taken today</u> on the governor's proposals, the legislation would pass.

    (A) If a vote were to be taken today

    (B) If a vote were taken today

    (C) If a vote was taken today

    (D) If a vote had been taken today

    (E) If a vote would be taken today

13 ____

IMPROVING PARAGRAPHS

Directions: The following passage is an early draft of an essay. Some parts of the passage need to be rewritten. Read the passage and select the best answers for the questions that follow. Some questions are about particular sentences or parts of sentences and ask you to improve sentence structure and word choice. Other questions refer to parts of the essay or the entire essay and ask you to consider organization and development. In making your decisions, follow the conventions of standard written English.

(1) According to author Alex Boese, the modern sophisticated human being, with all contemporary advantages, is probably as gullible as our ancestors, since people tend to trust rather than doubting. (2) This gentle, generally positive quality has encouraged massive mis-information, often being in the form of urban legends and hoaxes. (3) A number of the legends, like the alligator in the sewer, has no malicious intent and usually create no harm, but hoaxes on the other hand are deliberately misleading, often for purposes of financial gain. (4) P.T. Barnum perpetrated a number of hoaxes, like the Feejee Mermaid a merging of a monkey's body and the tail of a fish. (5) The Cardiff Giant, supposedly the fossilized body of a colossal early human being, brought its "discoverer" fame and fortune, as it turned out to be a modern statue chipped out of stone, with the chisel marks still upon it. (6) Perhaps people enjoy a good, harmless hoax, for even as of today, people flock to the Farmer's Museum in Cooperstown, New York, to see the "Giant."

(7) Popular culture is well supplied with hoaxes, some of them literary, others flourishing in the media. (8) In 1835, the *New York Sun* announced where life had been discovered on the moon and then provided detailed sketches of lunar landscapes and exotic creatures. (9) For sensationalism to attract gullible readers, some tabloid magazines today run stories of miraculous events and startling revelations, without any basis in fact.

(10) Financial hoaxes are costly to the public, as recent revelations of misrepresentation and fraud have shown. (11) Barnum's hoaxes were harmless, enjoyed by visitors, but investment hoaxes are felonies.

14. How may sentence 1 be improved?

    (A) Change *is* to *are*.

    (B) Insert *theirselves* after *ancestors*.

    (C) Insert *it seems* after *people*.

    (D) Change *tend* to *are tending*.

    (E) Change *doubting* to *to doubt*.

14 ____

15. How may sentence 2 be improved?

    (A) Change *generally* to *substantially*.

    (B) Change *has* to *may have*.

    (C) Insert *a great deal of* after *encouraged*.

    (D) Omit *being*.

    (E) Spell *urban urbane*.

15 ____

16. How may sentence 3 be improved?

    (A) Make sentence 3 the topic sentence of the paragraph.

    (B) Spell *alligator alligater*.

    (C) Change *has* to *have*.

    (D) Change *are* to *is*.

    (E) Omit *purposes of*.

16 ____

GO ON TO THE NEXT PAGE ⟩

17. How may sentence 4 be improved?

   (A) Insert *it may be told* at the beginning of the sentence.
   (B) Change *perpetrated* to *perpetuated*.
   (C) Add a comma after *Mermaid*.
   (D) Insert *which was* after *Mermaid*.
   (E) Put the apostrophe at the end of *monkeys*.

   17 ____

18. How may sentence 5 be improved?

   (A) Eliminate the capital letters from *Cardiff Giant*
   (B) Replace *supposedly* with *sensationally*.
   (C) Add *in size* after *colossal*.
   (D) Change *its* to *it's*.
   (E) Change *as* to *but*.

   18 ____

19. How may sentence 6 be improved?

   (A) Change *enjoy* to *are enjoying*.
   (B) Omit *as of*.
   (C) Insert *and* between *good* and *harmless*.
   (D) Change *for* to *and*.
   (E) Replace *see* with *visually appraise*.

   19 ____

20. How may sentence 8 be improved?

   (A) Change *where* to *that*.
   (B) Change *life* to *living forms*.
   (C) Insert *they* after *then*.
   (D) Insert *on the moon itself* after *landscapes*.
   (E) Insert *along with* before *exotic*.

   20 ____

WRITING THE ESSAY

Directions: Consider carefully the following excerpt and the assignment that follows it. Then plan and write an essay that explains your ideas as persuasively as possible. Keep in mind that the support you provide—both reasons and examples—will help make your view convincing to the reader.

S. I. Hayakawa declared, "The semantic environment is the world of words and images in which all human beings live. It is the environment of news and information, beliefs, attitudes, laws, cultural imperatives that constitutes your verbal world and mine. A quick way of describing the semantic environment is to say that it is part of the total environment which your pet lying on the rug has no inkling of."

Assignment: Is semantics, the study of word meanings as noted by Hayakawa, neglected in the school curriculum? Should it play a larger part in the English classroom? Should teachers spend less time on the names of things and more time analyzing how words function, how they manipulate, encourage, dismay, mislead, arouse, stimulate, console? Write an essay presenting your point of view, using examples to prove your point.

STOP

Mastery Test 2 / Writing

Directions: For each question, select the best answer from among the choices given and insert the correct answer at the lower right.

IDENTIFYING SENTENCE ERRORS

The following sentences test your knowledge of grammar, usage, diction (choice of words), and idiom. Some sentences are correct. No sentence contains more than one error. You will find that the error, if there is one, is underlined and lettered. Elements of the sentence that are not underlined will not be changed. In choosing answers, follow the requirements of standard written English. If there is an error, select the one underlined part that must be changed to make the sentence correct. If there is no error, choose answer E.

EXAMPLE

If the size of the brain is positively correlated with intelligence, the giant stegosaurus, with a brain the
A   B

size of a walnut, must of had difficulty fending off the voracious carnivores of the Jurassic period. No error
C   D   E

                                                           C

1. The music of many peoples owe a debt to the spiritual and secular songs of African-American balladeers ,
                          A   B   C   D
    composers, and unknown geniuses. No error
                              E

                                                           1 ____

2. Though I also enjoy an occasional egg or a corn muffin, pancakes and sausage is far and away my
   A   B   C   D
    favorite Sunday breakfast. No error
                        E

                                                             2 ____

3. So far this week Bongo chewed two socks, the tongue of Mike's left shoe , part of the drape in the
   A   B   C
    living room, and Fran's research paper. No error
      D   E

                                                             3 ____

4. At 22, Galileo becomes a professor at prestigious Pisa University and it was there that much of his
            A   B   C   D
    memorable work was done. No error
                        E

                                                             4 ____

5. As many of his followers suggested, George Washington could of become king, but his faith in
                                           A
    democracy and abhorrence of dictatorship caused him to reject the urging. No error
               B   C   D   E

                                                             5 ____

GO ON TO THE NEXT PAGE ⟩

6. A single deer came out of the clearing while three other <u>deer</u> , from the safety of the <u>forest edge</u> ,
 A B

watched <u>nervously</u> <u>as</u> two hikers plodded along the meadow path. <u>No error</u>
 C D E

 6 ____

7. Commander Dalgliesh, my favorite <u>among</u> the detectives in British <u>mysteries,</u> <u>don't</u> jump to the first
 A B C

easy solution that <u>presents</u> itself. <u>No error</u>
 D E

 7 ____

8. <u>If</u> you are interested in the new tennis program, <u>please note</u> that twenty dollars, not ten dollars
 A B

as previously <u>reported,</u> <u>are</u> the fee for the group lessons. <u>No error</u>
 C D E

 8 ____

9. For the children of several generations <u>ago,</u> <u>measles</u> <u>was</u> dangerous and even fatal <u>in some instances.</u>
 A B C D

<u>No error</u>
E

 9 ____

10. <u>During World</u> War II, the number of Navajo code talkers <u>were</u> increased <u>in</u> a successful operation
 A B C

<u>that</u> baffled enemy cryptographers. <u>No error</u>
 D E

 10 ____

11. <u>Despite</u> the <u>very vocal</u> objections, neither the Cayman Islands nor Barbados <u>were</u> included in this
 A B C

season's cruise <u>to benefit</u> cerebral palsy. <u>No error</u>
 D E

 11 ____

IMPROVING SENTENCES

> **Directions:** In each of the following questions, select the best version of the underlined part of the sentence.
> Choice (A) is the same as the underlined portion of the original sentence. If you think the original sentence
> is best, choose answer (A).

EXAMPLE

In its search for extraterrestrial intelligence, SETI patiently <u>listen's for whomever may be
transmitting out there, hoping</u> a meaningful signal will some day come through.

(A) listen's for whomever may be transmitting out there, hoping
(B) listens for whoever may be transmitting out there, and they hope
(C) listens for whoever may be transmitting out there, hoping
(D) is listening for whomever may be transmitting out there, hoping
(E) listens for whomever might be transmitting out there and hope

 C

GO ON TO THE NEXT PAGE ⟩

12. As a child, Bruce planned to become a chemist or a physicist, <u>but, as it turned out, that was impractical.</u>

  (A) but, as it turned out, that was impractical.
  (B) and, as it turned out, that was impractical.
  (C) and, as happens, his plan was impractical.
  (D) but, as it turned out, his plan was impractical.
  (E) and, as happens, he had an impractical plan

12 ___

13. At Waterloo, <u>in order that he might separate his foes, Napoleon</u> struck the Prussian army first.

  (A) in order that he might separate his foes, Napoleon
  (B) for the purpose of separating his foes, Napoleon
  (C) so separate his foes, Napoleon
  (D) so that he might separate his foes, Napoleon
  (E) after he had separated his foes, Napoleon

13 ___

IMPROVING PARAGRAPHS

Directions: The following passage is an early draft of an essay. Some parts of the passage need to be rewritten. Read the passage and select the best answers for the questions that follow. Some questions are about particular sentences or parts of sentences and ask you to improve sentence structure and word choice. Other questions refer to parts of the essay or the entire essay and ask you to consider organization and development. In making your decisions, follow the conventions of standard written English

(1) As a manned flight to Mars is a long way off, engineers are seriously considering the possibility of manned ventures beyond the solar system. (2) Having interstellar distances expressed in light years and space travel in the realm of science fiction, are these engineers serious? (3) Robert Frisbie, who is a scientist at Nasa's Jet Propulsion Lab, insists that with current technology and the emergence of new propellants, a spaceship might reach Alpha Centauri in a voyage of 12 1/2 years. (4) How is this even conceivable?

(5) In 1990, scientists declared that the sum total of human knowledge doubled every 7–8 years, and a little more than ten years later, it was theorized that knowledge had doubled in a span of just two years— 2000–2002. (6) This conclusion encourages the assumption that the expected increase in knowledge will solve those problems which are just beyond the range of current technology. (7) To approach closer to the speed of light rays, various plans have been proposed: nuclear fission, nuclear fusion, laser sails, and even exploitation of antimatter. (8) In the matter of essentials, most engineers believe that solutions to problems of food, water, air and gravity are within our grasp, but what of psychology and the unpredictable elements of human nature? (9) Can individuals be found with the "right stuff" to survive so many years of cabin fever, isolation, close quarters, and they might clash with other personalities?

(10) Landing a man on the moon seemed utterly beyond belief in 1950. (11) Is interstellar space travel equally "preposterous." (12) Only time will tell.

14. How may sentence 1 be improved?

  (A) Change *As* to *Though*.
  (B) Change *a long way off* to *absurd*.
  (C) Change *seriously considering* to *considering seriously*.
  (D) Replace *possibility* with *probability*.
  (E) Insert *they* after *engineers*.

14 ___

15. To improve sentence 2, which revision is most needed?

  (A) Replace *Having* with *With*
  (B) Replace *expressed* with *conjectured*.
  (C) Insert *incredible* before *light*.
  (D) Interchange this sentence with sentence 3.
  (E) Change *science fiction* to *fantasy*.

15 ___

GO ON TO THE NEXT PAGE ▷

16. What is the best revision for sentence 3?

    (A) Omit *who is*.
    (B) Change *insists* to *keeps insisting*.
    (C) Insert a semicolon after *propellants*.
    (D) Change *might* to *will*.
    (E) Insert a comma after *Alpha Centauri*.

                16 ____

17. How may sentence 5 be revised?

    (A) Change *declared* to *decreed*.
    (B) Insert *upward* after both uses of *doubled*.
    (C) Change *and* to *but*.
    (D) Change *than* to *like*.
    (E) Omit *2000–2002*.

                17 ____

18. How may sentence 6 be improved?

    (A) Omit *conclusion*.
    (B) Omit *that*.
    (C) Change *will* to *would*.
    (D) Omit *which are* after *problems*.
    (E) Replace *range* with *achievements*.

                18 ____

19. How may sentence 7 be improved?

    (A) Insert *As chance would have it* at the beginning.
    (B) Change *to approach* to *approaching*.
    (C) Omit *rays* after *light*.
    (D) Change *proposed* to *concocted*.
    (E) Change *even* to *actually*.

                19 ____

20. How may sentence 9 be improved?

    (A) Change *can* to *would*.
    (B) Change *with* to *possessing*.
    (C) Insert *who are able to* after *stuff*.
    (D) Change *so many* to *an incredible number of*.
    (E) Change *they might clash with other personalities* to *personality clashes*.

                20 ____

WRITING THE ESSAY

> **Directions:** Consider carefully the following excerpt and the assignment that follows it. Then plan and write an essay that explains your ideas as persuasively as possible. Keep in mind that the support you provide—both reasons and examples—will help make your view convincing to the reader.

Amidst the overwhelming barrage of television, there is one quiet, steady, reliable voice: Public Television. Though a few sponsors may be mentioned at the beginning of programs, PBS eliminates those annoying commercials that may take up to one-third of the broadcast time and interrupt the programs with sometimes clever, sometimes obnoxious commercials. Public Broadcasting presents programs that are shunned by commercial television and otherwise unavailable to discriminating viewers. It needs more government and public support.

Assignment: Have you watched PBS? Do their programs strike you as somewhat different from the run-of-the-mill? With only a handful of sponsors, without commercials, Public Broadcasting depends upon viewer contributions and whatever subsidy the government is willing to provide. Should the government increase its help to preserve this independent medium? Should the public provide more financial support? In an essay, present your arguments for or against Public Television.

STOP

Mastery Test 3 / Writing

> **Directions:** For each question, select the best answer from among the choices given and insert the correct answer at the lower right.

IDENTIFYING SENTENCE ERRORS

> The following sentences test your knowledge of grammar, usage, diction (choice of words), and idiom. Some sentences are correct. No sentence contains more than one error. You will find that the error, if there is one, is underlined and lettered. Elements of the sentence that are not underlined will not be changed. In choosing answers, follow the requirements of standard written English. If there is an error, select the one underlined part that must be changed to make the sentence correct. If there is no error, choose answer E.

EXAMPLE

If the size of the brain is positively correlated with intelligence, the giant stegosaurus, with a brain the
A · · · · · · · · · · · · · · · B
size of a walnut, must of had difficulty fending off the voracious carnivores of the Jurassic period. No error
· · · · · · · · · · · · C · · · · · · · · · · · · D · E

C

1. For a thoughtful reading of any book by James Michener, two weeks are too short a period . No error
   · · A · · · · · · · · · · · · · · B · C · · · · · · · · · D · · E

   1 ___

2. The shelfs in the library of Trinity University are confusing on a first visit, for the library uses a
   · · · · A · B · · · · · · · · · · · · · · · · · C
   classification system different from the Dewey decimal classification. No error
   · D · E

   2 ___

3. The skin of a snake has given it's name to a kind of leather distinguished by colorful geometric
   · · · · · · · · A · · · · · · · · · B · C · · · · · · · · · · · D
   patterns and striking colors. No error
   · · · · · · · · · · · · · · · · · · · E

   3 ___

4. Holly rushed in and declared breathlessly in typical Holly fashion , " Let's you and I plan a surprise
   · A · · · · · · · · · · · B · · · · · C
   party for Jenna this coming weekend ." No error
   · · · · · · · · · · · · · D · · · · · · · · · · E

   4 ___

5. As far back as C.E. 1400, German monks set up rows of clubs and then rolled stones at them , and soon
   · · A · B · · · · · · C
   it became a universal sport. No error
   D · · · · · · · · · · · · · · · · · · E

   5 ___

GO ON TO THE NEXT PAGE ⟹

6. Because of the long string of islands off <u>its</u> coasts, Alaska is the <u>only</u> state in the United States <u>what's</u>
                                   A   B   C   D

    in the eastern hemisphere. <u>No error</u>
                                E

        6 ____

7. Quoting Alexander <u>Woollcott</u> at the Golden Wedding Celebration, <u>Mr. Palmer</u> said that <u>for</u>
              A   B   C

    <u>a half a century</u> his wife had made life poetry <u>for him.</u> <u>No error</u>
                D   E

        7 ____

8. We <u>hadn't</u> barely started on our trip <u>to</u> the Canadian Rockies <u>when</u> our rebuilt Volkswagen motor
           A   B   C

    began <u>to cough</u> and sputter ominously. <u>No error</u>
              D   E

        8 ____

9. The robin <u>began</u> to eat the sunflower seeds which my little brother <u>had bought</u> <u>with</u> his allowance
                A   B   C

    and spread <u>them</u> on the bird feeder. <u>No error</u>
               D   E

        9 ____

10. A deserted goat <u>path steep</u> and <u>craggy,</u> <u>led from</u> the river to a meadow <u>aglow</u> with spring flowers
                    A   B   C   D

    and cedar trees. <u>No error</u>
                  E

        10 ____

11. A <u>museum with</u> an excellent collection of Egyptian <u>antiquities</u> is located <u>off</u> the beaten path in
         A   B   C

    Brooklyn, a <u>borough</u> of New York City. <u>No error</u>
          D   E

        11 ____

IMPROVING SENTENCES

Directions: In each of the following questions, select the best version of the underlined part of the sentence. Choice (A) is the same as the underlined portion of the original sentence. If you think the original sentence is best, choose answer (A).

EXAMPLE

In its search for extraterrestrial intelligence, SETI patiently <u>listen's for whomever may be transmitting out there, hoping</u> a meaningful signal will some day come through.

    (A) listen's for whomever may be transmitting out there, hoping
    (B) listens for whoever may be transmitting out there, and they hope
    (C) listens for whoever may be transmitting out there, hoping
    (D) is listening for whomever may be transmitting out there, hoping
    (E) listens for whomever might be transmitting out there and hope

        C

GO ON TO THE NEXT PAGE ⇨

12. Blaise Pascal was a brilliant mathematician, physicist, and he was also a philosopher, but he is almost as famous for observing that if Cleopatra's nose had been longer, the history of the world would have been different.

(A) physicist, and he was also a philosopher, but he is almost as famous for observing
(B) physicist, and he was also a philosopher, but he is equally as famous for observing
(C) physicist, and he was also a philosopher, but his fame is for observing
(D) physicist, and philosopher but his fame is for observing
(E) physicist, and philosopher, but he is almost as famous for observing

12 ___

13. Because George Washington was denied a commission in the regular British army in 1754, he became a planter and channeled his resentment ultimately by leading the American colonists to final victory.

(A) channeled his resentment ultimately by leading the American colonists to final victory
(B) resented his rejection and led the American colonists to victory at last
(C) channeled his resentment and ultimately led the American colonists to final victory.
(D) resenting the rejection, final victory was the ultimate revenge.
(E) channeled his resentment into leading the American colonists to victory.

13 ___

IMPROVING PARAGRAPHS

Directions: The following passage is an early draft of an essay. Some parts of the passage need to be rewritten. Read the passage and select the best answers for the questions that follow. Some questions are about particular sentences or parts of sentences and ask you to improve sentence structure and word choice. Other questions refer to parts of the essay or the entire essay and ask you to consider organization and development. In making your decisions, follow the conventions of standard written English.

(1) A jet passenger who is flying from the East Coast to the West should put his paper or magazine aside and just look out of the window. (2) After crossing the Mississippi, the interested traveler will begin to see a visual demonstration of an American achievement: like a vast checkerboard, the land is divided into huge squares of 40 acres each. (3) Out here in the Plains, the uniform patterns are visible. (4) In 1784, Thomas Jefferson had a dream: that we should divide the vast country into squares, each covering 36 square miles. (5) These townships could then be divided into one-mile-square sections, these parcels would be sold at auction, then subdivided as necessary.

(6) After the 1785 start, this visionary program was carried out with great difficulty, always in rugged mountainous terrain. (7) On the plus side, the mapping and surveying ultimately provided the basis for wide home-ownership and transforming the wilderness into manageable sections for settling.

(8) In 1862, Abraham Lincoln introduced the Homestead Act. (9) A settler who built a cabin and farmed it for five years was entitled to his land. (10) The ramifications were far-reaching: state universities, railroads, and ambitious settlers all benefited.

(11) As is often true in human affairs, there was a minus side, for having the progress and prosperity came at a cost. (12) Native Americans lost their ancestral hunting grounds and were settled on reservations.

14. In the context of the first paragraph, which revision is most needed in sentence 1?

(A) Do not capitalize *East* and *West*.
(B) Replace *who* with *which*.
(C) Replace *should* with *would*.
(D) Omit *just*.
(E) Omit *of*.

14 ___

GO ON TO THE NEXT PAGE

15. Which of the following is the best revision of the underlined portion of sentence 4 below? <u>Thomas Jefferson had a dream: we should divide the vast country into squares.</u>

    (A) Thomas Jefferson had a dream that was about dividing the vast country into squares.

    (B) Thomas Jefferson had a dream: to divide the vast country into squares.

    (C) Thomas Jefferson had a dream which included the division of the vast country into squares.

    (D) Thomas Jefferson had a dream. Dividing the vast country into squares.

    (E) Thomas Jefferson had a dream about dividing the vast country into squares.

15 ____

16. Which revision is most needed in sentence 5?

    (A) Change *could be* to *may be*.

    (B) Change *as* to *where*.

    (C) Begin a new sentence with *these parcels*.

    (D) Omit hyphens from *one-mile-square*.

    (E) Omit *then*.

16 ____

17. Which revision is most needed in sentence 6?

    (A) Put a colon after *start*.

    (B) Replace *visionary* with *foolish*.

    (C) Replace *carried out* with *avoided*.

    (D) Replace *always* with *especially*.

    (E) Replace *terrain* with *country*.

17 ____

18. Which revision is best in sentence 7?

    (A) Replace *plus* with *promising*.

    (B) Change *provided* to *provide*.

    (C) Change *transforming* to *transformed*.

    (D) Replace *ultimately* with *unexpectedly*.

    (E) Replace *manageable* with *acquired*.

18 ____

19. Which revision is most needed in sentence 9?

    (A) Change *A* to *Any*.

    (B) Replace *built* with *constructed*

    (C) Replace *it* with *the land*.

    (D) Put an apostrophe at the end of *years*.

    (E) Replace *land* with *deed*.

19 ____

20. Which revision is best in sentence 11?

    (A) Change *As* into *It is*.

    (B) Replace the comma after *affairs* with a semicolon.

    (C) Change *was a minus side* to *were minus sides*.

    (D) Omit *having*.

    (E) Change *came at a cost* to *had a cost*.

20 ____

GO ON TO THE NEXT PAGE

WRITING THE ESSAY

> **Directions:** Consider carefully the following excerpt and the assignment that follows it. Then plan and write an essay that explains your ideas as persuasively as possible. Keep in mind that the support you provide—both reasons and examples—will help make your view convincing to the reader.

The casual, the trivial, and the inexpensive are easily forgotten. *Smithsonian Magazine* ran an article on former pulp art, the covers of pulp magazines usually consigned to the trash bin but becoming increasingly expensive and collectible. Throwaway news sheets, posters, and placards of an earlier day are often more sought after than more typical and mainstream items like books. Items of this kind are rarely saved. What kinds of current material, now commonplace and unwanted, might become the gems of the future?

Assignment: As you look about, do you see commonplace worthless items that might be tomorrow's treasures? Which of these materials do you visualize as important for historians of the future? Write an essay presenting a view that what is under our noses now and unsought after might prove useful to a future historian. Use examples to accompany your opinion.

STOP

Division F

Answers

Answers to Complete Diagnostic Test for Critical Reading

Section 1

Pages 1–7

1. *(C)* The conjunction *when* implies both time and result. That the wall would be ten feet high and nine inches wide suggests that it would be **substantial**. Such a massive wall would lead to Sharon's **incredulity**. The other pairs are faulty, one word in the pair unacceptable or the connection absurd.

2. *(A)* The combination of *not only* and *but also* suggests that two items are being compared. **Compilation** and **repository** in this context are synonyms. None of the remaining pairs qualify.

3. *(E)* When we are stimulated, we tend to act. Try all alternatives in the slots. "Our actions are **determined** largely by conditioned responses to environmental stimuli" makes sense. Of all the other alternatives, *(C)* comes closest to making sense. You are not asked to select a *possible* answer. You are to choose the BEST answer. *Successes* is too broad a term. **Stimuli** is better.

4. *(B)* The sentence suggests a contrast to come. The **exquisite** Monterey coast is contrasted with the **sparse** stands of windblown trees. *Lush, murky, towering*, and *decaying* do not suggest that contrast. *Towering* might be possible, but its partner, *subtle*, does not fit as well with lyric words like *superb*.

5. *(D)* Expectations were disappointed when the bridge was closed down. The only word that suggests that inference is **disconcertingly**.

6. *(B)* If Noah Webster worked tirelessly, then the missing words should be positive. **Pertinacity...campaigned** fit the slots perfectly. At least one member in each of the other pairs is negative or absurd: *pathos, meditated, unawareness, procrastinated*.

7. *(E)* The slots suggest that words are being paired, either synonymous or at least associated. The only words that qualify are **gullibility** and **naiveté**.

8. *(C)* The limited diet of mare's milk and fat-tailed sheep suggests that the nomads' lives are hard. Only **inhospitable...subsist** suggest that harsh existence. Both words must qualify. *Rigorous* might be a temptation *(A)*, but its paired word, *nibble*, doesn't make sense.

9. *(A)* With a lively schedule of operas in 25 cities, we may reasonably infer that opera is far from dead. The only word that contradicts the negative assessments is **belies**.

10. *(B)* The answer lies in the expression *to be right within*. The expression *there's the point* is a specific clue. All the other examples are important, but they are prefaced by the subordinating expression *the next step*. A scientist is unconcerned with oratory *(C)*. *(B)* doesn't show a reasonable relationship.

11. *(D)* *(A)*, *(B)*, and *(C)* are details. *(E)* is not considered. *(D)* captures the major point of the selection. A process of elimination is wise, since several alternatives may seem possible. Always choose the BEST alternative.

12. *(B)* **Irony** suggests an opposition of ideas. The author is scornful of the concept that languages live and die. Euthanasia, mercy killing, suggests that scorn. Misguided philologists thought that if languages live and die, then some language elements could be killed mercilessly, by the "guardians of correct usage." Choose the BEST answer.

13. *(A)* The answer is a detail: lines (53–57).

14. *(C)* *Whale* is nowhere mentioned. The others are: *igloo* (58), *Arctic Circle* (35–36), *Egyptian hieroglyphics* (16–17), and *Latin* (18).

15. *(E)* The selection doesn't mention *(B)*, *(C)*, or *(D)*. The author disagrees with *(A)*. His open-minded approach to language throughout the selection suggests *(E)*.

16. *(E)* Native speakers have certain ideas "about the 'rightness' or 'wrongness' of whatever is said." A visitor might not realize that "only a few choices are acceptable at the moment."

17. *(A)* Elgin "despised himself." "He had become convinced that he was odd." "He laughed at himself." All these signal *(A)*.

18. *(B)* Several suggested titles are too broad: *(A)*, *(C)*, and *(E)*. *(D)* is wrong: he was "almost nineteen." *(B)*, which is a take-off on "love at first sight," adequately describes the situation.

19. *(C)* All but *(C)* are mentioned in lines 17–20.

20. *(D)* Elgin is clearly smitten, imagining a girl of his imagination, not a real girl. The other alternatives are either not mentioned or wrong.

21. *(E)* Once again, eliminating alternatives leads a reader to *(E)*. Nowhere is it stated or implied that Elgin may give up philology *(A)*, seek out the artistic in Ancient History *(C)*, or has decorated his home with prints *(D)*. His talents as an art critic are not considered *(B)*. His idealization of the girl suggests that he is in love with love, an abstraction rather than a real girl.

22. *(C)* "The Unpossessable Loved One" (line 103) parallels Elgin's own situation, as he appraises it.

23. *(A)* The girl may be striking, but we know nothing about her talkativeness *(B)*. She may be proud, but she has done nothing unkind *(C)*. She doesn't have blond hair *(E)*. Whether or not she is restless, is unknown *(D)*. She does seem to be healthy and self-confident: "arrogant self-satisfaction" *(A)*.

24. *(D)* "A number of his friends asked him if he was feeling ill" (lines 108–109).

25. *(E)* Elgin was dancing "with a girl who helped him on his German." When the next dance began, he left her.

Section 2

Pages 7–13

1. *(D)* The key word *fortunately* suggests that the effect of the sunflower seeds will be positive. The first blank should be positive; the second, negative. **Immunity** and **devastating** qualify best.

2. *(A)* The function word *if* means that the opening clause is conditional. Holmes is apologizing for saying something that may have been objectionable to his listener. *(E)* would require no apology. Stifling curiosity *(B)* and arousing wonder *(C)* have little to do with jogging memory. *Hostility* is too strong a word *(D)*.

3. *(C)* One of the blanks calls for something obviously visible and the other, audible. The word *slyly* suggests that Morris is happily conscious of his humorous comment. *(A)*, *(B)* and *(E)* are negative. *Catch* doesn't pair well with *wink (D)*.

4. *(E)* An incredible 100-mile run calls for strong blank completions. *(E)* immediately jumps out. *(D)* is contradictory. *(C) Serene* has the wrong connotation for Indians and terns. *Insulated (A)* is meaningless in the context. *(B)* is remotely defensible but clearly inferior to *(E)*. Always choose the BEST alternative.

5. *(E)* The key word *beneficial* suggests that the nematode's activities are positive for humankind. *Languid (C)* is scarcely a word for the attack upon harmful grubs, cutworms, and weevils. A strong word is needed. **Voracious** perfectly fills the bill and **exterminates** completes the statement. *Demolishes (B)* suggests the destruction but *fortuitous* makes no sense here. *Irritates (D)* and *outnumbers (A)* scarcely affect the grubs.

6. *(B)* The clause with the function word *when* combined with *even* suggests that the main clause will have an opposite or at least surprising revelation. *(A)* and *(E)* are almost meaningless. *(C)* and *(D)* don't suggest the opposite, surprising possibility. *(B)* suggests the unexpected result foreshadowed by *even when*.

7. *(B)* The linkage of *underestimated* with the two blanks suggests a sequence starting with that word. *Eulogized (A), Reappraised (C), Confirmed (D)*, and *Rehabilitated (E)* run counter to the sense of the sequence.

8. *(A)* The use of *so-called* and the *unearned reputation* suggest that this sentence is not a condemnation of the bees. The sequence must be increasingly negative, though the meaning of the sentence is positive. *(B)* and *(D)* are disqualified because they have a positive first word in each pair. Though *unrelenting (C)* is negative, *efficacious* loses the tone. *Feisty (E)* is too mild a word, and *unvarying* is meaningless here.

9. *(C)* The three tunnels suggest that after east-west traffic has been accommodated, one tunnel will be used for another purpose: a safety alternative and escape route in emergencies. The extra tunnel is obviously an alternative, not a process *(A)*, idea *(B)*, procedure *(D)*, or trial *(E)*.

10. *(B)* The tomato is linked with potato and corn, other foods from the New World. *Tantalizing (A)* doesn't match well with *bland*, nor does *aromatic* with *insipid*. *Inspired (E)* is scarcely a word associated with corn and potato. Using the adjective *starchy* for tomato *(C)* is a stretch.

11. *(D)* The opening sentence of each paragraph clearly indicates a strong preference. Physical contact *(A)* is not emphasized. The first paragraph doesn't mention the other sport *(B)*. Neither mentions any weakness *(C)* and *(E)* is nowhere suggested.

12. *(B)* The second sentence of Passage 1 emphasizes visibility *(B)*. The author doesn't make a graded comparison of the two plays *(A)*. Although the outfielders may play differently for a left-handed batter, the author doesn't claim superiority for him. *(C)* The length of the game is mentioned in *(D)* but not as a desired element. Though managers play a role, the author doesn't mention them *(E)*.

13. *(C)* The author of Passage 1 extols the lack of time constraints *(C)*. *(A), (B),* and *(D)* apply to both sports. *(E)* isn't mentioned.

14. *(E)* The author extols the "complexity of football" in the final sentence. *(A), (B),* and *(C)* are not mentioned. *(E)* doesn't make this comparison.

15. *(C)* The selection is devoted to the place of clocks and clockmakers in the development of science and advancement of machines. *(C)* covers this concisely. *(A)* and *(D)* are too narrow, details rather than generalizations. *(B)* is too broad. *(E)* doesn't suggest the clock as does *(C)*. The clock is at the heart of this selection.

16. *(E)* This is a detail mentioned in lines 20–21.

17. *(A)* The second sentence (lines 4–8) suggests the critical importance of those who created the clocks. *(E)* is obviously untrue. The clockmakers did NOT disregard previous knowledge *(B)*. The clockmakers were artisans, not businessmen *(C)*. The clock replaced wooden gears with metal *(D)*.

18. *(B)* Without flowery hymns of praise for clockmakers, the author writes his article directly, objectively, and effectively.

19. *(C)* The words *precisely* and *precise* in paragraph two, suggest the essential quality of precision.

20. *(D)* *Lathe* in line 53 suggests that this invention revolutionized clockmaking.

21. *(D)* Torriano is given credit: "Without such a device, it would have been impossible for clocks to be made in large numbers for the commercial market."

22. *(D)* The answer is stated: "...in the seventeenth century, when timepieces were reaching a wider market" (lines 63–65).

23. *(A)* Prototypes of the screw and the gear "go back to the time of Archimedes or before" (lines 73–74).

24. *(C)* "The introduction of the pendulum...made it possible for clocks to be ten times more accurate than they had been" (lines 20–23).

25. *(B)* Since the screw's "prototypes" go back to the time of Archimedes or before (lines 73–74) we may assume that prototypes are **original models**.

26. *(E)* "No wheel was made twice because it always came out right the first time." (lines 56–58).

Section 3

Pages 13–17

1. *(C)* Secret imprisonment is labeled a "more dangerous engine of arbitrary judgment," more heinous than death or confiscation. Although our own sense of fitness might place violence (D) and murder (E) at the top of the horror list, the paragraph is specific in considering secret imprisonment worse. (A) is also topped by (C). (B) is neither mentioned nor implied. Always base your answer on the selection, not on your own information or judgment.

2. *(B)* *Poisoned* suggests that a negative word is needed to fill the slot. *(A), (C),* and *(D)* are either neutral or positive and thus inappropriate. *(E)* may be considered reasonable, but a stronger word is required: **overturned**.

3. *(E)* The major thesis of paragraph 2 is the possibility that polls may sway the voters. Weisberger's quotation extends that concern to other countries: **voters may be influenced**.

4. *(C)* From the opening statement, with its use of the word *poisoned* Passage 1 has taken a negative view of polling. *(A)* is neutral. *(B)* Projection is a minor element in the discussion. *(D)* is a detail. *(E)* is too broad.

5. *(A)* "The polls...might run into First Amendment considerations in America" (lines 29–33).

6. *(C)* The author calls projections and polling "two separate elements" (line 28).

7. *(E)* The author of Passage 2 specifically says, "Perhaps the outstanding example of accuracy in polling was the Presidential election of 2000" (lines 111–113).

8. *(D)* The author emphasizes that the closeness of the polls "should have alerted election supervisors..." (lines 121–125).

9. *(B)* Metaphor is an implied comparison. Here the wind that blows straws suggests the direction of the political wind.

10. *(D)* "In the 1936 poll, an unrepresentative sample was counted" (lines 100–101).

11. *(D)* The author of Passage 1 might agree with *(B)*. The author of Passage 2 might agree with *(A)*. *(C)* is absurd. *(E)* is mentioned, but popular election is not proposed. That leaves *(D)* by a process of elimination, always a sound check of first choices. The author of Passage 2 actually mentioned the errors of polls. The author of Passage 1 takes a negative view of polls. We can infer a disenchantment with polls in general. In any event, this is the BEST answer.

12. *(C)* Paragraph 2 of Passage 1 discusses the effect of polling on voter apathy.

13. *(A)* Bernard Weisberger has reported the banning of polls in some countries. The word *even* suggests that this quotation follows a negative view of polling. Kathleen A. Frankovic says, "Polls both inform and elevate the level of public opinion."

14. *(B)* All other alternatives are incorrect because of Fremont *(A)*; James Buchanan *(B)* and *(C)*; and Cleveland *(E)*. Do not confuse James Buchanan with Pat Buchanan, a candidate in 2000.

Answers to Trial Tests for Division A, Vocabulary

Pages 26–27

1. *(B)* Since binoculars are being used, the answer must have something to do with seeing. The only answer that deals with seeing is *(B)*.

2. *(D)* If the explorers put the plan into operation, the answer must show that the plan is practical. The only answer that deals with this point is *workable*.

3. *(A)* If "calm settled over the city," hostilities must have stopped. The correct answer is *stopping*.

4. *(E)* If Charles was permitted "a few hours of sleep," the pain must have lessened. The correct answer is *lessened*.

5. *(C)* Since vinegar is sharp and sour, Bonnie's expression must have shown her unhappy surprise. The correct answer is *distorted face*.

6. *(E)* The back-and-forth nature of a tennis match provides the clue here. Linda returned the volley. The correct answer is *returned like for like*.

7. *(A)* If Mel "tripped awkwardly in front of Betty," he must have been embarrassed. The correct answer is *embarrassment*.

8. *(B)* Robins announce the coming of spring. Therefore a *harbinger* must be some kind of early messenger. The word that best suggests this definition is *forerunner*.

9. *(D)* If Pru worked throughout the night and finished her report in time, she must have worked hard. The correct answer is *industriously*.

10. *(A)* Jesse James is a famous outlaw who was involved in only one side of the battle against crime: the wrong side. The correct answer is *committed*.

Pages 31–32

1. *(B)* The word **flamboyant** is paired with "colorful." The word closest in meaning to both words in the pair is *showy*.

2. *(D)* **Acclamation** is paired with "obvious approval." The correct answer is *applause*.

3. *(E)* **Despicable** is paired with "mean." The correct answer is *unkind*.

4. *(A)* **Demurred** is paired with "disapproving." To demur is to disapprove. The correct answer is *objected*.

5. *(C)* **Reveries** is paired with "daydreams." Daydreams are *fantasies*.

6. *(D)* **Concise** is paired with "to the point." Something to the point is *brief*, not wordy.

7. *(B)* **Arduous** and "difficult" are paired. *Strenuous* means about the same.

8. *(A)* **Malign** is paired with "to tell an evil lie." The idea of evil suggests that the correct answer is *wrong*.

9. *(B)* **Privation** and "hardship" are paired. The correct answer is *want*. Here *want* is used as a noun.

10. *(E)* **Morose** and "ill-tempered" are paired. The word closest to describing such a state of mind is *gloomy*.

Pages 36–37

1. *(D)* "Rarely engaging in exercise" provides a definition of **sedentary**. Therefore the correct answer is *inactive*.

2. *(A)* **Subside** is explained by its appositive, "settle down." The correct answer is *calm down*.

3. *(B)* "Hitting a finger" and "sawing a crooked line" are given as examples of **ineptitude**. Since those activities show a lack of skill, the correct answer is *clumsiness*.

4. *(E)* **Velocity** is explained by its appositive, "speed." The correct answer is *rapidity*.

5. *(D)* **Predilection** is explained by its appositive, "taste." The correct answer is *preference*.

6. *(A)* **Harangue** is explained by its appositive, "endless lecture." The correct answer is *long, ranting speech*.

7. *(B)* If the **derisive** members "hooted and howled," we can assume the correct answer is *scornful*.

8. *(D)* "Presenting an obstacle" explains **protrudes**. The correct answer is *sticks out*.

9. *(C)* "Making unavoidable the mass slaughter" tells us that **precluded** means "made a peaceful solution impossible." The correct answer is *prevented*.

10. *(C)* "Miserly and thrifty to the point of excess" tells us what **parsimonious** means. The correct answer is *stingy*.

Pages 40–41

1. *(C)* "A wasp whose nest has been disturbed" is not likely to be happy. The comparison suggests that **irascibility** means *quickness to anger*.

2. *(E)* "A hammer smashing an eggshell" shows no "subtlety." Therefore Frank overwhelmed everyone. The correct answer is *bullied*.

3. *(C)* "Winter twilight" and "overcast sky" suggest darkness and gloominess. The correct answer is *gloomy*.

4. *(C)* "Endless drops from a leaky faucet" suggest a steady, annoying sound. The correct answer is *continuing*.

5. *(A)* "A startled lizard" moves rapidly. Therefore **alacrity** must mean *quick motion*.

6. *(C)* "An evening dress" is out of place "at a picnic." Therefore **incongruous** must mean *unsuitable*.

7. *(A)* "A corrosive acid" eats away substances. **Caustic** means *biting*.

8. *(E)* "A snake's trail" winds. Therefore **sinuous** means *winding*.

9. *(B)* "A scolding is disapproving speech. Therefore **tirade** must mean *denunciation*.

10. *(C)* "A tiger on a starvation diet" would be very hungry. Therefore **ravenous** must mean *hungry*.

Pages 44–45

1. *(B)* The opposite of "harmonious" is *conflicting*.

2. *(A)* When all participants share in decision making, the decision is not **unilateral** or *one-sided*.

3. *(C)* **Ludicrous** is opposed to "taking the proposal seriously." Therefore **ludicrous** must mean *laughable*.

4. *(E)* If "weak" and "changing" are opposites of **tenacious**, the correct answer is *persistent*.

5. *(B)* "Generous" is opposed to **penurious**. The alternative, which means the opposite of "generous," is *stingy*.

6. *(A)* The word "not" attached to **infallible** tells us that **infallible** means "the opposite of making many errors." The correct answer is *always right*.

7. *(B)* "Active" is contrasted with **dormant**. Therefore the correct answer must be the opposite of "active" or *quiet*.

8. *(C)* **Ephemeral** is contrasted with "lasting." Therefore the correct answer must be the opposite of "lasting" or *short-lived*.

9. *(D)* The wording shows that **cacophony** is contrasted with "blissful blending." Therefore the correct answer must be the opposite of "blissful blending" or *harsh sounds*.

10. *(E)* **Placate** is contrasted with "angered." Therefore the correct answer must be the opposite of "angered" or *soothe*.

Pages 48–49

1. *(D)* The wording suggests a change in degree from "slow" to **obtuse**. It even tells us that **obtuse** is like "slow"—only more so. The correct answer is *dull*.

2. *(C)* The change from **improvise** to "revise" suggests that improvise is freer, more spontaneous. The correct answer is *compose offhand*.

3. *(C)* "Steep" is high, but **exorbitant** is higher. The correct answer is *excessive*.

4. *(A)* The change from "irritating" to **obnoxious** suggests a downward trend. **Obnoxious** must mean "worse than irritating." The correct answer is *offensive*.

5. *(B)* The sequence suggests that **arduous** is harder than "challenging." The correct answer is *strenuous*.

6. *(E)* **Stereotyped** is obviously worse than "dull." The correct answer is *stamped from a mold*.

7. *(A)* **Irksome** is a lesser degree of "unbearable." **Irksome** is unpleasant but not unendurable. The correct answer is *annoying*.

8. *(D)* The wording, with "frightening," suggests that **gruesome** is a stronger word than frightening. *Unpleasant* and *bitter* are negative words, but we need a very strong word here. The correct answer is *hideous*.

9. *(B)* The wording suggests that **unparalleled** is not merely "magnificent." It is something greater, without any possible comparison. The correct answer is *incomparable*.

10. *(B)* The progression is from "wild" to something more wild. The correct answer is *frantic*.

Pages 54–55

1. *(E)* "Because" suggests the reason for the children's rebellion. The first four alternatives suggest no reason for rebellion, but the fifth does. The correct answer is *strongly controlling*.

2. *(B)* "If" suggests the reason for next year's dues increase. If the funds are inadequate, dues must be raised. *(A)*, *(C)*, and *(D)* make little sense. *(E)* is a remote possibility but unlikely. *Decrease* is the best answer.

3. *(D)* "But" tells us the drought was reversed. The rains *refilled* the reservoir with water.

4. *(C)* "Because" is the clue. Ted's friends "like to tell him wild stories" because he believes everything. The correct answer is *believing*.

5. *(A)* The words "in an attempt to" tell us the editor is trying to change the tired words and expressions, to make the report less *commonplace*.

6. *(D)* The key word "unless" shows a way out of the difficulty: "giving more help." If the speaker is uncertain about "the right course," he or she must be in a *state of uncertainty*.

7. *(C)* "Although" tells us we have contrasting ideas: *meticulous* and "careless." We need an alternative that is opposed to "careless." The correct answer is *very careful*.

8. *(C)* "Since" ties up the idea of the downpour with Beth's appearance. Rain does spoil people's appearances. The correct answer is *untidy*.

9. *(A)* "Until" suggests that the stables had been clean before rainwater leaked onto the dirt floor. The correct answer is *spotless*.

10. *(B)* The wording suggests that the speaker would like to correct a mistake or else resign as president. The correct answer is *correct*.

Pages 62–63

1. *(B)* *Flabby* is a word applied to weak muscles. The alternatives are unsuitable. *Delicate* may be applied to an aroma. *Flimsy* may be applied to the construction of a house. *Limp* may be applied to the way hair hangs. *Loose* is a general word with many applications. None of these words can appropriately be applied to muscles.

2. *(C)* The five alternatives are rough synonyms and may generally be applied to a word like "speaking." When camera shots are mentioned, however, the correct word is *candid*.

3. *(E)* All the alternatives have something to do with "make-believe," but the term used for characters in a novel is *fictitious*.

4. *(A)* All the alternatives can be said of winds, but the word "mild" limits the possibilities. Only a *breeze* is mild.

5. *(D)* All the alternatives have to do with *copying*, but they all have different applications. *Copying* is a general word that covers many situations. *Mocking* and *aping* are unflattering words, unsuitable here. *Imitating* and *matching* do not describe the writing process. The only possibility is *copying*.

6. *(B)* The word "stricken" tells us that the spectators acted from terror. All the alternatives but one are inadequate to express their actions. The correct answer is *panic*.

7. *(E)* The word "unreasonable" suggests that the owner expected *perfection*, which is not a reasonable expectation. The correct answer is *perfection*.

8. *(C)* The alternatives are rough synonyms, but only *familiar* suggests the appearance of a place we might return to. The correct answer is *familiar*.

9. *(A)* All the alternatives suggest a weakened hiker. The extent of his deprivation—a week without food and with very little water—calls for the strongest word among the alternatives. The correct answer is *haggard*.

10. *(E)* When three blocks of houses burn, ordinary words for fire are inadequate. The correct answer is *conflagration*.

Page 69

1. *(A)* Jean's quick action is compared with the action of a terrified mouse. Since the comparison uses **like**, this is a simile.
2. *(B)* The buds of the potato are compared with "eyes," but no comparison word is used. Metaphor.
3. *(G)* Obviously rainy weather and mosquitoes are not fun. Irony.
4. *(E)* Mr. Acton may have been angry, but he didn't hit the roof. This exaggeration is hyperbole.
5. *(D)* "Nose" is being used for the entire dog. Synecdoche.
6. *(C)* "Gloom" is here given human qualities. Personification.
7. *(B)* The error in reading is compared with actual stumbling in walking. Metaphor.
8. *(A)* This is an extended comparison with **as**. Simile.
9. *(F)* Six weeks of hospital stay is much more than an inconvenience. Understatement.
10. *(C)* "Love" is given human traits. Personification.

Pages 73–74

1. *(B)* *Constructed* is usually used for structures. *Created* is a general word applied to a wide variety of abstractions like ideas and fusses. *Prepared* is a general word for anything from arguments to meals. *Produced* is another general word, often applied to words like masterpieces or films. The word especially applied to music is *composed*.
2. *(D)* All the words suggest something long lasting, but the word reserved for flowers that last more than a season is *perennial*.
3. *(B)* All the words suggest opposition, but the word associated with justice is *obstruct*.
4. *(D)* *Glut, cloy, cram*, and *gorge* suggest excess. Since the words "very little" are used, the correct answer is a milder word, *satisfy*.
5. *(C)* *Catalog* is too comprehensive for something brief. *Enumeration, inscription*, and *register* are too grand. The correct answer is *memorandum*.
6. *(A)* All words suggest inner qualities, but the word for athletic ability is *native*.
7. *(B)* All alternatives deal with frequent activities, but the word for a special, repeated activity is *routine*.
8. *(D)* All alternatives suggest a coming together, but the word reserved for roads that come together at one point is *merged*.
9. *(A)* All alternatives deal with duplication. When books are exactly reproduced, the correct word is *facsimile*.
10. *(C)* All words suggest cockiness and self-assurance. The key word "charming" tells us we

need a word with pleasant connotations. The only word that qualifies is *pert*.

Pages 78–79

1. *(C)* *Song, rhapsody, hymn*, and *chant* are all musical forms. The word not associated with the others is **struggle**.
2. *(D)* *Dwell, lodge, reside*, and *occupy* have to do with living in a place. The word out of place is **support**.
3. *(E)* *Dye, stain, tint*, and *paint* all have to do with applying color to something. Though **sketch** might involve applying color, the basic meaning does not include that process. The correct answer is **sketch**.
4. *(A)* All the alternatives but **aid** have the idea of listening to someone.
5. *(D)* All the alternatives but **ballad** have the idea of a mixture.
6. *(C)* All the alternatives but **nervous** suggest boldness. **Nervous** is actually opposed in meaning.
7. *(E)* All the words but **violet** refer to parts of a tree.
8. *(C)* All the alternatives but **agree** suggest differences. **Agree** is the opposite, not associated with the others.
9. *(B)* *Majesty, grandeur, greatness*, and *splendor* are words suggesting magnificence. **Queen** and *majesty* may be associated, but this association does not account for the other three.
10. *(C)* All the alternatives but **scratch** have to do with drawing back.

Pages 82–83

3	hope	4	tasty
6	clearness	5	understanding
1	efficiency	8	unequal
2	certain	10	criticism
9	normality	7	thrifty

Pages 86–88

1. *(A)* There would be *noise and confusion* in such a hospital.
2. *(C)* A general would be associated with military *discipline*.
3. *(E)* If Machiavelli believed in possible deceit, *crafty* is the best answer.
4. *(E)* "Impossible feats" suggests Don Quixote was *impractical*.
5. *(B)* The unprotected heel was a *source of weakness*.
6. *(E)* Berserkers *raged violently*.
7. *(B)* "Strict rotation" eliminates the possibility of choice.

8. *(C)* The twisting, turning river suggests *wandering aimlessly.*

9. *(B)* Mesmer's powers suggest *hypnotic fascination.*

10. *(D)* Proteus's ability to change his shape suggests that **protean** means *extremely changeable.*

Pages 96–97

1. super	4. contra	7. retro	10. ante
2. ambi	5. dis	8. se	
3. post	6. ex	9. ab	

Pages 98–99

1. tri	4. bi	7. omni	10. mil
2. oct	5. semi	8. tri	
3. multi	6. uni	9. cent	

Page 103

1. cresc	6. flu	11. ag	16. cant
2. cogn	7. fer	12. fus	17. doc
3. dict	8. duc	13. gen	18. don
4. fac	9. dorm	14. curs	19. fug
5. fract	10. clam	15. ceed	20. cid

Page 105

1. mit	6. pos	11. mand	16. prehend
2. junct	7. ques	12. mers	17. puls
3. jud	8. port	13. mut	18. plaud
4. ject	9. lect	14. nasc	19. plac
5. grad	10. loqu	15. neg	20. pet

Page 107

1. tort	6. scrib	11. Tens	16. vol
2. strict	7. Sed	12. spect	17. vok
3. sta	8. tain	13. sequ	18. verg
4. vis	9. sect	14. volut	19. ven
5. vinc	10. rupt	15. turb	20. trus

Pages 110–111

1. digit	8. dent	14. corp	20. domin
2. Brev	9. ego	15. capit	21. ev
3. anim	10. equ	16. Centr	22. aqu
4. al	11. fid	17. dia	23. cur
5. culp	12. civ	18. ferv	24. arm
6. ann	13. cor	19. equ	25. cruc
7. ben			

Page 113

1. ment	8. man	14. mort	20. liter
2. labor	9. fin	15. liber	21. miser
3. Ign	10. fort	16. Grav	22. fum
4. Leg	11. loc	17. greg	23. grat
5. lev	12. mal	18. herb	24. flor
6. Mar	13. mater	19. min	25. foli
7. Magn			

Pages 115–116

1. nov	8. vok	14. Somn	20. vac
2. nox	9. par	15. son	21. termin
3. temp	10. plus	16. optim	22. sanct
4. norm	11. ped	17. terr	23. ocul
5. popul	12. sol	18. umbr	24. ver
6. reg	13. numer	19. Urb	25. verb
7. prim			

Pages 122–123

1. C	4. B	7. D	9. C
2. B	5. A	8. B	10. A
3. D	6. B		

Page 125

1. mis	6. pseudo	11. para	16. ana
2. iso	7. poly	12. peri	17. amphi
3. mega	8. an	13. micro	18. syn
4. cata	9. anti	14. neo	19. Hypo
5. auto	10. Hyper	15. pan	20. eu

Page 127

1. kilo	4. Tri	7. di	9. hexa
2. penta	5. tetra	8. deca	10. octa
3. mono	6. Proto		

Page 130

1. Hydr	8. heli	14. hetero	20. iatr
2. geo	9. cycl	15. lith	21. chron
3. Derm	10. bibli	16. graph	22. crat
4. erg	11. chiro	17. homo	23. crypt
5. arch	12. alg	18. Chrom	24. gam
6. bar	13. Anthrop	19. dem	25. Hem
7. dynam			

Pages 132–133

1. thes	6. morph	11. Soph	16. trop
2. the	7. onym	12. scop	17. typ
3. zo	8. Ortho	13. Tax	18. phan
4. tom	9. pyr	14. pod	19. path
5. neur	10. Phil	15. Tele	20. meter

Pages 137–138

1. A	4. C	7. D	9. B
2. B	5. D	8. A	10. C
3. B	6. A		

Pages 139–140

1. be	4. fore	7. Off	9. on
2. over	5. for	8. under	10. up
3. out	6. un		

Page 148

A	B
4	*make* systematic, arrange
9	*smallest* speck
6	*science* of production, distribution, and consumption of wealth
1	*place where* birds are kept
3	*having quality of* happiness
7	manual *skill*
8	*related to* light, clear
2	*one who* does good deeds
10	*in the manner of* a statue
5	*not able to* be reformed

Page 150

A	B
10	*having quality of* being annoying
6	*inflammation* of the stomach
3	*little* slice
2	*one who* is in charge of a museum or a library
5	*make* a speech of praise
7	*in the manner of* a greedy person
8	*place where* people work and experiment
4	*like* a horse
9	*diseased condition* of the mind
1	*quality of* unselfishness

Pages 153–154

A

1. American Indian	plants for food
2. French	fashion
3. Dutch	seafaring skills
4. German	science, chemistry
5. Arabic	science, mathematics
6. Spanish	opening up of the West
7. Persian	fruits and flowers
8. Italian	music
9. African	strange and new animals
10. American	technology and invention

B

10	China
15	England
5	England and Scotland
2	France
8	Germany
6	Hungary
3	India
4	Italy
9	Mesopotamia
13	Mexico
14	Morocco
11	Persia
12	Poland
1	Russia
7	Syria

Pages 161–162

1. abridged
2. tenuous
3. frisky
4. florid
5. severed
6. naive
7. aptitude
8. zealously
9. count
10. borne

Answers and Analysis for Vocabulary Diagnostic Test A

Pages 168–170

1. *(C)* The entire sentence (page 168) suggests a barrier in the climbers' attempt to reach the summit. The climbers are stuck during the period of the blizzard. We need a verb that suggests the climbers are facing a difficulty. *Impeded*, meaning "faced with a hindrance," fits the slot nicely. *Seriously* conflicts with *motivated (A)*. *Embittered* would be a possibility if *impeded* had not been included. You must choose the *best* answer. There is nothing to suggest that the climbers were physically *impaired (D)*. *Revolted (E)*, with its suggestion of disgust, is nowhere implied.

2. *(E)* The conjunction *but* (53) signals a contrast between what the clay was like before the sculptor began to work and what it was like afterwards. Since the sculptor is obviously artistically competent, we need a suitable word for the second blank. *Stubby (A)* is unlikely. The writer probably would not introduce a word like *stubby* to describe the sculptor's fingers. However, just to make sure, look at the first word in the pair. *Sodden* is not a good description of clay that is ready to be worked. This rather lengthy explanation intends to show that (a) one word of the pair may reject the alternative or (b) the two words in conjunction may fail to complete the picture obviously intended by the writer. The first word in *(B)* is obviously incorrect, as is the second word in *(C)*. The elimination of *(A)*, *(B)*, and *(C)* leaves us with two possibilities. If the sculptor has to shape the clay, it is probably not shapely when he first sees it. *(D)* can be eliminated, even though the second word in the pair is excellent. That leaves us with *(E)*. Here, both words fit. For extra satisfaction, you'll recognize the Greek root *morph* (131) in *amorphous*.

3. *(A)* Allusions of one kind or other (84–89) often help in getting the sense of a sentence. Hitler and Mussolini were notorious dictators, presumably known to every person who takes this test. There is another, confirming clue: *sweep democracy away*. That one clue immediately eliminates *(C)*, *(D)*, and *(E)* because of the faulty second word in each pair.

A choice must be made between *(A)* and *(B)*. Upon reflection, we must reject *namesakes*. The likelihood of a great many people named *Hitler* and *Mussolini* is slim. *(A)* fits the slot nicely. *Clones*, originally a word from biology, can be applied to any imitation.

4. *(D)* A plan that guaranteed benefits that could never be taken away must be comprehensive *(D)*, "all inclusive." Again the context of the entire sentence (24–30) is a clue to meaning. *(A)* is obviously absurd. *(B)* and *(C)* do not fit the meaning of the sentence very well. *(E)* suggests poor planning. Common sense dictates the right answer. *Comprehensive* is also covered in the section on Latin verbs (104).

5. *(B)* This is a vocabulary question that requires you to know the meaning of the key word. Sometimes all alternatives may be unknown to you. Then you must look to the words themselves. The context provides a clue. The key word must mean something like "lighten," "lessen," or "remove." Your memory of Latin roots (pages 101–102) recalls that *lev* means "light." *Alleviate* then must mean something like "lighten, lessen, partially remove."

6. *(D)* The sentence as a whole provides the clues (24–30). The answers are keyed to the clause "When it is time to return home." The best choice is *(D)*. Students achieve competence and then balk at returning. The phrasing suggests that the students are expected to return home to provide services in their homeland. That expectation is frustrated. The other choices fail to catch this point.

7. *(A)* Contrast provides the essential clue (43–47). *Merest* conflicts with *impressive*. The word modified by *merest* must contrast with *impressive*. *Quibble*, a "trivial objection," provides that contrast *(A)*. If you are uncertain about *quibble*, you can still get the right answer by concentrating upon the second word in the pair. *Impressive philosophical structure* calls for a strong negative word in the blank. *Topple* meets the need. A strong structure can be *toppled*. The other choices make little sense.

8. *(B)* The answer relies upon comparison (39–43).

Modern and ancient athletes are compared. *Triumphant (B)* best fits the sense for the first slot and *exploited* best fits the sense for the second. In the other choices, one or both words are unsuitable.

9. *(E)* A comparison is suggested between the schooling of Japanese schoolchildren and American schoolchildren (39–43). Students are paired (30–34) to sharpen the comparison. If Japanese schoolchildren go to school "240 challenging days a year," we may infer that their training is harder—more *intensive (E)*. The other choices do not concern themselves with that inference

10. *(B)* This is a sentence in which all five first choices fit the first slot and all five second choices fit the second slot. But only one pair fits. *Casual*, for example, would fit with *communication*, but *strategy*, the other word in the pair, doesn't make sense in the completed sentence. On the other hand, *strategy* might fit in the second slot, but the completed sentence would need a word other than *casual* to make good sense. The context of the sentence (24–30) requires the words in *(B)*. If *tactile* is unfamiliar, remember the *tact* root (106), meaning "touch."

11. *(E)* "Despite" warns us immediately that a contrast (pages 43–47) lies ahead. Something is being contrasted with the total success of the opening performance. The director did not expect the success. Therefore, he must have been worried. *Foreboding (E)* is the best choice. Note that in this type of question, many answers fit. The director might have been *excited* after the disastrous dress rehearsal. He might have shown *vigor* to bolster his morale. Choices *(A)* and *(D)* are not, however, as good as *(E)*. You are asked not merely to supply an answer that fits. You are asked to supply the answer that *best* fits the meaning of the sentence as a whole. In this sentence the likelihood is that the director was worried. If *foreboding* is unfamiliar, you might reach it by a process of elimination or

by analyzing the parts. **Bode** in "bodes no good" suggests bad possibilities. **Fore** obviously means "beforehand." *Foreboding* is thus a feeling that things will not turn out well. There are often many approaches to the right answer.

12. *(A)* Often, a key word will provide an essential clue. Here the key word is *inspiration*. The word is positive, suggesting a person worthy of being imitated, *emulated*, with the aim of equaling or surpassing the original. *(E)* makes a weak kind of sense, but it misses the essential tone of the statement. *(D)* is strong but inappropriate. Lionizing a former Senator is pointless. *(B)* and *(C)* make even less sense.

13. *(B)* The sentence describes an unusual achievement: the creation of a written language by one person. *(A)* is incorrect; no comparison is made. *(C)* is opposed to the sense of the sentence. *(E)* is not relevant. *(B)* and *(D)* are possible, but when listed with *(B)*, *(D)* is faulty. Singular, "unique," perfectly completes the sentence.

14. *(B)* Though it might seem more difficult to supply two words instead of one, actually supplying two words is often easier. Note how having two words, one of which is clearly wrong, helps us choose the right one. Choice *(A)* doesn't make sense. *Attentiveness* would have prevented the accident. Choice *(C)* provides a possible answer in *accepted*, but *boredom* does not fit the context. The word "although" clearly suggests a contrast (43–47), eliminating *boredom*. If "although" had been "because," the choice might have worked. *Dexterity* in *(D)* eliminates that possibility. The choices in *(E)* are farfetched and inappropriate. Choice *(B)* fits perfectly. The jury did not accept Mandy's disclaimer and decided she had been negligent.

15. *(C)* Comparison and contrast often provide clues (39–47). If Gorky, Smith, and Pollock died tragic deaths and de Kooning is unlike them, we may assume he *survived (C)*.

Answers and Analysis for Vocabulary Diagnostic Test B

Pages 170–171

1. *(D)* Though *cajoled* may be unfamiliar to you, a process of elimination suggests the answer. As often happens, a key bit of information provides a clue to a missing word (35). If Johnson sought party harmony, he wouldn't have done anything to alienate the Kennedy aides. On this basis alone, *(A)*, *(B)*, and *(C)* can be eliminated. *Distracted* doesn't sound much better. What would be the point? That leaves us with *cajoled*, "persuaded." *Cajoled* also has the suggestion of using flattery to win over a person.

2. *(A)* The entire sentence (24–30) provides essential clues to the correct answer. These are clues: the two months' delay and the successful result. One must be played against the other. Thus the blank must be filled with a word having negative connotations (60–65). *(B)*, *(D)*, and *(E)* may be eliminated because they are positive or neutral. We are left with *(A)* and *(C)*. *Sabotage (C)* has a negative connotation. Not only is there no hint of sabotage, but the nature of sabotage makes two months of it unlikely. Sabotage is usually an isolated action. Continuing sabotage on a program as heavily guarded as the shuttle flights would be unlikely. *Tribulations*, "distressful experiences," perfectly fits the slot.

3. *(E)* A quilting expert would not put down the very practice she is engaged in. This insight eliminates both *(A)* and *(B)*. Take the next step. Look at the second word in each pair and note the identical situation. The expert would not suggest that lap quilting is in any way out of step with American life-styles. With this realization, we can eliminate *(C)* and *(D)*. If you know the meaning of *espouses*, "supports," you might have used the process of elimination just to prove that you had chosen properly. If you did not know the meaning of *espouses*, you could still have solved the problem by the process of elimination explained above. Context (24–30) is a powerful ally.

4. *(B)* Knowing what *irony* (68) is supplies a quick answer to this problem. Irony suggests that reality is quite different from appearances.

The passengers thought that planes were more dangerous than trains. In this situation, the opposite proved to be true. *Wistfully (A)* is sentimental and inappropriate. *Prematurely (C)* makes little sense. *Realistically (D)* runs counter to the point of the passage. *Contradictorily (E)* has a general application, but *ironically* catches the nuances of the sentence as well as its literal meaning.

5. *(C)* The sentence context suggests (24–30) that if the protection of human rights had been missing from the Constitution, the slot must mean something like "clear," "obvious," "definite." The only word that carries this meaning is *explicit*, "clearly stated," "definite."

6. *(D)* The key to the sentence is *wasteful*. We are most concerned about waste when resources cannot be replaced. **Profligate** means *wasteful*, but even if the word is unfamiliar to you, the second word of the pair will help you choose the right pair.

7. *(C)* Be especially aware of function words that provide essential clues (pages 52–57). The word *though* tells us that a contrast is coming. We'd expect anything abnormal to be bad, but *though* tells us to expect the unexpected. Some **deviations** from abnormality may not be bad but **benign**.

8. *(E)* Though occasionally a word in a pair makes sense, only **native** and **extinction** both fit into the sentence. These are obviously correct, but an examination of all the other alternatives shows their unsuitability.

9. *(A)* If the signals are being scrambled, the static must be **disruptive**. The first word in the pair, *intermittent*, also fits perfectly into the sentence.

10. *(B)* If new world records have come about because of changes in swimming strokes, then the correct pair must complete a positive statement. Only **subtle** and **obsolete** make sense in this context.

11. *(B)* The pairing of "dead laboratory specimens" with "living creatures in the field" tells us contrast (pages 43–47) is a major clue. We can pinpoint the meaning by filling the first blank or the second. Since "dead" is being contrasted with "living," find a word that

appropriately describes living creatures. We can immediately eliminate *(A)* since *stodgy* is completely inappropriate. *Vibrant* and *active* seem the best possibilities. The other word along with *vibrant* is *scrutiny*. This word fits perfectly, but to be sure see whether the word with *active* fits: *carelessness*. This doesn't fit. The only pair that fits perfectly is *scrutiny* and *vibrant (B)*. Frequently one word in the pair will fit but not the other, as in *(E)*.

12. *(E)* The sequence of ideas (47–51) and the function words **from** and **to** (52–57) provide the clues here. In addition, there is a contrast (43–47) of "realism" and "abstract design." Trying the possibilities suggests that *(E)* is the correct answer. *Literal* provides a sound contrast with *abstract*. With such contrast, the diversity may well be *incredible*.

13. *(B)* **Although** tells us a contrast (43–47) is a clue. In addition, the blank before "intelligence" is paired with "outer space." This is intelligence from outer space. A word linked with "outer space" is *extraterrestrial (B)*. The

prefix **extra**, meaning "beyond" (95) and the root **terr**, meaning "earth" (115), tell us *extraterrestrial* means "beyond the earth," another expression for "outer space." Though words like *superior* and *galactic* may seem to fit also, their paired words do not fit. Neither *transfer* nor *broadcast* makes sense in the context. This sentence demonstrates that there are often many ways to ferret out the answer.

14. *(D)* The sentence as a whole (24–30) provides the needed clues here, but there is another, the pairing of "mysterious" and the blank. The only suggested word that can be reasonably paired with "mysterious" is *miraculous (D)*. Trying *limitless* in the first blank verifies our choice.

15. *(A)* What is the characteristic of a "meteor on an August night"? The trail is bright . . and brief. Here a comparison (39–43) provides the clues. The only word that fits the first blank is *blazed (A)*. *Faded* fits neatly into the second blank. All the other possibilities have one or both inappropriate choices.

Answers to Trial Tests for Division B, Reading Comprehension

Page 176

(C) The human mind ordinarily operates at a fraction of its capacity. Examine each of the statements in turn. Since William James' quote supports the Wilson point of view, *(A)* is incorrect. There is no suggestion in the paragraph that *The Mind Parasites* is other than an ingenious bit of fantasy, with no relation to the future. Therefore, we can discard *(B)*. That the human mind is idling most of the time is the point of view of the paragraph. Therefore, *(C)* is sound. Look at the other alternatives, just to be sure. Fatigue *(D)* inhibits achievement. It does not stimulate it. Wilson's point of view *(E)* was anticipated by James and others. The paragraph flatly says, "That we are all underachievers is not a new idea." The generalization stated in *(C)* is the only correct one.

Page 179

(D) Tadpoles survive under conditions that seem unlikely and inhospitable. The life cycles of fish and tadpoles are not compared. *(A)* is incorrect. *(B)* and *(C)* are correct statements, but they are details, not main ideas. They can be eliminated. *(E)* is incorrect. The passage specifically says that tadpoles could eat in ponds but could also be eaten. The paradoxical

nature of tadpole survival is the theme of the passage. *(D)* is the correct answer.

Page 182

(D) William F. Allen *(A)* was indeed a man for all seasons, but the paragraph is about time. His contribution, while important, is not the whole story. *(B)* is irrelevant, off the topic. The paragraph deals with time, not with the calendar. *(C)* deals with a single sentence in the paragraph and is a detail. The same objection holds for *(E)*. *(D)* tells what the paragraph is about. All sentences deal with this topic, beginning with a brief description of timekeeping before 1883. The central section deals with the transition from the old timekeeping methods to the new. The final section mentions the final victory of the four-zone agreement and comments on the importance of the change. Only *(D)* includes all three of these major sections.

Pages 184–185

(A) the mysterious appeal of mountain climbing. The pitfalls in answering this question resemble the pitfalls discussed in choosing titles. *(B)* is too narrow. Of course, the heroism of Joe Tasker is an important

element in the passage, but it does not deal with the passage as a whole. *(E)* is an inference based on a detail. It does not deal with the passage as a whole. In a sense, *(D)* is much too broad. It also fails to address itself to the major point of the passage. *(C)* is irrelevant to the point of the passage. Only *(A)* adequately sums up the point of the passage.

Pages 189–190

(B) The entire passage suggests the beginning of a storm, but there are more specific clues, too: the sudden whipping of the wind, the frantic activity of boat owners, the beginning of the rain. The full force of the storm has not yet struck, but its impact is beginning to be felt. We can infer from the clues that the worst is yet to come.

Page 192

(E) The major thrust of the paragraph is the danger in many common household substances. The summarizing statement suggests that the dangers require constant vigilance on the part of parents. This is the idea contained in *(E)*. The statement parallels a famous quotation: "Eternal vigilance is the price of liberty." Knowing the quotation adds interest to the question, but such knowledge is not necessary for the correct answer.

Page 195

(C) The last sentence of the selection gives the central idea. The best paraphrase of the idea is *(C)*: "Man's restless spirit, not his needs, brings advances." Note that both the original statement and the paraphrase say essentially the same thing.

Pages 197–198

(B) The selection is an extended comparison of the arguments for collecting two types of stamps: mint and used. Though all five choices suggest comparisons, only *(B)* states the essential comparison: the *arguments* for collecting the two types of stamps. *(A)* is incomplete. *(C)* and *(D)* are not touched upon. *(E)* is a detail only partially covered.

Pages 202–203

1. *(C)* The selection specifically says, "Over the protest of Arabella Huntington, Duveen persuaded Huntington to buy Reynolds' masterpiece, *Sarah Siddons as the Tragic Muse.*"

2. *(D)* The selection talks about "the two famous paintings often paired in the eyes of the public: Gainsborough's *The Blue Boy* and Lawrence's *Pinkie.*"

Page 206

(C) Statements I and V are nowhere stated or implied. Any answer with either of these can be dismissed at once. We can thus eliminate *(A)*, *(D)*, and *(E)*. *(B)* contains a correct statement, but since it says "IV only" it cannot be the desired answer.

Pages 209–210

(E) The last paragraph specifically says, "Some people may have a mild allergy to aloe vera." The statement goes on to say that most people find aloe beneficial. Yet this one drawback tells us that *(E)* is the right answer. No other paragraph mentions a disadvantage.

Pages 214–215

(C) This is a quiet sketch of a natural scene, emphasizing the subtle elements frequently overlooked in a cursory glance. This invites the reader to stand still a moment and recreate in imagination the stillness of a winter morning. The tone is *reflective*.

Page 212

(D) This is by no means a negative appraisal. Therefore, *(A)*, *(B)*, and *(C)* can be immediately rejected. It is positive, amused, interested in the behavior of the fans. It is not indifferent. Eliminate *(E)*. It does write with amused affection of the unusual characters who cheer on their football teams.

Page 223

(D) Since the selection deals exclusively with the activity *before* writing, the word *pre-writing* provides an immediate clue. The author plays down the critical faculties and self-criticism at the pre-writing stage. *(A)* and *(E)* are incorrect. Evans is introduced to make an opening point, but the purpose goes beyond Evans. *(B)* is incorrect. Phrases like *paralyze the will* and *freeze determination* suggest that writer's block is not trivial.

Pages 226–227

(C) This is a down-to-earth explanation of the importance of trees in the carbon cycle. It is strictly *expository*. It is too serious for *(E)*, too objective for *(A)*, too matter-of-fact for *(B)*. There is no indication of repetition *(D)*.

Pages 232–233

(C) Amphibian numbers are decreasing *even* in *unspoiled* places like national parks and mountaintops.

Page 236

(A) *Lumbering* suggests slowness and bulk. *Juggernaut* suggests a force that crushes every object in its path. All the answers but *(A)* are too specific. *Juggernaut* doesn't specify truck, bus, trailer, or ambulance.

Page 240

1. *(A)* Since trees do not depend on birds and weather for their defense, we can eliminate *(D)*. If the tree's chemicals "discourage or kill the invader," we can eliminate *(B)*, since the author clearly agrees. Trees and wildflowers handle insect infestations in different ways. We can eliminate *(E)*. "Warn their neighbors" tells us the author agrees with *(C)*. That leaves *(A)*. Since trees have defenses independent of man, the author would disagree with *(A)*. Therefore *(A)* is the right answer.

2. *(D)* The items mentioned in *(A)*, *(B)*, *(C)*, and *(E)* are specifically mentioned in the selection. Therefore these alternatives can be discarded. Nowhere in the selection are other insects mentioned as a check on insect growth. *(D)* is correct.

Pages 245–246

1. *(D)* The only advice that has not yet been tried is hitting the ball back to the opponent, at "the belt buckle." The backhand strategy has failed. *(A)* is incorrect. Frank has killed overheads. *(B)* is incorrect. There is no discernible reason for Frank to rush the net. *(C)* is incorrect. No mention has been made of the coach's presence, but more important: Ted is moving toward the ball. He has no time to look up into the stands. *(E)* is incorrect.

2. *(B)* There is no logical reason to suppose that Ted can turn the match around at this point. Though turnabouts sometimes occur, the law of averages (except in fiction) tends to suggest otherwise. Ted is in trouble, only one game away from defeat. The logical outcome is *(B)*. Thus we may eliminate *(A)* and *(D)*.

Pages 250–251

(D) The father starts with a generalization—that Labrador retrievers are good with children—and then concludes that a certain Labrador will be good for his children. If put in the form of a syllogism, the argument would look like this:

Major premise—Labrador retrievers are good with children.
Minor premise—This dog is a Labrador.

Conclusion—This Labrador will be good with my children.

The other arguments are all inductive, drawing conclusions from a series of incidents.

Pages 257–258

1. *(B)* The unusual behavior of Gant is touched upon throughout the selection, as the family revolves about him. *(A)* is all wrong. *(C)* might be inferred, but it's not the main idea. *(D)* is much too broad. *(E)* is nowhere stated or implied.

2. *(D)* That he kept choking on a fish bone says little for his ability to learn from experience. In some respects he may have been a devoted father *(A)*, but nothing is said about his credentials as a husband. He obviously didn't believe in moderation *(B)* and he did make the children nervous *(E)*. *(C)* is not stated or implied.

3. *(E)* Since Gant was doing nothing to help self or family, the author clearly disapproves of Gant's table behavior. *(A)* and *(B)* are incorrect. *(C)* is too strong. *(D)* is nowhere suggested.

4. *(A)* "Impregnable to the heavy prod of Gant's big finger" (lines 8–9) tells us he wanted to make sure Eugene was stuffed.

5. *(C)* The portions had to be large to fit Eugene's distending belly. *(A)*, *(B)*, and *(E)* are opposed to the meaning of the selection. *(D)* is not related. *Gargantuan* is a word from a name, the hero of a work by Francois Rabelais, a French writer.

Pages 263–264

1. *(A)* The problem arises because Molesworth's ticket was not in Trieste, but Venice. The other alternatives are for one reason or another inappropriate. The conductor was not vindictive, merely within his rights to ask for a ticket. *(B)* is wrong. Molesworth finally paid for a ticket, invalidating *(C)*. The telephone call never went through *(D)*. The narrator may have been embarrassed, but the details are presented objectively. *(E)* is, in any event, a weaker answer than the objectively provable *(A)*.

2. *(C)* Molesworth resolutely refused to take the ticket problem seriously. *(A)*, *(B)*, and *(D)* are off the mark. One might have chosen *(E)* *humorous* if the perfectly appropriate *stonewalling* had not been provided. The total effect was humorous, but Molesworth's strategy was to be unresponsive, as he clearly indicates in lines 8–10.

3. *(B)* The poor conductor is a slave of the system. Molesworth has no ticket; therefore, he can't ride. That there had been some human error did not matter. *(A)* is far too general. *(C)* is apparently untrue; the narrator and Molesworth are friends. There is no intercity conflict *(D)*. The railroad rules rather than national laws are the cause of the problem *(E)*.

4. *(D)* Molesworth is not sympathetic *(A)*, nor willing to speak the conductor's language *(B)*. He doesn't accept local train procedures *(E)*. That leaves *(C)* and *(D)*. Molesworth tends to be condescending toward the conductor. He drinks while dismissing the conductor's request, showing his contempt by his manner of speaking. The way in which Molesworth pays the 10,000 lire is a kind of put-down *(C)*, but calling the conductor by a completely inappropriate name is even more revelatory of Molesworth's scorn.

Since the conductor's first name is obviously unknown to Molesworth, we must assume that he is being snobbishly superior in using a familiar first name where none was indicated.

The episode with the lire occurs only once. It might display a momentary irritation with the conductor, but the use of the patronizing "George" three times is a continuing indication of Molesworth's attitude. Remember: when a strong case can be made for more than one answer, choose the BEST.

5. *(E)* The conductor's attitude is revealed by his reiteration of the "no ticket, no go" theme. At one point, he begins to perspire. Exasperation is clearly the answer. *Murderous rage (A)* is too strong. *(B)*, *(C)*, and *(D)* suggest a calm that the conductor obviously didn't display.

Pages 272–273

1. *(C)* Orwell, at least, failed to predict the disintegration of great states. *(A)* is incorrect. Lansing was involved in government but not Orwell. *(B)* is incorrect. The two men were not contemporaries. Lansing was of an earlier generation. *(D)* is incorrect. Lansing had nothing to do with writing *1984*. *(E)* is incorrect. Only *(C)* draws correct conclusions from the passage.

2. *(D)* The preceding sentence (lines 10–14) suggests that the three superpowers were repressive. The common prefix *mono* ("one") is another clue. The correct answer is *(D)*.

3. *(C)* In lines 42–47, the author notes that these nations had already demonstrated a capacity for nationhood in the years between World Wars I and II. *(C)* is correct.

4. *(B)* Any kind of warfare requires an enemy. *(B)* is correct.

5. *(A)* The next sentence provides the answer *(A)*.

6. *(B)* On the one hand, the author says, "Self-determination is a worthy ideal." In line 124, he says, "Sometimes good principles clash." *(B)* is correct.

7. *(E)* The following paragraphs mention the disintegrating, deteriorating situation because of rampant nationalism. *(E)* is correct.

8. *(A)* The key clues are *in* and *inside* (lines 75, 77). The prefix *en (in)* provides another clue. *(A)* is correct.

9. *(B)* Some of the tragic consequences of self-determination are *bloody civil war* (106–107), *human rights are often trampled upon* (127–128), *persecute new minorities* (129–130). *(B)* is correct.

10. *(D)* The partition of Yugoslavia was bloody (line 106 and following). The partition of Czechoslovakia was peaceful (105). *(D)* is correct.

11. *(C)* Both self-determination and human rights are excellent principles, but sometimes self-determination results in some loss of human rights (127–128). *(C)* is correct.

12. *(E)* The author suggests that there is a momentum that propels groups to seek nationhood. Lines 111 to 119 talk about further splintering. *(E)* is correct.

Pages 291–293

1. *(B)* In lines 16-20, the author says, "The first thing to learn . . . ours." We should not try to foist our own ideas and customs on others.

2. *(A)* "Curious speculation" is too shallow. An understanding of diversity has the most tremendous practical importance. That speculation is only a beginning. It may lead to a "deeper awareness," but there is no guarantee.

3. *(E)* The key to the answer is *non-interference*. We cannot expect our own rights to limit the rights of others.

4. *(E)* If no one has such insight, a rational solution is to keep an open mind, learning about the good ideas of others.

5. *(A)* The context clearly calls for a word with negative connotations, thus eliminating *(B)* and *(C)*. The word *pretension* suggests an assumption of superior wisdom. Such assumption would not necessarily require a loud voice *(D)*. *(E)* is nowhere hinted at.

6. *(B)* The message is simply given with the expectation that readers are reasonable people. The point is made without anxious pleading *(A)*. *(C)* is too strong. *(D)* is untrue. There is no attempt at humor *(E)*.

7. *(B)* Both passages make the point that each person is essentially concerned with his or her own values and meanings. "The meanings are there for the others, but they are not there for us." (6–7)

8. *(D)* Passage 1 takes a more serious view of human failings. It deals with larger problems than Passage 2, which is more forgiving.

9. *(A)* The author suggests that the lady's listener would not be interested in the collection of baby clothes and house linen (36–40).

10. *(E)* The final sentence emphasizes the importance of talking of ourselves or our own groups.

11. *(B)* Just as a jug cannot pour out anything that isn't in it, so a person cannot pour out, in conversation, anything not in the person.

Pages 304–305

1. *(B)* The opening sentence sets the humorous tone. Though those inanimate objects may seem aggressive, the writer is not. *(A)*. *Complacent (C)* and *contradictory (D)* overlook the humor. *Didactic (E)* is a remote possibility, but it loses the charm of the paragraph.

2. *(D)* *(D)* is correct because both II and V are reasonable inferences. *Medea* is mentioned in the sentence just after Euripides has been mentioned (II). The word *not* (applied to Sophocles) suggests that the other playwrights used the gods as essential to the plots (V). Euripides is mentioned as a current favorite, disproving (I). The operas of Euripides, not Sophocles, are referrred to (III). Aeschylus was the pioneer, not the last of the great Greek tragic writers (IV).

Answers and Analysis for Reading Diagnostic Test A

Pages 338–342

1. *(B)* The words *deciphered* and *cryptographers* imply (189–191) that cryptography (cryptanalysis) can assist in breaking the obscure codes *(B)*. The paragraph nowhere implies that solutions are hopeless *(A)*. The Minoan and Etruscan are linked as ancient languages, but the only actual Bronze Age identification was the Indus civilization *(C)*. The discovery of the Rosetta Stone made the decipherment of hieroglyphics different from other challenges *(D)*. The Rosetta Stone was a help, but the paragraph does not imply that it was the only road to solution *(E)*.

   Reminder: Base the answer solely on the text provided. Do not introduce information from other sources.

2. *(D)* The word *major* tells us we must draw a generalization (176) from the passage. Richard *(A)* is touched briefly. Queen Eleanor *(B)* is a detail. Energy *(C)* is one side of the Plantagenets. The deviousness of the Normans *(E)* is not in the passage. The contradictory personality of John is emphasized

throughout—for example, his rages and his cold intelligence, his greed and his generosity. The best choice is *(D)*.

3. *(B)* A question may require us to seek out details (202) in the passage, as here. John's cruelty is mentioned ("cruelties were conceived"), as is his intelligence ("a cold, inhuman intelligence"). *(B)* is clearly the correct choice. John was not gentle *(A)*, weak *(D)*, or stupid *(E)*. He is not called handsome *(C)* in the passage.

4. *(A)* This passage requires us to spot a detail (202) and then draw an inference (189). We read that "monkish chroniclers have emphasized his violence, greed, malice, treachery, and lust." We reasonably infer that these are "John's worst qualities" *(A)*. None of the other choices can be justified by the passage. They either state the opposite *(B)* or make a point not mentioned in the passage at all *(C)*, *(D)* *(E)*.

5. *(C)* The point of the selection is summarized in the last sentence: "The English-speaking world owe[s] far more to the vices of John than to the labours of virtuous sovereigns."

This says the same essentially as *(C)*. Finding generalizations (176) often requires you to draw inferences (189) as well.

6. *(E)* A title (181) must cover the subject, being neither too broad nor too narrow. The subject of the passage is not John Stark *(A)* but Scott Joplin. Stark is mentioned only as he plays a role in Joplin's life. *(B)* is too narrow. *(C)* is too broad—and partly off the subject. *(D)* is inaccurate. Other composers are not mentioned. *(E)* is the correct choice.

7. *(A)* The answer, a detail in the selection (202), is found in the opening sentence. The song was named after the Maple Leaf Club, where it was played *(A)*.

8. *(D)* Questions with *except* (239) reverse the usual challenge. Check off items actually mentioned in the selection. The one left is the answer. "He also wrote *songs, marches, waltzes*, and an elegant *tango*." Operas are not mentioned by name in the passage.

9. *(C)* An actual detail (202) in the passage provides the answer: "For several years, he appeared on vaudeville stages." The correct choice is *(C)*.

10. *(E)* Questions sometimes test your ability to define a word in context (24), as here. *Marginal* cropland is plowed but quickly abandoned because of soil depletion. We may reasonably infer (189) that such soil is poor. *(E)* is the correct choice. Note that *margin* usually means *border*. *Bordering* for *marginal* is an enticing choice, but it doesn't fit here.

11. *(B)* Questions sometimes test figurative language (66). Since straws are insubstantial and clutching at them quite ineffectual, we may assume that *(B)* is the correct choice.

12. *(B)* This is the key sentence: "Sustaining this nation's food- and fiber-producing capacity may become our most potent deterrent to international conflict." This suggests that the world may need America for food to survive *(B)*. This detail (202) is there in the text. The other alternatives are inaccurate, opposed, or even not mentioned. Though you

might be of the opinion that *(E)* is a reasonable answer, you cannot choose it, for it is nowhere mentioned in the selection.

13. *(D)* Dates are provided: 1644 for the overthrow of the Ming dynasty; 1662–1722 for the reign of K'ang-hsi. We may infer (189) from the details (202) that *(D)* is the correct choice. *(A)* is flatly incorrect. There is no justification for any of the other choices.

14. *(E)* The last sentence of the paragraph identifies those who "preferred to derive their art directly from nature" as individualists. The previous sentence tells us these same painters, "expressed a strong sense of dislocation and alienation in their works." Once again selecting details (202) and then drawing the proper inference (189) suggest that *(E)* is the correct choice.

15. *(C)* Identifying the main purpose of the author (222) is akin to finding the main idea (178). Let's evaluate each choice in turn. There is no attempt to glorify one school of painting at the expense of another. The author is quite neutral and objective. Therefore *(A)* is incorrect. There is no suggestion that "17th century artists" failed to paint from nature. Eliminate *(B)*. *(C)* expresses the central purpose of the author: to explain rather than criticize or take sides. *(C)* is correct. The individualists rather than the orthodox painters expressed nature through personal means. Eliminate *(D)*. As we have already seen in *(A)*, the author is not taking sides. Eliminate *(E)*.

16. *(A)* Sentence 2 supplies the key phrase: "after late Ming fragmentation." Spotting this detail (202) enables us to infer that *(A)* is the correct choice. The "early Ch'ing world" occurred right after the fall of the Ming dynasty. At this time orthodox painters aimed to recapture the "former glories of traditional painting." Thus we may infer that toward the end Ming art had been fragmented.

Answers and Analysis for Reading Diagnostic Test B

Pages 342–345

1. *(B)* The answer lies in the last sentence: "The whole cry of voices is on the other side" *(B)*

These voices are external, not inner voices *(A)*. The remaining alternatives are irrelevant.

2. *(C)* The episode is reported in utter seriousness, but the outrageousness of the events tells us the author's purpose (222) is to entertain *(C)*. Exaggeration, like its opposite, understatement, is often employed as a humorous device. The author's apparent hope to get the native killed is obvious exaggeration of a mild annoyance at the native's persistence.

3. *(E)* This question requires us to draw an inference (189). Though we are not told so directly, we can reasonably assume that Dan is being bothered for a silly whim. "As long as Dan has got a cent" suggests that Dan will not relish being relieved of all his money. The answer is *(E)*.

4. *(B)* This question requires us to look beyond the passage and predict outcomes (245). It also calls for an inference. Choices *(A)* and *(E)* are absurd. There is no suggestion the police are involved *(D)*. Dan hasn't said a word *(C)*. Elimination brings us to *(B)*, the most likely result.

5. *(D)* Finding details in the passages is a commonly tested skill (202). The sentence beginning "He crawled" clearly identifies the peg as the climber *(D)*.

6. *(A)* The author's attitude (218) is humorously irascible *(A)*. Note that *irascible* is related to *irate*. The other alternatives are unsuitable.

7. *(D)* Since the passage contrasts language and reality, the best title is *(D)* (181). *(A)* makes no statement about the contents of the passage or the relationship between words and things. *(B)* is too narrow. *(C)* is too broad. *(E)* is a detail.

8. *(C)* Korzybski uses an analogy that might be represented as follows:

map : territory :: language : reality

Thus *map* corresponds to *language* and *territory* to *reality*. The correct pairing is *language* and *map* *(C)*. Two skills are involved here: finding details (202) and drawing inferences (189).

9. *(B)* This question requires analyzing the author's use of language (232). The first two sentences of paragraph two contrast the "process nature of reality" with the static impression sometimes given by language. If reality is not *static*, it must be *changing (B)*.

10. *(A)* The passage says, "The usefulness of a map depends precisely on the degree to which it corresponds to the territory." Spotting this sentence (202) tells us *(A)* is the best choice.

11. *(E)* The passage flatly says, "We cannot do without generalizations." (176). Therefore *(E)* is correct.

12. *(C)* Shrinking the earth to a "wet ball" emphasizes its insignificance. (68–71; 189–191)

13. *(B)* The last two sentences, with the suggestion "cast out," conclude the paragraph on a quietly sad note. (218–222)

14. *(B)* This is a vocabulary question. (24–30) If the word *careering* is unfamiliar to you, try eliminating answers. *(A)* and *(C)* suggest motions nowhere hinted at. *(D)* suggests an image inappropriately descriptive of the solar system's movement. *(E)* makes little sense.

15. *(D)* When the solar system arrives "east of Hercules," it won't be "a place to call home." (68–71; 189–191)

16. *(E)* The metaphor of the dinner party, so obviously inappropriate for a wandering solar system, adds a note of humor in the sad context. (236–239)

Answers: Reviews, Review Tests, and Practice Tests

Review (pages 29–30)
1. C 2. D 3. A 4. B 5. D
6. A 7. B 8. E 9. C 10. B

Review (pages 33–34)
1. D 2. B 3. C 4. B 5. C
6. B 7. B 8. A 9. D 10. C

Review (pages 38–39)
1. B 2. A 3. C 4. B 5. C
6. E 7. A 8. D 9. A 10. B

Review (pages 42–43)
1. B 2. A 3. E 4. C 5. B
6. D 7. C 8. D 9. C 10. B

Review (pages 46–47)
1. B 2. D 3. A 4. D 5. C
6. C 7. A 8. D 9. B 10. C

Review (pages 50–51)
1. C 2. D 3. C 4. D 5. A
6. B 7. B 8. D 9. E 10. A

Review (page 56)
1. C 2. B 3. E 4. B 5. D
6. D 7. A 8. B 9. C 10. C

Review Test (pages 57–58)
1. deceit
2. excessive
3. nobody
4. punishment
5. equivalent
6. fortress
7. overcrowding
8. made poor
9. wearing away
10. timid
11. pierced
12. harsh
13. yellowish
14. soaked
15. noisy speech
16. hateful
17. poisonous
18. peculiarities
19. overelaborate
20. turned aside

Review (pages 64–65)
1. D 2. D 3. B 4. B 5. B
6. C 7. B 8. A 9. E 10. D

Review (page 70)
1. H 2. G 3. A 4. E 5. A
6. C 7. G 8. D 9. B 10. E

Review (pages 75–76)
A.
1. wound, damage, pain
2. pretty, beautiful, graceful
3. attained, won, earned
4. grotesque, witty, comical
5. wholesome, sanitary, healthy
6. title, pseudonym, name
7. antiquated, olden, elderly
8. achievement, feat, performance
9. quarrel, feud, strife
10. shrill, boisterous, loud

B.
1. recognized   6. scanned
2. scrutinized   7. peered
3. glowered   8. observed
4. gazed   9. distinguished
5. stared   10. surveyed

Review (pages 79–81)
A. 1. D 2. C 3. D 4. A 5. B
6. E 7. E 8. B 9. E 10. D

B. 1. B 2. D 3. E 4. A 5. C

Review (page 83)
2 pliable   10 mature
5 kindly   6 energetic
7 wealthy   1 assets
8 conflict   4 believable
3 important   9 buyer

Review (pages 88–89)

1. A	2. B	3. E	4. B	5. D
6. A	7. D	8. E	9. C	10. C

Review Test (page 90)

1. B	2. D	3. B	4. D	5. A
6. B	7. E	8. E	9. C	10. D

Review (pages 99–100)

1. medi	6. con	11. extra	16. re
2. oct	7. inter	12. circum	17. quadr
3. in	8. Pre	13. du	18. sub
4. de	9. dec	14. pro	19. trans
5. quint	10. ad	15. super	20. vice

Review (page 108)

1. rid	6. arbit	11. ora	16. tract
2. viv	7. prob	12. fac	17. pel
3. struct	8. sci	13. orn	18. cept
4. cred	9. clus	14. hib	19. mon
5. ora	10. aud	15. sent	20. tact

Review (pages 116–117)

1. apt	6. bell	11. naut	16. oper
2. fil	7. art	12. lus	17. sign
3. felic	8. cand	13. firm	18. via
4. Dom	9. Mor	14. maxim	19. Pac
5. dur	10. form	15. vulg	20. salut

Review (pages 119–121)

A.

1. C	2. A	3. B	4. E	5. B
6. A	7. C	8. C	9. B	10. D

B. Answers will vary.
This is a sample. Many other words are possible.

abject	defer	interrupt	prescribe
acclaim	dissolve	nonsense	prospect
antedate	extract	obtain	submerge
compel	extrovert	perfect	supervise
contradict	insult	postpone	transgress

Review (page 128)

1. hemi	6. hect
2. en	7. dys
3. dia	8. pro
4. Endo	9. Apo
5. meta	10. epi

Review (pages 133–134)

1. cosm	6. Psych	11. phos	16. dys
2. gen	7. Techn	12. log	17. pro
3. log	8. therm	13. dynam	18. epi
4. dot	9. Top	14. Trop	19. ec
5. nom	10. poli	15. chrom	20. apo

Review (page 135)

Answers will vary.
This is a sample. Many other words are possible.

autonomic	geography	photometer
chiropodist	microscope	telephone
cosmopolitan	neuralgia	theology
democracy		

Review (pages 141–142)

A.

1. C	2. D	3. A	4. A	5. A
6. D	7. B	8. A	9. B	10. E

B. Answers will vary.
This is a sample. Other combinations are possible.

background	homeless	snowstorm
dressmaker	lifeboat	sunstroke
eyesight	moonbeam	toothache
footstep	railroad	waterworks
gateway	sawmill	workman
goldfish	seasickness	wristband
handbook	skyrocket	

Review (pages 151–152)

1. C	2. B	3. A	4. E	5. C
6. B	7. B	8. D	9. A	10. C

Review (pages 156–158)

A.

1. E	2. A	3. D	4. C	5. E
6. C	7. B	8. D	9. A	10. B

B.

1. E	2. B	3. D	4. A	5. D
6. C	7. B	8. B	9. D	10. C
11. C	12. C	13. B	14. D	15. B
16. D	17. B	18. E	19. D	20. B

Review (page 164)

1. peer	8. humane	15. male
2. conceit	9. doled	16. feeble
3. sprite	10. hale	17. snub
4. venture	11. thin	18. clinch
5. guardian	12. florid	19. scuffle
6. antiques	13. thresh	20. Calipers
7. sample	14. abbreviation	

Review Test (pages 165–166)
1. A   2. C   3. B   4. E   5. D
6. E   7. B   8. B   9. E   10. A

Review (pages 177–178)
1. D   2. E   3. C

Review (pages 180–181)
1. B   2. A

Review (pages 183–184)
1. E   2. B

Review (pages 186–187)
1. D   2. A   3. E

Review (page 191)
1. A   2. C

Review (pages 193–194)
1. C   2. B   3. D   4. D

Review (pages 196–197)
1. D   2. C   3. A

Review (pages 198–199)
1. C   2. D   3. B   4. C

Review (pages 204–205)
1. E   2. A   3. E   4. B   5. D
6. A   7. D

Review (pages 207–208)
1. C   2. E   3. B   4. C   5. A

Review (pages 211–212)
1. C   2. C   3. C   4. E   5. A
6. E

Review (pages 216–217)
1. A   2. B   3. D   4. C   5. A
6. C   7. B   8. E   9. B

Review (pages 220–222)
1. E   2. B   3. E   4. A   5. C
6. C   7. B   8. B   9. A   10. D

Review (pages 224–226)
1. C   2. A   3. E   4. A   5. A
6. B   7. A   8. C   9. C

Review (pages 228–230)
1. D   2. D   3. A   4. D   5. B
6. B   7. C   8. B

Review (pages 234–235)
1. A   2. D   3. C   4. B   5. C
6. C   7. A   8. E

Review (pages 238–239)
1. C   2. A   3. C   4. A   5. D
6. C   7. B

Review (pages 241–243)
1. C   2. C   3. E   4. A   5. E
6. C   7. C   8. C

Review (pages 247–250)
1. B   2. A   3. A   4. C   5. E
6. E   7. D   8. C   9. D

Review (pages 253–255)
1. C   2. A   3. A   4. D   5. D
6. C   7. B   8. D

Review (pages 260–262)
1. B   2. C   3. A   4. B   5. E
6. C   7. D   8. E   9. B   10. C
11. E   12. E   13. A

Review (pages 267–271)
1. C   2. E   3. C   4. B   5. A
6. E   7. B   8. A   9. D   10. E
11. B   12. D   13. D   14. C   15. D

Review (pages 282–286)
1. B   2. D   3. E   4. C   5. B
6. B   7. A   8. A   9. E   10. B
11. E   12. B   13. D   14. A   15. D
16. A   17. C   18. A   19. E   20. D
21. B   22. C   23. A

Review (pages 287–290)
1. D   2. E   3. A   4. B   5. C
6. A   7. E   8. C   9. A   10. C
11. D   12. E   13. D   14. C   15. C

Review (pages 299–302)
1. B   2. D   3. E   4. A   5. D
6. B   7. C   8. C   9. A   10. D
11. C   12. D   13. B   14. E   15. A
16. D   17. D   18. C   19. A   20. D
21. D   22. A

Review Test (pages 306–307)
A

Practice Tests (pages 308–337)
A. D
B. E
C. D
D. 1.D   2. B
E.

1. B	2. D	3. E	4. A	5. C
6. C	7. B	8. A	9. E	10. C
11. E	12. D	13. A	14. B	15. D

F.

1. C	2. B	3. A	4. D	5. C
6. C	7. B	8. D	9. A	10. E
11. E	12. A			

G.

1. D	2. A	3. C	4. A	5. A
6. D	7. E	8. D	9. C	10. E
11. D	12. A	13. A	14. C	15. D
16. A	17. A			

H.

1. E	2. B	3. E	4. A	5. C
6. D	7. C	8. A	9. B	10. D
11. D	12. A	13. B	14. E	

I.

1. A	2. C	3. D	4. D	5. B
6. A	7. D	8. B	9. C	10. E
11. C	12. B	13. E	14. B	15. D

J.

1. C	2. B	3. E	4. D	5. A
6. A	7. D	8. B	9. E	10. C
11. A	12. D	13. C	14. B	15. E
16. B	17. C	18. D		

K.

1. B	2. A	3. B	4. D	5. E
6. A	7. C	8. B	9. C	10. E
11. D	12. E	13. A	14. C	

L.

1. C	2. C	3. D	4. C	5. C
6. A	7. D	8. B	9. B	10. E
11. B				

M.

1. C	2. D	3. E	4. A	5. B
6. D	7. C	8. B	9. A	10. E
11. B	12. C	13. A		

Answers to Mastery Test 1 / Critical Reading

Section 1

Pages 351–355

1. *(A)* The context tells us that *conventional* is being contrasted with another word. Both *theatrical* and **outrageous** provide such a contrast, but only **erratic** suitably completes the sentence. Though Denny's behavior may become *theatrical*, it would not then be *consistent*.

2. *(B)* If creatures are transferred to areas where they no longer occur, they are **reestablished** in the new area.

3. *(E)* If the arbitrator thwarted the efforts of the press to anticipate his decision, he didn't give things away. He was **noncommittal**.

4. *(D)* A favorable setting would hasten a person's recovery. Therefore his or her **recuperation** would be **accelerated**.

5. *(C)* Newborn infants are obviously too young to show *comprehension, condescension* or *magnanimity*. Both **equanimity** and *indifference* are possible, but only **penetrating** suitably completes the sentence. A newborn infant could scarcely be called *competent*.

6. *(D)* **Recluse,** "a person who leads a solitary life," fits the context here. Again, if you're not sure of the word, try eliminating the others. *(A)* and *(C)* can be dismissed out of hand. *(B)* is nowhere hinted at. Since Emily Dickinson speaks, *(E)* is inexact.

7. *(D)* The reviews had to be **derogatory,** "unfavorable," to turn a novelist to writing a different literary type.

8. *(C)* "Began to realize" suggests that Henry Jekyll was aware that Edward Hyde would take over. The context calls for a word that suggests a deep uneasiness: **foreboding**.

9. *(A)* The likelihood of such a coincidence is so slim that the answer must address this element. Only **minuscule,** "very small," fills the slot. The *min* root is mentioned on page 112.

10. *(C)* Stressing the sad fate that awaits all great singers, the author suggests both sympathy and sadness. The episode in question points up the inevitable loss *(C)*. The point is not the recollection, but the sadness of the occasion *(A)*. The author is sympathetic, not critical *(B)*. There is no basis for *(D)*. This is an objective report. The author's sympathy clearly eliminates apathy *(E)*.

11. *(E)* Mrs. E was not a cruel person, but her fussiness about the pocketbook showed an insensitivity to Mildred's feelings and a **lack of trust**.

12. *(D)* Although we hear only one side of the conversation, we can infer Marge's questions by Mildred's replies. These are the answers to Marge's questions:
    (A) "No, Marge. . . ." (6).
    (B) "I'd be more than glad . . ." (7).
    (C) "No, not those little novels . . ." (15).
    (E) "No, there's nobody there but me and her." (22–23)
    That leaves *(D)*, which is nowhere mentioned or implied.

13. *(B)* Mildred tells Marge to **keep working** as she tells her that hands aren't necessary for listening (29–30).

14. *(E)* Mrs. E has demonstrated a lack of trust, even when she and Mildred are the only ones in the house. The narrator gets in a double-barreled sting: Mrs. E's stinginess and suspicious nature.

15. *(B)* Despite her mean-spirited employer, Mildred retains a **sense of dignity**, without anger.

16. *(B)* Mildred sees an opportunity to let Mrs. E know how she has been bothered by the mistrust. That she waited a few minutes (38–39) indicates that she is setting up a situation to bring Mrs. E to her senses. The "gaspin' hard for breath" is part of the melodramatic act.

17. *(E)* The author mentions the *almost* appointment (7–8), says it "was not offered" (9), and mentions the "antagonism" (10).

18. *(B)* "Every plant and animal on Earth today is a symbiont, living in close contact with others." (29–30). The Greek prefix *sym* is mentioned on page 124. *Symbiont*, by derivation, means "living together."

19. *(D)* "You will never find life in isolation" (75–76). The examples of termites, spirochetes, and microbes stress the **interlocking associations**.

20. *(A)* The thrust of the passage is the interrelatedness of all things. When Margulis challenges the concept of the "rugged individual" (25), she is saying, in effect, "**we're all in this together**."

21. *(C)* "New Age types are drawn to her and then she busts them high, low and center for being softheaded" (21–23).

22. *(C)* "Margulis challenges the American myth of the rugged individual" (25). This question demonstrates the importance of basing your answer solely on the passage. Some Hollywood movies have blasted "the American myth of the rugged individual" *(A)*, but such information is irrelevant here. Stick to the passage.

23. *(D)* This kind of question requires that you skim the selection to identify the speaker. Certainly, Lynn Margulis could have spoken those words, but as it happens, the speaker is Gail Fleischaker (72).

24. *(B)* *(A)* is a waste of time. *(C)* puts the cart before the horse. First find the quotation. Margulis *might* have used the quotation *(D)* but she didn't. *(E)* is irrelevant. Only *(B)* suggests the most efficient method.

25. *(D)* The controversy over Margulis's work suggests that recognition doesn't come easily. *(A)* is untrue. *(B)* is not mentioned. *(C)* is the opposite of what is true. *(E)* is belied by the controversy over Margulis's work.

Section 2

Pages 355–359

1. *(D)* The use of *as well as* suggests a contrast between Simenon's failures and successes. A process of elimination suggests that **personal** *failures* is being contrasted with **professional** *successes*. The other alternatives do not provide the needed contrast.

2. *(E)* The context suggests a change in degree in the candidate's reactions. *Quiet* **pleasure** gives way to *expressive* **jubilation**. *Favorable* suggests that both words must be positive. The other alternatives all contain negative elements.

3. *(C)* Since most proponents of television insist its primary purpose is to *inform* or *entertain*, the emphasis on *sell goods* is clearly a **cynical** reaction. The other alternatives make no sense or contain contradictions.

4. *(B)* **Dependable, resilient**, and **inexhaustible** could fill the first slot. Therefore the second word in the pair is crucial. If the ecosystems cannot survive much tampering, they must be **fragile**. Thus, even if *resilient* is a new word for you, the clues for choosing *resilient . . fragile* are easy to find.

5. *(A)* Once again the second word in the pair is a major clue. Both the mastodon and the sabre-toothed tiger are extinct. A common idiom is *experience the fate*. **Experienced** fits the second slot nicely. **Stereotypes** fits into the first slot, and the modifiers *formerly accepted* make the choice certain. The stereotypes are as extinct as the animals.

6. *(E)* The parts of a collapsible telescope slide over and into each other, suggesting a condensing of its parts. In the same way, two words, *chuckle* and *snort*, were condensed to form one new word. Words like *chortle* are sometimes called "blends" or "portmanteau words." A portmanteau is a traveling case with two compartments, just as *chortle* is a word with two elements.

7. *(D)* The number and variety of uses for the Tower call for **checkered**, "diversified."

8. *(D)* A rich background and a knowledge of allusions (84–89) help here. An **odyssey**, an "extended wandering or journey," takes its name from the Greek warrior, Odysseus, who spent ten years wandering the seas in an effort to reach his native Ithaca, after the Trojan War.

9. *(C)* *But* tells us that the novel's success was in spite of negative qualities. Linking *wooden characters* and a(n) _____ plot suggests that the plot was not sparkling or scintillating. Of the alternatives, **hackneyed**, "trite," is the only one that logically completes the sentence.

10. *(C)* The policemen wouldn't have staged a strike against anything construed as positive or neutral. The sentence requires a word with negative connotations. **Servitude**, which implies a master-slave relationship, fits the slot.

11. *(A)* Passage 1 shows a love of dogs; Passage 2 for cats. The passages don't disdain the others' viewpoints *(B)*. Passage 1 would disagree with *(C)*. There are few if any "identical qualities" *(D)*. *(E)* is not mentioned.

12. *(B)* The second sentence from the end of Passage 1 specifically considers the length of time since domestication *(B)*. The other alternatives are irrelevant.

13. *(E)* Passage 1 refutes *(E)*, and is therefore "related to" the question.

14. *(C)* "An expectation of being served" suggests the servant-master relationship *(C)*.

15. *(D)* *Even as* suggests that Santayana was unaware of what he was doing. **Decried** means "condemned."

16. *(A)* As the opening paragraph, the Santayana quotation is intended to set the theme and tone of the passage. Interestingly, even though the paragraph espouses the principle of E-Prime, it actually uses *are* (4) in contradiction of the point of view expressed.

17. *(B)* The use of *is* can be deceptive. A statement of opinion has the same form as a statement of fact. *(A)* and *(D)* are too strong. *(C)* is opposed in meaning. *(E)* has nothing to do with the sentence.

18. *(D)* Even though *(D)* mentions E-Prime, its use of *is* disqualifies it as a sentence written in E-Prime.

19. *(C)* If "reality resists easy capture in words," no one can be sure just what the real world is, since our picture of reality is based on our verbal image, even if inadequate.

20. *(D)* Although E-Prime avoids the use of is and other linking verbs, it does use **traditional structure**, as in the present sentence.

21. *(A)* Looking for the smaller word within the larger (81-84) often helps on the SAT. **Perception** is the noun of the verb *perceive*, "recognize, take note of, become aware of." This method points to *insights* as the answer, but context also helps. Try out each alternative. "Sharpens insights" makes good sense.

22. *(B)* Three possibilities, all negative, may be eliminated at once: *(A)*, *(D)*, and *(E)*. The passage is not frivolous. We can eliminate *(C)*. It is informative, written in a readable style.

23. *(C)* All the sentences are subjective judgments except *(C)*. This sentence, though using the word *is*, eliminates one objection to writing that is not in E-Prime.

24. *(C)* The only **metaphor** (67) is contained in *(C)*.

25. *(B)* E-Prime attempts to avoid rigid classifications, especially those based on subjective judgments. Absolute words like *always* and *never* destroy this flexibility.

26. *(D)* The judgment word **boringly** makes this a subjective statement. Boring? How? According to whom? There are no objective yardsticks for measuring boredom.

27. *(C)* This is an objective statement of identity. All the other choices involve subjective judgments.

Section 3

Pages 360–362

1. *(A)* The major point of the paragraph is to contrast the abundance of available actors nowadays and the smaller numbers in Shakespeare's day (A). The other alternatives provide supporting details, but do not carry the central idea.

2. *(B)* Note how the wrong alternatives become quite apparent. In *(A)* no mention is made of climate. *More* than a half dozen leaders were responsible *(C)*. The mention of "great heroic dramas" (27) is a red herring. It uses dramas in a sense different from those in *(D)*. "Three or four times in history" rules out *(E)*. Only *(B)* properly fills the slot.

3. *(C)* Mention of "the whole world" identifies *(C)* as the answer.

4. *(A)* "The late sixth-century B.C." approximates the times of Buddha and Lao-tzu, a time described as the **"miracle of Ionia and Greece."**

5. *(E)* The author uses the phrase "larger than life" to emphasize their extraordinary impact on their period. *(A)* and *(D)* are opposed in meaning. Longevity is not mentioned *(B)*. Emphasis is not upon the spiritual nature of their achievements *(C)*. Only *(E)* captures the point of lines 22–24.

6. *(A)* The author suggests that the "heroic energy, confidence, strength of will and intellect" are visible in Durham Cathedral and the east end of Canterbury. *(B)*, *(C)*, and *(D)* run counter to the author's message. The author doesn't say *(E)* where Pope Urban announced the First Crusade (lines 25–26).

7. *(C)* The last sentence of the first passage says that goldsmith work and ivory carving **had been practiced**, though on a small scale.

8. *(E)* The smaller word *monument* within **monumental** is a clue, but note also that **monumental** is contrasted with "small portable objects." Monuments may be made of stone *(A)*, but not necessarily.

9. *(D)* The key is the statement "they totally contradict the dark Gothic style that preceded...them" (lines 62–64).

10. *(D)* The passage says, "**Learning** could be used to achieve a happy life" (87–88). This is a detail, not an inference.

11. *(E)* Passage 1 ranges the world; Passage 2 is devoted to Florence.

12. *(A)* The use of "suddenly" in Passage 1 (line 39) and "suddenly out of the dark" in Passage 2 (57–58) clearly signals the author's emphasis on the **"sudden bursts of glory."**

13. *(B)* "The extraordinary episode in the history of civilization known as the Renaissance" (lines 55-57) identifies *(B)* as the correct answer. *(A)* is too early, off the topic. *(C)* and *(E)* are much too broad. *(D)* is a minor detail. Only *(B)* satisfactorily completes the sentence.

Answers to Mastery Test 2 / Critical Reading

Section 1

Pages 363–367

1. *(B)* If we try every pair in the sentence, only **survival..inescapable** makes sense. *Harrowing* is much too strong a word in *(A)*. *Humdrum* in *(C)* makes little sense. *Captivating* is scarcely a word to be used with *fact (D)*. *Public contributions* wouldn't bring *audiences (E)*. *General* is a meaningless term.

2. *(D)* If the owl kills more prey than it can eat, it must be **ruthless**. When we try **predators** in the second slot, we find that it fits nicely. If you know only one word in the pair, you can often guess the pair correctly.

3. *(A)* The *hundred years* is a clue to **centennial** in the first slot. We need a positive word for the second slot, to go along with *great* and *innovative*. Only **creative** fits.

4. *(C)* *Uncomfortably warm* suggests that matters grew worse. **Unbearably** hot and **stifling** complete the expected sequence.

5. *(E)* The difference in dates, *1865* and *1886*, suggests that the project took a long time. **Conceived** suggests the beginning of the project.

6. *(A)* The use of *good or ill, both . . . and* suggests we need contrasting words. Though there is a contrast suggested in *(B)* and *(D)*, only *(A)* makes sense.

7. *(D)* *Accelerated* makes nonsense of *(A)*, *(B)*, and *(C)*. *Went* in *(E)* is too general. Besides, *sadly* makes no sense in the first blank.

8. *(E)* If Picasso had to use his drawings for firewood, the critical reception couldn't have been very good: **lackluster**. *(A)* and *(C)* run counter to the sense of the sentence. *(B)* and *(D)* are irrelevant.

9. *(B)* The clue lies in the important word *although*, which suggests a contrast. *Only 1.5 trillionths of a second* suggests an almost unimaginable brevity. The only contrasting word is **longer**.

10. *(D)* Both II and V are reasonable inferences. The word *outrageous* suggests that Miro's sculptures may have offended some (II). Miro actually "found" the elements that make up his sculptures (V). The paragraph nowhere evaluates the relative merits of Miro and his fellow artists (I). Nor did Miro evaluate his work critically (III). Mario Pei is quoted; Calder is not (IV).

11. *(D)* The author points out specific examples on modern **superstitions**—for example, tossing salt, walking around a black cat, or refusing the third light on a match.

12. *(E)* Skimming is the best strategy. *(A)*, *(C)* and *(D)* are mentioned in lines 20–22. *(B)* is mentioned in line 34. Only *(E)* is not mentioned.

13. *(A)* The answer is found in the last sentence.

14. *(D)* One of the best ways to find a vocabulary answer is to read the sentence with each alternative in place of the tested word. Doing so suggests that only **moderate** appropriately completes the sentence.

15. *(B)* We can laugh at man's stupidity, but we must realize that our own thinking has primitive foundations (38–40). We cannot feel superior since, in a sense, we all "live in glass houses."

16. *(B)* The smaller word *eradicate* suggests that *ineradicable* means "not able to be eradicated." *Eradicate* means "destroy, **tear out by the roots**." A *radical* idea uproots current ones.

17. *(D)* The passage contrasts pleasant, easygoing Mrs. Tylor with worried, tense, fearful Mrs. Harris. Mrs. Tylor is expecting a no-trouble, relaxed person like herself, but in reality she's getting potentially difficult neighbors because of the lifestyle of Mr. Harris. Mrs. Harris sets down some ground rules that may cause problems. The expectation is at odds with the reality, as slowly perceived by Mrs. Tylor.

18. *(B)* In an effort to be neighborly and agreeable, Mrs. Tylor sighs sympathetically, but she has no idea that Mrs. Harris will zero in on the radio and other "problems." As a result, Mrs. Tylor worries about the Tylor radio habits. Then come the other phobias: newspapers, movies, bridge. Prospects for a happy association are bleak. The Harrises have always been "unlucky" in their neighbors, but perhaps it was the other way around.

19. *(A)* Mrs. Tylor's feelings here are compared with her feelings when her car went dangerously out of control (28–31). The alternative that catches this feeling of no escape is *(A)*. The meaning of *irrevocably* is also derived from the sum of its parts: *ir*, "not" (95), *re*, "back" (95), *voc*, "call" (106), *able* (146). Putting the parts together defines *irrevocable*: "not able to be called back." The situation was getting out of control.

20. *(C)* Mr. Harris doesn't approve of neighbors' friendly gestures, the usual means of friendly communication. He's obviously a loner.

21. *(D)* Mrs. Harris says that the Harrises have at least *seen* a newspaper, "not like the movies at all." Apparently, the Harrises don't go to the movies.

22. *(B)* Mrs. Tylor, in an effort to be friendly with the new neighbor, at first is trying to be agreeable. Later she uses "of course" because she doesn't know what else to say. What Mrs. Harris is saying goes far beyond what Mrs. Tylor might consider reasonable. The phrase becomes a mechanical, knee-jerk reaction.

23. *(B)* Mrs. Harris's negative remarks about newspapers requires a negative answer: *corruption*. The other alternatives are neutral or positive. *Degradation* has an interesting etymology: *de*, "down" and *grad*, "walk." Because some Latin words have been in the language a long time, they acquire a metaphorical (67) meaning. Thus, *degradation* is a kind of "walking down," a lowering in quality, a good explanation of Mrs. Harris's appraisal of newspaper taste.

24. *(A)* Mrs. Harris calls the previous neighbors "unkind." Then she mentions what she considers a terrible deed: leaving the *New York Times* on the doorstep three times. Apparently, the "unkind" neighbors were trying to be neighborly, but Mrs. Harris imputed evil motives to them. When Mrs. Tylor says, "Good Lord," her astonishment is stirred, not by the "evil deed," but by Mrs. Harris's incredible reaction to it.

25. *(C)* This short sketch is a gem, allowing the interplay of characters. What starts out as a pleasant episode of a woman reaching out to a new neighbor turns into an increasingly neurotic explanation of the new family's antisocial quirks. The conversation, with its glimpse into a strange new world, has been a strain on Mrs. Tylor. Though she had obviously no intention of going to the movies (or even perhaps of letting Carol go), she seizes upon the movies for a return to normal behavior and a relief from Mr. Harris and his browbeaten wife.

Section 2

Pages 368–372

1. *(E)* A contrast is suggested between *disentanglement* and the insect's entrapment. The contrasting word here is **enmeshed**.

2. *(D)* The word *unlikely* is an important clue. Both *thrive* and **abound** fit the second blank, but *although* suggests that *favorable toward (A)* does not fit the first blank. **Alien to** and **abound** complete the sentence logically.

3. *(D)* The title, with its key word *stars*, suggests that the book is dealing with the major news anchors. Therefore **dominate** fits perfectly into the second blank. **Emphasis upon** neatly completes the sentence.

4. *(A)* The word *plentiful*, followed by *less and less* suggests that a contrast is called for. The essential word for the first blank is **abundant**. **Dry** perfectly completes the sentence.

5. *(B)* If the *initial reserve* disappeared, the missing word must suggest its opposite: **exuberant**. There is another clue: the activity of first-graders on a school playground.

6. *(A)* The quotation suggests that Congress take an active role in advancing the goals set up by Washington. Conferring rewards requires a strong word like **support**. The others are too mild, passive.

7. *(B)* If the current reputation has helped sell his works for millions of dollars, it cannot be negative, thus eliminating *(C)*, *(D)*, and *(E)*. A clue to the correct answer is the use of *lifetime*. His paintings didn't sell during his life, but they have sold well since his death. *Fanciful* is inappropriate, leaving **posthumous**, "after burial."

8. *(A)* If you know that **ascetic** means "austere, self-denying," you need go no further. If not, you still have a good chance. *Far cry* suggests a contrast between the teenage dandy and the mature leader of his people. *(B)* and

(D) are opposite to the intended meaning. *(C)* and *(E)* make little sense.

9. *(E)* A guide dog leads a blind person, doesn't follow *(A)*. That such dogs are gentle eliminates *(C)*. They are not encumbrances *(D)*. *(B)* is much too grandiose for the situation. Only *(E)* fills the slot appropriately.

10. *(D)* The fulfillment of a search would bring joy, satisfaction. *(A)*, *(C)* and *(E)* suggest the opposite. *(B)* makes little sense. An added proof is the prefix *eu*, "good, well" (124), suggesting that **euphoria** is "feeling good."

11. *(C)* Since the writer of Passage 1 doesn't rule out all space travel, he also realizes that the thirst for knowledge cannot be repressed. Passage 1 specifically rejects *(A)* and by implication *(B)*. Passage 1 mentions the *Voyager* successes *(D)*. Passage 2 might agree with *(E)*, but Passage 1 would emphatically disagree.

12. *(A)* Both Magellan and Lovell were courageous in their own ways. There is no suggestion of Lovell's *seamanship (E)*. The other alternatives are not suggested in either passage.

13. *(B)* There is a little difference in risk between driving on an Interstate and flying into space! The contrast is a humorous one *(B)*. The other alternatives are nowhere implied.

14. *(E)* The final sentence clearly mentions the expense as an extra objection to manned space flight.

15. *(C)* This opening section of the Constitution is not concerned with *(A)*, *(B)*, *(D)*, and *(E)*, all of which are considered in later sections.

16. *(A)* The context clearly calls for a word meaning "required, **essential**." Trying each alternative in the slot suggests *(A)*.

17. *(D)* The passage specifically mentions "**free persons**," a reference to indentured servants.

18. *(E)* Since the first national census was still in the future, "until such enumeration shall be made," the numbers of representatives had to be arbitrarily assigned.

19. *(C)* "The whole number of free persons" includes *(A)*, *(D)*, and *(E)*. "Indians not taxed" takes care of *(B)*. That leaves only slaves, for whom the three-fifths fraction was adopted.

20. *(D)* All are accounted for in the passage EXCEPT Rhode Island. The capital of Rhode Island, Providence, still retains the old name.

21. *(B)* The horror of war calls for a strong word here. *(A)* and *(E)* are too colorless. *(C)* and *(D)* are stronger, but still inadequate to describe war.

22. *(C)* The precisely parallel wording rules out accident, coincidence, or any other explanation. The opening was clearly based upon the much admired Constitution of the United States.

23. *(E)* The passage is not concerned with *(A)*, *(B)*, *(C)*, or *(D)*. The theme of peace predominates.

24. *(A)* The U.S. Constitution did not consider global problems. *(B)* and *(E)* are wrong. Neither *(C)* nor *(D)* is considered in either passage. The Constitution talks about "the blessings of liberty" (5). The Charter promotes "human rights" (54), "justice and respect" (58–59), and "tolerance" (65). Both point to *(A)* as the answer.

25. *(A)* The *not* is a caution sign. If you find one of the possibilities covered in the passage, eliminate it. Self-determination and human rights are mentioned in line 54. The rights of women are mentioned in 56. Treaties are mentioned in 59. International law is mentioned in 60. The Charter does allow the use of armed force "in the common interest" (70–71). You may find *(A)* directly or by a process of elimination. Sometimes one method works better than the other.

26. *(B)* The passage includes "unite our strength" to affirm the basic purpose of the U.N.: cooperation.

27. *(D)* The passage states that representation among the states shall be apportioned according to their respective numbers. The census is referred to as the "Enumeration."

Section 3

Pages 373–375

1. *(C)* All answers have a kind of plausibility suggesting that all the relationships are somehow linked together, but the correct causal connection is more clearly implied in *one reason (C)*. Always select the *best* answer. While it is true that wealthier persons have better health care, better nutrition, and may live longer, the paragraph does not clearly make that connection (A). Inferior inferences are demons demonstrated in the other alternatives.

2. *(B)* In irony, the surface meaning of a sentence is quite opposed to the deeper meaning. The dinosaur, foretelling the end of the cockroach, is long gone, but the cockroach is still with us!

3. *(C)* Since the major thrust of the passage is the control of insects, *(C)* is the only possibility. *Etymology*, the "study of word origins," is similar in appearance to *entomology* but an entirely different study.

4. *(D)* Odhiambo points to positive help, "obvious cases, like honey from bees" (55–56).

5. *(B)* The Emerson quotation perfectly describes Odhiambo, a person who made the ICIPE happen.

6. *(E)* The use of *seemingly* suggests that appearances are deceiving. Sandflies *seem* harmless but are "host to a deadly parasite" (94–95). Substituting each alternative in the sentence eliminates *(A)*, irrelevant; *(B)*, counter to the meaning; *(C)*, inappropriate as a contrast to *deadly*; and *(D)*, meaningless.

7. *(C)* Lines 82–83 reveal that "many methods, including a drastic scorched-earth policy, have temporarily halted the spread of the fly, or even, in a few instances, caused a retreat." The key to the answer is the word *temporarily*.

8. *(E)* To answer a question like this, you will probably have to skim, quickly spotting and checking off the insects mentioned. Remember that on the SAT test you may write on the question pages. The passage mentions sandflies (94), moths (93), tsetse flies (92), and mosquitoes (93–94). Only butterflies have *not* been mentioned.

9. *(A)* Substituting each alternative in the sentence points to *(A)* as the only answer.

10. *(D)* The author emphasizes Odhiambo's brilliance, his successes, his ability to work with people, all qualities that stimulate admiration.

11. *(B)* Odhiambo has many solutions: using insects for food (56–61), keeping blood parasites away from insects (86–87), providing new and better traps (88). His attack is inclusive, all embracing.

12. *(D)* Although all methods may have good results, you must base the answer solely on the passage. "New and better traps have been introduced and reduced the tsetse population by half over a 62-square-mile area" (88–90).

13. *(A)* The attitude of the author toward Odhiambo is entirely positive. *(C)*, *(D)*, and *(E)* may be eliminated. *(B)* implies an excited passage, filled with exclamation points. Actually, the passage presents a great deal of information in an objective way.

Answers to Mastery Test 3 /
Critical Reading
Section 1

Pages 376–380

1. *(A)* The falcon's action is compared to an airplane in a steep power dive. The verb that best expresses the comparison is **swooped**. **Scattering** suitably completes the sentence.

2. *(B)* *Though* tells us a contrast is called for between the good first act and the middle of the last act. The first word in the pair must be negative and the second positive. *Consternation* is a possibility for the first blank, but *contemplation* makes no sense. The only suitable pair is **desperation . . . . inspiration**.

3. *(C)* The context suggests that ecological habitats are being threatened. The only suitable word for the second blank is **doomed. Suitability** fits nicely into the first blank.

4. *(D)* *Not* tells us the first blank is opposed to *necessity*. The opposite of *necessity* is **luxury. Indulged** suitably completes the sentence.

5. *(E)* The key word is *relieved*, which suggests the heat must have been *uncomfortable*. The second clause supports the choice of **oppressive** in the blank.

6. *(E)* If *Associated Powers* is the original, but rejected, name, the needed word is **supplanted**, "replaced."

7. *(B)* The rigors of ballet require a muscular, lean body. Preparation would require a highly disciplined diet. The people of ancient Sparta had the reputation of living austere, highly disciplined lives. **Spartan** means "stoical, frugal, austere."

8. *(D)* A "continuing search for perfection" in an imperfect world is usually doomed to disappointment. Experts will be more than critical: **hypercritical**. *Hyper* (124) means "above, beyond."

9. *(C)* The clue here is a pairing of ideas (30–34). The word "inherited" is paired with the missing word. If something is inherited, it is part of the personality : **congenital** *(C)*. If *congenital* is a hard word for you, work through Latin prefixes and roots (92–118) or through a process of elimination. The other choices just don't fit.

10. *(A)* The second sentence implies that clocks had been in use but were not accurate on a moving vessel *(A)*. The passage suggests that longitude cannot be determined by astronomical observations *(B)*. Latitude has been easy to observe; longitude had not *(C)*. Though Harrison was labeled *important,* no comparison was made with Edison *(B)*. Radio is nowhere mentioned *(D)*.

11. *(E)* Under certain conditions, universal suffrage may "make it easy to seize the source of power" (27–28).

12. *(D)* "The absolute master of the Roman world *pretended* to rule . . . by authority of a Senate that trembled before him" (6–7).

13. *(C)* Freedom is the reality. All others mentioned are subject to abuse: constitution *(A)*(3), the privilege of voting *(B)*(11–12), popular elections *(D)*(3–4), republican institutions *(E)*(28–29). The substance of freedom is mentioned in line 10.

14. *(E)* Something to "stay the flood" (20) would be a *barrier.*

15. *(E)* "The deadliest enemies of nations ... dwell within their own borders" (41–42).

16. *(A)* The first passage points out that people may vote themselves into despotism. The other passage declares that an alert citizenry can avoid despotism. Both emphasize that the people determine their fate.

17. *(D)* The key to the answer is the word *concealment* (line 3). Although "no cover-up is intended" (4), she "only briefly alludes" (6–7) to "that secret inward-looking creature" (6) that is part of her personality.

18. *(D)* The Latin elements help with a word like *expatriate. Ex*, meaning "out of," combines with *patr*, "father," to suggest someone who has "left the fatherland." The other alternatives are correctly paired.

19. *(E)* Children do not usually abandon parties to "make up" stories. Though children are frequently creative, Edith Wharton's childhood creativity was beyond the usual. The answer may be confirmed by a process of elimination.

20. *(C)* In the "rigidly stratified society" (13), "there would not seem to be either the time or the place for a writer of fiction to emerge and to blossom" (20–21). Thus, literary activity would be a departure from the normal. Once again, the Latin elements help confirm the

choice. The prefix *ab*, "away," combines with the root *err*, "wander." An *aberration* "wanders away from the normal."

21. *(D)* When she discovered the lack of interest in her books, "her easy sophistication enables her to dismiss this" (25–26). She was indifferent, shrugging it off.

22. *(C)* "These novels have to do with the doomed attempts to challenge the social code" (77–79).

23. *(A)* Trying each of the alternatives in turn suggests that *soundness* makes the best sense. Though the attempts to challenge the social code are doomed, the challengers are strong persons with sound motives.

24. *(D)* "A very small child" is a literal statement with no comparison stated or implied. All the others contain metaphors (page 67).

25. *(C)* These are strong women (82) who were not afraid to challenge the rigid social code.

Section 2

Pages 381–385

1. *(D)* If events are being dropped and added, then the events are not unvarying. *(C)* presents an opposite meaning entirely.

2. *(A)* *Stop* tells us that the filibuster is unpopular. We need a negative word for the first blank. Only **interminable** fits. **Enforce** effectively completes the sentence. *(C)*, with *unexpected* in the first blank, seems possible, but *discussing* a rule wouldn't stop the filibuster; so **discuss** doesn't fit.

3. *(B)* *(C)*, *(D)*, and *(E)* refer to emotional reactions out of place with the quiet tone of the sentence. Since Captain Cook was an explorer, not a tourist, *outdid* makes nonsense out of *(A)*. Only **inevitably . . . preceded** makes sense within the sentence.

4. *(E)* Perpetual motion is an impossible dream. *Though* tells us the inventors refuse to accept this truth. The only word that makes sense is **undaunted**. The inventors are not discouraged by the cold reality.

5. *(C)* The first word of each pair in *(A)* and *(B)* is much too strong. *(D)* and *(E)* make little sense. If there is no *typical* "sled dog," we must have been surprised.

6. *(D)* The context suggests a contrast between *raw ability* and another quality. That quality is here linked with *single-mindedness of purpose*. *Talent* and *dexterity* are too close to *raw ability*. *Guile* and *egotism* are irrelevant. The only word that fits is **concentration**.

7. *(C)* The context suggests a contrast between *becoming a hero* and *becoming an object of* **criticism**. **Scorn** is too strong, and **typical** doesn't fit well into the first blank. Only *(C)* makes good sense.

8. *(A)* *But* tells us a contrast is needed. *Breakthrough* contrasts with only one word, **conventional**. **Technological** perfectly completes the sentence.

9. *(E)* *Clout, reward*, and *prestige* all fit into the first blank, but only **supposedly** suitably completes the sentence. *(D)* is the closest alternative, but when there are two possibilities, be sure to pick the better.

10. *(B)* "Putting a scalpel" suggests *cutting*, an **incision**. This new machine doesn't make an *incision*. Thus *(B)* is the correct answer. **Science fiction** fits neatly into the first blank.

11. *(A)* Phrases like "I remember" and "in early youth" suggest the impact of time. Passage 2 shows respect; 1 does not. *(B) (C)*, *(D)*, and *(E)* are too broad and must be rejected since *(A)* is clearly the superior answer.

12. *(D)* The final sentence almost paraphrases answer choice *(D)*. *(A)* and *(B)* run counter to the last sentence. *(C)* and *(E)* are not mentioned.

13. *(A)* Passage 2 finds worthy ideas from the past *(A)*. The opposite is true for Passage 1: old ideas may seem "feeble and conventional" *(B)*. As for *(C)*, Passage 1 takes an opposing position. Although Passage 1 has a negative attitude, Passage 2 is positive *(D)*. Thoughtful individuals are mentioned, not action heroes *(E)*.

14. *(C)* As for Question 12 above, the final sentence pays tribute to those mature men and women of the past who have made a contribution *(C)*. *(A)* is not stated. On the contrary, established customs are often positive *(B)*. The opposite may be true *(D)*. Judgment may improve with maturity *(E)*.

15. *(D)* All the statements are true, but the question calls for the main idea. The last sentence comes to the point, establishing *(D)* as the correct answer. The quotation at the end of paragraph 1 confirms it.

16. *(C)* Despite all efforts, the weather systems are beyond control, unpredictable. *(B)* is too specific. *(E)* is too positive. *(D)* is untrue. Since weather systems bring life and moisture as well as death and destruction, *(A)* is too one-sided. The systems are erratic.

17. *(D)* Breaks in the levee have occurred and will occur. We may thus eliminate *(A)*, *(B)*, and *(C)* because a *yes* answer is required for question 1. That leaves *(D)* and *(E)*. The fact that many communities are taking steps to minimize flood damage suggests that "not entirely" is a reasonable answer to the second question, identifying *(D)* as the correct answer.

18. *(E)* The author points out that building barrier jetties at the shore often has the same negative effect as building levees on rivers. In both places, manmade barriers prove harmful.

19. *(B)* Jetties and levees have both been designed as barriers to water flow. They have similar functions.

20. *(C)* If the seashore is easily eroded, our grip upon it must be weak, *slight*.

21. *(A)* "There had been four serious floods" is a literal, straightforward statement, with no comparison stated or implied. In *(B)*, catas- trophes "wait." In *(C)* floodplains are "safety valves." In *(D)* waters "roar." In *(E)* measures "take the sting out."

22. *(B)* *Not* tells us that we need a word opposed to *concentrated. Scattered* is a good antonym.

23. *(E)* Reinforcing levees is ultimately not the answer. The others are all mentioned as possible remedies.

24. *(A)* The first quotation, which suggests cooperation with nature, is in tune with the main idea of the passage.

25. *(B)* "We can't pick Des Moines up and put it on a hill" (81). This quotation by Harry Fitch sums up the problem, but alternative *(D)* uses the word *overlooked*, which eliminates that possibility. Riverside dwellers *(E)* accept short-term, ultimately inadequate, solutions: levees.

26. *(E)* "It's not a mystery," said Larry Larson. "We need to adjust human behavior to river systems." But most solutions have been shortsighted efforts that postpone realistic solutions. There is no mention of lack of neighborliness *(A)*. Insufficient levees *(B)* are just part of the problem. They also give residents a false sense of security. The key problem is shortsighted failure to cooperate with nature.

27. *(C)* Only *(C)* offers an example of an ecosystem that is untouched by human interference and allows natural checks and balances to work.

Section 3

Pages 385–387

1. *(A)* In making the surprising comment, the author suggests his wry amazement at the information about inactive bears and inactive people. The exclamation point makes the point *(A)*. Exclamation points do not look ahead, foreshadow *(B)*. The author offers no apology *(C)*. The informality of "couch potato" is suggested by quotation marks, not an exclamation point *(D)*. The author is factual, not exaggerating *(B)*.

2. *(D)* The clue to the answer is the sentence, "Send it to the lab." (2). If police officers send in something to the lab, it must be considered evidence.

3. *(C)* The author provides a clue: "Was it contempt?" (13) In line 17, Chee is angry. Both suggest that Leaphorn was being sarcastic.

4. *(B)* The sarcasm (question 3) and Chee's embarrassment, "flushing just a little," suggest that the two officers have a prickly relationship.

5. *(A)* "Chee believed in the poetic metaphor of the Navajo story of human genesis" (25-27). "He believed in the lessons such imagery was intended to teach" (29–30). His attitude is positive. The other alternatives are essentially negative.

6. *(C)* Leaphorn says, "If Yellowhorse says he's a medicine man . . . . , it is no business of the Navajo Tribal Police" (59–62). This quotation points to *(C)*.

7. *(A)* Chee has been complaining about "somebody cynically using our religion" (63–64). Leaphorn has summarily dismissed Chee's religious concerns. Such lack of concern is a disregard for sacred things *(A)*, a sacrilege.

8. *(D)* A specific detail, recognizable in a passage, takes precedence over inferences. The former is objective; the latter, subjective. Of course, SAT questions test inferences, but in these test items, no detail is there to override an inference. The specific quotation here is "No rule against it. No law" (62).

9. *(D)* Largo is identified as a captain in lines 83–84.

10. *(D)* The linkage with *flat* and the rest of the context suggest that the captain's order would be forthright, frank, and clear. The Latin elements in *unequivocal* tell a relevant story. *Voc*, "voice," and *equ*, "equal" suggest "equal voice." (106, 110) If two alternatives were presented at the same time, with equal authority, the message might be unclear. So here: *un* "not," is added to the two roots to mean "not of two equal voices."

11. *(B)* If you try *(A) (C)*, and *(D)*, you will waste valuable time. Your memory may be faulty *(D)*. Skimming is the best technique here.

12. *(A)* You might infer *(A)* immediately, but you can also eliminate the wrong alternatives. Leaphorn's sharp comments identify him as far from gullible *(B)*. He is cool, not hot-headed *(C)*. He's an old-timer, not a new-comer *(D)*. He believes in following rules *(E)* (62).

13. *(C)* Leaphorn is a major personage, not just local color *(A)*. There are no humorous episodes in the passage *(B)*. Leaphorn is not a tragic figure *(D)*. Leaphorn, a police officer, is nowhere suggested as a suspect. The conflict (35–38) adds zest.

Answers to Complete Diagnostic Test for Writing

Pages 391–395

1. *(A)* The subject, *neither*, is a singular noun and should be completed by a singular verb, *was (A)* Don't be misled by words, like *twins*, between the subject and the verb. *Though (B)* is a conjunction joining a subordinate clause to the main clause. The antecedent of *they, twins*, is plural, requiring a plural pronoun *(C)*. *As* correctly connects *possible* with *prepared (D)*.

2. *(E)* There is no error in the sentence. *Slow* may be used as an adverb as well as an adjective. The adverb *slowly* would also be correct.

3. *(D)* The accepted past tense of *bring* is *brought*, not *brung (D)*, *In (A)* introduces a gerund. *Flatly (B)* is an adverb modifying *declared*. *One (C)* is an indefinite pronoun used as object of the preposition *with*.

4. *(C)* *Whoever* is subject of the noun clause "whoever showed the most flexibility and resiliency." The entire clause is object of the preposition *to (C)*. *Whoever* plays a role in its own clause. *Whomever* would be correct in a sentence like this: "Give the award to whomever you prefer," Then it is object of the verb *prefer* in the noun clause. *Name-calling (B)* is correctly hyphenated. *Beleaguered (B)* and *resiliency (D)* are used correctly.

5. *(D)* *Any* should be *any other (D)*. Shakespeare was himself an Elizabethan dramatist and should not be compared with himself. *Despite (A)* is a correct proposition. *(B)* and *(C)* are correctly used.

6. *(A)* *Myself* is a reflexive pronoun and should not stand by itself *(A)*. *I myself* is acceptable. *Suggesting (C)* is a participle modifying *study*. *Well-being (D)* is correctly hyphenated. *Collaborative* modifies *report*.

7. *(E)* There is no error in this sentence. The singular *has (C)* is correctly used with the singular *each (A)*. The antecedent of *which* is *flaw*, a singular noun. Thus *causes (D)* is singular. *Shakespeare's (B)* uses the apostrophe correctly.

8. *(D)* *Pig* is an example of a faulty comparison *(D)*. The aardvark's snout should not be compared to the total animal, merely the snout. *Going (A)* is a gerund, object of *in*. *Suddenly* is an adverb modifying *pointed (B)*.

Aardvark's (C) is the correct possessive form.

9. *(B)* The correct plural of *mother-in-law* is *mothers-in-law*. The word being pluralized is *mother*, not *law (B)*. *On television (A)* is an accepted idiom. *Making (C)* is a participle modifying *caricatures*. *Spouses (D)* is object of *for*.

10. *(C)* The subject, *selection* is singular and should not take the plural verb *are (C)*. Though *essays* is close to the verb, it is object of the preposition *of*, not the subject *(B)*. *Mencken's (A)* uses the apostrophe correctly. *In (D)* introduces the prepositional phrase *in my study*.

11. *(A)* *Being that* is substandard; a conjunction like *since* would be acceptable *(A)*. *Doesn't (B)* uses the apostrophe correctly. *When (C)* is a conjunction introducing an elliptical clause: "when (it is) after a worm." The possessive pronoun *its (D)* does not have an apostrophe.

12. *(B)* *Kind* should be *kinds (B)*. *Those* is a plural modifier requiring a plural noun. *If (A)* introduces the adverbial clause. *Shoes (D)* is the object of *of*. The antecedent of *(D)* is *shoes (C)*, a plural noun.

13. *(B)* The problem is lack of agreement between subject and verb. The subject is *first*, a singular noun, requiring the singular verb *is*. Though *days* is closer to the verb, it is not the subject. rather the object of the preposition *of*. *(A), (C)*, and *(D)* include the incorrect *are*. Although *(E)* has the correct *is*, it unnecessarily changes the direct quotation to indirect quotation and inserts an incorrect comma after *declared*.

14. *(B)* The sentence as written is correct, but your job is to improve it. The original wording can be sharpened and improved by reducing the two adjective clauses to participial phrases. *(B)* replaces the *which* clause with the participle *planted* and the *that* clause with the participle *sent*. The remaining alternatives retain adjective clauses where participles would be more effective. *(E)* unnecessarily changes the tense from *had been sent* to *are sent*.

15. *(C)* Since the second clause provides a contrast with the first clause, *but* suggests that con-

trast better than *and (E)*. *Life (A)* is preferred here. *Life forms* is an unnecessary expansion. *Exist only (B)* is presented in correct order. *Only* is directly associated with *limits*. *There (D)* is the adverb, used correctly here. *Their* is a possessive pronoun. *Challenge (E)* more effectively suggests that the unusual information just presented goes against common sense.

16. *(C)* *Gram* is subject of the verb *may contain*, not object of an incorrect *in (C)*. *Those (A)* makes sense, but *the bacteria* effectively labels the organisms described in sentence 1. *So* effectively is linked with *that (B)*. *Quite* does not suggest the connection. *Will (D)* is too strong a word here. *Will* asserts; *may* suggests. Not all grams will be saturated with bacteria. A compound adjective *(E)* modifying a noun correctly uses a hyphen.

17. *(C)* The sentence in *(C)* correctly and concisely provides the needed information: that bacteria outnumber other types of organisms. *(A)* The subject of the sentence is properly *bacteria*, not *number*. *As separate individuals* modifies *bacteria*. *(B)* When a choice is possible, the active voice *outnumber* is preferable to the passive voice, *are outnumbered*, as here. The problem with *(D)* is the same as the problem with *(A)*. The subject, *bacteria*, is introduced by *there*, and is at a distance from the prepositional phrase that modifies it. The compound sentence in *(E)* does not suggest the effective subordination of ideas achieved in *(C)*.

18. *(E)* Inserting *in* after *even* balances the two other *in* prepositions *(E)*. *Everywheres (A)* is considered substandard. The colon *(B)* correctly suggests that a listing will follow. *Creatures* is plural; the plural *bodies* is correct *(C)*. *Of* is an unnecessary intrusion here *(D)*.

19. *(B)* *They* would constitute a double subject with *shots*, and should be omitted *(B)*. *And* is a satisfactory connective here and need not be replaced *(A)*. *But (C)* correctly suggests the contrast between control of harmful bacteria and mutations that threaten that control. *Course of natural selection* more gracefully expresses the situation than the replacement *(D)*. *That* provides the needed connection between the main clause and the noun clause. *And* is not needed *(E)*.

20. *(D)* *Either* should be placed next to *harmless (D)*. *As (A)* incorrectly states the relationship between the subordinate clause and the main clause. *Though* correctly suggests contrast; *as* does not. *Very (B)* is more low key, less theatrically dramatic, than *terrifying*. *Plurality (C)* is a term often used in voting where more than two candidates are entered in a race. There are only two categories here: harmful or harmless bacteria. As in *(B)* *astoundingly* is overkill here. *Even* makes the point more effectively *(E)*.

Part One – Answers to Review of Writing Skills

 **Section I:** Writing Skills— The Single Sentence

Trial Test (Page 396)
1. *(B)* It expresses the thought directly and clearly.
2. *(A)* It doesn't waste words.

Writing Exercise 1 (Answers may vary.) (Page 398)

Writing Exercise 2 (Answers may vary.) (Page 399)
1. My father refused to let me have the family car on Saturday night.
2. Please stay off the grass.

Writing Exercise 3 (Answers will vary) (Page 399)

Review (Page 400)
1. *(B)* It presents the essential message without the wordiness and pretentiousness.
2. *(A)* *(B)* has an unnecessary double subject *they*.
3. *(B)* It expresses the thought directly.

 **Section II:** Writing Clear, Forceful Sentences

(Note: For many writing exercises that follow, answers may vary.)

Trial Test (Pages 403–404)
1. In 1949, Molehill, West Virginia, changed its name to *Mountain*.
2. At this year's career conference, seniors could learn the requirements needed for beginners in ten different fields.
3. Since I can't use the Braves tickets, I'll give them to my brother.
4. My dream is to own a car like the Toyota Camry.
5. When pressed for an answer, the witness hesitantly answered *yes*.
6. Since tomorrow is a holiday, I'll take Jennie to the picnic.
7. Without Sylvia, we'll have to put Jennifer at forward.
8. We regret that we cannot fill your order as sent.

Writing Exercise 1 (404–405)
1. In the *Matrix* movies, robots seek to rule the world.
2. I'm sorry that I'll have to miss the class reunion.
3. Three Buccaneer linemen and two running backs were chosen for the Pro Bowl in Hawaii.

Writing Exercise 2 (Page 405)
1. Look before you leap.

2. Too many cooks spoil the broth.
3. The grass is always greener on the other side of the fence.

Writing Exercise 3 (Pages 407–408)
1. B   2. A   3. B   4. B   5. B

Writing Exercise 4 (Pages 408–409)
1. Sitting in her chair on the porch, Grandma loves to watch passersby.
2. Carl told his brother, "I've been accepted at Duke University."
3. Although Ellen had been away for the summer vacation, she still was able to return for Sandra's birthday party.
4. Because I misplaced my ticket, my chance of seeing the Bulls play the Lakers was slim.
5. The problem of driving to Craggy Gardens on the Blue Ridge Parkway was poor visibility.

Writing Exercises 5–7: Answers will vary.

Writing Exercise 8 (Pages 413–414)
1. We visited the Grand Canyon and then headed toward the Petrified Forest.
2. The Peace Corps helps Third World countries with their problems and broadens the lives of the volunteers.
3. Charles Babbage thought out the basic principles of modern computers but didn't have electronic solutions for his challenges.

Writing Exercise 9 (Pages 414–415)
1. Because the Navajo language is difficult to master, it was used as a code by the United States in World War II.
2. Although Berengaria, wife of Richard the Lion-Hearted, was Queen of England, she never even visited there.
3. Charlotte was weeding the vegetable patch while Dan was watering the extensive lawn.

4. Because they may yet provide cures for presently incurable diseases, we must support efforts to save wild plants.
5. Although Harry S. Truman was expected to lose the election, he won a smashing victory over Thomas E. Dewey.

Writing Exercise 10 (Page 416)
1. After studying Spanish for three years in high school, Paul nervously asked directions in Madrid.
2. Thomas Edison unsuccessfully tried hundreds of filaments for the light bulb before finding the perfect one.
3. To be chosen for Guinevere in *Camelot*, Tonya practiced the songs over and over.
4. Gathering the suspects together, Hercule Poirot identified the murderer.
5. Having discovered a keen interest in flower arrangement, I took a course in ikebana, the Japanese art of flower arranging.

Writing Exercise 11 (Pages 418–419)
1. The well-rounded tennis player has a good serve, a strong forehand, and a dependable backhand.
2. John F. Kennedy, the first U.S. President born in the twentieth century, didn't take office until 1961.
3. James Madison, the shortest President, was only five feet four inches and weighed only a hundred pounds.
4. A professional basketball player should be tall, agile, and courageous.
5. Although the Wright Brothers flew that first airborne plane four times, it was finally struck by a gust of wind, overturned, and wrecked.

Review (Page 419)
1. B   2. B   3. A   4. A   5. B

Section III: Writing the Paragraph

Trial Test (Pages 422–423)
1. The topic sentence is the second.
2. It uses details to support the topic sentence: easy to study and store, takes up little space, has broad appeal, is educational, provides international connections.
3. It uses connecting words like *first, second, third, finally; some others, still others.*

4. The beginning attracts attention. The end sums up the paragraph. It uses effective words like *hobby of kings* and *king of hobbies*.

Writing Exercise 1 (Page 423)
Sentence H does not belong. The rest of the answers in this section (and the next) will vary.

Part Two – Answers to Review of Common Usage Problems

 **Section I:** **Problems with Sentence Structure**

(For many exercises, answers will vary.)

Writing Exercise 1 (Page 434)
1. Keats and Shelley died young.
2. Theodore Roosevelt advocated the strenuous life and followed his own advice.
3. Sugar is a popular ingredient in food but lacks nutritional value.

Writing Exercise 2 (Page 435)
1. You may think of Dobermans as vicious dogs, but many of them are gentle.
2. For the perfect electric bulb filament, Thomas Edison experimented over and over, and he did not stop even at the 600th try.
3. Lightning struck the tree, and the bark peeled off in layers.
4. Pay your credit cards on time, or the interest will destroy your financial health.
5. The rain poured down, but the sun was shining.

Writing Exercise 3 (Page 436)
1. Although he was French
2. When a New York manufacturer of billiard balls offered a $10,000 prize for a substance to replace ivory
3. whenever an emergency occurs

Writing Exercise 4 (Page 437)
1. that had been formed by the action of the waves on sand, shells, and coral.
2. whose contribution helped found the Smithsonian Institution
3. where zircons can be found

Writing Exercises 5–9: Answers will vary

 **Section II:** **Problems with Nouns**

Writing Exercise 1 (Page 446)
1. babies
2. bunches
3. crashes
4. puffs
5. glasses
6. halves
7. misses
8. pinches
9. ponies
10. stones
11. stories
12. tanks

Writing Exercise 2 (Page 447)
1. heroes
2. feet
3. strawberries
4. textbooks
5. families
6. mouthfuls
7. cupfuls
8. brothers-in-law
9. potatoes
10. crises

Writing Exercise 3 (Page 448)
1. athletes'
2. cities'
3. salesmen's

4. mice's
5. months'
6. parents'
7. four-year-olds'
8. geese's
9. houses'
10. searches'
11. trees'
12. wolves'

Writing Exercise 4 Writing Possessives (Page 449)

1. book's books books'
2. man's men men's
3. box's boxes boxes'
4. lady's ladies ladies'

5. sheep's sheep sheep's
6. brush's brushes brushes'
7. rose's roses roses'
8. punch's punches punches'

Writing Exercise 5 (Page 449)

1. books
2. book's
3. sister's
4. sisters, houses
5. geese
6. geese's
7. daughters
8. daughters'
9. brothers, school's
10. doormen

Section III: Problems with Verbs

Writing Exercise 1 (Pages 450–451)

1. The 727 circled Greenville Airport and then headed toward Atlanta.
2. The players sneak up behind coach Bill Parcells and dump a bucket of Gatorade on him.
3. Dad handed the tiller to me and then ducked as the boom swung over.

Writing Exercise 2 (Page 453)

1. swam
2. brought
3. drew
4. eaten
5. caught
6. became

7. frozen
8. lain
9. did
10. shaken

Writing Exercise 3 (Page 456)

1. was
2. is
3. were
4. Were
5. Are
6. is
7. was
8. am
9. doesn't
10. helps

Section IV: Problems with Modifiers

Writing Exercise 1 (Page 457)

1. gently
2. regularly
3. well

Writing Exercise 2 (Page 458)

1. anywhere
2. anything
3. had

Writing Exercise 3 (Page 459)

1. wiser
2. somewhere
3. Those

Section V: Problems with Joining Words

Writing Exercise 1 (Pages 460–461)
1. Unless
2. Because
3. of
4. in December
5. good as

Section VI: Problems with Pronouns

Writing Exercise 1 (Page 463)
1. We
2. her
3. Tom and I
4. I
5. me

Writing Exercise 2 (Page 464)
1. its
2. his
3. her
4. his
5. are, its

Writing Exercise 3 (Page 465)
1. was
2. were
3. was
4. is
5. are

Writing Exercise 4 (Page 466)
1. her
2. hers
3. me
4. It's
5. Talbot and I

Section VII: Problems with Punctuation

Writing Exercise 1 (Page 469)
1. The spring garden features snowdrops, crocuses, aconites, hyacinths, and tulips.
2. Are you aware that George Washington, first President of the United States, served two terms?
3. William Henry Harrison, on the other hand, served only a month.
4. Two Adamses, two Harrisons, two Roosevelts, and two Bushes have been Presidents of the United States.
5. The sassafras, unlike most trees, has three different and distinct leaf patterns.

Writing Exercise 2 (Page 469)
1. "How did jazz start?" asked Cynthia.
2. Mark exclaimed excitedly, "Geraldine won the spelling bee by correctly spelling *syzygy*."
3. "Work is the best method for killing time," said William Feather.
4. "If you can come camping with me," said Tom, "bring your fishing gear."
5. "All cruelty," wrote the Roman philosopher Seneca, "springs from weakness."

Writing Exercise 3 (Page 470)
1. "The Most Dangerous Game" is a short story I have never forgotten.

2. The newspaper *Newsday* has many readers but not as many as the *Times*.
3. "Wagner's music," slyly declared humorist Bill Nye, "is better than it sounds."

4. One of the best movies of all time, in my opinion, is *Music Man*.
5. "They that know no evil," declared Ben Jonson, "will suspect none."

Section VIII: Problems with Capitalization

Writing Exercise 1 (Page 473)

1. My aunt, Colonel Andrea Langer, has just returned from a tour of duty in Iraq.
2. The Alamo, in the heart of San Antonio, Texas, is a major tourist attraction.
3. "Happiness grows at our own firesides," declared Douglas Jerrold, "and is not to be picked in strangers' gardens."
4. Tides along shores bordering the English Channel can be dramatically high and low.
5. The Department of Agriculture has charge of our national forests, and the Department of the Interior has charge of our national parks.

PRACTICE: Identifying Sentence Errors (Page 477)

1. *(D)* There is a lack of parallelism *(D)*. Inserting *must have* after *and* provides the parallel structure needed: *must be prepared* and *must have*. *Graduates (A)* is one of the verbs in the subordinate clause. *Away-from-home (B)* is correctly hyphenated. *Adjustment (C)* is object of the preposition *for*.

2. *(A)* *Compliment* is the wrong word *(A)*. *Complement* is the correct form here. *Staff members (B)* is object of the preposition *of*. *Offbeat (C)* is here used as a noun, object of the preposition *in*. *Out-of-the-way (D)* is correctly hyphenated.

3. *(B)* The correct word is *fewer (B) Less* is used for amounts not counted: *less lemonade*; *fewer* is used for amounts that can be counted: *fewer lemons*. *Were (A)* is part of the verb *counted* in the subordinate clause. *Than (C)* is a conjunction linking the subordinate clause with *less*. *Formerly*, not *formally*, is the correct form here *(D)*.

4. *(B)* The past perfect tense *had developed*, is needed here *(B)*. The action of the *developing* had been completed by the time the Spanish *arrived*. *By the time (A)* is a prepositional phrase modifying *arrived*. *That (C)* is a relative pronoun joining the adjective clause with its antecedent system. *Remarkably (D)* is an adverb modifying *efficient*.

5. *(C)* *Hadn't* is part of a double negative: *hadn't-but*. The correct form is *had (C)*. The comma *(A)* is correct after a long introductory phrase. *That (B)* is a conjunction introducing a noun clause object of *regretted*. *To give (D)* is an infinitive phrase modifying *life*.

6. *(B)* The adverb *well* is needed here, modifying the verb *does (B)*. *Unfortunately (C)* is an adverb modifying *is finding*. *Of a challenge* is a prepositional phrase modifying *more*. *(D)*

7. *(D)* *Showed discipline (D)* is not parallel with the adjectives *polished. (C)* and *witty. Disciplined* would be more grammatically correct. *Used to (A)* is an acceptable idiom. *Group's (B)* is a singular possessive form.

8. *(A)* *And* is unnecessary *(A)*. *Braved* is the verb in the subordinate adjective clause modifying *pioneer*. *Principally (C)* is an adverb modifying the participle *known (D)*.

9. *(C)* *It* has no antecedent. The logical antecedent, *ball*, is not in the sentence. If *it* is changed to *ball*, the sentence is grammatically correct *(C)*. *After (A)* is a preposition introducing an adverbial phrase. *Flying (B)* is a gerund, object of *after*. *Bleachers (D)* is object of the preposition *over*.

10. *(B)* The correct verb is *lying (B)*. *Poe's* has the apostrophe in the right place. *In plain sight (C)* is a phrase modifying *lying* (lying). *All along (D)* also modifies *lying*.

11. *(A)* The correct form is *ridden (A)*. *Rode* is a past tense form, not part of the past perfect tense. *So exciting (B)* modifies *found*. *Going (C)* is a gerund, object of *on*. *Despite (D)* is a preposition introducing a phrase modifying *insisted*.

12. *(B)* The subject of the sentence is *one*, requiring a singular verb *sends (B)*. The nearby *customers* is part of a phrase, not part of the subject. *According to (A)* is a preposition introducing a phrase modifying *send(s)*. *Thus* is an adverb introducing the gerund

providing. But (D) effectively suggests the contrast between *attractive* and *deceptive.*

13. *(D)* *Nowheres (D)* is unacceptable; *nowhere* is the accepted form. *All (A)* is a pronoun in apposition with the subject *we. Lying (B)* is the correct form. *To get out (C)* is part of an infinitive phrase, object of *wanted.*

14. *(A)* *I* is incorrectly used *(A).* The correct form, *me,* is part of the object of the preposition *Between. Are (B)* is the correct form. The nearer subject, *brothers,* determines the number of the verb. *Qualified (C)* is a predicate adjective *modifying brothers. Take over (B)* is an acceptable idiom.

15. *(E)* There is no error in this sentence. *Is (A)* is a singular verb because its subject, *selection,* is singular. *Misnomers* is object of a preposition and not part of the grammatical subject. The colon *(C)* is correct. It is a mark of anticipation. It says, "Something follows." The semicolon *(D)* is also correct. It provides a link between clauses that would otherwise run on.

16. *(B)* *Resedes* should be *recedes (B).* The comma after *wave (A)* sets off the appositive, *or tsunami. To do so (C)* is a prepositional phrase modifying *foolish. Could (D)* is part of the verb *could walk.*

17. *(A)* *Not only* should be placed after *was (A)* to create the parallelism with *but also (C):* "not only . . . a conductor . . . but also . . . a player." *Of (D)* is a preposition connecting its phrase with the noun *player.*

18. *(D)* *Literally* should be *figuratively, (D) Literally* would make the sentence impossible: the speaker would be dead. Both *teetering (B)* and *threatening (C)* are participles modifying *Harold Lloyd.*

19. *(D)* *Has* is incomplete *(D).* It needs a completer, something like this: ". . . has been successful for years." *Is (A)* the present-tense form, is often used in talking about a continuing literary body of work. *Creator (B)* is a predicate nominative referring to the subject, *Agatha Christie.* The comma after *Poirot (C)* sets off the appositive.

20. *(A)* *In my opinion* is redundant *(A). I think (B)* says the same thing. *For (C)* is a conjunction joining the two clauses together. *Tangible (D)* is an effective sensory word.

21. *(A)* A period is needed. The sentence is run on *(A).* The verb *was heard* has two adverbial modifiers: *in Bangkok* and *3,000 miles away (B). And (C)* connects its clause with the preceding clause. *Could see (D)* is the main verb in the last clause.

22. *(C)* *Subtlety (B)* and *economy* are nouns. A noun, *perceptiveness (C),* is needed for parallel structure. In titles, articles are not usually capitalized unless at the beginning of the title; *the* is correct *(A). Suggesting (D)* is a gerund, object of the preposition *in.*

23. *(E)* There is no error in this sentence. *More (D)* is the comparative, correct when two are being compared.

24. *(C)* *Must of* is an incorrect form; *must have* is correct *(C). If (A)* is a conjunction introducing an adverb clause modifying *must have had. The size of a walnut (B)* modifies *brain. Fending* off *(D)* is a correct idiom.

25. *(A)* *Three fourths* here is considered a single sum and should have the singular verb *is.* "Three fourths of the players *were* dissatisfied" would also be correct because the object of the preposition *of* consists of things that can be counted. *Assigned (B)* is part of the complete verb *are being assigned. Scrub-jay* is correctly hyphenated. *Habitat (D)* is object of the preposition *of.*

PRACTICE: Improving Sentences (pages 480–482)

1. *(B)* This alternative *(B)* avoids the double subject, *(Chopin . . . he),* in *(A)* and presents the information directly and economically. *(C)* and *(D)* use participles ineffectively. *(C)* inserts *so,* suggesting that an adjective clause *(that)* is needed, not a participle. *(D)* substitutes participles for main verbs, leaving the attempted sentence a fragment. *(E)* is correct, but is not as effective as *(B).* It subordinates the *taking* to the *incorporating. (B)* expresses the relationship more accurately.

2. *(D)* *Either* introduces *in Tuesday's paper. Or* introduces *in Wednesday's* The two connectives are correctly placed close to the words introduced. *Either* is out of place in the other choices.

3. *(D)* This alternative *(D)* demonstrates the advantages of simplicity and directness. It makes the same point as the other alternatives, but it does so with a minimum of unnecessary words, phrases, and partial sentences like *and one of these was,* as in *(A), (B)* and *(E). One of whom, (C)* is little better.

4. *(A)* This sentence uses the effective participle, *created. (B) unnecessarily* substitutes an adjective clause *(which . . .)* for the simple participle *created. (C)* generates a dangling participle. *Wandering* grammatically belongs with *Mahler,* not *success.* Though a possible solution, *(D)* uses the incorrect form

use to. (E) has Mahler discovering Lehar's gifts. The original stressed the intent, not the success.

5. *(C)* The usual idiom is "everybody and his..." *Everybody* is singular. The attempt to use a familiar idiom *(A)* fails here because the speaker has the incorrect *their* instead of *his* (or *her). (C)* omits the unnecessary distraction *and their mother. Everybody* is quite enough. The remaining alternatives struggle with the superfluous *mother.*

PRACTICE: Improving Paragraphs
(Page 482)

1. *(A)* *Either* and *or* are correlative (paired) conjunctions and should be placed close to the words joined: *staple-fossil (A). Perishable (B)* destroys the contrast with *fossil.* The insertion of *it is (C),* though not incorrect, is unnecessary. With its suggestion of finality, *ultimately (D)* strengthens the contrast mentioned above. *Fossil (E)* is strong; *experiment* is colorless and inaccurate.

2. *(B)* *Detractors* is already a negative word; insertion of *negative (B)* is overkill. The colon *(C)* correctly suggests an elaboration of the previous thought. *Newsweek* is sufficient in *(D); magazine* is redundant. *An endangered species* is a direct quotation from the article and requires quotation marks *(E).*

3. *(B)* Interrupting phrases require commas at both ends *(B).* If there had been no commas after *sitcoms,* the comma might have been omitted here. *Perverse (A)* is a judgment word not called for by the context. Though *jokes* is closer to the verb, the actual subject is *sitcom,* requiring the singular verb *has been (C). Only (D)* emphasizes the surprising decline. *Reflecting (E)* is unnecessary.

4. *(E)* *Last but not least (E)* is a wordy, unnecessary intrusion. The simpler word *back (A)* is preferable. *Can bring (B)* is less forceful than the simple *brings. Groundbreaking (C)* is specific, effective; *tremendous* is general, commonplace. *Which were (D)* makes the participle *followed* into a wordy clause.

5. *(B)* *More easier* is a double comparative; *more (B)* should be omitted. Sentence 6 begins a new thought and correctly begins a new paragraph *(A). It may be said (C)* is one of those useless phrases inserted to pad a sentence. *And* is perfectly acceptable *(D).* Why add words but no additional thought? Overuse of the exclamation point *(E)* is a stylistic error. The simple period is preferable here.

6. *(D)* *Theirselves (D)* is substandard; *themselves* is correct. The hyphen *(A)* between *character* and *driven* makes a comprehensible compound unit. *Having (B)* unnecessarily replaces the simple preposition *with.* The contrast requires the contrasting conjunction *but (C). Ensembles* here refers to the casts, not the staff *(E)*

7. *(B)* *Usually always (B)* is a double error. *Usually* conflicts with *always.* Both words can be omitted without harming the meaning. The subordinate clause *(A) because ... business* suggests a causal connection with the advice to producers. *Although* would make nonsense of that connection. *Let* is perfectly acceptable *(C).* Either version is acceptable *(D),* but why change when there is an actual error in the sentence. *For* is simple and direct *(E); inasmuch as* is pretentious and wordy.

Answers and Analysis for Writing Diagnostic Test A

Pages 484–489

1. *(E)* There is no error in this sentence.

2. *(D)* *Etc. (D)* is superfluous. A better usage would replace *etc.* with *other birds. While (A)* is a conjunction connecting its adverb clause with *identified. Walking* is part of the verb phrase *were walking,* serving as the main verb of the adverb clause. *Casually (C)* is an adverb modifying *identified.*

3. *(B)* *Every one (A)* is grammatically singular and takes a singular verb—*was* in this sentence *(B). Consensus (C)* is the subject of *disappeared. As (D)* is a conjunction connecting the adverb clause with *disappeared.*

4. *(E)* There is no error in this sentence.

5. *(A)* *Having found (A)* is a participle, but a main verb, *found,* is needed. *Through (B)* is a preposition introducing a phrase modifying

bursting. On his way (C) is a phrase modifying *eluding. To (D)* is a preposition joining its phrase to *way.*

6. *(C)* *They* is unnecessary *(C)*. The subject of *do advertise* is *that. That (B)* is a relative pronoun which connects the adjective clause with its antecedent *those. Displaying (D)* is a gerund, object of the preposition *by. Don't (A)* is the correct plural form with the plural subject *plants.*

7. *(D)* *Is* is singular *(D)*, but the compound subject (*running* and *participating*) requires the plural verb *are. Running (A)* is a gerund. *Three times (B)* is a phrase modifying *running. Iron-man (C)* is correctly hyphenated.

8. *(B)* *It was known as* should be eliminated as unnecessary *(B). Two-century (A)* is correctly hyphenated. *To cover (C)* is an infinitive modifying the infinitive *to be painted. Caused (D)* is a participle modifying *damage.*

9. *(C)* The modifier *only (C)* is misplaced; it belongs before *one. In all of (A)* is an acceptable idiom. *By (B)* is a preposition connecting *all his actions* with *proved.* The colon is correctly used: looking toward the information it anticipates: *the accumulation of money.*

10. *(A)* The adverb *infrequently (A)* is necessary to modify the verb *come. To restore (B)* is an infinitive phrase modifying the verb *come. After* is a preposition connecting its phrase with *to restore. Devastating (D)* modifies *season.*

11. *(C)* This is a run-on sentence. *Surprisingly (C)* is an adverb, not a conjunction, and cannot join together two clauses. It should begin a new sentence. *Presidents (A)* is a plural, not a possessive. *The long and the short of it (B)* is an acceptable idiom. *One-time (D)* is correctly hyphenated.

12. *(A)* *Irregardless* is substandard *(A). Desperate (B)* is correctly spelled. *Missing (C)* is a participle modifying *skiers. Days ago (D)* is an acceptable idiom.

13. *(E)* There is no error in this sentence.

14. *(A)* *Talking* is a dangling participle. The participle grammatically modifies the subject, *Warrick Dunn,* but the talker is obviously not Warrick Dunn, who is himself one of the runners *(A).* Making the subject the *coach* or a similar noun would remove the problem: "The coach was told that Warrick Dunn ..."

15. *(E)* There is no error in this sentence. *Were* is a correct subjunctive form suggesting a situation contrary to fact. He isn't taller.

16. *(A)* The wording as originally presented was concise and accurate. *(C)* is also concise, but

it omits essential information. The other alternatives add unnecessary words.

17. *(C)* Avoid *is when* or *is where.* Use a noun as predicate nominative after a *being* verb. *Discovery* is the predicate noun, meaning the same as the subject *moment.* The only other alternative that omits *was when* is *(E),* but this rephrasing loses the vital 90% information.

18. *(D)* All the alternatives but *(D)* struggle to present the information, adding all kinds of unnecessary words and clumsy expressions. The original wording has another fault: a lack of parallel structure. *Sketch* and *record* are infinitives (without *to*) parallel with *capture.*

19. *(B)* This revised sentence presents the original thought in clear and concise form. The original phrasing is unclear. It is **words** that have played the role and dazzled speakers *(B).* Sentence *(A)* had the speakers and listeners playing the role properly assigned to words. In *(C), role* hasn't been singled out as being in primitive and industrial societies. *Words* is more properly the subject. In sentence *(D), words, not role,* have dazzled. This sentence also has an error of agreement: *have* should be *has* since *role* is singular. Sentence *(E)* includes the dangling participle *playing.* It should modify *words,* not *speakers and listeners.*

20. *(C)* Making the *witches* the subject of the sentence suggests the point immediately and economically *(C).* Sentence *(A)* is unnecessarily wordy. *In order to* can be reduced to *to.* In *(B)* the important witches are attached at the end ineffectively. The actor Macbeth did not use the incantation *(D).* In sentence *(E),* the passive *are called* is less effective than the active *called. In the form of* is wordy.

21. *(D)* *Spells* is plural; *kinds* should also be plural *(D). As well as* adds nothing to the sentence; *and* is adequate *(A).* The insertion of *tend to* adds nothing and may actually weaken the statement. *Use* is strong here *(B).* The wordy, *so that they can cast* is far less effective than the simple infinitive *to cast (C).* Since magic words are the subject of the paragraphs, the quotation marks serve to emphasize the central point *(E).*

22. *(A)* The original sentence is run-on. *From* should begin a new sentence. *They* is unnecessary. The revision *(A)* makes the point directly. The revision in *(B)* contains a sentence fragment beginning with *and.* The revision in *(C)* subordinates the *satisfaction* to

the *delight* in sounds and words. In the preferred revision (A) the two are given equal weight. The conjunction *but* in (D) expresses contrast. The clause it introduces *adds* information and doesn't provide a contrast. *Finding* is not parallel with *delighted* (E) *Find* would provide suitable parallelism with *delighted* IF the *and* were omitted. *Finding* would be a participle modifying *children*.

23. (E) Revision (E) best expresses the point in simple, direct language. Sentence (B) is too wordy and includes a passive voice (*can be uncovered*) instead of the active *uncovers*. The second clause in (A) weakens the statement by presenting *wordplay* as a kind of afterthought. *Is revealed to have* is wordy

(C). It could be expressed by a simple word like *demonstrates*. *Qualities of* is completely unnecessary. The structure of (D) downplays *wordplay,* the central point of the statement.

24. (A) The subject is *relationships*, a plural noun, requiring the plural verb *are*. The second clause expands on the point of the first clause, providing examples, not contradictions. *But* (B) would incorrectly suggest contrast. *Replacing* (C) is concise, a gerund, object of the preposition *by*. The suggested alternative, *by replacement of*, is wordy. Substituting *every one* for *each* (D) would be unnecessary. If there had been no colon (E), *as in* would do the job. The colon makes *as in* superfluous.

Answers and Analysis for Writing Diagnostic Test B

Pages 490–494

1. (A) No comma is needed after *person* (A). *Whatever* (B) modifies *time*. *To be* (C) is an infinitive, object of the verb *wishes*. *Off* (D) is an adverb modifying the participle *stepping*.

2. (B) A period or semicolon is needed (B). There is no conjunction; the sentence is run on. *Has* (A) is part of the verb phrase *has been*, the main verb in the first sentence. *Worth his salt* (C) is an acceptable idiom. *Pays* (D) is the main verb in the second sentence.

3. (C) The adverb *easily* is needed to modify the verb *might win* (B). *Just when* (A) introduces the adverb clause. *Might* (B) is the correct verb form for a proper sequence with *appeared*. *Hit* (D) is the verb in the main clause.

4. (C) *Consequently* is an adverb, not a conjunction (C). It cannot connect the two sentences together. The second is run on. *Dynamite* (A) is figurative and correct. *Easily*, the adverb form (B), modifies the verb *pull*. *To shoot* (D) is an infinitive, object of *hesitates*.

5. (B) Regions of the country are capitalized. *West* is standard (B). *From early childhood* is a prepositional phrase modifying *wanted*. The semicolon (C) properly connects the two clauses. *City* and *state* are correctly separated by a comma (D).

6. (D) *University* should be capitalized (D). It is part of the full name *University of Florida*.

Weeks (A) is object of the preposition *after*. *Agonizing* (B) is a gerund, object of the preposition *of*. *Was* (C) is part of the verb *was accepted*.

7. (B) *Of today* is redundant; *modern* conveys the idea. *Wealth* (A) is part of the compound object of the preposition *in*. *A far cry* (C) is an acceptable idiom. *Schools* (D) is object of the preposition *from*.

8. (E) There is no error in this sentence.

9. (A) *Working* (A) is a dangling participle. Grammatically, it modifies the subject, *the Declaration of Independence*. Logically it belongs with *Thomas Jefferson*. Making *Thomas Jefferson* the grammatical subject solves the problem: "Thomas Jefferson wrote his masterpiece the Declaration of Independence, the rallying cry for the new nation." *Steadily* (B) is an adverb modifying *working*. *To produce* (C) is an infinitive modifying *working*. *Rallying cry* (D) is object of *became*.

10. (A) *Probably certain* is self-contradictory (A). *That* (B) is a conjunction introducing a noun clause in apposition with the subject *it*. *Rest* (C) is part of the verb phrase *would rest*. *Until* (D) is a conjunction connecting the adverb clause with the verb *would rest*. This sentence contains an adverb clause inside a noun clause.

11. (A) *By* is unnecessary. The proper subject of the verb *will offer* (B) is the gerund *studying*.

Western (C) is correctly capitalized—a region of the country. *Migrants (D)* is object of the preposition *of*.

12. *(C)* *Was when (C)* is substandard. *Occurred when* or *was the time when* would be acceptable. *Never-ending (A)* is correctly hyphenated. *Unimportant (B)* is correctly used with *trivia. Important trivia* might be considered an oxymoron. The phrase *38-minute (D)* is correctly hyphenated.

13. *(C)* *Passengers were taken*, not *the houseboat (C)*. If the subject were *passengers* then both verbs would be correct: "… *passengers on the houseboat were met by buses and taken* …" *During (A)* is a preposition introducing the phrase *during our trip. By buses (B)* is a prepositional phrase modifying *was met. Center (D)* is object of *near*.

14. *(B)* The needed word is *perpetuate*, not *perpetrate (B)*. A comma *(A)* is needed after *Copenhagen* to set off a lengthy phrase modifying *statue. Memory (C)* is object of *perpetrate (perpetuate). As (D)* is a conjunction joining the adverb clause with *greets*.

15. *(D)* The preferred idiom is either *tablespoonfuls* or *tablespoonful (D). When (A)* introduces an adverb clause modifying *be sure (C). That (B)* is a conjunction connecting an adjective clause with *recipe. This* is an adjective clause inside an adverb clause.

16. *(A)* The sentence as presented is correct. *Is*, a singular verb, agrees with the singular subject, *accessory. (B)* and *(C)* have incorrect plurals: *are* and *were, (D)* and *(E)* use the correct singular verb but leave the *commenting* distant from *designer*.

17. *(C)* *Hailed* is correctly parallel with *prevented (C)*. The *who* clauses in *(A)* and *(D)* lack parallelism. The participle *hailing* in *(B)* is also not parallel with *prevented. (E)* keeps the parallelism but uses the incorrect connective *and*. Van Buren's hailing the transfer was *in contrast* to his peaceful action in preventing the invasion of Canada.

18. *(B)* *Star* is singular. The pronoun, *her*, must agree with it *(B). (A), (C),* and *(D)* retain the incorrect *their. (E)* has the correct *her* but changes *which* unnecessarily to *what*.

19. *(E)* The subject of the verb in the *but* clause is *plays*, a singular noun, not the nearer *contemporaries*, the object of the preposition *by*. The adjective *who* clause is restrictive, requiring no comma *(A). Shakespeare* is singu-

lar; the apostrophe belongs at the end *(B)*. Changing *by* to *assigned to (C)* adds nothing but unnecessary words. An appositive *(D)* like *even a talented contemporary* is correctly set off at both ends.

20. *(C)* *So it is with early films* provides the best connection with the earlier mention of Shakespeare *(C)*. The remaining alternatives *(A), (B), (D),* and *(E)* talk about films but fail to link the Shakespeare sentence to the rest of sentence 2.

21. *(E)* *Oblivion* shows a lack of parallel structure. *Lost* and *stored* need a parallel construction: *discarded, (E)*. The present perfect, *have been preserved*, denotes an action begun in the past and continued into the present. *Are (A)* fails to suggest a continuing action begun in the past. *As have (B)* is acceptable, but *like* is more concise and effective. The second clause is contrasting the successful preservation of D.W. Griffith's films with the loss of other early films. *But (C)* expresses that contrast. *Mislaid (D)* is a weaker verb here than the direct *lost*.

22. *(A)* Cult films have been shown to be a special kind of film, not blockbuster successes. *Fill a niche for (A)* places the films in a special place, not the mainstream. The paragraphs nowhere limit fans' enthusiasm to *purchase films*. The remaining choices make sense, but the question calls for the more effective replacement. Since the selection emphasizes the unique appeal of cult films, *filling the niche* does the job best.

23. *(A)* *Although* incorrectly expresses the connection between the subordinate adverb clause and the main clause. *When (A)* correctly suggests the time connection. *When* the list was presented, *then* the readers sent in their lists. The quotation marks around *best* suggest that *best* is used in a special sense. *Including (C)* is more accurate: only two films are included in that "list." A comma *(D)* correctly separates an introductory subordinate clause from the main clause. *Their (E)* is the correct possessive personal pronoun. *There* is an *adverb*.

24. *(B)* Any of the alternatives would make sense, but *longevity (B)* best suggests the enduring life of cult films as kept alive by dedicated fans.

Answers and Analysis for Mastery
Test 1 / Writing

Page 489

1. *(A)* The gerund *taking*, not *Jerry*, is object of the preposition *to (A)*. Marilyn didn't object to *Jerry*. She objected to the *taking*. The correct form, *Jerry's*, is a possessive form of the noun modifying *taking (A)*. *Reins (B)* is figuratively used for *control*. *Departure (C)* is object of *after*. *Lame-duck (D)* is correctly hyphenated.

2. *(E)* There is no error in this sentence.

3. *(B)* *It's* should be eliminated *(B)*. It's a part of a double subject with *The Spoon River Anthology (A)*. *Frequently (C)* is an adverb modifying *sardonic (D)*, which modifies *epitaphs*.

4. *(C)* The second *that* is unnecessary *(C)*, adding nothing to the statement. *Start (A)* is the verb in an adverb clause. *Skidding (B)* is a gerund, object of *start*. *Best (D)* is a predicate nominative.

5. *(A)* *Seldom ever* is an incorrect idiom. *Ever* is unnecessary *(A)*. *Saturday's (C)* correctly uses the apostrophe. *All the more (D)* is an accepted idiom. *Crucial (B)* suggests the importance of the fumble.

6. *(A)* *Each* is singular and requires a singular pronoun, *its*, not *their (A)*. *Assessing* is a participle modifying *report (B)*. *Feasibility (C)* is direct object of the participle *assessing*. *Projected (D)* modifies *bypass*.

7. *(C)* The correct idiom is *couldn't care less (C)*. *Suicidal (A)* modifies *invasion*. *Demonstrated (B)* is the main verb of the sentence. *Contrary (D)* modifies *recommendations*.

8. *(D)* *It* has no antecedent *(D)*. Replacing it with *his promise* would remove the problem. *Would (A)*, a past tense, continues that past tense of *promised*, the main verb. All elements in *Golden Wedding Anniversary* are properly capitalized *(C)*. The plural *parents (B)* properly places the apostrophe after the *s* to indicate plural

9. *(A)* Who is *he*, Max or Oliver? The antecedent is ambiguous *(A)*. *Ought to attend* is a correct idiom *(B)*. *To forestall* is an infinitive modifying the verb *ought (C)*. *Opposition* is object of the preposition *by (D)*.

10. *(A)* *Wobbling* is a dangling participle. The logical subject of the sentence should be *penguins*. *(A) Grace* and *skill* don't wobble: They

do require the plural verb *are (C)*. *Ungracefully (B)* modifies *wobbling*. *Antarctic (D)* is properly spelled.

11. *(E)* There are no errors in this sentence. *Limit (D)* is the subjunctive form.

12. *(E)* The original *(A)* is wordy with a lack of parallel structure in *should study* and *to become*. *(E)* provides the information succinctly by using infinitives *(to study* and *become)* instead of unnecessary clauses. *(B)* is grammatically correct, but isn't as sharp and concise as *(E)*. *(C)* is even wordier than *(A)*. *(D)* makes Marla's decision less personal.

13. *(B)* *Was* or *were*? The rule is to use *were* if the *if* clause is contrary to fact. Actually, the vote wasn't taken today. *(C)* incorrectly uses *was*. *(A)* correctly uses *were* but includes the unnecessary *to be*. *(D)* and *(E)* use *had been* and *would be* in place of the acceptable, concise *were*.

14. *(E)* *Doubting* is not parallel with *to doubt*. The infinitive *to doubt* is needed for parallelism. The subject of the verb is *human being*, singular, not *advantages*, plural. *Is (A)* is correct. If needed, the correct form *themselves (B)* would be correct, but it is not needed. *It seems (C)* adds nothing to the presentation. The simple present tense *(D)* is sufficient.

15. *(D)* *Being* is an intrusive insertion *(D)*. *Substantially (A)* is too strong. The tenor of the selection makes clear that the definite *has* is preferable to the iffy *may have (B)*. Inserting *a great deal of (C)* is not only not necessary; it actually weakens the statement. *Urban*, pertaining to the city, is correct *(E)*.

16. *(C)* The subject, *a number*, takes a plural verb (*have*, here) when it is followed by a plural noun, *legends*, in the prepositional phrase *(C)*. If the sentence had read "the number of urban legends," the singular verb *has* would have been correct. This sentence *(A)* should not be the topic sentence. It is a development of the central idea suggested by the correct topic sentence (1). *Alligator (B)* is correctly spelled. The subject is *hoaxes*, not *hand*; *are (D)* is correct. *Purposes of (E)* adds nothing to the sentence.

17. *(C)* The comma is needed after *Mermaid*. It's the second in the pair, to set off the interrupting phrase. *Which was (D)* creates an unnecessary clause. The verbal *merging* adequately carries the thought. *It may be told (A)* is pretentious rubbish. *Perpetrated* "brought about," is the correct word here *(B)*. One monkey was used. The singular possessive, *monkey's* is correct *(E)*.

18. *(E)* *But* correctly suggests the contrast between reality and deception *(E)*. *Cardiff Giant (A)* is correctly capitalized. *Supposedly (B)* correctly suggests the intent to deceive. Inserting *in size* repeats part of the meaning of *colossal (C)*. The possessives of personal pronouns do not have apostrophes *(D)*.

19. *(B)* *As of* adds words without additional sense *(B)*. The simple present tense *enjoy (A)* adequately conveys the meaning. The comma makes *and* unnecessary *(C)*. *For (D)* correctly suggests the causal relationship. *Visually appraise (E)* is pompous and inflated.

20. *(A)* *That* correctly introduces the noun clause *(A)*. *Living forms (B)* adds nothing not covered by *life*. *Announced* and *provided* are parallel. Adding *they (C)* creates an unnecessary clause. *Lunar* makes the phrase unnecessary *(D)*. *Along with (E)* breaks the rhythm of the sentence. *And* does the job adequately.

Answers and Analysis for Mastery Test 2 / Writing

Page 503

1. *(A)* The subject, *music*, is singular and requires a singular verb *owes (A)*. *Peoples*, the word nearest the verb, is part of a prepositional phrase and is not the subject. *African-American (C)* is correctly hyphenated. *Balladeers (D)* is correctly spelled. *Secular (B)* modifies *songs*.

2. *(E)* There is no error in the sentence. *Pancakes and sausage* is a grammatically singular subject—one meal.

3. *(B)* The present perfect form, *has chewed*, is correct here *(B)*. The tense is used to represent a present situation resulting from action which began or occurred at some indefinite time in the past. *So far this week (A)* correctly sets the time of the action. *Living room* is usually written as two words *(D)*. *Mike's (C)* is the correct singular possessive form.

4. *(A)* The verb *was* is a past tense. *Becomes* should be *became* for the correct sequence of tenses *(A)*. *Prestigious (B)* is correctly used and spelled. *There (C)* rather than *their*, is the correct form. *Much (D)* is subject of *was*.

5. *(A)* *Could of* is a substandard version of *could have (A)*. *Abhorrence (B)* is correctly spelled. *Caused (C)* is the verb in the second clause of the compound sentence. *To reject (D)* is an infinitive used as object of the verb *caused*.

6. *(E)* There is no error in this sentence. *Deer* is the correct plural of *deer*.

7. *(C)* The singular subject, *Commander Dal-* *gliesh*, requires the singular verb *does (C)*. *Among (A)* is usually used for many items, *between* for two. *Mysteries (B)* is object of the preposition *in*. The antecedent of *that*, *solution* is singular; therefore *presents (D)* must be singular.

8. *(D)* Twenty dollars *(D)* is grammatically a single sum requiring a singular verb *is*. *If (A)* is a conjunction introducing the adverb clause. *Please note (B)* is an acceptable form. *As previously reported (C)* is a participial phrase modifying *dollars*.

9. *(E)* There is no error in this sentence. *Measles*, though a plural form, is usually considered a singular noun.

10. *(B)* The subject of *were* is *number*, a singular noun in this usage. *Was (B)* would be correct. When the article *a* is used before *number* followed by a plural, the plural verb is used: "A number of Navajo code talkers were used throughout the Pacific theater." *During (A)* is a preposition introducing the phrase "during World War II." *In (C)* is a preposition introducing the phrase "in ... operation." *That (D)* joins the adjective phrase with its antecedent *operation*.

11. *(C)* When subjects are joined by *neither-nor*, the verb agrees with the nearer subject—in this sentence *Barbados*, a singular noun *(C)*. *Was* would be correct. *Despite* is a preposition introducing the phrase "despite...objections." *Vocal* is an adjective modifying *objections; very* is an adverb modifying *vocal (B)*.

To benefit (D) is an infinitive phrase modifying *cruise*.

12. *(D)* In sentences *(A)* and *(B)*, *that* has no antecedent. *(D)* eliminates the problem by replacing *that* with *plan*. *(B)*, *(C)* and *(E)* have the incorrect connective *and* instead of *but*. The impractical plan is contrasted with the unattainable goals.

13. *(C)* Only *(C)* uses the infinitive *to separate* to present the information concisely. All the others are unnecessarily wordy.

14. *(A)* *Though (A)* expresses the contrast between the visionary flight to Mars and the plans for interstellar space travel. *Absurd (B)* is more pessimistic than the sentence suggests. There is no point to interchange *seriously* and *considering (C)*. The test requirement is to choose the *best* revision. *Probability* is too optimistic in the context *(D)*. Inserting *they* *(E)* would provide a double subject.

15. *(A)* Using *Having* instead of *With* creates a dangling element *(A)*. *Conjectured (B)* is an inaccurate replacement for *expressed*. The superlative *incredible (C)* is overdoing it. The facts speak for themselves. Sentence 2 *(D)* belongs where it is. It continues the engineer interest introduced in sentence 1. Science fiction and fantasy *(E)*, though having elements of imagination in common, are different genres.

16. *(A)* *Who is* is unnecessary *(A)*. The appositive *scientist (A)* adequately identifies the subject. *Insists* is simple; *keeps insisting* is an unnecessary embellishment *(B)*. A semicolon would bring about a more definite, but incorrect, pause *(C)*. The plan is still conjectural. *Might (D)* is more appropriate. Inserting a comma *(E)* would unnecessarily set off the phrase from the rest of the sentence.

17. *(C)* A period of two years is contrasted with 7–8. *But (C)* is preferred to suggest the contrast. *Decreed* suggests a legal process *(A)*. Inserting *upward* is superfluous *(B)*. *Than (D)* correctly continues the contrast. The span *2000–2002 (E)* adds specificity.

18. *(D)* *Which are* creates an unnecessary adjective clause *(D)*. *This* has no antecedent. Including *conclusion* avoids any ambiguity *(A)*. *That (B)* correctly introduces an adjective clause. *Expected* suggests the tentative nature of the prediction. *Will (C)* is preferable. *Range (E)* properly suggests the spread.

19. *(C)* *Rays* is unnecessary *(C)*. *As chance would have it (A)*, adds nothing relevant to the sentence. The infinitive *to approach (B)* is correct here. *Concocted* seems unduly frivolous *(D)*. *Even* effectively suggests a climax of possibilities *(E)*.

20. *(E)* The original phrasing lacks parallel structure. *Personality clashes (E)* is parallel with the other challenges: cabin fever, etc. *Can (A)* correctly suggests the challenge of the interstellar problem. *With (B)* is more simple and effective than *possessing*. *Who are able (C)* is unnecessary. The infinitive to *survive* modifies *can be found*. *So many (D)* is shorter and more effective than the suggested replacement.

Answers and Analysis for Mastery Test 3 / Writing

Page 507

1. *(C)* Though logically plural, *two weeks* is a singular span of time requiring the singular verb *is (C)*. *Of any book (B)* is a prepositional phrase modifying *reading*. *For (A)* is a preposition introducing the phrase "For … book." *A period (D)* is an adverbial modifier of *short*.

2. *(A)* The plural of *shelf* is *shelves*, not *shelfs (A)*. The plural subject takes the plural verb *are (B)*. *For (C)* is a conjunction joining the subordinate clause to the main clause. *Different from (D)* in a sentence like this is a standard usage.

3. *(B)* The possessive forms of personal pronouns (*ours, yours, hers, theirs, its*) do not have apostrophes. *Of a snake (A)* is an adjective phrase modifying *skin*. *Distinguished (C)* is a participle modifying *leather*. *Geometric (D)* is an adjective modifying *patterns*.

4. *(C)* The correct idiom is "Let's you and *me*" *(C)*. *Let (B)* is a verb with the object *us* (*'s*). *You* and *me* are in the objective case in apposition with *us*. *In typical Holly fashion (A)* is a prepositional phrase modifying *declared*. *This coming weekend (D)* modifies the verb *plan*.

5. *(D)* *It (D)* has no antecedent. For clarity, *it* should be replaced by something like this: "…soon their invention became a universal sport." *As far back as (A)* is an acceptable idiom. The antecedent of *them (B)* is *rows*. *Soon (D)* is an adverb modifying *became*.

6. *(D)* *What's* is substandard here *(D)*. *That's* would be acceptable. *Because of (A)* is a preposition joining its long prepositional phrase with *Alaska. Its (B)* is the correct possessive form of a personal pronoun – no apostrophe. *Only (C)* modifies *state*.

7. *(D)* *A half a century (D)* should be either *a half century* or *half a century. Quoting (A)* modifies the subject of the sentence, *Mr. Palmer (B). For (C)* is a preposition introducing the phrase "for . . . century."

8. *(A)* *Hadn't barely (A)* is a double negative. Eliminate the *n't. To (B)* introduces the prepositional phrase modifying *trip. When (C)* introduces the adverb clause that modifies *had started. To cough (D)* is an infinitive phrase, object of *began*.

9. *(D)* *Them (D)* is unnecessary. The object of *spread* is the relative pronoun *which. Began (A)*, not *begun*, is the correct form. *Had bought (B)* is one of the two verbs (*spread* is the other) that act as main verbs of the adjective clause. *With (C)* is a preposition introducing a phrase modifying *had bought*.

10. *(A)* A comma is needed after *path (A). Steep* and *craggy* are in the appositive position and must be set off by commas. The comma after *craggy (B)* is correct. *From (C)* introduces the adverbial phrase modifying the verb *led. Aglow (D)* is an adjective modifying *meadow*.

11. *(E)* There is no error in this sentence.

12. *(E)* The unnecessary *he was* eliminates *(A), (B)*, and *(C). (D)* is correct, but *(E)* better preserves the sense of the original sentence: "almost as famous."

13. *(E)* *(E)* is concise. The unnecessary *ultimately* and *final* are implied in *victory (A). (B)* avoids these words but includes the repetitive *ands*: "And channeled and led." *At last* is also unnecessary.

14. *(E)* *Of* is nonessential *(E)*. As regions of the country, *East* and *West* are properly capitalized *(A). Who* is correctly used for a person; *which* ordinarily refers to animals, ideas, objects *(B)*. As a suggestion, *should* is appropriate here *(C). Just* is an adverb modifying the verb *look (D)*. As another, optional revision, *who is* might also be omitted.

15. *(B)* The infinitive phrase *to divide* tightens the construction. Sentences *(A), (C)*, and *(E)* are as unnecessarily wordy as the original. *Dividing the vast country into squares* is a sentence fragment *(D)*.

16. *(C)* This is a run-on sentence. The first sentence correctly ends with *sections (C)*. The tense used throughout is the past tense. Therefore, *may* is inappropriate *(A)*. Though *where*

(B) might also be considered correct, *as* effectively conveys the meaning. Since this is a run-on sentence, you must choose the *best* answer. Compound adjectives that precede the noun modified are hyphenated *(D). Then (E)* is an adverb serving to indicate a time relationship between *at auction* and *subdivided*.

17. *(D)* Not all the surveying was done in the mountains; *especially* expresses the relationship best *(D)*. A comma, not a colon, is correctly used after an introductory adverb phrase *(A). Foolish* fails to express the forward-looking plan presented by Thomas Jefferson *(B). Avoided* changes the sense of the passage *(C). Country* would be an acceptable replacement for *terrain*, though not as apt *(E)*. The major point is that *always (D)* is the word best replaced.

18. *(C)* *Transforming* is not parallel with *provided*. A main verb, *transformed*, is needed, not the participle *transforming (C). Promising* is an unnecessary replacement for the effective *plus (A)*. Besides, *plus* contrasts with *minus* in sentence 11. The past tense is used throughout; the past tense *provided* is correct *(B). Ultimately* suggests the eventual positive results from an enterprise so difficult at its inception *(D)*. The original intent included some ownership; *unexpectedly* runs counter to the thought of the paragraphs. *Manageable* correctly suggests the convenient divisions of the planned surveys *(E)*.

19. *(C)* The nearer antecedent of *it* is *cabin*. The cabin isn't being farmed. Replacing *it* with *the land* expresses the meaning accurately *(C). A* and *any* are essentially interchangeable here. No change is needed *(A). Constructed* is a bit too grand for a cabin *(B). Built* is more in keeping with the context. *Years* is a plural, not a possessive. An apostrophe would be incorrect *(D). Land* better suggests the physical ownership. *Deed* is a legal term *(E)*.

20. *(D)* *Having* is an unnecessary intrusion. *Progress* and *prosperity* are more suitable as subjects of the verb *came* than as objects of the gerund *having (D)*. Replacing *As is* with *It is* creates a run-on sentence *(A)*. A new sentence would then begin with *there*. A semicolon does not separate a dependent clause from a principal clause *(B)*. A comma is correct. There is no reason to change the balance with sentence 7: *on the plus side; on the minus side (C)*. There is no semantic difference between *come at a cost* and *had a cost (E)*. Either one is acceptable, but keep in mind that *(D)* is the best answer.

HOW TO USE THIS GUIDE

The following outline of lessons has been planned for English Departments wishing to make preparation for the SAT a growth experience, rather than a quick cram course. Seen in this light, the SAT provides strong motivation for improvment in all language skills.

For both the Critical Reading and the Writing sections, the preparation materials have been divided into three major sections—for Grades 9, 10, and 11—with some suggestions for Grade 12. For those students taking the examination in the senior year, the early months of the year should be devoted to review and mastery tests.

In the Critical Reading section, lessons on reading alternate with lessons on vocabulary. In the Writing section, lessons on student writing are sandwiched between lessons on grammar and usage. Critical Reading and Writing lessons can be taught as alternating groups.

For each lesson that follows, the aim is stated. "Pages studied" might be assigned and then reviewed in class. The "Review and test" sections provide helpful summaries and checks of student understanding. Frequent review is sound pedagogy to offset student forgetting.

These suggestions are intended as a guide, not a rigid plan. Classes vary. The amount of previous preparation varies. While the following suggestions are inclusive, exploiting the resources of this book, they may be modified as needed: omitting lessons the class is already strong in or combining lessons in advanced classes. The pedagogy of the guides is sound. You will make the ultimate decisions as you appraise the needs of your class.

GETTING STARTED: SUGGESTED PLAN FOR LESSON 1

Aim: To get an overview of the SAT examination along with strategies for taking the test.

Materials: *Amsco's Preparing for the SAT in Critical Reading and Writing*

Motivation: You might introduce the study unit with remarks similar to the following:

"You have all heard of the SAT exam. A great many of you will be taking it. There are two general methods for preparing to take this exam. The more common and the less effective method is to cram for the exam, to try, in a short time, to learn how to take the test and memorize enough information to do well. The second and better method is to prepare for the exam over a period of months and years. During this time, you will be able to learn and practice the kinds of thinking strategies that work best for each type of question. (If you find out how the test *maker* thought, you can see how the test *taker* should think.) This method is of great value even for those who do not plan to take the exam.

"We are beginning a study plan that will lay the groundwork for taking the exam later on in high school. The plan will help improve your scores, but there is a more important value. The materials in our plan are skills units that are important in every phase of school life and will be important in the years to come—in college and in everyday life.

"As you progress day by day, your confidence in handling language will grow. You will learn new methods of increasing your word store. You will develop reading skills that will help you read everything, including magazines and newspapers, more effi-

ciently. You will review important information about grammar and usage. You will improve your writing skills."

Development:

The SAT that your students will take contains a new section, Writing. The test emphasizes the old three R's: reading, writing, and 'rithmetic. This book will prepare students for the first two. You may assign reading page 175 or go over the material without prior assignment. Emphasize that this book has been designed to seek improvement in *all* areas of language. It is intended as a preparation for college and for life afterwards. Spend some time on the organization of the textbook, p. xi.

After going over the introductory materials turn to Mastery Test 1, page 351, give students a quick overview of what the test looks like. Do not go into questions and answers at this time. On a separate day, do the same for Writing Mastery Test 1, page 499.

The lesson plans that follow teach both the critical reading and the writing materials. An organization is suggested in the pages that follow, but all classes are different. Adapt these suggestions to the needs of your classes.

Summary:

In conclusion, emphasize again that the goals of the SAT unit apply to all students, whether or not they plan to take the test. Remind them that "inch by inch, life is a cinch; yard by yard, life is hard."

For convenience in planning an effective program, these lessons have been divided into two groups: Critical Reading (vocabulary and reading) and Writing. Answers to Trial Test questions appear on pages 518–523; 527–532 (Critical Reading) and page 551 (Writing).

GRADE 9 STUDY PLAN

Critical Reading

Lesson 1

Aim: To get an overview of the SAT examination along with strategies for taking the test.

Pages studied: ix–xvi (See suggested lesson plan on previous page.)

Test for examination of format and content only, 351–362

Lesson 2

Aim: To familiarize students with sentence-completion test items.

Pages studied: 21–23

Review and test: Questions 1–5, page 9

Lesson 3

Aim: To introduce the idea of context as a course of vocabulary recognition and growth.

Pages studied: 24–30

Review and test: Questions 6–10, pages 29–30

Lesson 4

Aim: To understand how pairing of words often provides a clue to the meaning of an unfamiliar word in the pair.

Pages studied: 30–33

Review and test: 33–34

Lesson 5

Aim: To study some sentences that reveal word meanings by direct explanation.

Pages studied: 35–38

Review and test: 38–39

Lesson 6

Aim: To understand how comparison within a sentence often provides a clue to word meaning.

Pages studied: 39–42

Review and test: 42–43

Lesson 7

Aim: To understand how contrast within a sentence often provides a clue to word meaning.

Pages studied: 43–46

Review and test: 46–47

Lesson 8

Aim: To study sequence in a sentence to discover clues to word meanings.

Pages studied: 47–50

Review and test: 50–51

Lesson 9

Aim: To understand how seemingly unimportant function words can play a major role in word meaning.

Pages studied: 52–55

Review and test: 56

Lesson 10

Aim: To learn how to derive generalizations and main ideas from reading passages.

Pages studied: 176–177; 178–180

Review and test: 177–178; 180–181

Lesson 11

Aim: To study generalizations further through providing a title and a summary for a reading selection.

Pages studied: 181–183; 184–186

Review and test: 183–184; 186–188

Lesson 12

Aim: To understand what an inference is, what distinguishes an inference from a factual statement.

Pages studied: 189–190

Review and test: 191

Lesson 13

Aim: To continue the study of inferences with emphasis on supplying an interpretation.
Pages studied: 192–193
Review and test: 193–194

Lesson 14

Aim: To pursue the study of inferences with emphasis on paraphrases and comparisons.
Pages studied: 194–195; 197–198
Review and test: 196–197; 198–201

Lesson 15

Aim: To understand the part played by connotation and denotation in the meanings of words.
Pages studied: 60–64
Review and test: 64–65

Lesson 16

Aim: To understand how figurative language plays an important role in word meanings.
Pages studied: 66–70
Review and test: 70–71

Lesson 17

Aim: To realize that words similar in meaning still have individualized meanings of their own.
Pages studied: 71–75
Review and test: 75–76

Lesson 18

Aim: To understand how a person's vocabulary can grow through studying words in groups.
Pages studied: 77–79
Review and test: 79–81

Lesson 19

Aim: To break down larger words into smaller sections to derive word meanings.
Pages studied: 81–83
Review and test: 83–84

Lesson 20

Aim: To recognize the part played by allusions in understanding word meanings.
Pages studied: 84–88
Review and test: 88–91

Lesson 21

Aim: To spot specific details in a reading selection.
Pages studied: 202–204; 206–207; 210–212
Review and test: 204–206; 207–208

Lesson 22

Aim: To study how various reading skills may be tested in one question.
Pages studied: 209–211
Review and test: 211–212

Lesson 23

Aim: To learn important Latin prefixes for help in analyzing word meanings.
Pages studied: 92–96

Lesson 24

Aim: To continue study of Latin prefixes.
Pages studied: 96–99
Review and test: 99–100

Lesson 25

Aim: To learn important Latin verb roots for help in analyzing word meanings.
Pages studied: 101–103

Lesson 26

Aim: To continue study of Latin verb roots.
Pages studied: 103–105

Lesson 27

Aim: To continue study of Latin verb roots.
Pages studied: 106–108
Review and test: 108

Lesson 28

Aim: To review Latin prefixes and verb roots.
Pages studied: 92–108

GRADE 10 STUDY PLAN

Critical Reading

The Grade 10 study plan builds upon the groundwork laid in Grade 9. It continues the all-important study of roots, prefixes, and suffixes. It puts English in a world context. It continues, in reading, the part played by the author in a reading passage. It discusses attitude, purpose, and style. It also illuminates the language used in reading passages and looks beyond the reading for outcomes and application.

The opening lessons devote a great deal of time to roots, prefixes, and suffixes because these word elements are clues to thousands of words. They are worth memorizing, along with sample words to facilitate recall.

Lesson 1

Aim: To learn important Latin noun and adjective roots for help in analyzing word meanings.
Pages studied: 109–111

Lesson 2

Aim: To continue study of Latin noun and adjective roots.
Pages studied: 112–114

Lesson 3

Aim: To continue study of Latin noun and adjective roots.
Pages studied: 114–116
Review and test: 116–117

Lesson 29

Aim: To evaluate the author's tone in a reading passage.
Pages studied: 214–216
Review and test: 216–218

Lesson 4

Aim: To continue study of Latin noun and adjective roots.
Pages studied: 117–119
Review and test: 119–121

Lesson 5

Aim: To evaluate the author's attitude in a reading passage.
Pages studied: 219–220
Review and test: 220–222

Lesson 6

Aim: To evaluate the author's purpose in a reading passage.
Pages studied: 222–224
Review and test: 224–226

Lesson 7

Aim: To evaluate the author's style in a reading passage.
Pages studied: 226–228
Review and test: 228–230

Lesson 8

Aim: To learn important Greek prefixes and roots for help in analyzing word meanings.
Pages studied: 122–124

Lesson 9

Aim: To continue study of Greek prefixes and roots.
Pages studied: 124–128
Review and test: 128

Lesson 25

Aim: To study the special characteristics of the short (discrete) reading passage.
Pages studied: 304–305

Lesson 26

Aim: To study the paired passages.
Pages studied: 305–306
Review: 306–307

Lessons 25 and 26 may be combined.

Lesson 27

Aim: To give students a chance to request further explanation of any section covered in the text.
Pages studied: To be supplied by the students.

GRADE 11 STUDY PLAN

Critical Reading

Except for a brief vocabulary section and a study of outcomes and applications in reading, the Grade 11 study plan is basically a test-and-review plan. It provides for a diagnostic vocabulary test as well as diagnostic reading tests. It also provides for practice in taking Mastery Tests as preparation for the real thing.

Lesson 1

Aim: To realize how foreign words have entered the English language and added color.
Pages studied: 152–154
Review and test: 155–156 (A)

Lesson 2

Aim: To continue study of foreign words and their influence on the English language.
Pages studied: 154–155
Review and test: 157–158 (B)

Lesson 3

Aim: To study some of the ways in which the English language has been enriched.
Pages studied: 159–162

Lesson 4

Aim: To study the growth of the English language with special emphasis upon doublets and triplets.
Pages studied: 162–163; 165
Review and test: 164–165

Lesson 5

Aim: To review etymology as a guide to vocabulary building.
Pages studied: 166–167
Review and test: 165–166

Lesson 6

Aim: To study how longer reading passages are tested, with emphasis upon the single passage.
Pages studied: 272–282
Review and test: 282–290

Lesson 7

Aim: To study how paired reading passages are tested.
Pages studied: 291–299
Review and test: 299–302

Lesson 8

Aim: To complete or review Lessons 6–7.
Pages studied or reviewed: As needed.
Review and test: 287–290

It is always possible to assign some of the Practice Tests to be taken at home and discussed in class. Taking tests in class approximates test conditions. Home assignments save time. Both procedures may be followed throughout these lessons.

Some Practice Tests may be taken at home and analyzed in class. Answers are on page 537.

Lesson 9

Aim: Through Practice Tests to check on mastery of techniques taught earlier.
Review and test: 308–309 (A, B, C, D)

Lesson 10

Aim: Through Practice Tests to check on mastery of techniques taught earlier.
Review and test: 310–322 (E, F, G, H)

Lesson 11

Aim: Through Practice Tests to check on mastery of techniques taught earlier.
Review and test: 322–337 (I, J, K, L, M)

Lesson 12

Aim: To take a sample reading diagnostic test to check on progress and uncover weak spots in mastery.
Review and test: 338–342; 531–532 (A, B, C)

Lesson 13

Aim: To take a sample reading diagnostic test.
Pages 342–345
Analysis of answers: 533–534

Lesson 14

Aim: To review the textbook.
Pages studied: To be supplied by the students.

Lesson 15

Aim: To begin taking a Mastery Test for diagnostic and practice purposes.
Pages: 497–500
Analysis of answers: 562

Lesson 16

Aim: To take a Mastery Test.
Pages: 500–502
Analysis of answers: 562–563

Lesson 17

Aim: To take a Mastery Test.
Page: 502

Lesson 18

Aim: To take a Mastery Test.
Pages: 503–504
Analysis of answers: 563

Lesson 19

Aim: To take a Mastery Test
Pages: 504–506
Analysis of answers: 563–564

Lesson 20

Aim: To take a Mastery Test.
Page: 506

Lesson 21

Aim: To review Mastery Test strategy.
Pages: 497–506

Lessons 22–23

(If you prefer, Mastery Test 3 may be administered during two class periods under conditions resembling those at the SAT.) See also Grade 12 Study Plan.

Aim: To take a Mastery Test.
Pages: 507–511
Analysis of answers: 564–565

Lessons 24–26

Aim: To review important elements in the language study program. To go over areas in which students have shown weaknesses.

NOTE: A thorough review of the entire program is an excellent procedure at this point. Some of the material taught in Grade 9, for example, may well need reinforcing. A review of Latin and Greek roots may well pay dividends in student achievement.

GRADE 12 STUDY PLAN

Critical Reading

Lessons will be determined by the needs of the class. Reserving Mastery Test 3 for the beginning of the 12th year will provide insight into the needs and possible deficiencies of the students. The textbook should be used as a reference book, for frequent consultation throughout the high school career. The book is not intended as a one-shot attack on the SAT but as a teaching method and instrument for building language power.

PLANS FOR THE WRITING SECTIONS

GRADE 9 STUDY PLAN

Writing

Lesson 1
Aim: To take a diagnostic test to uncover student weaknesses.
Pages studied: 391–393

Lesson 2
Aim: To continue taking a diagnostic test.
Pages studied: 394–395

Lesson 3
Aim: To gauge students' ability to organize and write an essay.
Page studied: 395

Lesson 4
Aim: To appreciate a sound English sentence.
Pages studied: 396–399

Lesson 5
Aim: To practice writing sound English sentences.
Pages studied: 399–400

Lesson 6
Aim: To learn to write economically.
Pages studied: 401–407

Lesson 7
Aim: To write clear English sentences.
Pages studied: 407–410

Lesson 8
Aim: To write varied English sentences.
Pages 410–413

Lesson 9
Aim: To write unified English sentences effectively.
Pages studied: 416–420

Lesson 10
Aim: To write good paragraphs.
Pages studied: 421–423

Lesson 11
Aim: To write good paragraphs.
Pages studied: 423–424

Lesson 12
Aim: To write good paragraphs.
Pages studied: 424

Lesson 13
Aim: To review and write effective simple and compound sentences.
Pages studied: 433–435

Lessons 14 and 15
Aim: To write effective complex sentences.
Pages studied: 435–438

Lesson 16
Aim: To avoid sentence fragments and run-on sentences.
Pages studied: 438–444

GRADE 10 STUDY PLAN

Writing

Lessons 1 and 2 (if needed)
Aim: To take a diagnostic test to gauge progress.
Pages studied: 484–489

Lesson 3
Aim: To review writing the paragraph.
Pages studied: 421–424

Lesson 4
Aim: To review concepts studied in Grade 9.
Pages studied: 396–424

Lesson 5
Aim: To learn to write an essay to persuade.
Pages studied: 425–428

Lesson 6
Aim: To continue studying the essay to persuade.
Pages studied: 428–431

Lesson 7
Aim: To write the essay to persuade.
Pages studied: 431–432 (Writing Exercise 2)

Lesson 8
Aim: To review problems with nouns.
Pages studied: 445–449

Lesson 9
Aim: To review problems with verbs.
Pages studied: 450–456

Lesson 10
Aim: To review problems with modifiers and joining words.
Pages studied: 457–459

Lesson 11
Aim: To review and write an essay to persuade.
Page studied: 431 (Writing Exercise 3)

Lesson 12
Aim: To review problems with pronouns.
Pages studied: 462–466

Lesson 13
Aim: To review problems with punctuation.
Pages studied: 467–470

Lesson 14
Aim: To review problems with capitalization.
Pages studied: 471–473

Lesson 15
Aim: To review spelling.
Pages studied: 474–477

Lessons 16 and 17
Aim: To take the mastery test to check progress.
Pages 499–502; 562–563

Grade 11 Study Plan

Writing

Lesson 1
Aim: To take a diagnostic test to check progress.
Pages studied: 490–494

Lesson 2
Aim: To review the results of the diagnostic test.
Pages studied: 490–494

Lessons 3 and 4

Aim: To review the writing skills.
Pages studied: 396–431

Lesson 5

Aim: To practice writing an essay.
Page 432 (Writing Exercise 4)

Lesson 6

Aim: To review grammar and usage.
Pages 433–477

Lessons 7 and 8

Aim: To familiarize students with questioning techniques for "Identifying Sentence Errors."
Pages studied: 477–480

Lesson 9

Aim: To familiarize students with questioning techniques for "Improving Sentences"
Pages studied: 480–482

Lesson 10

Aim: To familiarize students with questioning techniques for "Improving Paragraphs.
Pages studied: 482–484

Lesson 11

Aim: To take a Mastery Test for assessment of progress.
Pages studied: 499–502

Lesson 12

Aim: To discuss results of Mastery Test in Lesson 11.
Pages studied: 563–564

GRADE 12 STUDY PLAN

Writing

By this time students should have familiarized themselves with SAT techniques, but a review is always sound pedagogy. Taking Mastery Test 3 at the beginning of the school year should reveal any remaining gaps and needs.

Pages 507–511

Lesson 1

Aim: to review content and technique.
Pages studied: 425–432

Lesson 2

Aim: To practice writing an essay.
Page studied: 432 (Practice)

Lesson 3

Aim: To discuss the results of the Mastery Test taken in Lesson 1.
Pages studied: 564–565

ACKNOWLEDGMENTS

Grateful acknowledgment is made to the following sources for permission to reprint copyrighted materials. Every effort has been made to obtain permission to use previously published material. Any errors or omissions are unintentional.

Page 3: "The Ecology of Language" from WORD PLAY by Peter Farb, copyright © 1973 by Peter Farb. Used by permission of Alfred A. Knopf, a division of Random House, Inc.

Page 5: Excerpt from "Sentimental Education" from FIRST LOVE AND OTHER SORROWS by Harold Brodkey © 1954, 1955, 1956, 1957, 1964 by Ellen Brodkey. Reprinted by permission of Henry Holt and Company, LLC.

Page 11: "Mother of Machines" from THE DISCOVERERS by Daniel J. Boorstin, copyright © 1983 by Daniel J. Boorstin. Used by permission of Random House, Inc.

Page 191: "The Scar" by William G. Christ, copyright © 1999.

Page 238: From ART AND ARDOR by Cynthia Ozick Copyright © 1983 by Cynthia Ozick. Reprinted by permission of Alfred A. Knopf, Inc.

Page 240: From "The Long Loneliness," *The Star Thrower,* by Loren Eisely, by permission of Times Books, a Division of Random House, Inc.

Page 257: Reprinted with the permission of Scribner, a Division of Simon & Schuster, Inc., from *Look Homeward, Angel* by Thomas Wolfe. Copyright © 1929 by Charles Scribner's Sons; copyright renewed © 1957 by Edward C. Ashwell, Administrator, C.T.A and/or Fred W. Wolfe.

Page 258: From *The Works of Robert Louis Stevenson in One Volume,* R. L. Stevenson.

Page 260: From THE SHORT STORIES OF KATHERINE MANSFIELD by Katherine Mansfield. Copyright 1923 by Alfred A. Knopf, Inc. and renewed 1951 by John Middleton Murry. Reprinted by permission of the publisher.

Page 263: From *The Great Railway Bazaar* by Paul Theroux. Copyright © 1975 by Paul Theroux. Reprinted by permission of The Wylie Agency.

Page 264: From *David Copperfield* by Charles Dickens.

Page 267: "Starlight," from *Floating* by Marian Thurm. Copyright © 1978, 1979, 1981, 1982, 1983, 1984 by Marian Thurm. Used by permission of Viking Penguin, a division of Penguin Putnam Inc.

Page 310: "The Mission of Jane," reprinted with the permission of Scribner, a Division of Simon & Schuster, Inc., from *The Selected Short Stories of Edith Wharton* by R. W. B. Lewis. (New York: Charles Scribner's Sons, 1991).

Page 319: Excerpt from *Pilgrim at Tinker Creek,* by Annie Dillard. Copyright © 1974 by Annie Dillard. Reprinted by permission of HarperCollins Publishers, Inc.

Page 326: From "How 'Bigger' Was Born," pages 232-233 in Ducas *Great Documents in Black American History* (Praeger Publishers, 1970), an imprint of Greenwood Publishing Group, Inc., Westport, CT. Reprinted with permission.

Page 330: "Spring Flight," from UNDER THE SEA WIND by Rachel L. Carson, illustrated by Bob Hines. Copyright 1941 by Rachel L. Carson. Copyright renewed © 1969 by Roger Christie. Illustrations copyright © 1991 by Bob Hines. A Truman Talley Book. Used by permission of Dutton, a division of Penguin Putnam Inc.

Page 332: From "Microbiological Mining" by Carole L. Brierley, in *Scientific American,* August 1982, page 44, by permission of Scientific American, Inc. All rights reserved.

Page 334: Excerpt from "The Five Layers of Ambiguity," BYTE Magazine, January 1993. By permission of CMP Media, LLC.

Page 338: From *The Birth of Britain,* by Winston Churchill, copyright 1956, by permission of Curtis Brown, Ltd., London.

Page 339: From "The King of Ragtime," by Brian McGinty from *American History,* by Brian McGinty. Copyright © 1983 by *American History.* Reprinted by permission of *Primedia Enthusiasts Publications* (History Group).

Page 340: From "Let's Stop Farming the System," by Rexford A. Resler, May 1984, *American Forests,* by permission of American Forestry Association, Washington, D.C. (www.americanforests.org)

Page 341: From "The Metropolitan Museum of Art Bulletin," Winter 1981-82, page 58, copyright © 1982, The Metropolitan Museum of Art, by permission of The Metropolitan Museum of Art, New York.

Page 342: From *Innocents Abroad,* by Mark Twain.

Page 343: Excerpt entitled "Structuralism in Reverse" is from the selection "General Semantics as a Tool to Investigate Scientific Empiricism" reprinted from *Et cetera,* Vol. 40, No. 4, by permission of the International Society for General Semantics.

Page 345: From *Teaching a Stone to Talk: Expeditions and Encounters,* by Annie Dillard, copyright © 1982 by Annie Dillard, reprinted by permission of HarperCollins Publishers, Inc.

Page 352: "The Pocketbook Game" by Alice Childress from *Like One of the Family.* Copyright © 1956. Renewed 1984 by Alice Childress. Used by permission of Flora Roberts, Inc.

Page 353: Excerpted from "A Biologist Whose Heresy Redraws Earth's Tree of Life," by Jeanne McDermott. From *Smithsonian,* August, 1989. Reprinted by permission of the author.

Page 360: Excerpts from *Civilisation* by Kenneth Clark. Copyright © 1969 by Kenneth Clark. Reprinted by permission of HarperCollins Publishers, Inc.

Page 365: From "Sophisticated Man Is Not Superstitious?" from *The Prevalence of Nonsense* by Ashley Montague and Edward Darling. Copyright © 1967 by M. F. Ashley Montague and Edward Darling. Reprinted by permission of HarperCollins Publishers, Inc.

Page 366: Excerpt from "Of Course" from *The Lottery* by Shirley Jackson. Copyright © 1948, 1949 by Shirley Jackson. Copyright renewed © 1976, 1977 by Laurence Hyman, Barry Hyman, Mrs. Sarah Webster and Mrs. Joanne Schnurer. Reprinted by permission of Farrar, Straus and Giroux, LLC.

Page 379: Excerpted from the Introduction, by Anita Brookner, to *The Stories of Edith Wharton.* Reprinted by permission of Simon & Schuster, London.

Page 386: Excerpted from *Skinwalkers* by Tony Hillerman. Copyright © 1987 by Tony Hillerman. Reprinted by permission of HarperCollins Publishers, Inc.

SAT questions selected from 6 SATs. College Entrance Examination Board, 1982. Reprinted by permission of Educational Testing Service, the copyright owner of the test questions.

Permission to reprint the above material does not constitute review or endorsement by Educational Testing Service or the College Board of this publication as a whole or of any other questions or testing information it may contain.

Index